THE AMERICAN PRESIDENCY

THE AMERICAN PRESIDENCY

Second Edition

JAMES W. DAVIS

PRAEGER

Westport, Connecticut
London

Library of Congress Cataloging-in-Publication Data

Davis, James W.
    The American presidency / James W. Davis.—2nd ed.
      p.   cm.
    Includes bibliographical references and index.
    ISBN 0–275–94874–9 (alk. paper).—ISBN 0–275–94875–7 (pbk. :
alk. paper)
    1. Presidents—United States. I. Title.
JK516.D38 1995
324.6'3'0973—dc20   95–7981

British Library Cataloguing in Publication Data is available.

Library of Congress Catalog Card Number: 95–7981
ISBN: 0–275–94874–9
      0–275–94875–7 (pbk.)

First published in 1995

Praeger Publishers, 88 Post Road West, Westport, CT 06881
An imprint of Greenwood Publishing Group, Inc.

Printed in the United States of America

∞™

The paper used in this book complies with the
Permanent Paper Standard issued by the National
Information Standards Organization (Z39.48–1984).

10 9 8 7 6 5 4 3 2 1

CONTENTS

PREFACE TO SECOND EDITION

Since publication of the first edition of this textbook, the Cold War has ended, the Soviet Union has disintegrated into a shadow of its former greatness, President Ronald Reagan has retired from office, the one-term presidency of George Bush is now history, and President Bill Clinton is already in his third year of his first term that, unless he can reverse his downward spiral in the opinion polls, threatens to be his only term in the White House.

In the 1994 off-year elections, Republicans regained control of both houses of Congress for the first time in forty years. After two short years of "unified" government—one party controlling both the executive and legislative branches—the nation has again reverted to the divided government that existed for twenty out of twenty-four years between 1968 and 1992.

Does the sudden resurgence of Republicans in Congress herald, as suggested by some political analysts, the return of Congressional dominance of the national government that persisted for most of the nineteenth century and surfaced again briefly in the Harding-Coolidge-Hoover era of the 1920s? This seems unlikely, for as explained in the first edition, the presidency remains the vital nerve center of the federal government. Indeed, whenever an international crisis erupts, endangering the security of the United States and its allies, or a domestic emergency upsets the daily lives of American citizens, the public first turns to the president to find a solution. Without question, the list of public expectations and demands placed upon the president has grown at such a frightening pace over the years that no president seems able to satisfy a majority of American citizens.

Three of the four most recent presidents—Ford, Carter, and Bush—have been turned out of office after a single term—victims of the exaggerated public expectations syndrome. This inability of American presidents to respond adequately to the rising level of public expectations is a recurring theme throughout the second edition, as it was in the original edition.

Highly unstable relations between the executive and legislative branches, it seems, have become the hallmark of our national government as we near the end of the twentieth century. It is in this context that I have approached the various constitutional and political roles handled by America's chief executive.

RECASTING CHAPTER TOPICS

Major revisions in the second edition include a new chapter on the emergence of "The Presidential Branch"—the White House staff—as the dominant decision-making agency, not the cabinet or the departmental bureaucracies, in the executive branch.

Another chapter is devoted to presidential-congressional relations, a topic that certainly cannot be ignored, especially in the era of divided government. In the concluding chapter, "The Road Ahead," I assess the mountainous obstacles that confront American presidents as the nation rapidly moves toward the twenty-first century: institutional checkpoints, weakened political parties, microscopic scrutiny by the mass media and opinion pollsters, well-funded political action committees, talk-radio hosts' anti-Washington diatribes, and Perot-inspired, direct-dialed "electronic town meeting" referenda.

ACKNOWLEDGMENTS

In preparing the second edition, I have been fortunate to have had the perceptive counsel of Professor William W. Lammers of the University of Southern California and Professor David Gray Adler of Idaho State University. Dr. Herbert E. Alexander, Director, Citizen's Research Foundation, whose encyclopedic knowledge of presidential campaign finance is invaluable to an understanding of presidential nominations and elections, has always been willing to lend a friendly hand in providing needed data.

Three veteran polling specialists—Leslie C. McAneny of the Gallup Poll, Margaret Ann Campbell of the NBC/*Wall Street Journal* Poll, and Pat Luevano of the University of Michigan's Institute for Social Research—have been unfailingly responsive to my frequent requests for polling data.

Frequent encouragement and support from Dr. Kenneth R. Hoover, Chairperson, Political Science Department, Western Washington University, has also contributed to the early completion of the second edition.

Mr. Peter Coveney, Senior Editor at Praeger, has been a steady influence and source of valuable guidance throughout the publication process. Margaret

Maybury, Jeanne Lesinski, and Terri Jennings all performed admirably in handling the editorial, copyediting, and production stages of the book, respectively.

My special thanks to Sue Scally of Western Washington University's Bureau of Faculty Research, who prepared the final manuscript copy for the publishers, and to the services of Geri Walker, director of this research office. David and Barbara Washburn were indispensable helpmates in processing the earlier draft of the manuscript. Kevin Short efficiently designed the graphics.

Finally, I would like to thank the three anonymous reviewers whose thoughtful comments and suggestions on an early draft have contributed significantly to whatever improvement the second edition may possess over its predecessor.

CHAPTER 1

INTRODUCTION

Five of the six most recent presidents of the United States—Johnson, Nixon, Ford, Carter, and Bush—have failed to win reelection, or have been driven from office by threatened defeat or impeachment. Only President Ronald Reagan completed two full terms, and even his tenure came under a dark cloud in his second term during the Iran-Contra "guns for hostages" investigation.

Is the United States destined to be governed by a string of one-term presidents for the remainder of the twentieth century and into the twenty-first? Have most of our presidents found themselves in a "no win" position that limits their tenancy in the White House to four years or less? Do we expect too much from our presidents? These are some of the questions that will frequently occupy our attention throughout this text as we examine and assess occupants of the highest office in the land.

EXAGGERATED PUBLIC EXPECTATIONS

Modern presidents, unlike their nineteenth- and early twentieth-century predecessors, are expected by the public not only to maintain the peace and security of the country, but also to maintain high employment and control inflation. If the economy turns sour, presidents are expected actively to fight the recession. Though the president's ability to manage the economy is minimal at best, the public nevertheless holds him personally accountable for the state of the economy. If he fails to maintain prosperity, voters may turn him out at the next election.

Undoubtedly the extravagant promises that presidential candidates make during their interminably long campaigns for the White House contribute to exaggerated public expectations once they reach the Oval Office. Typically, the public expects the president to anticipate problems. Failing that, the public expects the president to provide imaginative solutions. In truth, as the respected British commentator Godfrey Hodgson has put it: "The American people expect too much of their presidents. They demand more from them than any man or woman is going to be able to give."[1] It is this gap between limited presidential power and the all-encompassing responsibilities of the American chief executive—indeed, the impossibility of presidents' meeting many of these exaggerated expectations—that constitutes the central theme of this text.

An explanation for the public's lofty expectations of the president stems, in part, from a lack of understanding of the context in which presidential decision making takes place, especially with respect to his chief rival power base—Congress. As Richard E. Neustadt pointed out in his celebrated study, *Presidential Power*, first published in 1960, a president can rarely command; he must devote most of his time to persuading people to join, help, and vote with him.[2]

The phenomenon of rising public expectations for our president, it should be emphasized, is a twentieth-century development. Clearly, it is an outgrowth of U.S. emergence as a world power, the rapid industrialization and urbanization of the nation, the rise of the welfare state, and the remarkable growth of mass communications. Starting with Theodore Roosevelt and Woodrow Wilson, the American public has turned increasingly toward the White House to find answers to pressing national problems and to respond to recurring international crises. Most nineteenth-century presidents, by contrast, encountered few public demands.

The concept of exaggerated public expectations was never put better than by one of President Franklin D. Roosevelt's advisors, Louis Brownlow, more than forty years ago: "The nation expects more of the President than he can possibly do; more than we give him either the authority or means to do. Thus, expecting from him the impossible, inevitably we shall be disappointed in his performance."[3] The high presidential expectations syndrome, then, is a twentieth-century phenomenon.

Over the past two centuries, we have vastly multiplied the requirements for presidential leadership, but we have not matched this expansion by giving the president sufficient tools to do the job. In the words of Thomas E. Cronin: "We overestimate the powers of the office and underestimate the economic, social, and cultural factors that so often shape presidential performance and so greatly shape the people we place in the presidency."[4] Still, we are demanding more, not less, of our presidents. "It would take a political superman to do all the things Americans want their presidents to do" is the way Godfrey Hodgson, the British commentator, has assessed the president's responsibilities. Hodgson, who has observed presidents for more than three decades, has elaborated further on the overloading of the presidency:

> He must simultaneously conduct the diplomacy of a superpower, put together separate coalitions to enact every piece of legislation required by a vast and complex society, manage the economy, command the armed forces, serve as a spiritual example and inspiration, respond to every emergency.[5]

Yet, most Americans ignore or remain unaware of how limited are the formal constitutional powers of the president.

LIMITED PRESIDENTIAL POWER

More than one presidential scholar has noted the rather meager powers granted by the Constitution to the nation's top leader. The Framers, wary of the dangers of autocratic rule, prescribed only limited authority for the president in Article II:

> The executive power shall be vested in a President of the United States of America.
>
> The President shall be Commander in Chief of the Army and Navy of the United States. . . .
>
> He shall have power, by and with the advice and consent of the Senate, to make treaties. . . .
>
> He shall from time to time give to the Congress information on the state of the union, and recommend to their consideration such measures as he shall judge necessary and expedient. . . .
>
> He shall take care that the laws be faithfully executed. . . .
>
> He shall have power to grant reprieves and pardons for offense against the United States, except in cases of impeachment.

Beyond this minimal list of duties, the Framers expected the president to do little more than review legislative bills sent to him from Congress, collect excise taxes and tariff duties, conduct foreign policy, and protect the shores of the United States from invaders. Yet, from this original abbreviated list of executive powers, the nation's citizenry has come two centuries later to expect the president to perform near miracles whenever an emergency arises. Even though the president is the focal point of our expectations for public policymaking, he is not in a position to satisfy many of the needs of the electorate. Indeed, in recent years there has been a "substantial enlargement of presidential responsibilities, explicit and implied, but without a corresponding increase in presidential power."[6]

Less than a month before he was assassinated, President John F. Kennedy remarked: "The powers of the presidency are often described. Its limitations should be occasionally remembered."[7] Americans nevertheless want presidents to solve problems. But some foreign issues—for example, international terrorism, the pricing policies of the international oil cartel—are either beyond presidential influence or control, or involve such drastic responses that the high cost of undertaking them would not be commensurate with the risks wagered.

On the domestic front, the president's ability to implement policy is circumscribed by several factors: the separation of powers, a recently decentralized power structure in Congress, the number of cross-party coalitions needed to pass legislation, a slow-moving federal bureaucracy, and the potent influence of special interest groups opposed to the redistribution of power. The decline of political parties as vehicles for mobilizing presidential support has added to his woes. Consequently, modern presidents find themselves with a hard-core base of support that is smaller and less committed to the president's agenda. Also, the mass media, preoccupied with results, do not discuss how complicated the processes of governmental change are; nor do they convey the difficult tradeoffs often involved in important decisions.

Because some demands on the presidency are becoming more insistent at the same time as they are getting harder to meet, presidential nominees and recently elected presidents may sometimes overpromise and overextend themselves. Persistent expectations that a president can direct sweeping changes encourage presidents to attempt more than they can accomplish in any single term. In some cases, the negative impact of the public's high expectations of the president can be of his own making—and sometimes his undoing. Jimmy Carter, for example, was his own worst enemy in this matter. Of all the twentieth-century presidents, Carter made the most campaign pledges.[8] Repeatedly, he became the victim of his own excessive promises. Both before and after entering the White House, he set extremely high goals that probably no president could have fulfilled, certainly not in his first year in office. Yet Carter pledged during his election campaign to present a complete reform of the welfare system by the first of May of his first year in office. He promised to balance the budget and reduce unemployment to 3 percent by 1980, and to keep his administration free of scandal. But when the federal books did not balance by 1980 and unemployment stood at 7.5 percent, Carter was turned out of office.

President Reagan, too, promised to balance the budget during his 1980 election campaign and subsequently failed to do so, but the public did not seem to hold him up to the same high standards as President Carter because he had fulfilled two other campaign promises—to cut taxes and to step up military preparedness. Moreover, the economic recovery, which began in early 1983, and the continued reduction in the inflation rate (down to less than 4 percent in late 1984) also helped the Reagan administration shift public attention away from the still-unbalanced budget and the record-breaking deficits and return the movie-star-turned-president to office for a second term.

President Reagan, unlike Carter, developed a sophisticated strategy to avoid most of the political fallout from unfulfilled campaign promises. As Jeff Fishel has pointed out: "Reagan permitted some of his controversial proposals, the social issues, for example, to slide on and off the agenda, without seeming to alter the rhetoric of his conservative principles in supporting them. The White House packaged this stance as proof that he is still a 'strong' leader, undercut by a willful Congress that is dominated by irresponsible Democrats."[9] Furthermore, the Reagan administration did not openly and completely reverse itself on very many of its campaign promises, partly because Reagan made fewer concrete promises than many predecessors, and partly because "the administration opted for a strategy of deferring or not acting rather than clearly repudiating their commitments."[10]

President George Bush, on the other hand, failed to learn the painful lessons about the public's high expectation for handling the nation's economy experienced by Presidents Gerald Ford and Jimmy Carter during their reelection campaigns. Indeed, all three presidents were removed from office primarily for their excessive promises and their inability to turn the sluggish economy around—or to convince the public sufficiently that they were moving heaven and earth in an attempt to bring back prosperity.

More recently, it has been suggested that President Bill Clinton may come face to face with the same dilemma encountered by recent one-term presidents. Clinton the campaigner may have created unrealistically high expectations—universal health care, reduction of the deficit and unemployment, and major welfare reform—that Clinton the president may not be able to meet before reelection time in 1996. In assessing President Bill Clinton's early reelection prospects, after his surprising victory with the North American Free Trade Agreement (NAFTA), veteran Democratic power broker Robert S. Strauss observed: "If he's going to be re-elected, Clinton has to focus on domestic and foreign policy at the same time. He can't be just a domestic policy president any more than George Bush could be just a foreign policy President. The country expects the President to handle both."[11] Not many presidents, however, have been successful in both areas simultaneously.

CONTRADICTORY EXPECTATIONS

Paradoxically, public expectations of the president are not only high, but also frequently contradictory. Presidents, faced with contradictory expectations, find it difficult to escape criticism and loss of approval—no matter what course of action they take. Most voters want better education and improved health services but are against increased taxes; they favor economic development but without damage to the environment; they want inflation controlled but not at the expense of higher unemployment or interest rates—and so on. Despite the contradictions inherent in these expectations, the public nevertheless holds the president accountable for meeting them. That the public's expectations of the president are not only high but also contradictory does not seem to matter; the public holds the expectations anyway. Moreover, the greater the expectations of the chief executive, the more the potential for disappointment. While some presidents may succeed in educating voters to alter their expectations, George C. Edwards III has noted: "The public's views change slowly and usually the changes that take place only create additional burdens for the president."[12]

Lack of programmatic success usually translates into declining approval ratings in the opinion polls. Except for Eisenhower and Reagan, all post–World War II presidents have suffered a notable decline in approval ratings as their terms have drawn to a close (see Table 1.1).

In the age of television, presidents are portrayed and perceived as successful chief executives less frequently than in the pre-television era. Television has raised people's expectations of what the president can and should do, and it has made it more difficult for the president to measure up to these expectations. Presidential scholar Louis W. Koenig has commented: "Television also restricts the president's capacity to lay complicated issues before the public, to explain his proposals for action, and to perform the educative tasks of leadership."[13] Moreover, as political scientist Austin Ranney has observed, television "has made most government achievements seem transitory, unimportant, and even illusionary."[14] Ranney continues, "Presidents seem to be more vulnerable in the television age than they were before, and it may be that in the future it will be just as unusual for an incumbent president to be reelected as it used to be for one to be defeated."[15]

What kind of presidents receive high approval marks from the public? What type of leadership does it take to gain the generous approval of the American electorate? How does the nation's chief executive avoid becoming a victim of the high presidential expectations syndrome?

To predict successful presidents obviously requires more than a crystal ball. Perhaps there is no clear answer. But for a start, it may be worthwhile to examine various presidential leadership styles and models in search of an answer.

PRESIDENTIAL LEADERSHIP: STYLES AND MODELS

Presidential leadership styles have never failed to fascinate presidential scholars. In recent years some students of the presidency have focused on the personality of the president as a major factor in determining his performance in office. Political scientist James David Barber in his study, *The Presidential Character*, has used the so-called psycho-biographical or psycho-historical approach to explain presidential behavior in office.[16]

Table 1.1
Average Yearly Presidential Approval, 1953–1992

Year	Approval	Year	Approval	Year	Approval	Year	Approval
1953	68%	1964	75%	1975	44%	1986	61%
1954	66	1965	66	1976	49	1987	48
1955	71	1966	50	1977	63	1988	57
1956	73	1967	44	1978	45	1989	64
1957	64	1968	43	1979	38	1990	68
1958	54	1969	63	1980	42	1991	71
1959	64	1970	58	1981	58	1992	40
1960	61	1971	51	1982	44	1993	49
1961	76	1972	58	1983	44	1994	46
1962	71	1973	43	1984	56		
1963	65	1974	36	1985	61		

Sources: Data for the period 1953–1980 are from Gallup polls cited in George C. Edwards III, *The Public Presidency* (New York: St. Martin's, 1983), 22. Copyright © 1983. Reprinted with permission of St. Martin's Press, Incorporated; for the period 1981–1992 the percentages are from the *Gallup Poll Monthly*, January 1993 (No. 328), 8; figures for 1992–1994 supplied by the Gallup Poll, Princeton, New Jersey.

Barber's Typology

First published in the early 1970s, Barber's fourfold personality classification is conceptualized on two dimensions: the first is based on the degree of activity (active or passive) and the second measures the degree of affect or satisfaction (positive or negative) exhibited by the president (see Figure 1.1). Barber's objective is to create an analytic framework, based on several dimensions of personality, to categorize a president's psychological tendencies, and then use these categories to explain and predict presidential behavior. Barber suggests that presidential performance can be evaluated on the basis of character, style, and world view. These three components shape a person's behavior throughout life and are resistant to change. Consequently, Barber argues, they are extremely valuable not only in predicting how a president will perform in office but also in helping the public evaluate presidential candidates to determine which ones have the temperament, level of self-esteem, and vision needed to succeed in the White House. Barber also considers two environmental conditions—power situation and climate of expectations—as important factors affecting presidential success.

The "active-positive" president, Barber's first choice, is filled with self-confidence and vigorously pursues major goals. Active-positives enjoy their work and seek to use power to achieve beneficial results for others. If they encounter roadblocks, they are prepared to shift directions rather than accept a costly political defeat.[17]

Figure 1.1
Barber's Classifications of Presidential Personality Types

AFFECT	ACTIVE	PASSIVE
Positive	*Active-Positive*	*Passive-Positive*
	Franklin Roosevelt	William Taft
	Harry Truman	Warren Harding
	John Kennedy	Ronald Reagan
	Gerald Ford	
	Jimmy Carter	
	George Bush	
Negative	*Active Negative*	*Passive-Negative*
	Woodrow Wilson	Calvin Coolidge
	Herbert Hoover	Dwight Eisenhower
	Lyndon Johnson	
	Richard Nixon	

Source: Adapted from James David Barber, *The Presidential Character*, 4th ed. (Englewood Cliffs, NJ: Prentice-Hall, 1992). Used by permission of the author.

By contrast, the "active-negative" president considers life as a "hard struggle to achieve and hold power." As a result, this person derives relatively little satisfaction from his job as he attempts to overcome feelings of inadequacy. This person's high-level activity has a compulsive quality about it, as if he were trying to make up for lost time or "to escape from anxiety into hard work."[18]

The third category—the "passive-positive" president—also lacks self-confidence but endeavors to overcome a hostile environment by seeking affection or acceptance from other people. Barber notes: "This is the receptive, compliant, other-directed character whose life is a search for affection as a reward for being agreeable and cooperative rather than personally assertive."[19]

The fourth category—the "passive-negative" president—assumes office out of a sense of duty. Consequently, he finds little enjoyment in his work and contributes little to the office.

Passive-negative types are in politics because they think they ought to be. This dutiful service compensates for low self-esteem. "Their tendency is to withdraw, to escape vague principles (especially prohibitions) and procedural arrangements. They become guardians of the right and proper way, above the sordid politicking of lesser men."[20]

Barber expresses serious concern that "active-negative" presidents pose a major danger to the nation because they tend to overreact to crises and continue failed policies long after they have been rejected by the public. To be sure, the four active-negative presidents—Wilson, Hoover, Johnson, and Nixon—made significant contributions to the country before adversity struck. But their psychological makeup led them to pursue and continue policies that eventually cost the nation dearly.

Barber's favorite category—"active-positive" presidents—contains a group of outstanding leaders—Franklin Delano Roosevelt, Harry S. Truman, John F. Kennedy, and from an earlier period, Thomas Jefferson. All of these chief executives displayed qualities needed for the presidency that "enabled them to make that office an 'engine of progress.' "[21] Barber also perceives serious danger from both the passive-positive (Taft and Harding) and passive-negative (Coolidge and Eisenhower) presidents because they allow the nation to drift and neglect major social problems.

Critics of Barber's analysis, however, insist that his categories are too broad and ambiguous, that psychological tendencies do not each fit neatly into one and only one square, and that predictions of behavior are often self-fulfilling.[22] As political scientists George C. Edwards III and Stephen J. Wayne have commented, "None of these criticisms invalidates the model, but they do question its scope, application, and general utility as an explanatory and predictive tool."[23] For example, it seems questionable to categorize President Eisenhower as a passive-negative president who is, according to Barber, withdrawn, suffers from low self-esteem, and compensates for inadequacy by agreeing to work on behalf of his fellow citizens. Barber is so preoccupied with analysis of character that he takes little account of the existing climate of expectations and power relationships. Also, it seems increasingly questionable to write about individual behavior in the 1990s and pay virtually no attention to what has been learned about political processes since his first edition appeared more than two decades ago.

Burns's Classification Typology

James MacGregor Burns, a longtime student of the presidency and biographer of FDR and John F. Kennedy, has constructed three models of the presidency based on leadership style: Hamiltonian, Madisonian, and Jeffersonian.[24] In Burns's mind, the Hamiltonian model (named after President Washington's brilliant secretary of the treasury, Alexander Hamilton) emphasizes the use of heroic leadership within the separation of powers system. The activist Hamilton style depends upon a strong leader who relies upon manipulation, expediency, and political pressure to expand executive power.

The less activist Madisonian model, personified by the nation's fourth president, adheres to the Founders' checks and balances conception of government based upon bargaining among minority coalitions and limited presidential power. Burns argues that the Madisonian model leads to frequent deadlock and an inability to govern.[25]

The Jeffersonian model, Burns's preference, is based upon executive team-work and disciplined party organization. Majoritarian leadership in a vigorous two-party system, Burns argues, would generate wide public support and most likely lead to more responsible government.[26]

Hyman's Typology

In the 1950s, author Sidney Hyman developed a typology of leadership that ranged from active to passive extremes. Hyman's classification of presidents was based upon what he called the Buchanan, Lincoln, and Cleveland models.[27] The Buchanan category included not only the last pre–Civil War president but also William McKinley and Calvin Coolidge. These presidents rejected the idea of a president as a strong political leader; instead, they viewed their role as administrative in nature. They did not exert leadership over Congress, and they went to great lengths to avoid crises.

By contrast, the Lincoln-type president, which also included Jefferson, Wilson, and FDR, willingly accepted the challenges facing the country, drafted proposals to meet national crises, and accepted full responsibility for his actions.

Midway between the Buchanan and Lincoln models, Hyman selected President Cleveland as the prototype of the middle-of-the-road chief executive. Primarily administrators, these presidents were prepared to take action, if sufficiently pushed. Generally, however, they shied away from strong executive action. But they were prepared, if necessary, to resort to the veto power.[28]

Another standard classification of presidential leadership that has been around for many years divides chief executive into "Whig" and "Stewardship" models. Developed before the Barber or Burns models arrived on the scene, these leadership models have been described below.

The Whig Model

Depicted as the weak executive or Buchanan-type of presidential leadership, the Whig conception prevailed in the White House throughout the nineteenth century. These presidents all adhered to the strict construction of the Constitution. Indeed, President Buchanan viewed himself merely as executor or administrator of acts of Congress. "My duty," he said, "is to execute the laws . . . and not my individual opinions."[29] He shrank from initiating any positive action, even in the face of threatened Southern secession, and did nothing to prod Congress into national preparedness. In fact, he believed he lacked the legal power to use force against the Southern rebels.

The Whig view of the presidency includes subordination to the Congress and cautious use of those inherent prerogatives of the commander-in-chief and executive power. As one scholar observed: "In the Buchanan concept, the President has not undefined or residual powers of protecting the public welfare or dealing with national emergencies; he is limited to the powers expressly given him in the Constitution."[30] The result of this concept of a weak executive finding shelter in the status quo translated into minimal social change or political innovation—and a president with little influence on Capitol Hill. The Buchanan-type president rejects the idea that the presidency is a political office; instead, it is viewed as the administrative arm of Congress. President Taft spelled out the operative belief of the Whig president:

The true view of the Executive function is . . . that the President can exercise no power which cannot be fairly and reasonably traced to some specific grant of power as proper and necessary to its exercise. Such specific grant must be either in the Federal Constitution or in an act of Congress passed in pursuance thereof. There is no undefined residuum of power which he can exercise because it seems to him to be in the public interest.[31]

Briefly, then, Whig presidents will be reluctant to advocate or enforce policies that enlarge national power or that impinge on state or local authority.

The Stewardship Model

The second category of presidents is the strong executive, such as Lincoln, Jackson, Wilson, the two Roosevelts, Truman, Kennedy, Johnson, and Reagan. Frequently identified as the "Lincoln-type," most of the strong presidents have served in times of crisis—a war or a depression—and so have had the opportunity for the exceptional leadership that marked their administrations. Some have also served during periods of reform, such as the Progressive era and the New Deal. This too accentuated confident leadership. All were liberal in construing the Constitution; none hesitated to fill in the gaps with his own interpretation when the occasion arose. Supporters of the strong executive have often been labeled "presidentialists."

Theodore Roosevelt viewed the president as the "steward of the people." He believed that a president was obliged to act when circumstances demanded it, even if he could not find "some specific authorization to do it." As the Rough Rider president explained:

My belief was that it was not only his right but his duty to do anything that the needs of the Nation demanded unless such action was forbidden by the Constitution or by the laws. Under this interpretation of executive power, I did and caused to be done many things not previously done by the President and the heads of departments. I did not usurp power, but I greatly broadened the use of executive power.[32]

Confident of their leadership ability, the strong executives have been precedent-setters—sometimes stretching their powers to such an extent that the legality of their acts is questioned and even challenged in the courts. As described by one commentator, "the strong president advocates the extension of national authority and is untroubled by the decline of localism. He attempts to bridge the separation of powers, to join the political branches of government, and to direct the legislative process."[33]

The strong president must inspire confidence even in times of adversity, as FDR did during the banking crisis of the Great Depression. His warm voice came over the radio to say: "We have nothing to fear but fear itself," and a nation on the verge of panic moved forward.

Not all presidents, as we explained earlier, conveniently fit entirely in either major category. While the gradations of strength and weakness among presidents could probably be stretched into the two broad classifications outlined above, we have included another category to provide greater clarity.

The Benevolent Protector Model

Chief executives in this third category seek for the most part to remain above politics and to be "president of all the people." Two popular presidents—George Washington and Dwight D. Eisenhower—personify this type of presidential leadership.

Following General Washington's example, the benevolent protector presidents endeavor to rise above political divisions to build a national consensus. Author Sidney Hyman, writing with President Eisenhower in mind, has characterized the benevolent protector model as follows:

All men are by nature good. Government alone corrupts them. Therefore to the extent that governments can be reduced in importance, the natural goodness of men will assert itself in social cooperation voluntarily given. However irreconcilable rival interests may seem to be, once their representative men sit down and talk things over without intervention of government, natural goodness will resolve all difficulties. His own presidential function, then, was to be "the President to all the people."[34]

Both benevolent protector presidents were former generals. Unless either major party decides to turn to the military again for another nominee, it seems unlikely that we will see another president of this category in the foreseeable future.

But we are still left with the question of what type of president will provide the nation with the most effective leadership.

THE SEARCH FOR PRESIDENTIAL GREATNESS

Despite the various styles and models for assessing presidential leadership, national leadership selection since the early days of the Republic has remained essentially a game of chance. Since no foolproof system exists that would guarantee the nation effective leaders, probably the best recommendation that can be made is to review the list of great presidents, the near great, and the failed White House occupants to see if there are some unique qualities among past presidents that we should be looking for before we cast our ballots in future elections.

To simplify our task of evaluating presidents we have used a number of surveys conducted over the past five decades; also, we have borrowed their standard rankings: "great," "near great," "average," "below average," and "failures." Surprisingly, the results of these surveys show remarkably consistent agreement on the ratings of the presidents (see Table 1.2).

By way of background, the first modern survey was conducted by historian Arthur Schlesinger, Sr., in 1948.[35] In this pioneering survey, Schlesinger asked fifty-five eminent historians to rate the nation's chief executives. He repeated the poll in 1962, expanding his survey to a group of some seventy-five authorities, which included historians, political scientists, and journalists.[36] In evaluating the presidents Schlesinger asked the participants to use only one criterion—performance in office.

Eight years later, Gary Maranell and Richard Dodder conducted a far more comprehensive survey, asking over 570 historians to rate our presidents on the basis of (1) accomplishments, (2) strength in influencing government and events, (3) an active or passive approach to their administrations, (4) idealism, and (5) flexibility.[37] A number of other surveys were also conducted over the next dozen years, but the most notable and ambitious undertaking was done in 1982 by historian Robert Murray.[38] In his broad-gauged survey he asked approximately 900 historians to evaluate and rank presidents from Washington through Jimmy Carter. In the two Schlesinger surveys, only five presidents—Lincoln, Washington, Franklin D. Roosevelt, Wilson, and Jefferson—were termed "great." In the subsequent Maranell-Dodder and Murray surveys, as indicated in Table 1.2, the rankings varied only slightly from the earlier surveys.[39] Regretfully, the most recent president—President Bush was not evaluated. Nor were the abbreviated presidencies of William Henry Harrison and James Garfield included.

Because most of the great and near-great presidents served before the era of modern opinion polling, it is impossible to determine accurately if there is a direct correlation between high public approval and presidential "greatness." It is noteworthy, however, that all of the great and all but two of the near-great presidents—John Adams and James K. Polk—served two full terms or moved up from the vice presidency to fill an unexpired term and then won election on their own to a full term. Their electoral success indicates presumably that all enjoyed considerable public approval at least during most of their White House tenure.

If there is a special exception on the list of near-great presidents, it is Harry S. Truman, who left office with a public approval rating hovering around 23 percent—an all-time low. But the plain-spoken man from Independence, Missouri, has continued to grow in public stature each subsequent decade, as more historians and commentators have reassessed his outstanding accomplishments:

Table 1.2
Ratings of Presidential Performance

Schlesinger Poll 1948 N=55	Schlesinger Poll 1962 N=75	Maranell-Dodder Poll 1970 N=570	Murray-Blessing Poll 1983 N=900
Great	**Great**	**Overall Prestige**	**Great**
1) Lincoln	1) Lincoln	1) Lincoln	Lincoln
2) Washington	2) Washington	2) Washington	F. Roosevelt
3) F. Roosevelt	3) F. Roosevelt	3) F. Roosevelt	Washington
4) Wilson	4) Wilson	4) Jefferson	Jefferson
5) Jefferson	5) Jefferson	5) T. Roosevelt	
6) Jackson		6) Wilson	**Near Great**
	Near Great	7) Truman	T. Roosevelt
Near Great	6) Jackson	8) Jackson	Wilson
7) T. Roosevelt	7) T. Roosevelt	9) Kennedy	Jackson
8) Cleveland	8) Polk	10). J. Adams	Truman
9) J. Adams	9) Truman	11) Polk	
10) Polk	10) J. Adams	12) Cleveland	**Above Average**
	11) Cleveland	13) Madison	J. Adams
Average		14) Monroe	L. Johnson
11) J.Q. Adams	**Average**	15) J.Q. Adams	Eisenhower
12) Monroe	12) Madison	16) L. Johnson	Polk
13) Hayes	13) J.Q. Adams	17) Taft	Kennedy
14) Madison	14) Hayes	18) Hoover	Madison
15) Van Buren	15) McKinley	19) Eisenhower	Monroe
16) Taft	16) Taft	20) A. Johnson	J.Q. Adams
17) Arthur	17) Van Buren	21) Van Buren	Cleveland
18) McKinley	18) Monroe	22) McKinley	
19) A. Johnson	19) Hoover	23) Arthur	**Average**
20) Hoover	20) Harrison	24) Hayes	McKinley
21) Harrison	21) Arthur	25) Tyler	Taft
	22) Eisenhower	26) Harrison	Van Buren
Below Average	23) A. Johnson	27) Taylor	Hoover
22) Tyler		28) Coolidge	Hayes
23) Coolidge	**Below Average**	29) Fillmore	Arthur
24) Fillmore	24) Taylor	30) Buchanan	Ford
25) Taylor	25) Tyler	31) Pierce	Carter
26) Buchanan	26) Fillmore	32) Grant	B. Harrison
27) Pierce	27) Coolidge	33) Harding	
	28) Pierce		**Below Average**
Failure	29) Buchanan	* Harrison and Garfield not included due to abbreviated tenure.	Taylor
28) Grant			Reagan
29) Harding	**Failure**		Tyler
	30) Grant		Fillmore
	31) Harding		Coolidge
			Pierce
			Failures
			A. Johnson
			Buchanan
			Nixon
			Grant
			Harding
			Not Rated
			Bush
			W.H. Harrison
			Garfield

Sources: Arthur Schlesinger, Sr., "The U.S. Presidents," *Life* (1 November 1948), 65, LIFE Magazine © 1948 Time Inc. Reprinted with permission; Arthur Schlesinger, Sr., "Our Presidents: A Rating by 75 Historians," *The New York Times Magazine*, 29 July 1962, 12ff. Copyright © 1962 by *The New York Times* Company. Reprinted by permission; Gary Maranell and Richard Dodder, "Political Orientation and Evaluation of Presidential Prestige: A Study of American Historians," *Social Science Quarterly* 51 (September 1970): 41, (Table 1.2, "Ratings of Presidential Performance"). By permission of the author and the University of Texas. Robert Murray and Tim Blessing, "The Presidential Performance Study: A Progress Report," *Journal of American History* 70 (December 1983): 540–541. The rating of President Reagan was obtained in a separate poll conducted in 1989 by the Siena Research Institute, Siena College, Loudonville, New York. Tim H. Blessing, "Updating the Murray-Blessing Survey: The Presidential Performance Study Ranks Reagan," unpublished paper, Pennsylvania State University, 1991, in Harold Stanley and Richard G. Niemi, eds. *Vital Statistics on American Politics*, 3rd ed. (Washington, DC: CQ Press, 1992), 258–259.

leading the Allied nations to final victory in World War II, passage of the highly acclaimed Marshall Plan for post-war European economic reconstruction, the rapid development of the "containment" policy to block Soviet expansionism, especially military aid to Greece and Turkey, as well as the establishment of the North Atlantic Treaty Organization (NATO) and other regional collective security alliances in Asia and the Southwest Pacific. Thus, it seems fair to conclude that there is not always a direct correlation between high public approval and future presidential greatness. Moreover, it would seem prudent to guard against excessive reliance on popularity in determining presidential greatness. For example, when the Gallup Poll asked respondents in 1975 to rate the three presidents that they regarded as the greatest, John F. Kennedy topped the list. Abraham Lincoln was second and Franklin D. Roosevelt, third. Few students of the American presidency would agree with the evaluation of President Kennedy as number one on the list.

THE PERISHABLE NATURE OF PRESIDENTIAL POPULARITY

As noted earlier in the chapter, five of the six most recent presidents have failed to win reelection, or have decided not to seek another term, or have been forced from office by the threat of impending impeachment. Yet, all five of these presidents at some time early in their terms enjoyed high public approval—Bush (89 percent), Johnson (79 percent), Carter (75 percent), Ford (71 percent), and Nixon (67 percent). But high presidential approval and presidential power cannot be stockpiled or deposited in the bank like money. These assets must be constantly replenished. In a real sense, Presidents Johnson, Ford, Carter, and Bush were all victims of the presidential expectations syndrome.

Since presidential power and high public approval ratings are, in effect, two sides of the same coin, their market value can be expected to fluctuate throughout the presidential terms, as unanticipated international crises or compelling domestic issues impact heavily on the American public. But because of the mismatch between public expectations and the institutional constraints affecting all presidents, most White House occupants have been unable to maintain public support at a sufficient level to ensure political effectiveness. Only those presidents who can respond, or seem to respond, effectively to these crisis-laden domestic and international challenges throughout their tenure will be accorded a mark of greatness—or near greatness.

Looking to the future, the built-in constraints of the American constitutional system will probably prevent most presidents—unless a national emergency exists—from measuring up to most of the high expectations the American public holds of its chief executives.

In the chapters that follow we will examine the presidency from a variety of perspectives: nominating and electing presidents; the president as party leader;

the public presidency; the rise of the "presidential branch"; the president as chief administrator; the president's relationship with Congress; the president as commander in chief and chief diplomat; presidential interaction with the judicial branch; president's newer role as overseer of the economy; and the president's relationship with the vice president. We will also analyze a number of proposed reforms to improve the presidency and evaluate their viability.

NOTES

1. Godfrey Hodgson, *All Things to All Men* (New York: Simon & Schuster, 1980), 238–239.

2. Richard Neustadt, *Presidential Power* (New York: Wiley, 1980), 196.

3. Louis Brownlow, "What We Expect the President to Do," excerpted from his *The President and the Presidency* (Chicago: University of Chicago Press, 1949), 52–56, 62–76, reprinted in Aaron Wildavsky, ed., *The Presidency* (Boston: Little, Brown, 1969), 35.

4. Thomas E. Cronin, *The State of the Presidency*, 2nd ed. (Boston: Little, Brown, 1980), 2.

5. Hodgson, *All Things to All Men*, 239.

6. Robert Shogan, *None of the Above* (New York: New American Library, 1982), 13.

7. As cited in Ben W. Heineman, Jr., and Curtiss A. Hessler, *Memorandum for the President* (New York: Random House, 1980), 9.

8. Michael G. Krukones, "The Campaign Promises of Jimmy Carter: Accomplishments and Failures," *Presidential Studies Quarterly,* Vol. 15 (Winter 1985), 143; for further discussion see Jeff Fishel, *Presidents and Promises* (Washington, DC: CQ Press, 1985), 57–120.

9. Fishel, *Presidents and Promises*, 170.

10. Ibid., 173.

11. R. W. Apple, Jr., *The New York Times*, 19 November 1993.

12. George C. Edwards III, *The Public Presidency* (New York: St. Martin's, 1983), 187.

13. Louis W. Koenig, "Reassessing the Imperial Presidency," in Richard M. Pious, *The Power to Govern: Assessing Reform in the United States* (New York: The Academy of Political Science, 1981), Vol. 34, 31-34, reprinted in David C. Kozak and Kenneth N. Ciboski, eds., *The American Presidency: A Policy Perspective from Readings and Documents* (Chicago: Nelson-Hall, 1985), 576.

14. Austin Ranney, *Channels of Power* (Washington, DC: American Enterprise Institute, 1984), 74.

15. Ibid., 147–148.

16. James David Barber, *The Presidential Character*, 2nd ed. (Englewood Cliffs, NJ: Prentice-Hall, 1977).

17. Ibid., 12.

18. Ibid.

19. Ibid., 13.

20. Ibid.

21. Ibid., 20.

22. Alexander George, "Assessing Presidential Character," in Aaron Wildavsky, ed., *Perspectives on the Presidency* (Boston: Little, Brown, 1975), 110–111.

23. George C. Edwards III and Stephen J. Wayne, *Presidential Leadership*, 2nd ed., (New York: St. Martin's Press, 1990), 230.

24. James MacGregor Burns, *Presidential Government: The Crucible of Leadership* (Boston: Houghton Mifflin, 1966), 28–31.

25. Ibid.

26. Sidney Hyman, "What Is the President's True Role?" *The New York Times Magazine*, vol. 17, 7 September 1958, 108–109.

27. Ibid.

28. Wilfred E. Binkley, *President and Congress,* 3rd ed. (New York: Vintage, 1962), 142.

29. Ibid., 151.

30. William Howard Taft, *Our Chief Magistrate and his Powers* (New York: Columbia University Press, 1916), 139.

31. Theodore Roosevelt, *An Autobiography* (New York: Scribner's, 1924), 357.

32. "Introduction," in Robert R. Hirschfield, ed., *The Power of the Presidency* (New York: Aldine, 1982), 10.

33. Hyman, 108–109.

34. Arthur Schlesinger, Sr., "The U.S. Presidents," *Life*, 1 November 1948, 65.

35. Arthur Schlesinger, Sr., "Our Presidents: A Rating by 75 Historians," *New York Times Magazine*, 29 July 1962, 12ff.

36. Gary Maranell and Richard Dodder, "Political Orientation and Evaluation of Presidential Prestige: A Study of American Historians," *Social Science Quarterly* 51 (September 1970): 418.

37. Robert Murray and Tim Blessing, "The Presidential Performance Study: A Progress Report," *Journal of American History* 70 (December 1983): 540–541.

38. For an excellent discussion of these four surveys (as well as several others not covered in this chapter) and what they tell us about presidents and the presidency, see an original essay by Arthur B. Murphy, "Evaluating the Presidents of the United States," in David C. Kozak and Kenneth N. Ciboski, eds., *The American Presidency*, 437–448.

39. *The Gallup Opinion Index*, February 1976, 14–15.

CHAPTER 2

THE PRESIDENCY FROM WASHINGTON TO CLINTON

Since World War II, the president of the United States has become the most powerful leader in the free world. His military powers are so vast that they rival those of any modern dictator. Indeed, with the single push of a button, the modern American president could launch an intercontinental missile attack that would, in all probability, lead to a world holocaust. Contrast the magnitude of power exercised by the modern president with the limited authority wielded by the nation's first president, George Washington, in the newly established republic of three million people.

How the presidency of this infant American republic evolved over two centuries into an office of awesome power will be the main theme of this chapter. Our survey will also reveal that, for long periods in the nineteenth century, Congress clearly overshadowed a series of weak presidents. We will examine several factors that account for the rise of the modern presidency in the twentieth century, as well as the impact of two world wars and the development of nuclear weaponry on the nation's highest office. We will look closely at the "heroic" presidency of the 1950s and early 1960s and the growth of the "imperial presidency" in the Johnson-Nixon years. Also, we will assess the congressional reaction to an overreaching presidency and the Watergate investigation that led to the post-imperial presidency—some called it the "imperiled presidency." In a final section we will examine the resurgence of presidential power under Ronald Reagan, George Bush, and Bill Clinton, reconfiguring a thesis developed early in the chapter—that the presidency is a composite of the office, the occupant, and the dimensions of executive power that he exercises at any given time in our history.

ABSENCE OF EXECUTIVE LEADERSHIP: BEFORE 1787

The evolution of the American presidency began during the 1780s as the thirteen former colonies floundered in economic stagnation and interstate rivalries under the Articles of Confederation. Within the states, the former colonists insisted that power be centered in the legislature. In most states the American governor, or the president as he was called in several states, became a figurehead. His term was for one year, except in South Carolina (where it was two) and in Delaware (where it was three).[1]

Only in New York could the governor be termed a strong executive. Significantly, the New York governorship served as the chief model used by the Founding Fathers in outlining many of the powers and functions assigned to the future president of the United States.[2]

The Articles of Confederation had no chief executive. All decision making was handled by a five-member Confederation committee of representatives. Routine decisions on foreign policy, the levying of assessments against each of the thirteen states (since the Confederation had no power to tax), and the maintenance of the small armed force and navy were left to the committee.[3] But since any major decision required the agreement of nine out of thirteen states, decision making by the committee was, more often than not, hamstrung or postponed. The simmering feuds between states over the imposition of tariffs, the nearly worthless currency, and the threat to private property posed by the Shays' Rebellion (1786–1787) in western Massachusetts all generated concern over the viability of the newly established Confederation. To the more thoughtful state leaders, the weakest link in the confederation was the absence of an independent executive. State leaders were increasingly concerned about the inability of the Confederation to carry out the governmental responsibilities of the young nation. The general impotence of the Confederation government, the badly battered economy, and the threat of possible foreign intervention all pointed toward the compelling need for strong leadership within the young nation. It was this chaotic state of affairs that faced the Philadelphia convention when the Founding Fathers met in the late spring of 1787.

ESTABLISHING A CHIEF EXECUTIVE

Deploring the absence of leadership within the Articles of Confederation, several members of the convention expressed considerable misgivings about the excesses of the state legislatures during the American Revolution and afterward. Drawing from his observations of state legislatures during the period, James Madison stated: "Experience had proved a tendency in our government to throw all power into the legislative vortex. The executives of the states are in general little more than Cyphers."[4] Madison, who had been won over by the "presidentialists" during the course of the convention, viewed an independent executive as an essential counterpoise to an all-powerful legislature.

Most of the delegates to the Philadelphia convention, however, were "congressionalists," suspicious of executive power—a carryover from the days of the hated colonial governors. But several convention leaders—Gouverneur Morris, James Wilson, George Washington, and Alexander Hamilton—favored a strong and forceful executive. The ability of this minority of "presidentialists" to outmaneuver the dominant "congressionalist" majority and establish a greatly strengthened executive was undoubtedly the paramount achievement of the convention. But this goal was not easily reached. No problem was thornier or consumed more drafting time than the office of president.

The men of 1787 had several alternatives. One choice was to create a Council of States as a plural executive to run the new government. Historian Forrest McDonald tells us that one-fourth of the delegates to the Constitutional Convention favored a plural executive.[5] This type of weak executive would have assured a system of legislative supremacy. Another choice was to establish a president to be chosen by Congress. Indeed, throughout most of the convention proceedings legislative selection of the president seemed to be the preferred choice of many delegates, until the Committee on Unfinished Business addressed the still unresolved question of presidential selection. A third choice was to establish a strong executive with independent grants of power who might assume the functions, if not the form, of the British Crown. At least four major proposals for president were introduced at the constitutional convention, and "no fewer than eight methods for choosing a president were first and last suggested in the Convention."[6] (See Appendix 1 at the end of this chapter.)

One of the major contributions of the constitutional craftsmen at Philadelphia was the blending of two fundamental structural concepts: separation of powers and checks and balances. By establishing the president as an independent executive, the Framers prevented the president from being a mere tool of the legislative branch. Yet the Framers, with their fear of executive tyranny, imposed checks on the president to prevent him from overwhelming the legislative branch.

Although the presidency has become the keystone of the American governmental system, a careful reading of the Constitution would not reveal this central fact. The Founding Fathers, most historians agree, went to considerable lengths to avoid delineating the specific powers and duties of the president in order to calm the widespread fear of monarchy. They seemed to want a president of somewhat limited powers. They wanted a chief executive who would remain above parties and factions, enforce the laws Congress passed, negotiate with foreign governments, and help the states in times of civil disorder.

In a sense, the Framers sought to have it both ways: to create a president strong enough to match Congress, but not so powerful as to overshadow Congress. Gouverneur Morris put the problem this way: "Make him too weak;

the Legislature will usurp his power; make him too strong; he will usurp on the Legislature."[7] In the final draft, the Framers empowered the president to make treaties, provided two-thirds of the Senate concurred, and to nominate, with the advice and consent of the Senate, ambassadors, other public ministers and consuls, and justices of the Supreme Court. The president's term was set at four years with no limits on reelection. He was given the veto power, but Congress could override his veto by a two-thirds majority in both houses. The president was also made commander in chief of the armed forces.

It seems doubtful, however, if the Framers fully perceived in their deliberations in Philadelphia how much authority they had actually granted to the new chief executive. Article II contains only a hint of the potential power of this office. Does this cryptic statement merely serve as an introduction to the executive branch article, or does it confer a broad grant of inherent power to act in any way the president deems appropriate to protect the public interest? For two hundred years, this constitutional ambiguity has allowed presidents wide latitude in defining their executive duties. If they prefer, they can remain largely a ceremonial caretaker of the federal government, performing minimal duties and allowing Congress to determine the national agenda. But if they choose a bold course, they can grasp the reins of leadership, chart a course of action to lead the country out of a severe depression, ward off a totalitarian threat from abroad, or establish a new set of national priorities to deal with pressing domestic problems.

The constitutional flexibility of the office, in the words of one commentator, "has made the Presidency both the most dynamic and most dangerous of our political institutions."[8] Still, the record of the past two centuries shows that in no other nation has so much power been invested in one individual, nor have the constitutional restraints imposed on this office worked so effectively as in the United States.

A UNIQUE OFFICE

If two factors stand out above all others in the study of the presidency, they are that the presidency is a composite of the office and the incumbent, and that the "dimensions of the executive power at any given moment are largely consequences of the incumbents character and energy."[9] As a result, history shows that the development of the presidency is a discontinuous one, marked by periods of expansion, stasis, and contraction of executive power. All presidents, it should be emphasized, enter office with the same constitutional grants of authority, but the similarity usually ends there. Some presidents have employed the war power and the role of commander in chief to expand executive power. Others have used the "take care that laws be faithfully executed" clause to broaden the concept of executive authority. Still others have relied heavily on the position of party leader to exert strong executive leadership.

At the other end of the leadership continuum, a majority of presidents has taken a relatively passive view of executive power, satisfied to carry out the purely administrative and ceremonial duties of the office. Edward S. Corwin, for example, estimated in the 1950s that only one out of three chief executives contributed to the development of presidential power.[10]

How different the nation's history might have been if, say, the first president had been Martin Van Buren rather than George Washington, or if Andrew Johnson had been president when the first shots were fired at Fort Sumter in 1861. How different the history of the country would have been if Warren G. Harding had moved into the White House on March 4, 1933, instead of Franklin D. Roosevelt.

EARLY PRESIDENTS

Historically, Washington's conception of the presidency could be best described as a benevolent protector or a quasi-monarchical leader. Some Federalists viewed the president as an elected king without the trappings of monarchy. Washington's successor, John Adams, also adhered to a quasi-monarchical conception of the presidency. But "the Revolution of 1800," which swept Thomas Jefferson into the White House on a democratic tide, rapidly submerged this view of the presidency.

A strong president, Jefferson derived his power chiefly from his role as party leader and only secondarily as chief executive.[11] Through his control of the party caucus, Jefferson compiled a formidable legislative record. But his successors, James Madison and James Monroe, were both selected by the congressional caucus—a plan that had, in effect, been rejected by the Framers. The sixth president, John Quincy Adams, though not nominated by a congressional caucus, was nonetheless selected by Congress, since the election was thrown into the House of Representatives when no candidate received a majority of electoral votes in 1824.

The Jacksonian Legacy

Jackson's accession to the presidency four years later, however, checked any further enfeebling of the chief executive. As Edward S. Corwin interpreted the shift, "Jackson's presidency was, in truth, no mere revival of the office; it was a remaking of it."[12]

As a surrogate of the people, Jackson was clearly a stronger national leader than Jefferson. Beyond question, the tough-minded general-turned-president fundamentally altered the relationship between the executive and legislative branches.[13] In brandishing his veto of the Second United States Bank, for reasons other than constitutional, Jackson "notified Congress that they must consider his views on all bills *before* passing them or run the risk of veto."[14] In other words, Jackson was claiming in unmistakable terms the right to participate fully in the legislative process. Heretofore, the first six presidents (who had vetoed a total of nine bills) cited only constitutional grounds for their vetoes. Until Jackson's presidency a bill's unconstitutionality was presumed to be the sole ground upon which a president could reject legislation. But Old Hickory tossed this view aside. Instead, Jackson made the point of assuming a share of legislative power. In the process, President Jackson "was becoming the first among equals, not simply an equal partner with the other two branches."[15] Furthermore, Jackson's assertion of executive power in removing a cabinet member (for refusing to transfer deposits from the Second National Bank), without notifying Congress or asking the lawmakers' approval, added another dimension of executive power to the presidential office.

The predominant view of the Founding Fathers was that the legislative branch was the centerpiece of the government, the branch closest to the people and the most representative of their will. But Jackson disagreed. Not only did Jackson claim to serve as chief of state, but he soon declared that he, as president, represented all the people.[16] When the U.S. Senate censured him for removing deposits from the National Bank, Jackson responded in a "Protest" message, reminding the lawmakers that the "president is the direct representative of the American people." Not only was the president "elected by the people, but Jackson said he is responsible to them."[17] It may therefore be not surprising that the threat of a plebiscitarian president that sometimes lurks in the shadows along the Potomac can be traced rather directly to the doorsteps of Andrew Jackson. No wonder the historian Robert V. Remini recently observed: "The so-called 'Imperial Presidency' begins with him."[18]

Though Jackson's critics could do little to thwart his exercise of power while he remained in office, once he retired they mounted an all-out attack on executive autocracy. "The President," thundered Daniel Webster, "carries on the government; all the rest are subcontractors." Another of Jackson's opponents, Henry Clay, declared that the country was in the midst of a revolution "hitherto bloodless, but tending rapidly towards a total change of the pure republican character of the Government, and to the concentration of all power in the hands of one man."[19]

Presidential Decline

Even more responsible than these anti-Jackson critics for curbing executive power was the rise of the slavery question in the 1840s—an issue that seemed to call more for legislative compromise than executive direction. Moreover, the leaders of the two major parties—Democrats and Whigs (Democrats and Republicans after 1856)—selected a series of undistinguished nominees who could easily be dominated by Congress. The historic "two-thirds" rule in the Democratic party, which required that a nominee receive a two-thirds majority vote of the convention delegates, helped ensure the nomination of pliable presidential candidates.

The rise of the committee system in Congress also weakened the president's influence within the legislative branch. Except for the shrewd James K. Polk (1845–1849), the decline of the presidency continued without interruption until the election of the first Republican president, Abraham Lincoln, in 1860. But in the first eleven weeks after the fall of Fort Sumter, Lincoln pushed the inherent powers of the presidency to their constitutional limits and beyond.

Lincoln's Constitutional Dictatorship

To meet the challenge of secession, Lincoln called up and amalgamated the state militias into a ninety-day volunteer force, called 40,000 volunteers for three years of service, added 23,000 men to the regular army and 18,000 to the navy, purchased the needed supplies, and paid out $2 million from unappropriated funds in the Treasury to persons not authorized to receive it, without even bothering to convene Congress for authorization until midsummer.[20] Throughout this critical eleven-week period, Lincoln alone constituted the government of the United States. No president before or since has ever stretched the authority of the office to the degree that the Civil War president did during the country's darkest hours. Called a dictator by his critics, Lincoln nevertheless became the greatest defender of the Constitution in the nation's history. Lincoln set precedents for presidential power that all modern presidents turn to in times of emergency. Indeed, his legacy endowed the presidency with sufficient authority and power to meet any future challenge to national survival.

After Lincoln's "constitutional dictatorship," the presidency quickly contracted. Lincoln's successor, Andrew Johnson, came to the presidency destined to confront a Congress angered by the excesses of the Lincoln administration and determined to reassert its dominance. Radical Republican hostility to Johnson's moderate, pro-Lincoln Reconstruction policies toward the South eventually led to his impeachment trial. Though Johnson escaped impeachment by a single vote, the entire proceeding signaled the beginning of an era of congressional dominance of the United States government that would not be seriously challenged until the turn of the century.

THE ERA OF "POSTAGE STAMP" PRESIDENTS

After the Civil War, congressional aggressiveness seemingly placed the presidency in permanent eclipse. Three major reasons can be put forth to explain congressional dominance of the executive branch during this period. Congress, from the passage of the Tenure of Office Act (1867), which preceded the Johnson impeachment trial, through the next thirty years regularly challenged the chief executive over appointment and control of personnel in the executive branch. Congress insisted upon the advice and consent of the Senate in the selection of high officials as well as subordinates. Controllers and auditors in the Treasury, as well as coiners and even melters in local mints, were subject to Senate confirmation.[21]

A second major reason for congressional dominance during this period was its control of the purse and its careful specificity in legislation. Congress forbade the transfer of funds from one year to another. One observer of the period notes: "On the major legislation of the era—reconstruction, currency, tariffs, veterans' affairs, interstate commerce—Congress left a heavy imprint."[22] Congress intruded into day-to-day operations by attaching substantive legislation to appropriations bills which the president dared not veto.

Another major factor explaining congressional dominance during this era was the absence of emergencies and crises requiring presidential action. Depressions, urban and rural poverty, and the strikes and riots of the period were viewed as within the jurisdiction of state and local governments. Congress and the courts had excluded the national government from oversight of the industrial giants.

As a matter of fact, attempts were made during the post–Civil War period to cripple the presidency permanently. Horace Greeley championed a constitutional amendment to restrict presidents to one term in office. The Pendleton Committee proposed that cabinet members be authorized to sit in the House and Senate and be required to attend sessions twice a week for the purpose of supplying information. Had these proposals been successful, Congress would have upset the balance of power in the federal government and, as political scientist Leonard White concluded, "would have weakened the President's effective participation in departmental business by increasing the authority of Congress and its committees."[23]

In light of presidential domination of the American government during most of the twentieth century, it is difficult to envisage a period when the president of the United States played second fiddle to the legislative branch. But in post-Civil War America, Congress clearly set the national agenda. The office of the president, as one eminent historian has put it,

remained small in scale and limited in power, caught up more in the vicissitudes of party politics and patronage than in the formulation and conduct of public policy. Late nineteenth century Presidents had little to say over the estimates, appropriations, expenditures, and policies of government bureaus and departments. These agencies were much more responsive to the House Appropriations Committee and other organs of Congress than to the White House.[24]

Let's take a moment to look more closely at the post–Civil War presidency. Despite being overshadowed by Congress, late nineteenth-century presidents had one of the better jobs available in the country. The hours were good, and the salary was not too bad ($50,000 annually in an era of low inflation and before the federal income tax). Nor were the demands of the job oppressive.

With an annual national budget of approximately $400 million (not billion), the president had no trouble balancing the books. Indeed, throughout the period 1866 to 1893, the protective tariff provided a surplus every year. During the 1880s, for example, the annual surplus was $100 million.[25] Unlike the $270 billion military budgets of the present era, the post–Civil War budgets for the army and navy seldom exceeded $100 million. Just prior to the outbreak of the Spanish-American War, the standing army consisted of less than 29,000 officers and men.[26]

Foreign affairs were left to the secretary of state to manage, with only an occasional consultation with the president. Other members of the cabinet conducted their business routinely, with no huge White House staff looking over their shoulder, second-guessing their every move or preempting any newsworthy action reflecting favorably upon the president. Generally, the president spent most of the year right in the nation's capital, with an occasional train trip for a speech in Boston, New York, or a major Midwestern city. Foreign junkets were unheard of. If one were to select the standard model of the "postage stamp" or figurehead presidency, it would be Benjamin Harrison, whose single term (1889–1893) has all but been forgotten, even by most historians.

Toward the end of the century, however, the first signs of a more dynamic and assertive presidential style appeared during Grover Cleveland's first administration. His major weapon for displaying his independence from Congress was the veto. During his first term (1885–1889), he brandished his veto pen three times more frequently than all his predecessors combined. But this "government by veto" was essentially negative in nature and did not reflect broad policy initiatives from the White House.

Two Supreme Court decisions in the 1890s, however, significantly enhanced presidential power. In the case of *In re Neagle*,[27] the Supreme Court set forth a doctrine of inherent presidential power to defend the "peace of the United States."

The president's duty to see that the laws are faithfully executed, the Court said, is not "limited to the enforcement of acts of Congress . . . according to their *express terms*," but includes also "the rights, duties, and obligations growing out of the Constitution itself, our international relations, and all the protection implied by the nature of the government under the Constitution."[28]

Five years later, the Supreme Court upheld presidential intervention and the use of federal troops in a labor dispute case *In re Debs*.[29] In 1894, a strike by the railwaymen's union against the Pullman Company spread to trains using Pullman equipment, causing almost a complete stoppage on the railroads operating out of Chicago. President Grover Cleveland ordered federal troops into Chicago to restore order and get the trains running again. Eugene V. Debs and the other union officials were arrested for contempt of court in disobeying the injunction; they all received sentences of from three to six months. Debs's attorneys appealed for a writ of habeas corpus, but the Supreme court rejected the request, upholding the presidential action in a unanimous opinion.

THE PRESIDENCY COMES OF AGE: TR TO FDR

Several factors account for the rise of the modern presidency and the establishment of a new congressional-presidential relationship in the twentieth century: (1) growing federal regulation of the modern industrial state; (2) the emergence of the United States as a world power; (3) the concentration of authority in the executive branch during World War I; (4) the establishment of an executive-controlled budget in 1921; and (5) White House occupancy by two dynamic chief executives—Theodore Roosevelt and Woodrow Wilson.

Before 1885, few statutes had been passed to protect the public from the giant economic combinations that increasingly dominated national life. After the passage of the Interstate Commerce Act in 1887 and the Sherman Anti-Trust Act of 1890, however, no fewer than thirty-seven laws were enacted to give the national government regulatory power, albeit limited, over industry.[30]

Another major factor altering presidential and congressional relationships and adding to the power of the presidency was the emergence of the United States as a world power. Presidential responsibilities in the field of foreign affairs took a quantum leap at the turn of the twentieth century. By the end of the Spanish-American War (1898), the United States had suddenly become a world—and imperial—power. Though the country had always espoused a staunch anti-imperial bias, the acquisition of the Philippines and Puerto Rico and the establishment of an American protectorate over Cuba marked the beginning of a new era in American history.

From 1900 to the outbreak of World War I, Congress generally chose to watch quietly as United States military forces were used for numerous "expeditions" and "interventions" in such places as China, Haiti, Cuba, Nicaragua, Mexico, Honduras, and Panama. "Dollar Diplomacy" in the Caribbean and Central America was the centerpiece of American foreign policy. Public opinion seemed to favor military activity and Congress did not choose to intrude into this area of executive prerogative. At the turn of the century, for example, President McKinley sent American troops to China during the Boxer Rebellion, without congressional approval. In another instance, when Congress balked at an executive spending, Commander in Chief Theodore Roosevelt sent the fleet halfway around the world and left it up to Congress to buy enough coal to bring the ships back home. In the role of international statesman, President Roosevelt persuaded Russia and Japan, locked in a costly war in the Far East, to come to the peace table in the United States. The Treaty of Portsmouth (New Hampshire) was one of his proudest accomplishments. Both at home and abroad, according to one team of scholars, "Roosevelt extended executive authority to the further-est limit permitted in peacetime by the Constitution—if not further."[31]

In 1916, President Wilson did not hesitate to send American troops deep into Mexico without congressional approval in a vain attempt to capture Pancho (Francisco) Villa, a Mexican insurgent leader who had attacked several border towns in New Mexico. Two years earlier, American troops had temporarily occupied Vera Cruz, Mexico. Wilson's eminent biographer, Arthur S. Link, observed that the scholarly president intervened elsewhere in Latin America "on a scale that had never before been contemplated."[32]

World War I added greatly to the president's authority. Woodrow Wilson resorted to powers that had not been exercised since the Civil War—and to other powers that had never been exercised. Congress delegated to the president the authority to take over and operate the railroads, regulate and prohibit exports, commandeer factories, withhold fuel, and fix transportation priorities. Unlike Lincoln, Wilson sought and received from Congress express legislative authority for almost every unusual step he undertook. "The source of Lincoln's power was the Constitution, and he operated in spite of Congress," writes one presidential authority, "[while] the source of Wilson's power . . . was a batch of statutes, and he cooperated with Congress."[33] Even so, Wilson relied on his authority as commander in chief to create such agencies as the War Industries Board, the Committee on Public Information, and the War Labor Board. International events of the twentieth century and the enormous military strength of the United States, especially since World War II, have added greatly to the powers exercised by modern presidents.

Revised public expectations of the need for an expanded presidential role in directing the nation's domestic affairs and institutional changes within the federal government itself also help account for the president's emerging as the chief architect of public policy. Theodore Roosevelt is remembered as the first great reformer of the modern industrial era. He revealed in his autobiography that in the anthracite coal strike of 1902 he had planned to use army troops to run the mines if a settlement had not occurred. Taft, while less flamboyant than Roosevelt, was no less vigorous in his campaign against the giant industrial trusts and proposed the Sixteenth Amendment, which made a graduated income tax possible in 1913. This amendment opened a huge reservoir of funds for the federal government, which could be employed by future presidents to underwrite social and economic programs for the benefit of the entire nation.

President Theodore Roosevelt also ushered in the "rhetorical presidency," that is, the use of public speeches and White House press conferences—the "bully pulpit," Teddy's colorful phrase—as a principal technique of presidential leadership.[34] (This topic is discussed in detail in Chapter 6.)

The inability of Congress, through its numerous appropriations and revenue committees, to coordinate a comprehensive budget led eventually to an executive-controlled budget. President Taft's Commission on Economy and Efficiency first suggested a national budget system in 1912. Seven years later, a select committee of the House of Representatives proposed a national budget under presidential control, vested in a bureau of the Treasury. Finally, in 1921 the passage of the Budget and Accounting Act eliminated the freedom the departments had enjoyed to submit requests for money directly to Congress. Henceforth, budget requests would come from the president. The major impact of this centralization of budget making was to strengthen the president's hand in dealing with Congress and with the departments, agencies, and bureaus under his jurisdiction. By the New Deal era, the president's budget message had become a basis for presidential leadership. The institutionalized presidency was coming of age.

Woodrow Wilson firmly believed that the president's constitutional duty "to give the Congress information on the State of the Union and recommend to their consideration such measures as he shall judge necessary and expedient" could be used as a source of power. Unlike all presidents since Washington, Wilson delivered his State of the Union address in person, rather than merely dispatching it to Congress in written form. Wilson often went to Congress personally to deliver special messages.

For a twelve-year interim (1921–1933), Presidents Harding, Coolidge, and Hoover served in the White House with a general pledge not to be executive autocrats in their dealings with Congress. Herbert Hoover summed up his own belief and those of his two immediate predecessors about the misfortune of aggressive executive leadership by declaring: "The militant safeguard to liberty [is] . . . legislative independence. . . . The weakening of the legislative arm leads to encroachment by the executive upon individual liberty."[35] Faced with economic collapse during Hoover's administration, the nation demanded a president who would not be timid in leading Congress and the nation. The leader that the voters turned to in November 1932 was Governor Franklin Delano Roosevelt of New York.

WHITE HOUSE LEADERSHIP MODELS

Some presidential scholars mark the beginning of the modern presidency with Franklin D. Roosevelt, who will be found on all historians' lists of great presidents.[36] But few historians would deny that FDR constructed the modern presidency on building blocks first laid in place by Presidents Theodore Roosevelt and Woodrow Wilson.

The New Deal: The White House Takes Over

When Franklin D. Roosevelt won the election in 1932, the nation was in such desperate straits that the day after the president's inauguration Will Rogers, the renowned humorist, observed: "The whole country is with him just so he does something. If he burned down the Capitol, we would cheer and say, 'Well, we at least got a fire started.' "[37] The massiveness of the economic collapse of the

1930s can hardly be exaggerated. With a population only half the size of the nation in the 1980s, between 12 and 15 million persons were unemployed; 25 percent of the blue-collar workers were out on the streets competing for jobs that did not exist; one family out of seven was receiving public relief; 4,600 banks throughout the nation had shut their doors; automobile plants in Michigan and textile factories in New England were closed; farmers let crops rot in the fields because it cost more to harvest them than they could be sold for at the market. The economic chaos of the Great Depression and the desperate mood of the nation demanded action and vigorous leadership. Both were not long in coming under Roosevelt's administration.

On March 4, 1933, Roosevelt laid the challenge facing the nation before Congress in his inaugural address:

It is to be hoped that the normal balance of executive and legislative authority may be wholly adequate to meet the unprecedented task before us. . . . I am prepared under my constitutional duty to recommend the measures that a stricken nation in the midst of a stricken world may require. . . . But in the event that the Congress shall fail to take these courses and in the event that the national emergency is still critical I shall not evade the clear course of duty that will then confront me. I shall ask Congress for the one remaining instrument to meet the crisis— broad executive power to wage a war against the emergency as great as the power that would be given to me if we were invaded by a foreign foe.[38]

The president moved with breathtaking swiftness to deal with the crisis by calling for a special session of Congress to convene five days after his inaugural address. Then followed the famous "Hundred Days" during which more legislation was passed by Congress than at any other time in the history of the Republic.

Throughout the 1930s Roosevelt refined leadership techniques which had been employed less effectively by his predecessors. The first was the presidential message. His cousin, Theodore, had indicated to a critic the inadvisability of proposing details of a bill when a message was sent to Congress. Franklin Roosevelt, however, not only sent a flurry of messages to Congress, but also sent along carefully drafted bills (SEC, AAA, Social Security) to accomplish the purpose of the message. From 1933 to 1938, he sent over 120 special messages to Congress.

A second device employed by FDR to control legislation was the veto. At the close of his second term in early 1941, FDR had vetoed 505 measures—over 30 percent of all measures disapproved by presidents since 1792. That the veto is an effective device in the legislative process can be seen by the fact that from 1792 to 1941, only 49 of 1,645 vetoes were overridden by Congress. (Presidential vetoes are discussed further in Chapter 12.)

A third device of which Roosevelt made extensive use was patronage. Not since Woodrow Wilson, twelve years before, had a Democrat occupied the White House. In addition to the federal marshals, judges, postmasters, and high-level cabinet posts that were normally available, President Roosevelt was also able to appoint thousands to new offices in the relief and recovery agencies—all outside the merit system.

Mr. Roosevelt was the first president to master the techniques of modern communication. He talked directly with the people via radio. One observer notes: "In his fireside chats, he talked as a father discussing public affairs with his family in the living room."[39] FDR had occasional setbacks, such as when he tried to pack the Supreme Court in 1937; yet he knew how to rally people behind his leadership.

To mount his New Deal programs, Roosevelt had obtained authority from Congress by specific statutes. But the growing defense buildup after the fall of France in 1940 changed Roosevelt's approach to presidential power. To marshal the manpower and weapons needed to defeat Hitler, Mussolini, and the Japanese militarists, Roosevelt turned instead to his war-making and commander-in-chief authority—based upon sweeping emergency authority granted him by Congress—to mobilize a huge military machine of twelve million men and women, the total industrial plant capacity of the nation, and almost the entire civilian work force.

As Arthur M. Schlesinger, Jr., has commented:

War again nourished the Presidency. The towering figure of Franklin D. Roosevelt, the generally accepted wisdom of his initiatives of 1940 and 1941, his undisputed authority as Commander-in-Chief after Pearl Harbor, the thundering international pronouncements emanating from wartime summits of the Big Two or the Big Three—all these gave Americans in the postwar years an exalted conception of presidential power.[40]

THE HEROIC PRESIDENCY

After World War II, the United States, the first country to develop the atomic bomb, emerged as the most powerful nation in the world. Other nations, especially Britain and France, which had been bled white by two world wars in a generation, turned to the United States for international leadership. President Truman responded to the challenge by obtaining passage of the Marshall Plan to fund the huge reconstruction task in Western Europe. Meanwhile, the United States, under strong presidential leadership, became a powerful member of the United Nations and by the mid-fifties had pledged this nation in treaties to defend militarily forty-three nations around the world. With the onset of the Cold War between the United States and the Soviet Union shortly after the end of World War II, the president became, in one commentator's words, the "permanent commander-in-chief of the free world's militia."[41] With the final authority over control of the nation's huge arsenal of nuclear weapons, the president of the United States had at his fingertips the sole power to destroy in a matter of minutes entire cities and millions of lives behind the Iron Curtain.

The first two decades after World War II have been depicted by some writers as the era of the "heroic presidency," which might be described as an updated version of the stewardship concept. The heroic models—Washington, Jackson, Lincoln, Wilson, both Theodore and Franklin Roosevelt, and Truman—all boldly used the powers of the presidential office to meet the challenges and crises of their times. During the 1950s and 1960s, leading writers on the presidency extolled the dominant role of the American chief executive. The late Clinton Rossiter, for example, lauded the American presidency as "one of the truly successful institutions created by men in their endless quest for the blessings of free government."[42]

Adherents of the heroic presidency insisted that a strong president was needed to overcome Congress's innate conservatism and inability to respond to sudden crisis. The widespread use of executive authority has often been justified by defenders of the heroic presidency on the basis that the president more directly "represents" all the people, since members of Congress must be more responsive to the parochial interests of their districts and states.

Beyond doubt, the Cold War reinforced the growth and superordinate status of the presidency. Arthur M. Schlesinger, Jr., later to become the foremost critic of the "imperial presidency," conceded at the time that

the uncertainty and danger of the early Cold War, with the chronic threat of unanticipated emergency always held to require immediate response, with, above all, the overhanging possibility of nuclear catastrophe, seemed to argue all the more strongly for the centralization of control over foreign policy, including the use of armed forces, in the presidency.[43]

When North Korea invaded South Korea in 1950, Truman immediately used his powers as commander-in-chief and ordered U.S. armed forces to come to the aid of the South Koreans. His successor, President Eisenhower, relied more on traditional methods when faced with the task of aiding friendly governments overseas—he asked Congress to pass joint resolutions granting him broad authority to use the armed forces as he saw fit in the Middle East and in the Formosa Strait. Congress responded promptly, confident that General Ike would take care of any crisis in the same manner that he had handled the victorious Allied Forces in World War II.

Since 1950, presidents have ordered U.S. armed forces into Korea, Lebanon, the Dominican Republic, Vietnam, Cambodia, Laos, Grenada, Panama, the Persian Gulf, Somalia, and Haiti. They have ordered a naval quarantine around Cuba, approved undercover plots directed by the Central Intelligence Agency against the leaders of several foreign governments, dispatched military advisors to friendly countries, and even ordered aerial overflights of countries behind the Iron Curtain—all actions undertaken without obtaining advance congressional assent. Public trust in the president during the New Deal and post–New Deal eras remained high, even though presidents placed more demands on the citizenry in World War II than at any time since the Civil War.

During America's involvement in Vietnam, however, public confidence in presidential leadership began to wane, reaching an all-time low during the Watergate investigation in the early 1970s. While the seeds were planted earlier, the excesses of presidential power became evident soon after President Lyndon B. Johnson's landslide victory in the 1964 election. Complaints about President Johnson's "credibility gap" began to surface in 1965 and 1966 over his handling of the American intervention in Vietnam. Charges that he had lied, or at least misrepresented the facts surrounding the initial North Vietnamese attack on American ships in the Tonkin Gulf in order to obtain a blank-check authorization to deal with future attacks, echoed through the halls of Congress. Johnson's decision not to seek reelection in 1968, instead of halting the growth of the imperial presidency, accelerated a great concentration of authority in the White House during the Nixon years.

President Nixon's unilateral decision to invade Cambodia in 1970, his secret orders for stepped up bombing of Laos without telling Congress, as well as his impoundment of congressionally approved appropriations for programs he wished to see cut back or terminated, all helped reinforce the belief of many Americans that the President was moving ever closer to an "imperial presidency," a term coined by historian Arthur M. Schlesinger, Jr.[44]

THE IMPERIAL PRESIDENCY

President Johnson invariably pointed to the Gulf of Tonkin Resolution whenever his congressional critics alluded to his unilateral actions, such as expanding American troop deployment to 525,000 troops in Vietnam in 1965. But not until President Nixon mounted secret bombing attacks in Laos and Cambodia did congressional patience with the conduct of the Vietnam War eventually wear thin. Finally, in 1973, Congress voted to rein in the "imperial presidency" by passing the War Powers Resolution, a subject we discuss in greater detail in Chapter 9.

Arthur M. Schlesinger, Jr., in his book *The Imperial Presidency*, published in 1973, the same year as the Watergate hearings, contended that presidential power had been so expanded and abused by the early 1970s that it endangered our constitutional system. Two critical instruments—the commander in chief's role and presidential secrecy—were, according to Schlesinger, primarily responsible for the rise of presidential autocracy. The president's power as commander in chief, because it is an undefined office, not a function, is sufficiently ambiguous to allow him to stretch its meaning far beyond what the Founding Fathers intended. While the Framers expected that a president would respond to sudden attacks and act to protect the rights and property of American citizens, they did not envisage the president's resorting to undeclared wars. The ambiguous constitutional authority, Schlesinger argued, especially in the field of foreign policy, enabled presidents to arrogate to themselves the right to wage an undeclared war unilaterally, a power the Framers expected the president to share with Congress.

Schlesinger made a crucial distinction between the *abuse* and the *usurpation* of power. In his view, Lincoln, FDR, and Truman temporarily usurped power in wartime, but recognized that they had no intention of retaining this power in peacetime. By contrast, Presidents Johnson and Nixon abused power, even in peacetime, and saw this near-absolute power as a permanent prerogative of the presidency.

In reviewing the president's role in waging war from Washington's administration to Nixon's, Schlesinger perceived this power as culminating in an imperial presidency of the Johnson-Nixon type. Furthermore, this "plebiscitary" conception of the office, as propounded by President Nixon, justified his actions beyond foreign policy into domestic policy matters as well.

Members of the Democratic majority in both houses of Congress also objected strenuously to Nixon's practice of impounding (refusing to spend) appropriated funds for water pollution control, urban aid, and the emergency loan program of the Farm Home Administration. Lawmakers complained that by refusing to spend appropriated money, the chief executive was, in effect, exercising an *item veto* and thereby avoiding the use of a regular veto and the risk of a congressional override.

Other practices of the imperial presidency included excessive secrecy and the heavy reliance on the presidential prerogative known as executive privilege, a claim based on the constitutional separation of powers, which allowed the president or his designated officials to withhold information from Congress. Constitutional scholars, the courts, and Congress all concede that a president has the right to withhold certain diplomatic and military information when it is essential to national security—such as the Normandy invasion plans in World War II. Critics objected to the studied practice of Mr. Nixon, who withheld information on matters relating to military assistance and five-year plans and foreign aid for Cambodia—data that could scarcely be termed vital to national security.

Watergate

The imperial presidency continued to expand until it was finally halted by the emerging Watergate scandals in early 1973. Watergate is the name given to the constitutional crisis precipitated by a string of unlawful Nixon White House-sponsored acts. These ranged from illegal entry into the Democratic National Committee headquarters in the Watergate office-hotel complex near the Potomac River, to burglary, perjury, the misuse of the FBI and CIA to cover up illegal activity, the destruction of evidence, the creation of a White House secret police unit (the so-called plumbers' group), illegal wiretapping, and the illegal solicitation of corporate contributions for President Nixon's 1972 reelection campaign. These activities, many of them first reported in the *Washington Post* and widely publicized by the special Senate Watergate Investigation Committee, led to the prosecution and conviction of more than a dozen top-level White House aides, including Attorney General John Mitchell. The Watergate scandals cast the darkest shadow over the presidency since the impeachment of President Andrew Johnson after the Civil War. Even in Johnson's case, no charges of criminal activity were made against him or his aides. By the summer of 1974, President Nixon, facing an impeachment trial in the Senate, resigned from the presidency—the first chief executive in American history to be driven from office.[45]

Watergate had a profound effect on our view of the presidency.[46] Some contemporary observers declared that the presidency, discredited by abuses of power unparalleled in American history, had been irreparably wounded. But these observers underestimated the resilience and durability of the chief executive office. Once Mr. Nixon left Washington, the greatest constitutional crisis since the Civil War subsided. Congressional opposition to the imperial presidency had hastened the "deroyalization" of the presidency, as evidenced by the passage in 1972 of the Case Act (to curb the wholesale use of secret executive agreements by imperial presidents), the enactment of the War Powers Act of 1973, and the approval of the Budget and Impoundment Control Act of 1974. Congress thus reclaimed some of the powers its members had too easily and sometimes casually ceded to the White House over several decades. The emergency powers exercised by several presidents also came under scrutiny during the Watergate era.

THE PRESIDENT AND EMERGENCY POWERS

No emergency powers are granted to the president under the Constitution, but neither does the Constitution forbid the president to take appropriate action in times of national emergencies.

Except for Lincoln's drastic actions during the Civil War, the concept of national emergency is almost exclusively a twentieth-century phenomenon. During World War I, President Wilson exercised wartime powers nearly equal to those of a Roman proconsul. Indeed, during America's eighteen-month involvement in the European conflict, Congress was more than willing to pass measures giving President Wilson dictatorial powers over the American industrial system. But until President Franklin D. Roosevelt declared a national emergency the day after he assumed office on March 4, 1933 to forestall the collapse of the American banking system, the use of national emergency power had always been confined to wartime. Actually, Roosevelt's measures were pleasing to the banking community, and within a week the major banks reopened their doors. Both the Federal Reserve Board and the Reconstruction Finance Corporation came to the aid of the banking industry. When Congress convened four days later, the lawmakers passed Roosevelt's bank aid bill in a record four hours.

Shortly after the outbreak of World War II (more than two years before Pearl Harbor), FDR announced a "limited" national emergency. In May 1941, President Roosevelt announced an "unlimited" national emergency in the aftermath of Hitler's conquest of France. President Truman, following in the footsteps of FDR a decade later, put the nation on an emergency basis soon after our entry into the Korean conflict. No further national emergencies were proclaimed until President Nixon announced one at the time of the postal strike in March 1970. So impressed was Mr. Nixon with the dramatic effect of this national emergency declaration that he proclaimed another one in August 1971, in response to the perilously high deficit in the U.S. balance of payments.

Looking back in history, Roman proconsuls were granted dictatorial powers for a maximum of six months. But at no time in the six emergency declarations proclaimed by American presidents since the Great Depression has the American president ever specified the duration of his emergency declaration. Of these six national emergencies, only two were rescinded by the president—Mr. Truman in 1952 issued a proclamation terminating Roosevelt's national emergency declarations of 1939 and 1941.[47] The other four national emergency statutes (1933, 1950, 1970, and 1971) remained on the books until 1976.

In the aftermath of the U.S. invasion of Cambodia, a Senate Special Committee on the Termination of the National Emergency, chaired jointly by Senators Frank Church (D-ID) and Charles Mathias (R-MD) unearthed some 470 emergency statutes dating back to March 5, 1933 and ranging from suspending the writ of habeas corpus to placing the entire nation under martial law. Committee members discovered that since the early 1930s President Roosevelt and his successors had declared numerous separate national emergencies, but none had ever been rescinded. By passing the National Emergencies Act of 1976, Congress trimmed much of the president's historic freedom to declare national emergencies and simultaneously invoke sweeping powers.

The 1976 act repealed all the previous emergency acts; it also stipulated that future presidentially declared emergencies could be terminated by Congress by concurrent resolution (which is not subject to a presidential veto), or by a presidential proclamation. Furthermore, if the president declares a national emergency, he must inform Congress of the provisions of the law under which he acts. The president and the designated federal agencies must report to Congress all rules and regulations issued during an emergency, as well as expenditures. Congress, in turn, must at six-month intervals determine whether or not the emergency should be terminated.[48]

Significantly, the new law states that a majority vote in both the Senate and House can terminate the emergency at any time. President Ford termed this action unconstitutional and indicated that future presidents might turn to the courts to challenge this provision if Congress chose to invoke it.

THE RISE OF THE PRESIDENTIAL BRANCH

In the meantime, while the commentators and politicians were focusing their attention primarily on the "imperial presidency," a gradual transformation within the institutionalized presidency was taking place at 1600 Pennsylvania Avenue. Beginning with the Kennedy and Johnson administrations in the early 1960s, presidents began to centralize the policy control in the White House, relegating cabinet secretaries to a distinctly subordinate role. The "cabinet government" of the Eisenhower era held little appeal for the hard-driving Democratic presidents and their successors.[49]

So clearly has been this steady shift of decision making away from the cabinet governmental and executive departments to the White House that we now have, in effect, a separate and distinct "presidential branch" or new fourth branch of government.[50] This subject will be treated separately in Chapter Seven.

THE POST-IMPERIAL PRESIDENCY

In retrospect, passage of the War Powers Resolution of 1973, the Watergate hearings, and the forced resignation of President Nixon in August 1974 represented the high-water mark of congressional constraints against the imperial presidency. The congressional and public backlash against overreaching presidential actions temporarily halted further expansion of presidential power and prerogatives. Congressional resurgence was marked by increased skepticism of claims for presidential prerogative, careful scrutiny of presidential proposals, demands for more extensive consultation of congressional leaders by the White House, and more exacting confirmation of presidential appointments.

The elevation of the first appointed vice president, Gerald Ford, to the White House gave the country a short breathing spell from the repeated clashes between President Nixon and Congress. President Ford signaled that a *rapprochement* between the two branches would be the highest priority on his agenda. In his first address to Congress, delivered three days after taking office, Mr. Ford declared: "I do not want a honeymoon with you. I want a good marriage. As President, I intend to listen." Ford stated that his relations with Congress would be characterized not by confrontation, but by "communication, conciliation, compromise and cooperation."[51]

This presidential-congressional honeymoon lasted slightly over thirty days. It came to an abrupt halt the day President Ford pardoned former President Nixon for his complicity in the Watergate cover-up. Still, President Ford went a long way toward de-emphasizing the pomp and ceremony surrounding White House activities. Indeed, the country heard little about the "crisis" in the presidency and the "imperial presidency" after the resignation of Richard Nixon. Congress, now working with an appointed president, quickly reasserted some of its lost authority. Furthermore, by the establishment of the Congressional Budget Office in 1974 and the addition of a sizable professional staff of policy analysts, computer specialists, and economists, Congress gained an increased institutional capacity to participate to a greater degree in the "code-termination" of public policy and the maintenance of its legislative oversight function. Presidential power also may have been vitiated by the fact that Mr. Ford was an appointed, not an elected, president.

The Divided Government Era

The "post-imperial presidency" coincided with the resurgence of divided government. In twenty years out of twenty-four between 1968 and 1992, the executive branch and one or both houses of Congress were controlled by different parties. Except for President Jimmy Carter's single term, Republican presidents faced Democratic majorities in one or both chambers on Capitol Hill throughout this period. Divided government, in turn, frequently led to "government by veto." President Ford, for example, wielded his veto pen sixty-six times in less than thirty months (August 1974–January 1977), averaging more than two vetoes a month. Twelve of Ford's vetoes were overridden by the Democrats. President Bush, in his single term (1989–1993), vetoed forty-six Democratic-sponsored measures; only one veto was overridden. Throughout this era loud complaints of "gridlock" and "stalemate" echoed frequently from one end of Pennsylvania Avenue to the other. But the legislative output of Congress, according to the only comprehensive study available, did not differ significantly between the years of divided and "unified" government for the 1948–1988 period.[52]

By 1980—six years after Nixon's resignation—some political leaders and analysts began expressing concern that Congress had overreacted to Vietnam, the Watergate scandals, and President Nixon. While they conceded that some rebalancing was needed to restore equilibrium between the two branches, "presidential" supporters argued that Congress was carried away with its reform zeal. Passage of the War Powers Act, the Case Act (regulating executive agreements), the Budget and Impoundment Control Act, and other legislative constraints on the president, these critics claimed, so hobbled the president that he became a helpless giant. Before long, concern about the imperial presidency was replaced by apprehension about the "imperiled presidency."

The "Reagan Revolution"

When Ronald Reagan moved into the White House in 1981, many Washington observers were lamenting that we had entered an era of one-term presidencies. In the previous two decades they had seen John Kennedy assassinated, Lyndon Johnson pushed into political exile, Nixon forced to resign under the threat of impeachment, and both Gerald Ford and Jimmy Carter rejected by the voters.

President-watchers commented, not implausibly, that the pressures of the presidency were so intense and public expectations so much higher than its limited institutional authority that no incumbent could hope to be returned for a second term. Critics could see nothing but revolving-door presidencies in the years ahead. But President Reagan, soon after his election in 1980, undertook to strengthen the presidency by patching together a new constituency for presidential power and rebuilding the capacity of the chief executive to operate independently of Congress. By the time of President Reagan's reelection in 1984, most naysayers agreed that Mr. Reagan had restored the presidency to its central role in our governmental system. One respected national columnist concluded: "It is no exaggeration to say he has rescued the office."[53]

Reagan reasserted the prerogative of the president unilaterally to deploy military forces abroad. His invasion of Grenada and the bombing of Libyan dictator Mu'ammar Gadhafi's headquarters were textbook successes. Political scientists Benjamin Ginsberg and Martin Shefter assessed Reagan's actions this way: "In both of these episodes the duration of the American involvement was minimal, victory was assured, and hence support for the president was extremely high."[54]

President Reagan's second term, however, was seriously marred by the Iran-Contra scandal. In this series of events, it seemed evident to all but Reagan himself that, as president, he had condoned a White House secret operation to swap U.S. arms (indirectly through Israel) with Ayatollah Khomeini's Iranian government in return for the release of a half dozen United States citizens held hostage by Iranian-directed terrorists in Lebanon. Profits from this clandestine guns-for-hostages scheme were to be funneled—in violation of a congressional ban on military aid to Nicaragua (the Boland Amendment)—to the Contra guerrillas seeking to overthrow the leftist government of Nicaragua.

The Iran-Contra congressional hearings ended inconclusively, but Reagan's reputation—and the "Reagan Revolution"—were both badly tarnished. However, like a badly battered gambler, Reagan recouped most of his losses later in 1987 by negotiating an intermediate nuclear weapons ban with Soviet leader Mikhail Gorbachev. The joint signing, amidst the Reagan-Gorbachev handshakes and the whirring television cameras, of the Intermediate Nuclear Forces (INF) Treaty in Washington, DC in December 1987 demonstrated that the ever-confident Reagan had regained his master's touch. Reagan's deft handling of foreign policy had saved the day. He completed his final year in the White House with a strong finish—his final year Gallup poll approval rating was exceeded only by President Dwight D. Eisenhower's record high.

Overall, however, despite the early programmatic successes of the "Reagan Revolution," political scientist Theodore Lowi's assessment of the actor-turned-president at the time of his retirement is not far from the mark: "Reagan leaves no major institutional legacy."[55]

The Bush Years

President George Bush's four years in the White House have sometimes been called the "Reagan third term." Most of Mr. Bush's domestic policies were a continuation of "Reaganomics," with minimal federal government intervention in the economy. Bush's jingoistic foreign and national security policies differed little from Reagan's. The Bush-directed lightning attack on Panama in December 1989 to capture the drug-trafficking dictator Manuel Noriega matched President Reagan's highly successful invasion of Grenada, the Caribbean island, to overthrow a Marxist regime. President Bush's leadership in the Persian Gulf War to thwart Iraqi dictator Saddam Hussein's military invasion of Kuwait, an oil-rich sheikdom, won even louder plaudits from the American public. A Gallup poll conducted shortly after the "100 Hour War" victory, for example, showed Bush's approval rating at 89 percent—the highest in the polling organization's history. But this stratospheric rating proved to be short-lived as the American economy continued to stagnate into the 1992 presidential election year.

Even though the four-decade old Cold War had ended and the breakup of the Soviet Union occurred during President Bush's watch, the American electorate remained unimpressed with Bush's foreign policy successes. Voters in 1992 chose to focus their attention chiefly on the poor state of the domestic economy.

Thus, when the 1992 Democratic nominee, Bill Clinton, promised to move actively to get the domestic economy back on track, the fickle American voters rejected George Bush, the experienced chief executive and World War II hero. Instead, they turned to the forty-six-year old governor from Arkansas, who had no military experience, indeed, who had avoided military service during the unpopular Vietnam War. Clinton's election clearly signaled a new generation takeover of the nation's leadership.

Democrats Recapture White House

The first Democrat to occupy the White House in twelve years, President Bill Clinton had promised in his 1992 campaign to mount a new "One Hundred Days" legislative program, in the best tradition of Franklin Delano Roosevelt's historic program in 1933. But, choosing not to recognize the vast differences between conditions in the 1930s and the 1990s, Clinton had clearly over-promised. Indeed, his record during his first one hundred days in office was a pale carbon copy of FDR's. Clinton's $16 billion job-stimulus program, for example, was filibustered to death by the Republican opposition before the Easter recess. In mid-summer 1993—nearly 200 days into his new administration—President Clinton's five-year, budget reduction package was saved in the

Senate only by the tie-breaking vote of Vice President Al Gore. The same budget measure had passed the House of Representatives after frantic, last-minute lobbying by Democratic congressional leaders, with exactly the 218 votes needed to pass; one vote less would have torpedoed the entire Clinton budget program.[56]

President Clinton's inability to win public credit for some of his legislative successes can be attributed in part to his overloaded first-year agenda. Still, his first-year legislative record was far superior to President Kennedy's. But the residue of the Kennedy mystique invariably creates a public perception of higher ratings for the assassinated president.

Unlike Presidents Franklin D. Roosevelt and Lyndon B. Johnson, who both enjoyed solid working majorities in Congress at the height of their power, President Clinton found himself operating in the era of fragmented political parties, decentralized power in the House and Senate, and vast numbers of well-financed special interest groups. Nor has Mr. Clinton's task been any easier in national security affairs. Despite the recent end of the Cold War, the U.S. involvement in U.N.-sponsored peace-keeping actions in Bosnia, Somalia, and Haiti, especially the continuous televised coverage of these expeditions, has severely tested the national security policies of the inexperienced young commander in chief from Arkansas.

Every modern president is under intense pressure to succeed, but relatively few do. Why? Part of the reason is that in a time of declining economic resources and recognized national limitations, facts that became painfully evident both at home and abroad in the 1970s, it is the president who becomes the chief target for public frustrations. As a result, recent presidents often find the gap between public expectations and their ability to solve the nation's top-priority problems is unbridgeable. For most presidents this chronic disparity between hope and reality first arises during the nominating race for president—the subject of the next chapter.

APPENDIX 1: THE MAKING OF THE PRESIDENCY

A Chronology of the Creation of the Presidency at the Constitutional Convention, Philadelphia, 1787

May 29th

Virginia Plan, introduced by Edmund Randolph, provided for a "National Executive" to be chosen by Congress for a single seven-year term. (The original version of the plan left unresolved the question of whether this would be a person or a group.)

Virginia Plan granted national executive "general authority to execute the National laws." Chief executive would be aided by a Council of Revision, composed of "a convenient number of the National Judiciary," to examine acts of Congress before they become operative.

Note: Before the formal debate commenced the Convention adopted a rule that permitted its decisions to be reconsidered at even a single delegate's request. This explains why the convention voted five different times during the long, hot summer in favor of selecting the president by Congress.

June 2nd

James Wilson of Pennsylvania proposed "that Executive consist of a single person" (defeated, two states to eight).

Charles Pinckney of South Carolina proposed election of president by Congress annually; also proposed a Council of States advisory council to include heads of executive departments. (Plan was never debated.)

June 15th

The New Jersey Plan, introduced by William Paterson, provided for election of a plural executive by Congress for one term only.

June 18th

Alexander Hamilton offered plan for indirect election of President for life by electors chosen *ad hoc*.

Hamilton proposed executive powers to include veto, execution of laws, treaties, appointments, pardons.

Gouverneur Morris of Pennsylvania advocated qualified executive veto, subject to overruling by two-thirds of Congress. Absolute veto voted down, ten states to none.

June 19th

New Jersey Plan rejected. Amended Virginia Plan, which included a single executive, accepted as working document by Convention.

July 17th

Popular election of president proposal received vote of only one state—Pennsylvania.

July 18th

Nathaniel Gorham of Massachusetts proposed executive appointments to make with Senate's advice and consent, defeated by a tie vote.

July 24th

Convention flopped back to original Virginia Plan for selecting president by legislature and reaffirmed this vote two days later.

July 26th

Committee on Detail appointed, chaired by James Wilson of Pennsylvania.

July 26–August 6th

Convention in recess.

Committee on Detail actions included:

President granted the power to recommend legislation by Congress, make executive appointments, receive ambassadors from other nations, issue pardons, "take care" that the laws be executed, and command the armed forces.

Impeachment power placed in House and the power to try impeachment in the Supreme Court (later shifted to Senate as favor to small states).

Provision borrowed from New Jersey Plan, which stated that once war had been declared, war powers in prosecuting war were to be divided between president and Congress with the president serving as commander in chief. (The power of the president to serve as commander in chief was not much discussed, according to Madison's *Notes*.)

August 24th

John Rutledge of South Carolina moved to elect president by a joint ballot of House and Senate members. (Motion carried, seven states to four.)

Gouverneur Morris, to head off legislative selection of president, moved the selection be done by electors without specifying how they would be chosen (tie vote, four states to four, with two not voting).

Convention, warned of deadlock, postponed further consideration of presidential selection and then consigned the issue to the Committee on Postponed Matters. (This committee was heavily weighted with "separationists" who favored an independent executive.)

August 27th

The Convention without debate accepted the wording that the president should be "Commander in Chief of the Army and Navy of the United States."

August 31st

Committee on Postponed Matters (or Committee of Eleven) established (chaired by David Brearly of New Jersey), to resolve "unfinished business," chiefly the method of choosing the president. Choice ranged between those favoring election by the legislature and those favoring some form of popular election.

Committee invented the electoral college. Compromise proposal consisted of an electoral college with each state having the same number of electors as it had senators and representatives. The candidate who received the greatest number of votes, assuming a majority, would become president; the second highest would become vice president. (This was the first mention of the vice presidency at the Convention.) In case no candidate received a majority of electors, the Senate—later changed to the House—would select the President with each state having one vote. The Senate would still choose the vice president if the electoral college failed to produce a winner.

Many of the Framers were convinced that there would be so many candidates—after Washington retired—that in most cases, no one would receive a majority of electoral votes; consequently the House would probably make the decision in nineteen instances out of twenty.

Note: No fewer than sixty ballots were needed before the presidential selection process was finally decided. No fewer than eight methods of choosing the president were proposed at the Convention.

Committee agreed that term of office would be four years, with no limit on re-eligibility. Earlier seven-year term was rejected.

The Committee assigned certain responsibilities to the vice president, namely to serve as the presiding officer of the Senate, the right to cast tie-breaking votes, and to act as president if the office became vacant before the expiration of the president's term.

September 4th–September 7th

Committee agreed president should make treaties "with the advice and consent of the Senate" (two-thirds vote required). Senior appointments and Supreme Court justices were to be approved by majority vote of Senate.

Wilson's proposal that treaties also be approved by House of Representatives was defeated by a vote of one state to ten.

The Committee also included the proposal that the president was to be impeached by the House and, upon conviction by two-thirds of the Senate, removed from office on grounds of "treason or bribery or other high crimes and misdemeanors against the United States."

September 7th

Approved section that president "may require opinion in writing of the principal officer in each of the Executive Departments upon any subject relating to the duties of their respective offices."

George Mason of Virginia proposed a Council of State for the president, made up of six members—two from the Eastern, two from the Middle, and two from the Southern states—appointed by Congress or the Senate. (Proposal defeated, three states to eight.)

Convention accepted Committee on Postponed Matters Report.

Convention's final acceptance of separation of powers doctrine preserved independence of the president. "Separationists" convinced majority of delegates that the dangers of intrigue would accompany legislative selection of the President.

September 12th

Hugh Williamson of North Carolina moved that the president's negative vote (veto) would be overruled by two-thirds (instead of three-quarters) vote of Congress. (Convention approved by narrow vote.)

September 15th

Convention approved new U.S. Constitution.

September 17th

Document signed by 39 of original 55 members. Convention adjourned *sine die* and submitted document to Confederation Congress.

Sources: Catherine Drinker Bowen, *Miracle at Philadelphia* (Boston: Little, Brown, 1966 and 1986); Christopher Collier and James Lincoln Collier, *Decision in Philadelphia: The Constitutional Convention of 1787* (New York: Random House, 1986); Edward S. Corwin, *The President: Office and Powers, 1787–1957*, (New York: New York University Press, 1957); Max Farrand, *The Framing of the Constitution of the United States*, 4 vols. (New Haven, CT: Yale University Press, 1913); Michael Kammen, ed., *The Origins of the American Constitution: A Documentary History* (New York: Penguin, 1986); Richard B. Morris, *Witnesses at the Creation* (New York: New American Library, 1985); William H. Riker, "The Heresthetics of Constitution-Making: The Presidency in 1787, with Comments on Determinism and Rational Choice," *American Political Science Review*, 78 (March 1984): 1–16; Charles Warren, *The Making of the Constitution* (Boston: Little, Brown, 1937).

NOTES

1. This section draws heavily upon Everts G. Greene, *The Provincial Governor in the English Colonies of North America* (New York: Longmans, Green & Company, Vol. VII, Harvard Historical Series, 1898).

2. Edward S. Corwin, *The President: Office and Powers, 1787–1957*, 4th ed. (New York: New York University Press, 1957), 7.

3. Merrill Jensen, *The Articles of Confederation* (Madison: University of Wisconsin Press, 1940).

4. Corwin, *The President: Office and Powers*, 11.

5. Forrest McDonald, *Novus Ordo Seclorum: The Intellectual Origins of the Constitution* (Lawrence: University Press of Kansas, 1985), 240.

6. Corwin, *The President: Office and Powers*, 317, footnote 25.

7. As cited by Louis W. Koenig, *The Chief Executive* (New York: Harcourt, Brace & Jovanovich, 1961), 30.

8. Robert R. Hirschfield, ed., *The Power of the Presidency*, 3rd ed. (New York: Aldine, 1982), 3.

9. "Postscript," in Corwin, *The President: Office and Powers, 1787–1984*, 5th ed. Randall W. Bland, Theodore H. Hindson, and Jack W. Peltason, eds. (New York: New York University Press, 1985), 31.

10. Ibid., 30.

11. Corwin, *The President: Office and Powers*, 4th ed., 18.

12. Ibid., 20.

13. Robert V. Remini, "The Jackson Era," in Martin Fausold and Alan Shank, eds. *The Constitution and the American Presidency* (Albany: State University Press of New York, 1991), 33.

14. Ibid.

15. Ibid.

16. Ibid.

17. Ibid., 35.

18. Ibid., 43.

19. Corwin, *The President: Office and Powers*, 4th ed., 22.

20. Ibid., 264.

21. Leonard D. White, *The Republican Era: 1869–1901* (New York: Macmillan, 1948), 113.

22. James MacGregor Burns, *Presidential Government: The Crucible of Leadership* (New York: Avon Books Edition, 1967), 50.

23. White, *The Republican Era: 1869–1901*, 109.

24. Morton Keller, *Affairs of State* (Cambridge, MA: The Belknap Press of Harvard University, 1977), 297.

25. Ibid., 310.

26. Russell F. Weigley, *History of the United States Army* (New York: Macmillan, 1967), 295.

27. 135 U.S. 1 (1890).

28. Ibid.

29. 158 U.S. 564 (1895).

30. F.D.G. Riddle, *State and National Power Over Commerce* (New York: Columbia University Press, 1937), 117–119.

31. Samuel and Dorothy Rosenman, *Presidential Style: Some Giants and a Pygmy in the White House* (New York: Harper & Row, 1976), 123, as quoted by Sidney M. Milkus and Michael Nelson, *The American Presidency: Origins and Development* (Washington, DC: CQ Press, 1990), 192.

32. Arthur S. Link, *Woodrow Wilson and the Progressive Era* (New York: Harper & Row, 1954), 93.

33. Clinton Rossiter, *The American Presidency*, rev. ed. (New York: Mentor Books, 1960), 100.

34. Elmer E. Cornwell, Jr., *Presidential Leadership of Public Opinion* (Bloomington: Indiana University Press, 1965), 9; Jeffrey K. Tulis, *The Rhetorical Presidency* (Princeton, NJ: Princeton University Press, 1987), 97–116.

35. Wilfred E. Binkley, *The President and Congress*, 3rd ed. (New York: Vintage, 1962), 281.

36. Political scientists Sidney Milkis and Michael Nelson make a rather persuasive case that the modern presidency actually began with Presidents Teddy Roosevelt and Woodrow Wilson rather than FDR. See Sidney Milkis and Michael Nelson, *The Origins of the Presidency* (Washington, DC: CQ Press, 1993). To be sure, these two presidents ushered in a series of progressive reforms that made the federal government an active participant in regulating unfair competition and stabilizing the banking system (the Federal Reserve Act of 1913), upgrading

inspections in the meatpacking industry, and improving the general quality of life. But these reforms were modest in comparison to the major reforms of FDR's New Deal. Consequently, the present author has opted to follow the Greenstein time frame that places FDR at the beginning of the modern era.

37. Arthur M. Schlesinger, Jr., *The Coming of the New Deal* (Boston: Houghton Mifflin, 1958), 13.

38. As cited in Wilfred E. Binkley, *President and Congress*, 294.

39. William E. Leuchtenburg, *Franklin D. Roosevelt and the New Deal* (New York: Harper & Row, 1963), chap. 14.

40. Arthur M. Schlesinger, Jr., *The Imperial Presidency* (Boston: Houghton Mifflin, 1973), 122–123.

41. Thomas E. Cronin, *The State of the Presidency*, 2nd ed. (Boston: Little, Brown, 1980), 85.

42. Rossiter, *The American Presidency*, 13.

43. Arthur M. Schlesinger, Jr., "Congress and the Making of American Foreign Policy," *Foreign Affairs* (1972): 94–95.

44. Schlesinger, *The Imperial Presidency,* viii.

45. Cronin, *The State of the Presidency*, 195.

46. For a fascinating account of the Watergate story, consult Bob Woodward and Carl Bernstein, *All the President's Men* (New York: Simon & Schuster, 1974; see also Theodore H. White, *Breach of Faith: The Fall of Richard Nixon* (New York: Atheneum, 1975).

47. Cronin, *The State of the Presidency*, 267.

48. Public Law 94–412 National Emergencies Act, 94th Congress, September 14, 1976.

49. The term "cabinet government" should not be confused with its usage in the British parliamentary system. In the U.S. context the term, as explained by James P. Pfiffner, "refers to the delegation of a certain amount of authority to cabinet secretaries to the presidential consultation with the cabinet as a deliberative body." James P. Pfiffner, *The Modern Presidency* (New York: St. Martin's, 1993), 111.

50. Credit for coining the term "presidential branch" should go to Nelson Polsby, "Some Landmarks in Modern Presidential-Congressional Relations," in Anthony King, ed., *Both Ends of the Avenue* (Washington, DC: American Enterprise Institute, 1983), 20; see also his article, "Congress, National Security and the Rise of the Presidential Branch," in Howard Shuman and Walter Thomas, eds., *The Constitution and National Security* (Washington, DC: Notre Dame University Press, 1990), 202. For a more detailed discussion of this development, see John Hart, *The Presidential Branch* (New York: Pergamon Press, 1987). The second edition was published in 1994 by Chatham House Publishers, Chatham, NJ.

51. *The New York Times*, 13 August 1974.

52. David R. Mayhew, *Divided We Govern* (New Haven, CT: Yale University Press, 1991), 51–135.

53. David Broder, *Washington Post*, 21 January 1985.

54. Benjamin Ginsberg and Martin Shefter, "After the Reagan Revolution Post-Electoral Politics?" in Larry Berman, ed., *Looking Back on the Reagan Presidency* (Baltimore, MD: Johns Hopkins University Press, 1990), 248.

55. "Reagan Added Luster but Little Clout to Office," *Congressional Quarterly Weekly Report*, 7 January 1989, 3.

56. *The New York Times*, 6 August 1993.

CHAPTER 3

PRESIDENTIAL NOMINATIONS: THE GREAT AMERICAN STEEPLECHASE

If the Founding Fathers were to return to earth and view the presidential nominating system of the 1990s in operation, they would blink their eyes in amazement at its complexity—the long selection process, the incredibly high cost, and the dominant role of presidential primaries and television in singling out the eventual nominee. That the process should involve the participation of millions of rank-and-file voters and party members and be officially spread over half a year and unofficially over most of the four-year term would astound them, as would the huge expenditures of the two major parties ($104 million for the 1992 nominating races). Equally startling would be the discovery that an electronic tube, found in nearly every living room in America, has largely replaced the political party as the major decision-making agent in presidential nominations.

After a brief historical overview, we will survey the remarkable changes in the nominating process over the past two decades that have revolutionized the way we select presidential nominees: (1) the rapid spread of primaries to more than thirty-eight states; (2) the vital importance of money in campaigns; (3) the powerful impact of television; (4) the strategic role of public opinion polls; and (5) the fading influence of political parties.

We will pay special attention to the proliferation of presidential primaries and how the selection of national convention-pledged delegates by rank-and-file voters, not state party leaders, has taken away the decision-making power of state delegation leaders. As a result of this power shift, presidential nominees are now, in effect, chosen in the primaries. National conventions have become chiefly a ratifying body that anoints the popular favorite of the primaries. The chapter will also explain that running for president without a huge campaign bank account and sophisticated fund-raising machinery is a futile trip. Also, we will look closely at the role of the opinion polls and mass media in "handicapping" the various contenders in the pre-primary period and their *de facto* role as chief arbiters of the "winners" and "losers" during the primary season. Finally, it will be argued that the polls and the media have, to a large extent, displaced the political parties as major decision makers in the presidential nominating process.

PRESIDENTIAL NOMINATIONS: A UNIQUE SYSTEM

Beyond all doubt, the process by which American parties select their nominees for president is the longest, most convoluted, and most expensive in the Western world. The U.S. presidential nominating process is unique in another sense: it permits a degree of popular control and participation not found elsewhere in the free world, except in Canada.[1] In 1992, approximately thirty-six million Americans participated in the presidential primaries, more than double the number of participants in the 1968 primaries. That rank-and-file voters should have a voice in the selection of a national party leader seems bizarre to a foreign observer; in most Western democracies, there is a clear distinction between the nominating and electing processes. To be sure, the final choice of a national leader is left to the electorate in Western Europe and Japan, but the preliminary decision—the nomination that determines which candidate is to be selected as the party standard-bearer—belongs to the party.

THE IMPORTANCE OF THE NOMINATING PROCESS

Nineteenth-century New York political boss William Marcy Tweed once observed, "I don't care who does the electing just so I can do the nominating."[2] His sage observation underscores a basic political fact of life: Nominations are the decisive stage in the whole process of presidential selection.

Put simply, the presidential nominating process narrows the alternatives from a theoretical potential candidate pool of millions who meet the constitutional requirements to only two candidates, one Republican and one Democrat, with a realistic chance of winning the White House. Political scientist Donald R. Matthews has also noted: "The nominating decision is one of the major determinants of who wins in November."[3] Indeed, because electoral considerations usually take on greater importance in nominating decision making than calculations on probable performance in the White House, the presidential nominating process has as much effect, if not more, as the election itself in shaping the future of the country. The choice of Franklin Delano Roosevelt over Alfred E. Smith in the 1932 Democratic race, the Republicans' preference for Dwight D. Eisenhower over Senator Robert A. Taft in the 1952 contest, the selection of John F. Kennedy over Adlai Stevenson and Lyndon Johnson in the 1960 Democratic race, and the Republicans' choice of Ronald Reagan over George Bush, Howard Baker, Robert Dole, or John Connally in the 1980 race, and the selection of Bill Clinton over Paul Tsongas, Bob Kerrey, and Jerry Brown in 1992 are all cases in point.

The presidential nominating process has evolved through three basic systems. We have borrowed Thomas R. Marshall's classification outline: the congressional caucus system, 1800–1824; the brokered convention system, 1832–1968; and the system of popular appeal, 1972 to the present.[4] Each of those systems differs from the others in several respects: the type of candidate favored, the focus of the nomination, the role of party leaders and rank-and-file members, and the role of campaign funds and the media. In the course of our brief review of these systems, we will examine why the first two ultimately collapsed.

The Constitution says nothing about presidential nominations. Why? The Framers seemed to assume that the choice would be made by a council of notables—the Electoral College—and limited to a small number of obviously well-qualified men, with the best one being selected. Parties, it should not be forgotten, did not exist at the time of the Philadelphia Convention. Nor did the Framers foresee that the method of picking presidents would soon evolve into a two-stage process: first, the nomination of candidates, and second, an election between candidates from different parties.

The Framers assumed that after George Washington stepped down, the Electoral College votes would be so widely distributed (because each state would probably vote for its favorite son) that rarely would a candidate receive a majority of electoral votes, as required by the Constitution (Article II, Section 1). Instead, most presidents would ultimately be chosen by the House of Representatives. In other words, the members of the Electoral College would "screen" (nominate) the candidates, and the House of Representatives would make the final choice. This arrangement was a package of compromises. To placate large states, the Framers gave them an elector for each congressional seat, so that in the initial vote of the Electoral College the large states would have an advantage. But since it was assumed that most presidents would be finally chosen in the House of Representatives, with each state having one vote, the small states would have a greater voice in the final choice.

TWO CENTURIES OF PRESIDENTIAL NOMINATIONS

The first presidential nomination presented no problem, since George Washington was the unanimous choice of his countrymen. Eight years later, however, Washington's announcement that he would not seek a third term signaled the opening of the first presidential nominating contest. But his belated announcement in his farewell address left little time for potential contenders to organize campaigns. Rival factions in Congress—the Federalists and Democratic-Republicans—convened into newly formed congressional caucuses to select their nominee. The Federalists, aware that Washington was planning to step down, actually had already held caucuses during the summer of 1796 and chosen Vice President John Adams to be their nominee and Thomas Pinckney as his running mate. Thomas Jefferson was the choice of the Democratic-Republicans (later to be called Democrats) to head the ticket, and Aaron Burr was picked as his running mate. But this pre-party era of candidate selection soon came to an end with the emergence of the congressional caucus system.

Congressional Caucus System: 1800–1824

From 1800 to 1820, the Democratic-Republicans relied exclusively on their congressional caucus (the elected members of Congress) to pick the party standard-bearers—Jefferson, Madison, and Monroe. The congressional caucus (known as "King Caucus") had quickly become a centralized or national mechanism that contained some representation from all or nearly all the states.

By 1816, the Federalists had faded into history. The superficial unity of the congressional caucus, however, disintegrated in 1824 because there was no opposition party to force the reigning Democratic-Republicans, faced with a multi-candidate field, to unite and make a binding nomination.

The election of 1824 marked the end of an era—the demise of the congressional caucus and the short-lived one-party system. The system was abandoned because it smacked too much of aristocratic privilege; it violated the great touchstone of Jacksonian democracy—popular sovereignty. Another charge against the caucus, an argument that came to a head in 1824, was that it violated the separation of powers, a basic principle of the Constitution. Contemporary critics pointed out that the congressional caucus amounted, in effect, to the selection of the president by the legislative branch. This could lead, they said, to domination of the president by Congress or the corruption of Congress by presidents or would-be presidents.[5]

The demise of the congressional caucus, it has been pointed out, not only altered the character of the young political parties, but changed the constitutional system as well. From 1800 to the 1820s, "the main impact of caucus nominations was to convert the formal separation of powers between the President and Congress into a *de facto* 'fusion of powers' not unlike such parliamentary systems as the British."[6] But the collapse of the congressional caucus, the rise of the popular favorite Andrew Jackson, and the emergence of national conventions consisting of delegations chosen by state parties gave "him and succeeding Presidents a base of power independent of Congress . . . totally split Congress off from the presidential succession and established for the first time an institutionalized, *real* separation of powers."[7]

Brokered Convention Systems: 1832–1968

Presidential nominations shifted totally to the state level in 1828. State legislatures and party conventions selected "favorite sons," such as Andrew Jackson and President Adams, as their nominees. But state leaders were dissatisfied with this decentralized form of nomination, since it lacked a national mandate. Three years later, a small splinter group, the Anti-Masonic party, decided to experiment with a unique nominating mechanism—a national convention. Almost by accident, the Anti-Masons discovered that a national party convention, consisting of delegates chosen in most of the states, could serve as a popular forum to assess and discuss prospective presidential candidates before choosing a party standard-bearer. Though the Anti-Masons, caught in the Jacksonian electoral tide, did not survive to hold another national convention, this minor party will forever be credited with developing the unique American presidential nominating convention.

President Andrew Jackson, borrowing a page from the Anti-Masons, instructed his managers to convene a national convention in 1832 in order to ensure that his hand-picked vice presidential running mate, Martin Van Buren, would be nominated. Jackson chose this method rather than trusting to endorsement of Van Buren by various state legislatures. Jackson agreed, too, that a national convention would reinforce his great popular support. The newly formed National Republicans, consisting of former Federalists and disgruntled anti-Jackson Democrats, also decided to call a national convention in 1832. They chose Henry Clay to carry the party banner.

By 1840, the newly emergent Whig party (formed from the elements of the defunct National Republican party and anti-Jackson Democrats) had also adopted the national convention to pick its nominee. Sixteen years later, the newly organized Republican party also borrowed the convention idea. Since then, the national nominating conventions of the two major parties have been a regular part of the American scene. Clearly, the national convention was an idea well suited for the young, sprawling nation:

The national convention system has concentrated the electorate behind the two major party nominees, thus keeping the final selection away from Congress and giving the President a base of support independent of the legislative branch. Clearly, the national convention has strengthened the nominee's ability not only to lead his party but—if successful at the polls—to lead the nation as well. Thus, it can be said that the national convention, though it has escaped constitutional regulation, has profoundly shaped the nature of the Presidency as much as the party system itself has.[8]

By the mid-1840s, the national nominating convention had reached maturity. The convention system remained the only method of nominating candidates—both presidential and state and local candidates—until about 1910. Defenders of the national convention system insisted that it reflected the "popular will" because convention delegates had been chosen by caucus delegates originally selected in local precincts.

Late in the nineteenth century, however, critics began protesting that political rings were manipulating state nominating conventions and that the delegates attending these conventions and those chosen to represent the state at the national nominating conventions were often unsavory characters affiliated with the moneyed interests and the underworld. By the turn of the century, the reformers' charges against the party bosses and the vested interests who worked with them reverberated across the land. It was this rising discontent among the middle class—small businessmen, members of the professions, and independent farmers—that spawned the Progressive movement.[9] From this protest movement was to emerge the direct primary system and the first major reform of the national nominating convention in almost a century—the presidential primary.

Emergence of Presidential Primaries

The Progressives demanded that the state party "kingmakers" and political machines be replaced by popularly elected national convention delegates chosen in state presidential primaries. To sidetrack boss control of the presidential nominating process, the Progressives proposed giving rank-and-file voters the opportunity to elect national convention delegates and to express their personal preferences for president. Indeed, some of these reformers believed that the national party convention eventually should merely ratify the choice of president made in primaries held throughout the United States.

By 1912, a dozen states had adopted presidential primaries to pick delegates and, in some instances, to register their personal choice for president. Structurally, the Progressives' institutional plan called for shifting the locus of decision making in the nominating process from the national convention itself to the preconvention stage—the state presidential primaries. By 1916, more than two dozen states had experimented with some form of popular selection of delegates, but at no time were a majority of delegates chosen in the primaries. Indeed, the Progressive dream for a popularly selected nominee fell far short of the mark. The conservative reaction after World War I took the momentum out of the Progressive movement. By 1935, eight states had repealed their presidential primary laws, and the party regulars had moved back into the driver's seat.[10]

Until the 1960s, presidential candidates lined up support with state party leaders to win the nomination. While presidential primary victories were sometimes helpful for winning party support at the national convention, they never played a decisive role in obtaining the nomination. The reason was simple: most primaries were "advisory," that is, elected state delegates were not pledged to a specific candidate and the presidential preference vote (the so-called beauty contest) was not binding on the state delegations.

Demands for Reform within the Democratic Party

Insurgent Democrats supporting anti-Vietnam War candidate, Senator Eugene McCarthy of Minnesota, quickly discovered during the 1968 primaries that the delegate selection rules were heavily stacked against them. As they sought to wrest the Democratic nomination from Vice President Hubert H. Humphrey, the party insiders' choice after President Lyndon Johnson announced his intention not to seek another term, the McCarthyites found the door closed at every turn. Secret or closed caucuses, unpledged delegates who refused to support the winner of the presidential preference primary, and iron-clad state party leader control over the selection of at-large delegates by the state party organizations were typical barriers the McCarthy backers encountered in most of the caucus-convention and primary states.[11]

In 1968, for example, twenty-six states and three territories still selected their entire delegation to the national convention at state conventions. Four state Democratic parties—Arizona, Arkansas, Maryland, and Rhode Island—and the territory of Puerto Rico chose their entire delegations to the national convention by party committees. In two other states, Georgia and Louisiana, the chairman of the State Democratic Executive Committee chose the entire state delegation, with the advice and consent of the governor—in effect, the governor made the choice.

Although sixteen states and the District of Columbia used presidential primaries, in 1968 most of them were "advisory." Thus, Senator McCarthy won 78.5 percent of the 1968 Pennsylvania presidential preference vote, but collected only 18 percent of the uncommitted delegates.[12] For the McCarthy forces the ultimate miscarriage of justice occurred at the Chicago convention when Vice President Humphrey, who did not enter a single primary, won the nomination—1,760 votes to McCarthy's 601.

Widespread demands for reform of the delegate selection process echoed throughout the convention hall. In a belated response, the Democratic convention directed the Democratic National Committee to establish a commission to open up the nominating process to far more popular participation. Little did the Democrats realize, however, that with the appointment of the McGovern Commission, the party—in fact, American presidential politics—would never be the same again. (The task force name was later changed to the McGovern-Fraser Commission when Senator George McGovern resigned the chairmanship to run for president in 1971 and was replaced by Congressman Donald Fraser of Minnesota.)

McGovern-Fraser Commission Reforms

To avoid a repeat of the 1968 convention, the McGovern-Fraser Commission recommended that all state parties adopt and make readily available published rules on how delegates are to be picked. Secret caucuses and proxy voting were banned. Furthermore, the task force recommended that all delegates be given the opportunity to list their presidential preference on the ballot and that delegates be pledged to vote for their designated candidate or run uncommitted.[13]

Though the McGovern-Fraser Commission expressed no preference between the caucus-convention and primary systems for selecting delegates to future national conventions, one of the unintended consequences of the commission's report was to spawn a proliferation of presidential primaries. By 1980, the number of presidential primary states had risen to thirty-five (see Figure 3.1). Thus, nearly 75 percent of the convention delegates attending the 1980 Democratic convention (the figure was slightly lower at the GOP convention) were chosen by rank-and-file voters, and most of these delegates were pledged to specific candidates. In many states the Republican party, which had not been overly enthusiastic about party reform, was swept along by the Democratic reform tide, since state primary laws usually covered both parties. In 1992, approximately 77 percent of the Democratic delegates and nearly 68 percent of the Republicans were chosen in the primaries. (See Table 3.1)

With the rapid proliferation of primaries, presidential candidates now have no choice but to campaign in the primaries, if they hope to capture the nomination. For most presidential aspirants, however, the march toward the nomination begins long before the presidential primary season opens. Indeed, in some respects, the quest for the presidency has become a continuous four-year campaign.

System of Popular Appeal: 1972 to Present

Today, presidential nominations have become a vast national popularity contest and a delegate-hunting sweepstakes. Participatory democracy has become the watchword, and the number of Americans involved in the nominating process has risen steadily. Between 1968 and 1992 the number of participants in the Democratic primaries expanded from 12 million to more than 18 million.[14] During the same period the number of Republican primary voters grew from approximately 4.5 million to 12.7 million. Overall, however, the turnout in the primaries averaged less than 30 percent of the general election turnout.

Recent Shifts in Primary Schedule Alters Candidate Strategy

Because primaries have become the chief battleground for the nomination and because the early primaries have such a decisive impact on the outcome of

Figure 3.1
Growth of Presidential Primaries, 1968–1980

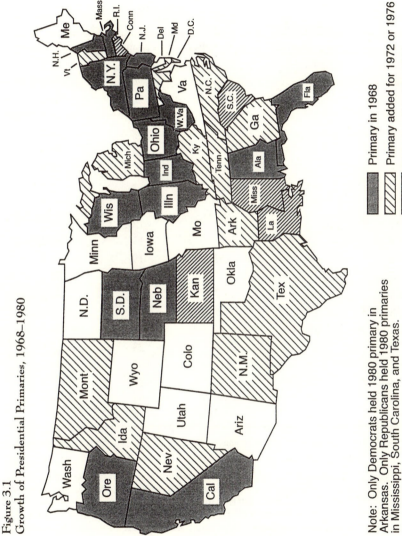

Primary in 1968

Primary added for 1972 or 1976

Primary added for 1980

Caucus-Convention States

Note: Only Democrats held 1980 primary in
Arkansas. Only Republicans held 1980 primaries
in Mississippi, South Carolina, and Texas.

Source: Congressional Quarterly Weekly Report, 2 February 1980, 283.

Table 3.1
Number of Presidential Primaries and Percentage of Convention Delegates from
Primary States, by Party, 1912–1992

	Republican		Democratic	
Year	# of primaries	% of delegates	# of primaries	% of delegates
1912	12	32.9	13	41.7
1916	20	53.5	20	58.9
1920	16	44.6	20	57.8
1924	14	35.5	17	45.3
1928	17	42.2	16	44.9
1932	16	40.0	14	37.7
1936	14	36.5	12	37.5
1940	13	35.8	13	38.8
1944	14	36.7	13	38.7
1948	14	36.3	12	36.0
1952	15	38.7	13	39.0
1956	19	42.7	19	44.8
1960	16	38.3	15	38.6
1964	17	45.7	17	45.6
1968	17	37.5	16	34.3
1972	23	60.5	22	52.7
1976	29	72.6	28	67.9
1980	31	71.8	35	76.0
1984	26	62.1	30	71.0
1988	37	66.6	37	76.9
1992	39	70.0	39	84.0

*Does not include Vermont, which held nonbinding presidential preference votes but chose delegates in
state caucuses and conventions.

Sources: 1912–1976, James W. Davis, *Presidential Primaries: Road to the White House*, 2nd ed.
(Westport, CT: Greenwood, 1980), 279–357. Copyright © 1980 by James W. Davis. Used by permission
of the publisher; Richard C. Bain and Judith H. Parris, *Convention Decisions and Voting Records*, 2nd
ed. (Washington, DC: The Brookings Institution, 1973); William Crotty and John S. Jackson III,
Presidential Primaries and Nominations (Washington, DC: CQ Press, 1985), 62–63; figures for
1980–1992 were supplied by the Democratic and Republican national committees.

subsequent primaries, two of the largest delegate states—California and New
York—recently moved up their primary dates to March 1996. ("Front Loading"
is the term given to this shifting to earlier dates.) By moving their primaries to
the early round, leaders from both parties in California and New York expect to

play key roles—perhaps the role of kingmaker—in selecting the party nominee. By late March 1996—nearly four months before the first national convention is held—over 80 percent of the Democratic party delegates will have been chosen, according to a source at the Democratic National Committee.[15] A similar proportion of GOP delegates can also be expected to be selected by that date.

Recent history shows that early primaries quickly sort out the winners and losers in a decisive manner. In the 1980 GOP nominating race, for example, Senators Howard Baker (R-TN) and Robert Dole (R-KS) were so badly wounded politically by their poor showings in New Hampshire that they soon pulled out of the Republican nominating race won by Ronald Reagan. In the 1988 primaries—the first time since 1960 that an open contest existed in both parties—the New Hampshire primary continued to perform its "winnowing" role with its usual efficiency. Within the Republican party former General Alexander Haig bowed out of the race several days before the New Hampshire primary; Delaware Governor Pierre DuPont soon followed suit, and Republican Congressman Jack Kemp lasted only through Super Tuesday in early March, leaving only Vice President Bush and Senator Bob Dole to fight for the nomination. In the 1988 Democratic race won by Governor Michael S. Dukakis of Massachusetts, former Arizona governor Bruce Babbitt withdrew shortly after his defeat in the New Hampshire primary, and 1984 Democratic runner-up, Gary Hart, lingered on for another three weeks, though his scandal-plagued candidacy was obviously dead in the water.[16] In 1992, two major Democratic contenders—Senators Bob Kerrey of Nebraska and Tom Harkin of Iowa—emerged from the New Hampshire primary so badly battered that they both threw in the towel by early March.

With the rapid spread of primaries, presidential aspirants have no choice but to enter primary contests for pledged delegates, since there is no longer an alternative route to the nomination. Moreover, the linkage between candidate preference and delegate selection is now so inextricably connected that the free agents of earlier campaigns—"favorite sons," bosses, and uncommitted delegates—have all but disappeared.[17] Only pledged delegates count in this era of binding presidential primaries.

CANDIDATES' STRATEGIC PLANNING

Most candidates in the out-of-office party now spend nearly two years gearing up for the big race, establishing fund-raising operations and lining up support throughout the country, with special attention focused on the early primary and caucus states. To win, however, they will first need to develop a strategic plan for their nominating campaign.

Candidate game plans depend upon a number of factors: their name recognition, their standing in the polls, and the availability of money and trained staff.

Generally, candidate strategies fall into two major categories: front-runner and outsider.

The Front-Runner Strategy

Leading contenders within the out-of-power party hope to score an early knockout victory. With their high name identification, efficient fund-raising operation, strong campaign organizations in the early primary and caucus states, skilled pollsters, and media experts, the front-runners try to drive their intraparty rivals out of the race early. By demonstrating widespread popular appeal and a big early delegate lead, they hope to persuade their opponents of the futility of continuing the race.

To be a front-runner in the presidential nominating race is both a blessing and a curse. The chief advantages in the out-of-power party (front-runner is defined here as the leader of the Gallup poll before the primary season begins) are widespread name recognition and a broader political base, plus favorable ratings in the early polls. The front-runner finds it easier to raise money, to set up campaign organizations in the major primary states, and to obtain endorsements from national and state party figures. But the front-runner's position creates expectations that he is a winner and should perform accordingly. Although a front-runner can overcome a limited number of defeats, he will find it difficult to survive a series of setbacks.

Few early front-runners have faced a rockier road to the nomination than Governor Bill Clinton in the 1992 Democratic primaries. Though he led in the early polls in New Hampshire, charges of marital infidelity surfaced in a national tabloid less than two weeks before the first-in-the-nation primary. This embarrassment, coupled with rumors of draft evasion during the Vietnam War, nearly knocked him out of contention. But a joint appearance with his wife, Hillary, on the popular CBS-TV *Sixty Minutes* network program blunted the allegations and helped him salvage a second place finish behind former Massachusetts Senator Paul Tsongas in the nation's first primary. Charges that Clinton had smoked marijuana while at Oxford University on a Rhodes scholarship also dogged his campaign. So concerned were national party leaders about nominating a candidate with as many negatives as Clinton that serious discussions were held in the nation's capitol to consider asking several potentially strong candidates who previously opted not to run in 1992 (viewing President Bush as a shoo-in winner) to reconsider.[18] But Clinton managed to weather this storm, too. Still not until Clinton won decisive victories in the Super Tuesday primaries in the South, followed by solid victories in Illinois, Michigan, New York, and Pennsylvania did his campaign pick up big momentum, clearing the way for his nomination. Political scientist Larry Bartels argues that momentum plays a decisive role in shaping the outcome of the nominating race, and the 1992 Democratic race was no exception.[19]

The Outsider Strategy

Over the past three decades, the road to the nomination has been littered with the bones of many defeated outsider candidates: Kefauver, McCarthy, Bayh, Shapp, Crane, Hart, Simon, Brown, Harkin, Kerrey, and Buchanan, to mention only a partial list of victims. But two outsiders—George McGovern and Jimmy Carter—captured the nomination, and Carter, of course, made it to the White House for one term.

In view of the recent "front loading" of primaries, especially in New York and California, the skyrocketing costs, and the exhaustive organizational demands of launching a national nominating campaign in a nation of fifty states, another successful presidential try by an outsider candidate can almost be ruled out. In 1976, however, former Georgia Governor Jimmy Carter proved with a carefully mapped campaign plan, sufficient access to funds in Georgia, and nearly 275 days of preprimary campaigning, mostly in Iowa, the year before the 1976 race opened, that an outsider candidate could follow this campaign route all the way to the White House.

One of Carter's aides readily conceded in a postconvention interview: "We organized only three states in depth—Iowa, Florida, and New Hampshire."[20] But by winning the early contests to become known nationally and pyramiding these victories into triumphs in the big-delegate states, Carter used his outsider strategy to win the presidency.

The Expectations Game

Mass media expectations of a candidate's performance in the primaries have become important, especially in the early phase of the nominating race. The mass media tend to give special attention to those candidates who do "better than expected." Thus, Senator Eugene McCarthy (D-MN) was viewed as the "victor" in the 1968 New Hampshire Democratic primary, even though President Lyndon Johnson received 49 percent of the popular vote to McCarthy's 42 percent. Four years later, Maine Senator Edmund G. Muskie was viewed as the "loser" in the New Hampshire Democratic primary because in winning he did not receive more than 50 percent of the total vote. Senator George McGovern of South Dakota, the eventual Democratic nominee in 1972, collected only 37 percent of the New Hampshire vote—but he did "better than expected." Similarly, in 1992 Governor Bill Clinton's staff labeled him "the comeback kid" in the New Hampshire Democratic primary and the media seemed to agree (even though he lost to former Massachusetts Senator Paul Tsongas) because he did "better than expected."

Renomination Strategy

If a president wishes to seek reelection, the old cliché still applies: "The presidency is the best place to campaign for President." Challenging an incumbent president seeking a second term has never been an easy task. In fact, no sitting president has been denied renomination—not even Herbert Hoover in 1932—in the twentieth century.

Who are the presidential nominees? What route have they followed to reach a point only one step removed from the White House? Let's take a moment to examine how an aspirant becomes a "presidential possibility" and assess what the prospects are of this person becoming the party nominee.

SERIOUS PRESIDENTIAL POSSIBILITIES

Political scientists William R. Keech and Donald R. Matthews found that between 1936 and 1972 only slightly more than 100 men (and one woman) emerged as "presidential possibilities"—serious candidates. Using the criterion of 1 percent or more of public support in the Gallup poll, Keech and Matthews calculated that sixty-two Democrats and forty-seven Republicans met this "presidential possibility" criterion during this period.[21] The recent plethora of candidates in the Democratic and Republican races obviously expands this number of presidential possibilities, but continued application of the Keech-Matthews criteria for the past five presidential races would not enlarge this list of presidential possibilities by more than three dozen. Indeed, this working list probably errs on the side of including too many potential candidates rather than too few.

During the 1928–1992 period, over 91 percent of all nominees have been elected officeholders—the only exceptions being Herbert Hoover (1928), a cabinet member in the Harding and Coolidge administrations; Wendell Willkie (1940), a businessman-lawyer; and retired five-star General Dwight D. Eisenhower (1952). The record during this period also shows that all presidential nominees who have held public office have been vice presidents, governors, or U.S. senators at the time of their nomination, or formerly held one of these offices (see Table 3.2). The exact route followed by each of the nominees for the 1928–1992 period is depicted in Figure 3.2.

Vice Presidential Success

One of the most significant trends in twentieth-century nominating politics has been the electoral success of vice presidents winning the White House outright after moving to the presidency upon the death of the incumbent. This represents a complete reversal from the nineteenth-century pattern.[22] Four twentieth-century vice presidents rose to the presidency: Theodore Roosevelt,

Table 3.2

Last Major Office Held before Presidential Nomination in Two Major Parties, 1868–1992

	1868–1892		1896–1924		1928–1968		1972–1992	
	%	(N)	%	(N)	%	(N)	%	(N)
Vice President to Presidency	----	----	18.1	2	28.6	4	44.4	4
Senate	10	1	9.1	1	14.3	2	11.2	1
House of Representatives	10	1	9.1	1	----	----	----	----
Governor	40	4	27.3	3	35.7	5	44.4	4
Federal apointive	20	2	27.3	3	7.1	1	----	----
State elective	----	----	9.1	1	----	----	----	----
None	20	2	----	----	14.3	2	----	----
TOTAL	100	10	100	11	100	14	100	9

Sources: Robert L. Peabody and Eve Lubalin, "The Making of Presidential Candidates," in James I. Lengle and Byron E. Shafer, eds. *Presidential Politics* (New York: St. Martin's, 1980), 55 for the period of 1868–1956. Copyright © 1980. Reprinted with permission of St. Martin's Press, Incorporated. The more recent calculations have been made by the present author.

Calvin Coolidge, Harry Truman, and Lyndon Johnson were nominated and elected president on their own. Only Gerald Ford, an appointed vice president, who won nomination to a full term after taking over the presidential duties from the deposed President Nixon (who had also previously served two terms as vice president), failed to retain his office. By contrast, all four nineteenth-century presidents who succeeded automatically to the presidency—Tyler, Fillmore, Johnson, and Arthur—sought renomination, but their parties dropped them from the ticket. This complete reversal of the nineteenth-century experience can probably be explained, in part, by the twentieth-century presidents' ability to capitalize on the expanded role of presidents as world leaders, the persistence of international crises, and continuing domestic problems. The expanded power and prestige of the White House has also helped the incumbents elevated from the vice presidency to keep most potential challengers at bay—at least for one term.

More recently, the vice presidency has become an important stepping stone to the nomination for president in yet another way. Since 1956, each time an incumbent president has stepped down, the incumbent vice president—Nixon in 1960, Humphrey in 1968, and Bush in 1988—has received the nomination of the party in power. In 1984, former Vice President Mondale, who had left office in 1981, won the Democratic nomination. Even serving as the party nominee for vice president in an unsuccessful venture or seeking the number

Figure 3.2
High Public Offices Held by Major Party Nominees, 1928–1992

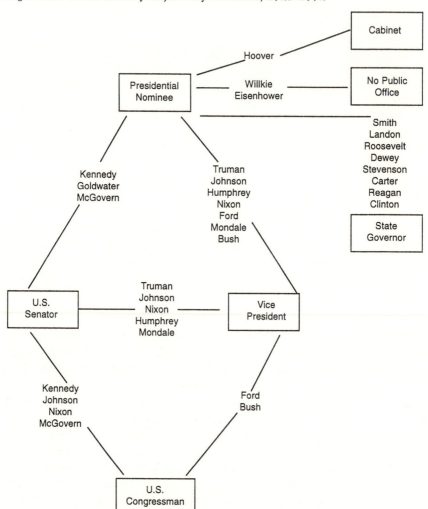

Source: John A. Crittenden, Parties and Elections in the United States (Englewood Cliffs, NJ: Prentice-Hall, 1982), 213. Adapted from William R. Keech and Donald R. Matthews, *The Party's Choice* (Washington, DC: The Brookings Institution, 1976), 20. Reprinted by permission of the Brookings Institution. Names of recent nominees were added by the author.

two spot can sometimes have future benefits. Franklin D. Roosevelt, for example, was the Democratic vice presidential nominee in 1920, twelve years before he won the presidency. In 1956, John F. Kennedy narrowly missed being selected the Democratic vice presidential nominee, but four years later he moved into the White House. The role of the vice president is analyzed more fully in Chapter 14.

As a result of the nationalization of American politics and the growth of the mass media centered in Washington, U.S. Senators have increasingly become prospective nominees for their party. They have found that they can become nationally known as experts on foreign affairs, energy, and military affairs, even in their first term, by appearing frequently on national television news and the regular news interview panels, such as *Meet the Press* and *Face the Nation.* Indeed, the rise of the mass media has made it possible for relatively junior senators to use subcommittee chairmanships to build up their standing in the national opinion polls and enhance their prospects for the nomination. However, the odds of senators capturing the presidency have not been encouraging in recent years. Since 1960, thirty-five sitting senators have sought the presidency, but only one has reached the White House—John F. Kennedy.

Governors and former governors should be included in our list of top presidential possibilities. Indeed, three of the more recent White House occupants—Jimmy Carter, Ronald Reagan, and Bill Clinton—all received their political apprenticeship in state executive mansions. See Table 3.2 for a record of the last office held by candidates winning the nomination for the 1868–1992 period.

But as political scientists Robert Peabody and Eve Lubalin have observed, "The patterns in the nominating process, patterns that obtained as recently as forty years ago, seem almost quaint in light of contemporary preconvention campaigns."[23] Clearly, the rapid expansion of the mass media, especially television, the decline of sectionalism, the proliferation of two-party competitive politics to a relatively large number of pivotal states, and the spread of presidential primaries to three-quarters of the states have all drastically changed the political landscape and the conditions under which candidates for the highest office have sought the nomination.

All presidential contenders, winners and losers alike, share one problem in common—the need for campaign cash. Let us now turn to this vitally important aspect of the nominating race, sometimes called the "money primary."

NOMINATING FINANCES

Financing presidential nominations has become a big business (see Table 3.3). Thirty years ago, a presidential contender could mount a respectable nominating campaign for $1 million. Senator John F. Kennedy, for example, reported spending only $825,000 in his successful 1960 nominating race.[24]

To have a serious chance of winning the party's nomination in the 1990s, however, a candidate must be prepared to raise and spend more than $20 million. This figure may seem high at first glance, but if a candidate is going to mount a nationwide, high-velocity campaign in more than thirty-five primaries, a big

Table 3.3
Republican and Democratic Candidate Expenditures in Nominating Races,
1952–1992 ($ Millions)

Year	Republicans	Democrats
1952	$5.8	$0.8
1956	$0.5	$2.5
1960	$0.5	$2.1
1964	$10.0	$1.0
1968	$20.0	$25.0
1972	$5.7	$32.7
1976	$26.2	$40.7
1980	$71.5	$35.7
1984	$27.1	$79.6
1988	$112.7	$89.7
1992	$49.9	$65.3

Sources: Figures for 1952 and 1956 are from Alexander Heard, *The Cost of Democracy* (Chapel Hill: University of North Carolina Press, 1960), 334–338; the data for 1960–1972 are from Herbert E. Alexander's studies: *Financing the 1960 Election* (Princeton, NJ: Citizens Research Council, 1966), and reprinted by permission of the publisher from Herbert E. Alexander, *Financing the 1968 Election* and *Financing the 1972 Election* (Lexington, MA: Lexington Books, copyright © 1971 and 1976, D. C. Heath and Company); figures for 1976 are from FEC Disclosure Series No. 7, *1976 Presidential Campaign Receipts and Expenditures* (Washington, DC: Federal Election Commission), 9; figures for 1980 are from FEC news release dated November 15, 1981; figures for 1984, 1988, and 1992 are from FEC data supplied to the author by Herbert E. Alexander, Director, Citizens Research Foundation, University of Southern California, Los Angeles.

exchequer is required. Maintaining a big staff for nearly a year before the national convention, underwriting candidate travel, and spending large amounts on television advertising in the primary states consumes huge amounts of cash. In 1992, for example, Governor Bill Clinton's pre-nomination costs exceeded $26 million.[25] Clinton's veteran fund-raisers, by collecting $3.3 million (not including federal matching funds) by the end of 1991, were able to exploit in a substantial way the federal subsidy program, which nearly doubled their treasury during the crucial early weeks of the primary season when each contender was vying for the front-runner spot.[26]

Campaign finance, it should be emphasized, has a much greater influence on presidential nominations than on general election campaigns. To be a serious contender for the nomination, a presidential candidate must establish sophisti-cated fund-raising operations early, long before the primary season opens, to collect money from a large number of small donors, since the 1974 Federal

Election Campaign Act limits individual contributions to $1,000. No longer can candidates rely on individual "fat cat" contributors.

Money-raising activity consists of a three-stage process in the nominating race. Generally, candidates first organize personal, "multi-candidate" political action committees (PACs), like George Bush's "Fund for America's Future," or Richard Gephardt's "Effective Government Committee" in 1988. These committees can be used to collect funds to pay for the candidate's early reconnaissance forays into key primary states, to build the infrastructure for a national campaign organization, and, in some instances, to contribute funds to friendly candidates for various state offices and Congress in the mid-term elections.

The second step is to establish a presidential "exploratory committee" shortly after the mid-term elections for the purpose of raising money to qualify for federal matching funds and help launch a formal campaign—if the candidate decides to jump into the race. Since passage of the Federal Election Campaign Act of 1974, presidential candidates must raise a minimum of $100,000 spread over twenty states ($5,000 per state with no donation of more than $250) to qualify for federal matching funds up to $10 million, plus fund-raising costs.[27] Money raised and spent by the exploratory committee before a candidate's formal entry into the race, it should be noted, is not counted against the overall federal spending limit imposed on announced candidates. Consequently, this "testing of the waters" period can be invaluable in helping a candidate get his campaign organization and fund-raising machinery established and ready to run in high gear.

Formal entry—the third stage of the nominating process—usually occurs a year or more before the presidential election. But fund-raising never stops for the candidate and his staff; indeed, many candidates spend nearly half of their daily campaign time raising money. Candidates are also aware that the news media view a candidate's big war chest as a sign of strength, especially in the prenomination period when reporters are busy assessing the winning prospects of the various contenders.

In recent years a shortage of campaign funds has plagued most presidential candidates in their bid for the White House. In fact, most of the failed candidates have found themselves caught in a vicious cycle during the nominating race. The inability to raise the huge sums (several million dollars) needed in the early primaries diminishes their chances of doing well in these preliminary elections. Poor showings in the early primaries, in turn, dry up the candidate's prospective sources of funds, since donors are not inclined to back losers. The inevitable result is that these cash-poor candidates are forced to the sidelines. A short list of recent presidential contenders who have been forced to drop out of the race, chiefly for financial reasons, would include John Glenn (D-OH), Richard Gephardt (D-MO), Jack Kemp (R-NY), Paul Tsongas (D-MA), Tom Harkin (D-IA), and Bob Kerrey (D-NE).

   With the steady increase by the state legislatures in "front loading" primaries during the first six weeks of the season, candidates in 1996 and future presidential nominating races will face an incredibly difficult task of raising more than half of their campaign funds by New Year's Day of the election year. In the ensuing weeks there is simply not enough time to raise the huge amount needed to organize for the Iowa caucuses, the New Hampshire primary, the multi-primary Junior Tuesday and Super Tuesday contests, and the big California and New York primaries—all to be held before the end of March. Formerly, the sequential nature of the primary system spread the races over a four-month period from mid-February to early June, enabling candidates to pursue a pay-as-you-go strategy.[28] But no more. Unless a candidate has several million dollars in the bank or secured loans (an unlikely prospect for most candidates) by New Year's Day, this candidate will soon be consigned to the "also ran" column. Clearly, the presidential primary nominating system has become money-driven, but this is the cost of greater participatory democracy.

   Since candidates must reach millions of voters in the more than thirty-eight primary states in a short period of time, they have no choice but to devote most of their campaign funds to television advertising.

THE POWERFUL IMPACT OF TELEVISION

   Television has revolutionized the presidential nominating campaigns. Over the past two decades, presidential contenders and their managers have all concluded that presidential nominating races simply cannot be conducted successfully without using the mass media, especially television, to communicate with countless thousands of voters in the primary states. Before the 1976 nominating campaign opened, Gerald Rafshoon, Jimmy Carter's media advisor, summed up the situation this way: "The media is an extension of the campaign." One campaign manager has gone even further: "The media is the campaign."[29] Richard Rubin, a perceptive observer of contemporary political parties, has noted:

The development of television, for example, has provided lesser-known challengers, shunned by established party leaders, with a quick and effective way to gain recognition among the party's mass electorate. And as a result, the rapid development of modern communications techniques together with the decline of patronage-supported organization workers have shattered the near monopoly over campaign resources once maintained by local machines in primary competition.[30]

   To win the attention of the national media's opinion makers and become better known has become the top priority of all presidential aspirants. As Christopher Arterton has put it: "Name recognition has become a critical ingredient in the calculus of electability."[31] Consequently, campaign operatives concentrate on media strategies to build candidate visibility and needed press coverage. Arterton reports: "Campaigners take the view that the press corps constitutes an alternative electorate within which they must campaign simultaneously with their efforts to gather votes."[32] Federal limitations on overall campaign spending in individual primaries have made it more imperative than ever that the candidate turn to the national and local media as early as possible to reach—hopefully through extensive use of the "free" media—the voting public.

Similarly, television has become so dominant, especially in the early primary and caucus states, that the television reporters have become the chief "handicappers" of the candidates. How the network reporters and national press rate a candidate's performance, or even his chances, in the early races, for example, can affect not only the amount of television coverage he receives, but also his standing in the opinion polls and the amount of financial support he can attract. Because the national media overemphasize the significance of the early primaries (especially the New Hampshire primary, whose voters number less than one-half of 1 percent of the American electorate), failure to run well in the early races spells disaster.[33]

Furthermore, early in the nominating campaign the voters' knowledge of the candidates is often meager; consequently they tend to rely far more heavily on the media in the primary season to assess the candidates and interpret the primary and caucus results. Prospective voters are more susceptible than in the fall campaign to media stories on the nominating race and to the candidates' paid spot ads. Voters are also more likely to be influenced by the "horse race" or game aspects of the nominating contests, as the television networks and local stations identify the real "winners" and "losers." The media also report on the national opinion poll standings of the various candidates, who is ahead and who is behind in the delegate count, and how the contenders compare in "trial heat" match-ups with the president or leading candidates in the opposition party.[34] Generally, the media give the front-runner more coverage, but also judge him more harshly than the long-shot candidates.

Many observers see the media taking over the intermediary function formerly performed by the party organization, such as informing voters about policy issues, structuring the decisions of voters and conventions, and in effect delineating both the nature and the limits of the nominating contest.[35]

Significantly, the media's influence seems to be the greatest during the period before the primary season opens and during the early primaries, a time when the public has relatively little information about the various contenders. Christopher Arterton notes: "The latitude of journalistic interpretation is also greatest at this time, when the indicators of growing or declining political support are at their poorest in predictive validity."[36] Nor would most observers dispute political scientist Thomas E. Patterson's assessment that "today's presidential campaign is essentially a mass media campaign."[37]

ELECTRONIC PRIMARIES

More than anything else, the 1992 presidential nominating campaign will be remembered by the rise of the "electronic primary"—the use of the television talk show and the morning news-entertainment shows by the presidential candidates, especially Bill Clinton and Ross Perot. Indeed, the feisty Texas billionaire devised a new kind of nominating process consisting of appearances on *Larry King Live*, a CNN talk show, *Donahue*, a popular afternoon talk show, and Ted Koppel's *Nightline* to launch his unconventional candidacy. Throughout the nominating season Mr. Perot bypassed the party structure, the primary contests, and even the semblance of traditional campaigning to become the first purely electronic media candidate.

Actually, the 1992 nominating races were covered by both the "old media" and the "new media."[38] The old media consist of the major television networks and their Sunday morning interview programs, the metropolitan newspapers, the news magazines, public television (PBS), and influential journals of opinion. But in 1992 these veteran newsmakers were seriously challenged by the new media: Cable News Network (CNN), C-SPAN (the cable public affairs network), the "infotainment" talk shows and satellite hook-ups to targeted local audiences. Indeed, these talk-show appearances seem to have become the new campaign centerpiece for some candidates.

While the mainstream political media still maintain their agenda-setting function early in the nominating race, they face growing competition from the new media, which are less analytical and more informal. Dubbed the "new news" by *Rolling Stone*'s media critic Jon Katz, the television talk shows have clearly become favorites among new-generation candidates. The talk-show forums allow the candidates—free of charge—to speak in more personal terms and offer the candidates an opportunity to address more directly the issues of the race, sex, and power as well as their personal lives, which is of more concern to many viewers.[39]

Unlike the "old news" of the network evening news programs, the new media help the candidate maintain greater control over the dialogue and agenda. Generally, talk-show hosts are more gentle with their guests, serving up a variety of "cream puff" questions. Tough questions and follow-ups are seldom asked, as evidenced by Arsenio Hall's polite treatment of Democratic nominee Bill Clinton. Most viewers only remember the youthful Clinton sporting his new "shades" and playing an Elvis Presley number on his saxophone, not his dialogue with Hall.

Despite the growing popularity of talk shows and late night interviews, some media analysts insist, however, that presidential candidates must still rely heavily on network news programs to reach large numbers of likely voters. Their reasoning is that the average viewership for the evening television news on all three networks is still approximately thirty million homes. Moreover, half the audience is fifty-five years old or over, the age group that is statistically more likely to vote than Arsenio Hall's younger viewership, which is one-tenth the size of the major network audience and contains more, far more, nonvoters.[40]

To win a presidential nomination, candidates must also do well in the public opinion polls. Let's take a moment to explore the important role of polls and pollsters and the growing influence of "focus groups" in presidential nominations.

OPINION POLLS AND FOCUS GROUPS

In this section we will discuss two kinds of polls: public and private. Public opinion polls, such as Gallup, Harris, and *The New York Times*/CBS News, are published periodically to reveal the latest sounding of the public's view of various candidates or other political phenomena. The distinguishing feature of the published polls is that they are conducted as a form of journalism to inform the public about the political world, and not for political intelligence. Private polls are those commissioned for the personal use of candidates and staff in charting campaign strategy and tactics.

Over the years, the Gallup polls have shown considerable evidence that a relationship exists between the candidate's standing in the polls, success in the primaries, and the likelihood of winning the nomination.[41] Since 1936, approximately three-quarters of the time the leader in the Gallup polls after the first major primary has gone on to win the nomination (see Table 3.4). No wonder high ratings in the early Gallup polls are so coveted by presidential contenders.

In the age of primaries, private polls can be as valuable to a presidential candidate as a campaign manager. Senator John F. Kennedy first popularized the use of private polls in the 1960 primaries. His pollster, Louis Harris, made a political reputation for his client and himself during the 1960 Democratic primaries. Surveys by Harris showed that Kennedy's chief opponent, Senator Hubert H. Humphrey, was vulnerable in Wisconsin and West Virginia, two important primary states. With this valuable data, Kennedy boldly entered the Wisconsin primary, thought to be Humphrey country since he lived in neighboring Minnesota, and won a decisive victory. Similarly, with favorable poll data available from West Virginia, Kennedy boldly entered the primary of this overwhelmingly Protestant state and proved that his Roman Catholicism was not a political liability by defeating Humphrey decisively.

Kennedy's West Virginia triumph persuaded many fence-sitting state leaders and national convention delegates that his religion was not a political handicap.[42] Since then, leading presidential candidates in both parties have regularly used private polls to identify voter attitudes on key issues, suggest the kinds of appeals to be made to targeted demographic groups, and help design a campaign to maximize campaign time and money. Frequent polling during the campaign allows the candidate to make adjustments in strategy and tactics.

Table 3.4
Public Opinion Polls and the Nomination, 1940–1992

Year	Party	Gallup Poll After First Primary	Final Gallup Poll Before Convention	Party Nominees
1940	D	Roosevelt	Roosevelt	Roosevelt*
	R	Dewey	Wilkie	Wilkie
1944	D	Roosevelt	Roosevelt	Roosevelt*
	R	Dewey	Dewey	Dewey
1948	D	Truman	Truman	Truman*
	R	Stassen	Dewey	Dewey
1952	D	Kefauver	Kefauver	Stevenson
	R	Eisenhower	Eisenhower	Eisenhower*
1956	D	Stevenson	Stevenson	Stevenson
	R	Eisenhower	Eisenhower	Eisenhower*
1960	D	J. Kennedy	Kennedy	Kennedy*
	R	Nixon	Nixon	Nixon
1964	D	----	Johnson	Johnson*
	R	Lodge	Goldwater and Nixon	Goldwater
1968	D	R. Kennedy	Humphrey	Humphrey
	R	Nixon	Nixon	Nixon*
1972	D	Humphrey	McGovern	McGovern
	R	----	Nixon	Nixon*
1976	D	Humphrey	Carter	Carter*
	R	Ford	Ford	Ford
1980	D	Carter	Carter	Carter
	R	Reagan	Reagan	Reagan*
1984	D	Mondale†	Mondale†	Mondale
	R	Reagan	Reagan	Reagan*
1988	D	Dukakis	Dukakis	Dukakis
	R	Bush	Bush	Bush*
1992	D	Clinton	Clinton	Clinton*
	R	Bush	Bush	Bush

D = Democrat; R = Republican; *indicates general election winner; †Mondale was the choice of Democrats—he trailed Hart among self-identified Independents.

Source: *The Gallup Poll, Public Opinion 1933–1971*, vols. 1–3 (New York: Random House, 1972); *Gallup Opinion Index* (Princeton, NJ: Gallup International, 1971–1980). Data for 1984–1992 are from various issues of the *Gallup Report*, the renamed Gallup monthly opinion report. (Princeton, NJ: Gallup International). Reprinted with permission.

Presidential contenders, it seems fairly clear, depend far more on private polls than on the widely circulated public polls, such as the Gallup and Harris polls. Indeed, it is unlikely that a presidential candidate will ever venture into a campaign again without a trusted private pollster at his side.

Because the Gallup and Harris polls have come to be considered reliable barometers of candidate popularity, all presidential contenders make it one of their main preconvention objectives to gain the top spot in the opinion poll ratings. Favorable ratings can be used to build momentum, raise campaign funds, and generate additional media coverage. Within the past decade presidential campaign managers have found another valuable adjunct to private opinion polls—focus groups.

"When the history of the 1992 campaign is written, it will be hard to find a policy position taken, a television ad broadcast, or a strategy shift executed that has not been approved by a focus group," wrote Elizabeth Kolbert, the news media specialist reporter for *The New York Times*, shortly after the national conventions.[43] Focus groups, an off-shoot of military research conducted during World War II to evaluate training films, are basically designed to probe an individual's response to a specific stimulus. Consisting of carefully selected small panels (ten to fifteen persons) of prospective voters, preferably relatively homogeneous participants—all men, all women, or all white or black—the focus groups are asked a series of specifically designed questions, or asked to monitor a candidate's taped speech with a thermometer-like gadget that measures the intensity of the respondent's feeling toward specific points in the speech. Panelists' reactions are also closely monitored from behind one-way mirrors by opinion experts and campaign professionals.

Though manifestly unscientific, focus group research nevertheless has become a remarkably effective tool for gauging public attitudes, to measure what voters are actually thinking. Long used by consumer marketing agencies to measure public preferences for products in grocery stores, or by Hollywood directors to determine which movie ending the focus groups like the best, focus groups are now utilized throughout both the primary and general election races. Foremost among the early findings of the Clinton panels in 1992, for example, was that President Bush had seemingly lost touch with ordinary Americans and their deep concern about the poor state of the economy. Focus group participants also gave President Bush's leadership in the Persian Gulf War a low-priority rating.

President Bill Clinton's pollsters began using focus groups even before their candidate had formally entered the nominating race in October 1991. Focus group findings were also invaluable to Clinton strategists in guiding their candidate through the dark days before the New Hampshire primary when charges of marital infidelity nearly shipwrecked his campaign. Subsequently, Clinton neutralized party rival, former Massachusetts Senator Paul Tsongas, and his austere economic program with a populist appeal in several southern states (relying heavily on focus group data). Clinton then demolished his last rival, Jerry Brown, in the New York primary by charging, based upon focus group data, that Brown's proposed 13 percent flat tax was clearly regressive and warned primary voters in New York that this tax would wreak havoc on the Social Security system.[44]

From focus group panelists the Clinton strategists learned belatedly that the public had little knowledge about the Arkansas Governor's personal background. Because Clinton attended Georgetown University, Oxford, and Yale, many voters assumed that he, like President Bush, was an Establishment candidate. Panelists did not know that Clinton had lost his father before he was born and that he had worked his way through college.[45] Focus group responses to this information helped Clinton and his managers correct public misperceptions about his background—and undoubtedly contributed heavily to winning the party nomination and his dramatic victory in November 1992. Clearly, focus group panels are here to stay.

PRIMARIES OVERSHADOW NATIONAL CONVENTIONS

Officially, presidential nominees of the two major parties continue to be nominated by delegates to national party conventions. But over the past three decades presidential primaries have, in effect, taken over the latent functions of convention balloting.

In the traditional national nominating convention, multiple ballots served the function of informing delegates about the relative strengths of the various contenders and of pointing to the likely nominee. In recent years, however, this balloting or informing function has been usurped by the presidential primaries.[46] Each primary, or set of primaries, serves, in effect, as a convention ballot, with the consequent shift in delegate strength among the candidates after each set primaries calculated and assessed by the national media. Unlike the typical four-day national convention, presidential primary elections have been stretched out over a four-month period. Winning a single primary is not enough to sweep the nomination. Instead, candidates usually acquire only a portion of delegates from each state, since the proportional vote rule applies in most states (all states for Democrats). Building a majority of national delegates to win the nomination has been a slow, incremental process.

If the primary returns do not point to a clear-cut winner, the delegates always have the option of using the convention as a "brokering" agency for arriving at a compromise choice. But this has not happened since 1952, when the Democrats went to three ballots before nominating Illinois Governor Adlai Stevenson. Instead, the national convention over the past four decades has been transformed from a decision-making body into a coronation that merely serves as a mechanism to legitimize the popular favorite of the primaries. Still, the national convention remains an important political institution.

NATIONAL NOMINATING CONVENTIONS

Though the presidential primaries, the television networks, and national opinion polls have in recent years pinpointed the eventual nominee of the out-of-power party long before the convention time, the final choice must still be made by the party's national nominating convention. Incumbent presidents seeking another term must also be formally renominated and voted by the convention delegates before they are officially authorized to carry the party banner again. Indeed, if a majority of convention delegates wishes, they can jettison an incumbent president in favor of a new face, though this has not occurred in the twentieth century. However, since 1968 four incumbent presidents—Johnson, Ford, Carter, and Bush—have all faced stiff intraparty challenges to renomination.

History shows that for over 150 years national conventions have nominated or renominated presidential and vice presidential candidates acceptable to most factions within each major party, except in 1860, 1912, and 1964 for the GOP, and 1924, 1968, 1972, and 1980 for the Democrats. Especially in a close nominating race, the convention has almost always in the past served to break the deadlock and "broker" a compromise candidate behind whom a majority of the delegates can unite.

National conventions have also hammered out party platforms each quadrennium for 140 years. The quadrennial conventions serve, too, as a campaign rallying mechanism for the national party and to help kick off the fall campaign. This function of arousing party faithful to unite behind the national ticket has long been recognized as a valuable attribute of the party conclaves. Television coverage of the conventions has also helped arouse the enthusiasm of the millions of home viewers for their candidate. Indeed, some critics argue that free television coverage of these conventions "poses an almost irresistible temptation to convention managers to concentrate on the mass rally aspect of the conventions at the expense of platform-writing, rules changes, and even bargaining over the vice presidential nomination."[47]

Sometimes, however, the national convention's televised activity can be counterproductive to the party's chances in November. The raucous, frequently out-of-control 1968 Democratic national convention in Chicago, which chose Vice President Hubert H. Humphrey as the party standard-bearer, produced such a harsh, negative reaction among television viewers across the country that it may have cost Humphrey the election. Scenes of the Chicago police clubbing anti-war protesters in Grant Park, hundreds of heavily armed Illinois national guardsmen patrolling outside the crowded convention hall, and television pictures of Mayor Richard J. Daley's henchmen beating up CBS-TV reporter Dan Rather all contributed to the public impression that the Democratic party was out of control and not deserving the continued stewardship of the country.[48]

More recently, the 1992 Republican convention in Houston appeared to have been hijacked by the Christian right wing of the party. The convention scene left the distinct feeling among millions of television viewers that the pro-life, anti-abortion forces were in the driver's seat at the GOP convention. Most political observers subsequently concluded that the right-wing extremist monopolization of the GOP agenda in Houston contributed significantly to President Bush's defeat in the November election.

In the years ahead, convention managers will undoubtedly continue to de-emphasize the conduct of party business and endeavor instead to capitalize on the rally functions (as exemplified by the nominee's acceptance speech) to persuade the national electorate—via the free network coverage of the convention—to vote for their party nominee in November. The national convention also offers the nominee the best opportunity to introduce himself to the nation, indeed for the first time for many Americans.

By 1972, an estimated 115 million people watched some part of the two nominating conventions as the three major networks covered the proceedings gavel to gavel. In the 1980s, however, the major networks began cutting back from the traditional coverage (because they concluded that the nominees had already, in effect, been nominated in the primaries). But the networks nevertheless continued to telecast "live" the convention highlights, especially the candidates' acceptance speeches.

National conventions also perform a number of latent (unintended) functions that are sometimes overlooked. First, over the years the quadrennial gatherings have performed a valuable legitimizing function for the nonconsensus candidate. Clearly, the conventions furnish a stamp of legitimacy for the nominee that tells all party members and the nation as a whole that the party stands behind the nominee as its standard-bearer. It has sometimes been overlooked, for example, that in 1976 Democratic nominee Jimmy Carter was the choice of only 39 percent of the primary voters nationwide before the national convention; yet once nominated, he was accepted by almost all party groups as the legitimate nominee.

Second, the evolution of the national convention as a nominating device is closely intertwined with the development of the president's independent power base. Indeed, these quadrennial party grand councils fulfill an indispensable role in helping to build and maintain the independent stature of the president in the American separation of powers system.[49]

Over the past century the national convention has profoundly influenced the evolution of the modern presidency. Had the congressional caucus by some quirk of fate survived as the method for nominating presidential candidates, the odds are high that the presidency would have but a faint resemblance to the powerful institutional chief executive that has emerged in the twentieth century.

Winning the presidential nomination, however, is only half the battle. The party standard-bearer cannot, of course, lay claim to the White House until he or she defeats the nominee of the rival party in the fall presidential election—the subject of the next chapter.

NOTES

1. For more background on the Canadian leadership conventions, see John Courtney, *The Selection of National Party Leaders in Canada* (Hamden, CT: Shoe String Press, 1973).

2. James W. Davis, *Presidential Primaries: Road to the White House* (New York: Thomas Y. Crowell, 1967), 15.

3. Donald R. Matthews, "Presidential Nominations: Process and Outcomes," in James David Barber, ed., *Choosing the President* (Englewood Cliffs, NJ: Prentice-Hall, 1974), 36.

4. Thomas R. Marshall, *Presidential Nominations in a Reform Age* (New York: Praeger, 1981), 17–64.

5. James S. Chase, *Emergence of the Presidential Nominating Convention, 1789–1832* (Urbana: University of Illinois Press, 1973), 294.

6. Theodore J. Lowi, "Party, Policy and Constitution in America," in William Nisbet Chambers and Walter Dean Burnham, eds., *The American Party System* (New York: Oxford University Press, 1967), 248, as cited by Austin Ranney, *Curing the Mischiefs of Faction* (Berkeley: The University of California Press, 1975), 173.

7. Ranney, 173–174.

8. James W. Davis, *The National Conventions in an Age of Party Reform* (Westport, CT: Greenwood Press, 1983), 31.

9. For an excellent discussion of the Progressive reforms, see James W. Ceaser, *Presidential Selection: Theory and Development* (Princeton, NJ: Princeton University Press, 1979), Chapter 5; see also Ranney, *Curing the Mischiefs of Faction*.

10. James W. Davis, *Presidential Primaries: Road to the White House*, 2nd ed. (Westport, CT: Greenwood Press, 1980), 43–44.

11. Ibid., 44–47.

12. The story of McCarthy's travels during the 1968 preconvention campaign is well summarized in Lewis Chester, Godfrey Hodgson, and Bruce Page, *An American Melodrama: The Presidential Campaign of 1968* (New York: Viking, 1969), 547–558.

13. *Mandate for Reform,* a report of the Commission on Party Structure and Delegate Selection to the Democratic National Committee (The McGovern-Fraser Commission), (Washington, DC: Democratic National Committee, 1970).

14. Although these figures reflect a greater turnout since 1968, this turnout rate (approximately 30 percent) is actually lower than what it was between 1948 and 1968. Austin Ranney, in a study of eleven states holding competitive primaries for the earlier period, found an average of 39 percent voting in the primaries and 69 percent in the general election. Austin Ranney, "Turnout and Representation in Presidential Primary Elections," *American Political Science Review* 66 (March 1972): 21–37.

15. *The New York Times,* 1 July 1994.

16. Rhodes Cook, "The Nominating Papers" in Michael Nelson, ed., *The Elections of 1988* (Washington, DC: CQ Press, 1989), 45–46; Jack W. Germond and Jules Witcover, *Whose Broad Stripes and Bright Stars: The Trivial Pursuit of the Presidency, 1988* (New York: Warner Books, 1989), 34–36.

17. James Lengle and Byron Shafer, "Primary Rules, Political Power and Social Change," *American Political Science Review* 70 (March 1976): 25–40.

18. "How He Won," *Newsweek* (Special Election Issue), November-December 1992, 33.

19. Larry Bartels, *Presidential Primaries and the Dynamics of Public Choice* (Princeton, NJ: Princeton University Press, 1988), 108–135.

20. "People don't know who I am," *Time,* 2 August 1976, 14; also see Richard Reeves, *Convention* (New York: Harcourt, Brace, Jovanovich, 1977), 180.

21. William B. Keech and Donald B. Matthews, *The Party's Choice* (Washington, DC: The Brookings Institution, 1976), 15.

22. The discussion in this section relies heavily upon Robert L. Peabody and Eve Lubalin, "The Making of Presidential Candidates," in James I. Lengle and Byron E. Shafer, eds., *Presidential Politics* (New York: St. Martin's, 1980), 50–68.

23. Ibid., 59.

24. Theodore H. White, *The Making of the President, 1960* (New York: Atheneum, 1961), 7.

25. This figure includes $12.5 million in federal matching funds. Candice J. Nelson, "Money and Its Role in the Election," in William J. Crotty, ed., *America's Choice: The Election of 1992* (Guilford, CT: Dushkin Publishing Group, 1993), 104.

26. *Washington Post*, 3 January 1992.

27. Frank J. Sorauf, *Inside Campaign Finance* (New Haven, CT: Yale University Press, 1992), 9-14.

28. Davis, *Presidential Primaries,* 2nd ed., 202–242.

29. F. Christopher Arterton, "Campaign Organizations Face the Mass Media in the 1976 Presidential Nominating Process." Paper delivered at the American Political Science Association annual meeting, Washington, DC, September 1–4, 1977.

30. Richard L. Rubin, *Party Dynamics: The Democratic Coalition and the Politics of Change* (New York: Oxford University Press, 1976), 153.

31. Arterton, "Campaign Organizations Face the Mass Media," 6.

32. Ibid., 1–4.

33. Davis, *Presidential Primaries*, 2nd ed., 78–110.

34. Thomas E. Patterson, *The Mass Media Election: How Americans Choose Their President* (New York: Praeger, 1980), 21–30.

35. William Crotty and John S. Jackson III, *Presidential Primaries and Nominations*, (Washington, DC: CQ Press, 1985), 77; see also Ronald Berkman and Laura W. Kitch, *Politics in the Media Age* (New York: McGraw-Hill, 1986), Chapter 5.

36. F. Christopher Arterton, "Campaign Organizations Confront the Media Environment," in James David Barber, ed., *Race for the Presidency* (Englewood Cliffs, NJ: Prentice-Hall, 1978), 4.

37. Patterson, *The Mass Media Election*, 3.

38. This section relies primarily on Jonathan Alter, "Between the Lines," *Newsweek*, vol. 120 (8 June 1992), 28.

39. Elizabeth Kolbert, *The New York Times*, 5 June 1992.

40. Ibid.

41. James R. Beniger, "Polls and Primaries," in Davis, *Presidential Primaries*, 2nd ed., 111–133.

42. James W. Davis, *Presidential Primaries* (New York: Thomas Y. Crowell, 1967), 62–64.

43. Elizabeth Kolbert, "Test Marketing a President," *The New York Times Magazine*, 30 August 1992, 18; for further details, see David W. Moore, *The Super Pollsters* (New York: Four Walls Eight Windows, 1992), 235–239.

44. See " 'Manhattan Project' 1992," *Newsweek*, vol. 70 (November-December 1992), 40–42.

45. Ibid.

46. Davis, *National Conventions in an Age of Party Reform*, 5–12.

47. Ibid., 273.

48. Theodore H. White, *The Making of a President*, 1968 (New York: Atheneum, 1969), 301–366.

49. Davis, *National Conventions in an Age of Party Reform*, 31.

CHAPTER 4

PRESIDENTIAL ELECTIONS

Winning the presidential nomination means the candidate is only halfway to the finish line. Although the party nominee will have campaigned in most of the more than thirty-eight presidential primaries and in a dozen caucus-convention states, delivered dozens of speeches, shaken thousands of hands, and spent nearly $25 million to become the party standard-bearer, he still faces a relentless general election campaign before he can hopefully lay claim to the grand prize.

In this chapter special attention will be focused on Electoral College politics, a widely misunderstood aspect of presidential elections. Equally important, the strategic environment in which presidential campaigns operate will be assessed, as well as the strategies for building a winning coalition. The prominent role that the televised presidential debates have come to play in presidential campaigns is also discussed. Additionally, the powerful impact of television on the way presidential campaigns are conducted and the media's preoccupation with the "horse race" aspects of the campaign, not major issues, will receive detailed treatment. The critical role of campaign finance and the growing importance of "soft" money in presidential campaigns will be closely analyzed. Also, we evaluate the pervasive influence of political polls in predicting presidential elections and especially the extensive use of "exit" polls to provide more detailed information on demographic voting patterns. Finally, we explore briefly the meaning of the election to the voters and to the newly elected or reelected president. Does the quadrennial election give the president a broad mandate, or is it to be considered primarily an instructional message from the people?

INTRODUCTION

In the United States presidential candidates generally do not use election campaigns to get the prior approval of the voters for solutions to the nation's problems. Instead, as explained by one veteran political scientist, "The candidate's first priority is to get elected and only then does he worry about the problems he'll face in office."[1] As Walter Lippman implied in *The Phantom Republic* nearly seventy years ago, elections are seldom decided by issues per se.[2] Indeed, presidential contests rarely formulate public policy, and the president-elect, once in office, may shift positions from those taken during the campaign. Two examples readily come to mind. New York Governor Franklin D. Roosevelt campaigned in 1932 on a platform of economy and major cuts in federal spending and then launched his New Deal reform program, which included heavy expenditures in public works, shortly after his inauguration. President Bill Clinton's abandonment in 1993 of a "middle-class tax cut" in the face of the harsh realities of continued mounting federal deficits is another case in point. Presidential elections are more like an ongoing referendum about the public's views on such matters as the state of the economy, the direction in which the country is headed, economic prospects for future generations, and so on.

Structurally, general election campaigns differ from nominating campaigns in a number of crucial aspects. Presidential nominating campaigns are aimed at winning national convention delegates; general election campaigns are aimed at winning votes. Since the general election contest is a battle between rival party adversaries, party identification and issue differences soon come into play. Moreover, the incumbent's record (if he is running for reelection), party ideology, personal qualifications, and "image" will all be weighed by the voters. While a majority of voters usually make up their minds before or soon after the party conventions (see Table 4.1), a sizable portion of the electorate will still remain undecided. It is on this large bloc of undecided voters that the two major party nominees will concentrate their attention "like a laser beam," while also seeking to reassure their own partisans that their votes too are needed in November.

Let's take a moment to trace the evolution of presidential campaigns.

HISTORICAL BACKGROUND

During the nineteenth century, presidential election campaigns were usually marked by torchlight parades, mass rallies, and plenty of hard cider—but presidential candidates rarely appeared on the scene. Abraham Lincoln, for example, was elected president without leaving the state capital in Springfield, Illinois. Presidential campaigns were decentralized. Candidates depended almost exclusively on party leaders in each state to manage and conduct their

Table 4.1
Reported Time of Vote Decision on President, 1960–1992

1. Knew all along, always vote same party, preconvention
2. At time of conventions
3. After conventions
4. Within two weeks of election, on election day

	1960	1964	1968	1972	1976	1980	1984	1988	1992
1.	31%	41%	35%	44%	33%	41%	52%	31.7%	29.6%
2.	31%	25%	24%	18%	21%	18%	18%	28.7%	14.4%
3.	26%	21%	19%	22%	22%	15%	17%	22.2%	21.8%
4.	12%	13%	21%	13%	24%	26%	13%	17.3%	34.2%

Note: The responses above were made to the standard question asked quadrennially by interviewers from the University of Michigan's Institute for Social Research: "How long before the election did you decide that you were going to vote the way you did?"

Sources: "Opinion Roundup," *Public Opinion* (December-January 1981), 26. Reprinted by permission of American Enterprise Institute for Public Policy Research. Data for 1980–1992 supplied by Institute for Social Research, University of Michigan, and reprinted by permission.

campaigns, while they issued an occasional lofty statement from their office or home on the major issues of the day—usually the tariff or a currency problem. Candidates devoted themselves largely to "front porch" campaigns. Biographer Margaret Leech has described a typical William McKinley front-porch perform-ance in 1896 at his home in Canton, Ohio:

He bade them welcome to his home and thanked them for the honor of their call. He said a few words on the campaign issues, adapting the discussion to suit the special interests of his audience. In conclusion, he expressed a desire to shake the hand of each and every one, and held an informal reception on the porch steps.[3]

Although Democratic nominee William Jennings Bryan in 1896 delivered more than 600 campaign speeches and traveled more than 18,000 miles by train in his first unsuccessful quest for the presidency, full-time campaigning did not become standard practice until Democratic challenger Franklin D. Roosevelt mounted a full-scale whistlestop campaign against President Hoover in 1932. FDR used his nationwide rail tour not only to castigate Hoover, but also to squelch a whispering campaign about his own health. Roosevelt had suffered a serious polio attack in the early 1920s that had incapacitated him for more than two years. His relentless attacks against the Republican incumbent forced President Hoover onto the campaign trail. As the first incumbent president to campaign actively, Hoover logged over 10,000 miles, speaking to audiences across the land.[4]

With the advent of radio in the late 1920s, candidates for the first time could also reach large audiences previously denied them. Whistlestop campaigning reached its zenith in 1948 when President Truman, a political underdog, launched the famous railroad speaking tour that carried him over 32,000 miles across the length and breadth of the land—and back to the White House for another four years. But air travel soon displaced this time-honored electoral train travel. By 1952 the age of television had arrived, and with the availability of this new communications medium, presidential campaigns entered the electronic era. More will be said about the impact of television later in the chapter.

ELECTORAL POLITICS

Most political bystanders view the presidential election as one gigantic swirling battle between opposing political forces. But in fact the presidential contests are really fifty separate, state winner-take-all elections for the electoral vote in each of the fifty states and the District of Columbia. The prime goal of a candidate and his staff is not to capture a majority of the popular vote, but to collect 270 out of the 538 votes in the Electoral College—a simple majority in this time honored electoral institution. Then, and only then, can the party nominee claim the presidency. It is therefore understandable that when candidates and their staffs map out an electoral strategy, they talk more in terms of carrying state electoral votes, not the national popular vote.

Generally, both major candidates concentrate their heavy firepower on the "battleground" states—California, New York, Illinois, Pennsylvania, Ohio, Michigan, New Jersey, Texas, and most recently, Florida—since winning these nine states will ensure 243 electoral votes, just twenty-seven short of the needed majority. During the fall campaign, the presidential and vice presidential candidates of both major parties cross and recross these states, stopping each time in one or more of the major media markets to obtain valuable television coverage.[5] The Electoral College also affects campaign strategy in another way: Candidates seldom campaign in states in which they have little chance of winning; nor do they waste time in those states in which they are considered sure-fire winners.

Electoral College politics is confusing to many Americans. It is a commonly held belief that if a presidential candidate receives a majority of the popular vote—or even a plurality (more than any other candidate)—he will automatically be elected president of the United States. Not so. The Founding Fathers, with their innate distrust of popular democracy, set up an indirect system of presidential election called the Electoral College. Under this system, each state is allocated a sum of electors equal to its total number of U.S. representatives and senators. Thus California, which has fifty-two U.S. representatives and two U.S. senators, is allocated fifty-four electoral votes (see Table 4.2); Montana, which has one U.S. representative and two senators, is allocated three electoral votes; New York has thirty-one U.S. representatives and two U.S. senators, or thirty-three electoral votes.

Under the Electoral College "ground rules" that have prevailed since the beginning of the nineteenth century, the candidate who wins a plurality of votes within the state wins all the state's electoral votes.[6] In other words, it is "winner-take-all" for the victor. Thus, when President Clinton in 1992 won California, Montana, and New York—as well as twenty-nine other states—he collected the ninety electoral votes from these three states and 280 electoral votes from the other 29 states. His grand total was 370 electoral votes to 168 for President George Bush, who carried eighteen states, including two "battle-ground" states—Florida (twenty-five votes) and Texas (thirty-two votes).

Ronald Reagan won landslide victories in 1980 and 1984 and George Bush in 1988, but the presidential elections of 1960, 1968, and 1976 were all cliffhangers. Indeed, the outcome of presidential elections would have been reversed or shifted to the House of Representatives with the switch of only a few thousand popular votes in two states. In 1960, for example, a combined shift of 9,241 votes in Illinois and Missouri would have denied the presidency to John F. Kennedy and shifted the election to the House of Representatives.[7] In 1976, a switch of less than 4,000 votes in Hawaii and less than 6,000 in Ohio would have given the election to Gerald Ford, despite his trailing Carter by 1.7 million votes in the popular vote figures.

Actually, under the Electoral College system, a presidential candidate can win the popular vote and yet fail to win a majority of the electoral vote and the presidency, as was the case with Grover Cleveland in 1888. Cleveland won a plurality of approximately 95,000 popular votes but only 168 electoral votes, compared to 233 electoral votes for the Republican Benjamin Harrison. Cleveland's loss of New York, his home state, by about 15,000 votes and Indiana, Harrison's home state, by about 3,000 votes cost him reelection. Four years later, however, former President Cleveland won a second term with a convincing 279 to 145 electoral-vote victory over President Harrison in their rematch. Significantly, no winning presidential candidate since 1888 has lost the popular vote.

What happens if no candidate wins a majority of the Electoral College vote? According to the U.S. Constitution, Article II, section 2, if no person shall have a majority, then the House of Representatives shall choose the president from the five highest persons (later changed to three by the Twelfth Amendment) on the list with each state having one vote. To become president when an electoral impasse shifts the election to the House of Representatives, a candidate must

Table 4.2
Number of Presidential Electors by State, 1992

State	Number	State	Number
Alabama	9	Montana	3
Alaska	3	Nebraska	5
Arizona	8	Nevada	4
Arkansas	6	New Hampshire	4
California	54	New Jersey	15
Colorado	8	New Mexico	5
Connecticut	8	New York	33
Delaware	3	North Carolina	14
District of Columbia	3	North Dakota	3
Florida	25	Ohio	21
Georgia	13	Oklahoma	8
Hawaii	4	Oregon	7
Idaho	4	Pennsylvania	23
Illinois	22	Rhode Island	4
Indiana	12	South Carolina	8
Iowa	7	South Dakota	3
Kansas	6	Tennessee	11
Kentucky	8	Texas	32
Louisiana	9	Utah	5
Maine	4	Vermont	3
Maryland	10	Virginia	13
Massachusetts	12	Washington	11
Michigan	18	West Virginia	5
Minnesota	10	Wisconsin	11
Mississippi	7	Wyoming	3
Missouri	11		
		Total	538

Note: The District of Columbia, which has no voting delegation in Congreess, was authorized membership in the Electoral College by the Twenty-third Amendment, ratified in 1961.

win a majority of the states (twenty-six votes) in the House. Prior to the passage
of the Twentieth Amendment in 1933, members of the old Congress, which
invariably included some defeated "lame duck" members, were eligible to
choose the president. But under the new amendment members of the newly
elected Congress, who take their seats on January 3, vote for the president, if
no candidate has received a majority of the electoral votes.[8] Also, the Twentieth
Amendment moved up Inauguration Day from March 4 to January 20.

Only once since the passage of the Twelfth Amendment in 1804 has the House
selected the president. In 1824, the House picked John Quincy Adams over
Andrew Jackson and William Crawford. In the presidential election Jackson
had collected ninety-nine electoral votes to eighty-four for Adams, forty-one

for Crawford, and thirty-seven for Henry Clay. In 1876, Democratic candidate Samuel Tilden, who led by 250,000 popular votes was denied the presidency when a special, congressionally appointed commission, consisting of eight Republicans and seven Democrats, was established to settle the question of disputed electoral votes in three states. By upholding the Republican claims in all three states—all under questionable circumstances—the GOP candidate, Rutherford B. Hayes, emerged victorious by a single electoral vote, 185 to 184.[9]

The Electoral College is often criticized as an anachronism—an eighteenth-century institution still functioning in the late twentieth century. But abolition of the Electoral College would have far-reaching consequences on the U.S. political system. Direct election of the president—the most frequently mentioned alternative—is discussed in chapter 15 on proposed reforms of the presidency.

THE STRATEGIC ENVIRONMENT

No two presidential elections are exactly alike, and only rarely do the same candidates square off against each other more than once, such as the Eisenhower-Stevenson matchups in 1952 and 1956. The Electoral College provides the legal framework and dictates the electoral strategy each candidate is likely to follow. The economy, unemployment rates, and international crises all affect the political climate.

To maximize their advantage within the strategic environment, candidates and their managers concentrate mainly on the elements that determine voter choice. Past research on voting behavior has shown that three major factors (which vary from election to election) have the greatest impact on voter decision making: party identification, issues, and the candidate's image.[10] No serious contender can entertain hopes of victory unless he includes all three factors in his strategic planning.

PARTY IDENTIFICATION

For more than three decades, party identification has been viewed as the most stable indicator of voter intentions. Party identification is the psychological attachment voters feel toward one party or the other. Generally, it is based upon family influence during childhood and later contacts with issues and candidates. When voters are undecided about issues and candidates, they usually make their choice, if they are not independent, on the basis of party identification.

Because Democratic party identifiers have outnumbered Republican identifiers since the New Deal era, Republicans tend to downplay their candidate's party affiliation. Thus, in 1984 President Reagan concentrated on such nonpartisan themes as patriotism, "America's back," a strong economy, and low inflation. So frequently did he identify with Democratic presidents such as

Franklin D. Roosevelt, Truman, and Kennedy that Democratic challenger former Vice President Walter F. Mondale repeatedly complained the president was trying to steal the Democratic heroes while never mentioning former GOP presidents, such as Hoover and Nixon. President Reagan also invited Democrats to defect to the GOP ranks, pointing out that he was once a Democrat who left the party only after it lost its moorings.

By contrast, the 1992 Democratic nominee Bill Clinton frequently invoked the names of Democratic greats Franklin D. Roosevelt and John F. Kennedy in his all-out effort to win back blue-collar Democrats who had defected to Ronald Reagan and George Bush in the 1980s.

ISSUES

Generally, issues surface in every presidential campaign in three forms. The first involves specific policy questions of the moment. In 1992, for example, the issues of the stagnant economy, high unemployment, and inadequate health care were foremost in the minds of most American voters.[11] Consequently, Democratic nominee Clinton hammered President Bush incessantly for his failure to deal with these substantial issues. The second form of issue concerns involve values, such as patriotism, morality, and democracy—valence issues. Generally, there is a broad public consensus on these valence issues, which are more basic than a position on a specific policy question. Valence issues can be powerful instruments for obtaining public support. Indeed, presidents often prefer to be judged on values and symbols than on specific issues—"America's back and standing tall," "It's morning in America again." Few experts would dispute that valence issues augmented President Reagan's standing in the polls.

The third form of issue relates to the public's verdict on the overall direction of the president's policy leadership or that offered by the challenger. Thus, it was not necessary for Franklin D. Roosevelt to have lifted the country out of the Great Depression by reelection time in 1936. Because a majority of Americans felt he was trying hard, moving in the right direction, and that his policies were preferable to those of his GOP predecessor, Herbert Hoover, they returned him to the White House for another term. Similarly in 1984, the opinion polls showed that the voters felt President Reagan was moving the country in the right direction, especially on matters of inflation and foreign affairs; therefore the voters supported Reagan, even though they did not always agree with him on specific issues.

CANDIDATE IMAGE

Favorable public perception of the incumbent president or his challenger will often tip the scales on election day. President Reagan was the chief beneficiary of candidate image in 1984, especially the image of leadership. According to the *Washington Post*/ABC News Polls, 72 percent of the respondents said the president has "strong leadership qualities." Only 49 percent held this view of Walter F. Mondale.[12] Reagan's strong leadership ratings helped him effectively neutralize Mondale's effort to make the future direction of the country a major issue in the campaign.

President George Bush in 1992, on the other hand, was unable to maintain his winning image for reelection. Why? Shortly after the victorious Persian Gulf War in early 1991, President Bush received the highest public approval rating in the polls (89 percent) since polling began in the 1930s. But over the next eighteen months he saw his approval ratings melt away to below 40 percent. In the face of a weak economy and persistent, high unemployment, many voters came to perceive President Bush as detached and uncaring about the fate of working men and women. This negative image clearly overshadowed his rosy forecasts about a rebounding economy. As a result of Mr. Bush's failure to develop a detailed plan to deal with the economic malaise, he found himself in mid-summer 1992, after the Democratic convention, trailing Governor Bill Clinton in the polls for the first time.[13] He never recovered.

OTHER KEY FACTORS

Financial resources and the mass media, two topics discussed later in the chapter constitute the principal instruments through which campaign objectives may be reached.[14] But time is another important factor that is sometimes overlooked. To have any serious hope of contacting a major segment of the potential voters, directly or most likely via television, requires a prodigious effort. Since the out-of-office party holds its national convention in mid-July, the party's nominee and his staff seldom have enough time to map a comprehensive general campaign strategy, allocate resources (especially the $55.2 million federal campaign grant), put key state managers in place, purchase television air time, and produce the commercials for an arduous fifty-state campaign.[15] For the in-power party, whether it renominates the incumbent or chooses a new standard-bearer, the time frame is considerably shorter. Incumbent party conventions are generally not held until the third week in August. Consequently, the incumbent or his successor have even less time to mount and execute their strategic plan. No wonder presidential campaign plans are often compared to the battle plans of rival field commanders.

All elements of the master plan must be carefully weighed and integrated into a grand strategy for the general election campaign. Failure to develop this plan early in the campaign can be fatal to the candidate's chances, as several defeated contenders have learned. Vice President Hubert H. Humphrey, for example, emerged from the strife-torn 1968 Democratic convention with the nomination in hand, but no campaign plan had been drafted; no television film was ready for commercials; and no money was available to purchase critical television time near election day. It took his campaign manager Larry O'Brien and the staff until the end of September to get back on track.[16] In the final five weeks Humphrey closed Richard Nixon's 43 percent to 25 percent Gallup poll lead to less than a point, but failed by a whisker to win the presidency.

President Bush and his staff committed the same error in 1992. Basking in the glow of his Persian Gulf War victory and his stratospheric poll ratings in early 1991, the overconfident Bush failed to get his campaign organization mobilized until mid-summer 1992, and even then it lacked focus and a grand strategy.[17]

ADVANTAGES OF INCUMBENCY

Although three of the last five presidents—Ford, Carter, and Bush—have all failed to gain a second term, the advantages of incumbency cannot be easily dismissed. First, the incumbent holds the highest office in the land and can capitalize on all the trappings and prestige that attaches to the office. As president, he enjoys instant recognition, dominates the news, and sets the national agenda. When the president emerges from the door of Air Force One to greet the waiting crowds, the nation stands proud and the television cameras capture every moment of the action. Generally, incumbents are viewed as experienced and knowledgeable. As head of state, greeting foreign dignitaries and participating in White House ceremonies, he can remain "presidential" throughout much of the campaign. Relying on his decision-making power, especially his commander in chief role, he can influence events both at home and abroad. Also, he has a huge, trained staff and numerous surrogates who can campaign for him around the clock. Federal windfalls in the form of defense contracts, grant money for urban transit, sewage treatment plants, and other priority local projects can be released in the weeks before election to help influence the outcome. Understandably, presidential incumbents point with pride to their accomplishments, note the unfinished work, and sound a "let us continue," "stay the course" theme.

On paper, at least, the incumbent president possesses so many advantages over a challenger that it seems a wonder that he should ever be defeated. Yet, within the past sixteen years three presidents have failed to win reelection. Why?

One of the chief reasons for this failure, other than those already indicated, is that in the age of television the gap between public expectations and performance has widened. Presidents are expected to solve the problems of inflation, high interest rates, and unemployment, and to extricate the country from foreign quagmires. Failure to halt inflation or the rise in unemployment, even though there is actually relatively little that a president can do alone on these issues, can wreck his chances for a second term. Failure to impress the public that he is a decisive leader on top of his job can be equally fatal. The excessively high public expectations placed on the president, especially in the economic sector, make the campaign task of the challenger much easier. Nevertheless, the challenger must demonstrate leadership potential and also appear "presidential."

Since the public knows far less about the challenger and his personal life, he must rely on the mass media to display his openness, decisiveness, and leadership potential for all America to see. Television and its exposure of any presidential shortcomings, it seems fair to say, has narrowed the margin an incumbent enjoys over the challenger. As Stephen J. Wayne has commented: "By appearing to be at least the equal of their incumbent opponents, the presidential images of the challengers are enhanced."[18] Other things being equal, however, the incumbent should generally be favored to win reelection. After all, in the twentieth century, fifteen incumbent presidents have run for reelection and ten of them have won. But that was not the case in 1992. Let's take a moment to review the campaign strategy of the Clinton and Bush campaigns and then offer a few observations on the Perot campaign plan.

THE 1992 PRESIDENTIAL ELECTION

The Clinton advisers designed a tough-minded campaign plan based upon the Democratic party vote in previous elections and current economic conditions, especially in the big industrial states. Predicated on a quick-fire start, the Clinton plan aimed to be fully mobilized before the Bush campaign even got off the ground. The Clinton-Gore team added a new twist to national campaigning by commencing an ambitious week-long, 1,240 mile, eight-state bus caravan tour—from Manhattan to Missouri—on the day after the Democratic national convention. This carefully orchestrated "buscapade," which generated almost as much national media attention as the Democratic convention itself, gave an added lift to the Clinton-Gore team—a sharp pickup that President Bush and his managers were never able to match.

With this surprising head start, the Clinton team hoped to build up insurmountable leads against Bush in key states needed for an Electoral College majority. Those states considered unwinnable were, in effect, written off, though no one on the Clinton staff would admit this publicly.

In the Clinton grand plan, according to political scientist William Crotty and others, the Arkansas governor's strategists divided the country into three major categories of states.[19]

- Category I, or "Top End" states—thirteen states and the District of Columbia: These were considered to be strong Democratic areas, to which the campaign devoted only the minimal resources needed to win. They included (in addition to the District of Columbia): Arkansas, Massachusetts, Rhode Island, West Virginia, Minnesota, and Hawaii, all heavily Democratic, and California, New York, Illinois, Washington,

Oregon, Vermont, and Connecticut, all reasonably competitive and all (with California being the extreme example) facing difficult economic times. Clinton won each of these.

- Category II, or "Play Hard" states—eighteen. A full court press could be applied to these states, which were considered to be more competitive and less predictable than those in the other two categories. The election would be won or lost here. These states were the battleground. They included: Delaware, Georgia, Maryland, Missouri, Pennsylvania, Iowa, Kentucky, Louisiana, Maine, Michigan, Colorado, Montana, North Carolina, New Jersey, New Mexico, Ohio, Tennessee (Gore's home state), and Wisconsin. Clinton lost North Carolina by one percentage point; he won every other state.

- Category III, or "Big Challenge" states—nineteen. These were divided into ten states in which minimal campaign effort, at best, was extended, and nine others that were worth "watching." The latter received a slightly higher priority and more, although still severely limited, campaign attention and resources. In the first group were: Alaska, Virginia, Mississippi, Indiana, North Dakota, Nebraska, Oklahoma, Wyoming, Idaho, and Utah. The second included: Alabama, Arizona, Florida, Kansas, New Hampshire, Nevada, South Carolina, South Dakota, and Texas. Clinton did make occasional forays into some of these states (Florida and Texas are examples) to test the waters, to force the Bush campaign to focus more on their base, or in an effort to help a local candidate, but overall these were the orphans, essentially conceded by the Democrats to the Republicans. Still, Clinton managed to win close races in New Hampshire (39 percent to Bush's 28 percent and Perot's 23 percent) and Nevada (38 percent to Bush's 35 percent and Perot's 26 percent). He lost the rest.[20]

Overall, the Clinton strategists concentrated on winning 376 electoral votes in thirty-two states, plus the District of Columbia—one hundred more votes than needed for victory in the Electoral College. Surprisingly, the Clinton campaign plan unfolded in almost clockwork fashion. Clinton won thirty of the thirty-one targeted states, plus New Hampshire and Nevada, for a smashing victory in November (see Figure 4.1).

President Bush's campaign, on paper at least, began his drive for reelection with significant advantages on the electoral map. Since 1968, the Republican ticket had carried a large bloc of states totaling 202 electoral votes for six straight presidential elections. Located in the Great Plains, Rocky Mountains, and Far West, these states constituted the bedrock foundation for a remarkable string of electoral victories. Another thirteen states, mostly in the South, with an additional 152 electoral votes had supported the Republican nominee in five of the

Figure 4.1
Electoral Votes by States, 1992

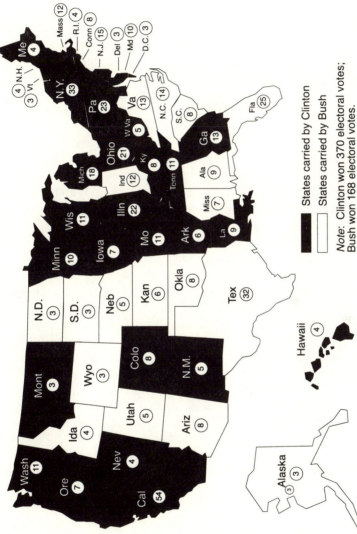

■ States carried by Clinton

□ States carried by Bush

Note: Clinton won 370 electoral votes;
Bush won 168 electoral votes.

Source: Paul R. Abrahamson, John H. Aldrich, and David W. Rohde, *Change and Continuity in the 1992 Elections* (Washington, DC: CQ Press, 1994), 87.

six most recent presidential elections. With this firm base of 354 electoral votes, the Republicans felt that they already had far more than the 270 votes needed to capture the White House and further opportunity to collect additional votes in other friendly states.

With these impressive electoral numbers in front of them, the Bush managers could scarcely be faulted for their optimism as they approached the 1992 campaign. But with the sudden end of the Cold War, the fall of the Berlin Wall, the disintegration of the Soviet Union, and a faltering economy across the land, the 1992 campaign was not to be a replay of the three highly successful Reagan-Bush campaigns of the 1980s. On election night Bush won only eighteen states with 168 electoral votes—a drop of 258 electoral votes and 16 percent of the popular vote from his one-sided victory over Governor Michael S. Dukakis in 1988.

The mercurial Texas tycoon, H. Ross Perot, was the wild card in the 1992 presidential election. Perot's strategy, when he re-entered the race on October 1, was based essentially on a television-driven campaign. During the final thirty-four days of the campaign, Perot spent approximately $60 million, mostly of his own money, to buy huge chunks of television advertising time on the networks and cable systems. Perot also made frequent appearances on the televised talk shows and the network morning news and information programs. Invited to participate in the three national television debates, the feisty Texas businessman proved to be a formidable adversary, especially in attacking President Bush and his handling of the deficit and the stagnant economy. But, alas, his rejection of conventional parties—Perot seldom left the television studios during his campaign—failed to win him the presidency, despite his huge outlay of campaign cash.[21] Perot's 19 percent of the popular vote, however, was the most votes a third-party candidate had collected since Teddy Roosevelt and his Bull Moose Party in 1912. But Perot captured no votes in the electoral college. Nevertheless, in most states west of the Mississippi, Perot received nearly a quarter or more of the votes cast, and he ran surprisingly well in the New England states. Clearly, the nation had not heard the last from H. Ross Perot.

One unpredictable factor in recent presidential campaign strategy has been the candidates' performance in the televised presidential debates—our next topic.

THE DEBATES

Presidential debates have come to represent the most important single campaign event of the presidential race, especially for the challenger. The debates provide a forum where the two contenders are placed on a relatively equal footing. Thus the challenger, though less experienced than the incumbent, is in an excellent position to counter charges that he lacks experience and presidential qualities. In any case, these confrontations can sometimes make or break candidacies in a single roll of the dice.

In the first series of nationally televised debates, held between Senator John F. Kennedy and Vice President Nixon in 1960, Kennedy was considered by those watching to be the winner of the opening round in the four-debate series. More than anything else, Kennedy's outstanding forensics performance—his crisp answers, his cool-headed demeanor, and his "presidential" qualities of decisiveness and conviction—was also thought to have turned him into the front-runner overnight. Curiously, most people listening to the first debate on radio rated the candidates about even or Nixon slightly ahead. But this reaction was almost completely ignored by the television commentators and many of the estimated 60 million viewers who lauded Kennedy's brilliant presentation. The results of the other three debates were judged to be nearly standoffs. But it did not matter because Kennedy had won the laurels on the opening night.[22]

No debates were held in the next three presidential elections because President Johnson refused to debate Senator Barry Goldwater in 1964, and Nixon declined to debate Vice President Humphrey in 1968 and Senator George McGovern in 1972.[23] But in 1976 challenger Jimmy Carter, according to most pollsters, benefited immensely in the second debate from President Ford's misstatement (and his subsequent refusal for several days to correct his remark) that Poland, a Soviet satellite, was not under the domination of the Soviet Union. This gaffe was thought by most observers to have halted Ford's remarkable fourth-quarter comeback (Ford had been listed nearly thirty percentage points behind Carter in the late August polls), which fell just short of victory on election day.

Four years later, challenger Ronald Reagan came up with a forensic victory against President Jimmy Carter in the single, winner-take-all encounter just one week before the election. (Previously, Carter had refused to debate both Reagan and third-party candidate John Anderson on the same platform.) Compared to the 1976 series, the Carter-Reagan confrontation was relatively low-keyed. There were no major rhetorical blunders like Ford's gaffe in 1976. Even though he was the incumbent, Carter was on the attack more than Reagan, the challenger. Reagan, however, had the last word with his famous summation: "Ask yourself, are you better off than you were four years ago?"

Most press observers at the Carter-Reagan debate rated it as fairly even. But the public scored it differently. A *New York Times*/CBS News poll taken the next day indicated that 44 percent of the viewers thought Reagan had won, while 36 percent picked Carter. Approximately 6 percent said they had changed their vote after watching the debate; these respondents went for Reagan by a two to one margin.[24]

In 1992 for the first time since the beginning of the presidential debates in 1960, the nation was treated to a three-way forensic contest among President Bush, Governor Bill Clinton, and Texas business tycoon Ross Perot.

Perot and Clinton shared top honors in the first and third debate (see Table 4.3). But Clinton's extemporaneous skills, most observers agreed, carried him to a solid victory in the second encounter. Throughout the three confrontations Perot more than held his own with his sharp wit and populist, anti-Washington responses.

President Bush did not begin to impress viewers until the final debate—too late in the minds of many analysts. Subsequently, Bush critics and some of his own staff members privately admitted that President Bush's negotiators made a serious blunder in delaying the debates until mid-October, and then telescoping three debates into an eight-day time frame, especially since Bush had been trailing Clinton by more than eight percentage points in the polls throughout the first six weeks of the fall campaign.[25]

Nationwide interest in these forensic contests may have reached new highs in 1992. Figures released by The Commission on Presidential Debates, the official host, reveal that the four encounters, which included one vice presidential debate, drew nearly 85 million viewers per debate.[26] Although it is impossible to calculate exactly how many of these viewers saw more than one debate, it is reasonable to assume despite the numerous repeaters, that more than 100 million Americans of voting age watched at least one debate. In other words, the overall size of the debate audience was approximately equal to or exceeded the 104.2 million Americans who cast ballots in the general election.

Exit polls on election day revealed that half of the respondents thought Clinton was the overall winner of the debates. The remaining half was split between Mr. Bush and Mr. Perot.[27]

CAMPAIGN FINANCE

Prior to 1972, all presidential campaign funds came from political parties and private donors. Early contests between the Republican and Democratic candidates were conducted at bargain basement rates. Abraham Lincoln, the first Republican president, spent only $100,000 in 1860 to capture the White House. Republican President James A. Garfield in 1880 was the first nominee to spend $1 million to reach the White House. But it was eighty years and twenty presidential elections later before another GOP candidate Vice President Richard M. Nixon in 1960 spent $10 million in his first, unsuccessful bid for the presidency.

The quantum leap in the cost of campaigning—national, state, and local—between 1952 and 1972 can be attributed mostly to television advertising costs. Clearly, the age of television profoundly changed the rules of the game. Television advertising costs, especially those for thirty-second spot ads, skyrocketed. Money, not campaign volunteers, became the most important commodity of campaigns. As Table 4.4 shows, the total cost of presidential spending—this includes prenomination, convention, and general election

Table 4.3
Winner of the 1992 Presidential Debates

Question: Which candidate do you think did the best job—or won—tonight's debate? (Asked of those who had watched or listened to each debate.)

	First	Second	Third
Clinton	30%	54%	30%
Bush	16%	25%	23%
Perot	33%	20%	30%

Source: CBS News/*New York Times* polls, as quoted in Kathleen A. Frankovic, "Public Opinion in the 1992 Campaign," in Gerald R. Pomper, ed. *The Election of 1992* (Chatham, NJ: Chatham House, 1993), 120.

Table 4.4
Presidential Spending: 1960–1992 (Adjusted for inflation, 1960 = 100)

Year	Actual Spending[a]	CPI (1960 base)	Adjusted Spending[a]
1960	30.0	100.0	30.0
1964	60.0	104.7	57.3
1968	100.0	117.5	85.1
1972	138.0	141.2	97.7
1976	160.0	192.2	83.2
1980	275.0	278.1	98.9
1984	325.0	346.8	93.7
1988	500.0	385.4	126.5
1992	550.0	446.9	117.8

[a]All spending figures are in millions of dollars and include prenomination, convention, and general election costs.

Source: Citizen's Research Foundation, reprinted from Herbert E. Alexander and Brian A. Haggerty, *Financing the 1984 Election* (Lexington, MA: D. C. Heath, 1987), 84. Revised 1984, 1988, and 1992 figures furnished by Herbert E. Alexander, Director, Citizen Research Foundation.

costs—doubled from $30 million in 1960 to $60 million in 1964. By 1972—the last presidential election before major campaign finance reform—the total cost of presidential spending more than doubled again from 1964. To be sure, the cost-of-living index had risen substantially, but even with this adjustment, presidential campaign spending jumped more than threefold between 1960 and

1972. As Table 4.4 shows, the spending spree by presidential candidates and their staffs has continued unabated into the 1990s.

The growing "professionalization" of campaign staffs, communication specialists, high-priced chartered jet air travel, and the inflated costs of phone banks, office space, computerized mailing lists, satellite downlink rentals, and campaign polling have all contributed to the zooming costs of running for the White House. Until Congress intervened in the 1970s, heavy reliance on "fat cat" contributors had become an integral part of presidential campaigns.

But in the early 1970s public financing of presidential campaigns replaced the private system. The Watergate investigation (1973–1974) revealed that the Nixon White House had collected huge illegal campaign contributions, nearly $50 million, from corporations (banned since 1907) and exerted heavy pressure on big individual contributors. Public outrage over these illegal activities led Congress to pass the Federal Election Campaign Act of 1974 (FECA).

This legislation, among other things, restricted the individual contributions to $1,000 for presidential candidates and provided for the option of full public funding of presidential elections, major party national conventions, and matching federal subsidies in the nominating race.[28] Thus, if candidates agreed to accept Uncle Sam's money for the general election campaign, they were prohibited from soliciting any private funds. Since then, all major party candidates have accepted federal money rather than go it alone, though in 1980 GOP candidate Ronald Reagan flirted with the idea of raising his own campaign funds. But he finally decided to put aside his personal bias against government intervention in the election process and accepted the federal funds. In 1992, President Bush and Governor Bill Clinton each received $55.2 million in federal funds for their campaigns.

Additionally, the 1974 law permits the major national committees to spend two cents per citizen of voting age in support of their presidential nominees. In 1992, this figure amounted to approximately $10.2 million each for the GOP and Democratic national committees.

Beyond question, the 1974 Federal Election Campaign Act marked the beginning of a new era in presidential election politics. First of all, the legislation equalized spending between the major party candidates, eliminating the traditional funding advantage the GOP had almost always enjoyed. By granting the money directly to the presidential candidates instead of the national party committees, however, the 1974 law has further weakened the political parties and fostered the growing trend toward a plebiscitarian presidency.

President Reagan in his 1985 tax reform plan proposed, among other things, that Congress end the current system of public financing for presidential elections by repealing the $1 checkoff allowed on individual tax returns. Congress, however, refused. Although Reagan had not used the $1 checkoff on his own tax return, it is noteworthy that he had accepted more federal money than any presidential candidate (until surpassed by George Bush in 1992) since the passage of the federal legislation—a grand total of $90.5 million in 1976, 1980, and 1984, according to federal records.[29]

The new champion fund-raiser is President Bill Clinton whose money managers in 1992 collected more private "soft" money than any contender in modern times—$71 million. "Soft" money refers to funds raised and spent outside the constraints of federal law. This sum shattered another record set in 1988 by less successful Democratic contender Michael S. Dukakis, whose finance chairman and staff raised $52 million, mostly "soft" money.[30] In 1992 President Bush's fund-raisers collected $62.4 million in "soft money" during the campaign.[31]

Party fund-raisers have been operating recently as if federal contributing and spending restrictions hardly existed. Both parties have unashamedly utilized loopholes in the federal law to collect huge amounts of "soft" money. Termed by critics as "sewer money," this extra-legal cash has become a vital supplement to the candidate's war chest. Indeed, within the last decade soft money fund-raising has grown from a relatively minor aspect of presidential campaigning to a dominant activity.[32]

Although federal election laws limit how much money can be given directly to campaign organizations, donors are advised that they can easily circumvent the limits by funneling the money instead to the Republican and Democratic national committees and to state and local organizations that work on behalf of presidential candidates. Similarly, federal campaign limits can also be easily circumvented through other "soft" money loopholes, which permit unlimited spending by state parties on such "party building" activities as voter registration, get-out-the-vote drives, and advertising that does not specifically use a candidate's name.

Beyond question, federal limits on campaign spending have failed miserably to halt large contributions by individuals and corporations, prompting some critics to label the federal legislation a farce. Significantly, more contributions larger than $100,000 were given in 1992 than in the extravagant Watergate era (1973–1974).[33]

Independent candidate Ross Perot immediately became a big stakes player in the three-cornered 1992 presidential race. Perot's financial outlay, according to preliminary reports from the Federal Election Commission (FEC), exceeded $65 million—all but a token amount came from Mr. Perot's own deep pockets.[34] Perot, it should be noted, was not bound by FEC limits because under the 1974 law he was ineligible to receive money in 1992 (since he and his "party" —United We Stand—had not participated in the 1988 election to establish his credentials as a candidate).

Ample funding is, of course, indispensable to a winning campaign, but presidential candidates also need to utilize the latest political technology, a topic that merits brief discussion.

POLITICAL TECHNOLOGY

Traditionally, the central task of a presidential campaign has been to put together a coalition of support among groups already predisposed toward one's candidacy and to add to this coalition enough political independents and disgruntled opposition party supporters until victory appears within reach.

To reach a potential electorate of 190 million individual voters, modern political campaigns require the latest political technology. Private polling, huge direct mail advertising campaigns, massive television advertising, and satellite downlinks, have all become key elements in the final drive for the White House.

The 1992 presidential campaign has been called the year of "talk show" politics; but, just as accurately, it should be termed the year of satellite dish politics. Aware that the television networks and local stations have faced scarcer resources to devote to political coverage, the presidential campaign teams in 1992 decided to get directly into satellite technology themselves. Both the Clinton and Bush managers sent their own equipment and crews to major events, including the presidential debates, and put the coverage on the satellite free for any station to use. At the debate sites, for example, the campaign teams set up production trailers filled with camera and editing equipment to beam their campaign messages to independent television stations across the country.

Why do the major campaigns spend their limited resources on satellite transmissions? The compelling reasons are that it gives the campaign managers a wider audience and more direct control over the news, enabling them to bypass the television networks to reach key "persuadable markets" where they think they will gain favorable treatment. Local television stations, pinched by low budgets, find these "free" telecasts hard to resist. Indeed, nearly half of all local television stations used satellite technologies to obtain live exclusive interviews with presidential candidates in 1992—a figure that more than doubled since the 1988 campaign.[35]

ROLE OF THE MASS MEDIA

With the advent of television, the nature of the entire presidential election campaign has also changed. Much of this transformation can be traced to the role of the mass media itself. As political scientists Thomas E. Patterson and Richard Davis have pointed out: "Most election coverage is devoted to the campaign contest itself rather than to what the choice of one candidate or the other may mean to the nation."[36] Patterson's studies of recent presidential elections have documented the media's concentration on the "horse race" or game aspects of the campaign—who's ahead? who's behind?—rather than the issues.[37]

Several causes underlie this shift in emphasis by the media. Because the campaign is so long, the candidate's position on the issues will be reported early on, but once reported, it appears to lose news value. Television reporters and even members of the "pencil press" would much rather update the players' strategies and their standings in the latest polls than rerun the candidate's policy statements and qualifications. Occasionally, the candidate will come up with a fresh proposal, a new issue—but once covered by the media, it will usually be relegated to the reporters' notebooks.

Opinion Polls

The steady growth of syndicated public opinion polls has helped tilt the mass media's emphasis on the game aspects of the presidential contest even more. As Patterson and Davis have noted: "The increasing availability of polls—many of them conducted by news organizations themselves—has elevated the probable outcome of the election to an everyday news subject, and thus this speculation has become a constant competitor with the election's substance for space in newspapers and time on television."[38] The same authors found, for example, that in the last week of the 1984 election (October 31–November 6, 1984) *The New York Times* ran fifteen stories—nearly a third of its election coverage stories—based wholly or in significant part on polls, mostly its own jointly operated with CBS News. Another quarter of its election stories made at least some mention of poll results.[39] No longer can there be much doubt that the election agenda centers on the "game," not the issues.

"Free" Media

The 1992 campaign also saw much more extensive candidate use of the "free" media—network morning news-talk shows, afternoon audience participation programs, such as *Donahue* and *Oprah*, the evening cable network interview call-in show *Larry King Live*, and Ted Koppel's popular ABC *Nightline* news-interview program. Although television network evening news programs are also considered to be part of the free media, candidate coverage has usually consisted of short, ten-second "sound bites," selected by the network news editors or the anchorman, not the presidential candidate.

Another type of free media would be the networks' weekend news-interview programs. But television viewers would have looked in vain for presidential candidates to appear on *Meet the Press*, *Face the Nation*, or *This Week with David Brinkley*—too many tough questions and follow-ups.

DECISION TIME

How much influence does the ten-week general election campaign by the major party candidates have on voter choice for president? Data collected over the past quarter century show that although over half the voters have decided on their candidate by convention time, voters appear to be delaying their choice until the last two weeks of the campaign (see Table 4.1). In 1980, for example, approximately 26 percent of the voters made their decision in the last two weeks of the campaign or on election day. In 1992, 34 percent decided in the final two weeks of the campaign.

While we can only speculate about the time sequence of voter decision making, it may be that the re-establishment of presidential debates in 1976 has offered prospective voters two or three additional opportunities to "size up" the presidential nominees before making a final choice. Furthermore, weak party loyalties characteristic of the contemporary electorate leave it inherently more volatile than previous electorates. This does not necessarily mean, however, that large numbers of voters will be in a state of flux every four years. In 1984, for example, an election day poll taken by the *Los Angeles Times* found that an extraordinary 47 percent of the voters stated that they had made up their minds on how they would vote before the first presidential primaries in February.[40] In any event, it is impossible to state precisely how many voters are persuaded by the general election campaign to change their choice of candidates, or decide whether or not to vote at all. But there can be no doubt that candidates have the undecided voters in their sights continuously.

VOTER TURNOUT

Although approximately 182.6 million Americans over the age of eighteen were eligible to vote for president in 1988, only 92 million Americans went to the polls—a 50.1 percent turnout. Ironically, as more and more citizens acquired the right to vote in recent years, voter turnout declined—until 1992. As Table 4.5 indicates, the estimated number of those eligible to vote has more than doubled in the past fifty years, but after reaching a peak in 1960 (62.8 percent) the percentage of citizens who actually cast ballots dropped for three decades. Voter turnout fell almost ten percentage points in the past seven elections. Between 1968 and 1972—the height of the Vietnam War—it fell by over 5 percent.

What has accounted for the drop in turnout? Political experts are still scratching their heads over this question because some of the most serious restrictions—stringent registration and residence requirements—have been relaxed. A low education level has always been equated with low voter turnout, but the level of education of American citizens was considerably higher in 1988 than in 1960. Lack of political information is another factor that research has shown reduces turnout; yet the availability of political information, especially via television, which can be found in over 98 percent of America's 84.5 million households, has never been higher. Close political races are thought to generate higher voter turnout, but the turnout in the Johnson landslide of 1964 was 61.9 percent without any presidential debates, while the tight Carter-Ford contest twelve years later, featuring three debates, was only 53.5 percent.

Table 4.5
Participation in Presidential Elections

Year	Total Voting Age Population	Total Presidential Vote	Percentage of Adult Voting Population
1824	3,964,000	363,017	9.0%
1840	7,381,000	2,412,698	33.0%
1860	14,676,000	4,692,710	32.0%
1880	25,012,000	9,219,467	37.0%
1900	40,753,000	13,974,188	35.0%
1920	60,581,000	26,768,613	44.0
1932	75,768,000	39,732,000	52.4%
1940	84,728,000	49,900,000	58.9%
1952	99,929,000	61,551,000	61.6%
1960	109,674,000	68,838,000	62.8%
1964	114,085,000	70,645,000	61.9%
1968	120,285,000	73,212,000	60.9%
1972	140,285,000	77,719,000	55.2
1976	150,127,000	81,556,000	53.5%
1980	162,761,000	86,515,000	52.6%
1984	173,936,000	92,032,260	52.9%
1988	182,628,000	91,594,693	50.1
1992	187,033,000	104,403,641	55.9

Note: Restrictions based on sex, age, race, religion, and property ownership prevented a significant portion of the adult population from voting in the nineteenth and early twentieth centuries.

Sources: Population figures for 1824 to 1920 are based on estimates and early census figures that appear in Neal R. Peirce and Lawrence D. Longley, *The People's President: The Electoral College in American History and the Direct Vote Alternative*, rev. ed. (New Haven, CT: Yale University Press, 1981), 206. Copyright © 1981 Yale University Press. Reprinted by permission. Population figures from 1932 to 1980 are from the U.S. Commerce Bureau of the Census, *Statistical Abstract of the United States* (Washington, DC: Government Printing Office, 1984), 262. Figures for 1984 are from *World Almanac and Book of Facts 1986* (New York: Newspaper Enterprise Association, 1985), 229–230. Figures for 1988 and 1992 are from Federal Election Commission press releases, 14 January 1993.

Extension of the right to vote to eighteen-year-olds by the Twenty-sixth Amendment in 1971 may be another explanation given for the decline in voting, since young voter turnout has been found to be lower than for those over twenty-four. Some experts attribute the lower turnout to the decline in party identification, which seems to suggest less psychological involvement in politics. Another explanation is a decline in the sense of political efficacy—that is, over recent decades fewer people have thought public officials care about their views, or that as citizens they have less and less voice in what the government does. Vietnam and the Watergate scandals are thought to have contributed heavily to this voter disaffection.

What accounts for the reversal of the downward trend in 1992? According to Steven J. Rosenstone and his associates, "Turnout rose in 1992 because the electorate was more extensively mobilized by campaigns, interest groups, and activists motivated by the closest presidential election in a decade."[41]

PREDICTING THE OUTCOME

As the clock ticks on to election day, public interest rises, much as it does before the World Series or the NFL Super Bowl. Who is going to win? How big will the margin be? Will the victor win or retain control of Congress? The poor track record of the early period opinion polls in predicting the winner, especially the 1948 Truman-Dewey miscall, still haunts some pollsters.[42] Since then, however, the Gallup poll has kept its prediction well within the sample's margin of error. Between 1952 and 1980, it averaged close to 1.6 percent from the actual vote.

In 1992, all of the major national polls were within three percentage points of winner Bill Clinton's 43 percent of the popular vote in their final sampling (see Table 4.6). The Harris poll was right on the money with Bush's total and missed Clinton's popular vote by one percentage point.[43]

Since 1976, election day excitement has become even more intense as the three television networks, using sophisticated "exit" polls, have raced to beat one another in making a "call" on the winner. In 1980, by 8:15 P.M. (Eastern Standard Time), fifteen minutes after the polls closed in many eastern states, NBC News projected Ronald Reagan to be the winner, even though less than 5 percent of the national vote had been counted.[44] Meanwhile the country was treated to the spectacle on all three networks of President Carter conceding the election to challenger Ronald Reagan at 9:45 P.M. (Eastern Standard Time)—more than an hour before the polls closed on the West Coast.

The greatly rising costs of exit polling and collecting election statistics in the mid-1980s and heavy cuts in network news department budgets finally forced them to call off their costly rivalry, especially on making early "calls" on projected winners. Instead they have pooled their assets and established the Voter Research and Surveys polling consortium (VRS). Under this arrangement all the television networks, including CNN, plus the wire services jointly use VRS to collect the voting data on election day.[45] Each member is still free to use the data as it sees fit. But since they all rely on the same voting data, there have been relatively little differences in their projections.

PRESIDENTIAL MANDATES

Despite the uncertainty about why the voters choose a particular presidential candidate, newly elected presidents quickly construct their own mandates. The

Table 4.6
The Final Polls, 1992

	Clinton %	Bush %	Perot %	Undecided or other
Actual Popular Vote	43%	38%	19%	
Gallup/CNN/ USA Today	44%	37%	14%	5%
Lou Harris	44%	38%	17%	1%
CBS News/New York Times	45%	37%	15%	3%
Washington Post	43%	35%	16%	6%
ABC News	44%	37%	16%	3%
NBC News/Wall Street Journal	44%	36%	15%	5%

Note: The 1992 presidential race narrowed during the final two weeks of the campaign, but all major polling organizations projected a winning margin for Clinton.

Source: Associated Press Wire Service, *Seattle Post-Intelligencer*, 3 November 1992.

vague guidance elections provide reelected presidents or the nation's new leader offer broad latitude in initiating public policies. Consequently, the victors frequently interpret the electoral mandate as a broad grant from the people to pursue the policies they personally favor.

Similarly, President-elect Ronald Reagan, after his resounding victory in 1980, promptly proclaimed that he was elected to implement his "supply side" economic program of tax cuts and a reduced federal budget, as well as his plan to rebuild national defense and to reverse nearly a half-century of governmental centralization. With this "mandate" in hand, he persuaded congress to approve the major part of his program in record time, much to the surprise of veteran Washington observers.

Did Ronald Reagan's victory in 1980 constitute a conservative mandate from the voters? It is doubtful. In a nationwide poll conducted by *The New York Times*/CBS News after the 1980 election, respondents were asked whether Reagan's victory was a mandate for more conservative policies or a rejection of President Carter and his presidency. Approximately 63 percent of the respondents saw it as a rejection of Carter, and only 24 percent viewed the election as a conservative victory.[46] Similarly, the National Election Survey polls, conducted at the University of Michigan, revealed that the "key to Carter's defeat was widespread dissatisfaction with his performance in office coupled with doubts about his competence as a political leader."[47] Reagan won, then, not primarily because of his conservative ideology, his policy positions, or his personal appeal, but because he was an acceptable alternative to Jimmy Carter.

Reagan's 1984 reelection victory was described as a "lonely landslide" by some commentators because, though he won forty-nine out of fifty states, he carried only fourteen GOP congressmen on his coattails and lost two U.S. Senate seats. Pollsters, however, had a difficult time measuring the depth of Mr. Reagan's second-term mandate because his campaign managers chose to have him avoid specific campaign promises.[48]

For a second-term chief executive, a presidential mandate means, it seems fair to say, what the president chooses to make of it. However, a first-term president will soon learn that his electoral mandate is not a blank check, cashable at any time in his term. Jimmy Carter discovered this early in his term. A president's mandate remains viable currency only so long as he can prevail upon a majority in both houses of Congress to support his programs and policies. Without strong legislative backing, the president's mandate will generally suffer gradual erosion.

Winning only 43 percent of the popular vote in 1992, Arkansas Governor Bill Clinton became the fifteenth President of the United States to be elected by less than a majority of the popular vote (see Table 4.7). But as a result of the "magnifying effect" of the winner-take-all Electoral College mathematics, his 43 percent share of the popular vote produced 370 electoral votes—68.7 percent of the Electoral College.

As a minority president, Clinton joined such noted predecessors as Abraham Lincoln, Woodrow Wilson, Harry S. Truman, and John F. Kennedy who all received less than a majority of the popular vote. Abraham Lincoln, generally regarded by historians as our greatest president, eked out a 39.8 percent popular vote victory in 1860 in a four-way contest among Stephen Douglas, John Bell, and John C. Breckenridge. Still, this low percentage of the popular vote translated into 59.4 percent of the Electoral College vote—a sufficient mandate in Lincoln's eyes to preserve the Union, in the face of Southern secession, no matter how high the cost.

Do minority presidents have a strong mandate to govern? In reviewing presidential history, the size of an incumbent's margin of victory does not seem, in most instances, to have affected a president's leadership ability. To be sure, there have been strong leaders and weak leaders among the fifteen minority presidents, but the fact that they received less than a majority of the popular vote and thus have, at best, a qualified mandate does not appear to have affected in the slightest degree the ability and determination of strong presidents to lead. Indeed, Abraham Lincoln and Woodrow Wilson never hesitated to use their presidential mandates to act forcefully when events dictated decisive action. But in the present era, the electorate's inflated expectations of what a president can achieve collides with the reality of our separation of powers system. Newly elected presidents proclaim broad mandates, but survey experts often experience great difficulty in discerning what a presidential mandate really means in

Table 4.7
Minority Presidents, 1824–1992

	Year Elected	Popular Vote	Margin of Victory	Electoral Vote
John Quincy Adams (NR)	1824	30.9%	-10.4%	32.2%
Abraham Lincoln (R)	1860	39.8%	+10.4%	59.4%
Woodrow Wilson (D)	1912	41.8%	+14.4%	81.9%
Bill Clinton (D)	1992	43.0%	+5.0%	68.7%
Richard M. Nixon (R)	1968	43.4%	+0.7%	55.9%
James Buchanan (D)	1856	45.3%	+12.2%	58.8%
Grover Cleveland (D)	1892	46.0%	+3.1	62.4%
Zachary Taylor (Whig)	1848	47.3%	+4.8%	56.2%
Benjamin Harrison (R)	1888	47.8%	-0.8%	58.1%
Rutherford B. Hayes (R)	1876	48.0%	-3.0%	50.1%
James A. Garfield (R)	1880	48.3	+.02	58.0%
Grover Cleveland (D)	1884	48.5%	+0.2%	54.6%
Woodrow Wilson (D)	1916	49.2%	+3.1%	52.2%
James K. Polk (D)	1844	49.5%	+1.5%	61.8%
Harry S. Truman (D)	1948	49.6%	+4.5%	57.1%
John F. Kennedy (D)	1960	49.7%	+0.2%	56.4%

Sources: Congressional Quarterly Weekly Report, 50 (31 October 1992): 3498; data for 1992 are from *The New York Times*, 5 November 1992.

terms of programs and policies, other than the public expects a president to display strong leadership, maintain a viable economy, and avoid war.

Whether newly elected presidents accept the challenges or not, high public expectations are the reverse side of presidential mandates. Prior to the age of opinion polls, public expectations were less precise. It seems doubtful, for example, that the American public envisaged a Rooseveltian "New Deal" when they elected the dynamic New York governor as president in 1932 at the bottom of the Great Depression, since Governor Franklin Roosevelt had campaigned on a platform of economy and reduced government expenditures. Most analysts concluded that the 1932 presidential vote was chiefly against the inept incumbent Republican President Herbert Hoover rather than *for* FDR. But newly elected President Roosevelt quickly sensed that the public expected him to do something to halt the downward spiraling economy. (The nation's unemployment rate approached 25 percent and the sick manufacturing sector was operating at only 50 percent capacity.) Soon "Happy Days Are Here Again" became the Democratic theme song, and the country under its new leader moved briskly forward.

In retrospect, life was less complicated in the pre–World War II era, and public expectations of the president were considerably lower than in the current era. Television coverage of the presidential campaigns has widened the gap between expectations and performance. By 1990, the nation's population had also nearly doubled (from 140 million in 1940 to 250 million in 1990), and the number of hopelessly complex issues confronting the contemporary president have more than doubled: nuclear proliferation, a $4 trillion national debt, skyrocketing health costs, urban blight, mounting levels of crime and violence, and so on. To add to the president's current difficulties, the steady stream of national opinion polls measuring public attitudes on every conceivable major issue, and the public's level of satisfaction or dissatisfaction with the president's performance in handling these issues means that the president is under constant scrutiny. As a result, the ever-rising public expectations that the president can solve these massive problems often places him in an unsustainable position. However, one major source of support that a president can turn to for help in his struggle to win popular approval remains his political party—a topic that will receive close study in the next chapter.

NOTES

1. Bruce Buchanan, *Seattle Post-Intelligencer*, 28 October 1992.

2. Walter Lippman, *The Phantom Public* (New York: Harcourt, Brace, 1925), 55–57. The discussion in this section relies extensively on John Kenneth White, "The General Election: Issues and Themes," in William Crotty, ed., *America's Choice: The Election of 1992* (Guilford, CT: Dushkin Publishing Group, 1933), 61–68.

3. Margaret Leech, *In the Days of McKinley* (New York: Harper & Brothers, 1959), 88.

4. Stephen J. Wayne, *The Road to the White House*, 2nd ed. (New York: St. Martin's, 1984), 168.

5. For a discussion of the big-state effect on the Electoral College in recent presidential campaigns, see Herbert Asher, *Presidential Elections and American Politics*, 5th ed. (Pacific Grove, CA: Brooks & Cole, 1992), 302–309.

6. The states of Maine and Nebraska are the sole exceptions. The electoral vote in these states is cast on the basis of the popular vote in each of its congressional districts.

7. In 1960, Senator Harry F. Byrd (D-VA) received fifteen electoral votes from segregationist Democrats in Alabama and Mississippi. Thus, if Kennedy had lost Illinois (twenty-six electoral votes) and Missouri (twelve electoral votes), he would have dropped from 303 votes to 265—less than the magic number of 266 needed to win. See, Neal Peirce and Lawrence D. Longley, *The People's President: The Electoral College in American History and the Direct Vote Alternative* (New York: Simon & Schuster, 1968), 106.

8. Under the new, so-called "Lame Duck" Amendment, defeated members of the House of Representatives who formerly served thirteen months after losing office (the lame duck members) are replaced by the new members on January 3, following the presidential election. Under the constitutional revision the new House members who take their seats on the third are thus available on January 6 to resolve an electoral deadlock, if no presidential candidate has

received an electoral majority. See the Twentieth Amendment in Appendix A. For additional details, see Neal R. Peirce and Lawrence D. Longley, *The People's President*, rev. ed. (New Haven, CT: Yale University Press, 1981) 106–108; Walter Berns, ed. *After the People Vote* (Washington, DC: The AEI Press, 1992), 20–22.

9. Peirce and Longley, *The People's President*, 52–57.

10. Angus Campbell, Philip Converse, Warren Miller, and Donald Stokes, *The American Voter* (New York: Wiley, 1960).

11. *The New York Times*, 4 November 1992.

12. Paul C. Light and Celinda Lake, "The Election: Candidates, Strategies, and Decisions," in Michael Nelson, ed. *The Elections of 1984* (Washington, DC: CQ Press, 1985), 91.

13. See "How He Won: The Untold Story of Bill Clinton's Triumph," *Newsweek*, vol. 120 (November-December 1992), especially 59–61, 92–95. This is a special electoral issue of the magazine.

14. George C. Edwards III and Stephen J. Wayne, *Presidential Leadership*, 2nd ed. (New York: St. Martin's, 1985), 53.

15. In discussing the differences between nominating politics and general election campaign, George McGovern's 1972 campaign director, Gary Hart (later a presidential aspirant himself in 1984 and 1988), listed the abbreviated time frame of the fall campaign as the chief difference. Gary W. Hart, *Right from the Start* (New York: Quadrangle/*The New York Times*, 1973), 249.

16. Theodore H. White, *The Making of the President: 1968* (New York: Atheneum, 1969), 334–342.

17. "How He Won," *Newsweek*, Special Election Issue, vol. 120, November-December 1992, 67–69.

18. Wayne, *The Road to the White House*, 2nd ed., 228.

19. William Crotty, "Introduction: A Most Unusual Election," in William Crotty, ed., *America's Choice: The Election of 1992* (Guilford, CT: Dushkin Publishing Group, 1993), 10–11.

20. Ibid.

21. Frank B. Feigert, "The Ross Perot Candidacy and Its Significance," in William Crotty, ed., *America's Choice: The Election of 1992* (Guilford, CT: Dushkin Publishing Group, 1993), 77–87.

22. Elihu Katz and Jacob J. Feldman, "The Debates in the Light of Research: A Survey of Surveys," in Sidney Kraus, ed. *The Great Debate* (Bloomington: Indiana University Press, 1962), 195–200.

23. Another stumbling block to holding debates was the "equal time" rule of the Federal Communications Commission requiring the networks to provide equal time to all presidential candidates, including minor party candidates. Rather than grant equal time to all the candidates, the networks refused to sponsor any presidential debates. In 1960, Congress had temporarily suspended the equal time rule to allow the Nixon-Kennedy debates. To avoid the equal time barrier in 1976 and subsequent elections, the League of Women Voters agreed to "sponsor" the debates. Then the networks could cover them as "news events" without running afoul of the equal time rule.

24. *The New York Times*, 30 October 1980.

25. "How He Won," *Newsweek*, vol. 120, November-December 1992, 85.

26. Reuters dispatch, *Seattle Post-Intelligencer*, 18 December 1992.

27. *The New York Times*, 4 November 1992.

28. Herbert E. Alexander, *Financing the 1972 Election* (Lexington, MA: D. C. Heath, 1976), 11–58.

29. *The New York Times*, 31 May 1985. According to the U.S. Treasury, approximately one-fourth of all taxpayers use the checkoff. In 1984, the checkoff system generated $35 million,

but the money builds over the four years preceding a presidential election. During 1984 the Treasury paid out $120 million to eligible presidential candidates and to the Republican and Democratic national committees, which received $8 million each for their nominating conventions.

30. Ibid., 15 November 1992.

31. Ibid.

32. Herbert E. Alexander and Monica Bauer, *Financing the 1988 Election* (Boulder, CO: Westview), 37–40.

33. *The New York Times*, 15 November 1992.

34. Ibid., 2 January 1993.

35. Survey of news directors by the Freedom Forum Media Studies Center at Columbia University, reported in *The New York Times*, 23 October 1992.

36. Thomas E. Patterson and Richard Davis, "The Media Campaign: Struggle for the Agenda," in Michael Nelson, ed. *The Election of 1984* (Washington, DC: CQ Press, 1985), 122.

37. Thomas E. Patterson, *The Mass Media Election: How Americans Choose Their President* (New York: Praeger, 1980), 22–25.

38. Patterson and Davis, "The Media Campaign: Struggle for the Agenda," 124.

39. Ibid.

40. As cited by Everett Carll Ladd, *The American Polity* (New York: Norton, 1985), 454, note 20.

41. Steven J. Rosenstone, John Mark Hansen, Paul Freedman, and Marguerite Grabarek, "Voter Turnout: Myth and Reality in the 1992 Election." Paper delivered at the 1993 annual meeting of the American Political Science Association, Washington, DC, September 2–5, 1993.

42. See Harold Mendelsohn and Irving Crespi, *Polls, Television, and the New Politics* (Scranton, PA: Chandler, 1970), Chapter 2.

43. *Seattle Post-Intelligencer*, 3 November 1992.

44. Theodore H. White, *America in Search of Itself*, (New York: Harper and Row, 1982), 411.

45. *The New York Times*, 4 November 1992.

46. Adam Clymer, *The New York Times*, 9 November 1980. *The New York Times*/CBS News exit poll on election day covered 12,782 voters.

47. Gregory B. Markus, "Political Attitudes During an Election Year: A Report of the 1980 NES Study," *American Political Science Review* 76 (September 1982): 538–560.

48. Gerald M. Pomper, "The Presidential Election," in Gerald M. Pomper, ed. *The Election of 1984* (Chatham, NJ: Chatham House Publishers, 1985), 81; see also Robert A. Dahl, "Myth of the Presidential Mandate," *Political Science Quarterly* 105 (Fall 1990): 355–372.

CHAPTER 5

PARTY LEADER

Speaking from the Oval Office to Representative Pat Williams (D-MT) on the phone as the House of Representatives neared the final vote on the Clinton 1994 budget and tax bill—and still two votes short of the 218 vote majority needed to win—President Bill Clinton finally pleaded: "Pat, I can't pass this without your vote, and my presidency depends on getting this thing through."[1]

President Clinton's desperate, last-minute politicking reflected only too well how weak the president's role as party leader is in the American decentralized party system. Though Williams remained undecided until the final fifteen-minute roll call vote, Clinton's critical phone call finally paid off. Williams supplied one of two crucial votes needed to put the Clinton budget plan over the top, 218 votes to 216, on August 5, 1993.

The next day President Clinton returned to the phone once again. This time he focused his political antennae on Democratic Senator Bob Kerrey of Nebraska, a Medal of Honor winner from the Vietnam War, to ask him to provide the decisive fiftieth vote on the Clinton budget plan in the Senate. Kerrey's vote, coupled with Vice President Al Gore's tie-breaking vote, would spell victory for President Clinton's budget plan. However, despite a ninety-minute visit at the White House the previous day, Kerrey remained uncommitted throughout the final hours of the Senate debate. Less than two hours before the cliffhanger roll call vote, however, Kerrey announced his decision to support President Clinton's plan. Kerrey's vote saved the 1994 Clinton economic package—and some commentators said the Clinton presidency.[2]

INTRODUCTION

Unlike a British prime minister whose electoral majority in the House of Commons virtually guarantees that the government's budget bill will pass automatically, the American president must work tirelessly in retail fashion, one-on-one with lawmakers, mostly from his own party, to line up the individual votes needed to carry the day in both the House and Senate. This same vote solicitation must be repeated by the president on nearly every major bill, since voting coalitions in the House and Senate seem to shift with almost lunar regularity.

In this chapter the president's role as titular leader of his party, limited as it is by the separation of powers, will be explained and assessed. The declining influence of presidential coattails—the ability of the president as head of the party's slate to draw votes for other candidates on the same ballot—as well as the president's relationship with the national party committee will be examined. We also focus on several factors that point to the reduced influence of the president in party matters: the reformed nominating system, entrenched congressional incumbency, party decomposition, decline in partisan voting, decreased political patronage, and the uncertainty of renomination. Finally, we will also direct our attention to a number of factors that have led to lower presidential dependence upon his party to achieve some of his major goals: the rise of instant communication between the president and the electorate via television, full federal government underwriting of the presidential election campaign, and the president's frequent use of national interest groups to pressure Congress to support his legislative program.

Still, it will be argued that a president can be an effective party leader, if he is favored with working party majorities in Congress, and if he understands how to operate the levers of power. All of the great presidents, except Washington, have been strong party leaders.

THE CONSTITUTIONAL BACKGROUND

The constitutional job description for the president of the United States does not include the title "chief party leader"—the main reason being, of course, that political parties had not yet emerged when the Founding Fathers convened in Philadelphia. Even if the parties had existed then, it seems doubtful that the men of 1787 would have included the duties of party leader in the nation's fundamental document, for they regarded partisan groups as instruments of dissension and discord. John Adams, the nation's second president, echoed George Washington's warning about the disruptiveness of parties by declaring: "Division of the republic into two great parties, each under its leader . . . is to be dreaded as the greatest evil under our Constitution."[3]

Despite the Framers' antipathy toward parties, the presidential election contest had, by 1800, become a battle between rival political leaders Thomas Jefferson and John Adams. But not until the rise of organized political parties in the Jacksonian era did presidential leadership have an opportunity to flourish. In James Sterling Young's words: "Converting the presidential office into a vehicle of leadership of Congress required basic changes in the style and structure of American national politics."[4]

THE NATIONAL CONVENTION AND THE
PRESIDENT'S INDEPENDENT POWER BASE

The emergence of the national party convention as the nominating agency for presidential and vice presidential candidates during the Jackson administration turned out to be a remarkable invention for facilitating party leadership by the chief executive. Instead of being politically indebted to the congressional caucus for the nomination, as was the case prior to the rise of the national convention, presidential candidates now owed their loyalty only to the convention delegates representing party membership in nearly all states of the Union. More than anything else, the national convention gave the presidential nominee an independent base of power separate from Congress and opened the door for the growth of executive leadership.

Andrew Jackson, the first chief executive to perceive the value of the national convention as a means of assimilating the party leadership function into the president's office, marshaled the power of the rapidly growing electorate into the Democratic party and used it as an instrument to reinforce his leadership. Moreover, the emergence of a popularly based political party gave President Jackson "a constituency and a role of citizen spokesmanship equal to that of Congress."[5] As party leader, Jackson could henceforth appeal over the heads of Congress to the electorate to have them pressure the lawmakers to follow the president's leadership.

From Jackson's time to the present day, the ability of the president to carry out his role as party leader has been the hallmark of effective government. Conversely, whenever presidents have failed to exert strong party leadership, the country has languished. The paucity of party leadership by the "postage stamp" presidents of the Gilded Age—Grant, Hayes, Garfield, Arthur, and Harrison—immediately comes to mind. Even President Grover Cleveland, who was viewed as one of the stronger presidents of the post–Civil War era, complained in late 1883 about Congress: "If a botch is made at the other end of the Avenue, I don't mean to be a party to it." On another occasion he insisted: "I did not come here to legislate."[6]

Cleveland's uninspired performance as party leader demonstrated another truism about presidential party leadership that led the late nineteenth-century scholar Henry Jones Ford to comment: "It is impossible for a party to carry out even a purely legislative programme unless it embodies a policy accepted by the President and sustained by the influence of his office."[7] Some years ago, another leading party scholar noted that presidents who tried to govern without the benefit of organized party support never succeeded well enough to inspire imitation.[8]

Political parties have enabled our strong presidents, especially Woodrow Wilson, Franklin D. Roosevelt, and Lyndon Johnson, to overcome some of the limitations that the constitutional separation of powers has imposed on the American system of government and to provide powerful national leadership. Political parties, however, are two-way vehicles. While they have given the president the means to exercise broad power and influence over public policy, they have also served as a restraining force, keeping presidents responsive to the concerns of rank-and-file voters, especially if the president wishes to seek reelection.

LIMITED POWER AS PARTY LEADER

In the age of fragmented political parties, well-heeled lobbyists, and political action committees, the modern president often finds himself outnumbered as party leader. Recent presidents no longer have the same political clout with Congress as their predecessors. Congressional lawmakers now operate essentially as individual entrepreneurs. Lobbyist Anne Wexler, who worked in the Carter White House, has noted that any modern president is dealing not with Democratic and Republican blocs in the Senate but with "100 separate political machines."[9] Similarly, the "subcommitteeization" of the House of Representatives has meant that the president must now interact with dozens of the "sub chairs" and their colleagues, not just a handful of powerful chairmen, as Presidents Wilson, Roosevelt, Truman, Kennedy, and Johnson did, to get congressional action on any major bills.

The president's influence over his party seldom extends to state or local parties, or to congressional committees; his dominance is limited to the party's national committee. Although strong presidents continue to campaign for party candidates and officeholders at the state or congressional level in the general election, presidents have learned that it is imprudent to intervene directly in party nominations or to become embroiled in state or local conflicts. Even Franklin D. Roosevelt, despite his great leadership skills and popularity, learned the hard way that intervention in state nominating politics is unwanted. In 1938, for example, FDR's efforts to "purge" more than a dozen anti–New Deal Democratic senators and representatives in primary elections ended in almost total failure.

Even party control of both the executive and legislative branches under our separation of powers system does not translate into the responsible party leadership mode of the parliamentary system. Consequently, the American president has only limited means for imposing his will on members of his party in Congress. Why? First of all, the president and Congress answer to entirely different constituencies. Both houses of Congress function through their own party organizations. Some years ago, James MacGregor Burns suggested that the congressional party organizations and the party organizations headed by the president and the opposition party leader are so distinct that in this country we have, in effect, four rather than two national parties.[10] Nor does the president have any direct control over the selection of his party leaders in Congress.

Party discipline in the United States is of limited utility to the president. Most presidents soon learn the distinction between a "paper" or party majority in Congress and a "working" majority. John F. Kennedy, for example, had party majorities in both houses of Congress during his brief tenure, but the Southern Democrat-GOP coalition usually held a voting majority on most domestic issues. Like his predecessors, Franklin D. Roosevelt (after his first term) and Harry Truman, Kennedy often found his domestic proposals stalled or blocked by the Southern Democrat-GOP coalition. President Clinton's Democratic party held a 258–174 margin in the House of Representatives in 1993, but he knew that he had to overcome a phalanx of approximately forty Southern "boll weevil" Democrats to win on the close votes.

Even though it is a common practice to refer to the president as the titular leader of his political party, the fact is that the president has no formal position in the national party structure. Even though he may have been elected by a large majority, the president has virtually no influence over the selection of his party's leaders in Congress. Nor is there any record in the twentieth century of a president openly trying to get rid of a Speaker or floor leader.

President Bill Clinton, if he had any doubts about his minimal leadership role of the Democratic party in the House of Representatives, had them removed in early summer 1993. Both House Democratic Majority Leader Richard Gephardt of Missouri and Democratic Majority Whip David Bonior of Michigan, holders of the number two and three leadership posts in the House of Representatives, both came out against the administration-supported North American Free Trade Agreement (NAFTA). Clinton's chief consolation was that House Speaker Thomas Foley steadfastly endorsed the pact and helped immensely with its final passage.

One presidential scholar has observed: "At most, the President can be only a quasi-party leader."[11] A combination of forces and pressures have dictated that the president be only a quasi-party leader. First of all, a president may face a Congress one or both of whose houses is controlled by the opposition party. During the 1952–1992 period, for example, the president of the United States encountered a divided government for twenty-six out of forty years. Clearly, the American system of separation of powers and frequently divided government impedes majority rule.

Deprived of a strong party organization in the decentralized American party system, the president must depend heavily upon his personal magnetism and ability to work with congressional leaders if he is to carry the day. Still, he cannot expect to achieve much success with Congress without the support of his party. Fortunately, the president's ability to lead his party is aided by the fact that congressional leaders of his party have the same team loyalties and a similar stake in developing an attractive legislative program. As Austin Ranney has put it:

Despite the often-mentioned weakness of their party ties, most congressmen still have some sense of belonging to one of two teams, and their team loyalty impels most of them to vote as a president of their party asks, except where such a vote would clearly go against what they perceive to be their constituents' interests or wishes.[12]

They want the president to succeed. Consequently, members of his party usually try to move the president's program through Congress. Failure of the president's congressional leaders to push his programs will, of course, signify serious trouble within the party and reflect unfavorably on both the lawmakers and the president. Political scientist Frank J. Sorauf has explained this mutually dependent relationship with the president this way: "Members of the president's party know that if they make him look bad, to some extent they also make themselves and their party look bad."[13] Thus, members of his own party will, for example, vote to sustain his veto even though their own legislative preferences may differ with their party leader. The late GOP House Minority Leader Charles A. Halleck, an arch-conservative Republican who often found himself in ideological disagreement with President Eisenhower, once summarized the party loyalist's view this way: "I do my arguing in the huddle, but when the signals are called, the argument ends. My only idea is to get the ball over the line."[14]

PRESIDENTIAL COATTAILS

Presidential party leadership has often been evaluated by its ability to affect other election outcomes. For many years "presidential coattails"—the ability of a presidential candidate to sweep into office, along with himself, many Senate and House members, governors, and elected state officials on the party ticket—provided an important incentive for lawmakers and state party leaders to work closely with the president. Since their fortunes were tied closely with those of the president's, party leaders and elected officials at the national convention invariably sought to nominate a contender who would help the entire party ticket. The names of McKinley, Wilson, and both Roosevelts helped party candidates to ride into office on the president's coattails. But times have changed (see Table 5.1). Indeed, as political scientist Austin Ranney has commented: "A president running for re-election these days leads his party's ticket only in the sense that he is the best known candidate, not in the sense that the electoral fate

Table 5.1
Presidential Coattails, 1932–1992

			Gains or losses of president's party	
Year	President	Party	House	Senate
1932	Roosevelt	Democrat	+90	+9
1936	Roosevelt	Democrat	+12	+7
1940	Roosevelt	Democrat	+7	-3
1944	Roosevelt	Democrat	+24	-2
1948	Truman	Democrat	+75	+9
1952	Eisenhower	Republican	+22	+1
1956	Eisenhower	Republican	-3	-1
1960	Kennedy	Democrat	-20	+1
1964	Johnson	Democrat	+37	+1
1968	Nixon	Republican	+5	+7
1972	Nixon	Republican	+21	-2
1976	Carter	Democrat	+1	+1
1980	Reagan	Republican	+33	+12
1984	Reagan	Republican	+14	-2
1988	Bush	Republican	-3	-1
1992	Clinton	Democrat	-10	0

Source: Harold W. Stanley and Richard G. Niemi, *Vital Statistics on American Politics*, 3rd ed. (Washington, DC: CQ Press, 1992), 124–125.

of his party's congressional candidates depends heavily on how well or how badly he does."[15]

Clearly, the advantages of congressional incumbency—greater visibility, the ability to attract large amounts of political action committee (PAC) money for the reelection campaign, the high cost of campaigning—have all sharply reduced the lawmaker's dependence on presidential help to win reelection. Federal lawmakers no longer believe that their electoral fortunes are closely tied to the president's or even their own party. Whether or not they win re-election will depend largely on their own success in providing what Morris P. Fiorina calls "nonpartisan, non-programmatic constituency service" and much less on national trends.[16] Although the two-party vote for president may fluctuate widely from election to election, most congressional elections (especially in the House) have become noncompetitive.

Voter ticket-splitting has caused presidential coattails to become shorter and shorter. The percentage of congressional districts splitting between presidential and House candidates increased from 19.3 to 34 percent between 1952 and 1972.[17] Ticket-splitting reached an all-time high of 45 percent in 1984 (see Table 5.2). In other words, voters in 196 out of 435 congressional districts cast their ballots for presidential candidates of one party and for a congressional candidate

Table 5.2
Split District Outcomes: Presidential and House Voting, 1900–1988

Year	Total number of districts[a]	Number of districts with split results[b]	Percentage of total
1900	295	10	3.4
1904	310	5	1.6
1908	314	21	6.7
1912	333	84	25.2
1916	333	35	10.5
1920	344	11	3.2
1924	356	42	11.8
1928	359	68	18.9
1932	355	50	14.1
1936	361	51	14.1
1940	362	53	14.6
1944	367	41	11.2
1948	422	90	21.3
1952	435	84	19.3
1956	435	130	29.9
1960	437	114	26.1
1964	435	145	33.3
1968	435	139	32.0
1972	435	192	44.1
1976	435	124	28.5
1980	435	143	32.8
1984	435	196	45.0
1988	435	148	34.0

[a]Before 1952 complete data are not available on every congressional district; [b]Congressional districts carried by a presidential candidate of one party and a House candidate of another party.

Source: Norman J. Ornstein, et al., eds. *Vital Statistics on Congress, 1989–1990* (Washington, DC: CQ Press, 1989), 62.

from the other major party. Incumbents, especially in the House of Representatives, have become increasingly secure in their constituencies—over 90 percent of House incumbents seeking reelection have won over the past two decades, no matter who is sitting in the White House. Because these incumbents usually outpoll presidential candidates in their districts, they feel little obligation or indebtedness to a president who enjoys less popular support than they do in their home districts.

As a matter of fact, when John F. Kennedy squeezed into the White House in the 1960 election, House Democrats lost twenty seats. Many of the defeated Democrats blamed the presidential campaign for their losses. Sixteen years later, Carter won the presidency with slightly over 50 percent of the vote, while 208 out of 292 House Democrats received more than 60 percent of the total vote in the districts—a clear demonstration of greater enthusiasm for the legislative party. This phenomenon prompted one British observer to remark: "If presidents no longer have coattails, there's no point in congressmen's clinging to them."[18]

Republican coattails appear to be stronger than Democratic ones, but usually not strong enough to aid the party for any length of time. In 1952, General Eisenhower's coattails were long enough to enable the GOP to gain narrow control of both the Senate and House. But these wafer-thin majorities melted away two years later, and Eisenhower's coattails in 1956 were not long enough to enable the GOP to regain control of either house of Congress. In 1972, Nixon's landslide victory over George McGovern helped House Republicans gain twelve seats, though not enough to control the chamber. Nixon's coattails also failed to help in GOP senatorial contests; the Republicans lost two seats.

Eight years later, Reagan's coattails helped the GOP win control of the U.S. Senate for the first time since 1954. The Republicans picked up twelve Senate seats for a three vote margin. In the House the Republicans gained thirty-three seats, but not enough to overcome the almost two to one margin the Democrats enjoyed at that time. Thus, over the past forty years the data show that Democratic congressional candidates do not need a strong presidential candidate to win office, but the GOP can be helped to some extent by presidential coattails. In 1992, on the other hand, President Bill Clinton had a slight "reverse" coattails effect on his party—the Democrats lost ten House seats, but none in the Senate.

In off-year elections presidents are of little value in helping members of Congress retain marginal seats. With the exception of 1934, the party in the White House has always lost seats in the mid-term elections. Presidents from Wilson to Clinton have discovered that their White House occupancy does not translate into off-year congressional victories for their party. One longtime Capitol Hill observer has put it even more bluntly: "National trends don't affect congressional races anymore."[19]

PARTY REFORM AND PRESIDENTIAL PARTY LEADERSHIP

In the past two decades the ties between the president and his political party have been weakened considerably by changes in the presidential nominating process, the financing of presidential nominating and election campaigns, and network television.

Prior to 1970, most presidents began to build their governing coalitions while in the process of winning the nomination. New York Governor Franklin D. Roosevelt and his advisers, for example, reached political "understandings" before and at the 1932 Democratic national convention with governors, U.S. senators, big-city mayors, state chairmen, and local party bosses. These party leaders controlled the selection of a majority of delegates during the convention balloting. FDR and his campaign manager even bartered away the vice presidency (to Speaker of the House John Nance Garner) in return for his delegates in Texas and California, in order to obtain the then needed two-thirds majority to win the nomination.[20]

As late as 1960, John F. Kennedy and his lieutenants built these same alliances on his way to the White House. Consequently, Governor David Lawrence of Pennsylvania and Mayor Richard J. Daley of Chicago, Kennedy's key preconvention supporters, always found the door of the Oval Office open when they went to the nation's capital seeking federal help for their state or city. Furthermore, these powerful Democratic leaders could be counted on, in response to President Kennedy's requests, to exert pressure on their state's congressional delegation to support the president's legislative proposals. In short, the process of building nominating coalitions was an important foundation for the subsequent process by which the presidential nominee constructed his governing coalition.[21]

But the president's party leadership role, especially in the Democratic party, changed after the wholesale reforms in the nominating process by the McGovern-Fraser Commission in the early 1970s. Clearly, the reform rules aimed at taking the nominating process out of the smoke-filled rooms by stripping the party bosses and power brokers of their control over delegate selection.

To win the presidential nomination in the 1990s, a contender must tirelessly campaign personally for nearly two years in most of the three dozen primary states as well as most of the remaining states that pick national convention delegates through the caucus-convention process. Television enables the presidential contender to communicate directly with huge numbers of primary state voters without the need for any party organization workers.

Since the advent of party reform in the 1970s, the party nominee can become the president-elect with relatively little or no contact with party leaders in Congress. In 1992, for example, Governor Bill Clinton shied away from close ties with many incumbent Democratic congressmen, since the House Post Office scandal and the 325 Representatives from both parties who cashed hundreds of overdraft checks in the House bank gave Congress an extremely bad image in the public's mind.

By winning the presidential election almost entirely without the aid of incumbent lawmakers, modern presidents owe these future working partners in Congress virtually nothing, and they in turn have no obligation to him. The end result of these changes has been to separate the process of campaigning from the process of building an effective coalition needed to govern. When a president takes office without any IOUs or political bills, and with limited acquaintance with congressional leaders, he must construct his governing coalition from ground zero, since he has reached the White House without creating any network of mutual obligations between himself and his party leaders in Congress. The nomination and election of political outsider Jimmy Carter in 1976 is, of course, the best-known example.

As presidents have lost their party leverage over Congress, they have come to rely more and more on the nonparty components of their leadership—popular nonpartisan appeals via national television, major out-of-town speeches, and closer ties to powerful interest groups. In the words of one commentator: "The nonpartisan direct television appeal has replaced the party rally." [22]

INTEREST GROUP SUPPORT

As parties have become more fragmented, presidents and their White House staffs have steadily focused more attention on developing direct contacts with leading national interest groups to bolster White House influence and bargaining power with Congress. Presidents such as FDR and Truman dealt with interest groups through their allies in Congress and the party's national committee. But with the decline of political parties in recent decades, presidents have turned increasingly to dozens of major interest groups to help mobilize mass support for the chief executive's legislative programs. More and more, presidents and their staffs have discovered that organized interest groups can exert needed legislative pressure on Congress that parties can no longer apply. [23]

As one team of authors commented recently: "Except on brief and infrequent occasions, neither political party today can command a coalition with the potential to form an electoral or governing majority." [24] Consequently, presidents and their White House staffs now cultivate close relations with these interest groups "in order for the president to find a majority to support each of his policy goals, to win reelection, or simply to maintain the foundation of support necessary for managing conflict in the nation." [25] Interest groups, it seems fair to say, have filled the vacuum created by the decline of political parties.

NONPARTISAN APPEALS

Until President-elect Bill Clinton arrived in the nation's capital, the political reality of the post-Watergate era showed that presidents have relied less and less on their party leadership role. Instead, they have sought to capitalize on their role as "president of all the people." This approach to presidential leadership was especially widespread in the Reagan-Bush years when divided government (Republican president and Democratic Congress, or a GOP Senate and Democrat-controlled House) existed in Washington. Indeed, divided government helped spawn the need for presidents constantly to locate additional political support outside the party structure.

Especially during the Reagan-Bush divided government era, presidents preferred to rise above politics and avoid partisan rhetoric for another good reason. Aware that approximately one-third of the American electorate now describes itself as independent, recent presidents have been "going public" much more frequently, both on television and before live audiences, to push policies that appeal to these middle-of-the-road voters—often the key to electoral victory or defeat. Furthermore, this type of nonpartisan appeal seldom makes enemies, and it will also help create the impression that the president's actions are not simply done with an eye on the next election.

BIPARTISANSHIP

Over the years bipartisanship has often been the only viable course of action to gain congressional acceptance of a presidential measure. Because on almost any major issue a president may lose the support of up to one-quarter of the votes from his own party, he must cultivate the support of some members of the opposition party to make up for these defections. This has been especially true for Republican presidents, for in the thirty-two years they have held the presidency from 1929 to 1992, they have had control of both houses of Congress for only four years (1929–1931 and 1953–1955).

Even strong presidents have recognized that they must pick up opposition party support on many major bills. Except for brief periods—the first terms of Woodrow Wilson, Franklin Roosevelt, and Lyndon Johnson—seldom have presidents had enough party support in Congress to affirm the principle of majority rule on a consistent basis. Generally the president must negotiate, conciliate, cajole, and compromise almost every step of the way to pick up needed votes, including some from the opposition party, to win congressional approval of his priority measures. As Austin Ranney has commented: "No president has felt that he could afford to be so completely partisan in word and deed that he could offend all the members of the opposition party so much that they would never support him on anything."[26]

PARTY LEADERSHIP—THE HISTORICAL RECORD

In reviewing the history of the American presidency, the record shows that all great presidents, except Washington who served before the rise of parties, have all been great party leaders—Jefferson, Jackson, Lincoln, Wilson, and Franklin D. Roosevelt. All of these great presidents used their political party to bridge the constitutional separation of powers to provide strong national leadership. Historian Thomas A. Bailey is also certainly correct in his observation "the successful President is the successful politician, at a high level."[27]

Unlike the British prime minister or German chancellor, who both serve dually as chief executives and party leaders in the House of Commons and the Bundestag, the American president operates from a center of power outside the legislative branch. Nevertheless, he is expected to serve as party leader, along with his other duties, such as chief executive, commander in chief, chief diplomat, and overseer of the economy.

If the foundation of the president's power has been weak from the start, what reasons can be advanced to explain how Presidents Jefferson, Jackson, Theodore Roosevelt, Wilson, Franklin D. Roosevelt, and in some instances Ronald Reagan became such effective party leaders?

Presidential success in party affairs has resulted from a combination of factors: personality, public popularity, ability to spell out goals clearly, and skill in developing political teamwork. Having effective partisan majorities in both houses of Congress clearly simplifies the president's party leadership tasks. Under these circumstances party discipline, limited though it may be, helps bridge the gap between the executive and legislative branches. But having partisan majorities, as explained earlier, is not of itself a guarantee of success, as Jimmy Carter demonstrated by his dismal inability to obtain strong party support in Congress during his four years in the White House. Democrats controlled the House of Representatives by nearly a two to one majority and the Senate by an almost three to two margin throughout Carter's single term.

History shows, however, that party and legislative success have generally gone hand in hand. "Of all the Presidents," according to one leading authority, "Thomas Jefferson is unsurpassed as party leader and in the fealty he commanded from state and local party organizations."[28] Though parties were still in a formative stage when Jefferson first moved into the White House, he quickly displayed a firm grasp of the party reins. When the first Congress in Jefferson's administration convened, Jefferson and his advisers had already seen to it that not only the Speaker of the House but the chairman of every committee was a personal lieutenant of his. Jefferson and his cabinet members drafted a legislative agenda and then turned to members of his party in Congress to implement the program.

Andrew Jackson also stands near the forefront of strong party leaders. Even before he occupied the White House, Jackson gathered about him a coterie of dedicated and accomplished politicians (Jackson's "Kitchen Cabinet") "who persistently sought the centripetal issues to hold intact the Democratic group coalition."[29] Though Jackson is best known for his frequent use of the veto to obtain his political ends, his adroit handling of Democratic party affairs kept the rival National Republicans and Whigs off balance throughout his two terms. Jackson's accomplishments as party leader transformed the office so extensively that he is sometimes called the first modern president.[30]

While Abraham Lincoln is always remembered for having saved the Union during the nation's bloodiest conflict, his party leadership talents have often been overlooked. But as Wilfred Binkley has noted: "No president entered the great office more adept in the high art of party politics than Abraham Lincoln."[31] Lincoln's skillful handling of his cabinet appointments for the new administration has seldom been equaled.

Soon after the outbreak of the Civil War, the composition of the Republican party began to change as more War Democrats came over to it. For the duration of the conflict, the Republicans and northern Democrats adopted the name the Union Party. Lincoln had no hesitancy in using party patronage extensively to help cement ties with the Union party in states, cities, counties, and precincts. Post Office appointments were generously distributed to Union partisans, and when the supply ran low, Lincoln turned to the creation of captaincies, colonelcies, and brigadier generalships to keep them out of the Democratic party. In Lincoln's mind, preservation of the Union justified his utilizing military patronage to achieve this supreme goal.

In 1864 Lincoln used party patronage blatantly to help secure ratification of the Thirteenth Amendment, which abolished slavery. Lacking one state to obtain the needed two-thirds vote, Lincoln sent Charles A. Dana on a special mission to win the support of two congressmen whose votes were necessary to get Nevada admitted to the Union—and to provide the extra votes required for ratification of the new amendment. As Dana recounted the event some years later, Lincoln declared: "Whatever promise you make to them I will do."[32] Subsequently, Nevada was admitted to the Union and the Thirteenth Amendment was ratified.

Not until the election of William McKinley in 1896 did the country see another consummate party chief in the White House. His successor, Theodore Roosevelt, was also a strong party leader. But the model party leader in the White House before the New Deal was Woodrow Wilson. Five years before his inauguration in 1913, Wilson the educator had noted the growing popular tendency to recognize the president "as the unifying force in our complex system, the leader both of his party and the nation."[33] A warm admirer of the British parliamentary system, Wilson had this advice for the White House occupant: "He must be the leader of his party. He is the party's choice and is responsible for carrying out the party platform. He therefore should have a large influence in determining legislation." Furthermore, Wilson stated that the president "cannot escape being the leader of his party except by incapacity and lack of personal force because he is at once the choice of the party and the nation."[34]

To be sure, Wilson's leadership task was simplified by a huge Democratic House majority, consisting mostly of first-term congressmen who were especially responsive to party discipline. His handling of the Underwood Tariff Act was particularly noteworthy. At his urging, the Ways and Means Committee began working on the bill weeks before the inauguration. Within three weeks after moving into the White House, Wilson had a complete draft of the bill and announced his full support of the proposed legislation. He consulted with the House Democratic caucus and after a thorough study there, the membership took it to the floor of the House. Without even a motion to limit debate, the bill passed virtually intact by a large majority. Unlike his predecessors, Wilson then personally addressed the Senate urging passage of the tariff bill.

Immediately after the address he appeared in the President's Room, just off the Senate chamber, to confer with the finance committee on the proposed legislation. Though the Democratic senators were far from united on the tariff question, the Senate Democratic Caucus declared the bill to be a party measure and urged all members to support it. The Underwood bill became law before the summer recess. In the words of one close observer: "President Wilson had quietly assumed leadership and secured a hold on his associates which astonished friend and enemy."[35]

Twelve years later, Franklin D. Roosevelt entered the White House as the most astute politician of his time. Blessed with solid Democratic majorities in both houses of Congress, FDR mounted the famous "Hundred Days" legislative program in 1933, which produced more social and economic legislation than the country had ever seen. When bills dealing with the economic crisis were pending, congressmen came to the White House seeking patronage rewards—but FDR held them off with the coyly whispered information: "We haven't got to patronage yet."[36] FDR was not prepared to dispense jobs and federal contracts until the lawmakers had earned them with their pro–New Deal votes. Also, the Roosevelt party organization made clear that a congressman's sharing of patronage might depend upon his answer to the question, "What was your preconvention position on the Roosevelt candidacy?" Democratic National Chairman James A. Farley, Roosevelt's patronage manager, was also reported to have kept a private list of "eligible" job applicants, each bearing the cryptic initials FRBC (for Roosevelt before Chicago).

Presidents were probably more effective as party leaders when the postmaster general, then a member of the cabinet, also doubled as national party chairman. In the early days of the New Deal, for example, Postmaster General Farley not only served as a key political adviser to President Roosevelt, but also acted as the middleman between the Democratic National Committee and fellow cabinet members, keeping them apprised of the latest political developments and their potential impact on the members' departments.

Roosevelt's party leadership became more systematic after the first Hundred Days, but by the time he was ready to announce his second-term reelection plans in 1936, his legislative accomplishments included the Social Security Act, the Wagner Act (authorizing collective bargaining), the Securities Exchange Act, the Federal Deposit Insurance Corporation, and a host of other New Deal measures. But as other chief executives before him have discovered, a president's party leadership influence seldom carries far into his second term.

Roosevelt's "court packing" plan, announced in 1937 after the Supreme Court had invalidated nearly a dozen of his pet New Deal measures, led to a rapid deterioration of his party influence on Capitol Hill. Many Democratic legislators, especially from the South, deserted the Roosevelt ranks. Indeed, the only major bill passed during Roosevelt's second term bearing FDR's special stamp of approval was the Fair Labor Standards Act of 1938 (which established a minimum federal wage and, in effect, abolished child labor). From that point on, Roosevelt shifted his major attention abroad to battle Nazism, Fascism, and the Japanese militarists.

Even so, FDR left a mark on the Democratic party that remained for nearly four decades. He had inherited a badly tattered minority Democratic party, consisting of big-city bosses and Southern and Western farmers, held together by states' rights doctrine and periodic spurts of Progressivism. From this base he built an alliance of Northern city machines, labor unions, blacks and other minority groups, intellectuals, and low-income farmers into a majority coalition that dominated the American scene, except for the Eisenhower interregnum, until the Vietnam War.[37]

No president since FDR has been his equal as party leader. Lyndon Johnson for a brief shining period in 1964 and 1965 almost matched Roosevelt in obtaining congressional support for a broad range of Great Society domestic programs and the two historic Civil Rights Acts of 1964 and 1965. But Johnson's rapid escalation of American involvement in Vietnam soon ended his string of legislative triumphs. By the 1966 midterm elections, Johnson's legislative magic had disappeared, and the Democratic party slipped forever from his grasp.

Nixon, Ford, and Carter never displayed firm mastery of party affairs, though Nixon and Ford were both veterans of Congress. Carter was the antithesis of a party leader. Upon reaching the White House, the former Georgia governor announced that he was beholden to no political or interest group, since he had won the party running as the anti-Washington candidate. And he was right. But Carter discovered over the course of his one-term presidency that his lack of strong ties with Democratic leaders on Capitol Hill undermined his ability to push through a comprehensive legislative program, especially in his favorite area of energy conservation. Carter's failure as party leader was a telltale omen that his entire presidency would also come to be viewed by many political professionals and a majority of the voting public as a failure, too.

Ronald Reagan, though not generally concerned with the intricacies of day-to-day party management, nevertheless displayed a firm grasp of party matters and legislative leadership. Although faced with a Democratically controlled House of Representatives, Reagan used his political skill to win over most Southern Democrats in the House and with the GOP-controlled Senate obtained passage of three high-priority agenda items—tax cuts, a reduced domestic budget, and increased military spending—during the first eight months of his administration.[38]

George Bush, the first national party chairman to be elected president of the United States, was a party man to the core. Bush's own experience in running for the House of Representatives (he served two terms) and the Senate (he lost to Texas Democrat Lloyd Bentsen in 1970) left him with a deep appreciation of what a Republican president can do to help his fellow GOP office seekers. As vice president, Bush spent eight years honing his organizational and fund-raising skills for his own future presidential candidacy and to help fellow Republicans. So eager was Bush to aid Republican candidates that on more than one occasion then and when he occupied the White House, he was known to have interrupted his summer vacation at Kennebunkport, Maine, to go out campaigning for GOP candidates in neighboring states.

President Bill Clinton's keen attention to party coalition-building on Capitol Hill closely follows the model of Woodrow Wilson, Franklin D. Roosevelt, and Lyndon B. Johnson. Only a handful of presidents have spent as much time as Clinton lavishing attention on Congress during his first year in office. And he certainly equaled Lyndon Johnson's hospitality record in inviting lawmakers and their spouses to the White House for dinner, entertainment, and political bridge building. Clinton first refined his party-building skills during his twelve years as governor of Arkansas. According to friends, he was known for practically camping out at the state legislature in Little Rock, seeking votes for his proposed legislation.[39] More than a fraction of the credit for Clinton's hairbreadth victories for his 1994 budget plan in the House and Senate can be attributed, as explained earlier in the chapter, to his assiduous courting of several dozen Democratic lawmakers who had serious doubts about the political wisdom of backing the Clinton budget plan and its increased taxes but who supported the young president on the basis of friendship and party loyalty.

CONTROL OF THE NATIONAL PARTY COMMITTEE

Presidential candidates become the titular leaders of their party as soon as they win nomination. Once elected, they assume undisputed leadership of the party for as long as they remain in the White House. This has not always been the case. In the nineteenth century, James MacGregor Burns reminds us, national conventions frequently refused to renominate incumbent presidents. Moreover, national party chairmen were independent of presidential control, and the national party apparatus was dominated by competing leaders or factions.[40] Most twentieth-century presidents, however, have maintained tight control over the national party organization.

But most presidents soon become preoccupied with affairs of state and relegate management of national party affairs far down on their list of priorities.

Indeed, several recent presidents—Johnson, Nixon, and Carter—permitted the national party committees, intentionally or not, to fall into a sad state of disrepair. Nixon, for example, followed the Johnson pattern to a remarkable degree: concentrating political power in the White House staff, running campaigns totally divorced from the party, relying on personal loyalists to fill the top executive branch jobs, and virtually ignoring the national committee after his first year in the White House.

Few party chairpersons of the president's party have enjoyed much influence. As Robert Strauss, former Democratic national chairman, observed: "If you're Democratic party chairman when a Democrat is president, you're a god-damn clerk."[41] Another reason why the national committees of the president's party atrophy is that strong chairpersons usually resign to take other presidential assignments (because their main party task—getting the party nominee elected president—has been completed). Sometimes their services are terminated by a president who may doubt their loyalty to the White House. For example, GOP national chairman Ray Bliss, widely acknowledged as a brilliant organizational tactician, apparently was dumped in 1969 by President Nixon for this reason.

Lyndon Johnson treated the Democratic National committee with equal contempt. At first, he placed Johnson loyalists (mostly Texans) in key positions on the national committee, but before long he began shifting committee operations to the White House. Columnist David Broder observed that Johnson often acted as if party obligations and functions were the enemy, not the instruments, of responsible government.

He [Johnson] did not see political parties as necessary vehicles for communicating the often inchoate preferences of the voters to those in power. Nor did he see the parties as instruments for disciplining the whims of the elected leaders and holding them accountable for their actions. Instead he saw them as unwanted intruders on the process of consensus government.[42]

Joseph Califano, one of Johnson's close aides, also later recalled: "In my years on Lyndon Johnson's White House staff never once did I hear him say that he wanted to leave behind a strengthened Democratic Party."[43] In fact, Johnson left the Democratic National Committee debt-ridden and in shambles long before he departed the White House for retirement at his Texas ranch.

Jimmy Carter's view of the Democratic National Committee was not much better. After his victory in 1976, Carter recommended to Democratic Party National Chairman Robert Strauss that the size of the Democratic National Committee staff be reduced by 70 percent. Shortly thereafter, the staff was cut down to only twenty full-time employees. Meanwhile, Carter campaign staffers held the chief positions at the Democratic National Committee and the Carter White House Staff kept the entire national party apparatus on a short leash. In the 1980 presidential campaign Carter used virtually all the money assiduously raised by the Democratic National Committee to underwrite his own reelection campaign, leaving virtually nothing for financing congressional or senatorial races or as "seed money" for future national party fund-raising endeavors.

Reagan's skillful handling of the Republican National Committee, on the other hand, kept the GOP national organization in fighting trim. Though Mr. Reagan quietly jettisoned his first GOP National Chairman Richard Richards after two years, reportedly for management inefficiency, the president used the Republican National Committee effectively in party fund-raising and in strengthening the national organization. To oversee the Republican National Committee operations, Reagan installed his close personal friend, Senator Paul Laxalt of Nevada, as "general" chairman of the GOP. By putting a trusted associate in charge of party headquarters, President Reagan removed any threat of the national party committee becoming an independent power base while he occupied the White House.

This control of the national committee was not unlike the method John F. Kennedy had used to run the Democratic National Committee in the early 1960s. Kennedy installed his close associate and campaign adviser, John Bailey, the Connecticut State Democratic chairman, as national chairman. Nor did he object to Bailey's retaining his Connecticut chairmanship while running the national committee.

President George Bush, who served briefly as national party chairman under Richard Nixon, was treated much of the time as an errand boy. Upon reaching the presidency, however, Bush decided, unlike Nixon, to shift GOP political operations from the White House back to the Republican National Committee headquarters. This move clearly demonstrated Bush's confidence in his new GOP National Chairman Lee Atwater, manager of his highly successful 1988 nominating campaign. A skilled political infighter, Atwater's hard-edged attacks on Democrats kept his opponents on the defensive most of the time. But Atwater's political career came to a premature and tragic end when he succumbed to a brain tumor in early 1991.[44] Without Atwater's skilled leadership, GOP party management deteriorated and soon reverted back to the White House for the remainder of Bush's term.

President Bill Clinton, from the day of his inauguration, kept national party management mostly at the White House. He moved Democratic National Chairman Ron Brown from party headquarters and appointed him secretary of commerce. His hand-picked replacement, David Wilhelm, from Illinois, helped maintain ties with the powerful Daley Democratic organization in Chicago. In January 1995, however, President Clinton shifted to the "dual chairmanship" arrangement developed by President Reagan. To replace Chairman Wilhelm, Clinton moved to have Connecticut Demoratic Senator Christopher Dodd selected "general chairman" of the Democratic National Committee. Donald Fowler, a veteran South Carolina Democratic activitist, was picked as party chairman to handle the daily operations of the party.[45] Under the Clinton regime the primary function of the Democratic National Committee continues to be fund-raising, especially tracking down large sums of "soft" money. More will be said about presidential fund-raising later in the chapter.

DECLINE OF PARTY INFLUENCE AT THE WHITE HOUSE

The traditional model of the presidency has generally held that the president should promote and fulfill the party platform, reward the party faithful, isolate the mavericks, carry the party banner on the campaign trail, respond to its interests, and solicit the advice of state party leaders. Above all, the president should be a party builder and expand the party ranks by communicating the party's message to the electorate. Presidents, in the words of one commentator, "should be as much the product of their parties as their leader."[46] Ideally, the relationship between the president and the party should be a two-way street, with the parties serving as a rein on the president to ensure presidential accountability; the president, in turn, would be expected to consult regularly with party leadership at the local, state, and national levels. Presidential behavior, however, today seldom matches this textbook model.

One of the major paradoxes of the presidency is that a president is expected by many Americans to be a neutral public leader, the symbolic head of the country, and avoid political and party considerations. At the same time he is supposed to lead his party, help other party members be reelected, and build political coalitions to win passage of his legislative programs. However, with the multiplication of presidential responsibilities in recent decades—chief spokesman of the free world, national security manager, overseer of the economy—the president's schedule is usually devoured by pressing matters that will not go away. As a symbolic figure representing the entire nation, the president is expected to share the nation's concern over flood disasters, hurricane damage, and drought in the agricultural regions by visiting these areas. Foreign leaders arrive in the nation's capital on the average of one a week. These heads of state must be given the red carpet treatment, with formal dinners, guided tours, and high-level meetings.

Under these circumstances the party's business can wait—or, more likely, be put on the back burner until more time becomes available, which seldom happens. Nor do some sitting presidents feel that they really need their party any longer. Since they have used their own independently organized campaign team, conducted most of their campaigns via television, and financed their general election race from the $55.2 million lump sum grant (1992 figure) from the Federal Election Commission, most presidents do not feel that a political party has been a major factor in their successful election campaign. President Kennedy, according to one source, was "personally wary of working through party professionals, many of whom he viewed as a collection of 'tired or tarnished holdovers from another era,' " and believed that "the Democratic party was something to win through, not govern through."[47]

Unlike nineteenth-century presidents, the modern president has the advantage of instant communication with the American citizenry via nationwide television. Network cameras enable the president to bypass the party structure and Congress whenever he wishes to seek support for his policies from the American public. Thus, one of the main functions of the party—serving as a source of information and communication between the citizens and their government—has been largely replaced by the electronic media.

With the rise of special interest groups who build direct ties with the White House, the president has less need for help from state and local parties. The interest groups—labor unions, business groups, teachers, veterans—once worked through party groups. Now they are organized on a national scale, generally with headquarters and a staff of lobbyists in the nation's capital. High-level White House staffers work directly with these interest groups' leaders, listening to their problems, seeking solutions, perhaps arranging a special meeting with the president. By working directly with these groups, the president and his staff have, deliberately or not, further short-circuited the party out of the decision-making process.

RENOMINATION

The next election is never far from the minds of most first-term presidents and their inner circle. Consequently, nearly all their major decisions will be made with one eye on the calendar. In the nineteenth century, sitting presidents, reflecting their limited role as party leader, were often rejected for renomination. Between 1840 and 1860, for example, no incumbent president was renominated. After the Civil War, GOP conventions failed to renominate Presidents Hayes and Arthur. During this period national party chairmen, who were usually independent of presidential control and working with state party leaders, in effect, hand-picked presidential nominees. Since 1896, however, the most important change affecting the nominating process within the incumbent party, according to political scientists David, Goldman, and Bain, "has been the rising position of the Presidency and the increased recognition accorded the President as party leader."[48]

Since the turn of the century, most presidents could be renominated by their party merely by asking. To be sure, William Howard Taft faced a tough fight in 1912 to win renomination before he beat down the challenge by former president Theodore Roosevelt. But he failed to win reelection in the three-way race among Wilson, Roosevelt (running as a third party candidate), and himself. Even President Herbert Hoover, running for reelection in 1932, with the country in the midst of the Great Depression, experienced no trouble in winning renomination. With the exception of the discredited Nixon, Hoover was probably the most unpopular president of the twentieth century; yet his party stood by him when he sought a second term. Presidential incumbents have usually had one special advantage over their intraparty challengers: Refusal to renominate a sitting president is a tacit admission of the party's previous failure to choose a qualified leader. Thus, the president's party can repudiate him only at the grave risk of losing the ensuing general election.

With the decline in party loyalty, it would appear that we may have reached a point where incumbent presidents can no longer be guaranteed renomination. Certainly, the resurgence of the presidential primary after World War II has provided ambitious incumbent party challengers with a potent weapon to attack a sitting president. With voters in more than thirty-eight state primaries electing nearly three-quarters of all national convention delegates, an incumbent party challenger can have a field day attacking the president's first-term record. The primary campaign becomes, in effect, a referendum on the president's first-term performance. Aided by nationwide television and the 1974 Federal Election Campaign Act, which can provide a challenger with nearly $10 million in federal matching subsidies, rivals can mount a well-financed attack upon a sitting president.

Unless the existing presidential nominating system is overhauled and shortened, future presidents can be expected to echo Lyndon B. Johnson's complaint made in the early months of 1968 before he renounced seeking another term. LBJ bitterly observed: "The old belief that a President can carry out the responsibilities of his office and at the same time undergo the rigors of campaigning is, in my opinion, no longer valid."[49] Ronald Reagan's successful renomination drive in 1984, however, is a refutation of the Johnson thesis. But President Reagan's successor, George Bush, was unable to avoid an intraparty challenge in 1992. President Bush beat back the challenge of former White House staff member-turned-television commentator Pat Buchanan, but Buchanan's vitriolic, conservative attacks early in the nominating race knocked Bush off stride, creating a party fissure within Republican ranks that Bush was unable to overcome in the general election campaign.[50]

PATRONAGE

Since the founding of the Republic, rewards for dedicated service to the president have taken the form of jobs—cabinet posts, judgeships, regional directorships of governmental agencies, ambassadorships. Thomas Jefferson and Andrew Jackson always rewarded their key supporters with federal jobs. "To the victor belong the spoils" was long the rallying cry within the party occupying the White House. No president in the nineteenth century, however, spent more time reviewing patronage requests and calculating how to distribute the "loaves and fishes" than Abraham Lincoln. A review of Lincoln's correspondence and official actions shows that the Civil War president spent a sizable share of each working day on patronage matters. Even the relentless demands of the war effort did not prevent him from dealing with political appointments.[51]

Early twentieth-century presidents were also not unmindful of the importance of patronage as political currency. The national party organizations were actively involved in the presidential appointment process. With strong party chairmen like Mark Hanna and James A. Farley, the president's party served as "the unofficial employment agency for filling certain jobs in the executive branch."[52] Farley, FDR's national chairman, for example, despite the civil service protection afforded most federal workers in the 1930s, was able to distribute an estimated 75,000 appointive jobs during President Roosevelt's first two terms.[53]

By World War II, the steady "blanketing in" of most of the three million federal employees left only a few thousand higher-level policymaking positions outside the classified civil service. Consequently, recent presidents no longer have the degree of political leverage their predecessors had in using patronage to reward party loyalists. Not all presidents have regretted the disappearance of the spoils system, for as President William Howard Taft lamented many years ago, each time he made an appointment, he created "nine enemies and one ingrate."

Unlike earlier presidents, recent incumbents have selected most of their cabinet members and national security advisers not on the basis of their political affiliation, but on their professional competence and experience. By the late 1960s, a nearly complete transfer of high-level appointment recommendations from the national committee to the White House staff had occurred.[54]

FUND-RAISING ACTIVITY

Presidential fund-raising appearances for Senate and House candidates at state party organizations are another form of patronage dispensed by party-oriented presidents. As the highest-ranking party chief in the nation, the president of the United States is a stellar attraction at any national or state fund-raising event. Indeed, a presidential appearance at a party function will almost automatically raise several hundred thousand dollars, and often the net proceeds will top a million. John F. Kennedy, for example, grossed over $1.3 million for Pennsylvania Democrats during the 1962 off-year election campaign at an outdoor fund-raiser, attended by more than 13,000 contributors, near Harrisburg.[55]

More recently, Reagan proved to be the biggest draw ever for his Republican party. In 1985, his appearance at a GOP fund-raising dinner in the nation's capital helped the Republicans raise nearly $6 million—a new record for a single event.

President Reagan's successor, George Bush, was equally proficient in fund-raising. In his first twenty months in office, Bush's tireless campaigning for GOP house, senatorial, and gubernatorial candidates netted more than $73 million—a new record.[56]

Table 5.3
Presidential Support by Party on Key Votes (in Percentage), 1953–1986

Year	President's Party	Democrat	Republican	Democrat	Republican
1953	R	41	69	42	76
1954	R	42	60	38	65
1955	R	40	50	27	76
1956	R	48	68	31	72
1957	R	52	66	46	74
1958	R	43	62	36	65
1959	R	32	77	33	74
1960	R	37	70	40	64
1961	D	72	16	67	31
1962	D	73	17	58	26
1963	D	78	19	71	40
1964	D	74	25	64	43
1965	D	75	28	71	50
1966	D	68	26	66	41
1967	D	69	28	68	57
1968	D	54	40	54	56
1969	R	43	62	41	51
1970	R	32	62	39	66
1971	R	43	66	33	77
1972	R	30	60	52	73
1973	R	31	68	23	68
1974	R	45	61	42	60
1975	R	34	64	26	59
1976	R	29	76	27	58
1977	D	61	29	70	19
1978	D	62	28	66	46
1979	D	61	28	61	34
1980	D	50	31	60	32
1981	R	32	73	41	80
1982	R	24	70	30	64
1983	R	26	75	34	67
1984	R	34	79	35	83
1985	R	34	71	27	80
1986	R	26	77	26	73

R = Republican; D = Democrat.

Source: George C. Edwards III, *At the Margins: Presidential Leadership of Congress* (New Haven, CT: Yale University Press, 1989), 41. Copyright © 1989 Yale University Press. Reprinted by permission.

President-elect Clinton proved to be a quick learner, especially in the art of "soft" money fund-raising (see Chapter 4). In the twenty-one months from July 1992 to March 1994 the Clinton-led Democratic National Committee raised $40,546,000 in soft money. From Mr. Clinton's inauguration in January 1993 to June 1994 the Democratic Party raised $20.5 million on Mr. Clinton's behalf.[57] Until the FEC changes its liberal interpretation of the 1974 campaign law or Congress eliminates the loopholes in the law, the collection and expenditure of political soft money by

Table 5.4
Aggregate Partisan Support for Presidents (in Percentage), 1953–1986

Nonunanimous Support

	House			Senate		
President's Party	Democrats	Republican	Difference[a]	Democrats	Republican	Difference
Democratic	69	28	41	61	39	22
Republican	38	65	27	35	68	33

Key Votes

	House			Senate		
President's Party	Democrats	Republican	Difference[a]	Democrats	Republican	Difference
Democratic	66	26	40	65	40	25
Republican	36	68	32	35	69	34

[a]Differences expressed in percentage points.

Source: George C. Edwards III, *At the Margins: Presidential Leadership of Congress* (New Haven, CT: Yale University Press, 1989), 42. Copyright © 1989 Yale University Press. Reprinted by permission.

the presidential candidates' surrogates will continue to mushroom—and may even soon exceed the FEC presidential campaign subsidy ceiling of $55.2 million given to each major party candidate in 1992.

THE PRESIDENT'S NEED FOR PARTY SUPPORT

If a president has no control over the nomination of members of Congress in the fifty state parties, and if he lacks most of the nineteenth-century type of patronage, one might rightly ask, how can the president be the genuine leader of his party?

Presidents must still look to their partisans in Congress to carry the ball for the White House. As explained by political scientist George C. Edwards III, "No matter what other resources a president has at his disposal, he remains highly dependent upon his party to move his legislative programs."[58] Fortunately for most presidents, lawmakers of his party have personal loyalties or emotional commitments to their party and their leader that can usually be translated into votes for the president's program (see Table 5.3).

Still, Table 5.3 shows that presidents can count on their own party members for support no more than two-thirds of the time, even on key votes. Clearly, there is a substantial difference between the level of support the president receives from his own party and the opposition. As Table 5.4 shows, this partisan gap ranges from 22 to 41 percentage points for the 1953–1986 period. Throughout this thirty-three-year span, which covers the administration of four Republican presidents and three Democrats, lawmakers consistently supported the president of their own party far more widely than presidents of the opposition party, no matter how varied the presidents' policies, personalities, or the political environment.[59] In some cases the mark of the successful president rests on his ability to reach out to members of the opposition party without alienating his own.[60]

In the final analysis, however, the symbolic support the president draws from his party enables him to go forth to the country with his plans and programs, knowing that a formidable array of the party faithful are prepared to reaffirm and back up his demands for action at the next election. No president, it seems clear, can expect to achieve his goals or withstand the assaults from the opposition without broad party backing. As Gary Orren has commented: "A President who must depend overwhelmingly on his personal image to sustain himself, who cannot count on the obligations of party elites to support him, is an isolated and vulnerable leader."[61]

In reviewing the history of the American presidency, the record shows that all great presidents, except Washington who served before the rise of parties, have been great party leaders—Jefferson, Jackson, Lincoln, Wilson, and Franklin D. Roosevelt. All of these great presidents used their political party to bridge the constitutional separation of powers to provide strong national leadership. Generally, presidents have found that if they work closely with their party, this partnership can be mutually beneficial to both the party and the White House occupant. The truth of the matter is that both the president and his party need each other. The president needs the party's support in order to enact a legislative program; the party needs the president's leadership and the prestige of his office to achieve its goals.[62]

Still, the president's lack of control over his party's members in Congress can sometimes sweep him toward a whirlpool of unfulfilled public expectations. Though the White House incumbent may have promised during the heat of the presidential campaign to avoid foreign entanglements, to lower taxes, to reduce the deficit, and to provide universal health care, the president-elect's inability to deliver consistently on his campaign promises can ultimately lead to a political dead end.

Enterprising presidents, however, have turned increasingly to their role as the public or rhetorical president to avoid this impasse. This process of "going public" will be the central theme of the next chapter.

NOTES

1. Laurence I. Barrett, "Going the Last Mile," *Time*, vol. 142, 16 August 1993, 22.

2. For an "insider" report of the Clinton-Kerrey negotiations, see Bob Woodward, *The Agenda* (New York: Simon & Schuster, 1994), 303–309.

3. Wilfred E. Binkley, *The Man in the White House*, rev. ed. (New York: Harper & Row, 1958), 95.

4. James Sterling Young, "The Presidency and the Hill," in Aaron Wildavsky, ed., *The Presidency* (Boston: Little, Brown, 1969), 430.

5. Ibid.; see also James W. Davis, *National Conventions in an Age of Party Reform* (Westport, CT: Greenwood Press, 1983), 28–32.

6. Richard Harmond, "The Presidency in the Gilded Age," in Philip C. Dolce and George H. Skau, eds. *Power and the Presidency* (New York: Scribner's, 1976), 58.

7. Henry Jones Ford, *Rise and Growth of American Politics* (New York: Macmillan, 1898), as quoted in Wildavsky, *The Presidency*, 433.

8. Arthur N. Holcombe, "Presidential Leadership and the Party System," *Yale Review*, 43 (1954): 321–335, as cited by John Crittenden, *Parties and Elections in the United States* (Englewood Cliffs, NJ: Prentice-Hall, 1982), 284.

9. R. W. Apple, Jr., *The New York Times*, 5 August 1993.

10. James MacGregor Burns, *The Deadlock of Democracy: Four-Party Politics in America* (Englewood Cliffs, NJ: Prentice-Hall, 1963).

11. Louis W. Koenig, *The Chief Executive*, 4th ed. (New York: Harcourt Brace Jovanovich, 1981), 149.

12. Austin Ranney, "The President and His Party," in Anthony King, ed. *Both Ends of the Avenue* (Washington, DC: American Enterprise Institute, 1983), 146.

13. Frank J. Sorauf, *Party Politics in America*, 5th ed. (Boston: Little, Brown, 1984), 377.

14. *The New York Times*, 5 March 1986.

15. Ranney, "The President and His Party," 140.

16. Morris P. Fiorina, *Congress: Keystone of the Washington Establishment* (New Haven, CT: Yale University Press, 1977), 37.

17. Norman J. Ornstein et al., eds., *Vital Statistics on Congress, 1989–1990* (Washington, DC: CQ Press, 1989), 62.

18. Anthony King, "A Mile and Half in a Long Way," in King, *Both Ends of the Avenue*, 249. For additional data on presidential coattails, see George Edwards III, *The Public Presidency* (New York: St. Martin's, 1983), 83–93.

19. Paul Pendergast, executive director of the Democratic Congressional Campaign Committee, as quoted in *Congressional Quarterly Weekly Report* 35 (19 March 1977): 489.

20. The century-old two-thirds rule was not repealed until the 1936 Democratic National Convention voted to switch to simple majority vote for nomination. Richard Bain, *Convention Decisions and Voting Records* (Washington, DC: The Brookings Institution, 1960), 249.

21. Ranney, "The President and His Party," 142–143.

22. Thomas E. Cronin, "Presidents and Political Parties," in Thomas E. Cronin, ed. *Rethinking the Presidency* (Boston: Little, Brown, 1982), 291.

23. For an excellent discussion of this phenomenon, see Lester G. Seligman and Cary R. Covington, *The Coalitional Presidency* (Chicago: Dorsey, 1989).

24. Martha Joynt Kumar and Michael Baruch Grossman, "The Presidency and Interest Groups," in Michael Nelson, ed. *The Presidency and the Political System* (Washington, DC: CQ Press, 1984), 284.

25. Ibid.

26. Ranney, "The President and His Party," 150.

27. Thomas A. Bailey, *Presidential Greatness* (Englewood Cliffs, NJ: Prentice-Hall, 1966), 188.

28. Koenig, *The Chief Executive*, 4th ed., 135.

29. Binkley, *The Man in the White House*, 96–97.

30. Robert V. Remini, "The Emergence of Political Parties and Their Effect on the Presidency," in Philip C. Dolce and George H. Skau, eds. *Power and the Presidency*, 32.

31. Binkley, *The Man in the White House*, 100.

32. Charles A. Dana, *Recollections of the Civil War* (New York: 1898), 174, as quoted by Wilfred E. Binkley, "The President as Chief Legislator," *Annals of the American Academy of Political and Social Science* 307 (September 1956), 92–105.

33. Woodrow Wilson, *Constitutional Government in the United States* (Columbia University Press, 1908), 54.

34. Ibid., 60–67.

35. Quoted in H. J. Ford, *Woodrow Wilson: The Man and His Work*, as cited by Binkley, *The Man in the White House*, 108.

36. Binkley, *The Man in the White House*, 109.

37. For a fascinating one-volume study of FDR, see Frank Freidel, *Franklin D. Roosevelt: A Rendezvous with Destiny* (Boston: Little, Brown & Company, 1990).

38. See Barbara Kellerman, *The Political Presidency* (New York: Oxford University Press, 1984), chapter 11.

39. Richard L. Berke, *The New York Times*, 6 March 1993.

40. James MacGregor Burns, *Presidential Government: The Crucible of Leadership* (Boston: Houghton Mifflin, 1966), 315.

41. Joseph A. Califano, Jr., *A Presidential Nation* (New York: Norton, 1975), 153.

42. David S. Broder, *The Party's Over* (New York: Harper & Row, 1971), 76–77.

43. Califano, *A Presidential Nation*, 159.

44. James W. Davis, *The President as Party Leader* (Westport, CT: Praeger, 1992), 106.

45. *The New York Times*, 22 January 1995.

46. Thomas E. Cronin, "The Presidency and the Parties," in Gerald M. Pomper, ed. *Party Renewal in America* (New York: Praeger, 1981), 178.

47. James MacGregor Burns, *The Deadlock of Democracy*, 308–309.

48. Paul T. David, Ralph M. Goldman, and Richard C. Bain, *The Politics of National Party Conventions* (Washington, DC: The Brookings Institution, 1960), 72.

49. As quoted by Cyrus R. Vance, "Reforming the Electoral Reforms," *The New York Times Magazine*, 21 February 1981, 16.

50. Ross K. Baker, "The Presidential Nominations," in Gerald L. Pomper, ed. *The Election of 1992* (Chatham, NJ: Chatham House, 1993), 46–47.

51. Binkley, *The Man in the White House*, 101–102.

52. Cornelius P. Cotter and Bernard C. Hennessy, *Politics without Power: The National Party Committees* (New York: Atherton Press, 1964), 138.

53. Ibid., 139.

54. Roger G. Brown, "Party and Bureaucracy: From Kennedy to Reagan," *Political Science Quarterly* 97 (Summer 1982): 282. Straight-out supporters of party patronage received a major setback from the Supreme Court. In a 1990 ruling, the High Court held that federal, state, and local governments cannot refuse to hire, promote, or transfer most employees because of their political affiliation or party activities. Many political experts view this ruling as weakening the value of, if not mitigating party patronage. See *Rutan v. Republican Party of Illinois*, 11 S. Ct. 2729 (1990).

55. *The New York Times*, 21 September 1962.

56. Chuck Alston, "Bush Ladles Gravy for GOP Mashed-Potato Circuit," *Congressional Quarterly Guide to Current American Government, Spring 1991* (Washington, DC: CQ Press, 1991), 94–96.

57. *The New York Times*, 22 June 1994.

58. George C. Edwards III, *At the Margins: Presidential Leadership of Congress* (New Haven, CT: Yale University Press, 1989), 34.

59. Ibid., 41.

60. Ibid., 53.

61. Gary Orren, "The Changing Styles of American Party Politics," in Joel L. Fleishman, ed. *The Future of American Parties: The Challenge of Governance* (Englewood Cliffs, NJ: Prentice-Hall, 1982), 41.

62. Roger G. Brown, "The Presidency and the Political Parties," in Michael Nelson, ed. *The Presidency and the Political System* (Washington, DC: CQ Press, 1984), 332.

CHAPTER 6

THE PUBLIC PRESIDENCY

The twentieth century marks the rise of the "public" or rhetorical presidency. This political phenomenon has been described as follows:

> Popular or mass rhetoric which Presidents once employed only rarely, now serves as one of their principal tools in attempting to govern the nation. Whatever doubts Americans may now entertain about the limitations of presidential leadership, they do not consider it unfitting or inappropriate for presidents to attempt to "move" the public by programmatic speeches that exhort and set forth grand and ennobling views.[1]

Prior to the twentieth century, political scientist Jeffrey Tulis reminds us that presidents preferred written communication with Congress rather than public addresses. But in this century presidents rely chiefly on the spoken word from the "bully pulpit" (Teddy Roosevelt's colorful term) rather than the written word to persuade the public to endorse his policies. Indeed, in the words of one commentator, "The presidency has become a seamless extension of campaigning, at a cost to the deliberative processes of government."[2] Clearly, modern presidents view their primary function to be the exercise of rhetorical leadership to mobilize public opinion, especially via television, in order to break the frequent gridlock on Capitol Hill. Only by a steady campaign of televised public addresses and unrelenting pressure on Congress do modern presidents believe that they can overcome the institutional separation of powers and the frequent deadlock produced in a large, pluralistic society with its countless interest groups, each seeking to protect its own turf and vested interests.

In this chapter we will explore how the leadership styles of presidents affect the form of presidential rhetoric. We will review how the nineteenth-century conception of the "head of state" presidency has been replaced by the rise of the public or rhetorical presidency in the twentieth century. The president's important role as the nation's agenda-setter will be examined. Also, the advantages and the downside of "going public" will be carefully weighed. Special attention will be given to Ronald Reagan's effective use of rhetoric and his communication skills. The significance of presidential oratory and the importance of presidential slogans and symbols are also evaluated. Another section is devoted to the potential threat of the "plebiscitary president" described by one commentator as a president who endeavors to build "a direct, unmediated relationship between himself and the American people" and who depends upon mass approval of his actions to maintain his standing as leader of the nation.[3] Spawned by the mass media and abetted by the decline of political parties in this country, the plebiscitary president may pose a more serious, long-range problem to democratic government than is presently realized.

BACKGROUND

More than anything else, the ability to communicate instantly with millions of American constituents via television differentiates twentieth-century public presidents from their nineteenth-century counterparts. Television magnifies the person and institution of the presidency. Indeed, no invention in the past fifty years has had a more profound effect on the American political environment than network television. Some years ago presidential chronicler Theodore H. White described television's influence in far stronger terms: "Television in modern politics has been as revolutionary as the development of printing in the time of Gutenberg."[4] The truly revolutionary importance of television for a president is that it enables him to communicate directly with the huge American public without any of his words and appeals being filtered through editing or an intermediary process.

Since the advent of television, Americans have become so accustomed to watching and listening to the president on the evening network television news programs, or turning to the around-the-clock Cable News Network (CNN), that the president has become an integral part of our daily life. Seldom does a day pass that the president's activities or public pronouncements are not fully reported across the land. In the words of Samuel Kernell:

The presidency's singular visibility allows its occupant to command the nation's attention; the office's broad constitutional mandate bestows upon him the authority to speak on any policy matter; and his acknowledged expertise requires that his arguments be weighed and, even if opposed, dealt with.[5]

Clearly, the president's growing ability to reach mass constituencies and penetrate an individual's life space with his rhetoric has marked a new era of presidential leadership.

The public presidency, however, has not always dominated the American scene. Prior to this century, one team of political scientists has reminded us: "Popular leadership through rhetoric was suspect."[6] Presidents rarely spoke directly to the people, and even if they wanted to, they lacked the magic of mass communication. But there is little evidence available to show that those earlier chief executives craved the opportunity to address the American people, or to go out frequently, in President Lyndon Johnson's words, "to press the flesh." Instead, they preferred written communication between the branches of government.

George Washington, who viewed his office as a "head of state" position, seldom delivered more than one major address per year and that one—the Annual Address (now called the State of the Union speech)—was virtually mandated by the Constitution. His audience was limited to the members of Congress and the handful of onlookers in the gallery. Thomas Jefferson, who conducted an "open" presidency compared to many of his successors, even ceased delivering the annual message in person—a precedent not broken until Woodrow Wilson decided to appear personally before Congress in 1913.[7] During this long hiatus the clerk of the House of Representatives read the speech to those lawmakers who chose to listen to him drone on. No television cameras, no radios. "Media opportunities" had not yet entered the American vocabulary.

The Washington-Jefferson "head of state" model, characterized by few public speeches, continued throughout the nineteenth century. Unlike the numerous "policy speeches" of the modern era, the oratory of nineteenth-century chief executives consisted mainly of patriotic orations, discussion of a constitutional issue, and perhaps the conduct of war. In current parlance, the president maintained a low profile. In one conspicuous exception to this rule—President Andrew Johnson's "swing around the circle" speaking tour in the summer before the 1866 off-year congressional elections—the campaign "not only failed but was considered highly irregular."[8] Most other nineteenth-century presidents were content to perform the routine executive duties of the presidency and defer to Congress on major policy issues. During this period presidents generally received less press coverage than Congress.

THE RISE OF THE PUBLIC OR RHETORICAL PRESIDENCY

Significantly, the emergence of the public or rhetorical presidency at the turn of the century coincides with the rise of mass circulation daily newspapers and the United States as a world power. Between 1875 and 1900 the daily circulation of newspapers throughout the country jumped from 2.6 to 15 million.[9] Undoubtedly the massive growth in population—from four million in 1790 to seventy-six million in 1900—also convinced some leaders, such as Teddy Roosevelt and

Woodrow Wilson that the traditional methods of indirect political discourse were no longer adequate in the modern state.

Theodore Roosevelt's stewardship theory of leadership style personified the new public presidency. The first modern president to recognize the power of the media, Teddy Roosevelt delighted in taking his messages "over the heads of Congress" directly to the people who he said are "the masters of both Congress and the President."[10] Unlike his predecessors, Roosevelt cultivated the Washington press corps. The "Rough Rider" president clearly recognized that the press was the primary link between himself and the American people. The national press, in turn, found the flamboyant Roosevelt to be good copy and delighted in telling readers about Teddy and his exploits. Roosevelt's considerable oratorical talents and his gifted pen—he didnt need the stable of speech writers that recent presidents view as indispensable—exemplified the new rhetorical presidency.

But it was Woodrow Wilson who brought public oratory to the forefront of American politics with his dramatic appearances before Congress—shattering more than a century's precedent of presidential nonattendance. That President Wilson chose to move into the national spotlight as soon as he had taken the oath of office should have occasioned few surprises, for he had spelled out his concept of the public presidency in a series of lectures he gave at Columbia University only a few years earlier:

His is the only national voice in affairs. Let him once win the admiration and confidence of the country, and no other single force can withstand him, no combination of forces will easily overpower him. His position takes the imagination of the country. He is the representative of no constituency, but of the whole people.[11]

Better than anyone, Wilson understood that when it comes to telling the country what it needs to hear, no one is in a better position than the president of the United States. Wilson's concept of the public presidency, however, did not always achieve the ends he had in mind. His famous post–World War I nationwide speaking tour to go over the heads in the Senate to win public support for United States membership in the League of Nations ended abruptly with his physical collapse in Colorado and the subsequent rejection by the Senate of the Treaty of Versailles (which included the League of Nations Covenant) in 1919.[12] Still, as James W. Ceaser and his colleagues have pointed out: "Wilson articulated the doctrinal foundations of the rhetorical presidency and thereby provided an alternative theoretical model to that of the Founders. In Wilson's view the greatest power in modern democratic regimes lay potentially with the popular leader who could sway or—to use his word—'interpret' the wishes of the people."[13]

Since the New Deal era, which also coincided with the golden age of radio, the presidency has become the most visible national office. President Franklin D. Roosevelt's press conferences altered the way the national media covered national politics. By the time of his death in April 1945, FDR had invited the press and radio correspondents into the Oval Office on 998 occasions.[14] Henceforth, the White House would become the center of the national political stage, and the president would always be in the news. And a permanent new role would be added to the president's job description: "communicator in chief."[15]

With this steady expansion in presidential visibility would come heightened expectations of presidential performance. Hand in hand with advances in communications has come the steady proliferation of interest groups organized to promote the demands of their membership. These people expect the president to respond to their needs. In many instances, the president may, in turn, need the support of these organized groups outside government in order to generate support for his policies on Capitol Hill. Consequently, his rhetorical appeals to these groups have become an important aspect of presidential leadership. Presidents are, of course, importuned daily to speak to trade and professional associations, conventions, university commencements, veterans groups, trade union conclaves, and local government associations. Indeed, as Samuel Kernell points out, "The real explosion in presidential talk has occurred in the class of minor addresses. Presidents Nixon, Carter, and Reagan all surpassed their predecessors use of such rhetoric by nearly fivefold."[16] Both Carter and Reagan averaged one speech a day.

The rhetorical presidency and the rise of mass communications grew in tandem, especially after Franklin D. Roosevelt's arrival in the White House in 1933. Earlier, Theodore Roosevelt and Woodrow Wilson had used the presidential "bully pulpit" to influence public opinion. But to reach the public, their channel of communication was restricted to the mass circulation of daily newspapers. Neither could hope to match the advantage FDR enjoyed with the new expanded radio networks. Between 1928 and 1932, the number of radio sets doubled—from nine to eighteen million. By 1935, the number had jumped to twenty-six million sets.[17] For the first time in history, a president's voice was within the reach of fifty to sixty million listeners. Moreover, the three major radio networks, NBC, CBS, and MBS (Mutual Broadcasting System) had enough affiliates to blanket the entire country and give simultaneous coverage to a single speaker.[18]

Network radio served as a nationalizing force in the news. Nationally covered stories, especially news of the president's programs and activities, enabled the president to exploit the new channel of radio communication and enlarge his potential audience throughout the United States. Instead of being one voice among many, the president's rhetoric became the dominant voice in the American political dialogue. Never again would the president have to operate in the shadow of the legislative branch.

Only six days after his inauguration, for example, FDR made his first radio "fireside chat" to the nation. In this folksy, informal speech Roosevelt explained to the American public why he had closed all the banks, what he planned to do to restore their financial health, and what cooperation he expected from panicky depositors. Within the next twenty-four hours many banks reopened, large amounts of hoarded currency were redeposited, the banking crisis was halted, and Roosevelt in this swift action had established himself as a close friend and concerned leader to each of millions of apprehensive listeners.[19] Overnight, the president had successfully exploited a new channel of communications with its huge audience. As explained by Richard L. Rubin:

Radio linked him personally and directly to the people. No interpretive screen mediated between Roosevelt and people receiving his voice, as it did with the print press. Radio gave Roosevelt the opportunity to present his program, his voice, and his personality directly to his constituency. For Roosevelt, radio served as an effective communications alternative, a mechanism of person-to-person contact by which he could bypass a hostile commercial press. It was in essence an electronic adaptation of Bryan's national lecture program, and it enabled Roosevelt to react to his audience directly and instantaneously.[20]

More than any of his predecessors, except possibly cousin Teddy, "Roosevelt recognized the importance of the presidency not only as the center of government but also as the center of *political information*."[21] Roosevelt's rhetorical presidency enabled him to communicate with the American public as no president had ever done, despite the overwhelming opposition of most newspaper publishers, especially the Hearst and Scripps chains.

FDR's skillful exploitation of radio enabled him to restructure political communications and make radio a counterforce to newspaper influence over public opinion on the editorial pages. As FDR used to say: "Just let me make the news on the front pages, and I don't care what they say on the editorial pages." Richard L. Rubin summed up FDR's rhetorical presidency as follows:

He established a faster more centralized and more direct circuitry between the mass public and the presidency than possible before him and used the unique personal qualities of radio to deeply penetrate into a vast new listening audience.[22]

The age of radio gave way to the age of television in the early 1950s. In less than a decade television viewing largely replaced radio listening as the nation's favorite pastime for millions of Americans. Television also soon became the chief source of political information for the American public. Republican and Democratic presidents alike quickly recognized the priceless value of televised communication to reach and influence millions of viewers.

The old maxim that a picture is worth a thousand words explains better than anything why television drastically changed the president's relationship with the American people over the next four decades. In the age of television, the size of the president's prime time audience generally averages fifty to sixty million viewers. Equally important, with a vastly increased audience the role of the speech itself has changed. Presidents have come to understand that it is the visual performance, not the tangible text, that creates the public image. With only slight exaggeration, James W. Ceaser and his associates note: "What is not seen or heard today does not exist."[23] No recent president has been more adept than Ronald Reagan before the cameras. His ability to clarify complex issues through a simple, straightforward, smoothly-delivered message has made him probably the most effective national leader since Kennedy.

THE PRESIDENT AS AGENDA SETTER

The rise of the rhetorical presidency has made the president the preeminent agenda-setter for the nation. Though the Founding Fathers may not have fully recognized how crucial the single chief executive could become in managing the federal government, they were aware of the need for unified action in times of crisis.

As manager, the president—not Congress—dictates the issues that will occupy the nation's attention. Indeed, writes Bruce Miroff, "Press or partisan criticism may challenge a president on the form or details of his actions, but the outline of reality that he has sketched is usually left intact." Miroff continues, "His words and actions receive far more coverage from the mass media than the efforts of other political actors or institutions."[24]

By initiating action, the president can immediately occupy the center of the national stage. Presidential pronouncements will set the terms for political discussion and debate, whether the issue is a domestic problem or a foreign policy question. This ability to control the public agenda, which is the hallmark of the rhetorical presidency, has opened the door to even greater presidential domination of the public's business.

THE PLEBISCITARY PRESIDENT

With the emergence of the rhetorical presidency, the marked decline of political parties, and domination of the mass media in presidential nominating and general elections over the past two decades, the country has been moving in the direction, in the words of Theodore J. Lowi, of a "plebiscitary presidency."[25] Under these changed conditions the president increasingly maintains a direct personal relationship via television and radio with millions of American citizens. To some readers, the term *plebiscite* evokes images of Roman emperors and French Bonapartism, of rulers who governed on the basis of popular acclaim, with the masses giving their enthusiastic assent in the Coliseum or in a national referendum. While the term *plebiscitary* may be an exaggeration, it is nonetheless not far from the mark in describing the American chief executive in the age of television.

Even during the presidential election campaign the rhetoric and "image" of the winner and loser is focused on building a personal constituency involving a direct and unmediated relationship between the candidate—or incumbent president—and the mass public. Especially in the age of television, these ties between the leader and his followers become more evident once the country moves from the electing to the governing process.

Once in the White House, the president shifts to the posture of the nation's chief guardian and protector. Aided by a huge White House staff to publicize the president's every achievement and his abiding concern for the welfare of all the citizenry, the president easily becomes the nation's foremost authority figure. His commanding presence and the constant attention that he attracts from the public enhances or reinforces his national stature. With the president's instant accessibility to an arsenal of rhetorical weapons—televised press conferences, regular and special messages to Congress and the American people, and numerous "nonpolitical" speeches to various professional associations and veterans groups—the president would seem to be moving ever closer to becoming a plebiscitary leader. The plebiscitary president, it seems fair to say, can be considered an advanced form of the public presidency.

As a chief tribune of the American people, the president enjoys a preeminent position to articulate his programs to the American public. Consequently, the opportunities for the emergence of a plebiscitarian president are probably greater today than at anytime in American history.

For the public president to be a political success, he must create a sense of drama and mystique. Perhaps it is a reflection of the age of television, but the American public expects its presidents to be exciting and upbeat, and leave the distinct impression that they are in charge of the government. By and large, a president's impact on the American public seems to hinge less on his policies than his public presence. Heavy emphasis upon the person rather than the office can be expected to foster further plebiscitarian tendencies within the White House.

THE ADVANTAGES OF "GOING PUBLIC"

With the steady decline of political parties, the fragmentation of Congress, especially the "subcommitteeization" of the House, and the frequency of divided government, the president can no longer simply implore his fellow partisans on Capitol Hill to support his program. Instead, he must resort to "going public." A term coined by political scientist Samuel Kernell, going public has been described by Kernell as the "class of activities in which presidents engage as they promote themselves and their policies before the American public."[26] Furthermore, Kernell continues, recent presidents "are more inclined to pursue the same public strategies that placed them in the White House."[27] For these presidents campaigning and governing are almost indistinguishable. Under these circumstances it is much easier for a president to go public and seek support nationwide on prime time television than relying on insider politics (see Table 6.1).

Going public helps the president indirectly build coalition support, even if it is for only one major vote in Congress. Coalition building in this age of the

Table 6.1
Presidential Television from Kennedy to Bush: First Nineteen Months in Office,
1961–1990

President	Number of Prime Time Appearances	Time on Air Prime Time (hours)	Total Number of Appearances	Total Time (hours)
Kennedy	4	1.9	50	30.4
Johnson	7	3.3	33	12.5
Nixon	14	7.1	37	13.5
Carter	8	5.1	45	32.2
Reagan	12	8.9	39	26.5
Bush	7	3.7	56	22.3

Note: Gerald Ford has been omitted from analysis since his first nineteen months in office cross into the reelection period.

Sources: For Kennedy, Johnson, and Nixon, data were supplied by the White House Press Office, quoted in *The New York Times*, 3 August 1970. For Carter, Reagan, and Bush data are from program logs at CBS News, New York. Data are for speeches (including inauguration) and press conferences broadcast live by the national television networks. Reprinted from Samuel Kernell, *Going Public*, 2nd ed. (Washington, DC: CQ Press, 1993), 98.

mass media, however, has become much more difficult because senators and representatives operate more as independent contractors and less as team players. As Thomas E. Mann explained, "Senators and representatives are in business for themselves." "Consequently," Mann continues, "they are all more likely to view themselves first and foremost as individuals, not as members of a party or as part of the president's team."[28]

By going public, the president can sometimes avoid bargaining with 535 individuals on Capitol Hill. By dealing with mass publics, the president can achieve an economy of effort. By going public the president can also sometimes gain the upper hand with Congress because many members do not want to risk being viewed by their constituents as uncooperative with the nation's leader.

The downside of going public constantly, however, is that the president risks over-exposure—at least FDR and JFK both worried about this factor. Second, the president faces the real risk of making a major push for his program and failing with the resultant loss of potential influence for future legislative battles. Third, going public too frequently can result in trivializing the presidency, as some critics insist President Clinton has done.

MOLDING PUBLIC OPINION

Strong presidents have never been content just to follow public opinion; rather, they have engaged in a variety of rhetorical approaches to lead the public. As Franklin D. Roosevelt, the master molder of public opinion in the twentieth century, put it: "All our great Presidents were leaders of thought at times when certain historic ideas in the life of the nation had to be clarified."[29] Sometimes the president's goals have been to gain long-term support for the administration's policies; at other times, he has been more interested in obtaining support for specific programs—Social Security, the Marshall Plan, the Peace Corps, the Civil Rights Acts of 1964 and 1965, the SALT II treaty, the MX missile program. Often both his long- and short-term goals will persuade the president "to go public."

To influence and mold public opinion, modern presidents must, of course, become "great explainers."[30] Invariably they turn to national television, since no other medium routinely gives them instant access to such a huge audience. But no matter how effective a communicator the president is, he must contend with the general attitudes of his audience. As George C. Edwards III has noted: "The public's general lack of interest in politics constrains the president's leadership of public opinion in the long run as well as on a given day."[31] Indeed, the president has to wait until the issues he wants to discuss are on citizens' minds, which generally occurs only when an issue in question is personally affecting their lives. Thus, although the president can use television to reach his multimillion-person audience, the president cannot turn to the American people every time an important issue crosses his mind. If he does, his televised rhetoric will become commonplace and lose its dramatic impact.

Despite the fame and effectiveness of President Franklin D. Roosevelt's fireside chats on radio, he made only thirty of them in twelve years. FDR felt that he would "wear out his welcome" if he went to the airwaves too frequently. President Reagan, on the other hand, believed that frequent television appearances to argue his case would be the more effective form of leadership. As a president in a divided government, President Reagan felt that he had no choice but to fall back on his chief weapon—public opinion—to win and maintain support for his policies. Reagan's eight major television addresses in 1981 (a month of which was spent convalescing from an attempted assassination) stands as a first-year record for all presidents.[32]

How successful are these nationwide presidential appeals? Generally, presidents have had less success with domestic issues than with foreign affairs. There are several explanations for these different results. In foreign policy questions the president is viewed as the leader of the nation rather than as a partisan politician. Foreign policy crises evoke an outpouring of national pride and patriotism that usually results in a surge (often temporary) of public support for the president. Foreign policy issues are more distant from the lives of most Americans. Generally, they are viewed as more complex and based on specialized knowledge. Consequently, the public tends to defer more to the president on these matters than on issues closer to home which they can relate to their own experience. On most domestic issues, Americans are basically individualistic and skeptical of authority, and therefore not notably favorable toward domestic policies, especially if it means higher taxes. Thus, while Americans have been prepared to sacrifice at great lengths during a period of national crisis, they do not like constraints on their lives in peacetime. If inflation is spiraling, for example, Americans want prices to be controlled but not suffer higher taxes.

Televised nationwide speeches may enable presidents to create or modify public opinion at critical points during their terms. Presidential speeches may also enhance his reelection chances. While these addresses are no guarantee of reelection, they can serve throughout his first term as an excellent opportunity to "run for office while in office."[33]

Going public is such a common occurrence in the recent era of divided government that the American public has come to accept it as a way of life for our presidents. A trip to China, a televised news conference, a speech before a business convention on the West Coast, a prime-time address to the nation, or a summit meeting in Moscow with Russian leader Boris Yeltsin, all these events are intended principally to place the president and his message before the American people in a way that raises his public opinion ratings and thus enhances his chances of success with Congress. As Samuel Kernell writes, "the ultimate object of the president's designs is not the American voter, but fellow politicians in Washington."[34] By going public, the president seeks to transfer approval of his performance to support for his policies. Rallying national public opinion is, therefore, the keystone of this new style of presidential leadership. In Samuel Kernell's words, "Going public represents little more than an extension of the process that placed the outsider in the White House."[35]

Over the past three decades, the frequency with which presidents have communicated with the American public has also risen steadily—the more recent the president, the more likely that he went public. Table 6.1 shows the record of television time utilized by presidents from Kennedy to Bush during their first nineteen months in office. The reader will note the almost steady upward trend in the number of public appearances by presidents from 1961 to 1990.

The persistence of divided government—twenty-six years out of forty-two between 1952 and 1994—has encouraged several incumbent presidents to escalate their public activities to help deal with an opposition Congress. For minority party presidents, going public is usually the preferred (probably the only) course of action in dealing with the opposition party in Congress since the president would be clearly outnumbered at the bargaining table. By turning to network television and extensive public speaking tours around the country to drum up support for his programs, the president can circumvent much of the time-consuming bargaining with opposition party leaders on Capitol Hill. President Reagan, for example, succeeded for several years in winning support for his anti-Communist, Contra-backed program in Nicaragua by persuading (or intimidating) a sufficient number of opposition party lawmakers not to end up on the "wrong side" of this anti-Communist issue.

For many Bill Clinton watchers, it has not been easy to discern when the presidential campaign ended and his new administration began. The personification of the public president, Mr. Clinton launched the first in a series of televised "town meetings" from suburban Detroit three weeks after taking office. The first televised meeting was a media planner's dream. Appearing on the Detroit ABC-TV network affiliate, and linked by satellite with ABC-television stations in Atlanta, Miami, and Seattle, Mr. Clinton's prime-time one-hour show was also broadcast over the Cable News Network (CNN), C-SPAN public affairs cable network, and on seventeen other independent stations in major media markets around the country. Mr. Clinton also appeared the same night on Ted Koppel's *Nightline* news program on ABC-TV. This program had an estimated audience of five million viewers. Clearly, Mr. Clinton's televised meeting dominated the national agenda and enabled him to speak directly to "the people" without having to deal with pesky questions from the Washington press corps. Although hundreds of national reporters followed the president to Detroit, none had an opportunity to ask Mr. Clinton a single question before or after the town meeting.[36]

THE DOWNSIDE OF "GOING PUBLIC"

The power of presidential communication is formidable, but it is not unlimited. As Samuel Kernell has observed, "Going public may allow a popular president to soar, but even as he does so, he creates the risk of eventual collapse."[37] Three of the past four presidents have failed to win reelection, despite access to the most far-reaching communication system in history: four major television networks, including approximately 1,488 affiliated and independent television stations, 305 public television stations, 4,988 AM and 6,036 FM radio stations, 1,611 daily newspapers, with a combined daily and Sunday circulation of 62,600,000 copies; 466 weekly periodicals, 371 semi-monthlies, 4,326 monthlies, and 2,143 bimonthly publications.[38] Additionally, cable network subscribers now exceed sixty million.

With the availability of this massive communications system, why does it also have a downside? First of all, the mass media can serve as a matchless channel for critics to blame the president for every ill, real or imagined, that afflicts the country. Two former, high-placed public servants, McGeorge Bundy and Edmund S. Muskie have put it this way:

Although television has expanded the President's symbolic role, the other side of the coin is that television makes the President a highly available scapegoat for the nation's disappointment and failures. When events take a downturn, the President is a ready object of blame. If foreign oil prices soar, it is easy to blame the President rather than a major culprit, the American motorist riding alone in his car at high speed.[39]

Another negative for going public is that the extraordinary attention showered on the president by the media magnifies his flaws. President Bill Clinton has not been the first recent president to discover how quickly the mass media's microscopic coverage can transform a president's favorable ratings into negatives within a matter of weeks. President Gerald Ford saw his initial 71 percent favorable rating tumble shortly after taking over the White House in August 1974 to 49 percent in less than thirty days. Ford's surprise pardon of former President Richard Nixon triggered this 29 percent drop—the sharpest decline in Gallup's polling history.[40]

President George Bush also learned belatedly that going public frequently is no guarantee that the president can win congressional approval of his legislative agenda—or reelection. President Bush, for example, set a new high in going public during his first year in office, but without marked success. In his first twelve months he visited eighty-seven cities, held thirty-three full-blown press conferences, and fifteen informal press gatherings, fifty-four interviews, and delivered 320 speeches (an estimated total of three million words).[41] Yet, throughout his term his success rate with Congress was low. During 1992, according to the *Congressional Quarterly* boxscore, his success rate was only 43 percent—the lowest of any first-term president since the rating system began in 1953.[42]

Unlike George Bush, President Bill Clinton for two years had the advantage of operating under one-party government with both houses of Congress controlled by his fellow Democrats. President Clinton's persistent "going public" strategy seems to have paid off during his first year in office. In 1993, Clinton's legislative success record with Congress was 86.4 percent, according to the *Congressional Quarterly* scorecard.[43] Only Presidents Eisenhower and Johnson had higher ratings than Clinton in their first year in office (see Chapter 12, Figure 12.2).

In the final analysis, the going public strategy can be considered primarily as a complementary tool to help build public support, not a fundamental policy agenda. Going public contains no magic guarantee that it will produce enough positive results to insure reelection for the White House incumbent against a formidable opponent—or opponents, as was the case in 1992. Going public cannot serve as a substitute for developing a basic presidential agenda for dealing with pressing domestic issues, threatening foreign crises, or poorly managing the White House staff. Even then, despite strong policies abroad, modern presidents seeking a second term may find themselves caught up in the midst of a sputtering economy that, no matter what course they pursue, will doom their reelection chances. One team of media specialists has pointed to a related dilemma created by going public. "By constantly drawing attention to the president, the strategy of going public produces *an attribution error*, in which politicians are held responsible for outcomes even when their decisions and policies have no bearing whatsoever on the outcome."[44]

To be sure, summit meetings, and Rose Garden ceremonies can generate favorable publicity for presidents. But television cannot readily depict or explain the ever-rising costs of entitlement programs or the failure to balance the federal budget. "As for the economy," *The New York Times* television critic Walter Goodman has noted, "Television is not the best medium for explaining anything more abstract than an unemployment line."[45]

In the age of television, the president conducts his office, it has already been suggested, as if he were still campaigning for it. This "permanent campaign" approach to operating the White House also entails a heavy travel schedule— our next topic.

PRESIDENTIAL TRAVEL

Before the age of jet travel, time constraints limited the president's ability to go public. As late as 1948, the train was the president's standard mode of travel. But since a round trip across the country and back to the nation's capital consumed at least seven days, the president usually tried to combine presidential duties with politics. The leisurely train travel enabled the president to make several speeches along the way, visit with governors and state party leaders, invite them to travel across their states in the president's special observation car, and then dedicate a federal project or two. FDR, who enjoyed train travel, used this approach successfully on several occasions, and of course President Harry Truman's 1948 cross-country campaign special was tailor-made for his uphill reelection bid. But this all changed with the arrival of jet aircraft.

President Ronald Reagan was a foremost practitioner of the "Marco Polo" approach to presidential politics. His frequent foreign excursions offered him a priceless opportunity to combine stagecraft and practical politics on foreign shores. Few voters would forget President and Mrs. Reagan's visit in the spring of 1984 to the Normandy Beach cemetery to commemorate the fortieth anniversary of the D-Day landings; nor did the White House staff overlook the unmatched photo opportunities this ceremony presented during the early phase of his 1984 reelection campaign. Another memorable episode on this same European trip was the Reagans' visit to Ballyporeen, the small Irish village of his ancestors in Tipperary. In this picturesque setting the 1,800-member traveling television and print media contingent accompanying the Reagans outnumbered the 350 villagers who turned out to greet the American president by more than five to one.[46]

President George Bush undoubtedly holds the record of being the most traveled single-term chief executive in history. During his first year in office, Bush covered 185,000 miles.[47] His journeys included three summits: on the island of Malta with Soviet leader Mikhail Gorbachev; in Brussels with NATO leaders; and in Paris the "Group of Seven" (G-Seven) gathering on economic issues with other Western leaders. That President Bush would continue to use heavy foreign travel as a means of maintaining his high post–Persian Gulf War popularity and keeping the opposition Democrats off balance was evident soon after he gave a nationally televised Gulf War report to a joint session of Congress in early March 1991. In his address, he also called upon lawmakers to approve his new crime control and transportation proposals within one hundred days. The president's message to the controlling majority party Democrats was crystal clear: if the United States government could win a ground war in one hundred hours, certainly it could enact a tough crime control law and an expanded transportation bill in one hundred days. (Congress did not meet this deadline.)

By keeping in almost constant motion, President Bush endeavored to maintain his agenda-setting dominance over opposition Democrats in Congress. As explained by one Bush aide, "When we are in Washington, we end up playing on the Congressional playing field. But when we get outside Washington, we have a better opportunity to convey our message to the public, and we are not forced to follow the Congressional agenda."[48]

Generally, foreign travel helps the president not only to dominate the news, but also leave many intractable domestic problems behind at home.

PRESIDENTIAL ORATORY AND RHETORIC

Most experts have rated only a handful of presidents as great orators—Lincoln, Wilson, Franklin D. Roosevelt, and John F. Kennedy. Just a shade below this foursome would be Theodore Roosevelt and Ronald Reagan.

Lincoln's place among the great orators is beyond challenge. Wilson's eloquence has also won him a high ranking among presidential orators, but his words failed him when he probably needed them most—to win popular support for the ratification of the Versailles Treaty after World War I and membership in the League of Nations. Franklin D. Roosevelt's memorable phrases, "We have nothing to fear but fear itself," "We have a rendezvous with destiny," and his ringing declaration, "A day that will live in infamy," which prefaced his request to Congress for a declaration of war against Japan in December 1941, have assured him a top rating among the all-time great presidential orators. These three presidential orators, it should be noted, all made their mark before the age of television, before the United States assumed its full responsibilities as a world power, and most important, before the nuclear age.

Of the post–World War II presidents whose oratory has exerted the most influence on world opinion, John F. Kennedy would most certainly rate at the top of the list. As the hero of the 1962 Cuban missile crisis, and newly recognized leader of the Western democratic alliance, Kennedy's powerful rhetoric never reached a higher point than during his famous visit to West Berlin—the then western enclave a hundred miles behind the Iron Curtain—in July 1963, four months before his assassination. It was estimated that almost half of West Berlin's 2.3 million people turned out to greet the smiling young president. In the words of Herbert S. Parmet, his biographer: "No conquering hero ever received a more enthusiastic reception."[49] Kennedy's address in the Rudolph Wilde Platz outside West Berlin's city hall will long be remembered throughout the free world. Mixing defiance and appeal to pride, Kennedy told the huge crowd what they wanted to hear; indeed, it was almost as if he were campaigning for reelection.

"Two thousand years ago the proudest boast was *civis Romanus sum*," he said right after the introductory remarks. "Today, in the world of freedom, the proudest boast is *Ich bin ein Berliner*." Then came the rhetorical challenge: "There are some who say that communism is the wave of the future. Let them come to Berlin. And there are some who say in Europe and elsewhere we can work with the Communists. Let them come to Berlin." He went on to tell them that they lived "in a defended island of freedom, but your life is part of the main," and in conclusion declared: "All free men, wherever they may live, are citizens of Berlin, and, therefore, as a free man, I take pride in the words *Ich bin ein Berliner!*"[50] The ovation was deafening. No German crowd had ever responded as warmly and emotionally as they did to Kennedy, according to one official of the West German government—not even to Hitler at the height of his power.[51]

Sometimes a president's rhetoric can produce remarkable results on the domestic front, too. President Lyndon B. Johnson made one of the most dramatic speeches of the twentieth century in March 1965 during the height of the civil rights protests. The nationally televised scenes of Reverend Martin Luther King, Jr., and his freedom marchers being brutally attacked by police dogs and mounted state troopers at the outset of their planned, peaceful fifty-mile march from Selma, Alabama, to Montgomery, the capital, in March 1965 horrified the nation and provoked President Johnson to demand prompt passage of federal voting rights legislation. So outraged was the American public at the scenes of Reverend King's peaceful marchers being bull-whipped and clubbed by local authorities that Johnson had no choice but to demand an immediate end to the brutal police action. No other American president introduced a civil rights bill—indeed, any domestic legislation—with such fanfare and rhetorical flourish.

Johnson had quickly sensed the mood of the public and Congress. But instead of immediately sending federal troops to Alabama and going on national television, he let the full impact of Bloody Sunday sink into the nation's conscience. In the midst of the turmoil, segregationist Governor George C. Wallace of Alabama asked for a meeting with Johnson, who granted the request. In the Oval Office they discussed, among other things, the question of federal troops. So persuasive was President Johnson in appealing to Governor Wallace's populist-leaning views and larger ambition that Wallace was reported to have said after the three-hour meeting, "If I hadn't left when I did, he'd have had me coming out *for* civil rights."[52] Two says later, Johnson "federalized" the Alabama National Guard as a necessary measure to halt further violence and to demonstrate that he was acting reluctantly but out of necessity.[53] Meanwhile, the Justice Department was putting together the final draft of the proposed Voting Rights Act.

Eight days after the brutal confrontation in Selma, Alabama, President Johnson addressed a joint session of Congress—and the American people. The three television networks quickly acceded to his request for prime-time coverage. All members of the cabinet were present for the address, as were members of the Supreme Court; leading members of the civil rights organizations and other prominent citizens were in the House gallery.

"I speak tonight," Johnson began, "for the dignity of man and the destiny of democracy."

At times history and fate meet at a single time in a single place to shape a turning point in a man's unending search for freedom. . . . So it was a century ago at Appomattox. So it was last week in Selma, Alabama. . . . There is no constitutional issue here. The command of the Constitution is plain. There is no moral issue. It is wrong . . . to deny any of your fellow Americans the right to vote. . . . This time, on this issue, there must be no delay, no hesitation, and no compromise with our purpose. . . . What happened in Selma is part of a far larger movement which reaches into every section and state of America. It is the effort of American Negroes to secure for themselves the full blessing of American life. Their cause must be our cause, too. Because it is not just Negroes, but really it is all of us who must overcome the crippling legacy of bigotry and injustice.[54]

At this point Johnson stopped. He raised his long arms and repeated four words from the old Baptist hymn, now the marching song of the civil rights movement: "And . . . we . . . shall . . . overcome!" Suddenly, as one observer described it "The whole chamber was on its feet. . . . In the galleries Negroes and whites, some in the rumpled sports shirts of bus rides from the demonstrations, others in trim professional suits, wept unabashedly."[55] All the emotional outpouring was picked up by the network cameras, and the national viewing audience had that rare opportunity to see and hear a presidential speech that would truly shape events for years to come.

Unlike the Civil Rights Act of 1964, which had been stalled by a Senate filibuster for nearly four months before its final passage, the Voting Rights Act of 1965 (which banned literacy tests and provided for direct intervention by federal attorneys, if needed, in voter registration cases) passed both houses of Congress within a matter of weeks. This historic bill reached Johnson's desk less than two months after his address to Congress. Rarely have a president's words had such an immediate impact upon the conscience of Congress and the American people as President Johnson's rhetoric following the confrontation in Selma. And never again would the nation accord Mr. Johnson the same ringing endorsement they gave him in the days immediately following this nationwide telecast, for within five weeks he went back to Congress to obtain financial backing that would ultimately send 525,000 American troops to South Vietnam. From that day forward, Mr. Johnson popularity began sagging, never to return to its former high mark. Even more serious, the credibility of President Johnson's rhetoric began to erode. Indeed, his "credibility gap" continued to widen to a point that by early 1968 it became, in the eyes of many national observers, a significant factor in his decision not to seek reelection.

Not since John F. Kennedy's eloquent addresses of the early 1960s would the nation be treated to such persuasive presidential rhetoric as when Ronald Reagan arrived in the White House in 1981. The secret of Reagan's success, most pundits have agreed, was to "concentrate on a few transcendent issues and let the details take care of themselves." During his first term his close associates said that he had only three priorities: "(1) economics, (2) economics, and (3) economics."[56] His second-term agenda, his close associates said, would be largely confined to three main items: arms control, tax simplification, and the federal budget deficit. Reagan's rhetoric generally contained no surprises, no bold new programs, but rather the reassertion of the standard conservative principles—the need for a smaller federal government, lower taxes, and a strong national defense. One critic, in evaluating Reagan's first inaugural address, entitled it "Shadow or Substance?"[57] The same title might be given to most of Reagan's public addresses.

Washington commentator Morton M. Kondracke contrasted President Reagan's rhetorical style in his State of the Union Message with that of his predecessor, Jimmy Carter.

If Jimmy Carter had sent Congress a budget as fraught with pain as Ronald Reagan's, his State of the Union Message would have brimmed over with—as one-time chief speech writer James Fallows puts it—"stern talk about tightening our belts, sharing the sacrifice, taking our medicine, and facing hard truths." It's all too possible, says Fallows, that Carter would have recited the list of impending budget cuts, pausing to lecture each interest group affected—farmers, small businessmen, college aid recipients, Medicare beneficiaries—on why reduced funding was the only fair outcome.[58]

What can be concluded from the Reagan rhetoric? Have we reached a point where, according to the late Marshall McLuhan, the Canadian high priest of communications, "the medium is the message?" Commentator Edward W. Chester concluded after evaluating President Reagan's first inaugural address, that "in Ronald Reagan, the former motion picture and television star and present day conservative Republican ideologue, the style and content meet in harmonious whole."[59]

CEREMONIAL RHETORIC

Presidents have always been able to capitalize on the chief of state ceremonial rhetoric to strengthen their leadership role, while remaining above politics. The president's use of ceremonial rhetoric reached new highs during Reagan's White House tenure. Who can forget his official opening of the 1984 summer Olympics in Los Angeles? The public probably does not recall his exact words of greeting to all the participants and the throng of 80,000 watching the opening event, but no matter. The incumbent Republican president's direct involvement in the Olympic festivities in the midst of a presidential election year was considered a political bonanza by the White House. Since campaign managers regard televised coverage of candidates in a nonpolitical setting as far more effective than paid commercials, Reagan's ceremonial rhetoric, heard cost-free by millions of Americans watching the Olympics, underscored once again the political advantage the incumbent president usually holds over a challenger.

As one veteran reporter has summarized Reagan's effective use of ceremonial rhetoric: "Few Chief Executives have rivaled him as the White House 'master of ceremonies,' beaming like a game show host and palming a small card of Oval Office announcement notes at each day's several minor ceremonies, all to help display the self-confidence that bolsters his approval rating in the polls."[60]

SLOGANS AND SYMBOLS

Political slogans and symbols can be an important aspect of presidential rhetoric and may be just the elements needed to launch a successful presidency. Indeed, as George Edwards III, and Stephen J. Wayne have emphasized: "If presidents can get a substantial segment of the public to adopt symbols favorable to them, they will be in a position to influence public opinion."[61] Franklin D. Roosevelt quickly dubbed his administration the "New Deal," and it will always be so remembered in the history books. Harry Truman, seeking to establish a special identity for his own administration, termed it the "Fair Deal." Each slogan symbolized a multitude of programs, but they reflected action amid a sense of concern for rank-and-file Americans.

Similarly, President Kennedy's "New Frontier" symbolized a sense of adventure and an innovative approach to national problems. President Lyndon Johnson's "Great Society" programs enjoyed a brief period of popularity, but with the steady escalation of United States involvement in the Vietnam War in 1965, and President Johnson's declining popularity, most of the Great Society programs lost their luster.

Presidents who fail to exploit slogans and symbols for their administrations can experience serious problems in relating to the public. In the case of the Carter administration, as Edwards and Wayne have pointed out: "Jimmy Carter faced a great deal of criticism for lacking a unifying theme and cohesion in the programs, for failing to inspire the public with a sense of purpose, and the idea to follow. Instead of providing the country with a sense of his vision and priorities, he emphasized discrete problem solving."[62]

The plain truth is that the administrations of Nixon, Ford, Carter, Reagan, and Bush all lacked popular symbols and slogans. But in the case of the Reagan administration, the absence of any catchy slogan or symbol did not seem to diminish Reagan's general popularity. Perhaps the fact that Reagan was a former movie idol filled this symbolic vacuum. Also, the overriding anti-government theme of Reagan's rhetoric, repeated week in and week out, came to symbolize the new direction of his administration. President Reagan fashioned himself as the chief guardian of the balanced budget, although he never submitted a budget to Congress that was even close to being balanced, and during his two terms he incurred a larger national debt than all forty previous presidents combined.

President George Bush, despite his heavy dependence on his role as commander in chief in the Panama invasion in December 1989 and the Persian Gulf War (1990–1991), never succeeded in building a symbolic foundation for his presidency. Some commentators called it the "third Reagan Administration."

President Bill Clinton, in his first year in office, has also failed so far to come up with a powerful symbol—a "New Frontier" credo—that would give his presidency a unique identity. All presidents, however, seek to capitalize on their role as surrogate of the American people—our next topic.

SURROGATE OF THE PEOPLE

Presidential monopoly over public space sometimes has taken the form of the president proclaiming himself the chief surrogate for the mass public. This concept that the president is the sole representative of the national constituency goes back to Andrew Jackson. The general-turned-president portrayed himself as the sole protector of the people, who individually were unable to take action against the selfish, corrupt elite.[63] The Jacksonian image of the president serving as the surrogate for the American citizenry has, of course, recurred throughout American history. Teddy Roosevelt's campaign against the "great malefactors of wealth," FDR's rhetorical war of words against the "economic royalists" bent upon sabotaging the people's gains from the New Deal, and Ronald Reagan's relentless campaign against "big government" that suffocates individual initiative are the best-known examples. As depicted by Bruce Miroff: "Presidential action thus becomes—in a symbolic sense—our action, a scattered, divided, uncertain people are made one and exercise their popular power through their surrogate."[64] Consequently, presidents seldom pass up the opportunity to serve as surrogate of the American people, such as inspecting hurricane or flood damage to see what victims are being taken care of and that federal relief is on the way. The nation expects no less from the president.

Furthermore, as the national leader responsible for the nation's security and domestic well-being, Miroff continues, "the president's singular national visibility, constitutional legitimacy, and acknowledged institutional expertise preserve for him a special place in public opinion. Citizens take note of his appeals, whether they like him or not."[65] This unique position of the president has, especially since the age of mass communications, fostered the growth of a potentially alarming development already discussed earlier in this chapter—the rise of the plebiscitary presidency.

POLITICAL PARTIES KEEP THE PUBLIC PRESIDENT ACCOUNTABLE

The public president and the plebiscitary president derive their power and influence from the same source—the public. The best protection against the rise of a plebiscitary president as a threat to democratic institutions still remains a strong party system. Only viable parties can keep presidents accountable to the public. As two close students of the presidency have put it, "Parties can be a major means for reflecting popular impulses in ways that inform and channel uses of presidential power. Thus, they are potentially one means of holding the presidency within appropriate bounds."[66] Whether American parties can survive as viable public agencies in an era heavily dominated by the media remains an unanswered question. However, to the extent that parties retain their vitality in the years ahead, the growth of the plebiscitary president will be held in check. Meanwhile, televised national addresses, press conferences, and even "electronic town meetings" have all become standard operating procedures for contemporary White House occupants to direct their messages to the mass electorate. Consequently, it is largely wishful thinking to believe that the public presidency will be kept accountable without political parties.

The same conditions that have fostered the public presidency—network television, party decomposition, fragmentation and the subcommitteeization in Congress, and divided government—have all led to greater centralization of presidential management in the White House, not the executive departments. This development, which became plainly evident during the Kennedy-Johnson years, has led, in effect, to the formation of a new branch of government—the presidential branch. This phenomenon, with its far-ranging implications on the management of the federal government, will be the subject of our next chapter.

NOTES

1. James W. Ceaser, Glen E. Thurow, Jeffrey Tulis, and Joseph M. Bessette, "The Rise of the Rhetorical Presidency," *Presidential Studies Quarterly* 11 (Spring 1981): 159.
2. George F. Will, "Rhetorical Presidency," *Newsweek*, vol. 121, 5 February 1993, 74.
3. Theodore J. Lowi, *The Personal President* (Ithaca, NY: Cornell University Press, 1985).
4. Theodore H. White, *America in Search of Itself* (New York: Harper & Row, 1982), 165.
5. Samuel Kernell, *Going Public*, 2nd ed. (Washington, DC: CQ Press, 1993), 167.
6. Ceaser et al., "The Rise of the Rhetorical Presidency," 159.

7. Jefferson, however, used his great rhetorical skill in his inaugural address in his attempt to reunify the country following the divisive campaign of 1800; see Dumas Malone, *Jefferson the President: First Term 1801–1805*, vol. 4 (Boston: Little, Brown, 1970), 17–21.

8. Ibid. This discussion of Johnson's "swing around the circle" is based on Albert Castel, *The Presidency of Andrew Johnson* (Lawrence, KS: Regents Press, 1979), as cited by Ceaser et al., "The Rise of the Rhetorical Presidency," 159.

9. Edwin Emery, *The Press and America: An Interpretive History of the Mass Media*, 3rd ed. (Englewood Cliffs, NJ: Prentice-Hall, 1972), 285.

10. As cited in Donald Bruce Johnson and Jack L. Walker, eds. *The Dynamics of the American Presidency* (New York: Wiley, 1964), 134–135.

11. Woodrow Wilson, *Constitutional Government in the United States* (New York: Columbia University Press, 1908), 68.

12. See Thomas A. Bailey, *Woodrow Wilson and the Lost Peace* (Chicago: Quadrangle Books, 1944).

13. Ceaser et al., "The Rise of the Rhetorical Presidency," 162–163.

14. Samuel Kernell, *Going Public*, 2nd ed., 66.

15. George C. Edwards III and Stephen J. Wayne, *Presidential Leadership* (New York: St. Martin's, 1985), 11.

16. Samuel Kernell, "The Presidency and the People," in Michael Nelson, ed. *The Presidency and the Political System* (Washington, DC: CQ Press, 1984), 241. Professor Kernell has also included several interesting tables listing the presidents' national televised addresses from 1952 to 1980 and the total number of public appearances from Hoover to Reagan; Ibid., 238–245.

17. Richard L. Rubin, *Press, Party, and Presidency* (New York: Norton, 1981), 132.

18. Erik Barnouw, *Mass Communications: Television, Radio, Film, Press,* 2nd ed. (New York: Holt, Rinehart & Winston, 1960), 34. In 1943, the Justice Department ordered the National Broadcasting Company (NBC) to break up control of both its Red and Blue networks, or face an antitrust suit. Subsequently, NBC sold off its control of the NBC Blue Network, and it became the American Broadcasting Company (ABC). Listeners could also tune in on a fourth radio network—the Mutual Broadcasting System (MBS)—a network of nearly five hundred stations.

19. Rubin, *Press, Party, and Presidency*, 133.

20. Ibid., 131–132.

21. Ibid., 125.

22. Ibid., 146. For those who doubt the effectiveness of radio as a communication tool, the Electronic Industries Association, a national trade association, reported that 52 million radios were sold in the United States in 1983. Manufacturers report that in the past thirty-seven years, more than one billion sets have been sold. The Radio Advertising Bureau reports that 99 percent of American households have at least one radio set and that the average number is 5.5 sets per household.

23. Ceaser et al., "The Rise of the Rhetorical Presidency," 164.

24. Bruce Miroff, "Monopolizing the Public Space: The President as a Problem for Democratic Politics," in Thomas E. Cronin, ed. *Rethinking the Presidency* (Boston: Little, Brown, 1982), 219.

25. See Theodore J. Lowi, *The Personal President*, 97–133.

26. Samuel Kernell, *Going Public*, 1st ed., viii; see also William W. Lammers, "Presidential Attention-Focusing Activities," in Doris A. Graber, ed. *The President and the American Public* (Philadelphia: Institute for the Study of Human Issues, 1982), 145–171.

27. Kernell, *Going Public*, 2nd ed., 9.

28. Thoman E. Mann, "Elections and Change in Congress," in Thomas E. Mann and Norman J. Ornstein, eds. *The New Congress* (Washington, DC: American Enterprise Institute, 1981), 53.

29. Emmet John Hughes, "Presidency vs. Jimmy Carter," *Fortune*, 4 December 1978, 62–64.

30. Michael Baruch Grossman and Martha Joynt Kumar, *Portraying the President* (Baltimore, MD: Johns Hopkins University Press, 1981), 314–315.

31. George C. Edwards III, *The Public Presidency* (New York: St. Martin's, 1983), 41.

32. Samuel Kernell, *Going Public*, 2nd ed., 93; see also William W. Lammers, "Presidential Press Conference Schedules: Who Hides and When?" *Political Science Quarterly*, 96 (Summer 1981): 261–267.

33. Lyn Ragsdale, "The Politics of Presidential Speechmaking, 1949–1980," *American Political Science Review* 78 (December 1984): 972.

34. Samuel Kernell, *Going Public*, 2nd ed., viii.

35. Samuel Kernell, "Campaigning, Governing and the Presidency," in John E. Chubb and Paul E. Peterson, eds. *The New Direction in American Politics* (Washington, DC: The Brookings Institution, 1985), 139.

36. *The New York Times*, 3 February 1993.

37. Samuel Kernell, *Going Public*, 2nd ed., 240.

38. Sources: Commercial and Public television and radio stations listed in *Broadcasting and Cable Market Place* (formerly *Broadcasting Yearbook*, New York: R. R. Bowker, 1992), daily newspapers and the various categories of periodicals are listed in *The Statistical Abstract of the United States, 1992* (Washington, DC: Government Printing Office, 1992), 557.

39. McGeorge Bundy and Edmund S. Muskie, *Presidential Promise and Performance* (New York: The Free Press, 1980), 66.

40. *The New York Times*, 12 September 1974.

41. Hugh Sidey, "Totaling Up Year One," *Time*, vol. 135, 5 February 1990, 23.

42. *Congressional Quarterly Weekly Report* 50, (19 December 1992): 3841.

43. Phil Duncan and Steve Langdon, "When Congress Had to Choose, It Voted to Back Clinton," *Congressional Quarterly Weekly Report*, 51 (December 18, 1993): 3428.

44. Stephen Ansolabehere, Roy Behr, and Shanto Iyengar, *The Media Game: American Politics in the Television Age* (New York: Macmillan, 1993), 203.

45. Walter Goodman, "Why Clinton Can't Go on TV and Fix Everything," *The New York Times*, 30 May 1993.

46. Hugh Sidey, "The New Style of Expose," *Time*, vol. 123, 18 June 1984, 37.

47. Hugh Sidey, "Totaling Up One Year," *Time*, vol. 135, 5 February 1990, 23.

48. *The New York Times*, 21 September 1991.

49. Herbert S. Parmet, *JFK: The Presidency of John F. Kennedy* (New York: Penguin, 1984), 322.

50. Ibid.

51. Ibid.

52. Doris Kearns, *Lyndon Johnson and the American Dream* (New York: Harper & Row, 1976), 228.

53. Ibid., 228–230.

54. Lyndon Johnson, "The American Promise," *Public Papers*, (Washington, DC: Government Printing Office, 15 March 1965), 281.

55. Eric Goldman, *The Tragedy of Lyndon Johnson* (New York: Knopf, 1969), 322.

56. Hugh Heclo and Rudolph G. Penner, "Fiscal and Political Strategy in the Reagan Administration," in Fred I. Greenstein, ed. *The Reagan Presidency* (Baltimore, MD: Johns Hopkins University Press, 1983), 39.

57. Edward W. Chester, "Shadow or Substance? Critiquing Reagan's Inaugural Address," *Presidential Studies Quarterly* 11 (Spring 1981): 172–176.

58. Morton M. Kondracke, "More than Blind Luck," *Newsweek*, 18 February 1985, 22.

59. Chester, "Shadow or Substance?" 175–176.

60. Francis X. Clines, *The New York Times*, 31 March 1985.

61. Edwards and Wayne, *Presidential Leadership*, 125.

62. Ibid., 127.

63. Miroff, "Monopolizing the Public Space," 223.

64. Ibid.

65. Kernell, "The Presidency and the People," 249.

66. Roger G. Brown and David M. Wellborn, "Presidents and Their Parties: Performance and Prospects," *Presidential Studies Quarterly* 12 (Summer, 1982): 302.

CHAPTER 7

THE PRESIDENTIAL BRANCH

For two centuries the Founding Fathers' establishment of a tripartite, separation of powers government—consisting of legislative, executive, and judicial branches—has been considered one of the most remarkable political inventions in history. But over the past fifty years a new fourth branch of the American national government has emerged: the presidential branch.[1]

Earlier in the twentieth century the federal bureaucracy—the permanent government—was often referred to as the "fourth branch" of government because the federal government could not function without thousands of civil servants within the executive departments faithfully performing their duties. In recent years, the mass media have sometimes been referred to as the "fourth branch" of government. More accurately, however the Executive Office of the President, especially the White House staff, has truly become the "fourth branch" of government. No close observer of the Washington scene can escape the conclusion that in recent decades the presidential branch has become the dominant force in the federal government. The presidential branch not only maintains tight control over federal policymaking but also oversees the operation of government programs, frequently using White House staff to supervise those programs of high presidential priority.

Strangely, in many American government textbooks, the reader will search in vain for a detailed explanation of the rise of the presidential branch. This emergent branch now eclipses the executive departments in terms of political clout and decision-making authority. Indeed, by the Kennedy-Johnson years the White House had become the "operational center" of the executive branch.[2]

In this chapter we will trace the emergence of the new presidential branch, explain the causes for its rapid growth, and discuss the reasons for the decline of cabinet influence in executive decision making. Also, the special functions performed in the Executive Office of the President by the White House staff, especially the chief of staff, will be closely examined. Since members of the president's staff operate largely outside the purview of Congress, an endeavor will be made also to find a new approach to increase public accountability of the White House staff's activities. Finally, we will explore the emergence of several of the nation's recent first ladies as "ministers without portfolio" within the presidential branch.

PRESIDENTIAL BRANCH DEFINED

Briefly, the presidential branch comprises six main units: the Executive Office of the President, the White House Office, the Office of Management and Budget (OMB), the National Security Council (NSC), the Council of Economic Advisers, and the Office of Policy Development. Four lesser units—the Council of Environmental Quality, the Office of Science and Technology, the Office of the United States Trade Representative, and the Office of Administration—also operate under the White House umbrella. Although the office of the vice president is not included in the official table of organization of the White House staff, recent vice presidents have in fact provided valuable staff assistance to the president. This emerging role of the vice president within the executive branch is discussed in Chapter 14. In this chapter the terms "presidential branch" and White House staff will be used interchangeably.

The president of the United States, it has been mentioned many times, has prodigious management responsibilities. He is directly responsible for managing an annual federal budget of approximately $1.3 trillion, overseeing thirty executive departments and agencies, his White House staff, supervising the performance of more than two million federal civilian employees and commanding an equal number of members of the armed forces, and sharing power with Congress in lawmaking and foreign policy. Consequently, the president has turned more and more to his White House staff to coordinate activities between and among all of these federal entities. Nor does the White House staff work end here. They must also coordinate activities that may impinge, directly or indirectly, upon fifty state governments, 3,041 county governments, and 19,205 municipal governments.[3] Overall, the presidential branch has an annual budget of slightly more than $100 million and a full-time staff of approximately 1,700 persons.

HISTORICAL GROWTH OF WHITE HOUSE STAFF

Since the early days of the Republic, presidents have had to rely on trusted staff members to handle special executive responsibilities. Thomas Jefferson used his private secretary as a link between members of Congress and the White

House. Throughout the nineteenth century most presidents relied on their private secretaries to handle presidential paperwork; sometimes the president assigned them to maintain contacts and review patronage requests from state party leaders. President William McKinley's private secretary, George Cortelyou (his title was subsequently changed to "secretary to the president") was considered one of the nation's most astute Republican politicians at the turn of the century. McKinley relied on Cortelyou to dispense hundreds of patronage jobs and to maintain good relations with Republican leaders across the land. Executive department functions, however, were directed by cabinet members. McKinley invariably consulted with his cabinet before undertaking major decisions on domestic policy and foreign affairs.[4] The concept of a "presidential branch" was still decades away.

McKinley's White House staff consisted of twenty-seven employees, including the telephone operator, the stenographer, and the gardener. President Woodrow Wilson's staff was slightly larger, but the austere president depended chiefly upon his experienced assistant, Joseph Tumulty, who had worked for Wilson when he was governor of New Jersey, and a shadowy private advisor, Colonel Edward House, for handling many special assignments. But Wilson still looked to his cabinet members to carry out the ambitious "New Freedom" programs initiated by the highly disciplined president.[5]

The birthdate for the presidential branch, if it could be accurately determined, would probably be commemorated with the passage of the Budget and Accounting Act of 1921. This legislation shifted for the first time responsibility for federal budget making from Congress to the president and established the Bureau of the Budget. (This new budget agency was originally placed in the Treasury Department.) Previously, the House and Senate appropriations committees hammered out the federal budget, after individual meetings with each cabinet head and his staff. The president was little more than a bench warmer in the process. The full impact of this far-reaching legislation was not felt immediately, however, because the federal budget remained unbelievably small by current standards.

Until World War I the federal budget exceeded $1 billion only during the Civil War; in the 1920s it never went above $5 billion. The entire civil service roster, including all the postal employees, totaled approximately 400,000 persons. At 1600 Pennsylvania Avenue, however, the White House staff was gradually beginning to expand. Nevertheless, presidents continued to operate with comparatively minimal White House staffs until the New Deal era of the 1930s. During Herbert Hoover's single term (1929–1933), however, Congress saw fit to authorize two additional senior White House staff positions to deal with the increased administrative burden at 1600 Pennsylvania Avenue. Still, when Franklin D. Roosevelt moved into the Oval Office in March 1933, the White House staff consisted of thirty-seven people, nine of professional rank.

WHITE HOUSE STAFF EXPANDS RAPIDLY UNDER FDR

During President Franklin D. Roosevelt's first administration (1933–1937), the enormous growth of government, especially the rapid proliferation of agencies to administer New Deal anti-depression and social reform programs, magnified the existing management defects within the executive branch. Faced with the burden of combating the Great Depression and responsible for the management of over one hundred new agencies, FDR decided in early 1937 to appoint a special three-member advisory commission— "The President's Committee on Administrative Management (better known as the Brownlow Commission)"—to consider the growing problem of administrative management.

The Brownlow Commission's leading statement, "The President needs help," finally convinced Congress that the President should be given additional staff. After intense debate and long delay, Congress finally passed the Reorganization Act of 1939. This new legislation formally established the Executive Office of the President and authorized the hiring of six new administrative assistants to "assist the President in such matters as he may direct, and at the specific request of the President to get information and to condense and summarize it for his use."[6]

Actually, the reorganization act did not significantly expand the size of Roosevelt's White House staff; the most important expansion had taken place in 1933 and 1934—in the heyday of the New Deal revolution. With the founding of each new program or alphabetical agency—the FERA, the WPA, the CCC, the PWA, and so on—FDR would temporarily "borrow" staff members from executive departments to help oversee the new programs and agencies from within the White House. According to veteran White House watcher Stephen Hess, "The importance of the Brownlow report was in legitimating what Roosevelt had been doing all along. It was a ringing manifesto for presidential supremacy, which had not been an accepted fact before the New Deal."[7]

Subsequently, FDR issued Executive Order 8248, a landmark document in the history of the modern presidency, which established five divisions within the new executive office. The most important two—the White House Office and the Bureau of the Budget—soon formed the inside command post of the executive branch. Indeed, it is from this 1939 legislation and administrative reorganization plan that the White House Office has gradually become the focal point of presidential leadership.

The Bureau of the Budget, transferred from the Treasury Department, flourished in the Executive Office. Under the leadership of Harold Smith (1939–1945), the budget agency rapidly grew from a staff of forty to more than 500. Not only did the Bureau of the Budget review the annual budget, but FDR also gave it "central clearance" responsibilities, meaning that all administration legislative proposals had to be funneled through this office for review before being forwarded to Capitol Hill. Also, it became the coordinator of statistical services and drafted reorganization plans for executive agencies. As noted by Hess, "the augmented Bureau of the Budget provided a significant presidential presence throughout the executive branch.[8] Especially during World War II, the White House Office, too, expanded far beyond the expectations of the Brownlow Commission and Congress. Beyond question, the presidential branch had become a reality.

OUTSIDE FORCES SPUR GROWTH OF PRESIDENTIAL BRANCH

Various forces and events since World War II have spurred the remarkable growth of the White House staff or presidential branch of government. The emergence of the United States as a superpower after World War II, the continuing growth of big government spawned by New Deal social welfare and government regulatory reforms of the 1930s were major factors. Clearly the establishment of the Pentagon and a huge permanent military machine during World War II, and the subsequent Cold War between the United States and the Soviet Union also helped account for the gradual emergence of the presidential branch as the executive command post in the nation's capital.

Nor should one overlook the impact of instantaneous communication technology upon the president as a crisis manager and his need for a highly professional White House staff. In the past quarter century global satellite communications have kept the president abreast of fast-moving developments in the far corners of the world. Also, he can monitor televised pictures of an outbreak of a civil war in Yugoslavia, review the aftermath of a terrorist attack in the Mediterranean area or Latin America, and other international flash points by watching Cable News Network (CNN) on the Oval Office television sets. Instantaneous communication, in turn, creates a continuous demand for instant decision making in the White House. Heavy pressure for an immediate presidential response disrupts the flow of information through traditional departmental chain of command. Throughout these crises, the president receives the very latest information directly from the field before anyone in Washington. Consequently, the president has a critical need to have close, trusted advisers who can provide quick and sound interpretations from a presidential perspective. Under these conditions, the president has no time to call a cabinet meeting.

In recent decades Congress itself has contributed directly to the growth of the presidential branch. Congress, under its broad powers to establish new executive departments and reorganize the government's administrative functions, has from time to time added more responsibilities to the White House. Starting with congressional passage of the Budget and Accounting Act of 1921, which shifted national budget-making responsibilities from Congress to the president, the lawmakers have assigned additional duties to the White House.

Subsequent growth of the Bureau of the Budget (renamed the Office of Management and Budget in 1970) has led to an enormous concentration of fiscal power in the presidential branch. Passage of the Employment Act of 1946 and creation of the Council of Economic Advisers (CEA) by Congress placed additional economic responsibilities on the president. A year later, Congress established another new staff agency, the National Security Council, as part of a major reorganization plan within the Executive branch. This legislation also merged the independent armed services into a single Department of Defense and set up the Central Intelligence Agency (CIA). At the time, President Truman was not noticeably enthusiastic about either of the staff agencies, since he viewed the congressional action as a less-than-subtle scheme by the lawmakers to encroach upon his presidential prerogatives and maintain their over-the-shoulder review of his economic and national security policies.

Nothing, of course, can compel the president of the United States to accept advice from a new staff agency created by congressional initiative. But there can be no doubt that the long-term trend has been to make these agencies the keystone of the presidential branch.

Many of the same factors that have contributed to the growth of the presidential branch of government may have led to the decline of "cabinet government" over the past three decades. Most presidents no longer rely on cabinet members as their chief advisers. Instead, they turn to their trusted White House aides. In addition, the "decomposition" of political parties and the rise of candidate-centered nominating campaigns, which have helped displace the coalition-building function of parties, have indirectly enhanced the power of the White House staff and undercut cabinet influence.

Formerly, presidents—even strong presidents, such as Teddy Roosevelt, Woodrow Wilson, and to a lesser extent, FDR—depended primarily on their cabinet members for advice and support to handle the onerous burdens of the presidency. Prior to joining the cabinet, most of these cabinet members had previously served as governors, U.S. Senators, state party leaders, or corporation executives. But since the era of John F. Kennedy, who was among the first of the candidate-centered nominees to occupy the White House, newly elected presidents have turned, more and more, to leading members of their campaign staff to handle top-level White House jobs. Meanwhile, they have selected more corporate managers, foundation directors, and government careerists—many of whom the president has not worked with previously or may never have met personally—for cabinet posts.

Because the president trusts and feels more comfortable operating with veteran staffers who have made the "long march" with him through the nominating and general campaigns to the White House, he understandably assigns many top-level duties to his former campaign lieutenants. Most presidents, it should be noted, however, still consult fairly regularly with members of their "inner cabinet"—State, Defense, Treasury, and Attorney General—for advice.

PRESIDENTS FROM BOTH PARTIES EXPAND PRESIDENTIAL BRANCH

Especially since the Kennedy-Johnson years presidents have favored a substantially enhanced White House staff role in administrative policy development and management because they have viewed the executive departments as unimaginative and entrenched in traditional ways of handling government business. As a result, in recent decades there has been a proliferation of functional offices or units within the White House that carry out presidentially directed plans. President Richard Nixon, a conservative, was also deeply distrustful of the bureaucracy and proposed (unsuccessfully) to tighten centralized White House control through the establishment of four new "super departments."[9] Early in his second term his reorganization proposal immediately ran into heavy opposition in Congress. Indeed, this highly centralized reorganization proposal soon collapsed like a house of cards under the weight of the Watergate scandals.

President Reagan, though a vocal opponent of big government, was nonetheless a staunch advocate—indeed vigorous practitioner—of centralized government in the White House. Even before he moved into the Oval Office, he instructed his new Office of Management and Budget (OMB) director, David Stockman, to place ideological conservatives in all cabinet and sub-cabinet level positions. Wasting no time, Reagan mobilized a major component of the Executive Office of the President—the OMB—to screen and select upper- and middle-level management types throughout the Reagan administration who would work toward presidential goals.[10] In other words, President Reagan utilized a key agency in the presidential branch to centralize the direction of the federal government by "infiltrating" the executive departments with loyal "Reaganauts" who would follow White House directives. Under OMB Director Stockman's direction, the Reagan administration also removed senior executive service career personnel from important slots and replaced them with White House loyalists. To be sure, other presidents—notably President Nixon—have sought to strengthen the presidential branch's control over the cabinet and executive department bureaucracy, but none matched Reagan's efforts to "presidentialize" the executive branch.

Because so many of the Reagan policy initiatives during the first year of his administration were purposely intertwined with the administration's budget-cutting strategy, the OMB quickly became the central participant in policymaking. Clearly, the OMB, under its director David Stockman, served as the president's eyes and ears for riding herd over the entire executive branch and putting Reagan's stamp of reduced government spending on all governmental agencies. President George Bush, it might be added, continued this policy, though with less fervor than Reagan. Nor has President Bill Clinton reversed the trend toward greater centralization of power in the White House Staff.

From the New Deal era in the 1930s to the late 1980s, the number of people employed officially in the White House, excluding the Office of Management and Budget, increased nearly twenty-five times—from thirty-seven staffers to approximately 900. Bradley H. Patterson, Jr., a former White House aide in the Ford and Reagan administrations, computed in 1988 the size of the White House Office at 568 people, the National Security Council staff at 190; the Office of the Vice President at 98; and that section of the Office of Administration providing direct support to the White House staff at 91.[11] Earlier, when President Nixon left office, the number of people employed in the White House offices was nearly twice that employed under President Johnson, just as Johnson's staff was nearly twice the size of FDR's.[12] The imprecise figures can be attributed to the sketchy data, and because no two sets of published figures agree on the numbers for a specific year. Moreover, those figures do not include a substantial number of "detailees"—White House officials on "lend-lease" from various departments who remain on the departmental (rather than the White House) payroll. If these detailees are included, political scientist Thomas E. Cronin, a former White House staffer, suggests adding another 20 percent to the White House figures.[13]

President Lyndon Johnson's penchant for expert "task forces," instead of cabinet departments, to generate policy proposals undoubtedly led to further growth of the White House staff. To oversee these working groups—the number reached fifty before LBJ left office—required additional hands in the White House.[14] While the task force approach seemingly avoided further institutionalization of the White House staff, the paperwork produced by the task forces put an extra burden on the president's assistants. A White House staff liaison person, for example, was attached to each task force. President Nixon's Domestic Council director, John Ehrlichman, had a staff of twenty-five to supervise the various programs managed by his office.

The growth of the White House staff and Executive Office has continued not only in terms of numbers and separate staffs but also in terms of the number of functioning units. As explained by one Washington observer, "The White House has become a complicated organization in its own right. In 1980, for example, the White House-Executive Office complex consisted of thirty-five different units and staffs reporting directly to the president."[15] That the White House should be better staffed institutionally to furnish policy direction to the executive branch can, of course, be traced directly to the Brownlow Commission report of 1937. But it seems doubtful that members of that task force could have anticipated the day when the large White House staff would have so many units that they risked bumping into each other or operating on each other's turf. Indeed, the Carter White House Domestic Council suffered from "too many cooks in the kitchen." Lester M.

Salamon reports that problems in the Carter administration "included a high degree of relatively unrestrained inter-agency rivalry and dissension . . . a tendency to bypass career personnel of the Executive Office as deals were made directly between agency advocates and the White House staff, frequently without analysis or historical patterns of long-run implications."[16]

The White House staff, as indicated earlier, prospered under President Reagan. As a result of the Reagan centralization policy, the presidential branch more than at any other time in history became the central command post in the national government. Unlike the decades when most federal decision making took place in the executive departments, the presidential branch—meaning chiefly the White House staff and OMB—under Reagan made all major policy decisions, whether they concerned domestic or foreign policy questions. This enhancement of the presidential branch's power did not, of course, begin under President Reagan; the trend was clearly evident in the Kennedy-Johnson era. But one respected political scientist has suggested that Reagan's politicization and centralization of the institutional presidency "could well establish him as the most administratively influential president of the modern period."[17] Whether true or not, there can be no doubt that the presidential branch under Reagan became the central decision-making body in the federal government.

Clearly, the presidential staff enables the nation's chief executive to undertake a wide variety of high-priority initiatives that for lack of time and resources, he would be unable to do on his own. Indeed, without a large, skilled, and dedicated White House staff, the modern president would be only a shadow of his present stature. In the words of Australian observer John Hart,

The Presidential Branch is now a structurally complex, functionally sophisticated, and politically powerful unit operating at the very heart of the governmental process and has clearly expanded the President's capacity for leadership.[18]

Another reason for the growth of the presidential branch is that coordinating plans and policies across executive departments are not easily managed by cabinet members. These department heads may sometimes be at odds with some of their colleagues. In some cases, departments may be engaged in turf wars and adamant about sharing policy prerogatives. Also, cabinet members often become more enmeshed in their own departmental responsibilities than in looking after the president's priority interests. Under these circumstances it is no wonder that the White House staff has come to occupy the commanding heights of the executive branch. As explained by John Hart,

Presidential staff have become powerful because they are, functionally, an extension of the President himself, and because the functions they perform place them in a strategically commanding position relative to other actors in the political process, particularly Executive Branch officials.[19]

PRESIDENTIAL BRANCH ECLIPSES CABINET

Traditionally, cabinet members have been considered the president's chief advisers. Most standard American government textbooks list them immediately below the President in the chain of command. But this analysis is superficial and clearly out of date. Since the Kennedy years, it has been generally recognized by Washington insiders that with few exceptions, cabinet members are subordinate to the White House staff. Bradley H. Patterson, Jr.'s recent study, *The Ring of Power*, lucidly explains why this transformation occurred.

It is the White House staff on whom modern Presidents rely to coordinate the development of their important policies, to control the flow of sensitive information, to keep a close watch on cabinet responses and to manage crisis actions.[20]

Thus, in this fast-moving global community, most major executive decisions are made not in cabinet meetings but in the president's Oval Office, with the assistance of his ever-present White House staff. Especially since the 1962 Cuban missile crisis, during which President Kennedy and his White House staff monitored events on a minute-by-minute basis, crisis management has been centered in the White House. Beyond question, today's international crises are such sensitive combinations of diplomatic-military interchanges that more and more operational control is forced upward into the hands of the president and his national security staff.

White House management of governmental policy is not confined to international crises. Especially Presidents Kennedy and Johnson were anxious to centralize the domestic policy process more fully in the White House because they considered the executive departments to be unimaginative, too slow to respond to presidential leadership, or too beholden to entrenched special interest groups. Indeed, most modern presidents have been suspicious of the executive departments. This lack of trust had led to the proliferation of functional offices within the White House, such as the Office of Economic Opportunity and units concerned with minorities, ethnic groups, veterans, and so on. Frequently, the White House staff members have carried out plans because the president does not have confidence in the bureaucracy to get the job done.[21] President Johnson's "Great Society" initiatives were almost all products of his White House staff. Joseph A. Califano, Jr., who was in effect domestic policy chief, has recounted how hundreds of proposals were whittled down to a manageable number of legislative suggestions and then handed to Johnson for his review.[22] Cabinet input on these ambitious programs was minimal at best.

Ironically, no recent president has praised cabinet government more effusively than Richard M. Nixon before and after reaching the White House; yet no president in the twentieth century did more to undermine the status of the cabinet collectively (or its individual members) and, correspondingly, to expand further the powers of the White House staff.

Before his inauguration, for example, Nixon even arranged to have all eleven cabinet members introduced on national television as soon as he completed his selections shortly after Christmas. Also, before the beginning of his second term in January 1973, Nixon emphasized the organizational talents of his new team:

The eleven men whom I have chosen as department heads in the new Cabinet are one of the strongest executive combinations ever put together here in Washington, in terms of management ability, personal integrity, and commitment to public service.[23]

But almost from the start, Nixon moved quickly away from cabinet government and toward a state of affairs in which the department heads were frozen "out of the loop," outside the White House decision-making processes. The resultant high turnover of cabinet members during the Nixon years seemed to be deliberately calculated by Nixon to replace strong-minded political leaders with organizational and management experts whose basic tasks were to oversee the huge bureaucracies and to implement policies that had been hammered out in the White House Office.[24]

Political scientist Nelson Polsby characterized Nixon's cabinet-building exercise in these words:

Mr. Nixon increasingly appointed people with no independent public standing and no constituencies of their own. In this shift, we can read a distinctive change in the fundamental political goals and strategies of the Nixon administration from early concerns with constituency building to a later preoccupation, once Mr. Nixon's re-election was assured, with centralizing power in the White House.[25]

President Reagan endeavored to revive the fiction of "cabinet government" when he reached Washington in January 1981. Establishment of seven "cabinet councils" at the beginning of his first term created the appearance that cabinet members would have serious input in policymaking. Outwardly, the setting up of the councils denied cabinet members the opportunity to complain that they were being excluded from the inner circle of power. Nonetheless, these councils were under the thumb of the White House staff and functioned chiefly "as an ingenuous mechanism for legitimating that control."[26]

Reagan's cabinet members discovered, just as Nixon's and Carter's had earlier, that when a conflict developed between them and the White House staff, the cabinet member did not often emerge the winner. During the early days of Reagan's second term, the original seven cabinet councils were consolidated into two larger councils under the direction of senior White House aides. But this move merely underscored further tightened control by the White House and the cabinet's obvious decline of influence.

Newly elected President George Bush made no move to strengthen cabinet influence when he moved into the White House, though he glowingly praised the new cabinet members which included several holdovers from the Reagan administration. Bush's appointment of New Hampshire Governor John Sununu, a hard-liner, as his chief of staff, sent a signal that policymaking and coordination of new initiatives would remain concentrated in the White House inner circle. Critics soon labeled Sununu as the "Assistant President."

Confirmation that decision making remained concentrated in the Bush White House staff, especially in matters relating to national health care, surfaced more than once. For example, the budget of the Department of Health and Human Services, the biggest in the federal government, accounting for 37 percent of all federal spending, with an operating budget of $525 billion for fiscal 1992—far exceeding that of the Pentagon ($291 billion)—was drafted by the Director of the Office of Management and Budget, Richard G. Darman, not the secretary of HHS Secretary Louis W. Sullivan.[27]

Similarly, in November 1991, Darman established a unit in his OMB shop to evaluate proposals for overhauling the nation's health care system while attempting to head off the Congressional Democratic leaders' attempts to pass a more comprehensive national health care program. OMB Director Darman and his staff reviewed all department regulations and rules, which had the force of law, before they were issued in final form. Meanwhile, Secretary Sullivan spent much of his time traveling and making speeches—his office log revealed that he had been out of the nation's capital for more than 100 days in 1991 and given speeches in at least thirty-three states.[28] Secretary Sullivan's chief role, it appeared, was to serve as a naysayer, criticizing Democratic proposals for comprehensive reform of the health care system. Throughout the year, he also appeared frequently on the television networks' weekend programs, CNN, and C-SPAN, defending the Bush administration's health care programs.

With rare exceptions, cabinet members in the Bush administration remained largely bystanders, while the White House budget office set policy and spending priorities. In other words, the presidential branch continued to expand and dominate the executive branch, while most cabinet members devoted the bulk of their time to traveling, making speeches, and meeting with special interest groups.

The "centralized presidency" has continued to be the *modus operandi* of the Clinton administration. With possibly one or two exceptions, President Clinton has operated in virtually the same fashion as nearly all presidents since the Kennedy-Johnson era in directing and overseeing executive policy implementation from the White House.[29] Indeed, no serious observer of the contemporary Washington scene can escape the conclusion that the presidential branch has superseded the cabinet and executive departments as the central policymaking and management agency in the federal government.

CRISIS MANAGER

Over the past several decades, the presidential branch has displaced the State Department and Pentagon as crisis manager whenever an emergency arises. Three basic factors, according to former White House staffer Bradley H. Patterson, Jr., push the White House into tactical management of crises:

1. The recognition that most crises are unequal and cannot be handled by the departments simply following routine patterns of response or preordained "contingency plans" (if such even exist).

2. The sense of the potential for catastrophe from lower-level actions that are well intentioned but wrong.

3. The knowledge that only the president is the constitutionally accountable decision-maker, being the commander-in-chief as well as the ultimate bearer of executive responsibility.[30]

Other factors can also trigger White House involvement: if the threat of massive violence is genuine; if the national media are focused on the crises and the potential political fallout would damage the administration; if U.S. armed forces could be directly involved; and if—at least until recently—any aspect of the crisis could impact directly on U.S.-Soviet relations.[31] It is not a coincidence that the "hot line" (officially the Direct Communications Link) between the White House and the Kremlin, established by President John F. Kennedy and Soviet General Secretary Nikita Khrushchev in 1963, was operated by the White House staff, not the Department of State.[32] Though the forty-year Cold War between the Soviet Union and the United States now seems in the distant past, the hot line guaranteed secure, instant communications between the two superpowers in an era when confrontation, not cooperation, was the order of the day.[33]

Similarly, it is in the White House Situation Room, not the State Department or the Pentagon, that the president, his National Security staff, and other top-level advisers huddle to review all the priority cable traffic during each crisis. Located one floor below the Oval Office, the Situation Room is the hub of a sophisticated communications network spreading worldwide, stocked with huge military data banks, floor-to-ceiling maps, and state-of-the-art projection equipment. Clearly, the Situation Room becomes the president's second home whenever an international crisis looms. Established in 1962 by President Kennedy to deal with the Cuban missile crisis, the Situation Room has become a "mini Pentagon" used by every president since then to weigh options in any foreign conflict or threat of aggression against the United States. One former White House insider writes, "The Situation Room is a powerful tool for the personal presidency—the symbol of a president in action."[34]

Can there be any doubt, in light of these developments, that the presidential branch has become a major component in our separation-of-powers system?

In recent years the White House Office has, in effect, become the "State Department" in many delicate foreign negotiations. During the Nixon administration, for example, National Security Adviser Henry Kissinger and the president ran foreign policy out of their hip pockets. The secret negotiations between Kissinger and officials in Communist China which led to the reopening of the door to the People's Republic of China after a twenty-three year hiatus are a classic case of White House management of foreign policy. Secretary of State William Rogers was not told of the mission until after Kissinger reached Beijing. Similarly, during the Carter administration, National Security Adviser Zbigniew Brzezinski operated so frequently as alternate Secretary of State that Cyrus R. Vance, the state department head, eventually resigned.

The same *modus operandi* continued in the Reagan years. Thus, Secretary of State Alexander Haig, who viewed himself as the "vicar of foreign policy," learned rather early that major foreign policy decisions were being made elsewhere. Haig, anxious to mediate the Falkland Islands dispute between Great Britain and Argentina, discovered when he met British Foreign Secretary Francis Pym to go over an important series of negotiating points that Pym had already learned the United States' position during a breakfast meeting with National Security Adviser William Clark. Like Pym, other foreign diplomats had recognized for some time that most major foreign policy decisions are made in the White House, not over in Foggy Bottom.[35] Haig's successor, George Shultz, gradually earned the respect of President Reagan and his staff over the next six years, but he often found himself at loggerheads, not so much with the White House national security adviser, but with Secretary of Defense Casper Weinberger, an old friend and staffer of Mr. Reagan's during his days as governor of California (1967–1975).

President Bush's close personal relationship with his protégé, Secretary of State James A. Baker III, reduced temporarily the influence of White House national security staffers in foreign policymaking. But Bush's National Security Assistant Brent Scowcroft was invariably seen at Bush's elbow, whether at the White House, Camp David, or Kennebunkport, Maine, Bush's summer home. Indeed, as Bradley H. Patterson, Jr. and many others have observed, the long-term trend toward White House direction of foreign policy and national security matters seems unmistakably clear:

Presidents, impelled by their own precedent-breaking agendas, concerned at having delicate instructions twisted by other hands, and apprehensive of leaks, are willing, often eager, to use senior White House staff as personal communicators and negotiators.[36]

Beyond question, in most areas of foreign policymaking the presidential branch—the new fourth branch—easily overshadows the executive branch.

CHIEF OF STAFF

The number-one duty officer in the presidential branch is the president's chief of staff. So powerful has the chief of staff become that one Washington correspondent has observed, "The role of Chief of Staff has evolved into a power center with more clout than that of all but the most powerful Cabinet Secretaries and Members of Congress."[37]

Since Sherman Adams, former governor of New Hampshire, served as President Eisenhower's first chief of staff, the power of this influential presidential assistant has continued to expand. With the exception of Presidents Kennedy and Johnson, who preferred to use a "spokes-of-the-wheel" advisory system, the top presidential assistant has often been the second most powerful individual in the Executive Branch. The chief of staff, among other things, coordinates all White House policymaking paperwork, prioritizes the president's agenda, serves as gatekeeper to determine who the president will see, and guards his daily schedule. Sometimes known as the "Abominable No Man" for screening out countless persons wishing to talk with the President, the chief of staff usually loses more friends than he makes while serving the president.

Each recent president has had, of course, his own management style, but all of them have delegated immense responsibilities to their chiefs of staff. President Nixon, who preferred to concentrate on foreign policy, handed almost carte blanche authority over domestic matters to his White House chief of Staff, H. R. "Bob" Haldemann, who continued to serve until the Watergate investigation forced his resignation.

President Reagan, by contrast, chose James A. Baker III, a former aide to Reagan's leading rival for the 1980 GOP nomination, George Bush, to be his chief of staff. But Reagan divided overall White House management duties three ways, among Baker and two former California aides, Edwin Meese III (later appointed attorney general) and Michael Deaver, a longtime personal aide and media specialist. Known as "the troika," these three Reagan assistants performed with a high degree of success throughout Reagan's first term. However, at the outset of his second term, Reagan, for some unexplained reason, agreed to a job switch between Chief of Staff Baker and Secretary of the Treasury Donald Regan (no relation to the president) that soon proved to be disastrous. Regan's arrogant management style and his fondness for concentrating power in his own hands eventually led to his forced resignation. Some of his critics placed much of the blame for the Iran-Contra fiasco on his head. Former Republican Senate Majority Leader Howard Baker of Tennessee, a veteran Washington insider, was brought in to pick up the pieces. Within weeks, White House staff activity was back to normal.

President Bush, who spent eight years as vice president observing the White House scene, had definite ideas on how he wanted his White House Office to function once he reached the Oval Office. Bush appointed a key nominating campaign adviser, Governor John Sununu of New Hampshire, to be his chief of staff. Cut in the mold of the brusque top Eisenhower assistant Sherman Adams, Sununu ran the White House Office with an iron hand. President Bush, like Richard Nixon, decided early in his administration to concentrate his energy on foreign affairs and national security issues. In the meantime Sununu's fingerprints could be detected on almost every top domestic issue involving the White House. Described as the White House point man on budgetary, environmental, energy, and educational matters, Sununu reviewed all top-level appointments. Reportedly he was instrumental in the selection of David H. Souter, a New Hampshire native, as associate justice of the Supreme Court.[38]

With the unexpected death of former Republican National Chairman Lee Atwater midway into Bush's first term, Sununu also assumed the role of Bush's principal political adviser. In the words of one seasoned Washington reporter, "Probably no White House Chief of Staff has been more deeply immersed in substance policy making than Sununu since Sherman Adams served in that exalted position under President Eisenhower."[39] Sununu's imperious manner and reports of his excessive use of government airplanes and limousines for personal business, however, triggered a firestorm of criticism from the press and lawmakers from both parties on Capitol Hill. Equally embarrassing, Sununu became the butt of merciless jokes by the late night television comedians and the *Saturday Night Live* show—a sure sign that a public figure is in trouble. Sununu survived these attacks for a number of weeks, but by late fall 1991, with President Bush's popularity dropping steadily in the opinion polls, the nation in a severe recession, and the mass media constantly harping on Sununu's political fumbles, the flak became too intense and Sununu "resigned." Before his firing, Republican loyalists had complained that Sununu's arrogant manner made it impossible for them to work with the White House chief of staff. Also, with the 1992 presidential reelection campaign just around the corner, President Bush concluded that Sununu had become a major political liability because a number of GOP campaign operatives refused, if Sununu remained at the helm, to sign on the Bush reelection campaign team.[40]

Once again, another chief of staff was thrown over the side so that the president could divert public attention away from the Oval Office and demonstrate to the American public that he was prepared to re-evaluate his policies and staff and begin anew. Sununu was succeeded by Secretary of Transportation Samuel K. Skinner. But Skinner, unable to turn around White House staff operations, lasted only six months. President Bush replaced him with his old friend and campaign manager, Secretary of State James A. Baker III, who gave up his cabinet portfolio in an eleventh-hour, unsuccessful effort to rescue the Bush presidency in the November 1992 election.

Most chiefs of staff do not enjoy long tenure. Recent history shows that on average the shelf life of a chief of staff is about the same as a cabinet member—slightly less than two years (see Table 7.1). Serving as chief of staff

Table 7.1
Recent Chiefs of Staff, 1979–1994

President	Chief of Staff	Length of Stay (Months)
Jimmy Carter	Hamilton Jordan	Jan. 1979-June 1980 (11)
	Jack H. Watson	June 1980-Jan. 1981 (7)
Ronald Reagan	James A. Baker, III	Jan. 1981-Feb. 1985 (49)
	Donald T. Regan	Feb. 1985-Feb. 1987 (24)
	Howard H. Baker, Jr.	Feb. 1987-July 1988 (16)
	Kenneth Duberstein	July 1988-Jan. 1989 (7)
George Bush	John H. Sununu	Jan. 1989-Dec. 1991 (35)
	Samuel K. Skinner	Dec. 1991-Aug. 1992 (8)
	James A. Baker, III	Aug. 1992-Jan. 1993 (5)
Bill Clinton	Thomas F. McLarty, III	Jan. 1993-June 1994 (17)
	Leon E. Panetta	June 1994-

Source: *The New York Times*, 28 June 1994, A–12. Copyright © 1994 by *The New York Times* Company. Reprinted by permission.

has been likened to the job of a major league baseball manager. If the team is winning, no problem. But if the team is faltering badly, the manager is the first to be fired—or kicked upstairs. The most recent episode of a change of White House managers involved the Clinton administration and the replacement of Chief of Staff Thomas F. "Mack" McLarty III by OMB Director Leon E. Panetta in June 1994. President Clinton then appointed McLarty, his boyhood friend, the presidential counselor—an undefined advisory position. In any event, most students of the presidency agree that a president does need a chief of staff, but one who emphasizes management and process rather than policy advocacy.

In summarizing the role of chief of staff, one former White House chief of staff was asked if his job more closely resembled a quarterback, a goalie, or a utility infielder. He responded, "More like being a javelin catcher."[41] Few of his successors would disagree.

Centralization of power in the presidential branch would have been next to impossible without presidential control of the federal budget process, our next topic.

THE EXECUTIVE BUDGET PROCESS

Without doubt, the roots of the presidential branch can be traced most directly to the management of the federal budget. The Constitution neither prescribes a budget process nor spells out a role in budgeting for the president. For more than 130 years Congress kept primary control over the entire budget process. Individual cabinet members went up to Capitol Hill, departmental budgets in hand, to testify before the House and Senate appropriations committees. After gathering the needed budget information from all the cabinet members and independent agency heads, the two congressional committees hammered out the entire federal budget. The president, though responsible for administering the entire federal budget, had no final voice, except the veto threat, in the size of the federal budget.

BUDGET AND ACCOUNTING ACT OF 1921

Before World War I this cumbersome system clanked along reasonably well, since the entire federal budget rarely exceeded $1 billion, and the size of the federal bureaucracy was only a fraction of its present level.

But shortly after President Warren Harding took office, Congress passed the Budget and Accounting Act of 1921, requiring the president to establish a comprehensive budget. In the words of one commentator, "The Budget and Accounting Act of 1921, by which Congress delegated power over the budget to the President, was a historical watershed. Many believe that the modern presidency began with it."[42] Under the new legislation, Congress imposed upon the presidency the responsibility not only for proposed expenditures of the executive agencies, but also proposals for financing the executive agencies. To facilitate this task, Congress established a Bureau of the Budget, functioning under a director appointed by and accountable to the president.

The central purpose of the 1921 act was to introduce into the federal government for the first time modern managerial procedures, but as Louis Fisher, among others, has noted: "The Budget and Accounting Act provided for an 'executive budget' only in the sense that the president initiated the budget and took responsibility for it."[43] The legislation still allowed members of Congress full freedom, either in committee or on the floor, to cut or increase the president's estimates.

BUREAU OF THE BUDGET

In 1939, the Bureau of the Budget was transferred from the Treasury Department to the new Executive Office of the President, as recommended by the Brownlow Commission. Henceforth, the bureau was expected to become the president's management arm. In the meantime President Roosevelt also assigned the Bureau of the Budget the additional tasks of clearing and coordinating the implementation of presidential programs in the interests of economy and efficiency.

For the first time, the president gained the upper hand in the financial management of the federal government. Thirty years later President Nixon further centralized White House control over the budget when he reorganized the Bureau of the Budget into the Office of Management and Budget (1970). Under his reorganization plan President Nixon transformed OMB into a White House staff institution with a variety of oversight and political functions. The OMB director became a high-level White House assistant supervising a team of politically appointed "program assistant directors" assigned to monitor the budgets and staffs of the various executive departments. In 1981 President Reagan appointed David Stockman, a Michigan Republican congressman, to head OMB and undertake major cuts in the federal budget and staff. Within seven months Stockman had slashed over $30 billion in domestic programs and abolished a host of social welfare and training programs designed to help low-income persons. From the start, OMB Director Stockman became President Reagan's chief fiscal manager, overseeing all federal budgets and expenditures. Since then, neither President Bush nor President Clinton has reduced the financial oversight responsibilities of the OMB director. Indeed, more than any other White House staffer, the OMB chief has reinforced the centralization of power in the presidential branch.

Part of President Nixon's reorganization plan in 1970, which Congress approved, included the establishment of the Domestic Council as a cabinet-level advisory body.

Domestic Council

Designed as a domestic counterpart to the National Security Council by President Richard Nixon, the Domestic Council was intended to serve as a forum for discussion and action on policy matters that cut across departmental jurisdictions. Before passage of this legislation, Nixon had complained to Congress that there had been no "organized, institutionally staffed group charged with advising the President on the total range of domestic policy."[44] The new agency was scheduled to be chaired by the president; its members consisted of the vice president and all the members of the cabinet except the secretaries of state and defense, and it was to be supported by a regular staff, headed by Executive Director John Ehrlichman.

The Domestic Council, as indicated above, was viewed as a parallel body to the National Security Council. But in the Nixon administration it rarely met as a group; instead, most of the work was done in smaller committees and closely managed by Ehrlichman and his staff. Beyond doubt, the Nixon White House used the Domestic Council merely as a formality; Ehrlichman made clear early on that the staff worked for the president not the council. Actually, the Domestic Policy staff performed many of the same type of duties handled by the twenty-one staff members in the Johnson White House.

Nixon's Domestic Council became one of the early casualties of the Watergate scandal, when Director Ehrlichman was forced to leave under a cloud after he was indicted for his involvement in the White House cover-up. The Domestic Council concept, however, gained a new lease on life in the Carter administration. Indeed, according to political scientist John Hart, "The Domestic Policy Staff represented a substantial strengthening of the Presidential Branch over that Executive Branch in the Carter Administration."[45]

In the Reagan administration, the Domestic Policy staff continued to operate, but under a new name, the Office of Policy Development. Soon, however, it was overshadowed by the more influential Office of Management and Budget (OMB) and the White House Office staff. This operational pattern, as indicated earlier, continued throughout the Bush administration.

Office of Public Liaison

Another key link to the president's various constituencies is the Office of Public Liaison (OPL). Established by President Gerald R. Ford and continued by Presidents Carter, Reagan, Bush, and Clinton, the Office of Public Liaison "lobbies the lobbyists." Its chief function is to maintain contact with important non-governmental interest groups, such as business, labor, ethnic, religious, veterans, and women's groups, to promote the president's policies and to build coalition groups to win votes in Congress. Perhaps the most successful OPL director was Anne Wexler, a Carter appointee. Reportedly in periodic contact with nearly 800 of these special interest groups, Wexler set a high standard of performance unequaled by her successors. The Public Liaison staff, though its title has since gone through two or three name changes, has become an integral part of the White House Office.

Congressional Liaison Office

In this era of big government and special interest group politics, presidential communication with Congress can no longer be handled by meeting occasionally with Capitol Hill leaders in the Oval Office as FDR did in the 1930s. Since the early 1950s, the relationship between the two branches has been regularized by the formation of a Congressional Liaison Office.

Established within the White House Office by President Eisenhower and subsequently expanded by succeeding presidents, the Congressional Liaison Office has become the president's eyes and ears on Capitol Hill. These White House operatives have become indispensable to the administration for winning votes on key issues. Directed over the years by such outstanding appointees as Kennedy's Larry O'Brien and Reagan's Max Friedersdorf, the staff lobbies and consults with dozens of congressmen, provides vital services and favors to members of Congress, and keeps the White House advised of any potential firefights. No president can operate successfully without a competent Capitol Hill staff. Conversely, an incompetent congressional liaison team can spell disaster for a chief executive, as President Carter discovered to his lasting regret.[46]

As long as the president remains as co-partner in the legislative process, the size of the White House staff cannot be expected to shrink significantly. In one sense the White House staff proliferation reflects the changing conditions affecting the White House relationship with Capitol Hill. Over the past three decades, the size of congressional staffs has increased threefold. Between the mid-1950s and the early 1980s, the growth of staff in Congress and its committees surged. The staff of the members' offices grew from 3,556 in 1957 to 11,432 in 1981. The number of committee staffers increased from 715 in 1955 to 2,865 in 1981.[47]

Because the president and his staff must deal frequently with the Capitol Hill staff's seventeen standing committees in the Senate, the twenty-two standing committees in the House, the staffs of almost every one of the 435 members in the House and one hundred senators, as well as individual lawmakers, presidential supporters argue that he can ill afford to "downsize" his congressional liaison staff.

OPERATING BEYOND CONGRESSIONAL CONSTRAINTS

In recent years, the presidential branch has with increasing frequency frustrated the legislative branch by thwarting Congress from attempting to intervene and control the policymaking process and to perform its legislative oversight function.

The Reagan administration, for example, by shifting key foreign policy operations, such as Iran-Contra arms sales, from the Departments of State and Defense to the White House National Security Council staff, promoted further centralization of power in the presidential branch—without the congressional oversight required by our checks and balances system.

The experience of President Reagan with the Iran-Contra "guns for hostages" swap, however, boomeranged after the reported deal surfaced in a Lebanese newspaper. President Reagan pleaded ignorance about National Security Council operative Lt. Colonel Oliver North's White House basement intelligence operation to secretly fund the Nicaraguan Contra rebels (from money collected via the Iranian arms swap) in defiance of Congress' Boland Amendment. Beyond question, the Iran-Contra investigation seriously undermined Reagan's credibility and his presidential standing. More important, the Iran-Contra hearings and the subsequent prosecution of Lt. Colonel North and several colleagues underscored the danger of unchecked activity within the presidential branch.

On the domestic front, President George Bush wasted little time in devising machinery to thwart or circumvent congressional regulatory legislation passed mostly by a Democratic-controlled Congress. In 1989, Mr. Bush established a White House agency, the Quayle Council (originally called the "Council on Competitiveness")—a handpicked group of White House appointees—to monitor and water down regulations issued by the Environmental Protection Agency (EPA), the Occupational Safety and Health Administration (OSHA), the Food and Drug Administration, and other regulatory agencies established by Congress. Frequently, the Quayle Council issued rulings—made without congressional authorization—directly contravening congressional intent in matters relating to air pollution, toxic waste, and preservation of the nation's wetlands.[48]

Heavy reliance on his White House staff enables the president to organize public support for his policies and thus frequently constrain Congress from reconfiguring these policies. As a result, involvement of the presidential staff in the implementation of White House policies has had the effect of placing a significant amount of foreign policy and domestic activity beyond the reach of congressional oversight, sometimes with unfortunate consequences for the president as well as the nation.

From a constitutional standpoint, the presidential staff can be viewed primarily as an extension of the president, possessing no separate identity of its own. His staff's actions are treated as if the president himself were carrying them out. Unlike other divisions of the executive branch, the White House staff has no constitutional or statutory obligations to any other branch of government beyond those specifically imposed upon the president. Yet with increased frequency White House aides—the presidential branch—have assumed operational responsibilities for government programs. This action has occurred, despite the fact that Congress (with few exceptions) gives authority directly to department heads, not the president to be redelegated to department heads.[49] Since by law executive department and agency heads, not the president, are formally responsible for the operation of public programs and regularly answerable to Congress and the federal courts, what can be done to make members of the presidential branch more accountable?

GREATER PUBLIC ACCOUNTABILITY NEEDED

Critics of White House Office staff proliferation oftentimes seem more concerned about the enlarged size of the staff than the broader problem: how do we hold senior staff with policymaking duties and decision-making responsibilities accountable for their actions? Except for Congress, the best hope of limiting the policymaking activities of the White House staff may be strong cabinet members. Even though they are in debt to the president for their tenure, cabinet members can—if they are held personally responsible by the president—furnish executive leadership somewhat removed from the smothering influence of the White House staff.

The late E. S. Corwin's proposal, drafted nearly a half century ago, that members of Congress be permitted to serve simultaneously as lawmakers and cabinet members may warrant reconsideration as a means of cutting down the domineering influence of the presidential branch.[50] Whether the "congressional cabinet" proposal would produce the needed checks on the presidential branch is not an easy question to answer. But it is difficult to imagine such strong senators as GOP Majority Leader Robert Dole, or Democratic Senator Sam Nunn of Georgia—if they were appointed to the Cabinet—taking their marching orders from an unnamed chief of staff or national security adviser. In any event, implementation of Corwin's cabinet proposal would require a constitutional amendment, removing Article I, Section 6, paragraph 2, banning members of Congress from holding a civil office of the United States, while simultaneously serving as a member of either house.

For the present, however, the bottom line on this matter has been well summarized by overseas commentator John Hart:

The White House staff has grown in power at the expense of the Cabinet because Presidents themselves have wanted it that way. Whatever the defects of the presidential staff system and however mistaken Presidents might be in their thinking about the presidential staff, most post-war Presidents have signified that it has served their purposes better than the Cabinet system.[51]

To scale down the influence of the White House staff, political scientist Graham Allison has advocated an executive committee of the Cabinet (he calls it "ExCab") as the main forum for discussing and debating major policy issues.[52]

Once the dust had settled in late 1987 after the Iran-Contra hearings, however, the scattered complaints over operational excesses in the presidential branch were pushed aside as the nation shifted its attention to the rapidly moving events in Eastern Europe, the crumbling Soviet empire, the United States invasion of Panama, and the Persian Gulf War. Few voices were heard across the land about the excessive concentration of power and influence and the absence of public accountability of the White House staff. In fact, over the past forty years, only a few commentators led by historian Arthur M. Schlesinger, Jr., have focused on the potential dangers that a corps of top-level unelected decision makers poses to the existing separation of powers system.[53]

Does the eclipse of the cabinet and executive departments by the White House staff spell trouble for the country in the years ahead? Does growth of the presidential establishment and the takeover of executive department decision making by White House operatives dangerously thwart congressional oversight and deprive lawmakers of the opportunity to review and scrutinize carefully how federal programs are being managed and federal funds spent? Has the presidential staff become too large, too powerful, and too unaccountable to assure a responsible functioning of the federal government? Except for routine hearings on Capitol Hill to review federal budgets and occasional confirmation hearings to consider a new cabinet nominee or agency head, members of Congress have largely overlooked the rapid institutional development of the presidential branch. For a brief period during the Watergate investigation and its aftermath, however, many members of Congress expressed grave misgivings about the rise of the "Imperial Presidency." Passage of the War Powers Act of 1973, the Budget and Impoundment Control Act of 1974, and several other measures to curb presidential power reflected this serious anxiety. But by the Reagan inauguration in 1981, most of these apprehensions seemed to have evaporated.

After the turnover of the four presidents between 1974 and 1981, the mood of Congress and the country seemed to indicate that the major problem facing the country was an "imperiled" not an "imperial" presidency. Instead, some critics insisted that measures were needed to protect the integrity of the presidency. Under these circumstances only a few members of Congress, the press, and a small cadre of academicians continued to warn the nation about the dangers of the unchecked expansion of the White House staff and its lack of accountability to anyone but the occupant of the Oval Office. The distinct choice between a strong president who charts a course largely independent of the legislative branch and a chief executive ever responsive to the checks and balances of our separation of powers system is one that Congress and the American public often seem either indifferent to or unwilling to make.

Unless Congress decides to exercise greater oversight and impose greater accountability on the presidential branch, this fourth branch of government will continue to displace the executive departments as major decision makers in the nation's capitol—which is just about what most recent presidents have wanted.

Our discussion of the presidential branch would not be complete, however, unless we take note of the emergence of the nation's first lady as an important participant in the governing process.

PRESIDENTIAL WIVES

First lady is not a constitutionally designated position, but first ladies are now regular members of the presidential branch. Indeed, some contemporary writers have gone so far as to label President Clinton's wife, Hillary, as "co-president."[54] While this title obviously overstates Mrs. Clinton's role, little doubt remains among members of the White House press corps that she wields enormous influence on the president's decision making, especially in handling health care legislation and the selection of his executive branch appointees.

The powerful role of several recent first ladies is in marked contrast to the subordinate position occupied by most presidential wives in the nineteenth century. Except for the renowned Abigail Adams (who actually served at the end of the eighteenth century, 1797–1801), Sarah Polk (1845–1849), and "Lemonade Lucy" Hayes (nicknamed because she served no alcohol in the White House), presidential wives served primarily as hostesses at official functions.

Mrs. Clinton is not, of course, the first presidential wife to exert major influence over her husband. But her duties in pushing President Clinton's universal health care plan is undoubtedly the most prominent official assignment undertaken by a presidential spouse in the nation's history. Still, students of the presidency might question whether the level of Mrs. Clinton's influence is any stronger than that exerted by President Woodrow Wilson's second wife, Edith, after Wilson suffered a paralyzing stroke in September 1919, following his failed nationwide speaking tour to win popular support for the Versailles Treaty and the League of Nations Covenant.[55]

With President Wilson bedridden, word soon spread throughout the nation's capitol that Edith Wilson was running the government. Vice President Thomas Marshall chose to stay on the sidelines. Cabinet members were reluctant to act without first receiving a favorable nod from the White House living quarters. Popular magazines reported that Mrs. Wilson "came close to carrying the burden of the First Man."[56] Complaints were heard also on Capitol Hill that the nation was operating under a "petticoat government" or as some critics viewed it, a "regency."

Mrs. Wilson was not, the evidence suggests, interested in policymaking, per se; instead, she exercised power negatively. By denying presidential access week after week to cabinet members and Wilson's advisers, including Colonel Edward House, Mrs. Wilson, in effect, brought the wheels of government to a near standstill. Memos and papers requiring the president's signature piled up at Wilson's bedside, appointed positions remained unfilled, foreign policymaking languished, but no matter. Mrs. Wilson's only concern was to protect her husband's fragile health.[57] The extent of the authority wielded by Mrs. Wilson, even though exercised behind the scenes, is especially noteworthy, in view of the fact that no woman served in Congress until 1917 and none in the cabinet until 1933. (The Nineteenth Amendment, granting women suffrage nationwide, was not ratified until August 1920.) To be sure, the circumstances surrounding President Wilson's prolonged illness were extremely unusual; yet, the perplexing problem of presidential disability was not directly addressed until the passage of the Twenty-fifth Amendment in 1967.

Several other twentieth-century first ladies have played significant roles on the national scene. Historians have rated Mrs. Eleanor Roosevelt (1933–1945), FDR's wife, as the most successful First Lady of the twentieth century (see Table 7.2).[58] Clearly, Mrs. Roosevelt "set a new standard against which all later First Ladies would be measured."[59]

Mrs. Roosevelt's activity with the Women's Trade Union League, the League of Women Voters, the National Youth Administration (which provided employ-

Table 7.2

Historians' Rankings of Twentieth-Century First Ladies

A. Background; B. Value to Country; C. Integrity; D. Leadership; E. Intelligence; F. "Own Woman"; G. Accomplishments; H. Courage; I. Public Image; J. Value to President.

Rank	First Lady	Score	A	B	C	D	E	F	G	H	I	J
1	Eleanor Roosevelt	93.3	1	1	1	1	1	1	1	1	1	2
2	Lady Bird Johnson	77.5	3	2	5	2	2	3	2	3	3	3
3	Rosalynn Carter	73.8	7	4	3	3	3	4	4	5	5	1
4	Betty Ford	73.4	9	5	2	5	5	2	5	2	4	5
5	Edith Wilson	71.8	5	3	8	4	4	5	3	4	11	4
6	Jacqueline Kennedy	69.5	2	6	17	6	6	6	6	6	2	7
7	Edith Roosevelt	65.4	4	7	7	7	8	9	7	8	7	9
8	Lou Hoover	63.5	6	8	6	9	7	8	8	10	12	12
9	Bess Truman	61.7	16	10	4	17	13	13	13	9	9	6
10	Ellen Wilson	61.5	8	9	11	10	9	11	11	11	13	13
11	Grace Coolidge	61.3	12	11	10	11	11	12	10	13	8	14
12	Helen Taft	61.0	10	12	13	8	10	7	9	12	14	15
13	Mamie Eisenhower	59.7	13	13	9	15	17	16	14	14	6	10
14	Pat Nixon	58.5	15	15	12	16	12	17	16	7	10	11
15	Nancy Reagan	57.4	11	17	15	14	14	15	17	15	17	8
16	Ida McKinley	57.0	14	14	14	13	15	14	12	16	15	16
17	Florence Harding	55.8	17	16	16	12	16	10	15	17	16	17

Sources: Results of poll conducted in 1982 by Professors Thomas Kelly and Douglas Lonnstrom, Directors of the Siena Research Institute, Siena College, Loudonville, New York. History professors in 102 colleges were asked to rate the first ladies. The professors came from 57 northern colleges and 45 southern colleges. It should be emphasized that the poll was conducted early in the first Reagan administration. Reprinted in Betty Boyd Caroli, *First Ladies* (New York: Oxford University Press, 1987), appendix, 389. Copyright © 1987 by Oxford University Press, Inc. Reprinted by permission.

ment for several hundred thousand young people), slum clearance projects, nursery schools, equal opportunity hiring, and countless humanitarian projects won wide recognition. Her tireless efforts made Mrs. Roosevelt, according to the leading newspaper columnist of the era, Raymond Clapper, "not only the most influential woman of our time but also a most active force in public affairs."[60] Her record of 348 press conferences will probably never be equaled by another first lady.

After Mrs. Roosevelt left the White House, the next two presidential wives— Mrs. Bess Truman and Mrs. Mamie Eisenhower—adhered to the more traditional ceremonial role of their nineteenth-century predecessors. But with the arrival of Mrs. Jackie Kennedy at the White House in 1961, wholesale changes occurred almost overnight. Indeed, the period of modern management of the first lady's public role began with the appointment for the first time of a separate press secretary for Mrs. Kennedy. Despite the recent birth of a son, Mrs. Kennedy instituted major changes in the first lady's White House activities.

Mrs. Kennedy assembled a staff of approximately forty persons to operate "the First Lady's Secretariat."[61] Clearly, the first lady's involvement in national affairs would no longer be relegated to the society section of the national capital's newspapers. Network television also enhanced the role and influence of the photogenic Jackie Kennedy and her successors.

Of the first ladies who succeeded Mrs. Roosevelt, Mrs. Rosalynn Carter, wife of the thirty-ninth president has been ranked by some commentators—at least until the arrival of Hillary Rodham Clinton in Washington—as "the most influential First Lady since Eleanor Roosevelt."[62] Described as a "surrogate, confidante, and joint policy maker," Mrs. Carter frequently attended meetings with President Carter's advisers, and in 1978, she began sitting in on cabinet meetings. President Carter pronounced her a "political partner" with whom he often discussed domestic and foreign policy issues.[63] Historian Lewis L. Gould had these words of praise for Mrs. Carter nearly a decade ago: "Beyond actually being president or having the institution of the First Lady formalized into the functioning of the office, Mrs. Carter took the role of surrogate, partner, and advocate to the current limits of capacity in our system of government."[64]

In the minds of many Washington pundits, Mrs. Nancy Reagan ranks near the top of the list of influential first ladies. Historians will have to wait, of course, before Mrs. Reagan's record can be more fully evaluated. But one Reagan insider, Michael Deaver, opined a few years ago that Nancy deserved "as much responsibility for [Ronald Reagan's] success as he."[65] Especially after President Reagan's cancer operation in 1985, Mrs. Reagan's influence continued to mount. Power in the White House, according to news sources, consisted of the triumvirate of the president, his chief of staff (Donald Regan), and the first lady. Subsequently, Mrs. Reagan was considered to have played a key role in having Chief of Staff Regan removed from office for his inept handling of the Iran-Contra scandal fallout. Also, Mrs. Reagan has been credited in some quarters with convincing her husband to reverse his uncompromising Cold War rhetoric—President Reagan had described the Soviet Union as an "Evil Empire" in one speech—and agree to getting the Russians to a summit meeting in Geneva, Switzerland in November 1985. This exploratory summit meeting eventually led to the historic signing of the Intermediate Nuclear Forces (INF) Treaty in Washington in December 1987. Even before this pact had been agreed upon by President Reagan and Soviet leader Mikhail Gorbachev, *The New York Times* had chosen to describe Nancy Reagan as having "expanded the role of the First Lady into a sort of Associate Presidency."[66]

Another first lady assignment, especially since the Kennedy New Frontier era, has been to participate in presidential campaigning. Actually, the entire Kennedy clan participated in the 1960 campaign, and next to JFK, Jackie Kennedy was viewed as the top crowd-pleaser in this famous family. Lady Bird Johnson, Mrs. Kennedy's successor, was also widely regarded by the press as a top-level campaigner for her husband. In her White House years, Mrs. Johnson made 700 public appearances, both during and between elections on behalf of her husband and her favorite nationwide highway beautification program.[67] It should not be surprising that the popular Mrs. Johnson was ranked in 1982 second only to Eleanor Roosevelt as the most successful presidential wife in the twentieth century, according to a leading poll of American historians (see Table 7.2).

In any event, a major transformation in the first lady's role has occurred, beginning with Mrs. Eleanor Roosevelt's years in the White House. The first lady's official position has been "transformed from ceremonial backdrop to substantive world figure."[68] At the very minimum, presidential wives can now be considered "ministers without portfolio." In light of this development and the broad impact of the feminist movement, it seems safe to predict that membership in the presidential branch inner circle will never again be regarded as an exclusive, all-male club—especially since the arrival of Mrs. Hillary Rodham Clinton at 1600 Pennsylvania Avenue.

By way of summary, the Founding Fathers, if they were to return for a visit, would be astounded at the rise and dominant influence of the presidential branch in the operation of our national government. But they would undoubtedly be pleased with the president's administrative direction of the executive branch, as provided for under the U.S. Constitution, for the Founders were profoundly disturbed that the then existing Articles of Confederation had no chief executive to conduct the day-to-day activities of the national government. Government by committee under the Articles of Confederation was rapidly driving the newly established Republic toward disaster. In the next chapter we will examine the president's role of chief administrator and evaluate the unique concept of shared executive powers with Congress constructed by the Founders to guard against abuse of executive power.

NOTES

1. The title of this chapter has been borrowed from John Hart, *The Presidential Branch* (New York: Pergamon Press, 1987).

2. William D. Carey, "Presidential Staffing in the Sixties and Seventies," *Public Administration Review* 39 (September-October 1969): 454, as cited by Stephen Hess, *Organizing the Presidency*, rev. ed. (Washington, DC: The Brookings Institution, 1988), 5.

3. For more details, see Bradley H. Patterson, Jr., *The Ring of Power: The White House Staff and Its Expanding Role in Government* (New York: Basic Books, 1988).

4. Margaret Leech, *In the Days of McKinley* (New York: Harper & Brothers, 1959), 127.

5. Arthur S. Link, "Woodrow Wilson," in Henry F. Graff, ed. *The Presidents: A Reference History* (New York: Charles Scribner's Sons, 1984), 438.

6. [Brownlow Committee] *President's Committee on Administrative Management, Report with Special Studies* (Washington, DC: Government Printing Office, 1937).

7. Hess, *Organizing the Presidency*, rev. ed., 34.

8. Ibid., 36

9. On the Nixon years, see Richard Nathan, *The Plot that Failed: Nixon and the Administrative Presidency* (New York: Wiley, 1975).

10. Terry M. Moe, "The Politicized Presidency," in John E. Chubb and Paul E. Peterson, eds. *The New Direction in American Politics* (Washington, DC: The Brookings Institution, 1985), 235–271.

11. Patterson, Jr., *The Ring of Power*, 339.

12. Hess, *Organizing the Presidency*, rev. ed., 5.

13. Thomas E. Cronin, *The State of the Presidency*, 1st ed. (Boston: Little, Brown, 1975), 119.

14. Norman C. Thomas and Harold L. Wolman, "Policy Formulation in the Institutionalized Presidency," in Thomas E. Cronin and Sandford D. Greenberg, eds. *The Presidential Advisory System* (New York: Harper & Row, 1969), 129.

15. Lester M. Salamon, "The Presidency and Domestic Policy Formulation," in Hugh Heclo and Lester M. Salamon, eds. *The Illusion of Presidential Government* (Boulder, CO: Westview Press, 1981), 186.

16. Ibid.

17. Moe, "The Politicized Presidency," 271.

18. Hart, *The Presidential Branch*, 214.

19. Ibid.

20. Patterson, Jr., *The Ring of Power*, 85.

21. Hess, *Organizing the Presidency*, rev. ed., 5.

22. Joseph A. Califano, Jr., *A Presidential Nation* (New York: Norton, 1976), 47.

23. *Public Papers of the President*, 1974, 5 as cited by Hart, *The Presidential Branch*, 122.

24. A valuable source on how President Nixon used his White House staff in the management of the executive branch is H. R. Haldeman, *The Haldeman Diaries: Inside the Nixon White House* (New York: G. P. Putnam's Sons, 1994). Haldeman served as Nixon's chief of staff until revelations of his complicity in the Watergate scandals forced his resignation in April 1973.

25. Nelson W. Polsby, "Presidential Cabinet Making Lessons for the Political System," *Political Science Quarterly* 93(1): 16.

26. Hart, *The Presidential Branch*, 211.

27. Robert Pear, *The New York Times*, 25 November 1991.

28. Ibid.

29. Michael Duffy, "The State of Bill Clinton," *Time*, vol. 143, 7 February 1994, 24–29.

30. Patterson, Jr., *The Ring of Power*, 66.

31. Ibid.

32. Ibid., 117.

33. Ibid., 117–118.

34. Ibid., 119–121.

35. Ibid., 116.

36. Ibid., 117.

37. Dom Bonafede, "The Ultimate Seduction," *National Journal*, 18 May 1991, 1205.

38. Ibid.

39. Ibid.

40. *The New York Times*, 4 December 1991.

41. Cited in Samuel Kernell and Samuel L. Popkin, eds. *Chief of Staff: Twenty-Five Years of Managing the Presidency* (Berkeley: University of California Press, 1986), 12.

42. Howard E. Shuman, *Politics and the Budget: The Struggle Between the President and Congress* (Englewood Cliffs, NJ: Prentice-Hall, 1984), 23.

43. Louis Fisher, *The Constitution Between Friends* (New York: St. Martin's, 1978), 175.

44. Quoted in Hart, *The Presidential Branch*, 83.

45. Ibid., 86.

46. Eric L. Davis, "Legislation Liaison in the Carter Administration," *Political Quarterly* 95(3): 287–301.

47. Norman J. Ornstein, Thomas E. Mann, and Michael J. Malbin, *Vital Statistics on Congress, 1984–1985* (Washington, DC: American Enterprise Institute, 1984), 121–124.

48. Charles Tiefer, *The Semi-Sovereign Presidency* (Boulder, CO: Westview, 1994), 95–117.

49. Hess, *Organizing the Presidency*, rev. ed., 6.

50. E. S. Corwin, *The President: Office and Powers*, 4th ed. (New York: New York University Press, 1957), 297–299.

51. Hart, *The Presidential Branch*, 192.

52. Graham Allison, "The Advantages of a Presidential Executive Cabinet," in Vincent Davis, ed. *The Post-Imperial Presidency*; see also *A Presidency for the 1980s* (Washington, DC: National Academy of Public Administration, 1980); and Hugh Heclo and Lester M. Salamon, eds. *The Illusion of Presidential Government* (Boulder, CO: Westview, 1981).

53. Arthur M. Schlesinger, Jr., *The Imperial Presidency* (Boston: Houghton Mifflin, 1973.)

54. The term "co-presidency" for Mrs. Clinton has circulated so widely that it scarcely needs documentation. For an early assessment of Mrs. Clinton's influence, see Margaret Carlson, "At the Center of Power," *Time*, vol. 141, May 10, 1993, 28–36. The analysis in this section relies heavily on Betty Boyd Caroli, *First Ladies* (New York: Oxford University Press, 1987). A more detailed, historical overview of presidential wives can be found in Carl Sferraza Anthony, *First Ladies: The Saga of the Presidents' Wives and Their Power*, 2 vols. (New York: William Morrow, 1990–1991); For a lighter treatment of first ladies, see Paul F. Boller, Jr., *Presidential Wives: An Anecdotal History* (New York: Oxford University Press, 1988).

55. For a detailed study of the controversial second wife of Wilson, see Judith L. Weaver, "Edith Bolling Wilson as First Lady: A Study in the Power of Personality, 1919–1920," *Presidential Studies Quarterly*, 15 (Winter 1985), 51–76.

56. Robert J. Bender, "Signed—Edith Bolling Wilson," *Colliers*, vol. 65 (March 1920), 5, as quoted in Caroli, *First Ladies*, 149.

57. Wilson scholar Arthur S. Link, however, has downplayed Mrs. Wilson's role in White House decision making after Wilson's stroke. According to Link, Joseph Patrick Tumulty, Wilson's longtime private secretary, assumed general oversight of executive office and various departmental offices when Wilson was unable to discharge his duties. Arthur S. Link, "Woodrow Wilson," in Henry F. Graff, ed. *The Presidents: A Reference History* (New York: Charles Scribner's Sons, 1984), 460–461; See also Judith Weaver, "Edith Bolling Wilson as First Lady," 56–60; Betty Boyd Caroli, *First Ladies*, 148–157.

58. Poll conducted by Professors Thomas Kelly and Douglas Lonnstrom, Directors of the Siena Research Institute, Siena College, Loudonville, New York, 1982, reprinted in Betty Boyd Caroli, *First Ladies*, Appendices, 389.

59. Caroli, *First Ladies*, 198.

60. Raymond Clapper, "Ten Most Powerful People in Washington," *Readers Digest*, May 1941, 45, as quoted in Caroli, *First Ladies*, 196.

61. Caroli, *First Ladies*, 222.

62. Ibid., 268.

63. Ibid.

64. Lewis L. Gould, "Modern First Ladies in Historical Perspective," *Presidential Studies Quarterly* 15 (Summer 1985): 537.

65. Lou Cannon, *Reagan* (New York: Putnam, 1982), 142.

66. *The New York Times*, 13 July 1986, 66, as quoted by Caroli, *First Ladies*, 278; see also James G. Benze, Jr., "Nancy Reagan: China Doll or Dragon Lady?" *Presidential Studies Quarterly*, 20 (Fall 1990), 777–790.

67. Caroli, *First Ladies*, 241.
68. Ibid., xxii.

CHAPTER 8

CHIEF ADMINISTRATOR

In the words of the late presidential scholar Clinton Rossiter, "The President is *leader of the Executive Branch*."[1] Another presidential scholar Louis W. Koenig, however, reminds us, "The executive branch has not one but two managers—the President and his rival, Congress."[2] But the veteran British commentator, Richard Rose, observes: "The President's title of Chief Executive is a misnomer; he can more accurately be described as a non-Executive Chief."[3] Ironically, all three statements from these presidential scholars are, in a sense, true.

In this chapter we will endeavor to clear up this ambiguity and spell out how the president as chief administrator operates within our separation of powers system. The dual role of the cabinet as an advisory body to the president and individual managers of the fourteen executive departments will be examined. The president's vital leadership role in executive budget-making receives close attention. Presidential efforts to reorganize the executive branch that emerge from time to time will be treated as well as the various management styles of presidents, especially those of our three most recent chief executives.

FRAMERS' AMBIGUOUS GUIDELINES

Most historians trace the ambiguous role of the president as chief administrator to the Framers' deliberate decisions at the 1787 Philadelphia convention to leave many questions about the scope and power of the president unanswered. The Framers did not want to give opponents of the newly drafted Constitution additional ammunition to fight ratification of the proposed new governing system. Instead, they wrote in the new U.S. Constitution, Article II, "the

executive power shall be vested in a President of the United States of America."
But they did not go beyond this single sentence in defining this grant of power.
Thus, the Framers left it to future presidents, Congress, and posterity to shape
the newly established presidency in response to the exigencies of the times.

Did the men of 1787 intend to invest the president with independent authority
beyond the parameters of congressional control, or did they intend to let him
function in this broad area as an agent of Congress? Nobody knows. Must the
president execute laws that in his judgment violate his oath requiring him to
"faithfully execute the office of President of the United States" and to "preserve,
protect, and defend the Constitution of the United States"? What about laws
that in his judgment invade his own constitutional prerogatives as chief executive? The Constitution sheds no light on these questions.

The Framers, with their innate distrust of concentrated power, did not hesitate
to divide responsibilities between president and Congress in some areas of
administration. Thus, while the president's position of chief of administration
is reinforced by a grant of broad appointive authority in the Constitution
blanketing all the more important categories of executive and judicial officers,
these appointments are nevertheless "subject to the advice and consent of the
Senate" (Article II, Section 2). Further, the enumeration of the specific subjects
on which Congress may legislate, in Article I, Section 8, supplemented by a
grant of authority to "make all laws which shall be necessary and proper"
appears to be a distinct reservation of authority to Congress to regulate by law
the manner in which the president should proceed in carrying out his Constitutional duties. The requirement in the same article that no money may be
withdrawn from the Treasury except "in consequence of appropriations made
by law" is an additional reinforcement of congressional authority in the area of
administration. This clause suggests that Congress may pass laws to implement
and, incidentally, control and restrict the president's discretion in carrying out
his responsibilities as chief of administration.

With the exception of the offices of president and vice president in the
executive branch, constitutional theory has held, since the founding of the
Republic, that administrative offices are brought into existence normally by
legislative act, not executive order. Indeed, the language of the "necessary and
proper" clause indicates that Congress may by statute dictate the organizational
structure of the executive branch.

The powers of the executive branch's operating departments are delineated
by acts of Congress, funded by congressional appropriations, and implemented
for the most part of career civil servants. In short, the mission and structure of
the executive departments are marked out by Congress. Lawmakers can also
give authority to subordinate career officials to act independently of the White
House. Congress can prescribe specific and detailed procedures for bureaus and
agencies to follow; and they may require Senate confirmation of bureau chiefs.

Also, Congress can, if it wishes, establish or abolish independent regulatory commissions, such as the Interstate Commerce Commission, the Federal Reserve Board, and the Securities Exchange Commission, all distantly removed from the president's direction and control. Since all agencies require annual appropriations from Congress, the lawmakers can maintain a watchful eye over departments, agencies, and commissions and make the final judgment on the size of their budgets. Furthermore, Congress may launch an investigation and overall review of a department's operations, if evidence of wrongdoing or gross mismanagement surfaces.

Constitutionally, the president is responsible for seeing that the 2.4 million civil servants faithfully carry out the laws of the land, as he and his staff direct. But presidents frequently discover that some executive department bureau chiefs do not follow orders. Nor do they seem to fear the president's sanctions, for they enjoy cozy relationships with key congressional chairmen and subcommittee chairs. Because the lawmakers control appropriations and may wish to see an agency or bureau's responsibilities retained or expanded, the departmental functionaries take their cues from Congress, not the president. No wonder one of President Kennedy's key aides, Ted Sorenson, remarked some years ago: "Any chief executive of a private business corporation has greater power over his subordinates than does the President of the United States."[4] Only a handful of presidents has dominated the executive department bureaucracies. Presidents Franklin D. Roosevelt and Ronald Reagan immediately come to mind, but even their battles with the bureaucracies were ongoing struggles.

Most presidents have assumed that any power or responsibilities delegated by Congress to executive departments become a part of the president's authority, an integral part of his executive power, needed to carry out the president's duty of executing the laws faithfully. "Congressionalists" have taken the opposite position that when the lawmakers delegate power directly to a government department or agency, the president is not to interfere with this delegation. The courts, seeking to achieve a balance, have come down on both sides of the issue, sometimes favoring the president and sometimes Congress. But in the final analysis, the courts have recognized, the same observer has commented, "two constitutionally established 'chains of command, and the doctrine of coordinate powers makes it clear that neither Congress nor the president needs to subordinate its authority to the other branch."[5]

Which view of administrative authority did a majority of the Founding Fathers really favor? No one, of course, can say definitely. Louis Fisher's assessment comes down on the side of the president:

The Framers shared a desire for greater efficiency and more reliable governmental machinery. Direct experience with state government and the Continental Congress convinced them of the need for a separate executive and interdepartmental checks. Chief among their concerns was the need to protect against legislative usurpations and to preserve the independence of the executive and judicial branches. Those were the dominant thoughts behind the separation of powers, not the doctrine of Montesquieu, fear of executive power, or a basic distrust of government. If the Framers had wanted weak government they could have had that with the Articles of Confederation.[6]

The American constitutional system, in fact, represents a blending and mingling of powers—a structure based on interdependence. Richard E. Neustadt has described it as "a government of separated institutions sharing powers."[7] Thus, while the president serves as the chief executive officer of the Republic, the power to organize and reorganize departments, including the Executive Office of the President, is assigned to Congress under the "necessary and proper" clause of Article I. Congress may exercise these powers, as it often does, or it may delegate them to the president through a law granting him authority to create or reorganize federal agencies. During wartime emergencies Congress has readily passed broad statutes authorizing the president to create, reorganize, or even abolish agencies, subject to certain legislative restrictions.

The Constitution does not specifically grant the president the power to remove government officials, but the Supreme Court has held that Congress cannot interfere with the chief executive's right to fire officials he has appointed with the Senate's approval.[8] However, during President Franklin D. Roosevelt's first term, the Court ruled that the president did not have the right to remove officials serving in administratively independent "quasi-legislative, quasi-judicial" agencies, such as the Federal Trade Commission.[9]

STAFFING THE EXECUTIVE BRANCH

The nation has had executive departments in operation since the first administration of President Washington. Departments are established (or restructured or abolished) by Congress. The number has grown from three in 1789 to fourteen in 1989. (The great bulk of the 2.4 million federal civil employees are appointed by the department heads in the executive branch through the civil service system.) Though the Constitution alludes to executive departments, no specific clause directs that they be established. Nor is the term "president's cabinet" mentioned in the Constitution. Unlike a corporate president who has a free hand in the choice of his subordinates, the president of the United States must, as indicated earlier, share this power with Congress. The Founding Fathers believed that the most effective way to check power was to share it. And in no area was this doctrine more evident than in the administrative power shared between the president and Congress.

While the president was granted authority to nominate the heads of the executive departments, the Founding Fathers required that these nominees be confirmed by the Senate. In short, the president of the United States must obtain the "advice and consent" of the Senate for all appointees to executive-level positions, except approximately sixty White House staff positions. Included in the executive-level category are 800 or more secretaries, undersecretaries, deputy secretaries, assistant secretaries of the executive departments, and administrators and deputy administrators for various independent agencies.[10]

In the final analysis, Congress determines if a position requires confirmation by the Senate. Formerly, for example, the president's chief business manager—the director of the Bureau of the Budget—originally did not require Senate confirmation. But Congress amended the Budget and Accounting Act of 1974 to require that the Senate confirm both the director and the deputy director of the Office of Management and Budget.

The separation of powers doctrine, however, prevents the Senate from attaching formal conditions to the consent it gives to presidential nominations. Nor may the chamber instruct the nominee, in his performance of his duties, if confirmation is granted. Thus, the power of advice and consent on appointments appears to differ from the apparently similar power of advice and consent of treaties. In contrast, the Senate may revise the draft of a treaty to which it grants consent through amendments. And on more than one occasion the Senate has attached reservations to its resolution interpreting the obligations of the United States.

Most executive-level nominations, it should be emphasized, are approved *pro forma* by the Senate. Ronald Reagan experienced little difficulty in obtaining congressional approval of his original cabinet. But when in 1984 he sought to replace Attorney General William French Smith with his White House counselor, Edwin Meese III, he encountered strong congressional headwinds. Several members of the Democratic party raised questions about Meese's fitness for office, in light of disclosures that he had received an interest-free loan from an acquaintance while trying to sell his California residence after moving to the nation's capital. He was also criticized for helping to obtain a government position for the same acquaintance who had aided him with the interest-free loan. After protracted hearings, Meese was eventually confirmed by the Senate.

In 1989, President Bush's first nominee for secretary of defense, former U.S. Senator John Tower (R-TX), was abruptly rejected by the Senate over questions of his sobriety and possible conflicts of interest with Pentagon contractors whom he had represented after leaving the Senate. More recently, President Bill Clinton found it necessary to have the names of two female prospective attorneys general withdrawn because they had failed to pay social security taxes on household help.

ROLE OF THE CABINET

The president's cabinet is an extralegal advisory body to aid the chief executive in fulfilling his administrative responsibilities. Because the cabinet as an organization has no constitutional status—the Founding Fathers expressly rejected the idea of an executive council—its function within the executive branch depends upon the president. Washington's four-member cabinet would be clearly overshadowed by the size of its modern counterpart. Today the cabinet consists of the president, vice president, the fourteen heads of the executive departments (see Table 8.1), the U.S. ambassador to the United Nations, and other top-level advisors that the president may wish to include.

Presidents are not required by law to form a cabinet, nor do chief executives have to take the advice of their cabinets. Unlike the British parliamentary systems, votes are not taken, and even if they were, the president would not be obliged to follow their advice. As Lincoln said on one occasion when his entire cabinet opposed him: "Seven nays, one aye—the ayes have it." Most recent presidents have preferred smaller conferences with one or two cabinet members to discuss a major issue, instead of a full cabinet meeting. President Kennedy, for example, regarded full cabinet meetings as a waste of valuable time.

Departmental secretaries operate on several levels. First of all, they are responsible to the president for managing the executive branch departments, with their numerous bureaus, and field offices. Second, departmental secretaries are expected to be effective political representatives for the president with the American public. Third, they are expected to be successful lobbyists with Congress, which controls departmental budgets and programs. Fourth, departmental secretaries are expected to manage effectively and provide leadership to the career officials and political appointees (assistant secretaries, counselors, special assistants, etc.) of the various agencies. Fifth, as members of the cabinet, departmental secretaries serve as advisers to the president.[11] In the words of Richard F. Fenno, Jr., the leading authority on the cabinet, a cabinet member's "formal responsibilities extend both upward toward the President and downward toward his own department."[12]

Modern presidents have held diverse views toward their cabinets. Eisenhower relied heavily on his cabinet, meeting with this advisory council some 230 times during his eight years in the White House.[13] President Nixon paid lip service to the cabinet as an advisory body in his first term, but seldom convened this group during his abbreviated second term. Carter met with his cabinet frequently— more than any president since Eisenhower. But in one hectic week in July 1979, he fired or accepted the resignations of four cabinet members. These wholesale firings, as might be expected, badly eroded the confidence of the electorate in President Carter. Reagan during his 1980 electoral campaign, as indicated earlier, promised to institute a cabinet government. In practice, however, Reagan and his senior advisers usually made the final decisions. "Cabinet government is an illusion," one administration official conceded.[14]

The presidential chain of command often breaks down within the executive departments because the cabinet heads, strange as it may sound, frequently do not control their own departments. Several factors explain the inability of some cabinet heads to dominate their departments. Many cabinet appointments are

Table 8.1
The President's Cabinet

| Cabinet Office | Year Est. | Number of non-civilian Employees | | Number of non-civil service positions |
		1980	1991	
State	1789	23,644	25,479	20,382
Treasury	1789	123,754	159,785	9,196
War	1789b			
Navy	1798b			
Interior	1849	79,505	71,290	9,813
Justice	1870	56,426	84,867	33,883
Post Office	1872c			
Agriculture	1889g	122,839	108,935	12,723
Commerce and Labor	1903d			
Commerce	1913	46,189	45,013	15,372
Labor	1913	23,717	17,337	766
Defense	1947	972,999	1,014,212	165,077
Health, Education and Welfare	1953e			
Health and Human Services	1979	158,644	123,348	15,190
Housing and Urban Development	1965	16,890	13,211	758
Transportation	1966	72,066	66,688	2,844
Energy	1977	21,729	17,900	1,736
Education	1979	7,370	4,676	605
Veterans Affairs	1989	235,501	249,957	100,528

[a]Dates are when the department achieved cabinet status. Offices of the Attorney General and Postmaster General were created in 1789, but executive departments were not created until later. The Department of Agriculture was established in 1896, but the commissioner did not achieve cabinet status until 1889; [b]Incorporated into Defense Department in 1947; [c]Indepenent agency as of 1971; [d]Split into separate departments in 1913; [e]Split into Health and Human Services and Education in 1979; [f]Figures are for the Veterans Administration. The agency was upgraded on March 15, 1989 to the Department of Veterans Affairs.

Source: Harold W. Stanley and Richard G. Niemi, *Vital Statistics on American Politics*, 3rd ed. (Washington, DC: CQ Press, 1992), 263–264.

made for political reasons, not on the basis of the administrative talents of the nominees. Some secretaries provide geographical balance, such as a Westerner being chosen for the Department of Interior. Other secretaries may be selected on the basis of race, sex, religion, or ethnicity, to appease various interest group constituencies throughout the land, whether or not they have any talent for administration. Some cabinet members are chosen to serve as ambassadors to various constituencies, especially the secretaries of the treasury, commerce, agriculture, and labor.[15]

Unlike the past, when most cabinet members were often longtime acquaintances of the president, he may now meet some of them for the first time during the transition period between administrations. John F. Kennedy, for example, had not met his proposed Secretary of Defense, Robert McNamara, president of a major automobile company, before interviewing him for the job. In the years ahead the lack of acquaintance with future secretaries, undersecretaries, and assistant secretaries will probably be the rule, not the exception. Unlike the British parliamentary system in which the prime minister fills his or her cabinet with members on the parliamentary party's front bench, all of whom he or she has worked with closely for years, the American presidential system frequently relies upon new, politically untested leaders to operate the government.

Below the cabinet level, the president and his advisers select approximately 1,500 political positions in the executive, noncareer, and noncompetitive category to operate the government bureaucracy. A wide variety of top jobs in regional offices, U.S. attorneys, and U.S. marshals are filled via "senatorial courtesy." A carry-over from the nineteenth century, senatorial courtesy appointments consist of three main types:

1. The president clears his nominees for positions with senators of his own party from the state in which the appointment will be made;
2. If no U.S. senators belong to the president's party from the state concerned, the appointment will be cleared with national committee members;
3. This traditional method of appointment will in exceptional cases be extended to influential senators from the opposition party—for example, President Kennedy and Johnson were unfailingly responsive to GOP Senate Minority Leader Everett McKinley Dirksen's patronage requests. Sometimes the president may extend some of this patronage to leaders in the House.

More often than not, the primary loyalties of these appointed officials in regional or local offices will rest with their congressional benefactors or state party leaders, not the national administration. Also, the president frequently nominates to top positions at the subcabinet level former lawmakers or lame duck congressmen and senators of his own party and even their senior staff assistants. Under these circumstances, team loyalty may be lacking.

Secretaries and top subcabinet officials have been depicted by one authority as "wasting assets whose value to the president depreciates during his administration."[16] The high turnover of cabinet members also limits their management effectiveness. For a time, their average tenure in office was forty months.[17]

During the Nixon administration, it was only eighteen months. In the first five years of the Nixon administration, the entire cabinet was replaced with a grand total of thirty appointees. Despite the high turnover, most cabinet resignations are not attempts to influence administrative policies, although Secretary of State Cyrus Vance resigned in early 1980 in protest against Carter's abortive Iranian rescue mission to obtain the release of the American hostages.

Because political executives rarely stay in office long enough to gain mastery of their departments, the incentive for career officials to make changes ordered by them is low. Frequently, bureau chiefs make end runs to Congress and their own constituencies to evade the presidential chain of command. While each side blames the other for conflict and delay, the business of the department goes on as usual. After all, presidents and cabinet heads come and go; career officials stay and stay until retirement.

Cabinet officers have limited resources and lack the clout to control departmental bureaus. Except for the secretaries of defense, state, and treasury—the so-called Inner Cabinet—most cabinet heads do not have much access to or influence with the president. Sometimes members of the Outer Cabinet—those departments considered to be less crucial to the administration—do not meet with the president for weeks on end. Some of these departments have been depicted as little more than holding companies—a conglomeration of bureaus, agencies, and offices handling a wide variety of functions and responsibilities.[18]

Presidents from George Washington to Bill Clinton have often discovered that the cabinets are not unanimous in the advice they offer. President Washington, for example, often found himself serving as an umpire between Secretary of the Treasury Alexander Hamilton and Secretary of State Thomas Jefferson.

President Andrew Jackson concluded that a better way to avoid cabinet dissonance was to utilize a variety of personal advisers who came to be known as the "Kitchen Cabinet." Before long this small band of gifted counselors, in effect, displaced the Jackson cabinet as an advisory body. But even this tight little group disagreed frequently among themselves on the advice to give the elderly general-turned-president.

Similar informal advisory groups emerged during later administrations, each responding to presidential wishes to obtain independent counsel from a variety of sources. President John Tyler, for example, relied on his "Virginia Schoolmasters"; Grover Cleveland had his "Fishing Cabinet"; Teddy Roosevelt had his "Tennis Cabinet"; Warren Harding sported a "Poker Cabinet"; Herbert Hoover sought advice from his "Medicine Ball Cabinet"; and Franklin D. Roosevelt quickly established his "Brains Trust."[19]

Over the years the cabinet's utility in providing advice to the president has declined for a variety of reasons, chiefly related to the political process. Before the rise of the open presidential primary system, presidents were often forced to bargain future cabinet posts at the national nominating conventions in return for support from "favorite son" candidates or state party leaders.[20] If the presidential candidate won in November, he paid off his political debts. Geography and the federal system as well as politics dictated that all areas of the country be represented in the cabinet. Thus, most secretaries of agriculture generally came from the Midwest and the South. Sometimes presidents picked cabinet members because of their close ties to special interest groups—labor, bankers, or veterans' organizations. Briefly, then for a variety of reasons, the president was sometimes forced to fill his cabinet with members who were not especially close to him personally.

Because departmental secretaries have often identified with particular interest groups throughout their careers, they have sometimes found themselves "captured" by these interests in their departments. No wonder President Nixon's White House aide John Ehrlichman complained some years ago that departmental secretaries often go off and "marry the natives." For all the reasons cited above, political scientist James P. Pfiffner has concluded "lack of absolute loyalty to the president by departmental secretaries is inherent in the American political system."[21] The centrifugal force operating in this set of circumstances has prompted presidents in recent decades to look more and more to their White House staffs to carry out presidential directives. This transformation from cabinet-directed executive departments to the White House-centered "presidential branch" has already been described in the previous chapter. Next, let us turn our attention to executive budget making—the president's foremost administrative task.

THE EXECUTIVE BUDGET PROCESS

More than anything else, the presidential budget message sets the legislative agenda for the year. Congress may whittle away at the president's proposals, shift some priorities, tack on additional appropriations for selective agencies, and refuse to fund some favorite presidential projects. But the legislative agenda is now the president's, not that of Congress, as the Founding Fathers intended.

As chief administrator, the president must use the executive budget as a political weapon to demonstrate to the country his ability to manage the federal household. President Gerald Ford put it this way: "The budget is the president's blueprint for the operation of the Government in the year ahead."[22] Clearly, the budget is a political document. To be successful, the president must package his multibillion-dollar budget in such a fashion as to convey his top priorities without splitting his own party or leaving himself vulnerable to heavy bombardment from the opposition party. To gain special political advantage, the president usually endeavors to project a frugal image. As explained by Richard M. Pious, "He underestimates revenues by projecting a booming economy. The purpose of these maneuvers is to lower the anticipated budget deficit. It also enables the president to blame Congress for "irresponsible spending proposals and for subsequent deficits."[23]

Ronald Reagan used this strategy against the Democratic members of Congress with stunning effect during the early days of his first term. One commentator depicted the Washington scene soon after Reagan's arrival in the nation's capital as follows: "Within forty-five days of his inauguration on January 20, 1981, he proposed the broadest, most radical, and most explicit agenda and economic and budgetary change that any president had ever presented to the American people."[24] To obtain the huge budget cuts he had promised during the presidential campaign, Reagan appointed, as mentioned earlier, a young, two-term congressman from Michigan, David Stockman, as director of the Office of Management and Budget and ordered him to slash the federal budget.

Aided by GOP control of the Senate for the first time since 1954, and the defection of forty or so southern "boll weevil" House Democrats on key votes, Reagan strategists relied on an innovative parliamentary device—"reconciliation"—to short-circuit the cumbersome congressional budgetary process to achieve huge budget cuts. (*Reconciliation* is a procedure whereby Congress votes an overall appropriations ceiling and then orders its committees to tailor specific programs to conform to this ceiling.)

Under the Reagan administration, budget decision making became far more centralized, both in the Office of Management and Budget and the White House. In other words, top-down budgeting replaced bottom-up or incremental budgeting. As a result, the role of cabinet secretaries and their departmental budget offices has been further curtailed. With the nation facing huge structural deficits year after year and the agenda dominated by spending retrenchment and possible tax increases, the White House's central role in national budget making vis-à-vis Congress has continued to be the president's chief domestic task.

Budget making continued to be highly centralized in the Bush administration. Throughout his term President Bush and his staff spent long days and nights battling the Democratic-controlled Congress on budget priorities, especially military versus domestic spending. The Bush-versus-Congress budget battle reached a fever pitch shortly before the 1990 midterm election. To win congressional support for his 1991 fiscal year budget, President Bush had to retract his 1988 campaign promise of "no new taxes." Congress, in turn, ceded substantial power to the Bush administration's Office of Management and Budget (OMB) to implement procedures developed in the $490 billion three-year deficit reduction package, The 1990 Budget Agreement. The compromise agreement worked out between President Bush and the Democratic leaders in Congress, in effect, supplanted the 1985 Gramm-Rudman-Hollings deficit-cutting law that proved to be unworkable.

Under a little-noticed section of the 1990 budget agreement President Bush and Congress agreed that federal spending caps would cover three broad categories: domestic, military, and foreign aid. Moreover, instead of subjecting the entire budget to automatic across-the-board spending cuts, if a specific budget category target was not met each year, the new system imposed automatic spending cuts only in the category where the breach occurred. Thus, cuts in the military budget could not be used to offset overruns in domestic programs, and vice versa.[25]

Further, under the 1985 Gramm-Rudman-Hollings law the Congressional Budget Office (CBO) and Joint Committee on Taxation, the Congress' in-house budget experts, were to share responsibility for calculating how much particular spending programs would cost and the amount of tax increases that would be needed to raise the necessary revenue. But the 1990 agreement assigned these decisions to the president's Office of Management and Budget. Moreover, if the congressional tax-writing committees decided, for example, to cut the Social Security tax, the administration's Office of Management and Budget, not Congress, would decide how much money needed to be raised elsewhere to offset such a cut. If a breach in the spending ceiling occurred, the OMB would dictate how much to cut and Congress would have to comply within fifteen days under the new ground rules.[26]

Few observers beyond Capitol Hill recognized how much power had been shifted by the 1990 budget agreement from one end of Pennsylvania Avenue to the other. While President Bush gave up his "no new taxes" pledge, the new agreement shifted a tremendous degree of control over spending caps from Capitol Hill to the White House. One former House Budget Committee aide noted that "the sheer amount of numbers and details that have to be maintained by the OMB to monitor Congressional spending action will give the administration extraordinary power over decisions normally left to Congress."[27]

President Clinton's 1994 Budget and Deficit Reduction Plan

Upon reaching the White House President Clinton wasted no time in tackling the federal budget. But he, too, discovered that dealing with the federal budget was a horrific experience. His first budget proposal, a $16 billion job stimulus package to help jump start the sluggish American economy, was filibustered to death by Senate Republicans before the 1993 Easter recess. Stung by this setback, President Clinton and his OMB Director Leon Panetta (a former California congressman) began their "hard sell" of the 1994 federal budget and spending program scheduled to take effect at the beginning of the 1994 fiscal year, October 1, 1993. Mr. Clinton's proposed five-year deficit reduction package, which included higher income taxes for top bracket taxpayers and a new 4.3 cents tax increase on gasoline, met widespread opposition in Congress and across the country. But Mr. Clinton's skillful arm twisting and lobbying on Capitol Hill finally netted him a single-vote victory in the Senate and a two-vote margin in the House in early August 1993.[28] But Mr. Clinton's 1994 budget agreement also contained the same tight spending caps imposed in the 1990 President Bush-Congressional budget agreement.

More than any single action in his new administration, Mr. Clinton's 1993 budget victory won him increased respect from Congress and across the country. Clearly, it also marked a short-term turnaround for Mr. Clinton in the opinion polls. This, in turn, led to further administration successes, especially in winning congressional approval of the North American Free Trade Agreement (NAFTA). By mid-December 1993 President Clinton's job approval ratings in the polls had climbed from a mid-summer rating in the lower 40s to 58 percent, as he neared the end of this first year in office.[29]

While the president remains the chief budget maker, his influence over the total federal budget is less today than it was twenty-five years ago. In the early post–World War II period, most of the federal budget, as drafted by the Bureau of the Budget, was spent by federal agencies. But as federal budget expert Allen Schick has noted, "Today, over three-quarters of the funds appropriated to agencies are passed through to outsiders who actually spend the funds provided by the government. Each year more than $100 billion is transferred to state and local governments, more than $100 billion to bond-holders, and tens of billions of dollars to contractors and other countries."[30] With the changing composition of the budget, more and more resources are allocated through legislative rather than budgetary decisions. Indeed, congressional legislation has shaped the great entitlement programs (Medicare, agricultural subsidies, unemployment benefits, etc.) that now consume more than three-fifths of the federal budget.[31]

Since 1974, the president and his OMB director have had to deal with the new competition on Capitol Hill—the Congressional Budget Office (CBO) and its staff of experts. President Ford encountered this problem soon after he entered the White House. Indeed, as Allen Schick has pointed out, "The new Budget Committee quickly became the marshaling point for congressional opposition to President Gerald Ford's tax and expenditure policies."[32]

Even after President Reagan arrived on the scene, the federal budget continued to grow larger—though at a slower rate of increase—each year. Still, the president and his aides found they had influence over only one-quarter of the budget. To be sure, Reagan's spectacular cuts, approved by Congress in 1981, demonstrated that a president, intent upon scaling down the size of the federal government and with a fresh mandate from the electorate, could still play a key role. But his triumph was short-lived. Heavy increases in military spending, coupled with the 1981 tax cut, soon led to ballooning annual federal budget deficits that averaged, despite a $95 billion tax increase in 1982, to more than $200 billion annually from 1985 onward. By the end of Reagan's second term the national debt had tripled to $3.1 trillion. So much for the Reagan reduced government spending plan.

Central Clearance

Presidential assumption of chief responsibility for budgetary agenda setting could not have taken place without major organizational changes in the executive branch. With the passage of the Budget and Accounting Act of 1921, Congress gave the president a valuable management tool. The lawmakers, recognizing their own inability to keep track of the increasing number of budgetary requests arising throughout the growing federal structure, willingly vested in the president authority to formulate the federal budget. Surprisingly, President Harding, who has generally been rated one of our weakest presidents, had the foresight to accept a suggestion made by the House Appropriations Committee to develop a central clearance system for all prospective budgetary proposals.

Under this new budget system, all agency proposals for legislation or plans on pending legislation that, if adopted, would carry a charge on the U.S. Treasury or commit the federal government to obligations which would later require funding first had to be submitted to the Bureau of Budget for review before they could be sent to Congress.

When FDR moved into the White House, central clearance was still viewed primarily as an adjunct to the budgetary control of the president. In order to keep pace with fast-moving events of the early New Deal, Roosevelt expanded central clearance procedures to include a review of all agency proposals affecting substantive policy. FDR also insisted that the Bureau of the Budget furnish him with recommendations as to whether he should sign or veto bills presented to him by Congress. Although many Washington observers may not have realized it at the time, Roosevelt's decision had far-reaching consequences, for it signaled his intention "to protect not just his budget, but his prerogatives, his freedom of action, and his choice of policies, in an era of fast-growing government and of determined presidential leadership."[33] Roosevelt, in short, converted the budget from a mere financial control mechanism into a policy-making tool.

During World War II, military planning priorities and the production of war material forced the suspension of central clearances procedures. But with the cessation of hostilities and the return to normal government operations, President Truman reestablished central clearance procedures to aid the development and measure the cost-effectiveness of his legislative programs.

President Truman assigned the Bureau of the Budget, working hand in hand with his own White House staff, the task of reviewing and coordinating into a comprehensive program all federal agency legislative and budgetary recommendations. As described by one commentator, "Formulation of a presidential legislative program thus became the end product of a careful audit of agency plans, reviewed and reduced into an integrated scheme conforming to the basic policy guidemarks set by the President himself."[34] Eisenhower's well-known predilection for a staff system and clear lines of authority made it easy for him to adopt the system of central clearance and program review of his legislative program, even though he initially offered only a relatively short list of legislative initiatives. Thus, by the mid-1950s it could be said that central clearance procedures had become an institutionalized part of the presidency.

Impoundment of Funds

From the time of George Washington, presidents have exercised some measure of spending control through the practice of impounding or returning appropriated but unspent funds to the U.S. Treasury. Presidents have routinely impounded funds to save money when appropriations have been insufficient to cover expenditures. They have withheld funds when authorized or directed to by Congress in order to establish contingency reserves or impose a ceiling on total spending. Since the New Deal era, presidents have also impounded some of the funds Congress has added, despite presidential objections to both defense and domestic programs. Sometimes these impoundments provoked congressional criticism, but they did not lead to full-scale confrontations until President Nixon resorted to wholesale impoundments in the early 1970s. Nixon withheld huge sums (more than $18 billion) that Congress had already appropriated for regular programs in agriculture, housing, and water pollution control. Nor did he make any secret of the fact that he was using impoundment as a weapon in his battle with Congress over domestic spending priorities.

Congress, as expected, reacted to this flagrant use of the impoundment process, charging that the president was acting arbitrarily and illegally in substituting his spending priorities for those established by Congress. Instead of bargaining with Congress, as his predecessors had done, Nixon refused to compromise. His actions triggered a series of lawsuits to compel the release of the impounded funds, which the president lost on statutory grounds.[35]

Congress also had the last word when it passed the Budget and Impoundment Control Act of 1974 to halt further massive impoundments. The new law limited impoundments to the establishment of contingency reserves and the saving of money that would otherwise be wasted. The legislation established procedures for congressional review and control of all future impoundments. Furthermore, the president was required to report all impoundments to Congress. Under the 1974 law, proposed recision (returning appropriated funds permanently to the Treasury) must be approved by both chambers within forty-five days.[36] While the statute is not a model of sound fiscal management, it has halted the unrestricted use of excessive impoundments as a political tool of the president against Congress. The law does not, it should be noted, block presidents from using impoundments to increase administrative efficiency. But it does put presidents on notice that they must act prudently and not flout congressional prerogatives.

From time to time presidents also invoke another means to improve efficiency—administrative reorganization. Lets take a brief moment to review the efforts of various presidents to tackle this complicated problem.

ADMINISTRATIVE REORGANIZATION

Before the New Deal era, administrative reorganization was confined almost exclusively to Congress' establishing new departments or dividing existing executive departments into new units. In 1939, however, following publication of the Brownlow Report, Congress authorized presidents to propose executive reorganization plans that would take effect after sixty days, unless disapproved by both houses.[37] Between 1939 and 1973, presidents submitted 105 reorganization plans to Congress; only twenty-three were disapproved. Truman won approval of 32 out of 48 such plans; Eisenhower, 14 of 17; Kennedy, 6 of 10; Johnson, 17 of 17; and Nixon, 8 of 8.[38] But in 1973 Congress, caught up in a continuing battle with Nixon over his efforts to centralize control in the executive branch, allowed this authority to elapse. Four years later, however, Carter requested from the Democratic-controlled Congress and received authority to reorganize executive branch agencies, subject to the veto of each house.

To achieve major organizational changes within the executive branch, the president generally asks Congress to pass a reorganization resolution. This legislation would normally provide that presidentially initiated reorganization plans will go into effect, if neither chamber disapproves by resolution within a specified period of time, usually sixty days. But the Supreme Court's invalidation of the legislative veto in 1983 will require that a new means be used to implement reorganization plans.[39]

Between 1789 and 1989, Congress approved the formation of seventeen departments (see Table 8.1). As a result of department splits, mergers, and other administrative changes, however, the executive branch now consists of fourteen departments. No attempt will be made here to survey all the administrative changes of independent agencies, corporations, and other nondepartmental agencies since the founding of the Republic. Indeed, the changes that have occurred within the Executive Office of the President during the 1939–1989 period constitute a formidable list. Thus, while the president has been able to effect some administrative reorganization of his White House staff on his own, he is not entirely the master of his own house.

If reorganization involves an executive department or major governmental agency, Congress decides this matter. Indeed, several recent presidents have seen some of their reorganization plans flatly rejected by Congress. Truman's planned Department of Welfare was tabled on Capitol Hill, though Congress subsequently created a new conglomerate department—Health, Education, and Welfare (HEW)—during the Eisenhower administration. (The name was changed to Health and Human Services in 1980 when a separate Department of Education was established.) Kennedy's proposed Department of Urban Affairs, though initially turned down by Congress, was subsequently approved two years after his assassination as part of Lyndon Johnson's Great Society program. Jimmy Carter's plan for a Department of Energy was eventually approved, but not until after it was substantially modified by Congress.

The president is not, however, entirely at the mercy of Congress in running his shop. Some units of the Executive Office of the President have been created by executive order of the president based upon his executive power, and he can organize and reshuffle his White House office staff as he sees fit, since Congress has approved these reorganization plans as a matter of comity between branches.[40] Other presidential agencies in the Executive Office of the President have been created by statute, based upon the "necessary and proper" clause of Article I. Still others can be or have been set up (or abolished) by reorganization plans. From time to time, *ad hoc* agencies or presidential task forces have been created by executive order to deal with special problems as they arise—for example, the Rockefeller Commission on the Central Intelligence Agency, or President Reagan's special commissions on social security and Central America.

If major executive departments or agencies are involved, however, Congress calls the tune. The lawmakers may specify the authority of the departmental officials, and they may decide to grant some autonomy to bureaus. Also, Congress may specify the powers and duties of specific officials in the departments and bureaus. Congress in its wisdom (or caprice), may decide to create independent agencies and commissions outside the departmental structure. Performing quasi-legislative and quasi-judicial functions, these commissions and agencies enjoy autonomous status that puts them beyond reach of presidential supervision, although the president selects the members of these commissions subject to Senate confirmation. To deal with complex administrative problems that cut across several departments, Congress may even decide to establish public corporations or quasi-public corporations with independent boards of directors, such as the Tennessee Valley Authority or the U.S. Postal Service.

While Congress has given presidents considerable latitude in reorganizing the executive branch, they have staked out firm outer limits. The lawmakers excluded independent regulatory commissions from 1939 to 1949. In 1977, the lawmakers prohibited the use of reorganization plans to eliminate enforcement of the statutory functions of a department or a federal agency. If a president wants to create a new department or eliminate or consolidate the functions of existing departments and independent agencies, he must persuade Congress to enact the proposal into law. One of President Reagan's last official actions was to persuade Congress to change the Veteran's Administration into a new Department of Veterans' Affairs. This new cabinet post was established in March 1989.

Despite presidential faith in the efficacy of governmental reorganization, recent history shows that reorganization does not necessarily result in greater effectiveness or clearer public accountability. Indeed, it would appear that there is no ideal form for a governmental agency, nor is there a set formula for structuring the executive branch. Herbert Kaufman is undoubtedly correct when he points out that the most far-reaching consequences of organizational change are not to be found in the "engineering realm of efficiency, simplicity, size, and cost of government," but rather occur in the areas of "political influence, policy emphasis, and communication of governmental intentions."[41]

Presidential reorganization plans often reflect a president's management style—a topic that deserves brief examination.

PRESIDENTIAL MANAGEMENT STYLES

Political scientist Richard T. Johnson, after analyzing the management styles of six presidents (Franklin Roosevelt through Nixon), concluded that they could be classified under three general approaches: competitive, formalistic, and collegial.[42] Johnson cautioned, however, that these descriptions oversimplify the complex reality of each chief executive's administrative style. Indeed, elements of two or three approaches may be present in different combinations at different times in each president. Still, these models help demonstrate the variations possible in managing the executive branch—and the costs and benefits of each. The three major models developed by Johnson and expanded upon by Alexander George are shown in Table 8.2. Let's examine each of them briefly.

Competitive Model

FDR's preferred management style was based on a competitive or dual principle of assigning two or more competing federal agencies to handle the same general management function. As described by historian Arthur M. Schlesinger, Jr.,

His favorite technique was to keep grants of authority incomplete, jurisdictions uncertain, charters overlapping. The result of this competitive theory of administration was often confusion and exasperation on the operating level; but no other method could so reliably ensure that in a large bureaucracy filled with ambitious men eager for power, the decisions, and the powers to make them, would remain with the President.[43]

Thus Roosevelt counterbalanced a Works Progress Administration (WPA) run by Harry Hopkins with a Public Works Administration (PWA) run by Harold Ickes, secretary of the interior. FDR parceled out electric power programs among agriculture, interior, and the newly established Tennessee Valley Authority (TVA), to mention only two examples of his unorthodox system of administration. That his subordinates might be at sword's point with one another did

Table 8.2
Presidential Administrative Models

Benefits	Costs
Formalistic Approach	
Orderly decision process enforces more thorough analysis.	The hierarchy which screens information may also distort it. Tendency of the screen process to wash out or distort political pressures and public sentiments.
Conserves the decision maker's time and attention for the big decision. Emphasizes the optimal.	Tendency to respond slowly or inappropriately in crisis.
Competitive Approach	
Places the decision maker in the mainstream of the information network.	Places large demands on decision maker's time and attention.
Tends to generate solutions that are politically feasible and bureaucratically doable.	Exposes decision maker to partial or biased information. Decision process may overly sacrifice optimality for doability.
Generates creative ideas, partially as a result of the "stimulus" of competition, but also because this unstructured kind of information network is more open to ideas from the outside.	Tendency to aggravate staff competition with the risk that aides may pursue their own interests at the expense of the decision maker.
	Wear and tear on aides fosters attrition and high turnover.
Collegial Approach	
Seeks to achieve both optimality and doability.	Places substantial demands on the decision maker's time and attention
Involves the decision maker in the information network but somewhat eases the demands upon him by stressing teamwork over competition.	Requires unusual interpersonal skill in dealing with subordinates, mediating differences, and maintaining teamwork among colleagues.
	Risk that "teamwork" will degenerate into a closed system of mutual support.

Source: Richard T. Johnson, *Managing the White House* (New York: Harper & Row, 1974), 238. Copyright © 1974 by Macro Publishing Corporation. Reprinted by permission of HarperCollins Publishers, Inc.

not bother FDR in the slightest. The administrative rivalry enabled Roosevelt to keep tight control of all final decision making in the Oval Office.

Formalistic Model

President Truman used a more formalistic approach, delegating authority to cabinet heads and relying on the traditional bureaucracy to manage the government machinery. Presidents Eisenhower and Nixon generally adhered to the formalistic approach to managing the executive branch. Cabinet members were given broad latitude. Both Eisenhower and Nixon favored structured decision making and an extensive staff system. All interdepartmental planning was coordinated and funneled through a chief of staff who reported directly to the president. Before the recommendations reached the Oval Office, all the pros and cons were carefully examined. Ultimately the president made his decision on the merits of the evidence submitted. Under the formalistic approach, broad policy considerations are heavily weighted and political considerations de-emphasized.

Collegial Model

This pattern of management aims to build a team of colleagues who work together to generate solutions which, ideally, fuse divergent viewpoints. The collegial approach recognizes the existence—and in fact, the value—of conflict. Indeed, conflicting viewpoints are treated as a resource. The principal strength of this approach is its potential for forging solutions that are substantively sound and politically acceptable. Its chief limitation stems from its dependence on people working together. Richard T. Johnson terms the Kennedy approach "collegial."[44] Unlike Presidents Eisenhower and Nixon, Kennedy distrusted the federal bureaucracy and placed far more reliance on his New Frontiersmen, the White House staff.

Lyndon B. Johnson's administrative style, though it tended toward the formalistic approach, might better be described as idiosyncratic. LBJ exhibited a preference for structured decision making, and he preferred to evaluate alternatives rather than participate in creating them. But more often than not, he pressured his subordinates to follow his self-designed policies, no matter what the cost. Even within his inner circle, where differences and dissent should have been encouraged, "Johnson's demands for consensus quilted his advisers into patterns of static harmony."[45]

Clearly, the competitive, formalistic, and collegial approaches to management oversimplify presidential modes of administration. But Richard T. Johnson's study demonstrates the usefulness of the three models. To the degree that a president follows one of these models, he can expect to incur the costs and reap the benefits that each approach generates. The costs and benefits are summarized in Table 8.2. As Johnson has explained, each president has used a different mixture of the formal and informal organizational approaches, and the result has been a corresponding set of strengths and weaknesses. Roosevelt's competitive management model generated a host of innovative policies, but created an immense amount of strife and tension within his administration. Eisenhower's formalistic mode of operation utilized bureaucratic resources, but at the cost of lost information. When Eisenhower decided on occasion to go outside of channels, his special staff came up with his imaginative "open skies" nuclear weapons inspection plan.[46] Kennedy's collegial approach retained flexibility and control, but sacrificed bureaucratic resources. In another instance, Kennedy's delegation of authority to Secretary of Defense Robert McNamara showed that a formalistic approach served the young president well when he resorted to a different administrative pattern.

How do our three most recent presidents—Reagan, Bush and Clinton—fit into the Johnson managerial style format? Both Presidents Reagan and Bush fit most closely into the formalistic model. Significantly, President Reagan's adoption of the seven "cabinet councils" in his first term to facilitate interdepartmental cooperation showed a special willingness to innovate within the formalist model. President Clinton, on the other hand, is a strong adherent of the collegial model. A veteran policy "wonk" in his own right, President Clinton enjoys working long hours with his White House staff to generate new approaches for solving pressing national problems. If one were to pinpoint the chief shortcoming of the Clinton decision-making process, near the top of the list would be the seemingly endless discussion and debate in the White House that is needed to reach closure—and then the issue may be reopened for further discussion. Like Presidents Kennedy and Johnson, Clinton has displayed more confidence in his White House staff than the federal bureaucracy to come up with workable solutions to critical national issues. Some critics of the Clinton White House decision-making process insist that the lack of focus during the administration's first two years in office can be traced directly to the fact that President Clinton frequently insists on serving as his own chief of staff, instead of delegating these duties.[47]

In the final analysis, executive administration is the product of both institutional and individual influence and tradeoffs. Policy outcomes are the result of both institutional constraints and individual administrative styles operating on a particular president at a particular time in history.

Minding the store is only one of the president's constitutionally prescribed duties. Equally and probably more important, his responsibilities as commander in chief and foreign policy manager can consume more than half of each workday, even in peacetime. The next two chapters will be devoted to these important duties.

NOTES

1. Clinton W. Rossiter, *The American Presidency*, rev. ed. (New York: New American Library, 1960).

2. Louis W. Koenig, *The Chief Executive*, 4th ed. (New York: Harcourt, Brace, & Jovanovich, 1981), 186.

3. Richard Rose, "The President: A Chief But Not an Executive," *Presidential Studies Quarterly* 7 (Winter 1977): 5–20.

4. Quoted by Rose, "The President: A Chief But Not an Executive," 5.

5. Richard M. Pious, *The American Presidency* (New York: Basic Books, 1979), 214.

6. Louis Fisher, *President and Congress* (New York: The Free Press, 1972), 26.

7. Richard E. Neustadt, *Presidential Power*, 1st ed. (New York: Wiley, 1960), 9–10.

8. *Myers v. United States*, 272 U.S. 52 (1926).

9. *Humphrey's Executor v. United States*, 295 U.S. 602 (1935).

10. Pious, *The American Presidency*, 218.

11. James P. Pfiffner, *The Modern President* (New York: St. Martin's, 1993), 119–120.

12. Richard F. Fenno, Jr., *The President's Cabinet: An Analysis in the Period from Wilson to Eisenhower* (Cambridge, MA: Harvard University Press, 1959), 218.

13. George C. Edwards III and Stephen J. Wayne, *Presidential Leadership* (New York: St. Martin's, 1985), 173.

14. *Washington Post*, 18 July 1982.

15. Pious, *The American Presidency*, 236–241.

16. Ibid., 238.

17. Ibid.

18. Ibid., 239.

19. Harold Relyea, "Growth and Development of the Presidential Office," in David C. Kozak and Kenneth N. Ciboski, eds. *The American Presidency: A Policy Perspective from Readings and Documents* (Chicago: Nelson-Hall, 1985), 111.

20. James W. Davis, *Presidential Primaries: Road to the White House* (New York: Thomas Y. Crowell, 1967), 125–143.

21. Pfiffner, *The Modern President*, 120.

22. Gerald Ford, "Budget Message of the President," *The Budget of the United States Government: Fiscal Year 1978* (Washington, DC: Government Printing Office, 1977), as quoted by Pious, *The American Presidency*, 256.

23. Ibid., 269.

24. W. Bowman Cutter, "The Presidency and Economic Policy," in Michael Nelson, ed. *The Presidency and the Political System* (Washington, DC: CQ Press, 1984), 483.

25. *The New York Times*, 30 October 1990.

26. Ibid.

27. Ibid.

28. Ibid., 6 August 1993.

29. Richard Morin, "Everything's Coming up Rosier for Clinton," *The Washington Post National Weekly Edition*, 20–26 December 1993, 37.

30. Allan Schick, "The Budget as an Instrument of Presidential Policy," in Lester M. Salamon and Michael S. Lund, eds. *The Reagan Presidency and the Governing of America* (Washington, DC: Urban Institute Press, 1984), 95; see also Lester M. Salamon, "The Presidency and Domestic Policy Formulation," in Hugh Heclo and Lester M. Salamon, eds. *Illusion of Government* (Boulder, CO: Westview, 1981), 179–182.

31. Ibid., 96.

32. Ibid., 101.

33. Richard E. Neustadt, "The Presidency and Legislation: The Growth of Central Clearance," *American Political Science Review* 47 (September 1954): 643–644.

34. Joseph E. Kallenbach, *The American Chief Executive* (New York: Harper & Row, 1966), 342.

35. Louis Fisher, *Presidential Spending Power* (Princeton, NJ: Princeton University Press, 1975), 189–192.

36. Ibid., 198–201.

37. Kallenbach, *The American Chief Executive*, 383.

38. Pious, *The American Presidency*, 214.

39. The legislative veto permitted one or both houses to veto or rescind a specific piece of legislation if it found that the president failed to carry out the legislative intent of Congress. The Supreme Court declared the legislative veto invalid in *Chadha v. Immigration and Naturalization Service*, 103 U.S. 2764 (1983).

40. Pious, *The American Presidency*, 215.

41. Herbert Kaufman, "Reflections on Administrative Reorganization," in Joseph A. Peckman, ed. *Setting National Priorities: The 1978 Budget* (Washington, DC: The Brookings Institution, 1977), 403.

42. Richard T. Johnson, *Managing the White House* (New York: Harper & Row, 1974), 1–8.

43. Arthur M. Schlesinger, Jr., *The Coming of the New Deal* (Boston: Houghton Mifflin, 1958), 527–528.

44. Johnson, *Managing the White House*, 6–8.

45. Ibid., 197.

46. Ibid., 112–114.

47. Richard N. Haass, "Bill Clinton's Adhocracy," *New York Times Magazine*, 29 May 1994, 41; See also Elizabeth Drew, *On the Edge: The Clinton Presidency* (New York: Simon & Schuster, 1994).

CHAPTER 9

COMMANDER IN CHIEF

Late Sunday evening in mid-September 1994, millions of Americans across the country were watching their favorite television programs when the networks suddenly cut in for a special message from the White House:

My fellow Americans, I want to announce that the military leaders of Haiti have agreed to step down from power. The dictators have recognized that it is in their best interest and in the best interest of the Haitian people to relinquish power peacefully, rather than to face the imminent action by the forces of the multinational coalition we are leading.[1]

Once again, the President of the United States, acting as commander in chief, and operating under the terms of the United Nations Security Resolution 940 had taken decisive steps to deal with a festering international crisis. President Clinton's announcement of the peaceful settlement of the Haitian crisis came shortly after sixty-one military C-140 transports carrying members of the 82nd Airborne Division had already lifted off the runways from Pope Air Force Base, North Carolina, on their way to an invasion of the Caribbean island. But when President Clinton received word from his high-level negotiating team, led by former President Jimmy Carter, that the Haitian military rulers had agreed to step down from power, Mr. Clinton ordered the paratroopers to return to their North Carolinian base.

Though the threatened invasion of Haiti was far from popular with most members of the American public and Congress, President Clinton on his own decided nevertheless that it was in the best interest of the United States and its allies to remove the ruling Haitian junta.

This action once again underscored the decisive importance that the president's constitutional role as commander in chief has had in our system of government over the past two centuries.

In this chapter we examine the president's duties as commander in chief—one of the Constitution's least-defined roles. Members of Congress can point to the specific language in the Constitution for their authority to declare war and appropriate funds for the armed forces, but the Framers clouded the legal sources of the president's military authority. Because the president can order troops abroad to counter aggression, the commander in chief can, as we take note, undertake military action before Congress can meet to act on any war declaration or measures short of war. Thus, the lawmakers may face a presidential *fait accompli*. Indeed, as the chapter shows, the history of the past two centuries has often seen the executive and legislative branches attempting to reconcile two fundamental powers: war declaring by Congress and war making by the president. The Framers intended that the two activities would operate in tandem, but more often than not, the president has taken action unilaterally and only later turned to Congress for retroactive approval and financial support.

Our discussion will show that especially since World War II (1941–1945) the constitutional position of the commander in chief has been strengthened by the creation of a massive, permanent military establishment and the ratification of a network of European and Asian mutual security treaties—pacts that call upon the United States to protect smaller, friendly nations throughout the free world from outside attack. Our discussion then turns to the "High Noon" confrontation between the president and Congress over the bombing of Cambodia in 1973 that led finally to the passage of the War Powers Act or resolution limiting unilateral presidential war-making actions. However, since this legislation has been on the books, the act has been only marginally effective in curbing presidential military actions. We conclude with the observation that the uneasy tension that has frequently characterized relations between the president and Congress will probably continue indefinitely. This should be no surprise, for the Founding Fathers wanted the best of both worlds—a forceful commander in chief to repel sudden attack against the country and a strong-willed Congress determined to keep the president within constitutional limits.

INTRODUCTION

Even a cursory reading of the Constitution will reveal how defense and security-conscious the Framers were. Approximately half the clauses in Article I, Section 8, listing the delegated powers of Congress are concerned with military matters and the conduct of war. But the Framers deliberately chose generalities over specifics in drafting the president's duties.

Though the men of 1787 devoted more time and energy to drafting Article II on the presidency than any other section of the Constitution, their decision to associate the function of commander in chief of the nation's military forces with the office of president was reached with minimal controversy. Reflecting in depth on their experience during the War for Independence, the Framers revamped the post of commander in chief of the Continental Armies occupied by George Washington during the Revolutionary War, made it permanent, and added to it a number of civil functions.

The statement that the president shall be commander in chief of the nation's armed forces is unique among the clauses delineating the powers and duties of the president in that it confers an *office*, rather than merely a function, upon the chief executive. Special significance has been attached to this clause by one constitutional authority, who stated some years ago: "The implication is that whatever powers and duties are necessarily associated with the exercise of supreme military command belong to the president by constitutional prescription and cannot be constitutionally diminished or controlled by statute."[2]

No part of Article II has been more broadly interpreted and shaped by presidential actions than the commander in chief clause. Indeed, ever since the Civil War, when President Lincoln cited the commander in chief clause as the constitutional source of his authority to undertake a broad range of acts far beyond purely military matters, the commander in chief clause has been stretched repeatedly by other strong presidents to such a point that the Founding Fathers might not recognize their original craftsmanship.

INTENT OF THE FRAMERS

Does the president as commander in chief have the final authority to commit U.S. troops abroad? Does this authority rest with Congress? Is this power shared? To try and answer these elusive questions we must first turn to the Founding Fathers at the Philadelphia convention for their interpretation and understanding of the war-making power. Then we must review our military history and presidential actions over the past two centuries for further clarification. Even then, the answers will most likely be inconclusive. The men of 1787, however, had no doubt in their minds over which branch of the government should control the war power—it should reside in the legislative branch. For evidence we turn to James Madison, whose reports of the proceedings are still our best source:

The Constitution supposes what the History of all Govts. demonstrates that the Ex. is the branch of power most interested in war and most prone to it. It has accordingly with studied care vested the question in the Legist.[3]

The Framers, however, placed supreme authority over the military in the hands of the chief civilian official—the president. This action was, of course, clearly in accord with the development of English constitutional history. The

Framers seemed not to have given a great deal of thought to defining the commander in chief's duties, since they believed that the new nation needed only a small standing army and limited naval forces for defensive purposes. Thus, the Framers probably did not foresee a pressing need to develop more fully the president's war-making power.

Still aware, however, that a president might become a military despot, yet conscious of the need for immediate action in case of national emergency, the Framers decided to divide the power of the United States to wage war between the legislative and executive branches. First of all, the authority to decide if and when the country would go to war was granted to Congress. But Article II of the Constitution states: "The President shall be commander in chief of the United States and of the militia of the several States, when called into actual service of the United States." Though the Framers had the same goal in mind—the means of making war—when they drafted the two separate sections of the Constitution, they could not foresee how the two branches might someday hold widely divergent views in interpreting their constitutional authority. Nor did they anticipate that the United States in the modern era would require a full-time commander in chief. Indeed, the content of the commander in chief clause has been shaped and expanded, far more than the Framers could have envisaged, by strong-minded presidents. And as one recent observer has commented, "The war powers issue has been complicated by the need for snap decisions created by nuclear weapons, by the increase in civil conflicts world-wide, by the growing popularity of 'peacekeeping' operations, and by the Orwellian euphemisms of modern politics, 'preemptive strike,' 'incursion,' 'cross-border operation.' "[4]

Although the Constitution states that the president is to act as the commander in chief of the armed forces, it seems reasonably clear that the Founders did not intend this role to confer special authority upon him to wage war. As Alexander Hamilton commented in the *Federalist* papers, "It would amount to nothing more than the supreme command and direction of the military and naval forces, as first general and admiral of the Confederacy."[5] In other words, the president was to be commander in chief of the armed forces once the nation was committed to battle, but the decision on whether or not to make war was to reside solely with Congress.

PRESIDENTS AND THEIR COMMANDER IN CHIEF RESPONSIBILITIES

Early presidents adhered scrupulously to the constitutional mandate that Congress should make the final decision on war or peace. When George Washington, for example, announced that the United States would remain neutral in the renewed war between Great Britain and France, some critics argued that his action, in effect, prevented Congress from exercising its prerogative to side with France in the conflict and to declare war against Great Britain. After some hesitation, Washington agreed, stating, "it rested with the wisdom of Congress to correct, improve, or enforce the neutrality."[6] Members of Congress, however, subsequently concurred with Washington's view that the country would be better served by maintaining a neutral posture between the two warring European powers.

Thomas Jefferson deferred to congressional prerogative after an American schooner was attacked by pirates from the Barbary States of North Africa. Despite the fact that the American warship disabled an enemy ship and captured its crew, Jefferson ordered the American commander to release the vessel and crew because the president believed that the commander "was unauthorized by the Constitution, without the sanction of Congress, to go beyond the line of defense." Subsequently Jefferson asked Congress if it would authorize measures to permit American vessels to take action against ships from the Barbary States. Hamilton, among others, felt that Jefferson may have bent over backward to acknowledge the right of Congress to declare war.

In another instance, however, Jefferson was less concerned about observing the letter of the Constitution. In 1807, after Congress had recessed, a British ship fired on an American vessel, the *Chesapeake*. Jefferson quickly ordered military supplies for the emergency. He did not report his actions until Congress reconvened. His message was directly to the point: "To have awaited a previous and second sanction by law," he wrote, "would have lost occasions which might not be retrieved."[7] While observance of the written law is a high duty of a public official, Jefferson insisted that it was not the highest. Self-preservation and national security rated higher.

President Monroe was far less cautious than Jefferson in repelling outside aggressors. In 1817, when Seminole Indians conducted raiding parties against American settlers in Georgia, Monroe ordered General Andrew Jackson to drive them back into Spanish Florida. Jackson wasted little time in carrying out this presidential order. Unlike Jefferson, Monroe issued his orders to send American troops into foreign territory without consulting Congress. This action, known as the "doctrine of hot pursuit," was subsequently invoked by several twentieth century presidents—Wilson, Truman, and Nixon—to justify military actions in Mexico, Korea, and Laos. Surprisingly, Andrew Jackson acted much more cautiously as president. While in the White House, Jackson ordered an American naval vessel to South America to protect American ships there from Argentinian raiders without first consulting with Congress, but he nevertheless promptly went before Congress and asked for "authority and means to protect our fellow citizens fishing and trading in these seas."[8]

In this early case and in several twentieth-century incidents, Congress exhibited little hesitancy in allowing presidents to commit American forces in dangerous situations that could lead to armed hostilities, provided that the protection of American lives and property was the justification. This course of action, as we know, came to be abused by several recent White House incumbents.

Nuclear Weapons

Toward the end of World War II, the commander in chief's military responsibilities suddenly took a quantum jump with the development of the atomic bomb. President Truman was the first chief executive to assume the awesome responsibility of deciding when, if ever, to use the vast destructive power of this new weapon.

Only the president, it should be emphasized, can give the order to launch nuclear weapons. This has been done only once in history—near the end of World War II when Truman ordered atomic bombs dropped on Hiroshima and Nagasaki, Japan. Later presidents have threatened to use nuclear weapons. Shortly after taking office, President Eisenhower threatened Communist China with a nuclear attack unless it supported a truce in the Korean conflict.[9] During the Cuban missile crisis in 1962, Kennedy, to demonstrate to the Soviet Union that the United States would not tolerate the placement of offensive missiles in Cuba, put the Strategic Air Command and its Air Force missile crews on maximum alert. During the 1973 Middle Eastern War, when there were signs that the Soviet Union might intervene to rescue entrapped Egyptian army units, Nixon approved an order to put U.S. armed forces—including the North American Air Defense Command (custodians of the nuclear arsenal)—on a general standby alert.

With the arrival of the nuclear age, presidents faced two momentous concerns. First, they wanted to avoid the possibility of an "accidental" nuclear war, triggered by false alarms—that is, erroneous reports of enemy missiles racing toward the United States, or malfunctioning computers at the defense command. Second, presidents wanted at all costs to prevent some hotheaded or mentally unstable field commander from giving an order to launch a nuclear attack against the Soviet Union, without clearance directly from the president of the United States. "I dont want some young colonel to decide when to drop an atomic bomb," President Truman was known to have said on more than one occasion.[10]

During the Cold War era (1946–1990) nine presidents—five Republicans and four Democrats—had it within their power to order nuclear strikes that could have well led to all-out nuclear war and the end of Western civilization. All nine, to their everlasting credit, have measured up to their responsibilities as commanders in chief without resorting to nuclear weaponry. To be sure, with the end of the Cold War the threat of a nuclear holocaust has been substantially reduced, especially by the disintegration of the Soviet Union into more than a dozen breakaway republics in the new Commonwealth of Independent States (CIS). Still, Russia, Ukraine, and one or two other republics continue to possess several thousand nuclear warheads that remain as constant threats to international stability. Until the United States can reach an agreement with these countries as well as others that reportedly possess nuclear weapons, prudence requires that the president and the armed forces remain ever on the nuclear alert.

Defender of the Free World

With the decline and virtual disappearance of the British empire and the end of French, Dutch, Italian, and Portuguese colonial territories in the post–World War II era, the responsibility for the security of noncommunist nations fell largely upon the United States. Ratification of the North Atlantic Treaty Organization (NATO) in 1949, which committed the United States to the defense of Western Europe and Canada, was followed by the signing of a series of regional and bilateral treaties pledging the United States to meet common external threats side by side with its treaty partners. Bilateral treaties between the United States and the Philippines (1951), South Korea (1953), and Japan (1960), for example, contained similar language and the same type of firm commitment to meet external aggression.

In reviewing these pacts—treaties, executive agreements, and congressional resolutions—the reader will search in vain for a definitive interpretation of the "constitutional processes" under which this country is to fulfill its military commitments. But in any action requiring military force it is the president as commander in chief who possesses the sole power of decision and execution.

CHECKS ON THE PRESIDENT

What, if any, are the limits of the war power of the commander in chief? Five decades ago, the late historian, Charles A. Beard, commented that

the war powers of the President are in fact so great and so indefinite that their nature will not be fully known until our Republic has passed through all its trials and ceased to be. The President's war power is the unexplored and dark continent of American Government.[11]

While this statement is somewhat wide of the mark, the constitutional definition of the president's war-making power did not receive a specific interpretation until Congress passed the War Powers Resolution of 1973. More will be said about this legislation later in the chapter.

Other constitutional and extraconstitutional checks on the president as commander in chief also exist. The Constitution, for example, requires that the commander in chief must ask Congress for military appropriations every two years. Congress, if it wishes, has the authority to cut off or eliminate military appropriations. The lawmakers, however, have always been extremely reluctant to use the power of the purse against the president whenever American troops abroad have been involved in hostilities.

In rare instances, the Supreme Court may be a check on the president. But in the historic Civil War case of *Ex parte Milligan* (1866),[12] which involved President Lincoln's suspension of the writ of habeas corpus, the Supreme Court did not rule against the president until a year after the end of the conflict and more than a year after Lincoln's assassination. During the Korean War the Supreme Court invalidated President Truman's action of taking over the steel mills to avert a nationwide strike.

Looking back in history, the wisdom of the Founding Fathers was never more evident than in their decision to place supreme authority over the military in the hands of the chief civilian officer of the nation. But should this much authority be vested in the hands of one official in a democracy? The late Clinton Rossiter, one of the nation's most astute presidential watchers, offered a perceptive response to this question with another query: "We have placed a shocking amount of military power in the President's keeping, but where else, we may ask, could it possibly have been placed?"[13]

MILITARY ACTION ABROAD SINCE 1776

Protecting American citizens and property abroad has been an important function of the president as commander in chief since the beginning of the Republic. Between 1798 and 1945, the United States, according to one authority, was involved in 149 separate military incidents.[14] Between 1945 and 1975, according to another source, the United States was involved in another 215 military incidents, police actions, or "shows of force," including two threats of nuclear action, with other countries.[15] Since 1945, according to another source, more than 100,000 U.S. military personnel have been killed in undeclared wars; more than 400,000 have suffered battle injuries.[16] In all these confrontations the president as commander in chief has been the decision maker, sending warnings to potential aggressors, deploying troops, or dispatching naval vessels to troubled areas. Members of Congress simply acknowledged that hostilities existed.

Congress, on the other hand, has authorized declarations of war only five times in our history—1812, 1846, 1898, 1917, and 1941. To be sure, in the more than two hundred cases that the president has committed the armed forces abroad, most have been minor incidents. Still in ninety-three cases hostilities have lasted more than thirty days, even though the president did not ask for a declaration of war.[17] Since passage of the War Powers Resolution of 1973, the president has used the armed forces to undertake a variety of military actions abroad on nearly a dozen separate occasions.

Since the founding of our nation, the constitutional prerogative of the president to serve as commander in chief has never been an empty title in times of crisis. Once the United States entered World War I, for example, President Wilson decided, as commander in chief, against merging American armed forces in France with those of the Allies on the Western Front. Instead, Wilson maintained an independent American command. A generation later, President Roosevelt in his grand strategy meetings with Churchill and Stalin, agreed to pursue the war against Hitler to a successful conclusion before mounting the final all-out attack against Japan. FDR also passed over more than thirty higher-ranked officers to select General Dwight D. Eisenhower as the Commander of the United States Armed Forces in the European theater in World War II. Subsequently, in 1943, President Roosevelt jointly agreed with Prime Minister Churchill to name Eisenhower the Supreme Allied Commander in Europe to lead the Normandy invasion and the march to final victory against Adolf Hitler.[18] Civilian supremacy over the military was reaffirmed once again in 1951 when President Truman removed General Douglas MacArthur for insubordination and failure to follow the president's military directives during the Korean War.

PRESIDENTIAL WAR MAKING

President James K. Polk, one of our lesser-known presidents, was the first White House occupant seriously to undermine the war-making authority of Congress. Determined to add Texas to the Union, Polk ordered General Zachary Taylor to proceed across the Nueces River into disputed territory and station his forces there —an obvious provocation to Mexico, which regarded all of Texas as its own territory. Mexico, however, showed remarkable restraint and declined to challenge the American action. Polk, thwarted by the Mexican government's cool-headedness, then decided to goad the Mexicans further. In January 1846, he instructed General Taylor to move to the banks of the Rio Grande.

Within a matter of days, the Mexicans attacked the American troops, whose presence they viewed as an invasion of their territory. The wily Polk, given the pretext he needed, immediately asked Congress to recognize that a state of war existed between the United States and Mexico. For the first time, an American president had precipitated a military incident and presented Congress with a *fait accompli* that made war virtually unavoidable. Thus, even though Congress had exclusive power to declare war, Polk had maneuvered events so that Congress had little choice but to go along with the president and declare war against the Mexicans. Several members of Congress, including a young Whig Congressman from Illinois, Abraham Lincoln, challenged the constitutionality of Polk's actions.[19] Two years later, the House censured Polk for "unnecessarily and unconstitutionally" starting a war; the Senate, apparently satisfied with the fruits of a victorious war, declined to support this move.

The outbreak of the Civil War in 1861 erased forever this narrow interpretation of the president's power as commander in chief. In the words of the leading authority on the presidency, "The sudden emergence of the 'Commander in Chief' clause as one of the most highly charged provisions of the Constitution occurred almost overnight in consequence of Lincoln's wedding it to the clause that makes it the duty of the President 'to take care that the laws be faithfully executed.' "[20]

In his resolve to save the Union, Lincoln cited the commander in chief clause as the constitutional source of his authority to undertake numerous actions going far beyond purely military matters. Lincoln held the firm belief that the commander in chief clause underlay the war power and authorized the president to prosecute the war against the secessionists with minimal congressional oversight. In his post as commander in chief, he carried out measures that would have been shockingly unconstitutional in peacetime.

Following the outbreak of hostilities, Lincoln ordered a naval blockade of the Confederacy—without calling Congress into session. Lincoln's authority to impose a blockade was ultimately challenged in the federal courts in a series of suits known as the *Prize Cases*.[21] The litigants argued that the naval blockade constituted an act of war under international law and because Congress had not declared war, the president had no right to impose a blockade. But the Supreme Court upheld Lincoln's action, ruling that an "invasion or insurrection created a state of war as legal fact." Consequently, the president did not have to wait for Congress to declare war before taking action against the southern states.

Lincoln, it might be noted, never claimed that the authority to take the nation into a war was a prerogative of the president. His sole justification, he repeatedly maintained, was that the very survival of the nation was at stake; hence he had no choice. To be sure, most of these acts were retroactively approved by Congress, but this assertion of presidential prerogative put an indelible imprint upon the commander in chief role that has made it, in the minds of many constitutional lawyers, the most powerful section of the Constitution.

The war-making power of Congress suffered further erosion at the turn of the twentieth century when President William McKinley, often considered a weak president by some critics, ordered 5,000 American soldiers to China to help other Western powers put down the Boxer Rebellion, directed against foreign nationals. To justify his actions, McKinley insisted that he was sending troops merely to protect American lives and property, even though his motives were apparently more political than military. McKinley did not see fit to ask Congress for authority, and congressional leaders raised no objection to the dispatching of the troops to foreign territory. Significantly, the Boxer Rebellion marked the first time that an American president unilaterally committed troops to combat against another country outside the Western Hemisphere.

Lincoln's virtually unlimited use of his power as commander in chief in the Civil War also became a prototype for presidential actions in World War I and World War II. President Woodrow Wilson, unlike Lincoln, who acted boldly on his own initiative, called upon Congress soon after the United States declared war against Germany in 1917 to grant him broad authority to wage total war. Congress quickly obliged by delegating vast powers to the president to mobilize the nation's resources for an all-out war against the Central Powers.

By quickly passing the Selective Service Act, Congress vested President Wilson with the authority to raise an army by conscription. The Trading with the Enemy Act gave him power to license trade with the enemy and his allies and to censor all communications by mail, cable, radio, or otherwise. Other statutes empowered the president to take over and operate the rail and water transportation systems of the country, to take over and operate the telegraph and telephone systems, and to redistribute functions among the executive agencies of the national government.[22] Nor did President Wilson ignore his own constitutional prerogative as commander in chief. His formation of the Committee on Public Information, the War Industries Board, and a War Labor Board all rested exclusively on this power.

Because U.S. involvement in World War I lasted slightly more than eighteen months (April 1917 to November 1918), and the armistice came before the American war machine had reached high gear, the full impact of total war and Wilson's role as commander in chief was not felt by many Americans. In assessing Wilson's role as commander in chief, World War I served, as Edward S. Corwin has commented, as a "prologue and rehearsal" for World War II.[23]

Six months before Pearl Harbor, FDR proclaimed an "unlimited national emergency" and with this edict cloaked a variety of forceful actions under his commander in chief authority. On June 7, 1941 for example, Roosevelt issued an executive order seizing the North American aviation plant in Inglewood, California, where P-51 Mustang fighter planes were being produced, because a strike had halted production. Two other strike-bound plants were also taken over under presidential order before Pearl Harbor, and four other strikebound concerns were put under federal control after America's entry into World War II by virtue of authority from the commander in chief.

To maintain the most effective mobilization of the nation's work force, Roosevelt issued an executive order in December 1942 transferring the Selective Service system to the War Manpower Commission and thereby vesting this agency with complete control over the manpower of the country not yet enrolled in the armed services. When labor disputes threatened to interrupt production as the United States approached final victory, Roosevelt directed the seizure of many of the nation's industries. According to one source,

The total number of facilities taken over is significant: two railroad systems, one public utility, nine industrial companies, the transportation system of two cities. . . . In addition, thereto the President on April 10 [1945] seized 218 bituminous coal mines belonging to 162 companies and on May 7, thirty-three more bituminous mines of twenty-four additional companies. The anthracite coal industry fared no better; on May 3 and May 7, all the mines of 365 companies and operators were taken away from the owners and on October 6 [nearly two months after the end of the war] President Truman ordered the seizure of fifty-four plants and pipelines of twenty-nine petroleum companies.[24]

Once again, all these actions were undertaken under the president's authority as commander in chief.

Are there limits to the president's power as commander in chief in wartime? Undoubtedly there are, but the reader will search in vain to find them among the Supreme Court's decisions handed down while a war is in progress. And not until passage of the War Powers Act of 1973 had Congress ever adopted any legislation that would seriously restrict a president's attempting to break the resistance of an enemy or seeking to assure the safety of American forces.

PRESIDENTIAL WAR-MAKING AUTHORITY AFTER WORLD WAR II

Roosevelt's bold actions as commander in chief before America's entry into World War II established a precedent that his successor, Harry S. Truman, found easy to follow. United States intervention in the Korean conflict and Vietnam civil war, however, raised a host of new questions about the breadth of the president's powers as commander in chief.

The skirmishing between the president and Congress over the president's authority to send American troops abroad without congressional consent actually began in 1948, when President Truman claimed the power to send troops to Palestine as part of a United Nations peace-keeping force. Although no troops were actually dispatched to the Middle East, the issue became a burning question in June 1950 when North Korean troops invaded South Korea. To counter this Soviet-inspired attack, President Truman decided suddenly on June 25, 1950, to send U.S. troops to Korea to repel the invaders.

Significantly, for the first time in American history, a president of the United States was asserting that his duties as commander in chief gave him sufficient constitutional authority, without consulting Congress, to take the country into a major war against another foreign state thousands of miles from American shores. Senate critics, led by Senator Robert A. Taft (son of former President William Howard Taft), argued that the president "had simply usurped authority in violation of the laws and the Constitution, when he sent troops to Korea to carry out the resolution of the United Nations in an undeclared war."[25] Taft questioned Truman's authority to commit troops on foreign soil without congressional authorization. But he and his small band of critics were vastly outnumbered by lawmakers who supported the president's actions.

The so-called great debate of 1951 concerning presidential versus congressional control over the dispatching of troops abroad to bolster NATO's defenses ended inconclusively. A "sense of the Senate" resolution approved Truman's sending four divisions to Western Europe, but the lawmakers said that no additional troops should be sent "without further congressional approval." Interestingly, Senator Richard M. Nixon of California was among the majority voting against inherent presidential authority and for the principle of congressional control of troop deployment.[26]

President Eisenhower, after a long career as a military officer, nevertheless viewed his authority as more limited than did his predecessor. On several occasions he showed hesitancy in requesting congressional approval for committing American troops to combat. But he asked and received joint resolutions from Congress authorizing him to use armed forces in defense of Formosa (Taiwan) and the Pescadores Islands in 1955 and to repel a possible Communist takeover in Lebanon in 1958. To illustrate how low Congress' concern over the war-making power had fallen during this period, leading members of the Senate and House denied that Eisenhower even needed to seek congressional authorization for his actions. Senate Democratic Majority Leader Lyndon B. Johnson, for example, stated: "We are not going to take responsibility out of the hands of the constitutional leader and try to arrogate it to ourselves."[27]

President Kennedy, despite his brief tenure in the White House, faced the gravest crisis of any president in the post–World War II era when he learned in the summer of 1962 that the Soviet Union was in the process of installing offensive missile bases in Castro's Cuba. Despite repeated Soviet denials that missile base construction was underway, U.S. Air Force reconnaissance photos showed that the missile bases were nearing completion. With this evidence in hand and after several days of consultations with his advisers, President Kennedy ordered American naval vessels to set up a blockade—the more euphemistic term "quarantine" was used—around the Caribbean island to prevent Soviet vessels laden with missile warheads from reaching Cuba.[28]

Though Kennedy's action could have led to a nuclear holocaust, he gave the order without any advice or consent from Congress. In this instance, the need for a swift response and the utmost secrecy in planning this decisive move dictated that the president act with both dispatch and surprise. To have consulted Congress prior to this action might well have led to a crucial delay and denied the Soviets the opportunity for the face-saving withdrawal of their vessels from the scene. Congressional leaders subsequently agreed, but some legislators complained that Kennedy had not acted forcefully enough to meet the Soviet challenge! Clearly, in this nuclear age the scales have tipped heavily in the president's direction whenever the United States has faced military threats from abroad.

THE VIETNAM QUAGMIRE

Further expansion of presidential prerogative power occurred within a year after President Johnson moved into the White House. The Gulf of Tonkin Resolution, rushed through Congress in August 1964 at Johnson's request (after alleged attacks on American destroyers off the coast of North Vietnam), opened the door to further aggrandizement of the president's powers as commander in chief. The Resolution, passed unanimously by the House and with only two dissenting votes in the Senate, gave the president authority to take all "necessary measures" to repel any armed attack against the forces of the United States and "to prevent further aggression." In short, the resolution gave President Johnson "blank check" authority to deal with the crisis in Southeast Asia as he saw fit.[29]

In his haste to win approval of the Tonkin Gulf Resolution, Johnson may have been less than truthful in dealing with Congress. The full story of the president's deception, however, unfolded slowly. In 1968, the Senate Foreign Relations Committee hearings, conducted by Senator J. William Fulbright (D-AR), reached the following conclusions:

1. That President Johnson failed to mention that the two American destroyers fired upon by the North Vietnam P.T. boats were, in fact, on a "snooper" mission to obtain electronic intelligence on radar stations along the North Vietnamese coast;

2. that the U.S.S. *Maddox* was between eight and nine miles from the coast, well within the twelve-mile limit claimed by North Vietnam as its territorial waters;

3. that a South Vietnamese naval operation near the North Vietnamese coast was taking place at the same time;

4. that American naval vessels had been deployed in the Gulf of Tonkin to reinforce the *Maddox* prior to the incident, indicating that the U.S. Navy officers expected that the North Vietnamese might respond with force.[30]

Johnson originally presented a case to congressional leaders in August 1964 that the North Vietnamese had engaged in unprovoked aggression against the U.S. naval forces. According to President Johnson, the American vessels were in international waters, sixty-five miles from the coast, when five North Vietnamese P.T. boats approached in a threatening manner. The *Maddox* fired warning shots, then fired directly at the fast-moving boats. The North Vietnamese fired torpedoes, which the *Maddox* evaded. Subsequently, planes from a U.S. aircraft carrier damaged two of the P.T. boats. The following day American planes attacked the North Vietnamese P.T. boat base, destroying or damaging at least twenty-five boats and the petroleum storage facilities.

As historian Arthur M. Schlesinger, Jr., has commented, "The role of Congress under the Johnson theory of the war-making power was not to sanction but to support the war—a role that nearly all of Congress, except for the indomitable Senator [Wayne] Morse and Senator [Ernest] Gruening, accepted until 1966, and most others accepted for a long time afterward."[31] Significantly, the federal judiciary refused to intervene when President Johnson relied on his authority as commander in chief to justify sending troops to Vietnam.

Lyndon Johnson's interpretation of his role as commander in chief and the dispatching of over 500,000 American troops to South Vietnam, without formal authorization from Congress, eventually produced a strong backlash throughout the country.

Johnson insisted that sufficient precedents set by previous presidents existed for him to take action in South Vietnam. Further, he claimed that any president had the right to repel a sudden attack. The Johnson administration's view was that in this modern age of jet aircraft and instant communication, the security of the United States could be endangered by military action thousands of miles from our coastlines. Under this open-ended doctrine, the president could order our armed forces into combat anywhere and anytime that he believed the security of the United States to be threatened. Schlesinger has observed: "Under this theory it is hard to see why any future President would ever see any legal need to go to Congress before leading the nation into war."[32]

If the Johnson theory of the presidency continued to expand the powers of the president as commander in chief, Nixon's concept of exclusive presidential authority to carry on the Vietnam War pushed it to new heights. By 1970, the Nixon administration had disowned the Tonkin Gulf Resolution.[33] Henceforth, in the words of Schlesinger, "The claim of exclusive presidential authority now rested squarely on the powers of the Commander in Chief, especially his power to do whatever he thought necessary to protect American troops."[34] "I shall meet my responsibility as Commander-in-Chief of the Armed Forces," Nixon said in his announcement of the invasion of Cambodia in 1970, "to take the action necessary to defend the security of our American men."

According to *The New York Times*, Nixon did not even ask the State Department lawyers to prepare the legal case for the invasion of Cambodia until four days after it began.[35]

As the Vietnam War continued on with no end in sight, Congress became increasingly restless. Despite claims by Presidents Johnson and Nixon that significant progress was being made—they "could see the light at the end of the tunnel"—anti-war critics in Congress sought to force the administration to extricate the United States from the quagmire in Indochina. Between 1966 and July 1973, Congress had 113 roll-call or teller votes on measures to limit or end combat activities, with ninety-four votes taking place during the Nixon administration.[36] Virtually all these resolutions failed to pass, since a coalition of Democratic "hawks," mostly from the South, and minority Republicans invariably prevailed.

THE WAR POWERS RESOLUTION: CURBING
PRESIDENTIAL WAR MAKING

Anti-war forces in Congress, after repeated failures, finally voted to put a legislative curb on presidential war-making power in the fall of 1973. At long last Congress finally decided it was time to do something about the imperial presidency—or, more accurately, the president's discretionary use of his commander in chief authority to order American troops into combat situations almost anywhere in the free world.

Passage of the act, called the War Powers Resolution (or War Powers Act), came in the midst of the Middle Eastern crisis with the Soviet Union over hostilities between Israel and Egypt (the Yom Kippur War), and at the very moment President Nixon was embroiled in the "Saturday Night Massacre" firing of Watergate Special Prosecutor Archibald Cox. Nixon vetoed the War Powers Resolution, declaring, "The restrictions which this resolution would impose upon the authority of the President are both unconstitutional and dangerous to the best interests of the Nation." But the vast majority of lawmakers, unimpressed with the president's reasoning, quickly overrode the veto.[37]

Proponents of the War Powers Resolution—perhaps too optimistically—saw it as a means of restoring the original intent of the Founding Fathers to place the basic decisions about war and peace in the hands of Congress. The War Powers Resolution spelled out three main procedures: presidential consultation with Congress, presidential reports to Congress, and congressional termination of military action.

Briefly, the War Powers Resolution stipulated that the president may commit the armed forces to combat only in the following circumstances:

1. In the event of a declaration of war;
2. With specific statutory authorization;
3. In the case of a national emergency created by an attack on the United States, its territories, its possessions, or its Armed Forces.[38]

Furthermore, the legislation urged the president to consult with Congress in "every possible instance" prior to committing forces to combat abroad, and it required consultation after such a commitment.

Specifically, the resolution required a written report to Congress within forty-eight hours of a commitment of American forces and required ending of the commitment within sixty days, unless further authorized by Congress. Moreover, the commitment could be extended for thirty additional days if the president certified to Congress that military conditions required continued use of the forces in order to ensure their safety. Finally, the resolution stated that Congress may by concurrent resolution, not subject to presidential veto, order the withdrawal of U.S. forces to the end of the first sixty days.

Critics, however, have noted that the resolution does not distinguish between a major attack and minor incident.[39] The resolution has enough leeway to permit the president to deploy forces in such a manner as to create an incident and then lead the country into war. Thus, if American troops were attacked by hostile forces operating from sanctuaries, the president could order the invasion of a neutral country without obtaining a declaration of war—in other words, a repeat performance of Nixon's decision to invade Cambodia in 1970.

Some critics have argued that the War Powers Resolution, passed originally to restrain the "imperial presidency," has unconstitutionally given the executive more war-making powers than did the Founding Fathers. Senator Thomas Eagleton (D-MO), for example, asserted that it gave the president virtually a blank check to conduct military action around the globe. In Eagleton's words, "By failing to define the president's powers in legally binding language, the bill provided a legal loophole for the President's broad claims of inherent power to initiate a war."[39] As congressional analyst Louis Fisher has commented on the sixty-to-ninety-day time restriction: "Presidents are allowed to use military force anywhere in the world, for any reason, for up to three months without a shred of advance congressional authority. The Framers would have been stunned at the thought of granting a president that scope of authority."[40]

The War Powers Resolution's reporting requirements are also incomplete. The resolution, as one close student of the presidency has pointed out, does not cover the following: "military alerts; naval quarantines or blockades in international waters; the use of naval vessels for convoys; the training, equipping, or transporting of mercenaries or guerrillas for combat on foreign territory; or the supply, financing, training, or transporting of forces of another nation into a combat in a foreign territory."[41]

RECENT PRESIDENTS' DIM VIEW OF THE WAR POWERS RESOLUTION

Since its passage two decades ago, presidents have made a mockery of the War Powers Resolution. Presidents from Ford to Bush have marginalized, evaded, or ignored its provisions, insisting that the resolution is an unconstitutional infringement on their powers as commander in chief. All of these presidents have routinely ignored the prior consultation clause of the resolution. Although the resolution requires him to consult "regularly," the wording does not specify whether or not continuous consultation is required. Since the War Powers Resolution did not specify with whom the president should consult in Congress, the matter remains unresolved. It is reasonable to assume, of course, that the resolution did not mean the entire membership of both houses. But does it mean the Speaker and majority and minority leaders in both chambers, or the chairpersons of the intelligence committees? No clear answer is evident.

Nor does the resolution define "consult." Presidents have chosen to assume—for their own convenience—that they are consulting if they simply brief congressional leaders after the fact, or just before a military action has been launched, not during the critical planning stage when the various options could be explored by leaders of both branches.[42]

President Bush, even before the sudden invasion of Panama in December 1989, reiterated the Reagan administration's view that the "timely fashion" notification language of the War Powers Resolution should be read to leave the president with virtually unfettered discretion to choose the right moment for making the required notification.[43]

Presidents have trivialized the resolution's reporting requirements. Congress cannot compel the president to forward a report within forty-eight hours of using force, especially if the president denies that the military action constitutes "hostilities" and, instead, insists that the armed forces are engaged in "peace-keeping" activities, "covert operations," or "anti-terrorist" activities. Even if the president decides to communicate with Congress, it can be in the form of a standard letter that contains no more pertinent information on the military action than can be found in a daily newspaper story or an evening network news telecast. Nor have presidents chosen to issue their reports "under the requirements of the War Powers Resolution." Instead, they have generally used other terms, such as "consistent with" or "taking note of" the resolution.

The War Powers Resolution's sixty-day "clock" or time limitation that presumably signifies the beginning of hostilities and which is supposed to limit the use of U.S. forces without subsequent congressional approval has been utilized only once (in Lebanon). In this instance, the time limit was extended to eighteen months by mutual agreement of President Reagan and Congress to keep it from becoming an issue in the 1984 election. Thus, if Congress wants to insist on a time limit, it would have to start the clock running itself—most likely just when the crisis is heating up and the American public is "rallying around the flag" in support of the president's bold actions.[44] Under these circumstances it is virtually certain that any action by Congress to blow the whistle on the president will be viewed as congressional meddling while the president attempts to deal with the crisis.

Presidents have also systematically ignored the War Powers Resolution's threat of congressional sanctions. The provision granting Congress power to end presidential war making by concurrent resolution (which does not require the president's signature) is probably unconstitutional, in light of the Supreme Court's ruling in *INS v. Chadha* (1983) invalidating such a "legislative veto."[45] In this case the High Court ruled that resolutions which are not presented to the president for his signature or veto are unconstitutional. In other words, the only way Congress could restrain the president would be by a joint resolution, which is subject to a presidential veto. (Congress has not yet chosen to amend the War Powers Resolution to provide for this course of action.) Even if Congress chooses to go the joint resolution route, a president who retained the support of one-third, plus one, of the members of either chamber could utilize his veto against a congressional resolution ordering him to withdraw American forces, confident that his veto would be sustained. If the restraining resolution should win two-thirds approval, the president might still decide to ignore the resolution, because it seems highly likely that the federal courts would dodge the issue by adjudging this conflict between the executive and legislative branches a "political question," or they might hold that other congressional legislation or actions displayed an intent to support the president's policy. Or the courts might determine that the president's powers as commander in chief had been infringed upon.

The Ford White House, for example, insisted some years ago that, despite the War Powers Resolution, the president's authority extended far beyond protecting American territory and the armed forces. Indeed, the Ford administration, according to Louis Fisher, argued that in at least six other situations the president has constitutional authority to introduce armed forces into hostilities, "to rescue American citizens abroad; to rescue foreign nationals where such action directly facilitates the rescue of American citizens abroad; to protect U.S. embassies and legations abroad; to suppress civil insurrection; to implement and administer the terms of an armistice or cease-fire designed to terminate hostilities involving the United States; and to carry out the terms of security commitments contained in treaties."[46] Nor did the Ford spokesperson believe that any listing would be a complete one.

THE WAR POWERS RESOLUTION IN OPERATION

Since passage of the War Powers Resolution in 1973, there have been nearly a dozen occasions in which the president has committed American combat forces to military action abroad. In flouting the resolution, Presidents Ford and Carter contended that the need for absolute secrecy precluded any prior consultation with Congress. The Carter White House staff also resorted to a unique argument that the aborted Iranian hostage rescue operation was a "humanitarian," not a military mission. This argument caused more than a few lifted eyebrows on Capitol Hill, especially in light of reports that had the mission succeeded, the second and third stages of the rescue plan called for taking military action against selected targets in Iran.[47] After the aborted mission, *The New York Times* asked: "Why not an ounce of genuine consultation before the raid to avoid a ton of contention and second-guessing afterward?"[48] In the aftermath of the abortive mission, the White House retreated from the specious humanitarian justification by filing a report to Congress, as the law required.

President Reagan went several rounds with Congress over the scope and authority of the War Powers Resolution. In 1981, however, Reagan did not even bother to report to Congress under any provision of the War Powers Resolution when he sent military advisers to El Salvador. The State Department declared that no report was necessary because the American servicemen were not being introduced into hostilities or imminent hostilities.

President Reagan's order to land American troops in Lebanon in September 1982 subsequently led to a heated war of words between Congress and the president over whether the president had complied with the provisions of the War Powers Resolution.

Instead of acting under the procedures of the resolution, Reagan subsequently wrote to Congress that he had deployed the U.S. peace-keeping force, pursuant to the president's "constitutional authority with respect to the conduct of foreign relations and as Commander in Chief of the United States Armed Forces."[49] Reagan insisted that since no hostilities had existed, he had fulfilled the requirements of the legislation by informing Congress in September 1982 that "I have authorized the armed forces of the United States to participate" in a multinational peace-keeping force in Lebanon, "to assure the safety of persons in the area and to bring an end to the violence which has tragically recurred."[50]

A year later, President Reagan again sent a status report to the speaker of the House and the president pro tempore of the Senate. Congressional critics, however, argued that with the death of the four marines, the president was required to do more than inform Congress. The critics said that the sixty-day clock should be running because the U.S. troops were in a combat situation, as defined by the War Powers Resolution. President Reagan's refusal to set the War Powers Resolution clock in motion meant that Congress had to pass legislation to invoke Section 4(a)(1).

As the constitutional crisis heated up, congressional leaders on both sides of the aisle and the White House worked feverishly to hammer out a compromise resolution that conceded a major point to each side: Reagan continued to express reservations about the War Powers Resolution, while congressional leaders said he had recognized its authority. The key to the compromise was that Congress would, on its own, determine that the War Powers Resolution is in effect. This meant that the White House would not have to send Congress formal notification under the act and as a result President Reagan would directly avoid acknowledging the validity of the act in the current situation.

Clearly the most important provision was the eighteen-month time limit. Supporters of the compromise argued if it were limited to six months, the Syrians and other hostile forces would simply wait for the Americans to withdraw. And if the date set were one year later, it would fall in the middle of the 1984 presidential election.

When President Reagan signed compromise legislation, he commented obliquely that he already possessed the authority to keep the U.S. Marines in Lebanon, even without congressional approval. Indeed, the White House made it clear that the president might continue to keep U.S. troops in Lebanon beyond the eighteen-month limit without reauthorization from Congress. But following the terrorist truck bombing of the U.S. Marine barracks near the Beirut airport, which took the lives of 241 U.S. servicemen in mid-October 1983, many members of Congress became convinced that the authorization was too long. President Reagan also began to have second thoughts about the continued stationing of U.S. troops near the poorly defended airport and its potentially dangerous impact on American public opinion during the 1984 presidential election. Suddenly, in February 1984, the White House announced that the marines would be withdrawn, and with their removal from Lebanon, the controversy over the War Powers Resolution ceased to be front-page news.

GRENADA AND BEYOND

Congressional muscle flexing resumed in late October 1983 after U.S. Rangers invaded the Caribbean island of Grenada, which the Reagan administration asserted was being turned into a Cuban-Soviet military bastion. Five days after U.S. forces landed on Grenada, the Senate voted sixty-four to twenty to adopt an amendment (a "rider" to a bill raising the national debt ceiling), declaring that the War Powers Act now applied to the fighting in Grenada. The House followed up this Senate action by passing overwhelmingly 403 to 23 a resolution that would apply the War Powers Act to the troops on the island and require that they be withdrawn in sixty days unless Congress granted a specific extension. Since President Reagan had previously announced the same week that the withdrawal had already started, the vote was motivated chiefly by the desire to assert Congress' disputed authority under the War Powers Resolution rather than to actually direct administration policy.

Because Reagan's Grenada venture was generally hailed as a major military-diplomatic success in blunting a possible future Cuban takeover of the island, further congressional criticism soon dissipated, especially after a congressional study group, appointed by Speaker Thomas P. O'Neill, Jr., announced after a three-day trip to Grenada that Reagan's move was justified.[51]

Few observers would quarrel with the postmortem issued by E. S. Corwin's editors:

The successful "invasion" of Grenada by the United States without reference to the War Powers Act or "formal" congressional approval clearly demonstrated the power of the president to both act unilaterally in his role as commander in chief and to disregard congressional limitations on his authority in matters of foreign policy concerning war and peace.[52]

Most Washington observers concluded that Reagan's role as commander in chief was enhanced by the Grenada operation, just as earlier presidents have capitalized on special military actions to reinforce their authority in commanding the nation's armed forces and to improve their national political standing. Reagan's policies, according to numerous Washington observers, represented a return to a traditional reliance on military force to achieve political objectives.

Advance consultation with Congress was never a high-priority item during the second Reagan administration, either. When President Reagan summoned congressional leaders to the White House for a late afternoon top-level meeting on April 14, 1986, to announce the impending air strikes against the Mu'ammar Gadhafi regime in Libya, the American F-111 bombers had already left their bases in Great Britain and were well on their way to Libya. The air strikes were scheduled to begin at 7 P.M. Washington time. Vice Admiral John M. Poindexter, the president's national security adviser, reportedly told the lawmakers at a White House meeting about 6:20 P.M. that "this is a consultation," and that the mission could be aborted if Congress demanded![53]

President Reagan flouted the War Powers Resolution again in July 1987 when he sent U.S. naval units into the Persian Gulf and put "reflagged" Kuwaiti oil tankers under the Stars and Stripes in the midst of the Iranian-Iraqi war zone.[54] Reagan refused to report the naval deployment to Congress (as required under Section 4 of the War Powers Resolution), since he insisted that the resolution infringed on his commander in chief duties. Several Democratic congressional leaders introduced resolutions declaring that the clock on the sixty-day notice requirement of the War Powers Resolution should be started. But the Democratic leadership soon decided, however, that it did not want to take the responsibility for undermining the president in the Persian Gulf crisis, so they decided to do nothing. Once again, the president treated the War Powers Resolution as a scrap of paper. With the end of the eight-year Iranian-Iraqi War in the summer of 1988, the United States reflagging operation was no longer deemed necessary.

President George Bush's Military Actions

During his four years in the White House, President Bush took his commander in chief duties far more seriously than any other responsibilities assigned to him by the Constitution. His secret actions abroad, however, created a high degree of nervousness and apprehension in the halls of Congress. On December 24, 1989, however, Bush's invasion of Panama to depose the drug-dealing dictator Manuel Noriega pushed the president's favorable Gallup poll ratings from 55 to 73 percent (a new record for a president at the beginning of his second year in office).

President George Bush's pre-Christmas emergency intervention in Panama in 1989 was so successful that by the time members of Congress returned to

Washington from the holiday recess, the Central American crisis had passed. Some members of the Democratic majorities in both houses grumbled about the failure of President Bush and his staff to consult with them. But on January 3, 1990, President Bush proudly announced:

I ordered U.S. troops to Panama with four objectives: to safeguard the lives of American citizens; to help restore democracy; to protect the integrity of the Panama Canal treaties; and, to bring General Manuel Noriega to justice. All of these objectives have now been achieved.[55]

Once again, another emergency intervention victory could be chalked up by an American president. Less than eight months later, however, another major crisis unexpectedly landed on President Bush's doorstep.

The Persian Gulf War

On August 2, 1990, Iraqi dictator Saddam Hussein and his battle-tested troops suddenly overran Kuwait, the small oil-rich sheikdom bordering Saudi Arabia. Five days later, Secretary of Defense Richard Cheney, after a hurried overseas consultation with King Fahd of Saudi Arabia, announced that the United States would defend Saudi Arabia in the event of an armed attack. This executive agreement was made by President Bush and his top emissary without any consultation with Congress. One commentator, Michael J. Glennon, a former legal counsel to the Senate Foreign Relations Committee, has described this pact as "an agreement more sweeping in its terms than any of the seven mutual security treaties to which the United States is a party, for none of these contains an ironclad commitment to go to war."[56]

Two days after the November 1990 midterm election, Bush abruptly announced, without any prior consultation with congressional leaders, a doubling of U.S. forces in the Middle East to over 400,000 troops and a shift in strategy to mounting "an adequate offensive military option."[57] This "November surprise," which signaled a change in strategy from economic sanctions to active military intervention, soon led to a growing confrontation between the president and Congress. Meanwhile, on the diplomatic front, the Bush administration successfully pushed through the U.N. Security Council a resolution setting a January 15, 1991 deadline for Iraqi withdrawal from Kuwait and authorizing any member state to use "all necessary means" after the deadline to ensure compliance.

With U.N. Resolution 678 in hand, President Bush maintained that on the basis of the U.N. action and his constitutional authority as commander in chief, he could go to war after January 15, 1991 without a formal declaration of war by Congress. The Democratic majority in both houses of Congress disagreed. Because of the refusal of congressional Democrats to endorse fully Bush's evident intention to initiate hostilities and drive Saddam Hussein's invaders out of Kuwait, President Bush was reluctant over the next several weeks to ask for congressional authorization for this military action for fear of losing the vote. Meanwhile, by mid-December the Bush administration concluded that it could then win a vote in Congress to authorize the use of force against Iraq.

The threatened confrontation between the president and Congress continued to simmer over the Christmas holidays. Finally, on January 8, 1991, President Bush requested legislative approval to use United States troops, in conjunction with the United Nations peace-keeping forces, to deal with Saddam Hussein's takeover of Kuwait. But the president did not acknowledge that statutory authorization was constitutionally required. Indeed, he asserted the next day, "I don't think I need it."[58] The disputed resolution reached the floor of the House and the Senate on January 11, 1991. Both houses, after two days of intense debate, marked by high drama, voted on identical resolutions "to authorize the use of United States Armed Forces pursuant to United Nations Security Resolutions." Though the Democratic leadership in both chambers opposed these measures, the resolutions nevertheless passed by bipartisan majorities of 250 to 183 votes in the House and a closer 52 to 47 vote in the Senate. Enough Democrats, mostly Southerners, supported President Bush to carry the day and give him bipartisan support for military action.[59]

Six weeks later, the famed "One Hundred Hours War" against Saddam Hussein freed Kuwait from the invaders. Once again, President Bush used his commander in chief role to reinforce his national leadership, despite strong congressional opposition.

The successful conclusion of the Persian Gulf War may leave the reader with the impression that the threatened constitutional storm between the president and Congress had blown over without any lasting damage. But several unanswered questions remain.

Constitutional Crisis Avoided

What if the U.S. Senate had voted down the Persian Gulf War authorization bill and rejected President Bush's request for approval to launch hostilities? What if the president had ignored the hypothetical congressional rejection and begun the war without congressional approval? This impasse could have led, it might be argued, to the most serious constitutional confrontation since the Civil War. How would this dispute have been resolved? Would the Supreme Court have agreed to rule on the inter-branch controversy, or would it have labeled it a "political question" and sidestepped this issue entirely? Nobody knows.

Clearly, the separation of powers system cannot provide an easy answer. Legal historian Michael S. Glennon argues that the Constitution's grants of war-making power to the president are minimal compared to its specific grants to Congress: to provide for the common defense, to define and punish crimes against the law of nations, to raise and support armies, to provide and maintain a navy, to make rules for the government and regulation of the land and naval forces, to provide for organizing, arming, and disciplining the militia, to call forth the militia to execute the laws of the Union, to suppress insurrections and repel invasions, and to declare war.[60] But as already indicated, the War Powers Resolution since 1973 has not been an effective instrument for Congress to assert its war-making prerogative.

THE NATION'S TOP CIVILIAN MILITARY LEADER: A RECAPITULATION

From Vietnam to Lebanon, Grenada, Kuwait, Panama, and the Persian Gulf, presidents have operated as if the War Powers Resolution were a mere legal hindrance. Many thoughtful lawmakers and commentators have concluded that the Resolution, in its present form, has been a failure. Several leading lawmakers—Senators Robert Byrd, Sam Nunn, and John Warner, and Senate Democratic Majority Leader George Mitchell—have urged the repeal of the "time limits." Senator Nunn argues that the time limit "gives foreign governments and renegade groups a lever for influencing U.S. policy debates. . . . Our adversaries believe they can simply out-wait us."[61] Furthermore, Nunn continues, "any congressional action is subject to veto;" it "encourages Lebanon-type compromises that limit the time of troop deployments," and it "encourages confrontation rather than consultation between Congress and the President."[62] Instead, Senator Nunn has urged the establishment of a consultative mechanism so that the president consults with Congress before taking military action, not afterward.[63] Similarly, Senator Mitchell has proposed that "a permanent consultative group" consisting of leaders of both houses, be established. This small group would meet in times of crisis and upon the introduction of the armed forces into hostilities by the president. It would be empowered to introduce legislation approving or rejecting the action. So far, however, no legislative action has been taken on this proposal. Nor, in view of President Bush's successful conclusion of the Persian Gulf War, does it seem likely that reform or modification of the War Powers Resolution will be a high priority item on the congressional agenda in the immediate months and years ahead.

Still, the frequent presidential-congressional clashes over military policy underscore the persistent need for the president to reach an accommodation with Congress. Unilateral actions, in the long run, are seldom successful enterprises. Generally, the president's power is at its lowest ebb when he undertakes actions that lack the support of Congress. Successful policy requires, at some point, that the president secure the support and cooperation of Congress. Indeed, as Justice Robert H. Jackson noted in the steel seizure case in 1952, presidential authority reaches its highest level when the president's actions are based upon congressional authorization.[64] President Eisenhower's adroit handling of the

Formosa Strait and Lebanese crises during the 1950s immediately come to mind as examples of successful executive-congressional consultation.

As a result of the War Powers Resolution, more than anything else, this uneasy tension between the President and Congress over American military and paramilitary activities abroad will probably continue indefinitely, or at least until the president takes congressional leaders into his full confidence. That this executive-legislative conflict persists should be no surprise, for as former Undersecretary of State George Ball testified at a congressional hearing nearly two decades ago, the War Powers Resolution represented an attempt by Congress to do something which the Founding Fathers thought they could not do—namely, draw the dividing line between the constitutional power of Congress to declare war and the constitutional power of the president as commander in chief.[65]

Plainly, the Framers wanted the best of both worlds—a forceful commander in chief, one able to move quickly to repel attacks against the United States, and a strong-willed Congress, one determined to keep the president within constitutional bounds. Almost two centuries later, maintaining a delicate balance between these twin goals still remains at the top of the American public's agenda.

NOTES

1. *The New York Times*, 19 September 1994.

2. Joseph E. Kallenbach, *The American Chief Executive* (New York: Harper & Row, 1966), 526.

3. Madison to Jefferson, 2 April 1798, Madison, *Writings*, Gaillard Hunt, ed. (New York, 1906), VI, 312–313, as cited by Arthur M. Schlesinger, Jr., *The Imperial Presidency* (Boston: Houghton Mifflin, 1973), 5.

4. Alan Tonelson, *Christian Science Monitor News Service*, as quoted in the *Seattle Times*, 11 March 1984.

5. *The Federalist*, no. 69. In an early case the Supreme Court too ruled that the president's duty and powers as commander in chief were "purely military." *Fleming v. Page*, 9 *Howard* 603, 615 (1815).

6. Schlesinger, *The Imperial Presidency*, 20.

7. The writings of Thomas Jefferson, V, 542–555, as cited by Louis Fisher, *Constitutional Conflicts between Congress and the President* (Princeton, NJ: Princeton University Press, 1985), 288.

8. Schlesinger, *The Imperial Presidency*, 28.

9. Louis W. Koenig, *The Chief Executive*, 4th ed. (New York: Harcourt, Brace & Jovanovich, 1981), 257; Dwight D. Eisenhower, *Mandate for Change* (Garden City, NY: Doubleday, 1963), 181.

10. Koenig, *The Chief Executive*, 257.

11. Charles A. Beard, *The Republic* (New York: Viking Press, 1943), 103.

12. 4 *Wallace* 2 (1866).

13. Clinton Rossiter, *The American Presidency* (New York: Harcourt, Brace, & World, 1956), 23. See also David Gray Adler, "The President's War Making Power," in Thomas E. Cronin, ed. *Inventing the American Presidency* (Lawrence: University Press of Kansas, 1989), 119–153.

14. James Grafton Rogers, *World Policy and the Constitution* (Boston: World Peace Foundation, 1945), 92–123.

15. Information collected by Barry M. Blechman and Steven S. Kaplan, *Force without War* (Washington, DC: The Brookings Institution, 1978), as quoted in Richard M. Pious, *The American Presidency* (New York: Basic Books, 1979), 373.

16. Norman A. Graebner, "The President as Commander in Chief: A Study in Power," in Joseph G. Dawson III, ed. *Commanders in Chief* (Lawrence: University Press of Kansas, 1993), 31.

17. Pious, *The American Presidency*, 374.

18. Stephen E. Ambrose, *Eisenhower,* vol. 1 (New York: Simon & Schuster, 1983), 144–182.

19. It is worth noting that during the Mexican War Lincoln, who was one of President Polk's severest critics, voted for the Ashmun Resolution, which declared the president had "unconstitutionally" begun the war with Mexico. Edward S. Corwin, *The President: Office and Powers, 1787–1984*, 5th ed., revised by Randall W. Bland, Theodore T. Hindson, and Jack W. Peltason (New York: New York University Press, 1984), 496–497, note 7.

20. E. S. Corwin, *The President: Office and Powers*, 5th ed., 264.

21. 2 *Black* 635 (1863).

22. E. S. Corwin, *The President: Office and Powers*, 5th ed., 235.

23. Ibid., 272.

24. Arthur T. Vanderbilt, "War Powers and Their Administration," in *1945 Annual Survey of American Law* (New York: University School of Law), as quoted by Corwin, *The President: Office and Powers*, 5th ed., 507–508, note 62.

25. Schlesinger, *The Imperial Presidency*, 138.

26. Ibid., 140.

27. Ibid., 160.

28. On the Cuban missile crisis, see Graham T. Allison, *Essence of Decision* (Boston: Little, Brown, 1971).

29. Schlesinger, *The Imperial Presidency*, 179.

30. Pious, *The American Presidency*, 387.

31. Schlesinger, *The Imperial Presidency*, 181.

32. Ibid., 184.

33. Congress revoked the Tonkin Gulf Resolution in January 1971; however, the repeal of the resolution did not direct the president to end hostilities.

34. Schlesinger, *The Imperial Presidency*, 187.

35. *The New York Times*, 30 June 1970.

36. *Congressional Quarterly Weekly Report*, 11 August 1973, 2205.

37. The House voted to override President Nixon's veto 284 to 135 (four votes more than needed for the two-thirds majority) on November 7, 1973; the Senate voted to override a few hours later, 75 to 18. The full text of the War Powers Resolution (Public Law 93-148, 93rd Congress, H. J. Res 542, November 7, 1973) is available in Pat M. Holt, *The War Powers Resolution* (Washington, DC: American Enterprise Institute), 43–48.

38. Ibid.

39. Thomas Eagleton, *War and Presidential Power* (New York: Liveright, 1974), 203.

40. Louis Fisher, "Less Than Meets the Eye: Foreign Policy Making and the Myth of the Assertive Congress," book review of Barbara Hinckley (Chicago: University of Chicago Press, 1994) in *American Political Science Review* 89 (March 1995): 207.

41. Pious, *The American Presidency*, 405.

42. This discussion closely follows the analysis of Richard M. Pious, "Presidential War Powers, the War Powers Resolution, and the Persian Gulf," in Martin Fausold and Alan Shank, eds. *The Constitution and the American Presidency* (Albany: State University of New York Press, 1991), 195–210.

43. Letter from President Bush to Senator David L. Boren, Chairman, Senate Select Committee on Intelligence, made available to Daniel P. Franklin, "The President is Too Powerful in Foreign Affairs," in Herbert M. Levine, *Point Counterpoint* (New York: St. Martin's, 1992), 182, note 10.

44. Pious, "Presidential War Powers," 201–202.

45. 462 U.S. 919 (1983).

46. Fisher, *Constitutional Conflicts between Congress and the President*, 313.

47. *Washington Post*, 24 August 1980.

48. *The New York Times*, 2 May 1980.

49. Wkly Comp. Pres. Doc., XVIII, 1232 (29 September 1982), as cited by Fisher, *Constitutional Conflicts between Congress and the President*, 317.

50. *The New York Times*, 3 September 1983.

51. "Getting Back to Normal," *Time*, 23 November 1983, 16–17.

52. Corwin, *The President: Office and Powers*, 5th ed., 301.

53. *The New York Times*, 16 April 1986.

54. Michael J. Glennon, *Constitutional Diplomacy* (Princeton, NJ: Princeton University Press, 1990), 106–107.

55. Quoted in Lyn Ragsdale, *Presidential Politics* (Boston: Houghton Mifflin, 1993), 297.

56. Michael J. Glennon, "The Gulf War and the Constitution," *Foreign Affairs* 70 (Spring 1991): 85.

57. Ibid., 86.

58. Ibid., 84–85.

59. *The New York Times*, 13 January 1991.

60. Glennon, *Constitutional Diplomacy*, 72–73; see also David Gray Adler, "The Constitution and Presidential Warmaking," *Political Science Quarterly* 103 (Spring 1988): 1–36.

61. Ibid., 119–120.

62. Ibid.

63. *The New York Times*, 24 October 1993.

64. *Youngstown Co. v. Sawyer*, 343 U.S. 579, 637 (1952).

65. Pat M. Holt, *The War Powers Resolution* (Washington, DC: American Enterprise Institute, 1978), 1.

CHAPTER 10

CHIEF DIPLOMAT

"The need for crisis management in international affairs has brought about a shift in the locus of decision making from the State Department to the presidential office."[1] This statement by foreign policy experts Cecil V. Crabb, Jr. and Kevin V. Mulcahy accurately describes how American foreign policymaking is handled by the president and his staff in the late twentieth century.

Most recently, President Bill Clinton demonstrated a sure-handed grasp of a relatively uncharted foreign-policy area—trade and international currency—that will increasingly become the focus of U.S. policymakers in the post–Cold War era. The episode began shortly before Christmas in 1994, when the sudden devaluation of the Mexican peso sent it into a free fall, threatening to collapse the Mexican economy and produce huge losses for American investors.

When congressional leaders turned down President Clinton's request for a $40 billion Mexican loan package to rescue the sharply devaluated peso (after initially pledging support for the complicated bailout plan), President Clinton invoked his executive authority to put together a $43 billion loan package (including major support from the International Monetary Fund and the Swiss-based Bank of International Settlements) to help rescue Mexico.[2]

Congressional leaders immediately breathed a sigh of relief, for while they did not want to underwrite a huge loan to Mexico, the lawmakers did not want the Mexican government to fail. If Mexico had been forced to default on $26 billion of its government bonds shock waves would have run throughout markets in Latin America and the U.S. investment community. Some U.S. business leaders had predicted that the Mexican default would have led to the loss of several thousand jobs in the United States that are closely tied to the Mexican economy.

While it is far too early to know if President Clinton's bold loan guarantee package will save Mexico from financial chaos, congressional leaders from both parties and leading members of the New York financial community were quick to praise President Clinton for his decisive leadership in coming up with an innovative rescue plan almost overnight. But as the value of the Mexican peso continued to slide in spring 1995, congressional enthusiasm for the Clinton rescue plan waned.

Recent presidents have authorized their national security advisers and their staffs to create a "little State Department" in the White House basement. This development is not necessarily a reflection on the low esteem that some presidents have had of the State Department, but rather a clear recognition that fast-moving events around the globe demand immediate responses. The fragmentation and competition among the State Department, the Department of Defense, and the CIA over the formulation of policy initiatives have also encouraged presidents to establish a "White House foreign ministry."[3] In recent decades this arrangement has also helped the president contend with the persistent intrusion by members of Congress to reshape and sometimes restrict American foreign policy.

In this chapter we will trace the early development of the president's direction of American foreign policy, explore the constitutional sharing of power between the president and Congress on treaty making, discuss the steady increase in presidential use of executive agreements, comment on the extensive use of presidential special emissaries, evaluate the National Security Council, discuss the shadowy role of the CIA, and assess Congress' continued role in foreign policy formation and oversight. Finally, a brief analysis is made of the president's use of the "two-track" or bi-level system in managing foreign policy: unilateral decision making by the president on one level, and the consultative, shared power approach with Congress on the second level.

CONSTITUTIONAL BACKGROUND

The Founding Fathers concluded that the best way for the young federal republic to avoid the same humiliating treatment from European diplomats experienced under the Articles of Confederation was to vest the president with the management of foreign affairs. Indeed, more than one historian has indicated that it was the ineffectiveness and mismanagement of foreign affairs by Congress under the Articles of Confederation that more than anything else led to the calling of the Constitutional Convention in 1787.

Without doubt, the Founding Fathers had profited considerably from the bitter experience of the Articles of Confederation that a government without an executive branch was impotent to deal with any serious foreign or domestic crisis. Under the Confederation the determination of foreign policy and control of foreign relations lay with Congress, or more accurately after 1781, with the Department of Foreign Affairs. But since no executive or council gave direction to the department, the results were chaotic. Clearly, the need for a single voice in negotiating with other countries had never been brought home more forcefully to the Framers than when the British foreign secretary disdainfully suggested to the American minister in London that if he sent one envoy to the Confederation, he would have to send thirteen.[4]

That the Framers vested the handling of foreign affairs in the hands of a president is not surprising, since their principal sources—Blackstone, Locke, and Montesquieu—were unanimous in contending that the power to conduct foreign relations must reside with the executive. Even so, under the Constitution the Framers granted the power to declare war to Congress, not the president. Under the Articles of Confederation, the power to declare war had also been vested in Congress. But the Framers required that treaties obtain the consent of the Senate, and by a two-thirds vote. The Senate's advice and consent was also required for the president's appointment of all ambassadors. Indeed, two close students of foreign policy have commented: "The Framers of the Constitution clearly intended that *virtually no international business should be conducted by the president alone*" (italics in source).[5]

This shared constitutional power over foreign affairs, it could be predicted, made conflict between the two branches almost inevitable. Especially granting authority to Congress to approve appropriations, which can be essential to the development and execution of foreign policy decisions and to confirm all ambassadorial appointments, was in the words of one leading authority: "an invitation to struggle for the privilege of directing American foreign policy."[6] Still, the president holds most of the trump cards in directing foreign affairs.

George Washington firmly established the principle of executive authority over foreign affairs at the inception of his presidency. His proclamation of neutrality in 1793 to avoid taking sides in the European conflict, based upon his prerogative to determine foreign policy, aroused the ire of several factional groups. Those sympathetic to the French Revolution were incensed, as were the unreconstructed anti-Federalists, who had all along distrusted the national government and its "elected king." Despite the vehemence of the attacks, Washington's view of presidential authority over foreign affairs prevailed and continues to the present to be the constitutional doctrine governing our relations with other nations.

Next to his duties as commander in chief and chief administrator, the role of chief diplomat is probably the third most important function performed by the president of the United States. In the past, however, the dominant voice in foreign policymaking has from time to time shifted between the Congress and the president. Clearly, the Spanish-American War was a congressionally sponsored war, heavily pushed by jingoist lawmakers and reluctantly acquiesced to by President William McKinley. Teddy Roosevelt, on the other hand, was an activist president determined to make the United States a first-class world power by his "big stick" diplomacy. To head off European intervention, Roosevelt moved American forces into Santo Domingo in 1904 to collect customs and duties for transmission to European creditors. A year later, Roosevelt agreed to offer his "good offices" and convene an international conference at Algeciras, a small seaport town in southern Spain near Gibraltar, to avert a major crisis between France and Germany over Morocco. Within a few months Roosevelt's diplomatic leadership in the Far East brought an end to the Russo-Japanese War in 1905. For his efforts in settling these two conflicts Roosevelt was awarded the Nobel Peace Prize in 1906. Woodrow Wilson also soon turned into a world statesman, but the Senate shattered his fondest dream—membership in the League of Nations—by rejecting the Versailles Treaty.

Throughout the period between the two world wars, isolationism dominated U.S. foreign policy. But Franklin D. Roosevelt's skilled diplomatic talents eventually enabled him to outmaneuver the isolationist-minded Congress and bring the United States to the aid of beleaguered Great Britain before America's entry into World War II.

Presidential domination of foreign policy continued after World War II, the Korean War, and through the early and middle period of the Vietnam War. But a congressional resurgence occurred with the passage of the War Powers Act in 1973. Since then, an uneasy power balance over foreign affairs has existed between the executive and legislative branches.

Despite frequent congressional involvement in foreign affairs, however, the president still remains the chief diplomat. There is no better recent example of this role than President Bill Clinton's decision to hold a summit meeting in December 1993 in Vancouver, Canada, with Russian President Boris Yeltsin to discuss helping the leader of the largest former Soviet republic to master the transition from the state-run economy to a more privately oriented economic system. Also, Mr. Clinton was anxious to tie up the loose ends of the unfinished START nuclear weapons reduction pact.

The president's power in foreign relations rests on both constitutional and international law, as well as his authority as commander in chief.

CONSTITUTIONAL PREROGATIVES

First of all, the Constitution designates the president as the official channel for communications to and from other countries. The president appoints all ambassadors and consular officials and through the diplomatic corps maintains contact and receives reports from abroad through the State Department. He may appoint special envoys to work in some of the international trouble spots. All official negotiations with foreign countries are conducted under his overall direction, though usually through the State Department. Some aspects of presidential power in foreign affairs go far beyond votes in Congress. The President's power to negotiate with foreign governments, for example, is an authority that is virtually unlimited by the Constitution.

Second, the power of recognizing foreign governments derives from the presidential role in sending and receiving diplomatic representatives as well as international law. Early in our country's history, Washington set the precedent in 1793 when he received Citizen Genet as the official representative of the French government and then some months later demanded his recall by France, without consulting Congress in either instance. Decisions on the timing and establishment of diplomatic relations, such as Franklin Roosevelt's decision to recognize the Soviet Union in 1933 and Nixon's decision to open a diplomatic dialogue with Communist China in 1972, after twenty-three years of nonrecognition following the Communist takeover of mainland China in 1949, are two examples of the president's control over foreign policy that immediately come to mind. More recently, President George Bush's decision on his timing to recognize the half dozen new governments formed as a result of the breakup of the Soviet Union helped launch these breakaway republics of the new Commonwealth of Independent States (CIS). But Mr. Bush, out of courtesy to departing President Mikhail Gorbachev, delayed supporting the new Commonwealth until after Mr. Gorbachev's formal retirement.[7]

Third, the president's constitutional authority as commander in chief gives him wide latitude in implementing his foreign policy. By use of the armed forces, the president can further his foreign policy goals and enforce American rights and interests abroad.

Shortly after the turn of the century, Theodore Roosevelt moved American naval vessels near the Isthmus of Panama, then under the suzerainty of Colombia, to prevent the Colombian army from putting down the Panamanian insurrectionists. Within days Roosevelt recognized the insurgent government and quickly signed the Hay-Bunau-Varilla Treaty, which contained such advantageous terms as to make the newly founded Panamanian Republic a virtual military outpost of the United States.[8] One wag reportedly quoted Teddy as claiming, "I stole Panama, fair and square!" Three years later Roosevelt sent the newly expanded U.S. fleet around the world to demonstrate American power and influence.

In March 1917, while the United States sought to maintain neutrality in World War I, Woodrow Wilson ordered the arming of American merchant vessels, despite congressional opposition, as a move to counter unrestricted German submarine warfare. In 1958, Eisenhower sent 10,000 American troops to Lebanon to maintain an uneasy truce between warring Christian and Muslim factions. The mammoth American intervention in Vietnam, which in 1965 saw over 525,000 soldiers sent to help try to save South Vietnam from a North Vietnamese takeover, ended in failure a decade later. But Lyndon Johnson's actions, even though "legitimized" by the congressional Gulf of Tonkin Resolution, underscored the broad authority that an American president can exercise to aid friendly countries. Indeed, the president can, by his management of foreign affairs and his use of American troops, so influence foreign policy and trigger events that Congress may have little choice but to support presidential actions, even to the extent of declaring war.

It is noteworthy that of all the wars in which the United States has been involved, only two—the War of 1812 and the Spanish-American War (1898–1899)—were clearly the result of congressional policy. Though congressional sentiment generally supported administration policies leading to the outbreak of hostilities, the development of these policies was basically a product of White House actions. More recently, President Reagan invaded the Caribbean island of Grenada. President Bush invaded Panama in December 1989, and then eight months later, quickly dispatched more than 200,000 American troops to Saudi Arabia as the initial step in evicting Saddam Hussein's Iraqi forces from Kuwait.

THE SUPREME COURT'S SUPPORT

Throughout American history the Supreme Court has been content most of the time to play a passive role in the foreign policy process. When the High Court has ruled on foreign policy cases (which it does only infrequently), it has almost always taken one of two positions: either it has declared foreign policy cases to be political questions that are not susceptible to resolution by the justices, or it has forcefully upheld the exercise of presidential power.[9]

Supreme Court decisions have repeatedly recognized the president's exclusive position as "the sole organ of the federal government in international relations." While this doctrine has long been accepted, the Supreme Court did not formally enunciate this position until 1936—almost 150 years after ratification of the U.S. Constitution in *U.S. v. Curtiss-Wright Export Corporation*.[10]

This case involved a joint resolution passed by Congress in 1934 authorizing the president by a neutrality proclamation to prohibit the sale within the United States of military equipment destined for Bolivia or Paraguay, then locked in the protracted Gran Chaco War. Franklin D. Roosevelt promptly issued such a declaration. The Curtiss-Wright Aircraft Company, which had shipped fifty machine guns to Bolivia, was convicted of violating the presidential proclamation and joint resolution. But in court aircraft company lawyers challenged the joint resolutions on the grounds that the statute constituted an unlawful delegation of legislative authority to the president because the action left "unfettered discretion" to the executive with no statutory guidelines to govern his decision. They felt confident that they would win their case because the Supreme Court had recently invalidated two New Deal NRA (National Recovery Administration) cases as an unconstitutional delegation of congressional authority.[11]

But in *Curtiss-Wright* Justice Sutherland differentiated this case from the previous NRA cases by pointing out that the two earlier cases had "related solely to internal affairs," whereas the "whole aim" of the neutrality resolution was "to affect a situation entirely external to the United States." In this latter area Justice Sutherland declared that the president possessed not only powers given to him by the statute, but also "the very delicate, plenary and exclusive power of the President as the sole organ of the federal government in the field of international relations."[12]

This definitive ruling on the plenary power of the president in foreign affairs was not seriously questioned for almost half a century—until the aftermath of the Iranian hostage crisis in 1981. But a section of President Carter's executive agreement on claims settlement with Iran, which canceled all attachments against Iranian assets in the United States and transferred from U.S. courts to an international tribunal all legal claims by American firms against Iran, was challenged by a number of American corporations that had done business with the former shah's government. The president's agreement, however, was upheld by the Supreme Court in *Dames & Moore v. Regan* (1981).[13] The Court ruled that the 1977 Emergency Economic Powers Act explicitly gave the president authority to void attachments against Iranian assets in the United States.

While the Court found no statutory authorization for the transfer of legal claims out of the United States, the justices held that Congress had "implicitly" approved Carter's action by a long pattern of acquiescence in permitting the presidential settlement of claims disputes with other countries. Once again, the Iranian claims decision reaffirmed the Court's support of broad presidential authority to resolve thorny international problems, even though no specific grant of this power is found in the Constitution.

More recently, the Supreme Court in 1984 again defended presidential action in foreign affairs. By a five to four vote, the High Court upheld a Reagan administration order designed to keep Americans from going to Castro's Cuba. The specific order was a Treasury Department regulation forbidding U.S. citizens to spend money on travel to Cuba.[14] Critics cited the ruling as another example of the Court's tendency to exalt presidential power. In this case, the justices did so by a strained interpretation of congressional statutes.

TREATY-MAKING AUTHORITY

The Founding Fathers envisaged treaty making as a joint presidential-congressional enterprise. But in practice the necessity of securing Senate consent by a two-thirds vote for the ratification of treaties has proven to be a sharp limitation on executive management of foreign policymaking. The men of 1787 thought the Senate would serve as a type of council with which the president would sit while treaties were being drafted and from which he would regularly obtain advice. As a matter of fact, Washington attempted to pursue this course of action, going directly in person to the Senate in August 1789 and presenting seven issues pertaining to a proposed treaty with the Southern Indians on which he sought "advice and consent." But the senators indicated that they wished to consult privately among themselves and then voted to refer the proposed treaty to a committee of five. Washington indicated his displeasure with the manner in which the Senate treated him as he left the chamber. Two days later, he returned to the Senate for an answer to his questions, but the entire episode proved so unproductive that no other president has repeated the experience.

When treaties are sent to the Senate in final form for ratification, their fate is often uncertain. Secretary of State John Hay, who served under Theodore Roosevelt, once wrote: "A treaty entering the Senate is like a bull going into the arena; no one can say just how or when the final blow will fall—but one thing is certain, it will never leave the arena alive."[15] While Hay's observation is, of course, exaggerated, treaties are frequently ruined by unacceptable amendments and reservations. Woodrow Wilson learned to his dismay that an intransigent minority in the U.S. Senate could scuttle a treaty no matter what the long-term consequences of the rejection might be. The Versailles Treaty, which would have provided for United States membership in the League of Nations, failed to receive the necessary two-thirds majority by a vote of forty-nine "yeas" and thirty-four "nays."[16] Still, throughout the course of American history the vast majority of treaties has been approved by the Senate. Between 1789 and 1982, for example, only nineteen treaties out of approximately 1,400 submitted to the Senate were rejected.[17]

Despite the president's wishes, the Senate can defeat a treaty entirely or consent to ratification with amendments. If the Senate tacks on amendments, the president must, if he still favors the treaty, secure the acceptance of these amendments by the foreign power(s) involved before the treaty can be ratified. A recalcitrant Senate may also attach reservations, which do not directly alter the content of the treaty, but which qualify or modify the obligations assumed by the United States under the treaty. In some instances, the Senate neither approves nor disapproves a treaty; the lawmakers simply refuse to act upon the pact. This inaction is equivalent to rejection. Also, the threat of an adverse vote can induce a president to withdraw White House support for a treaty under Senate consideration. This occurred in early 1980 when President Carter, in effect, withdrew the SALT-II arms control agreement with the Soviet Union after the Russians invaded Afghanistan.[18] Though SALT-II still remained, technically speaking, "before" the Senate, the agreement fell into limbo because President Carter ceased pressing for its ratification and then left office.

Some critics of the treaty ratification process have pointed out that senators representing 7 percent of the population—the seventeen least populous states—theoretically could block ratification of a major treaty. As an alternative, approval by a majority vote of both houses of Congress—or just the Senate—has been suggested. But this change would of course require amending the Constitution—no easy task.

By its general lawmaking authority, Congress can also frustrate or limit presidential foreign policymaking. In 1924, for example, Congress passed the Japanese Exclusion Act over the protests of President Coolidge and Secretary of State Charles Evans Hughes, with damaging long-range consequences on the relations between the two countries. In the 1930s, President Franklin D. Roosevelt's reciprocal trade agreements, especially with Latin American countries, came under increasing congressional scrutiny, requiring legislative approval every two or three years. More recently, Congress has also resorted to statutory bans on trade or aid to countries in congressional disfavor.

Legislative power can be used sometimes, however, to fill the breach caused by the Senate's rejection of a treaty. Following the defeat of the Treaty of Versailles ending World War I, Congress resorted to a joint resolution to bring American participation in the war against the Central Powers (Germany and Austria) to a legal conclusion in 1921. It is also noteworthy that to minimize the possibility of congressional rejection, American membership in the United Nations Organization was accomplished not by treaty but by congressional statute, the United Nations Participation Act of 1945.

EXECUTIVE AGREEMENTS

Presidents prefer to negotiate executive agreements instead of treaties. The reason is simple. A two-thirds majority vote of the Senate is needed for ratification of all treaties; executive agreements require no Senate action. Executive agreements are not mentioned in the Constitution, nor does the nation's fundamental charter allude to any independent power on the part of the chief executive to make international agreements. But in the twentieth century, executive agreements have frequently been used to handle matters of major importance.

One of the most famous executive agreements—the destroyer-bases deal—was concluded in 1940 between President Franklin D. Roosevelt and Prime Minister Winston Churchill. Under this pact the United States, then neutral, agreed to transfer fifty over-age destroyers to the hard-pressed British to help their anti-submarine campaign against Nazi U-boats. The United States, in return, received ninety-nine year leases on a string of British islands in the Caribbean to strengthen long-range defenses around the Panama Canal.[19] Two other major World War II international agreements—the Yalta and Potsdam pacts—were in fact executive agreements.

Over the years the executive branch has claimed four sources of constitutional authority to make executive agreements:

1. the president's authority as commander in chief;
2. his duty as chief executive to conduct foreign policy;

3. his authority to receive ambassadors and other public ministers; and

4. his duty to "take care that the laws are faithfully executed."

Attempts to distinguish the legal effects of executive agreements from treaties have generally failed. Nor has the contention that the force of an executive agreement terminates with the end of the administration which negotiated it been upheld in the courts.

The contention that executive agreements, unlike treaties, are not the "law of the land" unless approved by Congress has no standing in the courts. In *United States v. Belmont* (1937),[20] the U.S. Supreme Court specifically rejected this contention, holding that the recognition of Soviet Russia in 1933 and the accompanying executive agreements constituted an international compact which the president was entitled to sign without consulting the Senate. This case developed after President Roosevelt had agreed with the Soviet authorities that title to all nationalized properties of the Soviet Union in this country would be handed over to the U.S. government. Under the Litvinov Assignment, the United States would then decide which assets would be returned to the Soviet Union.

Furthermore, the Court ruled in *United States v. Pink* (1942),[21] that executive agreements have the same effect as treaties in superseding conflicting state laws. In 1955, however, the Supreme Court in *United States v. Guy W. Capps, Inc.* struck down an executive agreement, because it contravened an existing federal commercial statute with Canada.[22] Two years later, the Supreme Court in *Reid v. Covert* invalidated an executive agreement that permitted American military courts in Great Britain to rely on trial by court-martial for offenses committed by American military personnel or their dependents. The plaintiff's lawyer successfully argued for the constitutional right to a trial by jury.[23]

Continued unhappiness with the widespread use of executive agreements became a major issue in the United States Senate shortly after World War II. In the late 1940s and early 1950s, Senator John Bricker (R-OH) spearheaded a constitutional amendment drive to limit the scope of international treaties and to prevent the use of executive agreements to circumvent the role of the Senate in the treaty-making process. Supported heavily by isolationist Republicans from the Midwest—Bricker had been the vice presidential running mate of Thomas E. Dewey in the 1944 presidential race—and other senators opposed to strong presidential leadership in foreign affairs, the Bricker Amendment came within one vote in the Senate of securing the necessary two-thirds majority in 1955.[24]

Recent presidents have often used executive agreements to make end runs around the treaty process—sometimes without informing Congress of the content of those agreements. Although Congress passed legislation in 1950 requiring the secretary of state to publish annually all executive agreements concluded during the previous year, the executive branch in a number of instances withheld information on those agreements it considered to be sensitive to this country's national security.[25] News of these secret agreements did not come to light until the Vietnam War hearings. Members of Congress were told that America's commitment to the South Vietnamese grew in part out of executive agreements made between American presidents and the South Vietnamese government.[26] These startling revelations prompted Congress to establish a special committee to investigate the nature of American commitments abroad made via executive agreements. Congressional probes turned up a variety of important commitments that had never been revealed to the legislators. Included among these commitments were promises of American military support for the Ethiopian army, apparent or implied commitments for the defense of Thailand and the Philippines, and even a commitment to defend the far-right Franco regime in Spain against *internal* uprisings.[27]

Executive agreements now clearly outnumber treaties. During the first half century under the Constitution, sixty of the eighty-seven international agreements to which the United States was a signatory, and all the major agreements, were made in the form of treaties. In the next fifty years (1839–1889), the record shows that there were 215 treaties, again including the major pacts, and 238 executive agreements. Between 1946 and 1976, according to one team of researchers, the United States entered into 7,201 executive agreements with foreign countries (excluding over sixty secret agreements that the State Department reported to Congress between 1972 and 1977)—almost twenty times the number of treaties during this period (see Table 10.1).[28] Since the onset of World War II, executive agreements have become the standard method, not the exception, for implementing foreign policy, as Table 10.1 indicates. No wonder political scientist Louis W. Koenig concluded years ago that it became clear from the experience of Franklin D. Roosevelt's administration that "the President can accomplish by Executive Agreement anything that can be done by treaty."[29]

By the early 1970s members of Congress exhibited growing concern that the legislative branch had been excluded from participation in numerous major decisions affecting American commitments abroad. Many legislators felt, with considerable justification, that these secret agreements abridged Congress's foreign affairs power under the Constitution. To halt this erosion of authority and gain some control over these foreign commitments, Congress passed the Case Act. Signed into law in 1972 by President Nixon, the Case Act required that the president transmit all executive agreements to Congress within sixty days after they had been negotiated. The provisions of this act, named after its chief sponsor, Senator Clifford Case (R-NJ), further required that Congress must be informed of all executive agreements in effect at the time this act was passed. But the Case Act required that only the House Foreign Affairs Commit-

Table 10.1
Treaties and Executive Agreements

Period	Treaties	Executive Agreements
1789-1839	60	27
1839-1889	215	238
1889-1939	524	917
1940-1970	310	5653
1971-1977	110	2062
1978-1980	62	1052
1981-1990	151	3594
TOTAL	1,432	13,543

Sources: Louis Fisher, *President and Congress: Power and Policy*, 45. Copyright © 1972 by The Free Press, a division of Simon & Schuster, Inc. Reprinted with permission of the publisher; figures for 1971–1980 provided by the Department of State, Washington, DC; figures for 1981–1990 are from Harold W. Stanley and Richard G. Niemi, eds., *Vital Statistics on American Politics*, 3rd ed. (Washington, DC: CQ Press, 1992), 278.

tee and the Senate Foreign Relations Committee be informed of secret executive agreements.

Has the Case Act accomplished its objective? The short-hand answer is no. Despite passage of the Case Act, experience since the 1970s shows that Congress has not been able to impose effective limits upon the president's power to enter into agreements with foreign countries. The record shows that the executive branch has informed Congress only of those pacts that fall under its own definition of executive agreements. In fact, the Nixon administration failed to report a number of international agreements, notably several negotiated with the government of South Vietnam. Less than three years after passage of the Case Act, Congressman Les Aspin (D-WI) (more recently, Secretary of Defense in the Clinton Administration), estimated that the United States had entered into between 400 and 600 agreements with foreign governments, none of which had been reported to Congress.[30]

One of the most dangerous secret agreements to surface was President Nixon's letter to President Thieu of South Vietnam, in which he stated that the United States would "respond with full force should the settlement (i.e., the Paris Peace Agreement) be violated by North Vietnam."[31] Senator Case, among others, contended that this secret commitment constituted an international accord that should have been transmitted to Congress for review. Nixon's original failure to abide by the Case Act ultimately provoked Congress to refuse to authorize additional military aid for the South Vietnamese government following North Vietnam's final invasion of the South in 1975. Among the more controversial executive agreements are military base agreements with Spain, Diego Garcia, and Bahrain.

Several bills have been introduced in Congress to correct the omissions or ambiguities in the Case Act. These proposals have sought to clarify what constitutes an executive agreement and also provide that Congress may, if it wishes, reject such agreements within sixty days after they have been signed. But these proposals have not generated strong support. Presidents have pointed out with some justification that they cannot be effective negotiators if their hands are tied while trying to make firm commitments with foreign governments. Further, presidents have persuasively argued that carefully negotiated compromises might come unraveled while waiting for Congress to make up its mind to approve or reject such agreements.

Can the president terminate an existing treaty? While there is general agreement that treaty making is a shared power between the president and Congress, the president appears to have the authority to terminate a treaty without Senate consent. At the time President Carter moved to establish full diplomatic relations with the People's Republic of China, he announced his intention to terminate the American defense pact with the Chinese Nationalist government in Taiwan, as of January 1, 1980. As justification for his action, Carter could point to a provision of the treaty permitting termination after one year's notice. Since no mention was made of Senate participation in the terminating action, the president felt that he was on solid ground in unilaterally nullifying the pact. Moreover, precedent for treaty termination could be found in several nineteenth- and twentieth-century diplomatic actions.

No sooner had the treaty abrogation been announced, however, than Senator Barry Goldwater (R-AZ) and other administration critics declared that Senate consent was implicit in the Constitution and in the treaty. He pointed out that the Senate had passed a resolution in 1978 requiring the president to engage in "prior consultation" before making any changes in American foreign policy toward Taiwan. Under Goldwater's leadership, a "sense of the Senate" resolution condemning the president's action was adopted by a vote of fifty-nine to thirty-five, but it had no legal effect on the executive branch's establishment of diplomatic relations with Communist China. Opponents of Carter's actions then turned to the courts. Initially, Goldwater's argument was supported by a U.S. federal district court. But in late 1979 the Supreme Court, by a seven to two vote, reversed the decision, holding that President Carter had the constitutional authority to abrogate the defense pact with Taiwan, without Senate approval.[32] In 1981, Senator Barry Goldwater introduced legislation to require a two-thirds affirmative vote in the Senate to terminate defense treaties. But Congress thus far has not acted on this bill or any other clarifying legislation.

Presidents, it might be noted, may sometimes withdraw treaties from the Senate before a final ratification vote is taken. If the Senate attaches too many conditions or reservations to a proposed treaty, the president may decide not to go through with the ratification process. In 1912, for example, President Taft dropped further ratification plans for arbitration treaties with Great Britain and France, even though the Senate had approved them by a vote of seventy-six to three, after the Senate emasculated them by exempting from arbitration just about every question of importance that any other nation might want to arbitrate, including state debts and the Monroe Doctrine.[33] President Carter, as mentioned earlier, asked the U.S. Senate to drop further consideration of the Strategic Arms Limitation Treaty (SALT-II) after the Soviet Union's invasion of Afghanistan in 1979 made defeat of the treaty almost a certainty. Carter, however, insisted that the pact, which included limitations on heavy bombers and ballistic missiles, was still in the national interest.

THE NATIONAL SECURITY COUNCIL

Foreign policy and national security considerations rarely fit neatly into separate compartments. Since the end of World War II the president has had an additional coordinating agency—the National Security Council—for handling the frequently overlapping and sometimes chaotic aspects of American foreign policy. The National Security Council, established in 1947, was created to help the president coordinate the far-flung activities of the foreign policy bureaucracy, the military establishment, and the intelligence community. Since then, the National Security Council has on more than one occasion been the *de facto* foreign policy agency for the president. Intended originally as a coordinating agency for the president, the National Security Council under some of its ambitious directors—McGeorge Bundy, Henry Kissinger, and Zbigniew Brzezinski—has often overshadowed the State Department in formulating foreign policy.

Founded partly as a congressional reaction to the free wheeling manner in which President Roosevelt and the military chiefs had dominated policymaking during World War II, the National Security Council (NSC) was a major segment of the National Security Act of 1947, which unified the Army, Navy, and Air Force (established in the act as a separate service) into the single new Department of Defense. The 1947 legislation also created the Central Intelligence Agency. Congress prescribed the NSC's chief function as "advising the President with respect to the integration of domestic, foreign, and military policies relating to the national security."

Though President Truman was initially suspicious of a legislatively mandated advisory body, he wasted no time in establishing his authority over the National Security Council by integrating it fully into the Executive Office of the President. Further, he determined that the NSC should be dominated by the Department of State, not the Department of Defense, as sought by the first secretary of Defense, James Forrestal. Following the outbreak of the Korean War, Truman used the NSC as an advisory forum to coordinate military and political responses to the Soviet-backed North Korean challenge.

Eisenhower continued the policy established by Truman of using the NSC as an advisory forum, strictly under the wing of Secretary of State John Foster Dulles. Eisenhower, however, enlarged the staff and assigned the council responsibility for reviewing and analyzing agency positions. Especially significant was Eisenhower's creation in 1953 of the position of special assistant for national security, who in subsequent administrations became a major factor in military and foreign policy development.

Kennedy seldom used the National Security Council as a forum for obtaining policy advice. Probably the most significant structural development within the NSC during the Kennedy administration was the enhancement of the role of the special assistant and the NSC staff. Under Special Assistant McGeorge Bundy, the National Security Council became the principal policy adviser to the president, with the responsibility of managing day-to-day national security affairs and meeting regularly with President Kennedy. Equally important, the position of the special assistant and the NSC staff gained major influence over foreign policy at the expense of the secretary of state and his department. This development did not entirely displease Kennedy; the young president frequently expressed displeasure in private with the State Department's ponderous handling of foreign policy matters.

President Lyndon Johnson ignored the National Security Council as a major advisory council. Instead, he relied chiefly on the "Tuesday lunch group"—the secretaries of state and defense, the special assistant for national security affairs, the director of the CIA, and the chairman of the Joint Chiefs—for advice and counsel on foreign affairs and especially the conduct of the Vietnam War. Johnson, according to one source, "convened the full NSC primarily for 'educational, ratification, and ceremonial purposes.' "[34] But he depended heavily upon Special Assistant for National Security Affairs McGeorge Bundy, a holdover from the Kennedy administration, until Bundy left government service in 1966.

Nixon, with the guidance of Special Assistant for National Security Affairs Henry Kissinger, developed a highly formal White House-centered system for the management of national security policymaking and coordination. Kissinger, in effect, displaced Secretary of State William Rogers as the chief architect of American foreign policy. Kissinger's flamboyant "shuttle diplomacy" produced a flurry of activity and left Rogers shuffling papers in his Foggy Bottom office. Eventually Rogers resigned. Political scientists Richard A. Watson and Norman Thomas have commented: "The result of the Nixon-Kissinger system was to convert what had originally been a staff position, the special assistant, into a main line operator. . . . Also, the NSC staff assumed many functions involving policy implementation and interagency coordination formerly performed by the State Department."[35] Thus, while the National Security Council is not an independent arm within the executive branch, it has become "a major component of what has grown into a highly influential in-house presidential advisory system."[36]

When Kissinger became secretary of state in 1973 (while retaining the special assistant's portfolio), the controversy between a State Department-centered foreign policy and a White House-centered policy abated. But the rivalry resurfaced again during the Carter administration. Secretary of State Cyrus R. Vance and Zbigniew Brezezinski, the special assistant for national affairs, were publicly at odds, especially with respect to dealing with the Soviet Union. While Brzezinski did not eclipse Vance as the principal national security adviser to President Carter, he nevertheless enjoyed co-equal status with the secretary of state—a condition that sometimes created the impression of inept handling of national security-foreign affairs policies within the administration.[37]

Reagan's announced commitment to cabinet government and major policy roles for the secretaries of state and defense suggested that the primary responsibility for foreign policy implementation would return to the State Department. And so it appeared when the strong-minded former White House aide, General Alexander M. Haig, was appointed secretary of state. But Haig's resignation two years later over policy differences with the White House staff once again opened the door for a series of national security assistants—six during Reagan's two terms. Haig's replacement, former Secretary of the Treasury George P. Shultz, came into office with strong credentials as a problem-solving member in the Nixon and Ford cabinets. Secretary of State Shultz, however, had to contend not only with these shifting national security advisers, but also Secretary of Defense Caspar Weinberger, an old friend of President Reagan since their state government days in California, who often had the president's ear. President Bush appointed his old friend and political confidant, James A. Baker III, as secretary of state and left the daily management of foreign affairs in his hands. But Bush also listened closely to his national security adviser, General Brent Scowcroft, a veteran Washington insider since the Ford administration.[38]

For the first few months of the new Clinton administration, Secretary of State Warren Christopher appeared to be its leading voice in foreign affairs. His reputation rested heavily on his success during the Carter administration in winning the release of fifty-two American hostages from Ayatollah Khomeini's Iranian revolutionaries in early 1980, after more than a year of failed negotiations. But a series of diplomatic missteps, especially negotiations surrounding economic sanctions and a most favored nation clause in a proposed trade agreement with Communist China and the Serbian-Bosnia peace talks, badly tarnished Christopher's reputation. President Bill Clinton's preoccupation with domestic issues has given critics of his foreign policy a constant source of ammunition. By mid-summer 1994 Washington insiders were predicting a major shake-up on the Clinton foreign policymaking team, but nothing happened.[39]

The Secretary of State's Declining Role

Traditional nineteenth-century doctrine had it that the secretary of state made foreign policy. But the emergence of the United States as a world power at the beginning of the twentieth century led several presidents to become their own secretaries of state. Theodore Roosevelt, though blessed with two strong secretaries, John Hay and Elihu Root, nevertheless ran the ship of state with gusto. President Wilson, after his legislative successes in 1913 and 1914, increasingly turned his attention to foreign affairs. He became heavily involved in the growing crisis with Mexico and then sought to maintain American neutrality during World War I until unrestricted German submarine warfare led him to obtain from Congress a declaration of war against the Central Powers in April 1917. During this period one secretary of state, William Jennings Bryan, resigned, and his replacement, Robert Lansing worked in the shadow of Wilson.

Franklin D. Roosevelt chose respected Senator Cordell Hull of Tennessee to be his secretary of state, though he kept most of the foreign policy reins in his own hands. Harry Truman, in describing his duties to a group of White House visitors one afternoon, unabashedly announced, "I make foreign policy."[40] But this pattern of action flowed more from the conception of the office held by these presidents, rather than any structural changes in the management of foreign affairs. President Truman, it should be noted, worked very closely with his two outstanding secretaries of state—General George C. Marshall and his successor, Dean Acheson.

John F. Kennedy chose to use his trusted White House staff and Special Assistant for National Security McGeorge Bundy to maximize his own influence in foreign affairs. Johnson, as indicated earlier, retained Bundy as assistant for national security, and in the eyes of many observers, permitted Bundy to exercise authority equal to that of Secretary of State Dean Rusk and Secretary of Defense Robert McNamara.

Special Emissaries

Throughout our history presidents have from time to time employed special emissaries to handle delicate missions that, for various reasons, they did not wish to entrust to regular ambassadors. Unlike ambassadors and ministers, the special emissaries are appointed solely by the president, without Senate approval. Although not mentioned specifically in the Constitution, their appointment may be implied from the treaty power and the all-purpose executive power clause.

Early in our history, Thomas Jefferson sent future president James Monroe to the court of Napoleon Bonaparte to assist Robert Livingston with the crucially important Louisiana Purchase. Before World War I, Woodrow Wilson dispatched his special agent, Colonel Edward House, to Europe on a number of secret missions. During World War II, Franklin D. Roosevelt relied heavily on his personal confidant, Harry Hopkins, to conduct high-level negotiations with Prime Minister Winston Churchill and Soviet Dictator Josef Stalin.

To be sure, not all special envoys have succeeded in their tasks. Still, the publicity surrounding their mission often buys the president time to deal with political ramifications at home while the international crisis receives close attention from the president's hand-picked personal representative. Presidents also like to get fresh, first-hand reports from their emissaries, who have not been deeply involved in the internal politics of the host country and its neighbors. Heads of state and foreign ministers, in turn, like to deal with special envoys because they know their discussions will reach the president directly, not be filtered through several layers of the State Department bureaucracy. Furthermore, they are confident that the president of the United States will honor any agreements made by his personal representative.

THE CIA AND OTHER SECRET OPERATIONS

Presidents sometimes rely on covert operations conducted by the Central Intelligence Agency (CIA) to help achieve foreign policy objectives. Readers of *The New York Times* learned in early July 1983, for example, that the CIA was funding a CIA-backed anti-Sandinista guerrilla force of several thousand in an attempt to overthrow the Marxist government of Nicaragua.[41] Nor was this the first instance since its founding in 1947 that the CIA had been heavily involved in paramilitary and counterrevolutionary operations.

Though the National Security Act of 1947, which authorized the establishment of the Central Intelligence Agency, says nothing about paramilitary operations, the CIA has been involved in this activity sporadically almost from the day of its founding. Soon after the China mainland fell to the Communists in 1949, the CIA started providing military and logistical support to the Chinese Nationalists on Taiwan for mounting raids against the offshore islands and the China coast.

President Eisenhower had a reputation for straightforward diplomacy, but he frequently utilized the CIA's undercover activity to attain some of his objectives. The CIA's most notable "successes" during the Eisenhower administration included aiding the overthrow of the left-wing Arbas regime in Guatemala (1954) and of the anti-American Mossadegh regime in Iran (1955). But the CIA was much less successful in its efforts to install a friendly government in Indonesia in 1954. Information also came to light from various sources that the CIA in the early 1970s sought to destabilize the Marxist-oriented government of Chilean President Salvadore Allende by supporting various right-wing opposition groups within the country.

Testimony has also appeared that the CIA may have engaged in assassination attempts on the heads of foreign states, including Fidel Castro of Cuba. Some sources have even hinted that as a result of this anti-Castro plot, the assassination of President John F. Kennedy may have had a "Cuban connection." In any case, it has only been in the last two decades that American citizens have become more aware of how prominent a role the Central Intelligence Agency has played in presidential foreign policy.

Should the CIA engage in the subversion of foreign governments by supporting insurgent forces or engaging in various "dirty tricks" to topple unfriendly governments? Does this type of activity abroad coincide with the democratic ideals or pretensions of the American system of government? Many citizens and legislators are deeply troubled by the contradictions generated by these practices as this country confronts totalitarian forces abroad.

In 1980, Congress passed the Accountability for Intelligence Activities Act, signed by President Carter shortly before the general election. In essence, this legislation stated that the president will normally be required to provide Congress with advance notification of any covert operations planned by the CIA. The 1980 act also reduced to two the number of committees that must be informed of covert operations and further stipulated that these committees must be kept "fully and currently informed of all U.S. intelligence activities." But the legislation stated that the two committees could not veto intelligence operations reported to its members."[42]

Whether the Intelligence Activities Act of 1980 will sufficiently rein in CIA activities and assure adequate congressional oversight remains an unanswered question. Nor did Congress anticipate that President Reagan would, knowingly or unknowingly, permit the establishment of secret intelligence operations run out of the basement of the White House by members of the National Security Council staff, led by Marine Lt. Colonel Oliver North.

Revelations of the Iran-Contra secret dealings understandably triggered a furor on Capitol Hill because Congress had passed legislation in 1984—the so-called Boland Amendment—banning all shipments of arms to the Contras. Democratic demands for a full-blown investigation soon led to a joint House-Senate Iran-Contra investigation. These hearings, highlighted by Colonel North's ringing patriotic defense of his actions in fighting Communists, ended inconclusively. But the joint committee report contained harsh language condemning North's superior, National Security Adviser John Poindexter, for maintaining that he had taken full responsibility for the guns-for-hostages swap to shield President Reagan. "This kind of thinking is inconsistent with democratic governance," the report said. "The ultimate responsibility for the events in the Iran-Contra affair must rest with the president. If the president did not know what his National Security advisers were doing, he should have."[43]

President Reagan, to deflect public criticism of Irangate, appointed his own Special Review Board, headed by former Senate Armed Services Committee Chairman John Tower of Texas, to get to the bottom of this murky intelligence operation. The Tower Commission, after weeks of interviews with key Irangate participants, let President Reagan off the hook gently: "President Reagan's personal management style placed especially heavy responsibility on his key advisers."[44] Despite this reprimand, President Reagan continued his personal crusade against the Sandinista government until the day of his retirement.

SHARED POLICYMAKING

The Founding Fathers, it should be noted, also gave Congress important constitutional duties in the foreign policy field. Among the eighteen enumerated powers granted to Congress in Article I, Section 8, seven affect foreign policy directly; others are shared powers listed in Article II. Two important powers belong to the Senate alone: first, giving advice and consent to treaties; and, second, confirming the president's nominations of ambassadors and ministers. The other two major powers exercised jointly by the House and Senate are the power to raise and appropriate funds and the power to declare war. Significantly, history shows that since World War II, the most successful collaborative foreign policy activity between the executive and legislative branches has occurred when the president has taken Congress into his confidence and consulted closely with the legislators.

President Truman, never known for his docility, established a hallmark for successful congressional consultation on foreign policy as he faced the enormous task of aiding the postwar economic reconstruction of Europe. Even though the 1946 election had seen the Republicans take over control of both houses of Congress, the president nonetheless obtained bipartisan congressional approval of the multibillion-dollar Marshall Plan for European reconstruction. Truman's secret weapon was his alliance with an old Senate colleague, Republican Senator Arthur Vandenberg, the influential chairman of the Senate Foreign Relations Committee and former isolationist-turned-internationalist.

To obtain Vandenberg's support and that of a number of other internationalist Republicans for the huge Marshall Plan, Truman permitted Vandenberg to name the administrator—Paul Hoffman, a leading industrialist—for the new program. Moreover, Truman agreed that the European Recovery Administration would be established as an independent agency rather than a bureau of the State Department, and further that "businessmen," rather than diplomats, would administer the program.[45] Other presidents, too, before and after Truman, have discovered that they cannot always operate successfully in the field of foreign affairs without bipartisan support.

More recently, President Bill Clinton decided, in a bold move in early February 1994, to end the nineteen-year trade embargo against Communist Vietnam.[46] In a strange twist of fate, the controversial decision to let bygones be bygones with an enemy country ultimately responsible for the deaths of 58,000 American servicemen during the prolonged Vietnam War was made by a president who had avoided the military draft during the Southeast Asian conflict. President Clinton, however, did not make this controversial decision until after the U.S. Senate passed a bipartisan resolution—supported by three highly decorated Senators who had served in Vietnam—recommending that the trade embargo be lifted.

REASSERTION OF CONGRESSIONAL INFLUENCE

Some years ago, a former British ambassador was asked what impressed him most about the American political system, and he quickly pointed to the "extraordinary power of Congress over foreign policy."[47] In the past two decades the growing overlap between foreign and defense issues has produced a series of confrontations between the president and Congress. The legacy of the Vietnam War has encouraged Congress to take a more active role in monitoring foreign affairs. In contrast with the presidentially inspired post–World War II foreign policy initiatives—the Truman Doctrine, the Marshall Plan, American intervention in Korea and Vietnam, President Kennedy's limited nuclear test ban treaty and the opening of the door to China—the past two decades have been marked by growing congressional resistance to presidential leadership. Since passage of the War Powers Act of 1973—the outgrowth of congressional disillusionment with the Vietnam War and the "imperial presidency"—Congress has shied away from granting blank-check support of presidential leadership in foreign affairs. This is especially true if it appears that it may lead to hostilities and the sending of American troops abroad.[48]

Many thoughtful leaders on both sides of the aisle in Congress, however, recognize that the present 535 members of Congress cannot hope to serve as an alternate secretary of state. Nor is the congressional role in foreign affairs enhanced by the fact that fourteen of the sixteen standing committees in the Senate and seventeen of the standing committees in the House have some jurisdiction over at least some aspect of overseas activities. Finally, to a far greater extent than the president, Congress is susceptible to the persistent and unrelenting demands of various special interest groups—the Jewish and the Greek lobbies, the Farm Bureau, the AFL-CIO, major banking institutions with billions loaned to Latin American and Third World countries. Indeed, the list of special interest groups with axes to grind abroad would fill pages.

While increased congressional staffing in the past two decades has enabled legislators to monitor foreign affairs more closely, members of Congress began having second thoughts in the later 1970s about the restrictions they had imposed on the president over the previous decade. In September 1980, Congress passed legislation designed to allow the president and the CIA greater flexibility in the direction of covert activities abroad. In the aftermath of the imperial presidency of Richard Nixon and the trauma of Watergate, leading members of Congress seemed more willing to give the president greater latitude in foreign affairs. Continuing crises in Lebanon, Iran, Afghanistan, Central

America, Libya, and Chad; the rising tide of international terrorism; and the Soviet downing of a Korean Airlines 747 commercial airliner off the coast of Siberia in September 1983 all contributed to the feeling that the president must have a freer hand in managing foreign affairs. Unlike in the past, however, Congress continued to look frequently over the president's shoulder, checking to see if he might not be stretching the country's political and military commitments too far, possibly repeating a disastrous Vietnam type of intervention.

Does this recent round of presidential-congressional differences represent a swing of the pendulum back to the period in the nineteenth century when Congress was the leader and the president the follower in foreign policy formation? Highly doubtful. Historian Arthur M. Schlesinger, Jr., has characterized presidential-congressional rivalry for control over foreign policy as a "guerrilla war" that has "dragged along through our history."[49] But twentieth-century presidents, with their instant sources of communication and intelligence throughout the world and their awesome nuclear weaponry, occupy a unique leadership position that Congress is unable to match. Still, the checks and balances mandated by the Founding Fathers have not left Congress entirely powerless.

The power of the purse can make the president sensitive to congressional concerns. While control of the purse enables Congress to resist a president only after the fact rather than to initiate foreign policy, this power is formidable. In 1974, for example, Congress cut off military aid to Turkey after its invasion of Cyprus, despite President Ford's objections. Two years later, Congress took similar action to shut off CIA-directed military assistance to pro-Western factions fighting the Soviet- and Cuban-based factions in Angola.

Equally important, informal extra-constitutional powers also give Congress—notably congressional leaders—formidable influence on a president's foreign policy. Chairmen of major committees in both houses, party leaders, and other key people must constantly be consulted and informed by the president if his foreign policy initiatives are to bear fruit. To assure friendly support from Congress, shrewd presidents have appointed congressional leaders to serve on delegations to international peace conferences and the major international meetings. Franklin D. Roosevelt, unlike Wilson, who failed to include any U.S. senators on the American delegation to the Versailles peace conference in 1919, invited several influential opposition Republican leaders to the San Francisco conference in 1945 which established the United Nations.

The investigative powers of Congress should not be discounted as a tool to influence foreign policy. In 1966, the Senate Foreign Relations Committee, chaired by Senator J. William Fulbright, conducted a full-blown, network-televised investigation of America's Vietnam policy. A year later, the Foreign Relations Committee adopted a Fulbright resolution asserting that "the executive and legislative branches of the United States Government have joint responsibility and authority to formulate the foreign policy of the United States" and further asserted that in the future American armed forces should not be committed to hostilities on foreign territory "without affirmative action by Congress specifically intended to give rise to such commitment."[50] The Fulbright resolution, however, did not produce immediate results. But eventually Congress resorted to its control over appropriations to halt the escalating involvement in the Southeast Asian conflict.

Though used belatedly, Congress' vote in 1973 to cut off support for American forces in Cambodia was decisive. Indeed, in a series of statutory funding limitations, worded much like the Boland Amendment a decade later, Congress prohibited the use of any appropriated funds for military or paramilitary operations in, over, or off the shores of North Vietnam, South Vietnam, Cambodia, and Laos. Although the Nixon administration objected to these actions on policy grounds, Mr. Nixon never challenged the constitutional power of Congress to cut off funds. In the end, Congress used its power over the purse to terminate the Vietnam War.[51]

THE TWO-TRACK SYSTEM

Political scientist Louis W. Koenig, one of the nation's most experienced presidential observers, has suggested that, intentionally or not, the Founding Fathers provided for a two-track system in foreign affairs.[52]

The first track consists of a set of powers and practices that give the president a free hand and almost complete autonomy in shaping foreign policy. Secret diplomacy and under-the-table understandings reached between the president and foreign heads of state can be handled beyond the purview of the Congress. Seldom until after the fact do the lawmakers hear about the results of these negotiations. For example, the hour was late, before leading members of Congress were informed about the Bush administration's Middle Eastern strategy. Indeed, the Bush administration's secret planning was almost a repeat performance of the Panama invasion scenario eight months earlier. Again, Congress was not in on the takeoff for planning this operation but only on the landing. The same virtues of the presidency originally noted by Alexander Hamilton in *The Federalist*—secrecy, dispatch, and unity—were relied on by President Bush to mount these two successful foreign ventures while Congress remained essentially in the dark.

The second track, broadly constructed by the Founding Fathers, is characterized by an open dialogue and collaboration between the executive and legislative branches with the president leading the way while keeping Congress well apprised of his progress in foreign policy initiatives. Mutual respect and frequent communication are the building blocks for this type of shared foreign policymaking. President Harry S. Truman, for example, used this approach to win congressional approval and eventually public support for the ambitious Marshall Plan, which provided the needed funds and technical expertise for the reconstruction of the shattered economies of Western Europe after World War II. President Jimmy Carter's successful handling of the Panama Canal Treaty negotiations in 1978 is another example of shared diplomacy. By working closely with the Senate, including several leading Republicans, and arranging to transport several dozen undecided senators to the Canal Zone for first-hand contact with leaders of the Panamanian government, Carter eventually persuaded two-thirds of the senators to support the controversial treaty.

Clearly, the two tracks cover almost the entire domain of foreign policymaking and offer the president a relatively clear choice: either to pursue a closed, inside, secretive policymaking approach that ignores congressional input; or, second, to engage in an open, above-board process taking Congress into his confidence and opening up avenues to generate public support.

If the president is determined to follow the first track, he can negotiate executive agreements, which exclude Congress and the public from the process. An imperial-minded president can engage in armed intervention (e.g., Panama, under his powers as commander in chief and present Congress with a *fait accompli*). But the president also has the parallel option of the second track: he can consult Congress and secure its approval under the terms of a joint resolution as President Dwight D. Eisenhower wisely did twice in the 1950s in dealing with the crises in the Formosa Strait (between Taiwan and mainland China) and in Lebanon. Also, the president can negotiate treaties and consult with the Senate prior to seeking its approval of the pact. This shared power approach usually fosters a sense of cooperation and teamwork between the executive and legislative branches. Many of these treaties, it might be added, have survived for decades, and some, for generations.[53]

BEYOND THE COLD WAR

On the diplomatic front the president, it has been emphasized repeatedly, has broad latitude to move dramatically in times of rapidly shifting international developments. Thus, less than five weeks after the failed three-day military coup against Soviet President Mikhail Gorbachev in late August 1991, President George Bush produced a diplomatic announcement that reverberated throughout the world community. Without advance warning, President Bush suddenly announced that the United States would eliminate all tactical nuclear weapons on land and at sea in Europe and Asia, called off the twenty-four-hour alert of the long-range U.S. B-52 bombers, and offered to negotiate with the Soviet Union for sharp reductions in the most dangerous kinds of nuclear missiles.[54] President Bush's headline-producing diplomatic move, it might be noted, was merely in keeping with the actions of many of his predecessors who have risen to the challenges of the times.

Clearly, the modern president is in the foreign policy driver's seat, even though he knows that in the long run he must build a bridge of cooperation with

Congress if his policies are to succeed. Constitutional lawyer Louis Henkin's description of presidential-congressional relationships on foreign policy is perhaps closest to the mark: "In the end, while insisting on its constitutional autonomy, Congress has generally sensed that in the strange contraption which the Fathers created for conducting foreign policy, the Congress are the rear wheels, indispensable and usually obliged to follow, but not without substantial braking power."[55]

While this system must seem cumbersome, indeed sometimes unworkable, to the foreign observer, the overall record of this shared arrangement seems to have found favor with most Americans over the years. Significantly, of the seventeen amendments added to the Constitution since ratification of the Bill of Rights (the first ten amendments) in 1791, none has involved the management or the distribution of power over foreign affairs.

NOTES

1. Cecil V. Crabb, Jr., and Kevin V. Mulcahy, *Presidents and Foreign Policy Making: From FDR to Reagan* (Baton Rouge: Louisiana State University Press, 1986), 39.

2. "Don't Panic: Here Comes Bailout Bill," *Time*, 145 (February 13, 1995), 34–36; "Why the Mexican Crisis Matters," *Newsweek*, 125 (February 13, 1995), 28–29.

3. Crabb and Mulcahy, *Presidents and Foreign Policy Making*, 39.

4. Thomas A. Bailey, *A Diplomatic History of the American People*, 10th ed. (Englewood Cliffs, NJ: Prentice-Hall, 1980), 54.

5. Barbara Kellerman and Ryan J. Barilleaux, *The President as World Leader* (New York: St. Martin's, 1991), 37.

6. Edward S. Corwin, *The President: Office and Powers, 1787–1957*, 4th rev. ed. (New York: New York University Press, 1957), 171.

7. *The New York Times*, 26 December 1991.

8. The treaty was ratified by the U.S. Senate after a bitter flurry of opposition on February 23, 1904—slightly more than two months after the Panamanian revolt. Bailey, *A Diplomatic History of the American People*, 491–496.

9. Cecil V. Crabb, Jr. and Pat. M. Holt, *Invitation to Struggle: Congress, the President and Foreign Policy*, 4th ed. (Washington, DC: CQ Press, 1992), 1.

10. 299 U.S. 304 (1936).

11. *Panama Refining Company v. Ryan*, 293 U.S. 388 (1934); *Schechter Brothers v. United States*, 295 U.S. 495 (1935).

12. 299 U.S. 304 (1936).

13. 453 U.S. 654 (1981).

14. *Regan v. Wald*, 468 U.S. 222 (1984).

15. William R. Thayer, *The Life and Letters of John Hay*, vol. 2 (Boston: Houghton Mifflin, 1915), 393.

16. Bailey, *A Diplomatic History of the American People*, 622.

17. Crabb and Holt, *Invitation to Struggle*, 43.

18. Michael J. Glennon, *Constitutional Diplomacy* (Princeton, NJ: Princeton University Press, 1990), 175. Between 1947 and 1963 forty-five treaties were withdrawn from the Senate by the request of the president. Ibid.

19. Crabb and Mulcahy, *Presidents and Foreign Policy Making*, 28.

20. 301 U.S. 324 (1937).

21. 315 U.S. 203 (1942).

22. 348 U.S. 296 (1955).

23. 354 U.S. 1 (1957). For a further discussion of these cases and others relating to executive agreements, see Louis Fisher, *Constitutional Conflicts Between Congress and the President* (Princeton, NJ: Princeton University Press, 1985), 272–283.

24. This proposed amendment would have required that all treaties and executive agreements not be self-executing—that is, they could not be implemented without congressional approval. For details surrounding debate over the Bricker Amendment, see Joseph E. Kallenbach, *The American Chief Executive* (New York: Harper & Row, 1966), 510–512; C. Herman Pritchett, *The American Constitution*, 2nd ed. (New York: McGraw-Hill, 1968), 364–366.

25. *Congressional Quarterly Weekly Report*, 1 January 1971, 24.

26. Arthur M. Schlesinger, Jr., *The Imperial Presidency* (Boston: Houghton Mifflin, 1973), 200–201.

27. *Congressional Quarterly Weekly Report*, 1 January 1971, 24.

28. Crabb and Holt, *Invitation to Struggle*, 16.

29. Louis W. Koenig, *The Presidency and Crisis: Powers of the Office from the Invasion of Poland to Pearl Harbor* (New York: King's Crown Press, 1944), 26, as quoted by Crabb and Mulcahy, *Presidents and Foreign Policy Making*, 98.

30. *The New York Times*, 17 April 1975.

31. *Congressional Quarterly Weekly Report*, 2 August 1975, 1714.

32. *Goldwater v. Carter*, 444 U.S. 996 (1979).

33. Bailey, *A Diplomatic History of the American People*, 541.

34. Keith Clark and Lawrence Legere, *The President and the Management of National Security* (New York: Praeger, 1969), 37–54, as cited by Louis W. Koenig, *The Chief Executive*, 4th ed. (New York: Harcourt, Brace and Jovanovich, 1981), 192.

35. Richard A. Watson and Norman C. Thomas, *The Politics of the Presidency* (New York: Wiley, 1983), 353.

36. Crabb and Mulcahy, *Presidents and Foreign Policy Making*, 43.

37. Brzezinski, since leaving the White House staff, has argued that the primacy in the area of foreign affairs should not belong with the secretary of state. Instead, he recommends that the Office of Assistant to the President for National Security Affairs should be upgraded by designating it as the Office of the Director of National Security Affairs, comparable to the post of Director of the Office of Management and Budget. This reorganization would give the director and his staff the status and authority required for the coordination of national security recommendations as they emanate from the State and Defense Departments and the CIA. Brzezinski would also require that the Director of National Security affairs be made subject to Senate confirmation. This would mean that the director would be expected to testify from time to time before congressional committees and not avoid the hearings, as Henry Kissinger did when he served as the national security adviser. See Zbigniew Brzezinski, "Deciding Who Makes Foreign Policy," *New York Times Magazine*, 18 September 1983, 62–74.

38. Former Vice President Dan Quayle reports in his recent book that Scowcroft frequently outmaneuvered Secretary of State Baker in their turf battles. According to Quayle, Scowcroft capitalized on his daily access to the president to bring him around to the NSC position. Dan Quayle, *Standing Firm* (New York: HarperCollins, 1994), 101–102.

39. For a trenchant analysis of Clinton's foreign policy management, see Jim Hoagland, "Flaws and Fissures in Foreign Policy," *Washington Post National Weekly Edition*, 8–14 November 1993, 29.

40. Clinton Rossiter, *The American Presidency*, rev. ed. (New York: New American Library, 1960), 10.

41. *The New York Times*, 25 July 1983.

42. Robert C. DiClerico, *The American President*, 2nd ed. (Englewood Cliffs, NJ: Prentice-Hall, 1983), 54.

43. *The New York Times*, 19 November 1987.

44. *The Tower Commission Report: The Full Text of the President's Special Review Board* (New York: Bantam Books and Times Books, 1987), xviii.

45. Harold F. Gosnell, *Truman's Crises: A Political Biography of Harry S. Truman* (Westport, CT: Greenwood Press, 1980), 357. See also David McCullough, *Truman* (New York: Simon & Schuster, 1992), 562–565.

46. *The New York Times*, 4 February 1994.

47. Quoted in William D. Rodgers, "Who's In Charge of Foreign Policy?" *New York Times Magazine*, 9 September 1979, 49.

48. Daniel Yankelovitch, "Farewell to 'President Knows Best,' " *Foreign Affairs* (1979): 670–693.

49. Arthur Schlesinger, Jr., "Congress and the Making of Foreign Policy," in Thomas E. Cronin and Rexford G. Tugwell, eds. *The Presidency Reappraised*, 2nd ed. (New York: Praeger, 1977), 221.

50. As cited in C. Herman Pritchett, *The American Constitution* (New York: McGraw-Hill, 1968), 361.

51. Michael J. Glennon, *Constitutional Diplomacy* (Princeton, NJ: Princeton University Press, 1990), 289.

52. Louis W. Koenig, "The Modern Presidency and the Constitution: Foreign Policy," in Martin Fausold and Alan Shank, eds. *The Constitution and the American Presidency* (Albany: State University Press of New York, 1991), 191–192.

53. Ibid.

54. Andrew Rosenthal, *The New York Times*, 28 September 1991.

55. Louis Henkin, *Foreign Affairs and the Constitution* (Mineola, NY: The Foundation Press, 1972), 123.

CHAPTER **11**

THE PRESIDENT AS OVERSEER OF THE ECONOMY

Modern presidents, unlike their nineteenth- and early twentieth-century prede-cessors, are expected by the public not only to maintain the peace and security of the country, but also to maintain high employment and to control inflation. If the economy turns sour, presidents are expected actively to fight the recession. Though the president's ability to manage the economy is minimal at best, the public nevertheless holds him personally accountable for the state of the economy. If he fails to maintain prosperity, they may turn against him at the next election. The same double standard that holds the president responsible for domestic and foreign policy decisions while excusing Congress also prevails for economic policy. Strangely, the lawmakers are not held individually ac-countable by the voters for poor economic conditions, though members of Congress clearly share a major responsibility for the economy. Especially during economic downturns heightened citizen expectations of the president come home to haunt him, particularly if he has made lavish promises to fix the economy during his campaign for the White House.

INTRODUCTION

To read the Constitution, one would not have the faintest idea that the president is the chief overseer of the economy. Indeed, the Constitution seems to make economic policymaking a congressional responsibility, since Article II (on executive power) provides no enumeration of economic powers. Article I, however, grants broad economic powers to Congress: to levy taxes, borrow money, regulate interstate and foreign commerce, coin money and regulate its value.[1] Nevertheless, since the early days of the Republic, presidents have used their executive powers to make economic policy. President Andrew Jackson's decision to close down the Bank of the United States is a case in point.

In this chapter, after a brief historical review of the limited role presidents played in economic policymaking before the Great Depression, we will endeavor to show how presidents since the New Deal have sought to influence the general direction of economic policy through macroeconomic and microeconomic policymaking. The duties and influence of the president's economic team—the Council of Economic Advisers, the Secretary of the Treasury, and the Office of Management and Budget—are discussed. Special attention is focused on the autonomous Federal Reserve Board and its crucial influence on monetary policy and the general state of the economy. Presidential alternatives to fiscal policy intervention are discussed and evaluated. Electoral economics—the president's efforts to stimulate the economy before elections—also receives detailed treatment, as does the role of the "pocketbook" issue in elections. Also included in this chapter is Congress' major, though less recognized, role in economic policymaking. Finally, the president's major responsibility for dealing with the annual federal deficit and recent efforts to scale down the mounting sea of red ink are closely analyzed as well as the proposed balanced budget amendment. A brief sketch of President Clinton's multi-pronged, long-term economic plan rounds out the chapter.

BACKGROUND

Until the Great Depression (1929–1933), presidents did not play a significant role in economic policymaking. As political scientist Richard M. Pious bluntly put it, "There was no administration fiscal policy." Generally, presidents operated in the following fashion:

In good times a president maintained the confidence of the business community by appointing financiers to the Treasury, by intervening on the side of management in strikes (if necessary with federal troops), and by keeping "hands off" the economy. In bad times presidents reassured the public that conditions would soon improve, maintained public order, and bailed out the banking system with the resources of the Treasury. The economy was supposed to be self-regulating.[2]

Nor did this lack of federal government involvement have the far-ranging consequences it has today. Even if the president had discovered fiscal theory as a tool to influence the economy, the low levels of federal spending—especially government spending and taxation in proportion to the gross national product—would have had virtually no impact on the nation's economy.

Except for the wartime expenditures during the Civil War, the federal budget did not exceed $1 billion until the United States entered World War I in 1917. (President Clinton's 1994 budget called for expenditures of $1.5 trillion.) It should be noted that until passage in 1913 of the Sixteenth Amendment—the federal income tax amendment—this country had no federal income tax, except during the Civil War (1861–1865) and briefly in the 1890s before the Supreme Court declared it unconstitutional.[3] With small annual federal budgets of $500 to $600 million—the Pentagon, for example, did not come into existence until 1940—Uncle Sam relied chiefly on the tariff and excise taxes to operate the federal government. More often than not, the U.S. Treasury showed a surplus after the annual books were balanced.

President Calvin Coolidge's banal observation in the 1920s that "the business of America is business" lost its meaning, however, in the October 1929 stock market crash. For the next three years the nation floundered helplessly while the Hoover administration (1929–1933) chose to remain on the sidelines, for the most part, and let market forces take their natural course. But this traditional "hands off" policy changed with the inauguration of Franklin D. Roosevelt in 1933.

President Roosevelt and his New Deal had as its central premise the responsibility of the federal government to halt depressions and restore prosperity. This commitment, later formalized in the Employment Act of 1946, became a major source of presidential strength. Since the post-war economy kept expanding through the 1950s and 1960s, generating huge tax revenue that paid for defense and expanded domestic programs, presidents were more than eager to claim credit for the booming economy. Administration economists in the early 1960s were, it seems hard to believe now, speaking about putting an end to recessions. But this optimism came crashing down to earth in the late 1960s. The United States—along with most other industrialized countries—moved into a period of declining growth and spiraling inflation. More and more, presidents found it increasingly difficult to find any prosperity to take credit for. Thus, instead of gaining popularity and accolades by dispensing more federal benefits, a president had to put some distance between himself and the growing national deficit or risk being tarred as the culprit responsible for the nation's ills. President Lyndon Johnson's attempt to have both "guns and butter" during the Vietnam War, without a major tax increase, added billions to the annual deficit.

World events, such as the 1973–1974 Arab oil embargo, and the resultant shortages of gasoline and the skyrocketing price increases, are clearly beyond presidential control but can have a disastrous effect upon the domestic economy. Thus, the president can be blamed for the huge lines at the gas stations, but because the nation is heavily dependent on oil imports, he is virtually powerless to solve the country's short-term energy needs—that is, unless he wishes (with congressional approval in peacetime) to invoke rationing, a highly unpopular action. (President Reagan, it might be noted, was the beneficiary of declining world oil prices in 1983 and 1984, which helped cool inflationary fires and contributed to his reelection victory in 1984.)

As the economic problems have multiplied, the public has demanded that the government—meaning the president—"do something." Yet while a president is expected to come up with solutions within his four-year term, most of the causes of economic distress usually require long-term corrective measures. To add to the president's woes, he must contend with skyrocketing deficits and an eroding global economic order that makes drastic economic policymaking hazardous and often next to impossible. Thus, the president must contend not only with unpredictable economic conditions at home, but with shifting tides abroad involving international exchange, debt ridden Third World countries, and multinational corporations.

Except in wartime, the president lacks the power of an economic czar to block major shifts in our industrial system. But the American chief executive, no matter which party he belongs to, will face severe criticism if the continued erosion of American production facilities and the export of jobs to Asia and Latin America is not halted. Yet while the president is expected to maintain direction over the economy, the American chief executive has less control over the budget and monetary policy and the nation's central bank than the leader of any major Western democracy. Although the White House has the responsibility for preparing the budget, the final budget approved by Congress may not be recognizable by its originators in the Office of Management and Budget. Congress has its own budgetary and fiscal powers, and the lawmakers will often have economic goals that differ considerably from those of the president, especially during periods of divided government.

Furthermore, the structure of the budget permits far less flexibility to the president and Congress than would appear at first glance. "Uncontrollable" expenditures—approximately three-quarters of the federal budget—leave little maneuverability for either the president or Congress. Moreover, most entitlement programs are indexed to inflation and are thus subject to sizable and unpredictable increases almost every year. Roughly one-half of the federal budget is consumed by Entitlements—Social Security, veteran's pensions and benefits, federal retirement pensions, Medicare, Medicaid, agricultural price supports, and unemployment compensation. Nearly 15 percent of the federal budget—approximately $292.5 billion—was earmarked in fiscal 1993 for interest on the national debt. This sum now exceeds the total of all federal spending on education, science, law enforcement, transportation, housing, food stamps, and welfare.[4]

If a president attempts a shift in priorities or sharply reduces budgets in any programs or agencies, it will trigger rapid counterattacks from members of Congress, organized interest groups, and the federal agencies affected. "Iron triangles" is the term coined to describe these powerful groups. Each of these so-called subgovernments bitterly resist any budget or program changes unless they expand or enhance the constituencies affected.

The president has even less power over monetary policy. The responsibility for regulating the money supply, which most directly affects interest rates, production, and purchasing power, belongs not to the president, but to the independent Federal Reserve Board. To be sure, the president appoints, subject to Senate confirmation, members of the Federal Reserve Board whose seven governors serve fourteen-year terms; he also names the chairman and vice chairman for four-year terms. But the terms of the president and the "Fed" chairman are not coterminous. Beyond this appointing power, the president has no formal role in the Federal Reserve Board's policymaking activities. Unlike the leaders of other Western democracies who can exert direct influence on their country's central bank policies, the president of the United States can only sit on the sidelines and comment on the Fed's decisions after the fact. No wonder incoming presidents privately shake their heads as they attempt to wrestle with the federal budget.

FEDERAL RESERVE SYSTEM

Congress, at President Woodrow Wilson's request, established the Federal Reserve System in 1913 to help control the financial panics and depressions that afflicted the country from time to time throughout the nineteenth and early twentieth centuries. Congress, in one of its most far-sighted economic actions of the twentieth century, made its first major delegation of its constitutional powers "to coin money and regulate the value thereof" (Article I, Section 8) by establishing the Federal Reserve System (the "Fed") and empowering it to create and print money. Prior to that time, currency consisted mostly of federal and state bank notes. During the Fed's formative years the secretary of the Treasury served as chairman of the Fed's board of governors and the system almost came completely under the wing of the White House. But Congress decided in 1935 to move the Treasury secretary off the board. Since then, the Fed has come to assume its independent and dominant role in the American banking system.[5]

Unlike most central banks of Western Europe and Japan, the Federal Reserve Board is, as indicated above, not an arm of the executive branch; nor can the president direct the Fed to increase or decrease the money supply. Though ultimately responsible to Congress for its existence, the Fed does not take its marching orders from Congress. With its responsibility to regulate discount rates and the availability of credit, the Fed's action invariably has a sweeping impact on the nation's economy. Its actions can affect the rate of inflation, interest rates, economic growth, and indirectly the employment rate. Small wonder, the Fed is often the target of criticism from both the president and Congress and from Republicans and Democrats alike. But at no time since its founding has a majority in Congress seen fit to change the independent status of the Federal Reserve System.

MACROECONOMIC POLICY FROM FDR TO CLINTON

The rise of Franklin D. Roosevelt's New Deal in 1933 marks the dividing line between traditional laissez-faire economic policy and the rise of macroeconomic policy—the name given to the general management of the economy by the government. Although macroeconomic policies were in operation before the 1930s, they took a great leap forward during the New Deal era, and they have continued to be a central feature of government policymaking since then.

Macroeconomic policy has two broad purposes: first, to promote economic stability in place of widely fluctuating economic conditions; and second, to foster economic growth. President Roosevelt's emergence as the first public manager of the economy and his decision to use fiscal policy to correct imbalances within the economy came in the midst of the Great Depression. Actually, Roosevelt's discovery that government expenditures could have a major impact on the economy evolved more as a byproduct of his emergency relief and spending programs than as a planned effort on his part to turn the economy around. In the meantime, however, a leading British economist, John Maynard Keynes, whom FDR met in 1934, provided a theoretical framework for the phenomenon of economic response to fiscal stimuli.

Keynesian Theory

According to Keynes, economic decline is caused by a drop in the demand for goods and services. During a depression, the accumulators of capital prefer to put their money into savings rather than investment. If total output is falling because of insufficient consumption or investment in the private sector, Keynes argued that the government could stimulate the economy by stepping up its own expenditures. Moreover, Keynes insisted, the temporary deficits created by the fiscal expenditures could be underwritten by government borrowing and repaid by higher tax rates during periods of growth in the economy.[6]

Traditional Economic Theory

Keynes' theory flew in the face of traditional conservative economics, which viewed a balanced budget as the key to a sound economy. The conservative economists held that government deficits were dangerously inflationary and threatening to confidence in the monetary system. Faced with a downturn in the economy, conservative economic theory required reduced government outlays to balance the budget. The government's demonstration of fiscal integrity would then lead to the restoration of economic confidence. Even during panics or depressions, the government was not required to act—nor did the people expect the government to become actively involved. To be sure, noninterference in the affairs of individuals and lack of action to change economic conditions sometimes came at a high cost, but according to the traditional economic theorists, prosperity would return as soon as the depressions were, to use President Herbert Hoover's phrase, "left to blow themselves out."[7]

Franklin D. Roosevelt, convinced that laissez-faire economics was not the answer to the Great Depression, found considerable merit in the innovative Keynesian theory. But he did not become a full convert until the 1937 recession, which followed his ill-fated attempt to return the country to a balanced budget. When the recession wiped out almost half of the nation's hard-earned economic gains since the beginning of the New Deal—unemployment rose again to 19 percent in 1937—FDR's reservations about Keynesian economics seemed to vanish. However, the American economy did not fully recover its vitality until total mobilization and the huge governmental outlays for armaments during World War II furnished empirical validation of Keynes' countercyclical "pump-priming" theory to many economists.[8] Thus, it is only since the New Deal that business cycles have been directly influenced through public policy.

Keynesianism continued to be the dominant macroeconomic policy until its limitations became evident during the rampant inflation of the early 1970s. The chief flaw in the Keynesian theory was more political than economic. Invariably, the president and Congress found it easier to increase spending and tax cutting—Keynes' remedy for expanding the economy—since these policies would attract political support. But the policymakers bridled at Keynes' prescription for curbing inflation—cut spending and raise taxes. In other words, the president and Congress found only half of the Keynesian theory to be acceptable; they were unwilling to use the second half of the equation—raise taxes and cut government spending to cool down inflation—for fear of losing office. Furthermore, policymakers made little or no attempt to create a budget surplus during expansionary periods. Some commentators referred to this practice as "one-way" fiscal policy.[9] As a result of this political defect, Keynesianism lost some of its appeal to both policymakers and economists. Partly as a result of this disenchantment, two other schools of macroeconomics—monetarism and supply-side economics—emerged as possible courses of action for government policymakers.

Monetarism

The first post–World War II challenge to Keynesianism came from the monetarists, sometimes called the Chicago School because the chief theorist, Nobel Laureate Milton Friedman, and his followers served on the faculty at the University of Chicago. Monetarism is an economic theory which asserts that monetary policy or control of the money supply is the primary, if not sole, determinant of the nation's economy.[10] The core element of monetarist theory is based on the proposition that prices, income, and economic stability are a function of growth in the money supply, not of the proportion of public expenditures paid for by borrowed funds. Monetarists hold that as long as the money supply grows at a constant rate commensurate with the potential growth in gross national product, economic activity will expand without placing upward pressure on prices and wages. Management of the money supply to produce credit ease or restraint, monetarists claim, is the chief factor influencing inflation or deflation, recession or growth.

Monetarists dismiss fiscal policy (government spending and taxation) as ineffective in regulating economic activity. Since contraction of the money supply—the monetarist medicine for controlling inflation—results in higher interest rates and unemployment, monetarism has not been a popular economic policy at the White House or on Capitol Hill in recent years. By 1980, another theoretical approach to economic policy—supply-side economics—became popular among some conservative economists and especially some elected officials. The most prominent convert turned out to be none other than President Ronald Reagan.

Supply-Side Economics

Combining features of both Keynesianism and monetarism, supply-side economics is based on the belief that economic expansion will come from lower tax rates. According to supply-side economists Arthur Laffer and George Gilder, a reduction in taxes will increase supply by encouraging production, providing greater incentives to work, and stimulating the savings and investment needed to support economic growth.[11] Furthermore, a greater supply of economic growth would produce a slowdown in inflation. Suppler-siders insist that a tax cut will not, in the long run, reduce overall tax revenues because increased prosperity will offset the effects of lower tax rates.

Members of the supply-side school of economics are not bothered by the big budget deficits created by tax reductions. Supply-siders argue that the stimulative effect of tax cuts will create enough additional savings to finance the added deficits without an inflationary expansion of the money supply.[12] Eventually, according to the supply-siders, an expanded economy will produce enough added revenues at lower rates of taxation to balance the budget. In other words, the nation's prosperity will enable the country to "grow out" of its deficit. However, the supply-siders, including President Reagan, overlooked the fact that lower taxes tied to a federal budget with heavy defense spending and uncontrolled expenditures on entitlements (social security, Medicare, etc.) produced record-breaking deficits.

Liberal critics of the supply-side school argue that it is simply a new version of the discredited "trickle down" theory in which tax breaks for the wealthy are justified on the basis that these advantages will encourage new investment and thus generate additional economic activity and jobs. Conservative critics, on the other hand, fear that the willingness of the supply-siders to incur huge deficits will produce excessive rates of inflation and loss of confidence in the monetary system. Liberal and conservative critics alike question the economic assumptions of the supply-siders.

Above all, they seriously doubt that the deficits produced by the supply-sider tax cuts will vanish; in fact, the critics believe the deficits, unless curbed, will produce even higher interest rates. To fund the deficit, the supply-sider critics argue, it will be necessary for the federal government to gobble up most of the available credit funds just to refinance the government deficit, thus crowding out private sector investor opportunities. In short, excessive government borrowing tends to slow down private sector development. As the federal deficits grow, this adverse affect becomes even greater.[13] By the end of President Reagan's two terms, the size of the national debt had tripled to more than $3 trillion and annual budget deficits twice ran in excess of $200 billion (see Table 11.1). Small wonder that supply-side economists lost much of their credibility.

ECONOMIC POLICYMAKING AND THE ROLE OF THE FEDERAL RESERVE SYSTEM

Next to national security and foreign affairs, post–World War II presidents have spent more time wrestling with macroeconomic policy than any other government matter. Consequently, the two principal instruments of macroeconomic policy—fiscal policy and monetary policy—are never far from the top of the president's agenda.

Fiscal policy consists of the government's attempt to regulate the health of the nation's economic activity by shifting the level of taxes and spending in an effort to keep the economy on an even keel. Fiscal policy can be used in two ways: By increasing spending and reducing taxes, the economy can be expanded; conversely, it can be cooled off by increasing taxes and reducing spending. Budget deficits are expansionary and budget surpluses—a rarity these days—are deflationary. Fiscal policy, it should be noted, is made jointly by the president and Congress by budgeting and appropriating funds and through tax policy legislation.

Monetary policy consists of the government's attempt through its central bank (the Federal Reserve Bank in the United States) to regulate the supply of money. Established by Congress in 1913, the Federal Reserve Board uses three main devices to influence interest rates and to control the money supply: the discount rate, reserve requirements, and open-market operations.

The rediscount rate refers to the interest rate charged commercial banks to borrow from the Federal Reserve Bank, which in turn affects the availability of credit for business investment. By increasing the discount rate, the Fed, as the central bank is popularly called, tightens the availability of credit to member banks because it forces banks to charge a higher rate of interest to borrowers. If the Fed permits a reduction in the member bank's reserve requirement, it

Table 11.1
Federal Budget Deficits, 1965–1994

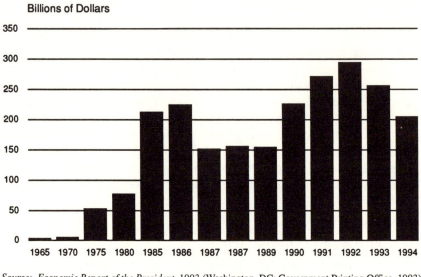

Billions of Dollars

Source: Economic Report of the President, 1993 (Washington, DC: Government Printing Office, 1993), 435.

increases the availability of credit to member banks who can then lend it to customers. Reserve requirements are the bank balances (usually 10 to 20 percent) that member banks must maintain on deposit at one of the regional banks in the Federal Reserve system.

To manage the money supply, the Fed uses open-market operations—buying and selling commercial securities from commercial banks. If the Fed wants to expand the money supply, it orders its regional reserve banks to purchase government securities on the money market, paying for them by drawing from Uncle Sam's account. As soon as the checks are cashed by the Treasury at commercial banks, the Treasury's account balance at the commercial bank increases. The commercial member banks can then present the checks at the regional Federal Reserve bank for redemption. The regional Federal Reserve banks credit the checks to the reserve accounts of commercial bank members. With this increased balance, the commercial banks can then lend to more private borrowers. Generally, they can lend amounts to, say, ten times the amount of the government securities the member has put on deposit at the reserve bank.

Conversely, the Fed's sale of government securities in the open market reduces the money supply and thus the availability of credit. From time to time, Congress has given the Fed temporary authority to fix terms of consumer credit. Federal Reserve banks also serve as depositories for government funds, clear millions of checks daily, and transfer funds among member banks. All of this activity, it should be noted, is conducted beyond the purview of the president and the White House staff.

While the Federal Reserve banking system generally works as its original sponsors planned, the President's Council of Economic Advisers and the Fed sometimes disagree on fiscal policy. Federal Reserve Chairman Arthur Burns in 1977 testified against the Carter administration's tax-cut proposals, again generating fears that the Fed might oppose administration policies. Clearly, the Federal Reserve's Board of Governors has the ability to counterbalance or aid attempts by a president or Congress to stimulate the economy.

From its inception, the Federal Reserve Board has intentionally been isolated from direct pressure from the president and Congress. Though it may have exceeded the expectations of its founders, the Fed has become a major economic policymaking institution that endeavors to provide national economic stability. Moreover, prevailing opinion in Congress and within the financial community has been to keep politics out of the Federal Reserve system.

More than one Fed chairman has clashed with the White House over the impact of the central bank's actions on fiscal policy. Some observers, however, have concluded that the Fed's independent authority serves as a convenient scapegoat for president and Congress alike. In a political sense, the Fed is in a "no-win" position, since its expansionary monetary policy can be attacked as inflationary and its restrictive policy can be said to contribute to recession and unemployment. In September 1980, the Federal Reserve drew loud complaints from President Carter after it raised its discount rate by a full point (from 11 to 12 percent) less than six weeks before the presidential election. Similarly, during the severe 1982 recession and the mounting deficits in fiscal year 1983, President Reagan and his Secretary of the Treasury Donald Regan could frequently be heard blaming the Federal Reserve Board monetary policy, not the administration's heavy defense spending and federal borrowing, for the record-breaking national deficits. Also, President George Bush often found himself at odds with Fed Chairman Alan Greenspan, a former head of President Gerald Ford's Council of Economic Advisers, for his refusal to lower the discount rate to help fight the recession. Mr. Bush conveniently overlooked the fact that Greenspan and the Fed had reduced the discount rate twenty-three times during the Bush presidency.[14]

President-elect Bill Clinton found no fault with Chairman Greenspan and the Fed during the 1992 campaign. During the presidential transition period he invited Mr. Greenspan down to Little Rock for a two-day visit, and the two policy "wonks" seemed to hit it off surprisingly well. More than a few eyebrows were raised at Mr. Clinton's first State of the Union Address when Mr. Green-span sat, front and center, between the president's wife, Hillary Rodham Clinton, and Vice President Gore's wife, Tipper. This was the first time in the eighty-year history of the Federal Reserve system that such an honor had been bestowed upon a Fed chairman.

Microeconomic Policy

Macroeconomic policy is always the central concern of the president and his advisers. But from time to time they will also devote considerable attention to microeconomic policy—a term used to describe government regulation of specific economic activity and antitrust policy. Twentieth century presidents, it should be noted, became involved in microeconomic policy long before they accepted the role of overall manager of the economy. Theodore Roosevelt and William Howard Taft pushed for vigorous enforcement of the Sherman Anti-Trust Act of 1890. In an attempt to preserve competition in the marketplace, Wilson, a Progressive Democrat, continued the Roosevelt-Taft tradition by obtaining congressional passage of the Clayton Anti-Trust Act of 1914 and the establishment of an independent regulatory agency, the Federal Trade Commission, to regulate and control unfair business practices. All three presidents believed the federal government had the responsibility and duty to prevent the excesses of trade restraints and unfair competition from suffocating the free-market economy.

The collapse of the American economy in the Great Depression, however, persuaded Franklin D. Roosevelt that legislation was needed to bring the operation of the stock market, private utilities, communications, and airlines under the watchful eye of the government. Congress, at Roosevelt's urging, established a series of independent regulatory agencies—the Securities and Exchange Commission, the Federal Communications Commission, the National Labor Relations Board, and the Civil Aeronautics Board—to halt abusive business practices and to serve as a referee among competing companies. FDR also turned his antitrust lawyers in the Justice Department loose to pursue certain big businesses—"economic royalists"—whose anticompetitive practices, the president said, were impeding the nation's recovery. A pragmatist of the first order, Roosevelt used a variety of governmental actions in his efforts to improve the health of the economy, discarding those that proved to be unproductive.[15] Beyond question, FDR should be credited (or blamed) for building up public expectations that the president is ultimately responsible for the state of the economy, even though his hands may be frequently tied by congressional opposition or inaction.

Post–World War II presidents—Truman, Eisenhower, Kennedy, and Johnson—pursued moderate microeconomic policies. Even Eisenhower, a moderately conservative Republican, chose not to dismantle the New Deal social reforms or disband the New Deal regulatory agencies established to monitor various sectors of the economy. Antitrust activity continued, but it was more of a "shotgun behind the door" threat than a serious campaign against monopoly or unfair competition.

The late 1970s marked a new era of microeconomic policy. Between 1976 and 1982, microeconomic policies included deregulation (in varying degrees) of surface and air transportation, stock exchange brokerage operations, financial markets, and interstate communications. These microeconomic policies, both Carter and Reagan insisted, would have a stimulating effect on the economy by throwing open to competition in markets that for decades had been subject to excessive governmental regulation.[16]

Most recently, President Bill Clinton has advocated the adoption of an industrial policy to help boost the American economy.

Industrial Policy

Widely ridiculed by mainstream economists when the concept first surfaced in the late 1970s, industrial policy has recently gained increased respectability. *Industrial policy* refers to governmental support or intervention to provide research aid and strategic planning guidance in the private sector for new technologies, especially those industries facing government-subsidized competitors abroad.[17]

Industrial policy proponents are, of course, almost 180 degrees removed from the laissez-faire theoreticians of the Reagan-Bush administrations. Critics of industrial policy argue that the government has no business moving into the middle of the private enterprise system. But the champions of industrial policy insist that unless the United States government takes an active role in helping underwrite research costs in the microchip, supercomputer, telecommunications, and biotechnology fields, and even the aircraft industry, the United States will eventually be left in the dust as foreign competitors—aided by the financial support of their governments—outresearch, outperform, and outsell American companies.[18]

In the Clinton administration, for the first time, industrial policy advocates have received a friendly hearing from the president and his advisers. But Clinton's industrial policy plans were still in the formulation stage after his first two years in office.

Until the end of World War II, White House economic policymaking was handled on an ad hoc basis. Franklin Roosevelt had no regular executive agencies, other than the Treasury, involved in economic policymaking. Instead, he asked Congress to establish a variety of special agencies to help stimulate the economy and put people back to work—the Public Works Administration (PWA), the Works Progress Administration (WPA), the National Youth Administration (NYA), and until it was declared unconstitutional, the National Industrial Recovery Administration (NIRA). However, once the United States entered World War II, FDR established a number of special agencies to provide overall direction to the economy—the War Production Board, the War Manpower Commission, the Defense Plant Corporation. When the war ended, Congress decided that the president needed a formal structure to oversee the economy, and it passed the Employment Act of 1946.

THE EMPLOYMENT ACT OF 1946

Although President Truman did not request the legislation, Congress for the first time in the Employment Act of 1946 officially gave recognition to macroeconomic policy and made the president general overseer of the economy. As Samuel Kernell phrased it: "The Full Employment Act of 1946 may have acknowledged overall government responsibility for managing the economy, but public opinion makes the president personally responsible."[19] Passage of this legislation represented still another transfer of authority and responsibility from Congress to the president.

In this new legislation, Congress stipulated that the president must prepare an annual economic report for the lawmakers. The net effect of this action was to elevate the Economic Report of the President to the level of the State of the Union address and the budget message. Also, Congress voted to establish a Council of Economic Advisers to serve, in effect, as the president's in-house advisory board on economic matters. This legislation, in effect, marked the acceptance of the Keynesian approach to management of the economy.

The Employment Act of 1946 greatly enlarged the macroeconomic responsibilities of the federal government by requiring it "to promote maximum employment, production, and purchasing power." The word "maximum," it should be noted, was substituted for "full" employment. It should also be pointed out that the legislation did not specify the means or policies that should be used to meet these goals. Nor did the act, for example, mention price inflation, or any central planning. In other words, the Employment Act of 1946 did not define public policy, but rather confirmed the federal government's commitment to macroeconomic policymaking.

THE PRESIDENT'S ECONOMIC TEAM

While many aspects of domestic policy can be delegated, the major questions of macroeconomics—employment, inflation, economic growth, participation in the international economy, and the interaction of fiscal and monetary policy—rest squarely on the president's shoulders. To handle this monumental and frequently frustrating task, all post–World War II presidents have relied on several agencies and advisers. The degree of influence wielded by these various members of the president's team varies from administration to administration, but the president's macroeconomic policymaking depends heavily upon the following agencies.

Council of Economic Advisers

Established by the Employment Act of 1946, the Council of Economic Advisers (CEA) has no line or operational responsibility; it serves exclusively as a staff arm to the president. This three-member team and small staff concentrate on gathering economic data, making forecasts, analyzing issues, and preparing the president's annual Economic Report to Congress. The relationship of the CEA chairman to the president will usually determine the degree of the CEA's influence on national economic policy. Truman found little use for the first CEA chairman, Edwin Nourse, who often privately lectured the president on economics and yet was reluctant to defend the president in public.[20] His second chairman, Leon Keyserling, a New Deal activist, was much more to his liking because he vigorously defended Truman's policies before Congress.

President Kennedy made CEA Chairman Walter Heller the "point man" for his administration's economic policies. Kennedy, for example, relied on Heller to float "trial balloons" or to defend still-to-be-formulated administration policies, such as an innovative tax policy that the president for political reasons was not yet prepared to adopt publicly.[21] Later, Kennedy received widespread approval for the special tax cut and the rapid depreciation write-offs, first advocated by Heller.

In recent years, it seems fair to say, the influence of the Council of Economic Advisers has declined as economic policy has become more political and as international economics and exchange rates have exerted greater influence on domestic policy.

National Economic Council

Creation of the National Economic Council, headed by Robert Rubin, a Wall Street financier (more recently appointed secretary of the Treasury in early 1995), has been viewed as one of the more innovative and successful moves by the Clinton administration. Considered a domestic counterpart of the National Security Council, the National Economic Council coordinates economic policy (as does the Domestic Policy Council), but since this unit has operated in low-profile fashion, its activities are not easy to assess.

Treasury Department

The role of the Treasury Department in economic policymaking should not be underestimated. The Treasury Department has the main institutional authority and responsibility for income and corporate tax administration, currency control, public borrowing, and counseling the president on such questions as the price of gold, the balance of payments, the federal debt, monetary matters in general, and international trade. And with the emergence of global economics there has been a blurring of the traditional distinction between domestic and foreign economic policy.[22] As a pivotal member of the cabinet, the secretary of the Treasury will have important ties with the nation's financial community; indeed, he will have often held a high position within that community before assuming his cabinet duties. Consequently, most presidents lean heavily on their secretary of the Treasury for advice. Some presidents depend heavily on the secretary to sell the administration's fiscal program to Congress and to keep the president's critics at bay.

Truman often turned to Treasury Secretary John Snyder, a Midwestern banker, for support and advice. Eisenhower, whose respect for Secretary of the Treasury George Humphrey, a former steel company executive, bordered on reverence, once described his trusted cabinet member this way: "In cabinet meetings I always wait for George Humphrey to speak. I sit back and listen to the others talk while he doesn't say anything. But I know that when he speaks, he will say just what I was thinking."[23] Kennedy, on the other hand, preferred to receive economic advice from a variety of sources. He encouraged a debate between his advisers and set the CEA against the Treasury Department. Nixon, who preferred to concentrate on foreign policy and found economic matters boring, virtually handed over authority to Treasury Secretaries John Connally and George Shultz to make major decisions.

Like Nixon, President Reagan during his first term gave almost free rein to Treasury Secretary Donald Regan in handling the president's international economic policies.

President George Bush relied far more heavily on his OMB director, Richard Darman, to handle economic policy. President Bill Clinton, recognizing that his innovative economic policies would need a strong defender on Capitol Hill, selected Senator Lloyd M. Bentsen (D-TX), chairman of the Senate Finance Committee, as Secretary of the Treasury. A successful Texas businessman before entering politics, Bentsen has had the respect of Wall Street and the business community.

The Office of Management and Budget

Since President Nixon upgraded the Office of Management and Budget (formerly the Bureau of the Budget) in 1970, this agency has moved into the inner circle of the president's economic policymakers. Though constituted originally to monitor departmental budgets and keep down the level of spending, the OMB has become the principal agency for shaping the spending component of fiscal policy. Presidents have differed in their level of confidence in the OMB, but Ford and Carter, for example, used it as a counterweight to the military budget prepared by the secretary of defense, and both upheld the OMB rather than the Pentagon on several crucial issues.[24]

Originally staffed with government careerists, the OMB since the Nixon years has become a political arm of the president. Top OMB officials have been recruited from outside the ranks of the civil service and now are clearly recognized as political assistants of the president. Furthermore, as one team of scholars has put it: "The budget has become as much a political weapon as a managerial tool or an instrument of fiscal policy."[25] President Clinton, to reinforce his influence on Capitol Hill, chose as his first OMB director Congressman Leon E. Panetta (D-CA), chairman, House Budget Committee. When President Clinton appointed Panetta as his new chief of staff in June 1994, he elevated Deputy OMB Director Alice M. Rivlin, former director of the Congressional Budget Office, to Panetta's vacated position.

FISCAL POLICY: MYTHS AND REALITY

Most students of the federal government have long concluded that fiscal policymaking is truly an inexact science. In recent years the administration's calculations on expenditures, receipts, and the anticipated deficit have, more often than not, been grotesquely wrong. When Ronald Reagan presented his first budget for fiscal year 1982, the deficit was put at $24.1 billion. When the 1982 fiscal year ended, the official deficit stood at $110.6 billion—off the mark by 358.8 percent. Why the gross miscalculations? In the case of fiscal year 1982, few economists foresaw the depth of the recession—the chief reason revenue fell approximately $85 billion short of the initial forecast. While over a sixteen-year period the average error for revenue has been 4.4 percent and for outlays 3 percent, even small errors in each of these categories can have a powerful effect on the deficit, especially when receipts and outlays move in opposite directions.

More recently, President Bush's OMB Director Richard Darman predicted in July 1991 that the 1992 fiscal year deficit (October 1, 1991 through September 30, 1992) would be as high as $315 billion—approximately $100 billion higher than projected a year earlier. The final figure for fiscal 1992 was actually $290.2 billion, surpassing the previous record of $269.5 billion reached in 1991.[26] It was the twenty-third consecutive year the government failed to balance its budget and brought the accumulated national debt to $3.97 trillion. The Bush administration predicted in October 1992 that the deficit for fiscal 1993 would be $341 billion; actually lower interest rates brought the 1993 deficit down to $254.9 billion.[27]

In assessing an administration's fiscal policy, outside observers should always remember that federal budgets are expressions of the president's political goals and hopes. Furthermore, the administration's budget is always biased on the side of optimism. According to one former congressional aide, "It has to be optimistic because it has to show things getting better because of what the President wants."[28]

Since 1974, the Congressional Budget Office (CBO) calculations on receipts, expenditures, and size of the deficit have injected more reality into the entire budgetary process. But even the CBO has had a tough time with its calculations because the inflation rate is so difficult to chart. Other factors—how many unemployed will be eligible for benefits or welfare? Will there be a drought or some other national disaster that will require increased payments to farmers? What will be the interest rate?—also make precise calculations next to impossible. Briefly, then, nobody really knows what the economy will be doing the next year.

Especially since the passage of the landmark Employment Act of 1946, the health of the nation's economy has been a major issue in presidential politics. Whether he wishes it or not, the president's political fortunes depend more on the state of the economy—the inflation rate, the prime interest rate, the rate of unemployment, and the consumer price index—than on whether the president understands the intricacies of the North American Free Trade Agreement (NAFTA) or is on good terms with the Japanese prime minister.

But as most post–World War II presidents have discovered, the labyrinth of the congressional committee structure, especially the massive growth of subcommittees since the mid-1970s, the proliferation of special interest groups that fight most reforms (except lower taxes) in economic policy, and the huge built-in entitlement costs for Social Security and Medicare all stand in the way of most presidential economic initiatives. Although the president is held fully accountable for managing the entire federal budget, his discretion now extends to less than 25 percent of the total outlays, since much of that budget, especially entitlements, has already been predetermined by decisions of his predecessors and earlier Congresses. With rare exceptions, presidents have formidable difficulties in getting Congress to pass their economic agenda or alter parts of their domestic programs.

President Bush, operating under a divided government, experienced little success in selling his modest economic program to Congress during his single term. President Clinton soon encountered stormy waters in the Senate over his proposed $16 billion stimulus package to jump start the sluggish economy. Republicans filibustered the bill to death before the Easter recess—the first serious setback for the new Democratic president. But after this initial setback, President Clinton mounted a concerted national campaign in the late spring to win approval of his 1994 deficit reduction-tax increase plan. This plan, which included a total of nearly $250 billion in increased taxes for individuals and businesses over the next five years, was approved in early August 1993. [29]

PRESIDENTIAL ALTERNATIVES TO FISCAL POLICY INTERVENTION

Presidents are not limited to fiscal policy intervention to try and keep the economy healthy—and reelection prospects upbeat. To provide more jobs in both the private and public sectors, he may propose various countercyclical employment and public works "pump priming" projects. Or he may prefer to push rapid tax depreciation write-offs, or to recommend tax credits to companies that employ the long-term unemployed, handicapped, unskilled, or those entering the job market for the first time. To control inflation, he may propose such microeconomic policies as deregulation of certain sectors of the economy, vigorous antitrust action in key industries, changes in tariff rates or special marketing agreements with friendly countries, such as the North American Free Trade Agreement (NAFTA), approved in November 1993.[30]

Generally, the president's task of trying to keep the nation's economy healthy requires that he should be a frequent oracle of good tidings. When the economy is booming, he should take the lion's share of the credit for the nation's prosperity; and when the economy is sliding badly, he should quickly find as many scapegoats as possible—the congressional budget process, the Fed, "special interests," excessively high wage settlements, and Congress' refusal to give him the constitutional weapons needed to fight unbalanced budgets (the line item veto and a constitutional amendment requiring a balanced budget). How successfully the president performs this economic high-wire act largely determines whether the electorate will give him a second term. Unfortunately, most macroeconomic and microeconomic problems the president encounters have no easy solutions, but the American public's expectations of his solving these problems remain high.

ELECTORAL ECONOMICS

The relationship of macroeconomic policy and electoral politics has long been recognized, especially by national politicians and high-level economic advisers. They fervently believe that the economy affects the electoral fate of the incumbent party. Several articles of this faith have been summarized by political scientist Edward R. Tufte:

1. Economic movements in the months preceding an election can tip the balance and decide the outcome of the election.
2. The electorate rewards incumbents for prosperity and punishes them for recessions.
3. Short-run spurts in economic growth in the months preceding an election benefit incumbents.[31]

What truth is there to this political business cycle thesis? Do electoral cycles actually exist? Have presidents and congressional majorities successfully manipulated economic policy to improve their electoral standing with the voters? Tufte has argued that administrations will manipulate short-term economic conditions with expansionary fiscal policies, even if it generates more inflation or increased rates of unemployment after the election. In his studies Tufte has discerned a distinct improvement in the economy in presidential election years.

Tufte discovered two distinct electoral-economic cycles between 1948 and 1976, except during the Eisenhower administration.[32] The first two-year cycle, which meshed with congressional elections, showed that real disposable income per capita rises in even-numbered years and drops in the odd-numbered years. Tufte points out that stepped up benefits in Social Security, farm programs, and other domestic programs as well as tax cuts have been used to boost income before elections. The second cycle, which occurs over a four-year period and synchronizes with presidential elections, involves a drop in unemployment in the months preceding the election and a rise in layoffs over the next twelve to eighteen months.

Tufte has also concluded that *"the greater the electoral stakes, the greater the economic improvement."*[33] Presidents often try to ensure that the economy is booming with high employment and rising personal income in presidential election years.[34] According to Tufte, "Real disposable income increased an average of 3.4 percent in years when the incumbent president sought reelection, 2.6 percent in midterm election years, 2.0 percent in those years where the incumbent president did not seek reelection, and a dismal 1.5 percent in off-numbered years."[35] These findings held for the entire set of elections from 1946 to 1976, including the Eisenhower years. Recently, political scientist Samuel Kernell updated Tufte's data on unemployment and inflation through 1992; his findings do not differ significantly from Tufte's.[36]

REELECTION ECONOMIC STRATEGY

Most recent presidents going into the year of their reelection campaign have taken strong actions to show the country they are trying to turn the economy around or to keep it on a sound footing. In 1963, President John F. Kennedy, acting on the advice of his Council of Economic Advisers, and looking ahead to a reelection bid in 1964, pushed for the biggest tax-cut package in American history up to that point. President Nixon, with an eye on his upcoming 1972 reelection campaign, persuaded Congress in 1971 to grant him authority to impose wage and price controls, which he did with disastrous effect. In 1991 President Bush again pushed (unsuccessfully) for a reduction in the capital gains tax to help revive the sputtering economy.

Also, to give his reelection campaign a little extra lift, President Bush ordered his Treasury Department early in 1992 to lower the income tax withholding rate for taxpayers. This action was expected to pump an extra $20 to $25 billion or so into the troubled economy and help Mr. Bush's reelection prospects.[37] Initially, this extra economic "shot in the arm" won some favor with voters, but obviously it was not enough to swing the 1992 election in his favor.

Failure by a first-term president to deal effectively with the economy invariably leads to job termination after four years. President Jimmy Carter's inability to revive the faltering economy and reduce high interest rates is a recent example; President George Bush is another.

Mr. Bush was, of course, not the first president to be turned out of office during a recession. History shows seven times in the past century that when the economy was in recession in the fall of a presidential election year, the opposition party challenger has been elected president. The winners were Grover Cleveland (1884), William McKinley (1896), Warren G. Harding (1920), Franklin D. Roosevelt (1932), John F. Kennedy (1960), Ronald Reagan (1980), and Bill Clinton (1992).[38]

Another way of looking at economic conditions and presidential success is to examine the unemployment rate. Political scientist Michael S. Lewis-Beck has found that all five times since World War II when the unemployment rate was falling in the second quarter of the election year, the incumbent party nominee has won: Truman (1948), Johnson (1964), Nixon (1972), Reagan (1984), and Bush (1988).[39] Conversely, when the unemployment rate was rising or flat during the April through June second quarter in six election years, the incumbent party lost five out of six of those elections—1952, 1960, 1968, 1976, and 1980. The 1992 election can also be added to this list. The only exception was in 1956, when President Eisenhower won reelection.

ECONOMIC POLICYMAKING AND THE POCKETBOOK ISSUE

A conventional view in American politics is that ratings of the president are affected strongly by personal economic circumstances. According to this view, people "vote their pocketbook." What this maxim means is that the voters consider presidential elections to be referenda on the incumbent administration's management of the economy. Voters are more likely to approve of the president if they feel they are prospering personally than if they feel they are not. Echoing this line of thinking, Lyndon Johnson, according to one of his aides, believed, "The family pocketbook was the root-and-branch crucial connection to all of his plans and hopes for the future."[40]

Recently however, some scholars have articulated a somewhat different perspective of presidential approval, insisting that citizens evaluate a president on the basis of broader views of the economy than merely their self-interest.[41] That is, rather than asking what the president has done for them lately, citizens ask what the president has done for the nation. Political scientist Donald R. Kinder, who uses a "sociotropic" research approach that reflects voter concerns about societal needs, contends: "In evaluating the president, citizens seem to pay principal attention to the nation's economic predicament, and comparatively little to their own."[42] Kinder continues, "They vote the country's pocketbook, not their own."[43]

George C. Edwards III, another close student of presidential popularity, has also concluded: "There is substantial support for the assertion that general evaluations of the economy are more important influences on voting than are the narrow self-interests of the voters.[44] In other words,

Citizen's evaluations of the president's handling of unemployment, inflation, and the economy in general are related strongly to overall presidential approval. In sum, the public evaluates the president's role in the economy more on the basis of his performance than on its view of the state of the economy. [45]

If a president can point to his success in handling economic policy, especially in the third and fourth years of his first term, he will be on his way to reelection, as Ronald Reagan clearly demonstrated in 1984. The Reagan prosperity cycle, financed by ever-mounting deficits, continued well beyond his retirement into the Bush administration—the longest period of uninterrupted economic growth in the twentieth century. But the day of reckoning arrived in the fall of 1990, with the onset of U.S. military intervention in the Persian Gulf. Economic uncertainty and the threatened disruption of Middle Eastern oil supplies pushed the nation into a recession that persisted, despite President Bush's upbeat pronouncements of economic recovery, until the third quarter of 1992. The upturn of the economy, however, came too late to help President Bush's reelection campaign.

In the final analysis, the 1992 electorate's response seemed to confirm another leading academic model of electoral behavior: "Future expectations count and count very heavily among contemporary American voters."[46] Many voters turned from a judgment of past economic performance to future prospects.

CONGRESS AND ECONOMIC POLICYMAKING

Despite the fact that the nation holds the president accountable to keep the nation's economy healthy, Congress plays an equally major role in formulating national macroeconomic and microeconomic policy. Nevertheless, over the years Congress has assigned the president increased economic responsibilities through the Budget and Accounting Act of 1921, the Employment Act of 1946, and the Budget and Impoundment Control Act of 1974, and the Budget Enforcement Act of 1990. But the lawmakers always retained their power over the purse.

Until passage of the Congressional Budget Office Act of 1974, however, the two chambers operated more as if they were overseeing the management of a department store, not an organizational structure with more than two million employees and a budget that exceeded $100 billion by 1968.

Congressional decision making on taxing and spending has reflected essentially the fragmented structure of the committee system, the absence of party discipline, and the special interest orientation of committee chairpersons and ranking minority members. As political scientist David E. Price has put it, "In both houses the appropriations committees have become, in effect, holding companies for thirteen largely autonomous subcommittees, and in areas like health, public works, and defense, norms of fiscal austerity have tended to give way to those of client and constituent service."[47]

Not until passage of the Budget and Impoundment Control Act of 1974 could it be said that Congress had begun to put its own financial house in order. The legislation also created House and Senate Budget Committees with jurisdiction over the budget resolutions, and a Congressional Budget Office (CBO) to serve as a staff agency with a full complement of computer analysts, economists, and statisticians. No longer would Congress have to depend on the expertise of the executive branch for advice on anticipated tax revenues, projected deficits, interest on the national debt, and so on. Clearly, the 1974 law strengthened the hand of Congress in its budgetary interaction with the president. But presidents enjoy an initial advantage because they are responsible for putting together the annual budget for presentation to Congress.

The Reagan Revolution

Newly elected presidents soon discover how vitally important it is to have their fiscal policy plans—indeed, the major outlines of their full legislative program—etched out soon after they take the oath of office. Presidents Lyndon Johnson and Ronald Reagan wisely concluded that major legislation, whether it affects fiscal policy or not, must be passed by Congress in the first year. Otherwise, it runs the risk of becoming mired in the off-year congressional campaign, the third-year doldrums, or in the next round of presidential combat.[48] Thus, within seven weeks of taking office in January 1981, President Reagan sent a full-blown budget to Capitol Hill containing his proposals for a reduction in personal and corporate taxes, a big cut in nondefense spending, and a huge increase in the defense budget. By skilled maneuvering on Capitol Hill and two nationwide televised appeals for popular support of his program, Reagan managed, despite divided government, to get the heart of his "Reaganomics" fiscal program passed before the August 1981 summer recess of Congress—less than seven months after arriving in the nation's capitol.[49]

President Bush had much less success than President Reagan in dealing with Congress on budget issues. By 1990, the inability of President Bush and Congress to reach agreement on budgetary issues led to the third revision of the Gramm-Rudman-Hollings deficit reduction law in five years.[50] After a long, drawn-out series of meetings between President Bush's representatives and congressional leaders, both sides finally hammered out a compromise agreement, known as the Budget Enforcement Act of 1990. To obtain passage of this legislation, President Bush agreed to abandon his "no new taxes" pledge made at the 1988 GOP National Convention in New Orleans.

The Budget Enforcement Act of 1990

For all practical purposes, the 1990 law superseded that 1974 Budget and Impoundment Control Act, which had taken authority away from President Nixon's OMB and given Congress greater authority to shift budget priorities.

The Budget Enforcement Act of 1990 grants still more authority to the president to impound or sequester funds he believes will breach the budget ceiling.[51] Indeed, in this instance, it appears that the very authority Congress took away from President Nixon during the Watergate era to impound or withhold appropriated funds in the Budget and Impoundment Control Act of 1974, the lawmakers have now given back to the president. Under the 1990 law the president is now authorized to reduce, veto, or impound funds that he estimates will exceed the spending ceilings or pay-as-you-go provisions of congressional appropriations, such as entitlements. But critics of the 1990 law remained dissatisfied with its deficit reduction features. Instead, they have proposed the adoption of a balanced budget amendment to halt the ever-mounting annual deficits.

Balanced Budget Amendment

During fiscal year 1992 the United States Treasury was hemorrhaging in red ink at the rate of almost $1 billion a day, or $11,574 per second. No wonder a growing number of lawmakers became convinced that the only way to halt the further flow of red ink is a balanced budget amendment.

Proponents of the balanced budget amendment argue that such an amendment is necessary to curb the profligate spending habits of Congress and presidents who continue to run the country deeper and deeper into debt. Without a balanced budget amendment, its advocates insist, powerful lobbies and private interest groups will continue to overwhelm the defenders of fiscal soundness and run up Uncle Sam's debts ever higher.

Some economists oppose a balanced budget amendment on the grounds that it would tie the government's hands if the nation fell into a recession. They argue that it would eliminate fiscal policy as a tool for fine-tuning the economy, especially the use of job-creating, stimulus spending that has been available since the New Deal era to counteract cyclical downturns in the economy. Critics of the amendment declare that under these circumstances it would prevent the federal government from spending revenues to pay unemployment benefits or to stimulate demand or purchasing power, and thereby impede a recession from deepening into a full-blown depression. In other words, the opponents argue, the amendment would deny the federal government flexibility in dealing with recessions, national disasters, or unforeseen international crises.

Economists point out that if the balanced budget amendment were passed and put into effect while the annual deficit remains at astronomical levels, then major spending cuts or tax increases would have to be implemented to balance the budget. Under these circumstances Robert D. Reischauer, formerly director of the Congressional Budget Office, told lawmakers recently, "The Congress would be faced with the Hobson's choice of enforcing the new rule and inducing a deep recession or waiving the rule from the start, which would clearly be an inauspicious beginning for the new era."[52]

Even more important, critics of the proposed amendment have pointed out that the amendment does not provide a mechanism to break deadlocks if the president and the Congress cannot agree on a balanced budget for the upcoming fiscal year. Under these circumstances, the critics say, the unelected federal judiciary might well be called to intervene and could conceivably end up managing the budget.[53]

Among the first items of business of the Republican-controlled 104th Congress was passage of the Balanced Budget Amendment. The House of Representatives, in late January 1995, passed the amendment overwhelmingly, 300 to 132 votes. But the Republicans had less success in the Senate. After more than a month of debate, the Senate narrowly defeated the proposed amendment with 66 to 34 votes—one vote short of the required two-thirds constitutional majority. Actually, the final vote was 65 to 35 votes after Senate Majority Leader Bob Dole, in a cleaver parliamentary maneuver, switched his yes vote to a nay vote. Under Senate rules this final vote count will allow him to move to reconsider the amendment at any time during the 104th Congress.[54]

CLINTON ECONOMIC PLAN

President-elect Clinton's promise to return the country to prosperous times was the top item on his 1992 campaign agenda, and it has remained there since he moved into the White House.

The multi-purpose Clinton economic plan included several objectives: a five-year plan for deficit reduction, infrastructure modernization, and increased taxes in the upper tax brackets and a gasoline tax.

Although criticized by many conservatives, Mr. Clinton's economic plan has been described by Dr. Herbert Stein, President Nixon's chairman of the Council of Economic Advisers as "probably the most far-reaching effort ever made by a President to control the budget deficit."[55] Still, the American public has given President Clinton barely a passing grade on his handling of the economy, even though more than four million new jobs were created during his first eighteen months in office. Once again, Clinton has become a victim of the rising expectations syndrome: no matter how hard he has worked to improve the economy, he cannot do enough to satisfy the public. Nor did President Clinton's economic plan receive much help from the Federal Reserve Board, which raised the central bank's discount rate seven times in the twelve-month period from February 1994 to February 1995.

To recapitulate, no area has a greater gap between presidential responsibilities and public expectations than the economic domain. Still, as Richard M. Pious has noted: "The public expects the president to provide full employment, stable prices, and a rising standard of living."[56] Yet, the president must take a backseat to the Federal Reserve Board on monetary policy. Also, he has virtually no control over entitlement spending (more than 50 percent of the Federal budget). Furthermore, the president must contend with the unpredictable nature of the business cycle, the highly complex nature of our economic system and the global economy, as well as decisions made by earlier administrations.

Even when the president is on an economic course of action that seems to offer promising results, the clanking congressional machinery sometimes moves so slowly that by the time the president's program is enacted, most of the "window of opportunity" may be lost. For example, the tax cuts recommended by President John F. Kennedy in late 1962 were not passed until sixteen months later—five months after he was assassinated. In this instance, JFK's compensatory fiscal policy was delayed so long by Congress that its full impact was lost. Also, the president's budget is prepared so many months (upward of sixteen months) in advance of its enactment into law that it is unclear what the state of the economy will be when it passes and what exactly the impact of the budget will be upon it.

The president also has even less control over the private sector of the economy, which far overshadows the public sector. The truth of the matter, in short, is that the president has only limited influence over economic policy. Yet the public expects him to be a miracle worker, especially in times of adversity.

NOTES

1. U.S. Constitution, Article I, Section 8.

2. Richard M. Pious, *The American Presidency* (New York: Basic Books, 1978), 294–295.

3. *Pollock v. Farmer's Loan and Trust Company*, 158 U.S. 601 (1895).

4. *World Almanac and Book of Facts 1995* (Mahwah, NJ: Funk & Wagnall's, 1994), 109.

5. Howard E. Shuman, *Politics and the Budget: The Struggle between the President and Congress*, 3rd ed. (Englewood Cliffs, NJ: Prentice-Hall, 1992), 183.

6. John Maynard Keynes, *The General Theory of Employment, Interest, and Money* (New York: Harcourt Brace, 1936).

7. As cited by Howard E. Shuman, *Politics and the Budget* (Englewood Cliffs, NJ: Prentice-Hall, 1984), 132.

8. The record shows that it took a mammoth eightfold increase in wartime spending from $9.1 billion in 1940 to $79.4 billion in 1943 to provide relatively full employment in the American economy and recovery from the Great Depression. *Supplement to Economic Indicators, Historical and Descriptive Background*, 90th Congress, 1st Session (Washington, DC: Government Printing Office, 1967), 35, 127, as cited by Shuman, *Politics and the Budget* (1984), 139.

9. For a readable discussion of Keynesian economics, see Herbert Stein, *Presidential Economics*, 2nd rev. ed. (Washington, DC: American Enterprise Institute, 1988), 37–53.

10. Milton Friedman, *Studies in the Quantity Theory of Money* (Chicago: University of Chicago Press, 1956).

11. Generally, most of the dialogue on economic theory takes place within the academic community, but as noted by one team of Washington observers, "Supply-side economics was a peculiar addition to the economic scene of the 1970s in that it grew up outside mainstream economics and its propositions were debated in the popular press rather than in academic journals." Hugh Heclo and Rudolph G. Penner, "Fiscal and Political Strategy in the Reagan Administration," in Fred I. Greenstein, ed. *The Reagan Presidency* (Baltimore: Johns Hopkins University Press, 1983), 26.

12. See Bruce Bartlett, *Reaganomics* (Westport, CT: Arlington House, 1981).

13. As one commentator put it, "President Reagan's contention that economic growth will eliminate the burden of the debt appears to put the cart before the horse by reversing the causality between public debt and economic growth. It neglects the damage that swelling public debt can do to long-term capital formation and economic growth." Leonard Silk, *The New York Times*, 20 February 1985.

14. *The New York Times*, 3 July 1992.

15. Arthur M. Schlesinger, Jr., *The Coming of the New Deal* (Boston: Houghton Mifflin, 1959).

16. See Alan Stone and Richard P. Barke, *Governing the American Republic* (New York: St. Martin's, 1985), 416–417; Perry D. Quick, "Businesses: Reagan's Industrial Policy," in John L. Palmer and Isabel V. Sawhill, eds. *The Reagan Record* (Cambridge, MA: Ballinger, 1984), 304–312.

17. See Robert Kutner, "Facing Up to Industrial Policy," *The New York Times Magazine*, 19 April 1992, 22.

18. Ibid., 26.

19. Samuel Kernell, "Explaining Presidential Popularity," *American Political Science Review* 72 (June 1978): 520–521.

20. Pious, *The American Presidency*, 307.

21. Ibid., 308.

22. Erwin C. Hargrove and Michael Nelson, *Presidents, Politics, and Policy* (Baltimore, MD: Johns Hopkins University Press, 1984), 186–189.

23. Roger B. Porter, "The President and Economic Policy: Problems, Patterns, and Alternatives," in Hugh Heclo and Lester M. Salamon, eds. *The Illusion of Presidential Government* (Boulder, CO: Westview, 1981), 206.

24. Richard H. Rovere, "Eisenhower: A Trial Balance," *The Reporter*, 21 April 1955, 19–20, as cited by Thomas E. Cronin, *The State of the Presidency*, 2nd ed. (Boston: Little Brown, 1980), 28.

25. Pious, *The American Presidency*, 267.

26. Richard A. Watson and Norman C. Thomas, *The Politics of the Presidency* (New York: Wiley, 1983), 380.

27. *World Almanac and Book of Facts 1995*, 40.

28. *The New York Times*, 5 February 1985.

29. Ibid., 7 August 1993.

30. Ibid., 21 November 1993.

31. Edward R. Tufte, *Political Control of the Economy* (Princeton, NJ: Princeton University Press, 1978), 9.

32. Ibid. Two other authors, however, have cast serious doubt on the effectiveness of presidential attempts to manipulate economic policy to enhance their approval rating. "The long and uncertain lags in the use of macroeconomic policy, coupled with the political risks and liabilities of miscalculation, weaken the underlying logic of the political business cycle thesis."

See David G. Golden and James M. Poterba, "The Price of Popularity: The Political Business Cycle Reexamined," *American Journal Political Science* 24 (November 1980), 696–714.

33. Ibid., 22–27.

34. On the other side of the coin, one respected economist has even hypothesized that presidents try to cause recessions early in their terms so that the economy will be rebounding again at reelection time. William Nordhaus, "The Political Business Cycle," *Review of Economic Studies* 41 (1975), 169–190, as cited by Paul J. Quirk, "The Economy, Economists, Electoral Politics, and Reagan Economics," in Michael Nelson, ed. *The Elections of 1984* (Washington, DC: CQ Press, 1985), 158.

35. Tufte, *Political Control of the Economy*, 24.

36. Samuel Kernell, *Going Public*, 2nd ed. (Washington, DC: CQ Press, 1993), 212–214.

37. Michael Duffy and Dan Goodgame, *Marching in Place: The Status Quo Presidency of George Bush* (New York: Simon & Schuster, 1992), 244–246.

38. Allan J. Lichtman and Ken DeCell, *The Key to the Presidency* (New York: Madison Books, 1990).

39. Quoted in *The New York Times*, 9 October 1991.

40. Jack Valenti, *A Very Human President* (New York: Norton, 1975), 151, as quoted by George C. Edwards III, *The Public Presidency* (New York: St. Martin's, 1983), 226.

41. See Donald R. Kinder, "Presidents, Prosperity, and Public Opinion," *Public Opinion Quarterly* 43 (Spring 1981): 1–21.

42. Ibid., 17.

43. Ibid., 3.

44. Edwards, *The Public Presidency*, 227.

45. George C. Edwards III and Stephen J. Wayne, *Presidential Leadership* (New York: St. Martin's, 1985), 114.

46. Morris Fiorina, *Retrospective Voting in American National Elections* (New Haven, CT: Yale University Press, 1981), 197; see also Michael S. Lewis-Beck, "Economics and the American Voter: Past, Present, Future," *Political Behavior* 10 (1988): 5–21.

47. David E. Price, "Congressional Committees in the Policy Process," in Lawrence C. Dodd and Bruce L. Oppenheimer, eds., *Congress Reconsidered*, 3rd ed. (Washington, DC: CQ Press, 1985), 170–173.

48. Paul C. Light, *The President's Agenda* (Baltimore, MD: Johns Hopkins University Press, 1982), especially chapters one and two.

49. See Robert W. Hartman, "Congress and Budget-Making," *Political Science Quarterly* 97 (Fall 1982): 381–402.

50. Lance T. LeLoup and Steven A. Shull, *Congress and the President: The Policy Connection* (Belmont, CA: Wadsworth, 1993), 184–185.

51. Susan F. Rasky, *The New York Times*, 30 October 1990.

52. Ibid., 7 May 1992.

53. Ibid., 8 May 1992. This unanswered question resurfaced once again during the prolonged debate over the Balanced Budget Amendment in February 1995. Senator Sam Nunn (D-GA) declared that he would not support the Balanced Budget Amendment unless it contained a special provision to prohibit federal courts from having power to become involved in any case arising under a constitutional amendment requiring a balanced budget. To obtain Nunn's crucial vote, Senate Majority Leader Bob Dole agreed to add a section to the proposed Balanced Budget Amendment banning the federal courts from intervening in disputes between the executive and legislative branches on deficit reduction issues. The Nunn-sponsored amendment was approved by the Senate 92 to 8 votes, but the final vote on the Balanced Budget Amendment still fell one vote short of the needed two-thirds majority required by the U.S. Constitution. Ibid., 1 and 3 March 1995.

54. Ibid., 3 March 1995.
55. Herbert Stein, "Let's Work with Clinton's Plan," *The New York Times,* 24 February 1993.
56. Pious, *The American Presidency,* 293.

CHAPTER 12

THE PRESIDENT AND CONGRESS

Historian Arthur M. Schlesinger, Jr., and one of his colleagues observed some years ago: "The relationship between the Congress and the presidency has been one of the abiding mysteries of the American system of government."[1] Part of the continuing mystery is inherent in the Constitution, which enumerates specific powers for Congress as well as those "necessary and proper" to carry them out. By contrast, the Framers used such vague and imprecise phraseology in sketching out the president's power that, intentionally or not, the resultant ambiguity has allowed presidents wide discretion in interpreting their constitutional responsibilities. But how were the powers and responsibilities of these two separate branches to be blended together into a functioning government?

Once again, the Framers left the question unanswered. Historical experience shows, as one commentator has noted, "The relations between Congress and the president at any given time are a simultaneous and shifting mixture of cooperation, comity, and conflict."[2] Over the past two centuries the relations between the presidential and congressional branches have been marked by long periods of uneasy cooperation, brief spurts of remarkable harmony, and for the most part since 1968, frequent gridlock.

BACKGROUND

During most of the nineteenth century Congress held the upper hand and most presidents, except Jackson, Polk, and Lincoln, were content to follow the lead of Capitol Hill lawmakers, and devote most of their time to a light load of administrative and ceremonial duties. In the twentieth century, however, with the rise of the industrial state and the emergence of the United States as a world power, presidents, led by Theodore Roosevelt and Woodrow Wilson, grabbed the leadership reins from Congress. Since then, with a few exceptions, presidents have generally dominated relationships with Congress. However, relations between the president and Congress, as the chapter points out, have also been marked by frequent clashes over national priorities, the direction of the domestic economy, and in recent years, foreign policy. Indeed, given the nature of their constitutional relationship, conflict between president and Congress is almost inevitable.

In this chapter our discussion will focus on the unique American presidential-congressional shared governance system. The various patterns of presidential-congressional policymaking will be analyzed as well as the uneasy power balance between the two branches. Attention will also be devoted to the various obstacles standing in the way of closer cooperation between the White House and Capitol Hill. The emergence of the president as chief legislator and the various strategies used by White House incumbents to win passage of their major programs, including the veto power, will be carefully examined. Also, the level of presidential success in dealing with Congress will be assessed, including the impact of divided government upon executive-legislative relations during most of the past quarter-century. Finally, a short discussion of President Bill Clinton's brief two-year era of one-party government, followed by the return of divided government, will round out the chapter.

SEPARATE INSTITUTIONS—SHARED POWERS

The United States is virtually alone among the Western democracies in having an executive branch that must share power with a co-equal independent, legislative branch. By contrast, within the British parliamentary system the executive and legislative branches are, in effect, fused or melded together in the Cabinet, which operates the government. Divided government between the Cabinet and Parliament rarely exists in Great Britain because, except in wartime, the Cabinet consists solely of members from the majority party in Parliament.

Unlike the president of the United States whose political base rests on a nationwide constituency, the British prime minister derives his authority from his position as leader of the majority party in Parliament. As long as his party retains control of Parliament and his colleagues approve of his brand of leadership, the prime minister's policies will prevail in the House of Commons.[3] But under the American separation of powers system, the president and members of Congress are each independently elected within the fifty states but must share the power of governing. As one British observer has commented, "A national election in the United States is really two separate elections, one to elect local representatives to Congress and the other to elect a President."[4] No wonder the continuing constitutional tension in the United States that marks the normal relations between two independently elected branches of government—the president and Congress—is unique among the Western democracies.

Equally important, the transformation of the American presidency from a constitutionally modest office in the early days of the Republic to the dominant institution of today's national government is one of the most fascinating chapters in the nation's history. Factors responsible for this transformation include the expansion of presidential activity in foreign affairs; presidential constitutional duties as commander in chief; the uncovering of "inherent" executive powers; the strategic use of veto power; the emergence of a major presidential role in policy initiation; extensive delegation by the Congress to the president of broad discretionary authority, especially in budget management; the rise of the institutional presidency or presidential branch; and the pervading influence of mass communications.

In face of these powerful forces, it is no wonder that congressional dominance of the national government that characterized most of the nineteenth century has now been overshadowed by the rise of the modern presidency.

Over the years, however, Congress has not served as a mere junior partner to the president. Especially during the past two decades lawmakers have frequently resorted to their constitutional powers over the purse and foreign affairs to constrain presidential actions. The truth of the matter is that Congress shares much of the constitutional responsibility for the fate of all the president's legislative programs. Presidents who have refused to consult or include Congress in their plans have suffered serious, occasionally grievous, reverses. This list includes Woodrow Wilson, Harry S. Truman, Lyndon B. Johnson, and George Bush.

FRAMERS DEALT PRESIDENT A WEAK HAND

From a constitutional viewpoint, the president has been given few trump cards in dealing with Congress. Indeed, the formal legislative powers of the president reveal little about his real influence in securing passage of important legislation. To be sure, the president possesses veto power, but the formal powers conferred upon the president by the U.S. Constitution are few compared to the extensive grants of legislative power to Congress. Nevertheless, presidential legislative influence and agenda-setting power have been greatly expanded in the twentieth century through custom and practice—and television. To be highly successful, the president must rely heavily on informal methods, especially his powers of persuasion. The president, it should be reiterated, does not command senators and members of Congress; he attempts to persuade them. In the words of former presidential advisor Richard E. Neustadt,

The essence of a president's persuasive task with Congressmen and everybody else is to induce them to believe that what he wants of them is what their own appraisal of their own responsibilities requires them to do in their interest, not his.[5]

Presidents can also use the "bully pulpit" to make nationally televised appeals and TV "town meetings" to rally the public around their priority programs and thereby pressure Congress to support the White House agenda. In addition, presidents can try to build public coalitions by working closely with private interest groups, senior citizens, trade associations, union members, and ethnic groups to support key legislation and pressure Congress to support the president's agenda. But the president's task, as White House occupants know, is a back-breaking job every step of the way.

The list of potential obstacles and sources of conflict between the president and Congress is formidable: different constituencies; different timetables; staggered terms of election; conflicting responsibilities; varied legislative priorities and policy differences; and, divided government. All of these barriers to presidential-congressional cooperation will be analyzed in the course of our discussion. Despite this imposing list of obstacles, however, strong presidents have usually been able to overcome, at least in their first terms, the formidable institutional barriers built into our Madisonian-shared powers system to achieve major policy breakthroughs.

Some observers have depicted the policymaking relationship between the president and Congress as an executive-legislative seesaw, when one side of the teeter-totter is up, the other side is down, and vice versa. This, however, is not an accurate description because it ignores the fact that it is entirely possible to have an era of both a strong president and a strong Congress; likewise, it is also possible that the country may experience an era of both a weak president and a weak Congress. In other words, there may sometimes be win-win or lose-lose outcomes.[6]

PATTERNS OF PRESIDENTIAL-CONGRESSIONAL POLICYMAKING

Over the past two hundred years, in which forty-two presidents have served, the policymaking relationships between the president and Congress have ranged from consensus and close cooperation to nearly open political warfare. The variations in policymaking have generally fallen into one of the following four major patterns: presidential dominance, congressional dominance, consensus-cooperation, and deadlock/extraordinary-resolution.[7] (See Figure 12.1 for recent illustrations of the various patterns of presidential-congressional policymaking.)

What form of policymaking is best? Scholars and politicians will undoubtedly disagree, depending upon their perspectives. Perhaps the soundest descrip-

Figure 12.1
Patterns of Presidential-Congressional Policymaking

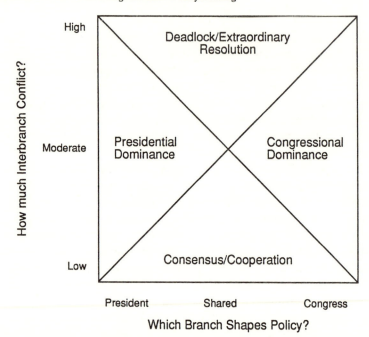

Which Branch Shapes Policy?

Source: Lance T. LeLoup and Steven A. Shull, *Congress and the President: The Policy Connection* (Belmont, CA: Wadsworth, 1993), 12. Copyright © 1993 Wadsworth Publishing Co. Reprinted by permission.

tion of joint policymaking has been suggested by political scientist Mark A. Peterson, "The policy connection between Congress and the president is one of tandem institutions sharing power and responsibility for both foreign and domestic policy."[8]

AN UNEASY POWER BALANCE

Several factors continue to affect the executive-congressional power balance: individual presidents and leading senators and congressmen, the dominant issues of the day, international crises, and the party balance in Congress. Even during periods when one branch seems to be in eclipse, the actual state of affairs in specific policy areas may be unresolved or shifting. Thus, the mid-1960s and early 1970s, which have been described as an era of the "Imperial Presidency," found Congress playing a distinct role in legislating the Great Society programs but also expressing serious reservations about the wisdom of U.S. military involvement in South Vietnam.[9] Indeed, the early 1970s constituted an interlude marked by widespread disillusionment with presidential power. Congressional backlash led to a resurgence of legislative assertiveness, especially the power of the purse and legislative oversight of intelligence gathering and secret executive agreements.

By the mid-1970s, Congress had also "successfully established its independence of the executive branch for information policy analysis, program evaluation, and legislative advice."[10] Formerly, Congress was at the mercy of the executive branch whenever questions about anticipated tax revenue, the size of the deficit, or the estimated cost of new weaponry were raised. Before 1974, the only budget figures the lawmakers had to work with were supplied by the President's Office of Management and Budget (prior to 1970, the Bureau of Budget). But with the establishment of the Congressional Budget Office (CBO) in 1974, Congress hired its own staff of budget specialists, statisticians, computer operators, and economists to provide the needed background for dealing with administration spokespersons during the hearings on the federal budget. Indeed, in projecting figures on the annual budget, the CBO experts were invariably closer to the mark than the administration's Office of Management and Budget to predicting anticipated tax receipts, the level of the federal deficit, annual economic growth, and the rate of inflation.[11] Thus, within a span of a few short years Congress had provided itself with the needed staff and data to establish a level playing field during budgetary discussions with the executive branch.

Especially since the 1930s and World War II, big government has led to the expansion of power in both branches. While the executive and legislative branches have sometimes enlarged their responsibilities at different levels and different time frames, both have had to address the problems emerging from the Cold War, domestic issues such as social welfare, health care, civil rights, and threats to the environment.

More recently, the end of the Cold War and the collapse of communism in Eastern Europe have forced both the president and Congress to reevaluate international and domestic priorities. In any event, our separate institutions-shared powers system provides plenty of room for both president and Congress to initiate policies jointly or separately, and to co-exist as powerful and active branches of government. Indeed, our constitutional system demands mutual accommodation.

THE PRESIDENT AS CHIEF LEGISLATOR

The president's legislative role derives from Article II, Section 3, of the Constitution. "He shall from time to time give to the Congress information on the state of the union, and recommend to their consideration such measures as he shall judge necessary and expedient." Delivered in person since President Wilson's first term, presidential addresses to Congress especially since the age of television, focus attention, publicize priorities, and mobilize public debate.

The president supplies to Congress something that its fragmented, decentralized structure seems to prevent it from sometimes providing itself—an agenda.

Congress, with its numerous committees, subcommittees, informal caucuses, and party conferences, is not structured for executive leadership. In the twentieth century, especially since the New Deal era, Congress has increasingly turned to the president to provide direction and goals. Thus, through special messages, communications, and appeals, "presidents highlight priorities, provoke public debate, stimulate congressional deliberation, and exhort for attention and support."[12] Furthermore modern Congresses expect the president to translate executive branch proposals into draft bills or give specific guidance on proposed legislation that does not originate in the White House.

President Harry S. Truman commenced the modern tradition of sending the administration's legislative agenda to Capitol Hill, but he simply did not come up with this idea one afternoon in the Oval Office. He discovered that when he asked for anti-inflation legislation from Congress in 1947, he was upbraided for not including a draft bill to carry out his recommendation. "If the President wants to tell the people that he stands for a certain thing," complained Senator Homer Ferguson (R-MI), "he ought to come out with his proposal. He ought to come to the House and Senate with a message. And he ought to provide a bill if that is exactly what he wants."[13]

The Eisenhower administration encountered a similar complaint a few years later when the Republican chairman of a House committee reportedly chided an administration witness before his committee for failure to offer a specific proposal: "Don't expect us to start from scratch on what you people want. That's not the way we do things here—*you* draft the bills, and *we* work them over."[14] As a result of this complaint, President Eisenhower, a strict constructionist of the president's duties under the Constitution, soon ordered his staff to prepare detailed legislative proposals for Congress on a variety of issues. All of his successors have followed this practice.

Political scientist James MacGregor Burns remarked some years ago, "The classic test of greatness in the White House has been the chief executive's ability to lead Congress."[15] History bears out this cogent observation. Twentieth-century presidents who have done the most to expand the power of the presidency— Wilson, Roosevelt, Truman, and Johnson—have been those who were most successful in leading Congress. The ability to lead the most powerful legislative body in the free world is no small task. But those presidents who have vigorously taken up this challenge have generally been ranked by scholars as among the "great" and "near great." While one may quibble about including Lyndon B. Johnson in this esteemed group, Johnson's legislative accomplishments with his Great Society reforms and his leadership in promoting civil rights legislation certainly rank him next to FDR and Wilson as a leader in domestic reform.

Presidential success in leading Congress should always be evaluated in light of the constraints the president operates under, for he must always share power with 535 elected members of the two houses of Congress, each chamber of which has the capacity to check the actions of the president. Undoubtedly this is what Lyndon B. Johnson had in mind when he lamented one afternoon:

I've watched the Congress from either the inside or the outside, man and boy, for more than forty years, and I've never seen a Congress that didn't eventually take the measure of the President it was dealing with.[16]

And one would also find it hard to disagree with political scientist Michael L. Mezey's historical overview that, "no president, not even the greatest, succeeded in leading the Congress for his entire tenure in office, that few succeeded in doing so for more than a year or two, that all went through periods of intense congressional resistance to their priorities and proposals."[17]

Over two centuries ago, one of the Founding Fathers, James Madison, pointed out one of the chief sources of conflict between the president and Congress: different constituencies.[18]

Different Constituencies

While the president is chosen in a nationwide election, each member of Congress is elected within a congressional district or statewide election and represents a different geographical interest. To win the presidency, a nominee must appeal to a far more diverse electorate and put together an electoral coalition representing a far wider variety of constituencies than any member of Congress. Furthermore, the staggered election structure in the U.S. Senate means that two-thirds of all U.S. senators are not elected at the same time as the president. One-third of the senators are picked two years before the president and another third two years after his election. Consequently, they are often responsive to somewhat different moods and points of view. Since the term of House members is only two years, after the midterm election presidents have to deal with a legislative body containing many new members and, possibly, controlled by the opposition party.

Because the two branches represent such diverse constituencies, their different perspectives surface at many stages of policymaking. Members of Congress often subscribe to the view that "What's good for Seattle is good for the nation"; presidents are more likely to say "What's good for the nation is good for Seattle."[19] Congress is frequently responsive to the desires or pressures of narrow constituencies. For example, key congressional committee chairpersons, who may represent oil-producing or tobacco-growing states, can exert tremendous pressure on tax legislation or agricultural policy far in excess of their numbers.

Different Timetables

The president and Congress also operate on different timetables. The president, according to the Constitution, is limited to two terms, or a maximum of ten years if he completes the unfinished term of a predecessor. Members of the House, once reelected, can usually expect to retain their seats for a long time. Senate terms are six years, and the odds are better than ever that the incumbent will win reelection.

Modern presidents have discovered that if they are to make a mark in history, they must get their programs off the ground in a hurry, usually during their first year in office. President Lyndon Johnson, who knew the inner workings of Congress better than almost any president in history, understood the need to get moving early in his term, for he believed that a president's impact is short-lived. This is how he put it in his memoirs:

The President and Congress run on separate clocks. The occupant of the White House has a strict tenancy. . . . A President must always reckon that this mandate will prove short-lived. . . . For me, as for most active Presidents, popularity proved elusive.[20]

Johnson's legislative record was made during his first eighteen months in office. Then Vietnam preempted most of his time and interest, and opposition to the war within his own Democratic party undermined the prospects for further legislative reform. President Reagan, profiting from the experience of his predecessors, wasted no time in pushing his tax and spending cuts programs through Congress in the weeks following his inauguration. But after this legislation was signed into law in August 1981, Reagan had much less to show for his efforts.

By contrast, Congress has a much slower timetable—or at least it did until newly elected Speaker of the House Newt Gingrich, with his ten-point "Contract with America" manifesto, arrived on the scene. Most members of Congress have viewed their congressional service, if they continue to be successful at the polls, as a lifetime career—or at least until the term-limits movement recently began sweeping the country. Consequently, they have lacked the compulsion to push proposed legislation through the congressional machinery quickly. Reluctant legislators, hesitant to follow the president's lead, recognize that if they resist or delay long enough, someone else will be sitting in the White House. Though perhaps not a typical example, the case of the late Representative William Natcher (D-KY), chairman, House Appropriations Committee, illustrates the point. Natcher, who arrived in the nation's capital in 1953 at the same time as newly elected President Dwight D. Eisenhower, had seen eight presidents come and go, and he was serving with the ninth—President Bill Clinton—when he died in early 1994.

Because the responsibilities, demands, and expectations now inherent in the modern presidency have outstripped the powers of the office, presidents must increasingly rely heavily on persuasion and informal bargaining skills to accomplish their goals.

The Personal Equation

From his first day in office the president can use several kinds of personal attention to win support from members of Congress. First, he can arrange to meet personally with them—a highly flattering and to some lawmakers a rather intimidating experience—to persuade them on the basis of argument and friendly appeal to support his policies.

Another valuable kind of attention involves consultation. The president can consult with both supporters and opponents, sometimes jointly, on a key bill, soliciting recommendations to improve proposed legislation. Presidents Kennedy, Johnson, and Reagan were all very good at this type of small group one-on-one discussions. President Jimmy Carter, on the other hand, was not very successful with this approach because he was perceived as never interested in real consultation with lawmakers.

A third type of attention involves catering to lawmakers' egos by inviting members of Congress to the White House for bill-signing ceremonies and the accompanying photo sessions, to be shown on network television or hometown newspapers. The president can often score points by calling them on the phone, writing complimentary letters that are released for publication, sending them autographed pictures, and inviting lawmakers and their spouses to the White House for dinner and evening entertainment. President Lyndon B. Johnson, in his prime, was past master as White House host, wining and dining his guests, dancing with their wives, and also engaging in some old-fashioned politicking, LBJ style.

President Ronald Reagan always had an ample supply of such items as "presidential cuff links," social invitations to the White House, and tickets to the presidential box at Kennedy Center. Most notably, he used those treasured items to win over Democratic defectors to support his budget-cutting proposals. Little courtesies can often mean a lot to members of Congress.

Fourth, a president can offer direct campaign help to loyal members of the House and Senate facing tough reelection battles. His personal appearances can be used both to sway votes and help raise campaign funds. A single presidential stopover in a large state can often generate nearly $1 million or more. Presidents Kennedy and Reagan were always top draws. Sometimes a president may agree not to campaign against supportive members from the opposition party. President Reagan always found this approach to be helpful, especially among Southern "boll weevil" Democrats.

Bargaining

If the president and Congress are often at loggerheads, the reason is under-standable. As James L. Sundquist has readily explained, "A branch made up of 535 equals has a hard time bargaining with a branch whose authority is concentrated in one executive."[21] But Sundquist continues, "The president and Congress are compelled to live together in a marriage arranged by matchmakers of a long-gone era, a marriage that, however loveless, is without the possibility of divorce."[22]

Political scientist George Edwards III, is undoubtedly correct in observing, "Legislative skills may be most significant at the margins of coalition-building, that is gaining the last few votes needed to pass a program."[23] No president since World War II has been better at collecting these last few votes needed to win than Lyndon B. Johnson.

LBJ also traded in wholesale lots. Looking for votes in 1964, Johnson came up with the idea of trading votes for the food stamp program for his farm bill. He phoned members supporting each program and asked them to support the other. Both passed.

Nor was President Ronald Reagan, the budget cutter, above supporting expensive programs in exchange for votes for his tax and budget reduction programs. Reagan reportedly agreed to raise sugar support payments to induce Democratic congressmen from Louisiana to vote for his 1981 budget cuts. Also, he promised to continue producing A-10 attack bombers in exchange for the support of Republican lawmakers from Long Island, where the aircraft was assembled, for his 1981 tax cuts and budget reduction program.[24] If all else fails the president can always turn to the veto, or threat of a veto—our next topic.

THE VETO

Described as the "third house of Congress" by Woodrow Wilson three decades before he reached the White House, the presidential veto has become one of the most powerful weapons in the president's domestic arsenal. As analyst James L. Sundquist has observed, "It is the possession of the veto that makes the executive branch a full partner in the legislative process."[25] Political scientist Richard A. Watson reminds us that "among all the elected leaders of the major democratic nations of the world, only the American president pos-sesses the executive veto power and uses it in the process of policy-making."[26]

It seems evident that the Framers probably did not anticipate the dramatic increase in the number of presidential vetoes and the infrequency of congres-sional overrides. Yet, the record shows that between 1789 and 1995 the president used his veto pen 2,509 times (see Table 12.1). Of this total, 1,056 were "pocket vetoes," not subject to congressional override. Of the 1,453 regular vetoes that Congress has had the opportunity to override, the lawmakers have been suc-

Table 12.1
Presidential Vetoes, 1789–1994

	Regular Vetoes	Pocket Vetoes	Total Vetoes	Vetoes Overridden
Washington	2	--	2	--
Madison	5	2	7	--
Monroe	1	--	1	--
Jackson	5	7	12	--
Tyler	6	3	9	1
Polk	2	1	3	--
Pierce	9	--	9	5
Buchanan	4	3	7	--
Lincoln	2	4	6	--
A. Johnson	21	8	29	15
Grant	45	49	94	4
Hayes	12	1	13	1
Arthur	4	8	12	1
Cleveland	304	109	413	2
Harrison	19	25	44	1
Cleveland	43	127	170	5
McKinley	6	36	42	--
T. Roosevelt	42	40	82	1
Taft	30	9	39	1
Wilson	33	11	44	6
Harding	5	1	6	--
Coolidge	20	30	50	4
Hoover	21	16	37	3
F. Roosevelt	372	261	633	9
Truman	180	70	250	12
Eisenhower	73	108	181	2
Kennedy	12	9	21	--
L. Johnson	16	14	30	--
Nixon	24	19	43	5
Ford	44	22	66	12
Carter	13	18	31	2
Reagan	37	39	76	9
Bush	40	6	46	1
Clinton (1993–1995)	1	--	1	--
TOTAL	1,453	1,056	2,509	82

Sources: Presidential Vetoes: 1789–1976, compiled by the Senate Library (Washington, DC: Government Printing Office, 1978), ix; *Congressional Quarterly Almanac* (Washington, DC: CQ Press, 1981), 7; Norman L. Ornstein, Thomas E. Mann, and Michael L. Malbin, *Vital Statistics on Congress, 1989–1990* (Washington, DC: CQ Press, December 1990), 162. Figures for the Bush administration are from Congressional Reference Service and supplied to the author by Congressman Al Swift, 2nd District, Washington.

cessful in only 104 cases—approximately 7 percent of the time. Generally, beleaguered presidents turn to the veto more frequently. Post–Civil War President Andrew Johnson, Lincoln's successor, has the dubious distinction of suffering the highest number of overrides—fifteen in less than four years. President Gerald Ford, the only unelected chief executive in history, had twelve overrides in less than thirty months. Presidents Johnson and Kennedy, on the other hand, never experienced a veto override. President Bush, serving in a divided government, suffered only one override among forty-six vetoes. President Clinton did not veto his first bill until early June 1995—878 days after assuming office.[27] Not since Millard Fillmore left the White House 142 years before had a president waited so long to cast a veto.

Pocket Veto

Less well understood, the pocket veto is a special legislative power exercised by the president after Congress has adjourned (see U.S. Constitution, Article I, Section 7, paragraph 2). Bills that a president does not sign within ten days of congressional adjournment do not become law and cannot be returned to the chamber of origin for a possible override. In effect, by this action the president "puts the bill in his pocket" and the bill thus fails to become law.

The Line-Item Veto

Presidents, starting with Ulysses S. Grant in 1876, have asked Congress to grant a line-item veto. But it was President Ronald Reagan who popularized the idea, which would enable presidents (like governors of most states) to reject part of a spending bill while accepting the remainder. Until the arrival of the Republican-controlled 104th Congress (1995–1996), passage of the line-item veto seemed unlikely. Indeed, there has been at least 200 attempts to pass some form of the line-item veto in one or both houses of Congress, and they all failed. The main reason for the opposition was that many members of Congress believed that the line-item veto would shift too much budgetary power to the president, who could selectively remove pet spending projects of senators and representatives while approving only those expenditures he favored. As one senator observed during the March 1995 floor debate, the president could select an item of critical importance to a senator's home state and then threaten to veto that item if the senator did not, for example, vote to confirm a Supreme Court nominee. With the line-item veto that president, as another senator declared, could "hold a gun to the head of members of Congress."[28] In any case, these lawmakers believed that they would become, in effect, hostages of the president on appropriations bills. Until now, presidents have had to sign or veto appropriations bills in their entirety.

However, part of Republican House Speaker Newt Gingrich's "Contract with America," the widely publicized Republican manifesto for the 104th Congress, included a legislatively enacted line-item veto. Speaker Gingrich and the newly selected House leadership insisted that the line-item veto—called "enhanced recision"—was an essential tool for the president to help reduce the annual deficit and whittle down the $4.5 trillion national debt. Among the first legislative actions taken by the new Republican majority, the House approved the line-item veto legislation, 294 to 134, in early February 1995.[29]

Senate Republicans, until they approved the line-item veto legislation in late March 1995, had been divided among themselves about which version of a selective line-item veto would attract enough votes for passage of the legislation. Several Senate Democrats, on the other hand, questioned the constitutionality of a legislative version of the line-item veto. These Democratic lawmakers insisted that a constitutional amendment would be required to modify the president's veto power (U.S. Constitution, Article I, Section 7, Paragraph 2).

Senator Bob Dole, Republican majority leader, however, unveiled a new selective line-item veto plan, which allowed the president to veto any of thousands of separate items in the massive federal spending bills. Under his proposal, after Congress passes appropriations bills, the president would be authorized to withhold money on certain spending, tax, and future entitlements. To sidestep a constitutional conflict, Senator Dole's amendment required congressional clerks to break each appropriations measure into separate bills before they reach the president. The president would then have twenty working days to act on each of the mini-bills. If the president failed to meet the deadline, the appropriation would stand. To override a presidential veto would require a two-thirds vote by each chamber on each item.

Senate Democrat minority leader Tom Daschle of South Dakota ridiculed Dole's proposal, declaring that the president "better have a very strong hand if he is to sign into law 1,700 or 1,800 individually enrolled items each and every time we pass on an appropriations bill."[30] With the passage of the line-item veto legislation, opponents can soon be expected to challenge it in the federal courts on the grounds that the legislation violates the U.S. Constitution (Article I, Section 7) on the veto power. Their lawyers will unquestionable argue that only by adopting a constitutional amendment can the line-item veto be added to the legislative process.

Although the line-item veto is found in some form in forty-three state constitutions, it is not a panacea. Many governors are reluctant to use it because it can backfire. The line-item veto, especially where it may be used to reduce as well as strike out appropriations for specific purposes, is an open invitation for legislators to pass appropriations in excess of projected revenues in the expectation that the governor will have to bear the onus of disallowing them. Also, state legislators have displayed considerable ingenuity in frustrating governors by manipulating the language of items in appropriation measures in such a way as to blend objectionable and unobjectionable funding in the same sentence. Former Senate Majority Leader Howard H. Baker, Jr. (R-TN) undoubtedly had this legislative ingenuity in mind when he once observed: "I really am afraid if we had line-item vetoes Congress would start sending [the President] appropriation bills with [just] one line."[31] As an alternative, Baker suggested that Congress consider strengthening the president's power to rescind or impound appropriations. It is noteworthy that the 1995 version of the line-item veto cannot be applied to entitlement programs such as Social Security or mandated legal obligations such as the $225 billion plus annual interest on the huge $4.5 trillion national debt.

President Bill Clinton is also a member of the item veto club. Though he did not make a big issue of the item veto during his 1992 presidential campaign, he has indicated his continued support for a limited item veto, such as he exercised as governor of Arkansas. More recently, President Clinton encouraged the congressional Republican effort to come up with the item veto legislation, saying Congress should give him "the strongest possible line item veto."[32]

Veto Threat

Presidents have found the veto as one of the most viable means of communicating his intentions to Congress. But presidents have also learned that the mere threat of a veto can be useful in defining his willingness to compromise with Congress or drawing a line in the sand. On more than one occasion FDR was heard to tell his aides, "Give me a bill that I can veto," as an admonition to keep Congress in line on his main legislative goals. By threatening a veto the president can declare in advance what he will and will not accept and thus more likely avert a legislative showdown. Selective use of the veto threat can sometimes be a means of avoiding or reconciling conflict with Capitol Hill. But the record of President George Bush conveys a mixed message. During his first year and one-half in office Mr. Bush issued 120 veto threats.[33] Bush's threats sometimes resulted in minor modification in legislation concerned with social welfare, the environment, and civil rights. On several of these issues Bush ultimately signed legislation that was more to his satisfaction, even in some instances signing bills previously vetoed but measures which in fact differed only a millimeter from the originally drafted bill.

PARTY TIES

Unlike a parliamentary system, a shared party label by the president and the majority leaders of both houses of Congress in the United States does not necessarily guarantee a cooperative approach to public policymaking. The president, it should be remembered, has no voice in the selection of his party's House and Senate leaders; it is done by the lawmakers themselves.

Structural makeup and norms stand in the way of close teamwork, even when the executive and legislative branches are controlled by the same party. Composed of numerous semi-autonomous power centers, Congress defies centralization. The countervailing forces of seniority, the committee system, the more than seventy informal caucuses (the Hispanic Caucus, the Textile Caucus, the Sunbelt Caucus, etc.) and the very nature of the complicated congressional lawmaking process all serve to disperse power. As a result, the president and his staff must constantly remain in touch with many of these power centers, if the White House is to succeed in pushing ahead its legislative agenda. Presidential insensitivity to these subgovernmental leaders invariably spells inaction or defeat. Asked how he dealt with Congress, President Johnson, with his usual locker room candor, said,

There is but one way for a President to deal with the Congress, and that is continuously, incessantly, and without interruption. If it's really going to work, the relationship between the President and Congress has got to be almost incestuous. He's got to know them even better than they know themselves. And then, on the basis of this knowledge, he's got to build a system that stretches from the cradle to the grave, from the moment a bill is introduced to the moment it is officially enrolled as the law of the land.[34]

Presidents and congressional leaders have met informally to discuss pending bills ever since the First Congress (1789–1790). President George Washington frequently solicited advice from fellow Virginian, Representative James Madison. President Thomas Jefferson kept close tabs on his party's congressional leaders, having dinner with them several evenings a week. But regular meetings between the president and congressional leaders did not become standard practice until President Theodore Roosevelt's administration (1901–1909). The "Rough Rider" president thrived on the give and take with Republican Capitol Hill leaders, most of whom were far more conservative than the young president. Since then, especially since Franklin D. Roosevelt's years in the White House, the two-way dialogue has been conducted on a weekly basis, with the president discussing his top agenda items and collecting the latest political intelligence from Capitol Hill. Presidents John F. Kennedy and Lyndon B. Johnson were constantly in contact with lawmakers. But another Democratic president Jimmy Carter learned little from the martyred president about getting along with the members of Congress. A House Democrat recalled:

When I came here President Kennedy would have six or seven of us down to the White House every evening for drinks or conversation. Johnson did the same thing, and they created highly personal, highly involved relationships. With Carter, he has 140 people in for breakfast and a lecture.[35]

President Reagan's "secret weapon" on Capitol Hill was Senate Majority Leader Howard Baker, Jr. (R-TN) whose advice and counsel was regularly solicited. With the Democrats controlling the House of Representatives and the Republicans in control of the Senate, Baker became the "point man" in negotiating bargains for the White House. As explained by White House Chief of Staff James A. Baker III (no relation to the senator), "Before we move on anything up there, we pick up the phone and get Howard's judgment on what will and won't fly."[36]

More recently, President Bill Clinton appears to have picked up where FDR, JFK, and LBJ left off, meeting regularly with Democratic lawmakers. By the end of four weeks in office Clinton had invited every Democratic member of the House (in groups of thirty or so) to the White House to discuss the new Clinton economic plan. Furthermore, in the tradition of Woodrow Wilson, Clinton also traveled to Capitol Hill twice in one week to meet with Democratic congressional leaders to cement closer political ties and discuss his pending economic plan and budget.

But a president should not always count on loyalty from his party members in Congress to back his presidential legislation. In 1990 President Bush suffered the embarrassment of a majority of House and Senate Republicans failing to support the Bush-backed Budget Reconciliation Act of 1990 compromise package, which reduced deficit spending by $490 billion over a five-year period. In working out the compromise legislation with the Democratic leadership, Bush agreed to drop his "no new taxes" pledge made at the 1988 GOP convention. Nonetheless, House Republicans opposed the tax increase-deficit reduction agreement by 126 to 47 votes, and GOP senators opposed it by 25 to 19.[37] Without Democratic majority votes in both chambers, the Bush-supported measure would have gone down in flames.

Presidents, even when their party has majority control of both houses of Congress, still rely on bipartisanship from time to time to help push through their legislative programs. Indeed, regional, ethnic, or economic pressures within their districts may cause some members of the president's own party to defect on critical issues. Even the "Grand Champ," FDR, despite heavy party majorities in both houses of Congress, sometimes turned to opposition Republicans for help. In perhaps the most crucial, single vote of his presidency, the one-year extension of the Selective Service Act in 1941—four months before Pearl Harbor—more than a dozen internationally minded Republicans from New England supplied the needed votes for a one-vote margin of victory, 203 to 202 votes, for the Roosevelt administration.[38] These critical GOP votes offset defections from isolationist, urban House Democrats (mostly Irish-Americans) from several Eastern cities. Failure to continue the military draft would have crippled America's military preparedness as Imperial Japan and Nazi Germany stood poised for further aggression.

President Lyndon B. Johnson relied heavily on moderate Republicans to help pass the landmark Civil Rights Act of 1964, banning discrimination in restaurants, motels, and public places. Throughout the House debate and the Senate filibuster by Southern Democrats, Johnson worked closely with GOP Congressman William McCullough (R-OH), ranking minority member on the House Judiciary Committee and several of his colleagues, and with Senator Everett M.

Dirksen (R-IL), the Senate Minority Leader, to collect more than enough votes to offset Southern Democrat defections. Without GOP support in 1964, President Johnson would have lost the vote on this historic legislation.[39]

Presidents who serve in a divided government are forced by mathematics, if nothing else, to depend heavily on a bipartisan approach to win approval of their legislative agenda. President Ronald Reagan, generally a highly partisan Republican conservative, shed his partisan mantle while seeking public support for his tax cut bill in 1981. Since Reagan required the votes of three dozen or more Democrats in the House of Representatives to pass his bill, he wanted voters, no matter what their party affiliations, to apply pressure on their congressmen to support the bill. Consequently, he went to great lengths to present his plan as bipartisan. In his televised address to the nation, Reagan described his tax cut plan as "bipartisan" eleven times in the span of a few minutes.

More recently, President Bill Clinton had been in office less than seven weeks when he paid a special visit to Capitol Hill for the specific purpose of meeting and courting opposition party Senate and House Republican lawmakers. Mr. Clinton's willingness to meet with opposition party members astounded many congressional observers. As noted by one veteran reporter, "It is virtually unheard of for a President to go to Capitol Hill expressly to call on lawmakers from the rival party. Congressional veterans said they could not recall a similar session in recent years."[40] One Republican senator suggested that Mr. Clinton's long-range goal was probably to determine what kind of bipartisan support he could expect down the road for his health care plan, welfare reform, and a second-year budget, if he needed bipartisan support on this future legislation.

WHITE HOUSE-CONGRESSIONAL LIAISON

Presidents, since Washington's first administration, have always maintained informal contacts with Congress to follow and shape pending legislation. Washington dispatched Treasury Secretary Alexander Hamilton to consult with lawmakers.

Woodrow Wilson, the first modern president to be an active lobbyist on Capitol Hill, was regularly found in the President's Room near the Senate chamber, discussing the legislative matters with Democratic congressional leaders. Franklin D. Roosevelt often dispatched top-level aides such as Tom Corcoran and James Rowe to Capitol Hill to lobby for his New Deal measures. But it was not until the Truman administration in 1949 that any president established an office to maintain ties with Congress. Truman's Capitol Hill liaison consisted of two persons inexperienced in legislative politics. Since then, White House liaison with Congress has become more formalized.

President Eisenhower institutionalized the president's legislative role by establishing a formal structure to help carry out this responsibility, the White

House-congressional liaison office. Lawrence (Larry) O'Brien, special assistant to the president for congressional affairs under John F. Kennedy and Lyndon Johnson from 1961 until late 1965, perfected the bridge-building activities first formalized by the Eisenhower White House. O'Brien's close ties to JFK made his job much easier. As explained by O'Brien, "For the first time, someone from the White House could sit in the Speaker's office with the congressional leadership and be recognized as a spokesman for the president. You weren't an errand boy or head-counter, you had the authority to speak for the president."[41]

Lobbying on Capitol Hill during the Carter administration, on the other hand, was generally rated below average. First of all, Carter selected an untutored fellow Georgian to be his congressional liaison chief. Most of the other members of the Carter liaison staff also lacked a basic knowledge of the legislative process. Poor coordination between the White House staff and congressional leaders frequently led to a breakdown in communication.

By contrast, President Reagan's lobbying staff received excellent grades from the start. Unlike President-elect Carter, whose problems with Congress began during the transition period, President-elect Reagan's transition period was smooth and efficient. Even before the inauguration, the White House-congressional liaison staff began making visits to Capitol Hill, working closely with members of Congress. Phone calls from members of Congress were returned promptly, and all correspondence was to be acknowledged in short order. All these actions created a favorable climate for Reagan's program in Congress. President Reagan held bipartisan breakfasts at the White House, met with key Senate Republicans, and even invited Democratic Speaker Thomas P. (Tip) O'Neill, Jr., to two private dinners in the White House—a marked contrast to the treatment the Speaker had received at the beginning of the Carter presidency. (Carter had been panned in January 1977 for allegedly, according to Washington gossip, denying Speaker O'Neill extra tickets to the inauguration. Reagan gave the Democratic Speaker an ample supply—and let it be known to everyone in the Washington press corps.)

PRESIDENT'S IMPACT ON CONGRESS

How much impact does the president actually have on Congress in winning support for his legislative agenda? Political scientist George C. Edwards III, in a series of careful studies, has concluded that there is apparently relatively little relationship between presidential legislative skills and measurable support for presidential policies. Relying on four different measures of support for the president during the 1953–1986 period, Edwards concluded that the impact of presidential leadership on congressional action (or inaction) was marginal (see Table 12.2).[42] Solid congressional majorities, he believes, are the key to presidential success.

Table 12.2
Presidential Support by Party, 1953–1986

Year	President's Party	Democrats	Republicans	Democrats	Republicans
1953	R	45%	70%	42%	66%
1954	R	34%	74%	36%	74%
1955	R	42	52	37	70
1956	R	38	72	35	69
1957	R	48	52	44	69
1958	R	52	55	37	66
1959	R	34	72	28	73
1960	R	46	64	41	66
1961	D	73	26	68	31
1962	D	72	30	64	31
1963	D	75	21	63	37
1964	D	78	26	63	56
1965	D	75	24	64	44
1966	D	67	20	53	35
1967	D	70	28	56	42
1968	D	63	36	46	41
1969	R	48	57	42	65
1970	R	41	60	35	63
1971	R	41	71	33	65
1972	R	46	68	34	66
1973	R	31	65	24	64
1974	R	38	59	31	53
1975	R	37	68	36	67
1976	R	32	67	29	62
1977	D	61	32	62	39
1978	D	65	34	64	36
1979	D	64	26	67	39
1980	D	63	31	60	38
1981	R	39	72	33	81
1982	R	30	61	35	72
1983	R	28	71	39	73
1984	R	32	66	31	74
1985	R	28	68	27	76
1986	R	23	72	26	80

Note: On roll-call votes on which the winning side was supported by fewer than 80 percent of those voting. R = Republican, D = Democrat.

Source: George C. Edwards III, *At the Margins: Presidential Leadership of Congress* (New Haven, CT: Yale University Press, 1989), Table 3.1. Copyright © 1989 Yale University Press. Reprinted by permission.

Two other political scientists, Jon R. Bond and Richard Fleisher, in a parallel quantitative study, which also examined the explanatory power of public approval, party and presidential leadership, plus ideology, found "little support for the theory that the president's perceived leadership skills are associated with success on roll call votes in Congress."[43] It is far more important, they argued, to have working majorities in both houses of Congress.

If these observations are correct, how do we account for landmark reforms contained in Woodrow Wilson's New Freedom (1913–1914), Franklin D.

Roosevelt's New Deal (1933–1937), and Lyndon B. Johnson's Great Society (1964–1965) programs? Quantitative or aggregate data are not available to measure Presidents Wilson and Roosevelt's success rate, but a study conducted by Edwards in 1980 revealed that Lyndon Johnson's legislative support scores did not differ appreciably from those of President Jimmy Carter, whose performance in office has been judged by most critics as unimpressive.[44] What accounts for this seeming discrepancy in presidential ratings? The explanation seems to lie in the fact that the scholarly studies of presidential legislative records are calculated on quantitative or aggregate data rather than the quality or importance of legislation. Clearly, a comparison of average congressional support for Presidents Johnson and Carter suggests the limitations of aggregate data.

What are the most important factors that account for the success or failure of a president to win congressional support for his legislative proposals? The bottom line for presidential success, of course, is to have working majorities, not simply party majorities, in Congress. But there are additional factors that help explain presidential success. Generally, they include all of the following: the content of his agenda, timing, popular support across the country, and an upbeat presidential style in dealing with Congress.

President's Legislative Agenda

Legislative priorities and sound strategy, if handled properly, will most likely affect his success with Congress. The contrast between President Jimmy Carter's and Ronald Reagan's handling of their agendas during their first year in office underscores the importance of priorities and focus. President Carter sent an overfilled plate of more than two dozen legislative proposals, including a top-priority energy-saving program, to Capitol Hill the first year and came up nearly empty handed. President Reagan, by contrast, sent only three top-priority items—budget reductions, tax cuts, and a huge increase in the Defense Department budget. Within eight months Reagan had pushed all three of these proposals through Congress, signed the budget- and tax-cutting measures, and returned to his California ranch for a summer vacation. Reagan received high marks for his performance and Carter was given a failing grade.[45] Reagan's ability to prioritize his agenda, limit the number of items, and focus on quick passage spelled success. In contrast, Carter overloaded congressional circuits, failed to prioritize key proposals, with a resultant gridlock on Capitol Hill.

Timing

Stockbrokers and politicians alike believe that timing is everything. Presidents who can sense the mood of the country have generally been successful, as history demonstrates. President Franklin D. Roosevelt, who campaigned and won the presidency in 1932 on a platform pledged to austerity and reduced government spending, quickly sensed that the country wanted him to take drastic action against the Great Depression. In response, FDR reversed course and produced the sweeping New Deal reforms.

Three decades later, President Lyndon B. Johnson, recognizing the depth of congressional and national grief following John F. Kennedy's assassination, called upon Congress to pass President Kennedy's unfinished agenda on civil rights and federal aid to education as a living memorial to the fallen president. LBJ also sent a host of his own Great Society proposals, one at a time, to Congress in the months that followed. Congress, except for a four-month Senate delay with the 1964 Civil Rights Act filibuster, responded with enthusiasm and warm support.

In commenting on presidential timing, political scientist Paul C. Light has observed: "Presidents are expected to recognize the moment of greatest impact; to hold the agenda like a poker hand, revealing the cards at the moment of maximum impact."[46] The importance of timing by the president has been colorfully described in the Southwest vernacular by Lyndon Baines Johnson:

Congress is like a dangerous animal that you're trying to make work for you. You push a little bit and he may go just as you want but you push him too much and he may balk and turn on you. You've got to sense just how much he'll take and what kind of mood he's in every day. For if you don't have a feel for him, he's liable to turn around and go wild. And it all depends on your sense of timing.[47]

While presidents are expected to possess that sixth sense of timing in exerting legislative leadership, relatively few in the twentieth century have had it— Teddy Roosevelt, Wilson, FDR, Johnson, and Reagan. And all these chief executives achieved most of their programming objectives in Congress during their first or second year in the White House. Why is the first year so important? Paul C. Light has put it well:

The answer rests on the cycle of decreasing influence. Presidents and staffs are painfully aware that their most valuable resources dwindle over the term. They understand that the essential resource, capital evaporates over time, that the first year offers the greatest opportunity for establishing the domestic program. Though information and expertise are rarely at a peak in the first year, capital does not keep, and Presidents must take advantage of whatever momentum they have; to wait is to squander the most important advantage.[48]

In recent years, the growth of congressional independence has heightened the pressure on executive leadership during the president's first year in office. Furthermore, the growing complexity of legislation on such matters as the environment, energy, Social Security financing, missile weaponry, communications, consumer protection, and medical care has meant that the president must strike quickly on his legislative program, for he will face delays enough in the labyrinth of the congressional committee apparatus as he seeks to move proposed legislation through both houses. Clearly, the longer a program must wait to be put in the legislative hopper, the greater potential for organized opposition.

Popular Support

Political scientist and former White House staffer Richard E. Neustadt has argued that the president's prestige or popular support affects the level of congressional support for his policies.[49] Neustadt and others have pointed out that a highly popular president enjoys considerable leeway in relating to Congress. George C. Edwards III has commented, "The likelihood that the president will obtain congressional support for his policies increases considerably if the president stands high in the polls and members of Congress either are concerned with how voters evaluate their support of the White House or use presidential approval ratings as indicators."[50]

Two other political scientists, Douglas Rivers and Nancy Rose, have also found that the more popular a president, the higher the proportion of their legislative proposals are passed.[51] Even after adjusting for factors such as the partisan composition of Congress, Rivers and Rose found that on average an increase of eight points in the president's approval rating boosted his legislative success rate by two points in the years between 1954 and 1974. In their view, "public opinion is an important source of presidential influence."[52]

If the president has lost popularity, the lawmaker will likely put some distance between himself and the president. In recent years, several presidents have encountered this "fair weather" treatment. Jimmy Carter, suffering from a continuing decline in popularity, discovered in the 1980 election campaign that a number of Democratic lawmakers sought to disassociate themselves from him. During their reelection campaigns they would be "out of town," if Carter were campaigning in their state. President George Bush, after he agreed to break his "no new taxes" pledge in 1990 to help get a compromise agreement for the 1991 federal budget, suddenly discovered that a number of GOP congressmen facing reelection in the off-year did not want to be seen on the same platform with him. Similarly, in 1994 President Bill Clinton had to accept the fact that many Democratic members of Congress campaigning for reelection did not want him to campaign in their states or districts.

Presidential Style

How a president deals with Congress has long been viewed as a major factor in determining legislative success. Does he actively seek cooperation from Congress through frequent meetings with congressional leaders and groups of lawmakers or is the president withdrawn and relatively inaccessible? The answer to this question will likely dictate the level of presidential success.

Clearly, modern presidents have varied considerably in their manner of relating to Congress. Presidents Kennedy, Johnson, Reagan and Clinton, as already indicated, all encouraged an open presidency, with frequent personal meetings with members of Congress. In John F. Kennedy's first year in office, for example, the young president held thirty-two Tuesday morning meetings with congressional party leadership, ninety private conversations with congressional leaders that lasted an hour or more, coffee hours with five hundred lawmakers, and bill-signing ceremonies with a host of legislators. During his abbreviated presidency he had 2,500 separate contacts, exclusive of correspondence.[53] Few presidents have been more popular on Capitol Hill than the fallen president.

President Johnson's nonstop style of communication with Capitol Hill—both by phone and personal meetings—is legendary. LBJ kept the phone lines humming to Capitol Hill as he lobbied, cajoled, browbeat, and bargained with lawmakers to nail down support for his Great Society bills. Nor did LBJ confine his Capitol Hill contacts to Democrats. Johnson gave the same preferred treatment that he gave to Democratic Majority Leader Mike Mansfield to opposition Republican Minority Leader Everett M. Dirksen. According to one White House aide, Johnson phoned Dirksen as often as ten times a day.[54]

No president is likely to match the intensity of LBJ, but both Presidents Reagan and Clinton have pursued an active courtship of Congress. Even during the presidential transition period in 1980 and 1981 President Reagan took a lively interest in building bridges with members of Congress, spending considerable time on Capitol Hill, stroking Republicans and Democrats alike. In fact, one Reagan transition leader reported in an interview, "We had to lasso him to keep him off the Hill."[55] During President Reagan's first one hundred days in office, his Capitol Hill liaison chief arranged sixty-nine Oval Office sessions in which 467 lawmakers participated. Also, he brought in sixty Democratic lawmakers for a personal White House visit with Reagan in the week before a critical vote on the Reagan-proposed budget cuts.[56] But after passage of his highly publicized tax and budget cuts in 1981, President Reagan's close involvement with Capitol Hill lawmakers tailed off considerably.

President Richard M. Nixon, though an avid campaigner, became reclusive after reaching the White House. Preferring to focus his attention on foreign affairs, Nixon was inaccessible most of the time. Whenever possible, he delegated this congressional "handholding" to his chief assistants, H. R. (Bob) Haldemann and John Ehrlichman. By the time the Watergate investigation was underway in the late spring of 1973, his contacts with Republicans on Capitol Hill had dwindled to a new low and his legislative proposals were dead in the water.

President George Bush, a former member of the House as well as vice president, began his term cultivating close ties with Congress. But as the continued executive-legislative gridlock in a divided government began to take its toll, Bush distanced himself more from Capitol Hill, especially from the opposition Democrats in control of both houses. Preoccupied with the Persian Gulf War, the disintegration of the Soviet Union, and the end of the Cold War, Bush seldom engaged in congressional lobbying, except to line up sufficient votes to sustain many of his forty-six vetoes. Between New Year's Day and mid-April 1992, for example, he did not have a single meeting with the Democratic congressional leaders.[57] By then, of course, he was in the midst of his renomination campaign and the pervading executive-legislative gridlock halted further meaningful dialogue on the White House legislative agenda.

President Bill Clinton's operating style with Congress has been vividly described by one veteran Washington reporter as follows:

Clinton gets a late start in a fight for one of his top priorities. The opposition gets a big jump on him. He sets up a war room to shape public opinion. He brings Democratic lawmakers to the White House by the busload. He pleads that his presidency is on the line. He bargains like a rug merchant for votes. He wins in sudden-death overtime.[58]

The "Two Presidencies"

Generally, Congress has tended to be more supportive of presidential initiatives involving foreign and defense policy. Political scientist Aaron Wildavsky, in a classic study in the 1960s, concluded that there are actually "two presidencies," one for foreign and defense policy and one for domestic policy. From 1948 through 1964 Wildavsky discovered that Congress approved 59 percent of the president's foreign policy initiatives and 73 percent of the president's defense requests, but only 40 percent of his domestic policy proposals.[59] Fifteen years later, however, political scientists Lance LeLoup and Steven Shull made a follow-up study and found that the gap in these two areas had narrowed. Presidential success rates, according to their calculations, were 50 percent foreign policy, 61 percent defense policy initiatives, as opposed to 46 percent in domestic proposals.[60] Another parallel study by political scientist Lee Sigelman also showed that "there has been only a slight differential in congressional support on domestic as opposed to foreign and domestic issues."[61]

Reasons suggested for greater presidential influence with Congress in foreign and defense policy than in domestic policy include the president's greater visibility as a world statesman, his constant access to the latest intelligence information, and his role as commander in chief. Also, there are fewer powerful interest groups involved in trying to push and prod the president in foreign policy matters than domestic issues, fewer constitutional restraints on his overseas actions, and public opinion is usually less concerned about foreign and military policy issues, except in times of crises, when the public generally "rallies around the flag" in support of the president.

PRESIDENT'S LEGISLATIVE SUCCESS WITH CONGRESS

Measuring White House influence over legislation is a hazardous occupation. Presidents Woodrow Wilson and Franklin D. Roosevelt were both remarkably successful in pushing legislation through Congress early in their terms. President Wilson's New Freedom program included, among other things, the Federal Reserve Act of 1913, the Clayton Anti-Trust Act, and the Federal Trade Commission. President Franklin D. Roosevelt's host of New Deal reforms, passed almost entirely in his first term, represented the most far-reaching economic and social reforms in the nation's history. But systematic records of presidential success are only a post–World War II phenomenon.

Political scientist Paul C. Light has compiled a box score of presidential success for the 1961–1980 period (see Table 12.3), focusing on bills deemed by the president—as opposed to the executive branch—to be centrally important to the president's legislative agenda. Two important facts stand out prominently in this table. First, the number of bills on the president's high-priority list is small, keeping in mind that Congress deals with thousands of bills in each session. The second fact that stands out is that presidents serving in a one-party government enjoy a greater degree of success than those in a divided government.

The success rate of the president on votes taken in the House and Senate on which he has indicated a clear position is another way of measuring presidential effectiveness. For the past four decades the *Congressional Quarterly* has been keeping score on presidential success with Congress (see Figure 12.2). With the exception of President Kennedy, the data show that presidents have won fewer votes as their terms wore on. The declines were notable in the cases of Eisenhower, Johnson, Nixon, Ford, and Reagan. Carter lost support only slightly during his single term.

As Figure 12.2 shows, the highest rate of success on House and Senate votes occurred in 1953 for President Eisenhower and in 1965 when Lyndon B. Johnson won approximately 88 percent of all votes on which he took a position. The low ratings came near the end of the terms for Eisenhower (52 percent in 1960), Nixon (51 percent in 1973), Ford (54 percent in 1976), Reagan (44 percent in 1987), and Bush (43 percent in 1992).[62] Generally, the higher scores came in the years in which the presidency and Congress were controlled by the same party and the lower scores came during the years of divided government.

President Bush's low batting average can, it seems fair to say, be attributed in large part to divided government—a topic that merits further discussion.[63]

Table 12.3
Light's Presidential Agenda Box Scores, 1961–1980

Year	President	Requested	Passed	Percent
1961	Kennedy	25	15	60
1962	Kennedy	16	7	44
1963	Kennedy	6	3	50
1964	Johnson	6	3	50
1965	(1st Term)	34	28	82
1966	Johnson	24	14	58
1967	(2nd Term)	19	8	42
1968	Johnson	14	4	29
1969	Johnson	17	7	41
1970	Nixon	12	3	25
1971	(1st Term)	8	2	25
1972	Nixon	3	1	33
1973	(2nd Term)	20	8	40
1974	Nixon	5	2	40
1975	Ford	10	3	30
1976	Ford	6	2	33
1977	Carter	21	14	67
1978	Carter	8	3	38
1979	Carter	8	2	25
1980	Carter	4	1	25

Source: Paul C. Light, "The Focusing Skill and Presidential Influence in Congress," in *Congressional Politics*, ed. Christopher J. Deering (Chicago: Dorsey, 1989), 247. Copyright © 1989 Wadsworth Publishing Co.

DIVIDED GOVERNMENT

Between 1968 and 1992 the country experienced divided government for twenty out of twenty-four years. During this time span the Republicans controlled the White House for twenty years and the Senate six years, while the Democrats maintained uninterrupted control of the House of Representatives for the entire twenty-four year period. Yet, the American public did not seem to object to this truncated arrangement. According to several national polls, more members of the American public throughout the 1980s preferred divided government to unified government—the White House and Congress in the hands of the same party (see Table 12.4). The main reason given by the respondents for this view was that the president could prevent the Democratic-controlled Congress from passing unneeded, expensive legislation, and the Congress could, in turn, keep in check President Reagan's foreign policy

Figure 12.2
Presidential Success on Congressional Votes, 1953–1993

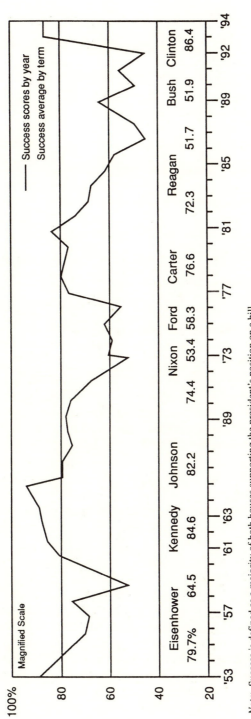

Note: Success is defined as a majority of both houses supporting the president's position on a bill.

Source: Congressional Quarterly Weekly Report, 50 (17 October 1992), 3249; 51 (27 November 1993), 3254.

Table 12.4
Public Opinion on Divided Control of Federal Government, 1981–1994

1. Do you think it is better for the country to have a president that comes from the same political party that controls Congress, or do you think it is better to have a president from one political party and Congress controlled by another?

	Nov. 1981	Sept. 1989	Apr. 1992	Oct. 1994
Same Party	47%	35%	30%	36%
Different Parties	34%	45%	60%	55%
Don't Know or No Opinion	19%	20%	10%	9%

Sources: The New York Times/CBS New poll surveys, cited in Gary C. Jacobson, *The Electoral Origins of Divided Government* (Boulder, CA: Westview, 1990), 121. Reprinted by permission of Westview Press, Boulder, Colorado; *The Wall Street Journal*, 17 April 1992; News/*Wall Street Journal* Poll, NBC-TV newscast, 19 October 1994.

adventures and protect social welfare programs. Two presidents later, as recent polling results in Table 12.4 indicate, the American public still seems to favor divided government.

Divided government, it should be noted, often results in different policy priorities between the two branches, generally producing a stronger resistance to presidential leadership from Capitol Hill and promoting a more independent, assertive role for Congress.[64] Since the mid-1970s Congress has increasingly demonstrated a determination to set the national agenda as a co-equal branch and to challenge the president's agenda. But divided government also obscures accountability and increases constant finger pointing between the president and members of Congress.

The Reagan-Bush years of divided government spawned another presidential stratagem to circumvent congressional oversight—executive orders. First developed by the Reagan White House, executive orders were used extensively to countermand congressional statutes by promulgating executive instructions inconsistent with the purpose of the legislation. One of the better-known examples was the establishment of the Quayle Council to monitor and blunt the effectiveness of the Clean Air Act of 1990. Created by a Bush executive order, the Quayle Council quashed several key congressional regulations imposing stricter controls on toxic waste, waste disposal, air pollution, and management of the nation's wetlands. In other words, the Quayle Council—without authorization from Congress—undermined congressional regulations to control industrial pollution. The Bush administration, for example, twisted the intent of the Clean Air Act of 1990 by promulgating rules that clearly let industrial polluters off the hook. As explained by Charles Tiefer, "In effect, the White House had exercised the sovereign prerogative to grant dispensation from obedience to the law."[65] Tiefer continues, "The Quayle Council represented an administration's strategy for exercising greater power outside the channels of checks and balances."[66]

Does divided government lead to endless gridlock in policymaking? Not always. Recently, political scientist David Mayhew discovered that over a forty-year period (1948–1988) the amount of legislation passed during periods of divided government does not differ appreciably from periods of unified government.[67] Why? The chief reason seems to be that neither the president nor Congress wish to be blamed for the rapid deterioration of the environment, failure to pass needed health care legislation, or failure to reduce the annual national deficit. Consequently, both sides attempt to take action and bargain a compromise settlement rather than face public displeasure over failure to deal with pressing problems. This, in turn, enables both sides to "take credit" for coming up with a solution.[68]

With the inauguration of President Bill Clinton on January 20, 1993, twelve years of divided government came to a close in the nation's capital. Instead, it was replaced with one-party government—the presidency and both houses of Congress in the hands of the same party, the Democrats. Did this spell the end the executive-legislative gridlock in Washington? Several Washington pundits claimed they could hear the chains of gridlock creaking and shattering after only a few months into the Clinton administration. But the end of the executive-legislative stalemate turned out to be short lived.

President Bill Clinton's legislative success with Congress for the first year in office was the third highest since the Washington-based *Congressional Quarterly* started calculating legislative support scores in 1953. Only President Eisenhower's rating (89 percent) in 1953 and President Lyndon Johnson's rating (88 percent) in 1964 topped Clinton's (86.4 percent). Understandably, White House officials hailed Clinton's first-year record as the most productive session of Congress in a generation or more (see Figure 12.2).[69] Surprisingly, President Clinton's legislative success continued at the same exact rate during his second year in office, despite his failure to win enactment of health care reform—a high-priority item on the Clinton agenda. Part of the reason for Clinton's high legislative success rate in 1994 under the *Congressional Quarterly* scoring system was that several other big ticket items also.did not make it to the floor for a vote—legislation on welfare reform, telecommunications, superfund, clean water, and campaign finance reform. However, with the return of divided government in the November 1994 midterm election, after the Republican Party took control of both houses of Congress, President Clinton began shifting toward a defensive strategy similar to that used by President George Bush during most of his four White House years of divided government.

If recent history repeats itself, the nation can expect in 1995 and beyond to see a resurgence of institutional combat between the executive and legislative branches. Divided government, in the minds of one team of observers, creates a pattern that "undermines the governing capacities of the nation's institutions, diminishing the ability of America's government to manage domestic and foreign affairs, and contributing to the erosion of the nation's international political and economic standing."[70] As the new 104th Congress convened in early January 1995, Republican Speaker of the House Newt Gingrich and his conservative-oriented "Contract with America" legislative program appeared to be on a collision course with Democratic President Bill Clinton and his Democratic allies in the House and Senate. How well a Republican-dominated Congress, especially for a party that has not controlled both houses for forty years, will cooperate with a Democratic president will of course show with time.

TOWARD A NEW LEGISLATIVE POWER BALANCE

Future legislation, it seems safe to predict, will continue to bear the strong imprint of both president and Congress—shared legislation. While the president can focus national attention on his legislative initiatives, he obviously cannot hope to enjoy many triumphs unless he can carry Congress along with him.

Congress will continue to enjoy co-equal status in domestic legislative matters, even though the president dominates the public forums. With its recently enlarged professional staff, especially the Congressional Budget Office and its corps of computer analysts, technicians, and economists, the lawmakers are now in a better position to evaluate the potential impact of the president's proposals and meet the president's spokesmen head to head on virtually all controversial issues.[71] No longer will the lawmakers have to rely exclusively on the president's facts and figures at congressional hearings. Consequently, Congress has become more competitive in challenging presidential initiatives and substituting its own version of bills before they reach the floor of each chamber.

Clearly, the Budget and Impoundment Control Act of 1974, the War Powers Resolution, and the growth of congressional oversight all signal congressional determination to exercise a greater share of political power. Indeed, it seems highly doubtful that the executive branch will ever again be accorded the special open-arms treatment that Franklin D. Roosevelt's New Deal measures or Lyndon B. Johnson's early Great Society proposals received on Capitol Hill.

In any event, the power balance between the executive and legislative branches is a dynamic process, ever changing as new presidents occupy the White House and the 535 members of Congress each react and evaluate their relationship with the new chief executive at 1600 Pennsylvania Avenue.

NOTES

1. Arthur M. Schlesinger, Jr., and Alfred de Grazia, *Congress and the President: Their Role in Modern Times* (Washington, DC: American Enterprise Institute for Public Policy Research, 1967), 1.

2. Robert Connery, "Preface," Harvey C. Mansfield, Jr., ed. *Congress against the President* (New York: Praeger, 1975), vii.

3. Philip Norton, *The British Polity*, 2nd ed. (White Plains, NY: Longmans, 1991), 202–232.

4. Richard Rose, *The Postmodern President* (Chatham, NJ: Chatham House, 1988), 65.

5. Richard E. Neustadt, *Presidential Power: The Politics of Leadership from FDR to Carter* (New York: Wiley, 1980), 53.

6. Lance T. LeLoup and Steven A. Shull, *Congress and the President: The Policy Connection* (Belmont, CA: Wadsworth, 1993), vii.

7. These categories, originally formulated by Randall Ripley, have been refined by LeLoup and Shull, *Congress and the President*, 12–17.

8. Mark A. Peterson, *Legislating Together: The White House and Capitol Hill from Eisenhower to Reagan* (Cambridge, MA: Harvard University Press, 1990), 4–6.

9. Arthur M. Schlesinger, Jr., *The Imperial Presidency* (Boston: Houghton Mifflin, 1973).

10. James L. Sundquist, *The Decline and Resurgence of Congress* (Washington, DC: The Brookings Institution, 1981), 407–408.

11. Randall B. Ripley, *Congress: Policy and Process*, 4th ed., (New York: W. W. Norton, 1988), 254–255.

12. Roger H. Davidson, "The Presidency and Congress," in Michael Nelson, ed. *The Presidency and the Political System* (Washington, DC: CQ Press, 1984), 201.

13. Joseph E. Kallenbach, *The American Chief Executive* (New York: Harper & Row, 1966), 340.

14. Richard E. Neustadt, "Presidency and Legislation, Planning the President's Program," *American Political Science Review*, 49 (December 1955): 1015.

15. James MacGregor Burns, *The Lion and the Fox* (New York: Harcourt & Brace, 1956), 186.

16. Eric Goldman, *The Tragedy of Lyndon Johnson* (New York: Knopf, 1969), 307.

17. Michael L. Mezey, *Congress, the President and Public Policy* (Boulder, CO: Westview, 1988), 82.

18. *The Federalist*, No. 46.

19. Roger H. Davidson and Walter J. Oleszek, *Congress and Its Members*, 2nd ed. (Washington, DC: CQ Press, 1985), 302.

20. Lyndon B. Johnson, *The Vantage Point: Perspectives of the Presidency* (New York: Holt, Rinehart & Winston, 1971), 441, 443.

21. James L. Sundquist, "Congress and the President: Enemies or Partners?" in Lawrence C. Dodd and Bruce I. Oppenheimer, eds. *Congress Reconsidered* (New York: Praeger, 1977), 227.

22. Ibid., 240.

23. George C. Edwards III, *At the Margins: Presidential Leadership of Congress*, (New Haven, CT: Yale University Press, 1989), 187.

24. Laurence I. Barrett, *Gambling with History* (New York: Penguin, 1984), 160–161, as quoted in Edwards, *At the Margins*, 190. See also David Stockman, *The Triumph of Politics* (New York: Harper & Row, 1986), 208–265.

25. James L. Sundquist, *Constitutional Reform and Effective Government* (Washington, DC: The Brookings Institution, 1986), 208.

26. Richard A. Watson, *Presidential Vetoes and Public Policy* (Lawrence: University Press of Kansas, 1993), 1.

27. *The New York Times*, 8 June 1995.

28. Marianne Means, *Seattle Post-Intelligencer*, 31 March 1995.

29. *The New York Times*, 7 February 1995.

30. Ibid.; Senator Robert F. Byrd (D-WV), a bitter opponent of the line-item veto, estimated in the floor debate that if the Dole proposal had been in effect for the fiscal year 1995, a total of 9,625 mini-bills would have been necessary rather than thirteen appropriations bills.

31. Ibid.

32. Ibid., 21 March 1995.

33. *Congressional Quarterly Weekly Report*, 22 September 1990, 2991.

34. Doris Kearns, *Lyndon Johnson and the American Dream* (New York: Harper & Row, 1976), 226.

35. Quoted in Davidson and Oleszek, *Congress and Its Members*, 300.

36. Ibid., 297.

37. *Congressional Quarterly Weekly Report*, 3 November 1990, 3764, 3769.

38. *The New York Times*, 11 August 1941. For a brief report on this crucial draft extension vote, see Ronald D. Elving, "The Contest of a Century: Vote Stirs Old Questions," *Congressional Quarterly Weekly Report* 49, 6 April 1991, 869–872.

39. Charles and Barbara Whalen, *The Longest Debate: A Legislative History of the 1964 Civil Rights Act* (Arlington, VA: Seven Locks, 1985).

40. Richard L. Berke, *The New York Times*, 3 March 1993.

41. Patrick Anderson, *The President's Men* (Garden City, NY: Doubleday, 1969), 307.

42. George C. Edwards III, *Presidential Influence in Congress* (San Francisco: W. H. Freeman, 1980), 197–199; Edwards, *At the Margins*, 176–178.

43. Jon R. Bond and Richard Fleisher, *The President in the Legislature* (Chicago: University of Chicago Press, 1990), 218.

44. Edwards, *At the Margins*, 39–44.

45. Courtney Shelton, "How Reagan Rates with Congress," *U.S. News and World Report*, 12 October 1981, 27.

46. Paul C. Light, *The President's Agenda: Domestic Policy from Kennedy to Carter* (Baltimore, MD: Johns Hopkins University Press, 1982), 41–42.

47. Kearns, *Lyndon Johnson and the American Dream*, 227.

48. Light, *The President's Agenda*, 41–42.

49. Richard E. Neustadt, *Presidential Power and the Modern Presidents* (New York: Free Press, 1980), especially chapter 5.

50. Edwards, *At the Margins*, 219.

51. Douglas Rivers and Nancy Rose, "Passing the President's Program in Congress," *American Journal of Political Science* 29 (1985): 183–196.

52. Ibid., 194.

53. John F. Manley, "Presidential Power and White House Lobbying," *Political Science Quarterly* 93 (Summer 1978): 270.

54. Joseph A. Califano, Jr., *A Presidential Nation* (New York: W. W. Norton, 1975), 160–161.

55. Stephen J. Wayne, "Congressional Liaison in the Reagan White House: A Preliminary Assessment," in Norman J. Ornstein, ed. *President and Congress: Assessing Reagan's First Year* (Washington, DC: American Enterprise Institute, 1982), 50.

56. "A Win for Blue Max," *Newsweek*, 18 May 1981, 27.

57. James W. Davis, "Presidents as Party Leaders," *Vox Pop*, newsletter of Political Organizations and Parties, American Political Science Association, published by the Ray C. Bliss Institute of Applied Politics, University of Akron, Akron, Ohio, vol. 11, no. 1, (1992), 11.

58. Janet Hook, "Clinton's Months of Missteps Give Way to Winning Streak," *Congressional Quarterly Weekly Report* 51 (November 27, 1993): 3245.

59. Aaron Wildavsky, "The Two Presidencies," *Transaction* 4 (December 1966), 7–14, reprinted in Aaron Wildavsky, ed. *Perspectives on the Presidency* (Boston: Little, Brown, 1975).

60. Lance T. LeLoup and Steven A. Shull, "The 'Two Presidencies' Reconsidered," *Social Science Quarterly* 59 (March 1979): 704–719; see also, Steven A. Shull, ed., *The Two Presidencies: A Quarter Century Assessment* (Chicago: Nelson-Hall, 1991).

61. Lee Sigelman, "A Reassessment of the Two Presidencies Thesis," *Journal of Politics* 41 (November 1979): 1195–1205.

62. "Bush's Sway with Congress Hits Record Low in 1992," *Congressional Quarterly Weekly Report* 50 (17 October 1992): 3247–3250.

63. For a new analysis of the Bush legislative track record, see Charles Tiefer, *The Semi-Sovereign Presidency: The Bush Administration's Strategy for Governing without Congress* (Boulder, CO: Westview, 1994).

64. For further discussion of divided government, see Gary W. Cox and Samuel Kernell, eds. *The Politics of Divided Government* (Boulder, CO: Westview, 1991); Morris Fiorina, *Divided Government* (New York: Macmillan, 1992); and Gary C. Jacobson, *The Electoral Origins of Divided Government* (Boulder, CO: Westview, 1990).

65. Tiefer, *The Semi-Sovereign Presidency*, 70.

66. Ibid., 87.

67. David R. Mayhew, *Divided We Govern* (New Haven, CT: Yale University Press, 1991).

68. Timothy J. Conlan, "Competitive Government: Policy Escalation and Divided Party Control," Paper prepared for delivery at the 1990 Annual Meeting of the American Political Science Association, San Francisco, CA, August 30–September 2, 1990, 13–14.

69. Janet Hook, "Clinton's Months of Missteps Give Way to Winning Streak," *Congressional Quarterly Weekly Report* 27 November 1993, 3243–3244; Steve Langdon, "Clinton's High Victory Rate Conceals Disappointments," *Congressional Quarterly Weekly Report*, 31 December 1994, 3619–3623.

70. Benjamin Ginsberg and Martin Shefter, *Politics by Other Means: The Declining Importance of Elections in America* (New York: Basic Books, 1990), 161.

71. Roger H. Davidson and Walter J. Oleszek, *Congress and Its Members*, 245–247.

CHAPTER 13

THE PRESIDENT AND THE SUPREME COURT

The Founding Fathers, as they groped toward constructing a constitutional framework that could protect the executive and judicial branches from a domineering Congress, were undecided about how much power should be given to the judiciary. For a time they considered joining the president and Supreme Court in a Council of Revision, with veto authority over legislation passed by Congress as well as state legislatures.[1] Part of the Virginia Plan offered at Philadelphia, this idea was eventually rejected after being put to a vote three times, for fear it might lead the Supreme Court to follow too closely the views of the president.

THE THIRD BRANCH

In the end the Founders left open the basic question that from time to time has been a major source of potential conflict between the executive and the Supreme Court: Who has the final authority to interpret the Constitution? Chief Justice John Marshall may have thought he answered this question once and for all in favor of the Supreme Court in his famous *Marbury v. Madison* (1803) decision which established the doctrine of judicial review. But as the dean of American scholars on the presidency, the late Edward S. Corwin reminded his readers: "Jefferson, involving the principle of the Separation of Powers, denied that the President and Congress were bound by the views that the Supreme Court adopted of the Constitution any more than the Court was bound by their views."[2] President Andrew Jackson held the same view.

Furthermore, Corwin writes: "Lincoln argued that to identify the Court's version of the Constitution, formulated perhaps for the purpose of deciding a single private lawsuit, with the Constitution itself was incompatible with the idea of popular government."[3] In retrospect, the tug-of-war between the president and the Supreme Court that sometimes emerges over the issue of final authority on interpreting the Constitution was probably what the Framers intended, since they viewed occasional conflict as an essential means of keeping the branches in their proper places.[4] During the recent era of divided government, a major source of interbranch conflict involving the Supreme Court has been between a Republican president and a Democratic-controlled Senate over the confirmation of conservative jurists to the High Court. However, the election of a Republican Congress in the 1994 mid-term election means that the sides will simply be reversed, with Democratic President Bill Clinton facing a Republican-controlled Senate in the confirmation process.

In this chapter our attention will be focused, first of all, on how the doctrine of judicial review has affected relationships between the president and the Supreme Court over the past two centuries. Throughout most of our history, the Supreme Court has done far more to expand than to restrain presidential power. We explore as well the Court's support of the president's powers as commander in chief, along with the justices' tendency to sidestep critical issues until after the crisis subsides. Overall, we will show that generally the Supreme Court leans over backward to protect presidential prerogatives.

But the Supreme Court, it will be pointed out, has not hesitated to blow the whistle on the president, if the justices believe he has exceeded his authority. President Truman discovered this to his surprise when he took over the steel mills during the Korean War. And the Court has made it abundantly clear that no president is above the law, as Richard Nixon learned when he sought to withhold certain White House tapes needed as evidence in a criminal trial arising from the Watergate investigation. Our discussion will indicate that the Court, when faced with a tough call on a question involving presidential-constitutional relations, may sometimes term the issue a "political question," though this now happens less frequently than it did formerly.

The confirmation process and the increasingly confrontational nature of these proceedings, especially during periods of divided government, are carefully reviewed. The type of nominees presidents select for the Supreme Court and whether they measure up to presidential expectations are also examined. Finally, it will be noted that the influence of the president's Supreme Court appointments on the future direction of the federal government endures long after the president leaves the White House.

OVERVIEW: RELATIONS BETWEEN THE PRESIDENT
AND THE SUPREME COURT

Taking American history as a whole, the Supreme Court has not been unduly harsh on the office of president. The record shows that during the 1789–1977 period, the Supreme Court decided against the president in only sixty-one cases in the domestic category and in only eight foreign policy cases.[5] Especially noteworthy is the fact that during the last hundred years the Supreme Court has decided against the president in only two foreign policy cases. According to political scientist Michael A. Genovese, the Supreme Court has ruled against the president in fifty-one cases during normal times and against presidents eighteen times during emergency periods between 1789 and 1979.[6] Most of the emergency cases occurred during the Civil War and Great Depression years. As Table 13.1 shows, the Supreme Court decided against President Nixon in twenty-five cases (36 percent of all cases); Franklin D. Roosevelt is second with eight cases, and Lincoln is third with five.

Significantly, the president and the Supreme Court have been embroiled in only two grand confrontations in the twentieth century: the anti–New Deal decisions of the Hughes Court in the mid-thirties and the anti-Nixon rulings during the Watergate investigation of 1973 and 1974 by the Burger Court. Otherwise the president and the Supreme Court have generally seen eye to eye on the major social and economic issues of their era.

COURT SUPPORT OF PRESIDENTIAL ACTIONS

Since the founding of the Republic, the Supreme Court has done far more to expand than to restrain presidential power. In a number of instances, the Founding Fathers' lack of clarity in defining presidential authority has enabled the Supreme Court to interpret presidential power broadly. Respect for the president and a desire to avoid embarrassing clashes with executive authority have, for most of U.S. history, characterized the Supreme Court's behavior toward the nation's leader. Indeed, the Court has invalidated less than a dozen major presidential decisions in almost two centuries.

As Edward S. Corwin, the dean of presidential scholars, observed some years ago, "While the Court has sometimes rebuffed presidential pretensions, it has more often labored to rationalize them; but most of all it has sought on one pretext or other to keep its sickle out of this 'dread field.'" Corwin also pointed out the tactical circumstances have been such that it has been more difficult for the Court to challenge the president than the Congress because "the Court can usually assert itself successfully against Congress by merely 'disallowing' its acts, [whereas] presidential exercises of power will generally have produced some change in the external world beyond ordinary judicial competence to effect."[7]

Table 13.1
Supreme Court Rulings against Presidents, 1789–1994

President	Number of Decisions
Jefferson	2
Madison	3
Monroe	1
Tyler	1
Filmore	1
Lincoln	5
A. Johnson	2
Hayes	1
Arthur	2
Cleveland	1
Wilson	2
Harding	2
Coolidge	3
Hoover	1
F.D. Roosevelt	8
Truman	3
Eisenhower	3
L. Johnson	2
Nixon	25
Ford	3
Carter	2
Reagan	6
Bush	1
Clinton	0
TOTAL	80

Sources: Michael A. Genovese, *The Supreme Court, the Constitution, and Presidential Power* (Lanham, MD: University Press of America, 1980), 264. Data for Presidents Lyndon Johnson, Carter, and Reagan's first term have been furnished by Professor Robert L. Dudley, George Mason University. Data for Reagan's second term, Bush, and Clinton supplied by John Killan, American Law Division, Library of Congress.

Chief Justice John Marshall was one of the first to recognize the judicial untouchableness of the president operating in the sweeping field of executive action. Speaking of the president's "important political powers," Marshall said the principle is that "in their exercise he is to use his own discretion, and is accountable only to his country in his political character and to his own conscience."[8] The Supreme Court has deferred to presidential actions in several broad areas. Jefferson's Louisiana Purchase, a bold action of the type not mentioned in the Constitution, could have provided the Supreme Court with an opportunity to constrain presidential authority. Opposition Federalists viewed

Jefferson's purchase of the vast Louisiana territory as an unconstitutional act. What happened? Nothing. The Court remained silent and, in effect, acquiesced to Jefferson's executive action. More than a half century later, the court upheld Lincoln's imposition of a blockade of Confederate ports without congressional authorization during the Civil War.[9]

Less than four years later, the Supreme Court reaffirmed its recognition of the president's broad executive powers in two post–Civil War cases. In *Mississippi v. Johnson* (1867), the state of Mississippi sought to restrain President Andrew Johnson from enforcing certain Reconstruction acts on the grounds of their alleged unconstitutionality. Mississippi lawyers sought to minimize the seriousness of the state's request to the Court by contending that President Johnson, in enforcing these laws, was performing a "mere ministerial duty" requiring no exercise of discretion. The Court rejected this line of argument and asserted that the president's duty to see that the laws were faithfully executed was "purely executive and political."[10] A similar attempt by Georgia to enjoin Johnson's secretary of war and the generals commanding the Georgia military district from enforcing the Reconstruction acts was also thwarted by the Court, which ruled that the military officials represented the executive authority of the government.[11]

In several later cases the Court attributed powers to the president that were not specifically granted by statute or expressly stated in the Constitution. In the case of *In re Neagle* (1890), the Court ruled that the president had inherent power to defend the "peace of the United States."[12] Neagle, a U.S. marshal, was assigned by the attorney general's office to protect a Supreme Court justice whose life had been threatened by a litigant. When the marshal killed the litigant after he attempted to attack the jurist, the marshal was arrested by state authorities. U.S. attorneys obtained a writ of habeas corpus ordering Neagle to be transferred from state to federal custody. Though this action was challenged by the state of California, the Supreme Court upheld the writ, stating that the president's duty was not limited "to the enforcement of the acts of Congress or of treaties of the United States according to their express terms," but also included "rights, duties, and obligations growing out of the Constitution itself, our international relations, and all the protection implied by the nature of the government under the Constitution."

In assessing this unique case, one constitutional authority has commented: "The compelling aspect of this case was the 'thesis' advanced by Justice Miller that there is a 'peace of the United States' and that it is the President who is to serve as the keeper of that peace. The Neagle case can serve as justification for almost any presidential act to halt domestic disorder."[13]

Five years later, the Supreme Court upheld the power of President Cleveland, acting through a U.S. attorney in Illinois, to obtain an injunction from a U.S. circuit court to keep the trains operating during the Pullman strike. This action enjoined the strike led by Eugene Debs because the labor dispute threatened to interfere with interstate commerce and the transportation of the U.S. mail.[14] The late Clinton Rossiter, recognizing the far-ranging implications of these two decisions, wrote:

> In light of the Debs and Neagle cases, it might be easily argued that there are no judicial limits to the President's real or alleged "inherent power to protect the peace of the United States."[15]

Delegation of legislative authority to the executive reached its zenith during World War II. To aid President Franklin D. Roosevelt in mobilizing the full resources of the country, Congress delegated sweeping authority to the chief executive. Some critics felt that Congress had abdicated its lawmaking function in handing over virtually unlimited authority to the president, but the Supreme Court had no problem in sustaining these broad delegations of legislative authority. In *Yakus v. United States* (1944), the Court upheld the power of the Office of Price Administration (OPA), a special wartime agency established by President Roosevelt, to fight inflation and fix maximum prices for consumer goods under the Emergency Price Control Act of 1942. In a companion case, *Bowles v. Willingham* (1944), the Court also sustained the Office of Price Administration's authority to establish rent controls. These wartime delegations by Congress, as the late Edward S. Corwin commented, exceeded "any previous pattern of delegated legislation touching private rights directly."[16]

A few years later, the court upheld President Truman's seizure of the coal mines to prevent a nationwide strike on the basis of the president's power to seize property in wartime (the Korean War).[17] Throughout the Vietnam War the Court steadfastly refused to entertain suits that challenged the constitutionality of the president's actions or the United States intervention in the Southeast Asia conflict. Indeed, in the words of one constitutional authority:

> Since Vietnam, the Supreme Court has intervened consistently across the spectrum of United States foreign policy interests to tip the balance of foreign policy-making power in favor of the president. Whether on the merits or on justiciability grounds, the courts have ruled for the president in these cases with astounding regularity.[18]

In 1978, the Court approved President Carter's decision to terminate a U.S. defense treaty with Taiwan, despite objections from several U.S. senators.[19] Also, the Court upheld Carter's executive agreement with the revolutionary government of Iran, the regime that held fifty-two Americans hostage for more than a year, to establish an international commission to settle debts owed by the former regime to American businessmen.[20]

In recent years the Supreme Court has been especially jealous in preserving the separation of powers doctrine and executive prerogative. In 1976, for example, the Court in *Buckley v. Valeo* ruled that the president could not share his appointment power with Congress in selecting members of the six-member bipartisan Federal Election Commission.[21] Under the original 1974 statute the

House, Senate, and president were each given authority to select two members of the commission. But after the Court's decision, Congress was required to revise the law, stipulating that the president, with the advice and consent of the Senate, must select all six members. More recently, the Court invalidated a section of the Gramm-Rudman-Hollings Balanced Budget and Emergency Deficit Control Act of 1985, which had assigned executive branch budget-cutting duties to the General Accounting Office's comptroller general, an agent of Congress. Following the Court's decision in *Bowsher v. Synar* (1986), Congress revamped the law—later termed Gramm-Rudman-Hollings II—assigning the deficit reduction and spending cap management duties exclusively to the president's director, Office of Management and Budget.[22]

COURT REBUFFS

In assessing the power relationships between the Supreme Court and the president, one authority on the presidency, Robert J. Sickels, has observed:

One reason the Court has kept its great power . . . is that it avoids serious clashes with the president. History suggests that presidents will retaliate if they are not treated with deference by the Court. Only when the president is out of office or merely hanging on is the Court likely to attack his programs and decisions.[23]

There is considerable validity to the assertion that the Court often sidesteps highly charged issues until the danger has passed, or the president has left office—or has died. The Supreme Court, for example, did not rule against Lincoln's suspension of the writ of habeas corpus in areas where the civil courts were open during the Civil War (*Ex parte Milligan*) until more than a year after Lincoln's assassination.[24]

Franklin D. Roosevelt, however, found a conservative Supreme Court to be a major roadblock in his efforts to combat the Great Depression during his first term. By late 1936, the Supreme Court had declared unconstitutional nine measures which were at the heart of his New Deal program.[25] Included among the judicial casualties were the National Industrial Recovery Act, the Farm Mortgage Act, the Agricultural Adjustment Act, the Bituminous Coal Act, the Railroad Pension Act, and the Municipal Bankruptcy Act.

COURT-PACKING PLAN

Deeply frustrated by the series of Supreme Court setbacks, FDR decided nevertheless that his landslide victory in the 1936 election gave him a mandate to take action. In early 1937, Roosevelt unveiled what was to become known as his "court-packing" plan. FDR's scheme aimed to force the Supreme Court majority to reverse its position on key New Deal legislation by enlarging the size of the Supreme Court. Roosevelt proposed that when any judge of the High

Court who failed to resign within six months after his seventieth birthday, the president would be allowed to appoint up to six additional judges to fill the vacancies. Defending his plan in one of his famous "fire side chats" to the nation, FDR declared that his proposal was necessary to bring into the judicial system "new and younger blood" and that it would "save our National Constitution from hardening of the judicial arteries."[26] If this proposal had been approved, it would have, of course, enabled Roosevelt to put enough friendly justices on the Court to halt the repeated rebuffs the president had suffered from the Court's conservative majority. Nationwide, the reaction to the court-packing plan was heavily negative.

Conservative critics screamed that FDR was determined ultimately to destroy the Supreme Court and judicial review as an integral part of the American separation of powers system. But as explained by political scientist William Lasser, FDR did not want to eliminate the Court, he merely wanted to capture it![27] FDR believed that his court-packing plan was far less radical than any of the several proposed constitutional amendments being circulated by pro–New Dealers to modify the jurisdiction or vote of the Supreme Court. In Roosevelt's view his plan would preserve the Court and judicial review, while neutralizing the elderly justices whose outdated views, he felt, threatened democracy itself. After several weeks of protracted hearings, the Senate in July 1937 soundly rejected FDR's court plan.

In the meantime, however, Chief Justice Charles Evans Hughes and Associate Justice Owen Roberts began having second thoughts about some of their earlier opinions overturning New Deal legislation. Indeed, in voting to uphold the Wagner Labor Relations Act, which was a revamped version of Section 7A of the Court-invalidated National Recovery Administration (NRA) Act in the midst of the Court-packing crisis, the new Court majority clearly displayed a more sympathetic attitude toward remodeled New Deal legislation. The specific case involved the protection of collective bargaining (*National Labor Relations Board v. Jones & Laughlin Steel*).[28]

Whether or not FDR's "threat" to increase the size of the Court had a direct impact on the justices' better-late-than-never thinking has never been fully documented. But legal scholar Thomas Reed Powell's witty observation "A switch in time saved nine!" may have captured the essence of the FDR-Supreme Court controversy. Pundits in the nation's capital and elsewhere concluded that although Roosevelt had lost the court-packing battle, he had won the legislative war.

Before the Court's 1937 summer recess, arch-conservative Justice Willis Van Devanter retired; within eighteen months two other conservative justices followed suit. By then, the new court's majority had produced an almost complete reversal on New Deal laws—a tacit recognition, some said, that the Court follows the election returns.

In a major post–World War II case, *Youngstown Sheet & Tube Company v. Sawyer* (1952), the Court ruled, however, in a split six-to-three decision, that President Truman lacked the authority to take over the nation's steel mills to avert a nationwide steel strike during the Korean War.[29]

Although Justice Black's opinion recognized no inherent power at all in the executive, the history of the presidency reveals that presidents have many times acted on their own with the blessing of the Court. Moreover, the weakness of Black's argument was further undermined by the fact that a majority of the justices (counting the separate opinions of six concurring and dissenting members) agreed that under some circumstances the president might exercise inherent or emergency powers. Chief Justice Fred Vinson, speaking for the three dissenters, argued that the constitutional grant of "executive power" to the president and his constitutional responsibility to execute the laws provided inherent power needed for his seizure of the steel companies. To underscore his argument, the chief justice cited a series of historical examples: Washington's vigorous suppression of the Whiskey Rebellion, Jefferson's initiative in negotiating the Louisiana Purchase, Lincoln's wholly unauthorized Emancipation Proclamation, and more recently, President Roosevelt's pre–World War II nonstatutory seizures of aircraft and industrial plants.

Had the Court recognized that a full-scale national emergency existed—which it did not in this instance—and if President Truman had been in the first or second year of his first term and not hovering near an all-time low in the public opinion polls, one may wonder if the Court's view of his steel company seizures would have been different.

President Nixon, though he appointed four members to the Supreme Court, suffered more serious judicial reversals (four major cases) than any president in American history. Nixon's first major setback came in the case *The New York Times v. United States*[30] when the Court rejected the administration's argument that the executive had an inherent constitutional right "to protect the nation against publication of information whose disclosure would endanger the national security." The case grew out of the unauthorized publication by *The New York Times* and the *Washington Post* of the "Pentagon Papers," an official documentary history of the Vietnam War. By a six-to-three vote, the Court rejected a presidential claim to inherent power that was unsupported by statutory authorization.[31]

The second Nixon setback came a year later in *United States v. United States District Court*,[32] when the Supreme Court ruled that warrantless electronic surveillance in a domestic security case was unconstitutional because it impinged on First and Fourth Amendment values. The Nixon administration argued that this surveillance was a reasonable exercise of the president's power to protect national security. The Court disagreed. The justices denied clearly and unequivocally the existence of any "inherent" independent presidential power in instances of suspected subversive domestic elements. Significantly, the majority opinion was written by Justice Lewis F. Powell, Jr.—a Nixon appointee.

Other than wait (in vain, as it turned out) until he could appoint a majority to the Court, Nixon could only fulminate against the liberal majority. Finally, with his back to the wall as he faced impeachment over his involvement in the Watergate scandals, Nixon claimed a right of "executive privilege"—as all presidents have—not only to withhold information from the press, but even from Congress and the Courts if, in the president's judgment, its release would jeopardize national security or interfere with the confidentiality of advice given to the chief executive.

President Nixon's third major judicial setback came in the celebrated case that led to Nixon's forced resignation, *United States v. Nixon* (1974). The Supreme Court held unanimously (Mr. Justice Rehnquist, a recent appointee and former Department of Justice staff member, did not participate in the case) that a president is subject to judicial subpoena for material relevant to a criminal prosecution.[33]

In this historic case, a unanimous Court ordered the president to turn over tapes of White House conversations with his advisers for use in a criminal case against several of his subordinates, despite Mr. Nixon's argument that executive privilege, considerations of national security, and presidential prerogative protected the confidentiality of these conversations. As the impeachment proceedings moved ever closer to a trial, Nixon may have hoped that the four justices he appointed would come to his rescue. But they did not. Significantly, for the first time in the nation's history, the Supreme Court decided a matter directly involving the president as a party to a case. Furthermore, executive privilege was a novel constitutional doctrine that had never previously been pled before or acknowledged by the High Court.[34]

While sanctioning executive privilege, the Supreme Court rejected the president's claim to *absolute* executive privilege and the idea that the president, rather than the judges, has the final word about what information to release and what to withhold. The justices held that neither the doctrine of separation of powers nor the alleged confidentiality of executive communications barred the federal courts from access to presidential tapes needed as evidence in a criminal trial of several Nixon subordinates. Commenting on the historical importance of this case, one team of legal scholars observed: "In constitutional theory and political consequences, *United States v. Nixon* is among the most remarkable decisions in the Court's history. Vindicated was the ideal 'government of laws and not of men.' "[35] Another legal scholar, Martin Shapiro, while conceding that the case drove the beleaguered president from the White House, suggests that "in the long run the case will be remembered as pro-presidency, the first that acknowledged the constitutional validity of the executive privilege doctrine."[36] In a sense, it was a case of the Court deciding against an individual president while adding to the power of the office.

Subsequently, however, the Supreme Court, in *Nixon v. Fitzgerald* (1982), upheld the absolute immunity for the president in civil cases. The Court majority held the immunity "a functionally mandated incident of the president's unique office, rooted in the constitutional tradition of the separation of powers and supported by our history."[37] The justices also expressed concern about the "dangers of intrusion on the authority and functions of the Executive Branch."[38]

Nixon lost his fourth major decision after he was driven from office. Less than a year after departing the White House, the Court ruled in *Train v. City of New York* that a president could not impound (refuse to spend) money duly appropriated by Congress for specific social programs.[39] In retrospect, Justice Robert Jackson was indeed close to the mark in his observation, made in a concurring opinion in the steel company seizures case, that presidential power was "at its lowest ebb" when the president "takes measures incompatible with the express or implied will of Congress."[40]

JURISDICTIONAL PARAMETERS AND PRESIDENTIAL COMPLIANCE

Robert Scigliano reminds us that Americans should take heart from the fact that "no president, so far as we know, has continued to enforce a law after the courts have definitely ruled it to be unconstitutional, nor has any president argued that he has such a right."[41] Have presidents ever refused to do as the courts have ordered? In a few cases, yes. Thomas Jefferson refused to appear in person at the Aaron Burr conspiracy trial, or furnish the requested documents, or even answer the court's subpoena. But Jefferson did forward some papers to the government attorney with permission to use them as he saw fit.

Frustrated sometimes by the Supreme Court, several presidents have threatened to disregard judicial commands. In most instances they sought to anticipate confrontations that never happened.[42] It seems doubtful that Jefferson would have delivered a commission to William Marbury, one of the so-called "midnight judges," if the Supreme Court had ordered it in the case of *Marbury v. Madison* (1803). But Chief Justice Marshall avoided this head-on collision by ruling that although Marbury was entitled to the commission, the *writ of mandamus* was issued by a court that lacked jurisdiction under the Judiciary Act of 1789.

Chief Justice John Marshall also had a major encounter with President Andrew Jackson during his final years on the bench. In the wake of a famous case, *Worcester v. Georgia* (1832), where the Supreme Court decreed that a state lacked power to pass laws affecting Indians living on Indian land within that state, President Jackson refused to provide military force to overcome Georgia's noncompliance with the High Court's ruling. The circumstances surrounding the dispute remain rather cloudy. But the case is best remembered because Jackson, an old Indian fighter of some renown, is purported to have said, "John Marshall has made his decision; now let him enforce it." Whether apocryphal or not, "Old Hickory's" belligerent retort reflects the Court's heavy dependence on the executive branch for help in enforcing its decisions.[43]

Lincoln ignored several judicial decisions ordering him or his field commanders to release disloyal persons from military custody. In the most famous case, *Ex parte Merryman*, Lincoln refused to order his field commander to turn over Merryman, who had been engaged in secessionist activities, to civil authorities. Though Merryman was subsequently indicted for treason, the case against him was eventually dropped. As Glendon Schubert has commented, this Civil War case makes it "abundantly clear" that "the civil courts have no power to interfere with or control the actions of the Commander in Chief if he wills otherwise."[44]

Franklin D. Roosevelt reportedly threatened to disobey the Supreme Court on two separate occasions, but each time the Court's decision turned out to be acceptable to the president. The first instance occurred when the Court was considering cases that challenged Roosevelt's authority to take the country off the gold standard. But the Court's decision in *Norman v. Baltimore Railroad Company* (1935) upholding the president's action by a five-to-four vote averted a showdown. The second time occurred during World War II when the Court decided, much to Roosevelt's chagrin, to rule on whether he could appoint a special military tribunal to try eight Nazi saboteurs landed from submarines off the American east coast.[45] Since the Court upheld FDR's action, the threatened test of strength between the two branches never materialized.

More recently, Nixon hinted during the Watergate hearings that he might not turn over the White House tapes, no matter what the Supreme Court ruled. But when the Court ruled against him unanimously, he concluded that he had no choice but to comply.[46] Information on the released tapes constituted the "smoking gun" evidence of Nixon's complicity in the Watergate investigation cover-up. Remaining support by fellow Republicans for Nixon against the impeachment charges quickly evaporated after the tapes became public. Within three days Nixon announced his resignation.

Over the Republic's two-century history the number of confrontations between the president and the Supreme Court has been relatively low. Only five presidents—Jefferson, Jackson, Lincoln, Franklin D. Roosevelt, and Nixon—have been engaged in direct conflict with the High Court. And only the Nixon administration was frequently involved in litigation. More recently, more members of the Reagan administration often inveighed against the Court's "abuse of power." This little guerrilla war actually began during Reagan's presidential campaign and erupted intermittently, throughout his eight years in the White House. Although there was no direct collision between the Supreme Court and the presidency during his administration, criticism by high Reagan officials was frequently heard about specific rulings, especially those involving affirmative action and abortion. But by the time president Reagan had placed his third appointee on the High Court in late 1987 and elevated Associate Justice

William Rehnquist to be chief justice, the complaints subsided. President Bush, who added two more conservative justices to the Supreme Court, found relatively little to complain about the Rehnquist Court's decisions.

By and large, recent presidents have fared well with the federal judiciary. In over 400 federal cases involving the presidency from 1949 to 1984, according to judicial scholar Stephen J. Wasby, approximately 70 percent were decided in the president's favor.[47] President Lyndon Johnson had the highest batting average with 92 percent of the cases decided in his favor. President Nixon, as might be expected, had the lowest average—58 percent.[48]

POLITICAL QUESTIONS

Many presidential actions do not easily lend themselves to litigation, for they involve broad questions of leadership, foreign policy, or national security. Jefferson's decision to purchase the Louisiana territory, Roosevelt's decision to build the atomic bomb, and Reagan's decision to invade the Caribbean island of Grenada are all cases in point. The Supreme Court will not review executive discretion; consequently, it will not intervene in presidential decisions of "political questions"—disputes beyond the competence of the Court. In one of the earliest cases, *Luther v. Borden* (1849), the Supreme Court refused to intervene in a case involving rival factions for control of the government of Rhode Island.[49]

Since then, the Supreme Court has from time to time furnished operational definitions of what constitutes political actions that are beyond the Court's review. Generally, these include the acquisition of foreign territory by presidential proclamation; the recognition of both foreign and our own state governments; the declaration of national emergencies; the declaration of martial law; "federalizing" the state militia (national guard); and the formal validity of legislative enactments and constitutional amendments.

The fine line between a judicial issue and a political or policy issue is not always clear. But because the Court retains this option, it can make the distinction and thereby declare an issue to be a political question if it wishes to avoid ruling against a presidential or congressional action. During the Vietnam War, for example, a Federal Court of Appeals used this approach in a 1973 case (*Holtzman v. Schlesinger*) to avoid ruling on the constitutionality of the presidential war being waged in Cambodia.[50]

In recent years, however, the Supreme Court has taken a more assertive role when faced with questions involving another branch of government. As Robert Scigliano has noted: "The Supreme Court has discarded large parts of the doctrine of 'political questions' since the 1950s."[51] Some court critics continued to argue that the Supreme Court avoids "tough calls" on disputes between the president and Congress or Congress and the states by deeming the controversies "political questions." In one recent case, however, the High Court could have dodged a volatile controversy involving congressional reapportionment, but instead the justices chose to face the issue directly. In *U.S. Department of Commerce v. Montana* (1992), the Court was confronted with the highly charged issue of reapportionment of congressional seats among the fifty states after the new decennial census.

Although President Bush's solicitor general argued that the allocation of congressional seats was a political question to be left to the discretion of Congress without interference by federal judges, the High Court rejected this argument, finding the dispute to be one that is appropriate for judicial resolution. Justice John Paul Stevens, speaking for a unanimous Court, declared that while the Court has "respect for a coordinate branch of Government," it nonetheless had to exercise its jurisdiction to decide whether Congress had acted "within the limits dictated by the Constitution."[52] The Court upheld the congressional action on reapportionment. Still, it should be kept in mind, as Michael A. Genovese has cogently observed:

Political questions do provide the courts with a safe escape when they are asked to resolve conflicts which present a "no win" situation to the courts. There are political conflicts which might place the courts in the middle of the two branches. Alienating either the President or Congress could prove to be dangerous. The courts occasionally use the "political question" logic to bow out of the conflict and let the "political branches" fight it out.[53]

Judicial avoidance of a thorny controversy is more likely to occur in foreign affairs and national security matters. Three times during the Reagan administration federal courts avoided umpiring disputes between Congress and the White House by ruling that the issues were either political questions or not yet "ripe" for judicial determination.

Most recently, in *Lowry v. Reagan* (1987) a federal district court dismissed the challenge by 110 members of Congress to President Reagan's alleged violation of the 1973 War Powers Resolution, stemming from the "reflagging" of Kuwaiti tankers in the Persian Gulf. The plaintiffs sought to have the Court require President Reagan to submit a written report to Congress on the status of the reflagging operation, in accordance with the War Powers Resolution. The federal court, however, dismissed the suit by ruling that the case represented a political question.[54] The Supreme Court decided to take no action on the case.

On matters affecting national security it seems fairly clear that national administrations bent on pursing aggressive foreign policy initiatives, free of congressional interference, can usually count on the federal courts to term these actions political questions not subject to review by the judiciary. In any event, the type of cases the Supreme Court may decide to hear is sometimes determined by the type of nominees the president decides to put on the High Court.

PRESIDENTIAL NOMINEES SHAPE DIRECTION OF
THE SUPREME COURT

Over the years there has been little doubt among most students of American government that presidents, especially if they serve two terms, can usually exert a major influence over the direction of Court policy—and public policy—with their Supreme Court appointees. Franklin D. Roosevelt's appointment of Hugo Black, William O. Douglas, and Felix Frankfurter reinforced the Court's switch from opposition to endorsement of the New Deal's broad-scaled social welfare reforms. President Richard Nixon's appointment of four conservative justices— Burger, Blackmun, Rehnquist, and Powell—slowed down or reversed several Warren Court decisions affecting criminal procedures, school desegregation, and other minority rights.

President Ronald Reagan during his two full terms (1981–1989) set an all-time record for the number of federal judges appointed to the bench—389 judges, or nearly half of all judges in the federal courts. Even though President Franklin D. Roosevelt occupied the White House for more than twelve years (1933–1945), he fell far short of Reagan in the number of appointments to the federal judiciary (see Table 13.2). Major reasons for the huge number of federal judges appointed by Reagan was not only the high turnover over eight years, but also legislation by Congress increasing the number of federal judgeships— nearly 100 new positions—to handle the heavy case overload that developed in the 1980s. In 1990, Congress created eighty-five additional positions at the federal district and court of appeals level. Especially the $30 billion federal anti-crime bill of 1994, approved by the 103rd Congress, is expected to generate hundreds of new cases for the federal courts. The decade-long trend of trans-forming many drug and gun infractions—historically the province of state courts—into federal offenses will undoubtedly require even more federal judges.

Congress, especially the Senate, has seldom hesitated to create additional judicial positions because it presents a welcomed opportunity for Senators, if their party occupies the White House, to reward loyal supporters with federal judgeships. Also, the argument for additional federal judicial appointees is unassailable as a campaign promise to deal firmly with criminal issues.

President Bill Clinton, even if he should serve only a single term, is expected to have the opportunity to fill nearly a quarter of all federal judgeships before his term is over. Among the existing 828 federal judgeships in March 1993, there were 115 vacancies. (These judgeships included several dozen positions left vacant when the Democratic Senate majority refused to confirm several dozen Bush-appointed nominees in 1992; this was done in hopes that a Democrat would win the White House in November and thus be able to submit a new list of Democratic nominees.) President Clinton nominated more federal judges—129 jurists—in his first two years than any president in history.[55]

Table 13.2
Presidential Nominees to the Federal Bench, 1933–1994

	Supreme Court	Circuit Court	District Court	Special Courts[1]	Total
FDR	9	52	137	14	212
Truman	4	27	102	9	142
Eisenhower	5	45	127	10	187
Kennedy	2	20	102	2	126
Johnson	2	41	125	13	181
Nixon	4	45	182	7	238
Ford	1	12	52	1	66
Carter		56	206	3	265
Reagan	4	78	290	10	382
Bush	2	37	148		187
Clinton*	2	19	108		129

*Appointments made through October 1994; [1]Includes Customs, Patent Appeals, and Court of International Trade.

Sources: Stephen J. Wayne, G. Calvin Mackenzie, David M. O'Brien, and Richard I. Cole, *The Politics of American Government* (New York: St. Martin's, 1995), 562. Copyright © 1994. Reprinted with permission of St. Martin's Press, Incorporated.

We should not underestimate the impact of the president's appointment power on the judiciary. As judicial scholar Sheldon Goldman has reminded us, "When we elect a President, we're electing a judiciary."[56] Also, Robert Dahl perceptibly noted some years ago that the appointment power helps esure

that the policy views dominant on the Court are never for long out of line with the policy views among the lawmaking majorities of the United States. Consequently, it would be unrealistic to suppose that the Court would, for more than a few ye--s at most, stand against any major alternatives sought by the lawmaking authority.[57]

Presidents invariably look to the Court, especially their own appointees, to legitimize the executive and legislative policies they have developed—though the record shows that the Court's decisions sometimes run counter to the president's preferences.

Since 1789, presidents have appointed 108 judges to the Supreme Court (see Table 13.3). Approximately 80 percent of the nominees formally sent by the president to the Senate have been confirmed.[58] But approximately one out of five has been rejected. Most of these rejections, however, occurred in the

Table 13.3
Presidential Appointments to the U.S. Supreme Court

President	Dates in Office	Number of Appointments
Washington	1789-1797	10
J. Adams	1797-1801	3
Jefferson	1801-1809	3
Madison	1809-1817	2
Monroe	1817-1825	1
J.Q. Adams	1825-1929	1
Jackson	1829-1837	6(5)*
Van Buren	1837-1841	2(3)*
W. H. Harrison	1841-1841	0
Tyler	1841-1845	1
Polk	1845-1849	2
Taylor	1849-1850	0
Filmore	1850-1853	1
Pierce	1853-1857	1
Buchanan	1857-1861	1
Lincoln	1861-1865	5
A. Johnson	1865-1869	0
Grant	1869-1877	4
Hayes	1877-1881	2
Garfield	1881-1881	1
Arthur	1881-1885	2
Cleveland	1885-1889; 1893-1897	4†
B. Harrison	1889-1893	4
McKinley	1897-1901	1
T. Roosevelt	1901-1909	3
Taft	1909-1913	6
Wilson	1913-1921	3
Harding	1921-1923	4
Coolidge	1923-1929	1
Hoover	1929-1933	3
F.D. Roosevelt	1933-1945	9
Truman	1945-1953	4
Eisenhower	1953-1961	5
Kennedy	1961-1963	2
L.B. Johnson	1963-1969	2
Nixon	1969-1974	4
Ford	1974-1977	1
Carter	1977-1981	0
Reagan	1981-1989	4
Bush	1989-1993	2
Clinton	1993-19__	2

Notes: *Jackson nominated Carton, but was not confirmed until Van Buren had taken over; †Two in each of his two terms, which was split by Harrison's single term; Although the number of appointments totals 112, four of the Chief Justice appointees—White, Hughes, Stone, and Rehnquist—previously served on the Supreme Court. Thus, the actual number of High Court appointees is 108.

Sources: *The Judicial Process: An Introductory Analysis of the Courts of the United States, England, and France*, 6th ed. by Henry J. Abraham, 55. Copyright © 1993 by Henry J. Abraham. Reprinted by permission of Oxford University Press, Inc.; David G. Barnum, *The Supreme Court and American Democracy* (New York: St. Martin's, 1993), 318–319.

nineteenth century. Only seven rejections—two were President Nixon's nominees—have taken place in the twentieth century. On average, a Court vacancy has occurred about almost every eighteen months since 1937 (approximately every twenty-two months since 1789). Thus, as mentioned earlier, a two-term president can normally expect to appoint close to a majority of the justices before he leaves the White House.

Four Republican presidents—Nixon, Ford, Reagan, and Bush—made eleven consecutive appointments to the Supreme Court over the 1969–1993 period before Democratic President Bill Clinton appointed Federal Court of Appeals Judge Ruth Bader Ginsburg to the High Court in June 1993. Judge Ginsburg was the first Supreme Court justice to be appointed by a Democratic president since President Lyndon B. Johnson selected Thurgood Marshall to the High Court in 1967. A year later, Mr. Clinton made his second appointment—Court of Appeals Judge Stephen G. Breyer—to replace retiring Justice Harry Blackmun.

The number of High Court appointments, it seems, seldom rests on any actuarial tables. Taft, a one-term president, appointed six justices, but Woodrow Wilson appointed only three justices during his two full terms. Franklin D. Roosevelt, who served in the White House for slightly over three terms, holds the runner-up position to Washington, who selected the entire original Supreme Court, plus four replacements (ten in all). FDR appointed nine justices; Jimmy Carter, on the other hand, did not have the opportunity to appoint a single member to the Supreme Court—the first full-term president in history to be denied that chance.[59] Plainly, the appointment power gives most presidents the opportunity to exert a major influence on a co-equal branch of the federal government.

Who does the president appoint to the highest court in the country? Top-drawer legal minds are usually at the head of the list. The names of John Marshall, Joseph Story, Roger B. Taney, John M. Harlan, Oliver Wendell Holmes, Jr., Louis D. Brandeis, and Felix Frankfurter immediately come to mind. Political strategy sometimes dictates a judicial appointment. Franklin D. Roosevelt, probably one of the most partisan chief executives of the twentieth century, opted for statesmanship rather than partisanship when he elevated Associated Justice Harlan F. Stone to chief justice in 1941, six months before Pearl Harbor. Roosevelt picked Stone, a former Republican attorney general nominated to the Court by President Calvin Coolidge in 1923, over Democratic Attorney General Robert M. Jackson, thought to be FDR's first choice, as a gesture toward national unity in the face of a growing war crisis.

Retiring Chief Justice Charles Evans Hughes urged FDR to promote Associate Justice Stone (who had been one of Roosevelt's professors at Columbia Law School) on the basis of his record. Hughes also suggested that Roosevelt consult Mr. Justice Frankfurter, a Roosevelt appointee, regarding the chief justiceship. Frankfurter advised the president:

When war does come, the country should feel you are national, the Nation's President, and not a partisan President . . . [to bolster this assessment] you [should] name a Republican, who has the profession's confidence, as Chief Justice.[60]

Personal friendship has sometimes been a significant factor, though obviously not the only consideration, in judicial appointments. William Howard Taft's appointment of Justice H. H. Lurton rested heavily on personal friendship. Both Taft and Lurton had served together for eight years on the U.S. Court of Appeals for the Sixth Circuit, where they became fast friends. Lurton, a Tennessee Democrat, had been elevated to chief judge when the future president went to the Philippines as governor-general. Later, President Taft called the nomination of his former colleague "the chief pleasure of my administration."[61]

President Truman's choice of Fred Vinson to be chief justice was based heavily on their long friendship. Vinson was serving in the cabinet as secretary of the Treasury when Truman elevated him to the chief justiceship. And John F. Kennedy's choice of Byron F. (Whizzer) White, a former all-American football player and Rhodes scholar, probably was based as much on friendship as legal qualifications.

Geographical representation on the Court has in the past been a prominent factor in presidential choice, such as Lincoln's choice of a trans-Mississippi lawyer, Samuel F. Miller, to the bench during the Civil War, and the concern to have a Southerner or a Westerner in one of the Court seats. President Harding's choice of Pierce Butler of Minnesota, a nominal Democrat, represented only the second justice born west of the Mississippi. President Nixon's choice of Lewis F. Powell, Jr., of Virginia, was, in current parlance, a "twofer"—he obtained at least two pluses from his appointee. Powell, a southern Democrat, was viewed by the president also as a strict constructionist.

Ethnicity, religion, and gender in recent years have become more important factors than geography in making appointments. Legal scholars and politicians now commonly refer to a "Roman Catholic seat," a "Jewish seat," a "black seat," and, most recently, a "woman's seat" on the Court. Robert B. Taney's appointment in 1835 by Jackson marked the first Catholic appointment. Since the turn of the century, there has been a Roman Catholic sitting on the bench almost continuously. The first Jewish seat was filled in 1916 with Wilson's appointment of Louis D. Brandeis, followed by Benjamin N. Cardozo (Hoover, 1932), Felix Frankfurter (Roosevelt, 1938), Arthur Goldberg (Kennedy, 1963), and Abe Fortas (Johnson, 1965). But until the recent appointment of Justice Ruth Bader Ginsburg by President Clinton, no members of the Jewish faith had served on the Court since Fortas's resignation in 1969.

Two years earlier, President Johnson's solicitor general, Thurgood Marshall, became the first black ever to be appointed to the Supreme Court, suggesting perhaps that there may come to be a reserved seat for a black jurist. Perhaps in the future there may also come to be a "Hispanic seat." While it seems doubtful that the makeup of the Court will always reflect all of these considerations, it is a virtual certainty that most of these constituencies will continue to be represented when the Court begins its annual session each October.

Despite the growing diversity on the Court, most members have been male Protestants of Anglo-Saxon heritage, upper-middle "establishment" background, who have held positions in the federal and state court systems and who previously were often involved politically. Significantly, approximately 85 percent of federal court appointees have come from the same political party as the president.[62] The last president to select a Supreme Court justice from the opposition party was Richard M. Nixon, who appointed Lewis F. Powell, Jr., a Democrat in 1971.

CONFIRMATION PROCESS: THE PRESIDENT VERSUS CONGRESS

During the height of the nationally televised coverage of the Senate's confirmation hearing of Supreme Court nominee Clarence Thomas in October 1991, Democratic Senate Majority Leader George Mitchell observed: "The confirmation process has become uncomfortable and demeaning for all concerned. It has taken on the trappings of a political campaign."[63] Few Washington commentators would disagree. Indeed, the nationwide campaign mounted by special interest groups against the confirmation of Judge Thomas and, in 1987, against Court of Appeals Judge Robert H. Bork reached a level of intensity seldom seen in the nation's capital. Judging by the huge number of phone calls to U.S. Senators, letters, personal visits to senators' offices, advertising in big-city newspapers, an outsider might easily conclude that the confirmation process of Supreme Court nominees is now barely indistinguishable from a political campaign. In previous eras prolonged investigation and questioning were just not the style. Chief Justice William Howard Taft and Justices Sutherland, Brynes, and Burton were confirmed the same day they were nominated and their names sent to Capitol Hill. The Senate took only two days to put Oliver Wendell Holmes, Jr. on the bench; and it required only eight days for Charles Evans Hughes to be confirmed the first time he was nominated.[64]

That the confirmation process has become increasingly confrontational over the past quarter century is beyond dispute. During the 1968–1987 period, six nominees were rejected or asked that their names be withdrawn. This turbulent era began when President Lyndon B. Johnson, nearing the end of his tenure in the White House, nominated his old friend and confidant, Associate Justice Abe Fortas to fill the seat of retiring Chief Justice Earl Warren. However, Republican opponents in the Senate, criticizing Fortas's continuing practice of privately advising President Johnson on various policy matters, his liberal opinions while an associate justice, and acceptance of questionable honoraria, filibustered his nomination for more than twelve weeks in late 1968. When his Senate supporters failed to win a closure vote to end the filibuster, Justice Fortas eventually asked that his name be withdrawn.[65]

Two of President Nixon's six Supreme Court nominees—Clement F. Haynesworth and G. Harold Carswell—were rejected by the U.S. Senate, controlled by the Democrats. Both rejectees were conservative, federal courts of appeals judges from the South whose positions on segregation, civil rights, and labor—and charges of "ethical insensitivity" in Haynesworth's case—were enough to sink their confirmation hopes.

President Reagan, the first chief executive to appoint a woman jurist (Sandra Day O'Connor) to the Supreme Court, later encountered a firestorm over his nomination of Circuit Court of Appeals Judge Robert H. Bork in 1987. A staunch conservative jurist who had written widely on the law, Bork discovered that his widely publicized conservative judicial philosophy made him a sitting target for Senate opponents. They succeeded in framing two major questions that proved to be fatal to his nomination: whether he would "turn the clock back" on civil rights and other pressing issues, especially abortion, and whether he was "out of the mainstream" of modern legal thought. After two raucous weeks of hearings and debate, the Senate rejected Bork by a vote of fifty-eight to forty-two.[66]

President Reagan then announced his intention to nominate Court of Appeals Judge Douglas H. Ginsburg, but within a week Ginsburg asked that his name be withdrawn. Disclosures about his personal and ethical conduct—most notably his admission that he had smoked marijuana with his students at Harvard Law School—and his actions as a Justice Department official in handling a television cable company dispute while he held stock in the cable company spelled the end of his candidacy.

Reagan's next nominee, Court of Appeals Judge Anthony Kennedy of California, on the other hand, breezed through the entire confirmation process with only token opposition. So did President Bush's first nominee, a little-known New England Court of Appeals Judge, David Souter, who was dubbed the "stealth" candidate because his track record as a judge and New Hampshire attorney general was almost invisible.

President Bush's second appointee, Court of Appeals Judge Clarence Thomas, however, triggered a series of vitriolic exchanges between Republican and Democratic members of the Senate Judiciary Committee. Millions of viewers watched on nationwide television as Judge Thomas, a black, denied charges of sexual harassment by a former black female employee who later became a law professor at the University of Oklahoma. Judge Thomas's complaint about being subjected to a "high tech lynching" by the Judiciary Committee reverberated across America as panel after panel of pro- and anti-Thomas advocates filled the PBS network and C-SPAN channels in a marathon fourteen-hour Sunday session. After a full-scale debate, during which President Bush brought heavy pressure on wavering senators and the public flooded Capitol Hill with phone calls and telegrams, the Senate voted fifty-two to forty-eight to confirm Thomas. Eleven Democrats joined forty-one Republicans in supporting the second black jurist to be appointed to the High Court.[67]

Critics of the confirmation process, including President Bush, insisted that another way must be found to avoid a repeat performance of the divisive Thomas proceedings. But these critics might look no further for an answer than the increasing frequency of divided government in the United States. During the twenty-four years between 1968 and 1992 the country experienced twenty years of divided government, with the Republicans occupying the White House and the Democrats controlling one or both houses of Congress.

Other commentators have suggested that the best solution for avoiding confirmation donnybrooks may be for the president to take the Senate's "advice" as seriously as its "consent" and consult beforehand with the lawmakers about who should be nominated. As put by law professor Walter E. Dellinger III of Duke University, "The President has it in his power to avoid this whole debacle by recognizing that in a time of divided government, it would be appropriate to nominate a consensus candidate of true distinction."[68] Indeed, this proposal is not as far-fetched as it might seem at first blush. In 1932, for example, President Herbert Hoover, a conservative Republican, named Benjamin N. Cardozo to the bench largely at the recommendation of leading senators from both parties. Cardozo, though far more liberal than Hoover, subsequently became one of the most distinguished justices of the twentieth century. Similarly, in the late nineteenth century President Grover Cleveland, a Democrat, consulted with Republican leaders who controlled the Senate before filling High Court vacancies.

Unless both ends of Pennsylvania Avenue are occupied by the same party or some common ground can be found between presidents and senators on selecting prospective nominees, the confirmation process is likely to remain more confrontational than consultative.

Most recently, however, the confirmation process for President Clinton's second nominee, Judge Stephen G. Breyer, was described by several reporters as a "lovefest." Breyer sailed through three days of hearings in mid-July 1994 with barely a ripple of criticism. He received the unanimous endorsement from the Senate Judiciary Committee. The Senate approved his nomination by a vote of eighty-seven to nine.[69]

PRESIDENTIAL EXPECTATIONS

Do presidents get value received from the individuals they appoint to the Supreme Court? While it is impossible to measure with precision how every president has felt about every major issue decided by the courts, the record shows that presidents have obtained—approximately 75 percent of the time—what they wanted from their appointees.[70]

Despite a few well-publicized exceptions, presidents have generally not been disappointed with the voting records of the people they appoint. Evidence that a president usually gets what he wants from his appointees began showing up early in our constitutional history. President John Adams was not unhappy with John Marshall's strong national views and his defense of private property. As a matter of fact, both Washington and Adams restricted their court choices to persons who were firm adherents of Federalist doctrine—strong supporters of the broad exercise of power by the national government, especially relating to commerce and industry, and who would limit the power of states to interfere with these and other national goals. As Robert Scigliano has noted, "Their appointees hardly ever deviated from these policies, and two of them, John Marshall and Bushrod Washington, espoused them in careers of more than thirty years service on the Court.[71] Indeed, the record shows that no Federalist justice dissent was ever recorded against landmark Federalist decisions of the first forty years of the Republic.[72]

Most of the justices appointed by Jackson, Van Buren, and Polk and other Democratic presidents of the pre–Civil War period were usually faithful to the states rights views of their benefactors. Lincoln had no reason to be disappointed with the five justices he put on the Supreme Court. His first four appointees voted to uphold the Union blockade of southern ports, and at the same time withheld the status of belligerent power from the Confederacy (*The Prize Cases*, 1863). All of Lincoln's justices voted to invalidate a state bank tax that would have severely hindered the federal government's financing of the war effort (*Bank of Commerce v. New York*, 1863); moreover, they refused to take jurisdiction of cases challenging legal tender legislation (*Roosevelt v. Meyer*, 1863) and the military arrest and trial of southern sympathizers in areas outside the perimeter of war (*Ex parte Vallandingham*, 1864).[73]

Nor was President Ulysses Grant disappointed with his two appointees, who filled vacancies after the Court had originally denied Congress the power to issue paper money. Indeed, Grant's two appointees joined three of Lincoln's to promptly overturn this ruling—one of the key decisions of the post–Civil War era. Most post–Civil War presidents, however, had their hands full finding appointees who would be acceptable to the Senate, which usually was closely divided or opposition controlled. President Cleveland, for example, had his first two nominations to the Court rejected before Edward D. White received Senate approval.[74]

Theodore Roosevelt, on more than one occasion, expressed his "bitter disappointment" over his nomination of Oliver Wendell Holmes, Jr., to the bench. But among his contemporaries it seems doubtful if Teddy would have been entirely satisfied with any justice, unless he were a clone. His distant cousin, Franklin D. Roosevelt, had no reason to be displeased with his judicial appointees (nine in all). As explained by Robert Scigliano, "Not one of Roosevelt's justices ever took the position in a case against the New Deal or against a state tax or business regulation on the grounds that the state enactment was not permitted by the due process clause of the Fourteenth Amendment."[75]

Until the Watergate hearings collapsed over Richard Nixon's head, the four justices he appointed all voted to cut back on criminal defense rights, the only Court issue, according to some observers, that seriously interested him.

Dwight D. Eisenhower, on the other hand, was deeply disappointed with two of his appointees—Chief Justice Earl Warren and Justice William J. Brennan, Jr.—who turned out to be "closet" liberals. Asked if he had made any mistakes during his presidency, General Ike reportedly replied, "Yes, and they are both sitting on the Supreme Court."[76]

Generally, presidents who serve two full terms not only leave an indelible mark on the Supreme Court, but they also put a heavy imprint on the entire federal judicial system. Between Presidents Reagan and Bush, these two chief executives appointed approximately 70 percent of the nation's sitting federal judges during their twelve-year occupancy of the White House (1981–1993). It could be argued that the Supreme Court appointees Presidents Reagan and Bush have made will be the most lasting and significant actions of their presidencies. Barring a nuclear holocaust or an epidemic, a large share of the Reagan and Bush appointees will still be sitting on the bench well into the twenty-first century. Many of President Bush's nominees—overall the youngest crop of federal jurists in the past three decades—could readily sit on the federal bench through the next six or more presidential terms, since they are appointed for life. Supreme Court Justice Clarence Thomas, for example, was only forty-three years old when President Bush nominated him in the summer of 1991.

Like President Reagan, Bush's appointees were generally white, wealthy, male, and almost uniformly conservative lawyers. True to the key tenets of the conservative judicial agenda, the Reagan-Bush judges have tended to construe laws as narrowly as possible, and they have generally favored law enforcement of officials over criminal defendants. Typically, they have also deferred to Congress in deciding close constitutional issues.[77] Not since Franklin D. Roosevelt's administration have two presidents had such an open-ended opportunity to transform the federal judiciary. Nor are presidents unmindful of the importance of lower court appointments. Approximately 80,000 cases are decided in lower federal courts annually, compared with nearly 150 that are decided by the Supreme Court. Because it is from the twelve courts of appeals and the ninety-four district courts that the Supreme Court gets most of its business, the president's ability to affect decisions of the lower courts by the appointment power can often affect the issues the Supreme Court decides to consider.[78]

According to a study by Sheldon Goldman, one-quarter of Reagan's judicial appointees during his first term were millionaires. Their average age was fifty years. Approximately two-thirds had judicial experience, suggesting that the

White House placed heavy emphasis on appointees with judicial track records.[79] In picking federal district judges, President Reagan usually followed the long tradition of accepting candidates recommended by the home state senators of his party. Nevertheless, Washington sources reported a surprising number of unpublicized cases in which the White House rejected a Republican senator's choice as too liberal or unqualified.

There is little reason to doubt that President Reagan's centralization of control in the "presidential branch" included judicial appointments. To carefully screen all prospective federal judicial appointees, Reagan's staff created the Committee on Federal Judicial Selection.[80] Consisting of the president's chief of staff, one or more presidential counselors, the presidential assistant for legislative affairs, the attorney general and several of his deputies, this committee closely scrutinized every prospective judicial nominee for his or her conservative ideological purity as well as general competence and character.

Sheldon Goldman, a leading authority on judicial selection, has argued that no administration in history more systematically reviewed individual appointees with respect to questions of public policy, patronage, and legislative relations.[81] Stories persisted in the nation's capital that the committee or its staff interrogated candidates, subjecting them to "litmus tests" on their policy views, for example, on abortion and other constitutional issues.[82] Indeed, some sitting federal district judges being considered for "promotion" to the federal court of appeals reported having been asked to defend some of their decisions.[83] Clearly, the record shows, according to Goldman, "that what the Reagan administration did in its systematic attempt to shape the judiciary went beyond anything we have seen in American history."[84] President Bush followed in President Reagan's footsteps in selecting conservative jurists to the High Court. Twice, he elevated Reagan-appointed federal courts of appeals judges to the Supreme Court. Most recently, President Clinton, too, has elevated two federal courts of appeals judges to the Supreme Court, but both appointees have been moderate Democrats.

By way of summary, a quick review of the nation's history shows that the Supreme Court generally gives great weight to the president's own interpretation and construction of the scope of his own powers. Indeed, the Supreme Court has seldom been a major barrier to the extension of presidential power. The Supreme Court is more likely to overrule a president on domestic matters than in the field of foreign policy and much less likely to thwart a president in times of national emergency.

Since the fine line between a judicial issue and a political or policy issue is not always clear, the Supreme Court may exercise the option of declaring a sticky issue a "political" question and thereby avoid ruling against a presidential or congressional action. In recent years, however, the Court has resorted to this option less frequently. The recent action invalidating the legislative veto in 1983 is a case in point.

Presidents exert a major influence over the Supreme Court by their choice of nominees. Political affiliation (belonging to the president's party), ideological compatibility with the president's views, ethnicity, religion, and gender are all factors that presidents weigh before sending their nominees to the Senate. The historical record indicates that presidents have been pleased with their choices in about three-quarters of the cases.

If a president serves two full terms, the chances are better than even that he will have an opportunity to pick nearly a majority of the justices in the federal judiciary—and thus leave a lasting imprint on the entire federal system.

NOTES

1. Christopher Collier and James Lincoln Collier, *Decision in Philadelphia: The Constitutional Convention of 1787* (New York: Random House, 1986), 220.

2. E. S. Corwin, *The President: Office and Powers, 1787–1984*, 5th ed., Randall W. Bland, Theodore T. Hindson, and Jack W. Peltason, eds. (New York: New York University Press, 1984), 329.

3. Ibid.

4. Robert Scigliano, *The Supreme Court and the President* (New York: Free Press, 1971), 15.

5. Michael A. Genovese, *The Supreme Court, the Constitution, and Presidential Power* (Lanham, MD: University Press of America, 1980), 242.

6. Ibid. Political scientists Craig R. Ducat and Robert L. Dudley have found a high level of support for presidential power among votes cast by federal judges at all levels—federal, district, court of appeals, and Supreme Court—in 531 cases decided between January 1949 and June 1984. "Of the 1337 votes cast, two-thirds (67 percent) favored the exercise of presidential power." Craig R. Ducat and Robert L. Dudley, "Federal Judges and Presidential Power: Truman to Reagan." Paper delivered at the Midwest Political Science Association annual meeting, Chicago, April 9–12, 1986, 7.

7. Corwin, *The President: Office and Powers*, 4th ed., 16, 25.

8. Ibid., 25.

9. *The Prize Cases*, 2 Black 635 (1863).

10. 4 Wall. 475 (1867).

11. *Georgia v. Stanton*, 6 Wall. 50 (1868).

12. 135 U.S. (1890).

13. Genovese, *The Supreme Court, the Constitution, and Presidential Power*, 153.

14. 158 U.S. 564 (1895).

15. Clinton Rossiter, *The Supreme Court and the Commander in Chief* (Ithaca, NY: Cornell University Press, 1976), 41.

16. Edward S. Corwin, *Total War and the Constitution* (New York: Knopf, 1947), 45.

17. *U.S. v. Pewee Coal Company*, 341 U.S. 114 (1951).

18. Harold H. Koh, *The National Security Constitution* (New Haven, CT: Yale University Press, 1990), 134.

19. *Goldwater v. Carter*, 444 U.S. 996 (1979).

20. *Dames & Moore v. Regan* (1981). See also Chapter 8.

21. 424 U.S. 1 (1976). See also Frank J. Sorauf, *Money in American Elections* (Glenview, IL: Scott, Foresman & Company, 1988), 246–248.

22. 478 U.S. 714 (1986). See also Robert J. Spitzer, *President and Congress: Executive Hegemony at the Crossroads of American Government* (Philadelphia: Temple University Press, 1993), 110–111.

23. Robert J. Sickels, *The Presidency* (Englewood Cliffs, NJ: Prentice-Hall, 1980), 268.

24. 4 *Wallace* 2 (1866).

25. Genovese, *The Supreme Court, the Constitution, and Presidential Power,* 169–170.

26. Speech of March 9, 1937, Senate Report No. 711, 75th Congress, 1st Session, as quoted in David G. Barnum, *The Supreme Court and American Democracy* (New York: St. Martin's, 1993), 198.

27. William Lasser, *The Limits of Judicial Power* (Chapel Hill: University of North Carolina Press, 1988), 156.

28. 301 U.S. 1 (1937).

29. 343 U.S. 579 (1952).

30. 403 U.S. 713 (1971).

31. Ibid.

32. 467 U.S. 297 (1972).

33. 418 U.S. 683 (1974).

34. Martin Shapiro, "The Supreme Court: From Warren to Burger," in Anthony King, ed. *The New Political System* (Washington, DC: American Enterprise Institute, 1978), 184.

35. Alpheus Thomas Mason, William M. Beaney, and Donald Grier Stephenson, *American Constitutional Law,* 7th ed. (Englewood Cliffs, NJ: Prentice-Hall, 1983).

36. Shapiro, "The Supreme Court," 184.

37. 457 U.S. 749, as cited by Louis Fisher, *Constitutional Conflicts Between Congress and the President,* 3rd ed. (Lawrence: University Press of Kansas, 1991), 75–76.

38. Ibid.

39. 420 U.S. 35.

40. 343 U.S. 579 (1952).

41. Robert Scigliano, "The Presidency and the Judiciary," in Michael Nelson, ed. *The Presidency and the Political System* (Washington, DC: CQ Press, 1984), 410-411.

42. Ibid.

43. Lawrence Baum, *The Supreme Court,* 3rd ed. (Washington, DC: CQ Press, 1989), 231.

44. Glendon Schubert, *The Presidency in the Courts* (Minneapolis: University of Minnesota, 1957), 185.

45. Scigliano, "The Presidency and the Judiciary," 411. See *Ex parte Quirin,* 317 U.S. (1942).

46. Theodore H. White, *Breach of Faith* (New York: Atheneum, 1976), 313–343.

47. Stephen J. Wasby, *The Supreme Court in the Federal Judicial System* (Chicago: Nelson-Hall, 1988), 314.

48. Ibid., 317.

49. 7 *Howard* 1 (1849).

50. Richard A. Watson and Norman C. Thomas, *The Politics of the Presidency* (New York: Wiley, 1983), 240.

51. Scigliano, "The Presidency and the Judiciary," 414.

52. *The New York Times,* 1 April 1992.

53. Genovese, *The Supreme Court, the Constitution, and Presidential Power,* 166.

54. Michael J. Glennon, "The Gulf War and the Constitution," *Foreign Affairs* 70 (Spring 1991): 99.

55. *The New York Times,* 17 October 1994.

56. Quoted in Howard Kurtz, "The Ideology of Federal Judgeships," *Washington Post,* Weekly Edition, 15 April 1985, 10.

57. Robert A. Dahl, "Decision-Making in a Democracy: The Supreme Court as a National Policy-Maker," *Journal of Public Law* 6(1) (1958): 285.

58. Henry J. Abraham, *The Judicial Process*, 4th ed. (New York: Oxford University Press, 1980), 80.

59. For a list of appointments to the Supreme Court from 1789 to 1992, see David G. Barnum, *The Supreme Court and American Democracy* (New York: St. Martin's, 1993), Appendix A, 318–319.

60. Abraham, *The Judicial Process*, 74.

61. Silas Bent, *Justice Oliver Wendell Holmes* (New York: Garden City Publishing, 1932), 248, as cited by Abraham, *The Judicial Process*, 71.

62. The figure is even higher for appointees to the federal district and appellate courts—approximately 94 percent of the appointees have been of the same political persuasion as the president. Henry Abraham, *Justices and Presidents: A Political History of Appointments to the Supreme Court* (New York: Penguin, 1974), 59.

63. *The New York Times*, 17 October 1991.

64. Hughes was the first put on the Supreme Court by President Taft in 1910; he resigned in 1916 to become the Republican nominee for president and lost to President Wilson in a cliffhanger election. Fourteen years later, President Herbert Hoover nominated Hughes in 1930 to the chief justice position to fill the vacancy created by the death of Chief Justice Taft—the only high official to serve both as president and Chief Justice of the United States.

65. Baum, *The Supreme Court*, 67–68.

66. Barnum, *The Supreme Court and American Democracy*, 224.

67. *The New York Times*, 16 October 1991.

68. Ibid.

69. *The New York Times*, 30 July 1994.

70. Scigliano, *The Supreme Court and the President*, 146. This section relies heavily upon this excellent text.

71. Ibid., 126.

72. Ibid.

73. Ibid., 131.

74. Ibid., 158.

75. Ibid., 137.

76. Abraham, *Justices and Presidents*, 246.

77. Barnum, *The Supreme Court and American Democracy*, 99–100.

78. Robert H. Birkby, "The Courts: Forty More Years?" in Michael Nelson, ed. *The Elections of 1984* (Washington, DC: CQ Press, 1985), 250.

79. Kurtz, "The Ideology of Federal Judgeships," 9.

80. Walter F. Murphy, "Reagan's Judicial Strategy," in Larry Berman, ed. *Looking Back on the Reagan Presidency* (Baltimore, MD: Johns Hopkins University Press, 1990), 210.

81. Sheldon Goldman, "Reorganizing the Judiciary," *Judicature* 68 (1985): 313, 315–316.

82. Walter F. Murphy, "Reagan's Judicial Strategy," 211.

83. Ibid.

84. Sheldon Goldman, "Judicial Appointments and the Presidential Agenda," in Paul Brace, Christine B. Harrington, and Gary King, eds. *The Presidency in American Politics* (New York: New York University Press, 1989), 41.

CHAPTER 14

THE VICE PRESIDENCY

Somewhat surprisingly, the United States is the only major nation among the western democracies that has a designated officer—the vice president—whose chief function is to be the ready successor to the chief executive in the event of a presidential vacancy. Other leading Western democracies either await a vacancy before designating a new leader or make some designated officer a caretaker pending the outcome of a special election.[1] When a British prime minister dies in office or resigns, for example, the ruling party immediately chooses a successor. But in the United States the vice president fills the remainder of the president's unexpired term. What is the reason for this unusual succession procedure? Was this constitutional arrangement just an afterthought of the Founding Fathers? Or was it a special insurance policy to protect the nation in the event of a sudden vacancy in the presidency?

Of greater importance have been recent institutional developments in the vice presidency. In the past two decades more institutional changes have occurred in the vice presidency than in any single office in the federal government. As noted by Paul C. Light, in his recent study of the vice presidency, "After two hundred years as errand-boys, political hitmen, professional mourners, and incidental White House commissioners, Vice-Presidents can now lay claim to regular access to the President and the opportunity to give advice on major decisions."[2] For a position that has often been the butt of political jokes, what reasons can be ascribed to the rising importance of the nation's second-highest office?

No single explanation, it seems clear, can be given to account for the rapid growth of vice presidential influence. But a number of factors have undoubtedly contributed to the rise of the modern vice presidency; they will be discussed later in the chapter. Another goal will be to analyze the constitutional background and operation of the second highest office in the land. The vice presidential selection process and its shortcomings will be discussed, and we will give special attention to the vice president's role in case of presidential disability. Though the original flaws in the Constitution on this problem were thought to have been resolved once and for all by passage of the Twenty-fifth Amendment, recent experience during the Reagan administration indicates that loopholes still exist. Let's turn first to the establishment of the vice presidency.

EVOLUTION OF THE VICE PRESIDENCY

Historically, the evolution of the vice presidency can be divided into five fairly distinct periods: (1) the founding period, which covers the years from the Constitutional Convention of 1787 until adoption of the Twelfth Amendment in 1804; (2) the nineteenth century, which can be described as the era of anonymous vice presidents; (3) the early modern era of the first half of the twentieth century, which began with the abbreviated six-month vice presidency of Theodore Roosevelt in 1901 and extended to the end of World War II; (4) the modern period which began in the eighty-two-day vice presidency of Harry S. Truman in 1945 and spanned the years to the Watergate investigation era of the early 1970s; (5) the institutionalized vice presidency, which emerged late in the Nixon administration and continues to the present.[3]

The Founding Period

The Framers, concerned with the problems of succession in the event of the death, removal, resignation, or inability of the president to perform his duties, decided that the runner-up in the presidential selection process should be designated vice president. Early in their discussions, they had considered proposals that, in the event of a vacancy in the presidency, would shift power to the president of the Senate, the chief justice, or a presidential council. The men of 1787 first accepted the idea that the presiding officer of the Senate should be designated as the president's successor if the position should become vacant. But when the principle of legislative selection of the president was finally dropped in favor of having a special body of electors, the Framers decided to have the vice president selected in the same manner. This proposal was accepted with little objection, as was the proposal to have the vice president serve ex officio as the presiding officer of the Senate.[4]

Even the Constitution's staunchest defenders, however, must have recognized that the vice presidency was a fundamentally weak office, with clear boundaries defining both the range of activities it could perform and the extent of the influence in government it could achieve.[5]

John Adams, the first vice president, wrote to his wife Abigail: "My country has in its wisdom contrived for me the most insignificant office that ever the invention of man contrived or his imagination conceived." Little did Adams realize that the vice presidency was at the peak of influence during the period he served.[6] Prior to the passage of the Twelfth Amendment, the vice president was the recipient of the second highest number of electoral votes and widely considered to be the logical heir apparent. Furthermore, as the dean of presidential scholars, Edward S. Corwin, pointed out some years ago, "before the Twelfth Amendment the Vice-President was in a sense—a fact not overlooked by Adams—'the constitutional equal of the President,' having been voted for by the Electors, not for 'Vice-President' but for 'President.' "[7] It was therefore not surprising that the nation's first and second vice presidents, Adams and Jefferson, became the second and third presidents. Also, because the Senate was still a small deliberative body and tie votes reasonably likely, Adams was able to cast a record twenty-nine tie-breaking votes.[8]

In the pre–Twelfth Amendment era it was also possible for the vice president to be a member of the opposition party (read faction), and that is exactly what happened in 1796 when Thomas Jefferson received sixty-eight votes—three less than President-elect Adams but nine more votes than Adams's running-mate, Thomas Pinckney of South Carolina.[9]

The real crisis in the vice presidency came to a head in 1800 when the anti-Federalist Republican ticket of Jefferson and Aaron Burr received an equal number of votes in the Electoral College, but Aaron Burr refused to accept second place and acknowledge Jefferson as the president-elect. With a tie vote in the Electoral College, the presidential election, as required by the Constitution, moved into the House of Representatives, with each state casting one vote. For a time it appeared that the Federalists, to square old accounts with Jefferson, might shift their support to Aaron Burr and thus prevent Jefferson from moving into the White House. However, Jefferson's old cabinet adversary, Alexander Hamilton, concluded that Burr was far more unscrupulous than Jefferson and should be blocked from the presidency. Following a long series of inconclusive ballots, Hamilton finally prevailed upon a number of Federalist representatives to cast enough blank ballots so that Jefferson received a majority of votes—and the presidency—on the thirty-sixth ballot.[10]

The Twelfth Amendment

To avoid another constitutional crisis over tie voting in the Electoral College, Congress passed the Twelfth Amendment. Ratified by the required three-quarters of the states in 1804, the new amendment stipulated that Electoral College members cast a single ballot for a joint ticket of president and vice president. During the debate over the proposed amendment, several members of Congress were unusually prescient in predicting the bad side effects the amendment would have on the vice presidency. Because "the vice president will not stand on such high ground in the method proposed as he does in the present mode of a double ballot," William Plumer admonished his colleagues that the chief concern in picking the vice president would be "to procure votes for the president."[11] For the next century, the vice presidency was viewed as a one-way ticket to political oblivion.

The Nineteenth Century—Era of Anonymous Vice Presidents

Ratification of the Twelfth Amendment (1804) and the gradual emergence of political parties left the vice presidency in a badly weakened condition. Since party leaders, not the presidential candidates, chose the nominees for vice president in the "smoke-filled rooms" at the national conventions, the selection process usually boiled down to "balancing the ticket." Party chiefs sought to use the vice presidential nomination as a consolation prize to placate the faction or region most dissatisfied with the presidential selectee, or to win a key, populous state in the general election. Consequently, some leading politicians were unwilling to accept the nomination for the number two spot on the ticket. Daniel Webster, in declining the Whig party vice presidential nomination in 1848, declared, "I do not propose to be buried until I am dead."[12]

Significantly, none of the four nineteenth-century vice presidents elevated to the presidency—Tyler, Fillmore, Andrew Johnson, and Arthur—was nominated for a subsequent term. Political scientist Michael Nelson has described the list of undistinguished nineteenth-century vice presidents as "a virtual rogue's gallery of personal and political failures."[13] Because the office was so seriously devalued, only over-the-hill politicians seemed interested in the job. Six vice presidents died in office, all of natural causes. Several others became embroiled in financial or personal scandals. Schuyler Colfax and Henry Wilson, for example, were implicated in the *Credit Mobilier* scandal in the 1870s.[14]

The Early Modern Period

The era of the anonymous vice president ended with the close of the nineteenth century. The emergence of mass circulation newspapers and magazines at the turn of the century, coincided with the arrival on the national scene of a new GOP vice presidential nominee, the flamboyant young governor of New York, Theodore Roosevelt. Recently returned from his heroic service in Cuba during the Spanish-American War, Colonel Roosevelt generated headlines whenever he traveled on the campaign trial. While President William McKinley waged a sedate "front-porch" campaign during the 1900 election, TR was on the stump almost nonstop. He gave 673 speeches to three million listeners in twenty-four states.[15] But Roosevelt served as vice president for only six months before McKinley's assassination put TR in the White House.

Although all four nineteenth-century successor presidents had been rejected by their party at the next national convention, the popular Roosevelt easily won the nomination and was elected to a full term in 1904.

Also, starting with James S. Sherman in 1912, all first-term vice presidents who sought a second term have been nominated. Probably no vice president who followed Teddy Roosevelt could have matched his charisma and energy, but most twentieth-century vice presidents held fairly prominent political positions before their nomination. The colorless Calvin Coolidge, who succeeded Harding, had gained national recognition in 1919 as governor of Massachusetts when he put down a policemen's strike in Boston. Charles Curtis (1929–1933), Hoover's running-mate, had been Senate majority leader. John Nance Garner, FDR's first vice president (1933–1941), had been speaker of the House; Harry S. Truman, Roosevelt's third vice president, headed a prominent Senate investigating committee during World War II, and Truman's running mate in 1948, Senator Alben Barkley, had been Democratic majority leader. Still, most duties performed by these vice presidents were chiefly ceremonial.

The Modern Vice Presidency

The sudden shock of President Franklin D. Roosevelt's death in the closing months of World War II awakened the nation as never before to the vital importance of an experienced vice president. Roosevelt's successor, Harry S. Truman, had occupied the nation's second highest office for less than three months when news of Roosevelt's death reached him in the nation's capital. Uninformed about the final war plans for the Allied victory, and unaware of the development of the first atomic bomb, President Truman faced a series of decisions and national crises unmatched since the Lincoln presidency. To the surprise of many skeptics, President Truman, despite his lack of executive experience, more than measured up to these monumental wartime challenges. Soon after the Japanese military surrender in August 1945, Truman also encountered the rapid escalation of the Cold War between the Soviet Union and the United States.

For the next three years and nine months, Truman served without a vice president. Congress did not address this vacancy directly, but at Truman's insistence the lawmakers in 1947 changed the presidential succession law. They put the speaker of the House and the Senate pro tempore next in line to the presidency, instead of the secretary of state and other ranking cabinet members, in the event both the presidency and vice presidency suddenly became vacant.[16] It was not until the Johnson administration, however, that Congress and the states approved the Twenty-fifth Amendment in 1967 to deal with presidential disability and a vice presidential vacancy.

With the arrival of the television age in the 1950s, vice presidents gained increased visibility across the country. Vice presidents were also given more special assignments—foreign visits, party-building and campaign duties, and appointments to a variety of government commissions. Yet, for another two decades it was mostly business as usual for the vice presidency until a significant restructuring of the staff occurred in the early 1970s.

The Institutionalized Vice Presidency

Surprisingly, the expanded Watergate investigation of the Nixon presidency after the 1972 election spawned the institutionalization of the vice presidency. President Nixon, pressured by the growing scandal that threatened to engulf the White House, agreed to increase the vice presidential budget as an inducement to get House Republican Minority Leader Gerald Ford to accept the appointment to the vice presidency, following Vice President Agnew's forced resignation. As a result, newly appointed Vice President Ford's personnel budget included staff slots covering press relations, speechmaking, scheduling, and administration.

This new executive budget allowed the vice president's office to expand from twenty aides in 1960 to seventy people during Nelson Rockefeller's brief term. From scattered offices in several locations, the vice president's staff is now consolidated in the Old Executive Office Building next to the White House, and no longer on Capitol Hill. With a regular budget and table of organization, vice presidents are also now in a position to attract and retain high-quality staff. In fact, explains Paul C. Light, "The Vice-President's office is now a replica of the President's office, with a national security adviser, press secretary, domestic issues staff, scheduling team, advance, appointments, administration, chief of staff, and counsel's office."[17]

As a result of these recent institutional changes, Vice President Walter Mondale—unlike Lyndon Johnson—was able to bring virtually all his Senate staff with him to the vice president's office. No wonder one former White House staffer recently observed, "The Office of the Vice-President—a staff of over ninety persons—is a significant new center of participation in White House decision making."[18]

President Jimmy Carter pushed ahead the institutionalization process further by bringing Vice President Mondale directly into the White House. He provided Mondale with a well-appointed office only a few doors away from the Oval Office. Furthermore, Mondale was given full access to the flow of all papers to and from President Carter. More important, Carter soon made him a top adviser on virtually all matters of politics and public policy. Since then, Presidents Reagan, Bush, and Clinton have all adhered to the Carter pattern of a close presidential-vice presidential relationship.

VICE PRESIDENTIAL NOMINEES—POLITICAL AFTERTHOUGHTS

The odds are fairly good that the vice president may become president—fourteen out of our forty-two presidents (one out of three) have reached the White House from the office of vice president. Despite this fact, political parties and the party nominee over the years displayed an extremely casual attitude toward picking candidates for the second highest office in the land.

Until World War II, vice presidential nominations remained, for the most part, in the hands of state party leaders meeting at their respective national conventions. Since both parties spent little time in screening their vice presidential nominees, there is little wonder they so consistently came up with mediocrities. Most of these vice presidents have been long forgotten—Daniel Tompkins, George Dallas, Hannibal Hamlin, William Wheeler, Levi Morton, and Garret Hobart, for example. On more than one occasion the parties took an almost cavalier attitude toward the vice presidential nomination. In 1912, for example, the GOP convention renominated Vice President James S. Sherman, even though the Republican leaders knew he was gravely ill—indeed, he died less than a week before the general election.[19]

Fortunately for the country, these weak nominees have been counterbalanced several times in the twentieth century by well-qualified candidates—Theodore Roosevelt, Harry Truman, Lyndon Johnson, Gerald Ford, Nelson Rockefeller, Walter Mondale, George Bush, and Al Gore.

In 1940, however, as the war clouds swept ever closer to the United States, President Franklin Roosevelt, who was tacitly seeking an unprecedented third term, insisted that he be allowed to pick his own running mate. Since FDR and Vice President Garner had had a political falling out over Roosevelt's Supreme Court-packing plan and his attempt to purge conservative Democrats in the 1938 congressional election, Roosevelt decided that he wanted a different running mate. Actually, the falling out between FDR and Vice President Garner opened the door for an important modification of the vice presidential selection process and would foster greater harmony between presidents and vice presidents.

First of all, the repeal of the historic two-thirds rule in the Democratic party (requiring presidential candidates to collect two-thirds of the national convention vote for the nomination) at the 1936 Democratic national convention meant that presidential candidates no longer had to engage in extensive trading of delegate votes for vice presidential nomination and various posts in order to win two-thirds of the convention vote needed for the nomination. With this century-old rule out of the way, FDR was in the position to seize the party leaders' traditional role of selecting the vice presidential running mate and make it his own choice. Roosevelt's audacious tactic caught the old party chiefs off guard.[20] When they turned to him desperately to accept an unprecedented third-term nomination in 1940, he said that he would refuse, unless the national convention accepted Secretary of Agriculture Henry A. Wallace as his new running mate. State leaders were loath to put the left-leaning Wallace on the ticket, but they concluded they had no choice—if FDR were to lead them to victory again. Since the 1940s, presidential nominees in both parties have been accorded the prerogative of handpicking their own running mate, unless they choose not to exercise this option.

Since then, conventions have routinely approved their choices. Except for 1956, when Democratic nominee Adlai E. Stevenson threw open the choice of the vice presidential nominee to the convention, presidential nominees have personally picked their choice or asked their advisers to come up with a "short list" from which a vice presidential nominee could be picked.

With the onset of superpower politics and the nuclear age it would seem prudent for both parties to devote far more attention to selecting the nominee for the second highest job in the land. But the record of the two parties on this point has been uneven. In 1964, the Republicans chose Congressman William Miller of New York at the request of the GOP nominee, Senator Barry Goldwater of Arizona, to give geographical balance, but also because, according to Goldwater: "He drives Johnson nuts."[21] Four years later, GOP nominee Richard Nixon decided that Governor Spiro Agnew of Maryland "would do the least harm to the ticket." Nixon's first preference according to several sources, would have been to run without a vice presidential candidate! Five years later, Vice President Agnew resigned from office rather than face impeachment for tax evasion and involvement in financial kickbacks while he was a county executive and governor in Maryland.

Although three of the four most recent presidents have been governors before moving to the White House, most Washington observers agree that the vice presidency is "the prime route to the presidential nomination."[22] Nor would many students of the vice presidency disagree with political scientist Joel K. Goldstein's observation that "the new importance of the presidency has forced parties to nominate people of higher caliber for the second spot."[23] Yet, because it is almost universally accepted that the presidential nominee's choice for running mate will be approved by the national convention on a routine vote, there is little formal campaigning for the vice presidency. Stephen J. Wayne has summarized well the dilemma of vice presidential contenders, "There are no vice presidential primaries and no government matching funds for vice presidential candidates. Only one 'vote' really counts—the presidential nominee's."[24]

FLAWS IN THE SELECTION PROCESS

Some critics say the existing vice presidential selection process is undemocratic because it allows one person—the presidential nominee—to pick his running mate. Other opponents of the existing system contend that the selection process is based on purely political considerations, not the relative merits of the various contenders. Still other critics state that another flaw in the selection system arises from the haste with which the nominee must sometimes be picked at the national convention.

Under the existing rules of both major parties, the vice presidential selection process must be undertaken less than twenty-four hours after the presidential nominee has been chosen. To be sure, the selection process is less complicated today than two decades ago by the fact that the presidential nominee is now usually "selected" in the presidential primaries long before convention time. However, unless the nominee has received the party nod in the primaries, he and his staff must begin a frantic search for a running mate at the national convention. But after three full days and nights of meeting most or all of the fifty state delegations, making prospective bargains with party or factional leaders, and rehearsing his acceptance speech for television, a presidential candidate will often be physically and emotionally drained. Yet he must immediately begin screening prospective running mates.

Although the 1952 Republican national convention is no longer typical, the Republican nominee, General Dwight D. Eisenhower, had only three hours between the balloting for president and vice president. Eisenhower assembled his close circle of advisers and handed them a list of seven names from which to choose a nominee. His aides, worn out from the bitterly fought nomination battle against Senator Robert A. Taft of Ohio (Eisenhower won the first ballot count by less than fifteen votes), proceeded to cull the list. The first two names, Taft and Senator Everett McKinley Dirksen, were discarded. The next name on the list—Senator Richard M. Nixon of California—provoked no objection, and when several of those present spoke well of him, the group agreed without further discussion to go along with Nixon. They immediately called Eisenhower with their recommendation. General Ike replied, "That's fine with me."[25]

In 1960, Senator John F. Kennedy, expecting a hectic twenty-four-hour search for an acceptable running mate, was surprised when his first choice, Senate Majority Leader Lyndon B. Johnson, his chief adversary in the fight for the nomination, unexpectedly accepted his offer for the number two spot on the ticket. But eight years later GOP nominee Richard M. Nixon and his aides deliberated into the wee hours of the morning before agreeing to sleep on their decision for about four hours before announcing their choice—Governor Spiro Agnew of Maryland. If Nixon and his staff had had more time to review the background of Governor Agnew and his activities in Maryland, perhaps they might have uncovered some of the incriminating evidence that ultimately led to his hasty resignation five years later.

Nor was former California governor Ronald Reagan the model of a decisive nominee in picking his running mate at the 1980 Republican national convention in Detroit. Though Reagan had safely locked up the GOP nomination more than two months ahead of the convention, he failed to conduct an exhaustive search for a running mate. Some Reagan insiders had hoped to persuade former President Gerald Ford to team up with Reagan on a "dream ticket" to drive Carter out of the White House.

Since public opinion polls prior to the conventions showed Reagan and Carter running neck and neck, Reagan's inner circle felt that Ford would be a valuable asset in the general election campaign. But this proposed ticket fell apart in the closing hours before the presidential balloting was scheduled to get under way. According to several insiders, it collapsed when Ford insisted that former Secretary of State Henry Kissinger be reappointed to his old post in the new Reagan administration and that Ford's economic adviser be given the secretary of treasury slot. This inflated asking price was, according to party insiders, too much for Reagan. The soon-to-be-nominated Reagan was also astounded to hear some of Ford's exorbitant demands publicly aired during a live, televised interview between Ford and CBS-TV anchorman Walter Cronkite in the network booth high above the convention area.

By 9:00 P.M. Ford reportedly scaled down his demands, but his insistence on veto power over two cabinet appointments—secretary of state and secretary of defense—further soured Reagan's attitude toward the former president. Instead, two hours later, amid convention rumors that Ford would be Reagan's choice as vice presidential nominee, Reagan abruptly selected George Bush—his chief rival during the hard-fought primary season.[26] In retrospect, Ronald Reagan apparently concluded that presidential power could not be shared, and he was not prepared to deal away the powers of the presidency to improve his chances of winning in November. By choosing Bush, Reagan scored points with the moderate wing of the GOP, especially in the East; he also added an experienced politician to the ticket. Bush had held five different national party and government posts over the previous ten years.

In the past two decades, however, the hectic last-minute selection of a vice presidential nominee has not usually been the case. Jimmy Carter, who had clinched the 1976 Democratic nomination almost two months before the convention, devoted over four weeks to screening the backgrounds of a half-dozen prospective running mates. After carefully scrutinizing their records, he invited each of them to his home in Plains, Georgia, to discuss their conceptions of the office and possible future working relationships. He renewed these discussions at the Democratic convention in New York City before announcing his choice—Senator Walter F. Mondale of Minnesota—on the morning after he had received the party nomination.

Eight years later, Walter F. Mondale, who had the Democratic nomination safely in hand more than a month ahead of the San Francisco convention, followed the procedure used by Jimmy Carter. A week ahead of the convention Mondale announced his choice for running mate—Representative Geraldine Ferraro of New York, the first woman in history to be selected as a vice presidential nominee.

In 1988, prospective GOP nominee Vice President George Bush unexpectedly handpicked Indiana Senator Dan Quayle for his running mate on the second day of the Republican convention in New Orleans. Many of the surprised GOP delegates had never heard of Senator Quayle. But Mr. Bush's choice was routinely ratified by the Republican convention. Most recently, prospective 1992 Democratic nominee, Arkansas Governor Bill Clinton, announced his choice for running mate, Senator Al Gore of Tennessee, more than a week before the Democratic delegates convened in New York City. Clinton defied conventional wisdom by picking a fellow Southerner to serve on the Democratic ticket—the first time in history that two candidates from below the Mason-Dixon line would share the Democratic ticket.

To inject more popular participation into the selection process for the vice presidential nominee, it has been suggested that the rank-and-file delegates of the national conventions be given a larger voice, instead of being presented with a *fait accompli* by the presidential nominee.

Other suggested reforms include changing the convention schedule to provide a day or two between the nomination of the presidential candidate and his running mate. The main objective would be to avoid a hurried or unwise vice presidential choice in the midst of the tumultuous proceedings. Another would delay the vice presidential nomination for several weeks after the convention, and then have the nominee submit his carefully selected choice to the party's national committee.

Another more radical reform would be to postpone the choice of the vice president until after the general election. The president-elect would then, on due reflection, submit his nominee's name to Congress to be confirmed within a specified time period either by a majority vote or by Congressional failure to act on the presidential choice during the period. Advocates of this procedure argue that it would eliminate the pressure of the blatant political considerations that the nominees weigh in hopes of strengthening the ticket and enhancing their own chances of winning the White House. Under this plan, it is also argued, the president-elect "would be freer to choose the individual in his judgement best qualified to assume the presidency, if necessary, and to assure continuity of his policies."[27]

The chief objection to this post-election proposal is that it would mean the vice president selected by Congress would not be popularly elected. Former Vice President Mondale is certainly on the mark when he argues that without the "dignity of a public plebiscite" placing a vice president in office, he would most likely have a "half-way house status" and "would not be the public's choice, but the politician's choice."[28]

Some critics of the present vice presidential selection process have suggested having national candidates run in the presidential primaries as a team ticket.[29] Under this plan the vice presidential running mate would obtain state-by-state exposure while his credentials are undergoing public and media scrutiny. But the negative side of this joint slate proposal is that it would rule out the selection of a defeated presidential candidate as a vice presidential running mate, even those possessing outstanding qualifications. This proposed scheme would, of course, have ruled out George Bush as a running mate for Ronald Reagan on the 1980 GOP ticket. Nor would a presidential candidate necessarily have an easy time finding a suitable running mate, since he would offer no guarantee of his own nomination, and some prospective partners might prefer to take their own chances at competing for the top spot on the ticket.[30]

THE MODERN VICE PRESIDENT—HEIR APPARENT

Clearly, the vice presidency is no longer regarded as a political dead-end job. From the day of his election, the modern vice president is considered a potential presidential nominee. Furthermore, an unanticipated consequence of the Twenty-second Amendment has also enhanced the stature of the vice president. The amendment, though aimed at curbing the tenure of the president to two terms, has focused the spotlight increasingly on the vice president during a president's second term. The vice president has become, in the minds of many citizens and politicos, the heir apparent. Actually, however, all modern vice presidents (except George Bush) who have become president owe their advance first to succession rather than election.

In recent decades the growth in importance of the presidency has also helped elevate the stature of the vice president. In Joel K. Goldstein's words, "The gravitational pull the strengthened presidency exerts has drawn the second officer into the executive orbit."[31] Both major party presidential nominees and the national convention delegates have come to recognize the necessity of nominating individuals of high caliber for the second spot. As a result, modern vice presidents have generally been more experienced, competent political figures—usually leading U.S. senators or House members—than their nineteenth-century counterparts. Many have been considered presidential timber before their nomination, and most have been so regarded after taking office.

Unlike their nineteenth-century predecessors, recent vice presidents have been more closely identified with the president and his policies. Goldstein has also pointed out that, in light of the continuing expansion of presidential responsibilities, especially in foreign affairs, "The growth of the presidency creates an obligation to keep the second officer current."[32] Though the office of vice president has often been downgraded, it is worth noting that five of our last ten chief executives were once vice presidents.

THE INSTITUTIONALIZATION OF THE VICE PRESIDENCY

For more than 150 years, vice presidents performed essentially ceremonial roles—except when in times of emergency the nation called upon them to fill a vacancy in the White House. Generally, vice presidents did little more than hold down duties as presiding officer of the U.S. Senate and make an occasional appearance at a federal dedication ceremony.

Franklin D. Roosevelt charted a new course for his second vice president, Henry A. Wallace, by sending him to foreign lands as a goodwill ambassador. Presidents Eisenhower, Kennedy, and Johnson continued this practice, but there is no evidence that they gave serious consideration to assigning more substantive responsibilities to their second in command.

As Vice President Gerald Ford wrote in 1974 only weeks before Nixon's forced resignation:

> The Vice-President is a Constitutional hybrid. Alone among federal officials he stands with one foot in the legislative branch and the other in the executive. The Vice-President straddles the Constitutional chasm which circumscribes and checks all others. He belongs to both the President and Congress, even more so under the Twenty-fifth Amendment, yet he shares power with neither.[33]

Though assigned presiding duties in the Senate by the Constitution, the vice president has often been viewed by members of Congress as an interloper. It was not until President Kennedy made office space available for Vice President Lyndon Johnson in the Executive Office Building, next to the White House, that the vice president was accorded a direct symbolic connection with the executive branch. But the vice president was still put on short rations. Unlike his former post as Senate majority leader with a full staff, Johnson had only a handful of staff members and a limited budget. Most of his former staffers chose to stay on Capitol Hill and retain their regular positions and salaries, rather than take up unspecified duties in the vice president's office. In some instances, Johnson (and later Humphrey) managed to retain some veteran staffers by hiding them on the payrolls of several executive agencies. Until Gerald Ford became vice president, occupants had been forced to rely completely on White House administrative support. Vice President Humphrey, for example, had to have all his travel manifests and vouchers signed by the White House chief of staff.

The institutionalization of the vice president's office also makes the incumbent less vulnerable to changes in presidential moods or capricious presidential aides. Vice presidents are now in a position to protect their staffs against arbitrary budgetary cuts. No longer do they have to beg for the use of White House jet aircraft, rely on presidential advance teams, or turn to White House speech writers. To be sure, vice presidents still clear all major speeches with top White House staff, but they have their own speech writers and foreign policy advisers and their own Air Force Two jet. To monitor domestic matters more effectively, Vice President Mondale also established his own domestic policy staff—a smaller version of President Carter's staff. Thus, the vice president is now in a better position to offer independent advice to the president.

Symbolic of the growing stature of the vice presidency was the purchase of a vice presidential mansion—the Naval Observatory on Embassy Row—in the early 1970s. For the first time in history the vice president was provided with an official residence. By contrast, Vice President Agnew and his wife lived in a residential hotel during their five years in Washington. Clearly, the establishment of an official residence enhanced the stature of the vice president in the status-conscious Washington community.

With a staff of over ninety members, the vice president's office is now hierarchically organized with chains of command and function. With specialized subdivisions to supply administrative, political, and policy support, the staff can now maintain ongoing operations, even when the vice president is traveling. Inasmuch as the vice president may spend up to 30 percent of his official time on the road, a regular White House-based staff provides continuity to the management of his office. Formerly, most of the vice president's aides traveled with him on his journeys.

Other benefits have accrued to the vice president in recent years. As Paul C. Light has pointed out, "Part of the institutionalization of the Vice-President's office involved regular access to presidential information—gaining a position in the White House paper loop."[34] Vice presidents now receive most of the paper traffic and briefing papers that go across the president's desk. Although they lack decision-making authority to act on this information, they are nonetheless kept fully apprised of major domestic and international developments and, if asked, can give the president their best judgment on these matters.

Keeping the vice president fully informed on national security matters should not be underestimated, especially in case of temporary presidential disability or the death of the chief executive. With the recent institutionalization, it is unlikely that any future vice president will find himself or herself in the same position as Vice President Truman at the time of President Roosevelt's death in 1945. According to Emmet John Hughes, Truman had only two appointments with Roosevelt during his eighty-two days in the vice presidency before taking over the reins of government.[35]

Institutionalization is, of course, an ongoing process, with each new vice president adding or subtracting some aspect of the second highest office in the land. But how does one explain the recent transformation of the office from an essentially bench warmer position to a prominent advisory role to the president? Undoubtedly, the lengthening presidential nominating race, the growing fragmentation in Congress, the decline of the national parties, the rise of a new set of complex policy issues, and continuing international crises have all affected the growth of vice presidential influence.

Beyond doubt, Watergate was the major catalyst in the growth of vice presidential influence. As Paul C. Light has commented, "The rise of an independent vice presidential staff, the freedom to organize and reorganize the office, the arrival of greater administrative and political support, even the growth of an institutional identity, all coincided with Watergate."[36]

Other factors also account for the growth of vice presidential influence at the White House. The election of two *outsider* presidents—Carter and Reagan—coincided with the election of two *insider* vice presidents, Mondale and Bush. As Paul C. Light has noted, "The President's inexperience creates vacuums for advice. Presidential outsiders—candidates with little Washington experience—have more use for active Vice-Presidents than presidential insiders."[37] President Carter, a newcomer to the nation's capital, needed former Senator Mondale's advice and understanding of the legislative process to get his new administration off the ground. Equally important, President Reagan quickly utilized Vice President Bush's executive and foreign policy experience.

As policymaking has become concentrated in the White House, and not in the executive departments, recent vice presidents and their staffs have been brought into more and more White House senior staff meetings. In Paul C. Light's words, "As presidential doubts about executive branch loyalty grew, the Vice-President's stock also increased."[38] Indeed, recent vice presidents "have come to resemble senior members of the White House staff."[39]

To President Jimmy Carter belongs a major share of the credit for maximizing the influence of the vice president. As mentioned earlier, Carter deliberately aided the institutionalization of the vice presidency by inviting Mondale to take a West Wing office. The acquisition of an office within the White House itself was probably the most important single factor in upgrading the vice presidency, for it brought the number two constitutional officer within immediate proximity of the president and moved the vice president into the center of the decision-making process. In the first year of the Carter administration, for example, Mondale met regularly with the president, averaging three to six hours a day in both public and private forums.[40]

But despite the expanded role of the vice president over the past fifteen years, the vice presidential job description "remains highly dependent on the President." As Light emphasizes, "The Vice-President's work is still largely whatever the President makes it."[41]

VICE PRESIDENTIAL DUTIES

Five hundred and thirty-seven officials—the president, the vice president, 100 U.S. senators, and 435 representatives—are sent to the nation's capital by American voters. Five hundred and thirty-six have a reasonably clear idea of their duties and responsibilities. But, as Thomas E. Cronin has explained, the vice president is never sure, except for his constitutional duties as the presiding officer of the Senate and successor to the President, what responsibilities the president may from week to week assign him. In recent decades the number of tasks assigned to him has grown. On paper at least, they seem fairly formidable. Cronin has summarized them as follows.

1. President of the U.S. Senate
2. Member of the National Security Council
3. Chair of several national advisory councils
4. Diplomatic representative of president and United States abroad
5. Senior presidential adviser
6. Liaison with Congress
7. Crisis coordinator
8. Overseer of temporary coordinating councils
9. Preside over cabinet meetings in absence of president
10. Deputy leader of the party
11. Apprentice available to take over the job of the president, either on an acting or full-time basis
12. Future presidential candidate[42]

While modern vice presidents are far busier than their nineteenth-century predecessors, their expanded duties are often tentative in nature. So long as a president lives, the vice president has no authority to make policy. Additional assignments depend entirely upon the president. Job assignments, it should be noted, are not permanent. As the late Hubert H. Humphrey once put it, "He who giveth can taketh away and often does."[43] Humphrey had learned, as have other recent vice presidents, that the constitutional position of the vice president may constrain a president from assigning continuing responsibilities to the number two officeholder. The chief reason: The vice president is the only major subordinate the president cannot remove. Understandably, the president may be reluctant to entrust duties of an official over whom he lacks this leverage.

Goodwill Ambassador

President Nixon, in his eight years as vice president, visited fifty-four countries in Latin America, Africa, Western Europe, the Far East, and the Soviet Union. Nixon's most publicized foreign encounter was undoubtedly his "kitchen debate" with Soviet dictator Nikita Khruschev over the relative merits of the American and Soviet systems.[44] As vice president, Lyndon Johnson undertook more than thirty special overseas assignments for President Kennedy. Johnson visited Southeast Asia to consider the possibility of increasing military aid to the anti-Communist government of South Vietnam; he allayed the fears of the West German government after the Soviet Union's erection of the Berlin

Wall in 1961; and he also informed the governments of Greece, Turkey, Cyprus, and Iran of impending reductions in foreign aid.[45]

Two recent vice presidents—Walter Mondale and George Bush—have handled a variety of foreign assignments in Canada, Latin America, Western Europe, and the Soviet Union. Mondale logged over 600,000 miles during his vice presidency. In early 1983, Vice President Bush traveled to the Soviet Union for the second time to represent the United States at the funeral of Soviet leader Yuri Andropov. By early March 1985, Bush had logged 610,000 miles on official government business when news suddenly reached Washington that Soviet leader Konstantin Chernenko had died. President Reagan asked Bush, who was visiting the starving refugees in Ethiopia, to attend the Soviet leader's funeral—the third funeral of a Soviet head of state that Bush had attended since assuming the vice presidency in 1981. The frequency with which U.S. vice presidents attend state funerals led columnist William Safire to quip, "You die, I fly."

On his return trip home, Bush made a side trip to Brazil for the inauguration of a new civilian government. By the time Bush reached Washington, DC again, he had traveled more than 29,600 miles. While in the Soviet Union Bush also had the opportunity to meet the new Soviet leader, Mikhail S. Gorbachev. Most Washington observers, with one eye on the 1988 Republican presidential nominating race, concluded that Bush had comported himself nearly flawlessly on this long pilgrimage. As a result, he had strengthened his early front-runner position to succeed President Reagan, who was ineligible to run for another term.

Legislative Liaison

Despite his constitutional role as president of the Senate, the major activity of the vice president on Capitol Hill is not his official capacity as presiding officer of the Senate, but his informal role as administration lobbyist.[46] Because the Constitution places the vice president with one foot in the executive branch and the other in the legislative chamber, he would seem to be ideally suited to serve as the president's lobbyist on Capitol Hill. But this does not necessarily follow. A few twentieth-century vice presidents—John Nance Garner, Hubert H. Humphrey, and Walter F. Mondale—have performed these duties in an effective manner; the others less so.

Vice presidential involvement in legislative activity dates only from the New Deal era, for only since this period has the president assumed the responsibility for presenting Congress with a comprehensive legislative program. The record of effective vice presidential lobbying over the past half-century should be higher than most critics rate it, for since 1933 ten of the thirteen vice presidents served previously in one or both houses of Congress.[47]

Vice President Garner, a former speaker of the House, performed yeoman service on Capitol Hill during President Roosevelt's first term. Though a southern conservative Democrat, Garner is generally credited with playing a major role in pushing New Deal measures through Congress. Shortly after Roosevelt's reelection in 1936, however, he and Garner had a falling out over FDR's court-packing plan. Garner also became disenchanted with the growing national deficit and made no secret of his displeasure in the halls of Congress. By 1940, the break between FDR and his vice president had become irreparable. Garner announced that he would seek the presidency, even before Roosevelt made his own intentions about a third term known. When Garner failed to win several presidential primaries against favorite son and Roosevelt stand-in candidates, however, he bowed out of the race and retired to his Texas ranch.

Vice President Richard Nixon, though a relative newcomer to Capitol Hill, served as a go-between for the Eisenhower White House and Senator Joseph McCarthy, the professional anti-Communist crusader of the 1950s. He persuaded McCarthy to drop his plans to investigate the CIA and also his drive to block several Eisenhower nominations. Along with other Eisenhower staffers, Nixon negotiated with Senator John Bricker over changes in his proposed constitutional amendment to curb presidential executive agreements and treaty-making power.

Vice President Humphrey, before he was consigned to the presidential doghouse for his opposition in a cabinet meeting to President Johnson's policy on bombing North Vietnam, was one of the more active vice presidential lobbyists on Capitol Hill; he helped push through a number of Johnson's Great Society programs during 1965. Vice President Walter Mondale was particularly valuable to President Carter and his staff because, as new arrivals in the nation's capital, they had so little experience in dealing with members of Congress. But the overall record of vice presidential lobbying, according to Larry O'Brien, Kennedy's congressional liaison chief, is not impressive.[48]

In many other ways, the vice president is operating against great odds. His legislative role offers him no bargaining power, for as Vice President Theodore Roosevelt noted many years ago, he has few favors to trade. Even though he is the presiding officer of the Senate, the vice president must be sensitive to senatorial prerogatives. His relationship with the Senate can become especially precarious if he lobbies too vigorously at the wrong time. As Goldstein has noted, "The Vice-President may offend Congressional leaders if he appears to compete with their operations. Humphrey's efforts apparently upset Senate Majority Leader Mike Mansfield."[49]

Party Worker

Vice President Nixon set a record of party service in the 1954 off-year election that has seldom been equaled. His forty-eight-day campaign schedule included visits to ninety-five cities in thirty-one states, 204 speeches, and more than 100 conferences.[50] Vice President Spiro Agnew, who resigned in 1973, was one of the more politically active vice presidents. His withering attacks on members of the Democratic opposition and national media— "the nattering nabobs of negativism"—may, however, have been counterproductive in the long run.[51]

Walter F. Mondale, in the first three years of his vice presidency (1977–1981), visited forty-eight of the fifty states, frequently to help fellow Democrats win public office. By campaigning on behalf of various candidates, Mondale created a number of valuable "IOUs" redeemable later. Undoubtedly, his work in the political vineyards for President Carter was a major factor subsequently in helping him win the Democratic presidential nomination in 1984.

Republican Vice President Dan Quayle, although widely criticized as a political lightweight, proved to be one of the party's most proficient fund-raisers. During the 1990 off-year election campaign Quayle visited nearly all fifty states and by some estimates raised more than $15 million to help fellow Republicans in their campaigns.[52]

While the vice president is serving as the president's surrogate, he is also reaping some benefits for himself. His public appearances bring the vice president into contact with numerous groups and acquaint him with a wide variety of regional and local issues. Additionally, he is gaining media exposure for a possible future run for the top spot on the ticket.

SEVERAL RECOMMENDATIONS

Despite the wide variety of presidential assignments given to vice presidents, however, many presidential scholars have until recently considered the vice president one of the most underutilized officials in the executive branch. Although presidents have delegated special assignments to their vice presidents—attending the funerals of foreign dignitaries, conducting goodwill trips abroad, speaking at fund-raising dinners, and so on—presidents have, over the years, generally relied on their trusted aides for most top-level duties. The special assignments given to Harry Hopkins, Clark Clifford, Joseph Califano, Jr., and H. R. Haldemann completely overshadowed the ceremonial functions performed by the vice presidents during the White House years of FDR, Truman, Lyndon B. Johnson, and Nixon. However, as a result of the recent institutionalization of the vice presidency, and especially the establishment of a vice presidential office in the West Wing, three of the most recent vice presidents—Mondale, Bush, and Gore—have become major policy advisers to the president.

A major reason for Mondale's and Bush's successful vice presidencies was their willingness to operate primarily behind the scenes to help the president. They did not attempt to steal credit from the president. Political scientist Paul

C. Light, based on his observations of vice presidents over the years, has suggested four rules to be followed if vice presidents are to be influential:

1. Never complain to the press. One of Rockefeller's continuing problems in the Ford administration was his high profile in the press. Leaks were easily traced to the vice president's office.

2. Never take credit from the president. The vice president must remember who is president and who is not. According to Mondale, once Carter made a decision, "I wouldn't rag him."

3. Fall in line. No matter how much the vice president opposes a presidential decision, he or she must support the final policy. The vice president does not have to become a vocal supporter or lobbyist, but must fall in line like any other staffer.

4. Share the dirty work. Though the vice president may not like the endless travel (and nights in Holiday Inns, as Mondale once complained), it is all part of being a team player. Mondale, for example, was on the road 600 days during his term.[53]

Vice presidential involvement in the activities of the various executive departments, however, has seldom been productive. As Thomas E. Cronin has observed, "The departmental secretaries preside over congressionally authorized departments; hence a vice president is very much an intruder, unless a problem arises which is definitely interdepartmental."[54]

Some reformers have recommended that vice presidents be given cabinet portfolios, such as secretary of defense or attorney general, but no president has opted for this suggestion. Nor is it likely that cabinet members would look with favor on this recommendation. As Cronin has pointed out, "Critics of this suggestion say existing cabinet members are already tough to make responsive to the White House. As an elected departmental official, a vice president who served also as a cabinet secretary/departmental head would be even tougher to get around or to 'fire.' "[55]

Far more important, however, than finding additional jobs for the vice president to perform is the task of delineating the precise role the vice president must perform in the event the president suffers a major physical or mental disability.

THE ISSUE OF PRESIDENTIAL DISABILITY

For some unexplained reason, the Founding Fathers never addressed the problem of presidential disability and the vice president's stand-in role during such a period. Would the vice president become "acting" president? Or would the vice president become merely a substitute for the chief executive? Nor did the Founders spell out the powers of the vice president if he succeeded a president who had died or resigned. Did only the "powers and duties" shift to the president? Or did the office transfer to a new president?

The question of transfer of the office was actually resolved first, though the initial test did not come until the death of President William Henry Harrison in 1841—only one month after his inauguration. His successor, Vice President John Tyler, insisted that he became president and not "acting president." Although opinion on this glaring ambiguity was divided at the time, all seven other accidental vice presidents who have succeeded to the presidency have made the same claim as Tyler—and it has been sustained. As a result, when Presidents Garfield, Wilson, and Eisenhower suffered from clear disabilities, their vice presidents refused to assume presidential responsibilities. They feared that any action would make them appear to be usurpers of the office. The country therefore drifted in a state of semi-paralysis during periods that sometimes extended over several weeks and sometimes months. Nothing was done about this dangerous gap in the constitutional system until President Eisenhower's second term.

In 1957, President Eisenhower proposed a constitutional amendment that would permit the vice president, with the advice of the cabinet, to decide when a stricken president was unable to carry out his duties, provided the president was unable to make the decision himself. Congress failed to act on Eisenhower's proposal.[56] The following year, however, President Eisenhower, after recuperating from the third of three serious illnesses, which included a heart attack and a mild stroke, decided to formulate a set of extralegal guidelines. Eisenhower and Vice President Nixon agreed that the president would inform the vice president of his disability, if possible, at which point the vice president would act as president. If such communication were impossible, the vice president "after such consultation as it seems to him appropriate under the circumstances" would decide whether to act as chief executive. In any event, the president would decide when he was capable of resuming his duties. Significantly, this type of agreement was subsequently adopted by Kennedy, Johnson, and Humphrey.[57]

While this type of pact was a distinct improvement over the previous ambiguous condition, it was nonetheless an inadequate stopgap measure in a crisis-ridden modern world. Furthermore, it lacked legal sanctions so that the right of the vice president to sign laws, appoint and dismiss officials in the executive branch, or act as commander in chief was not beyond constitutional challenge.[58] Equally important, the Eisenhower-Nixon agreement depended solely on the president's judgment that he could function.[59] No wonder that as late as 1964 Professor Clinton Rossiter could still describe the problem of presidential disability as "a situation that has no easy solution, perhaps no solution at all, except patience, prayer, and improvisation."[60]

In the same year, Richard M. Nixon, who had served eight years as vice president, called the clause in Article II on presidential disability "this one great defect in an otherwise remarkable document."[61] A combination of circumstances—Eisenhower's three major illnesses, the death of President John F. Kennedy, concern over the state of President Lyndon Johnson's health (he had suffered a heart attack in 1955), and the long-recognized constitutional hiatus on presidential disability—all prompted Senator Birch Bayh (D-IN) and some of his colleagues to draft the proposed Twenty-fifth Amendment to the Constitution to deal with the issues of presidential disability and vacancies in the office of vice president.[62]

THE TWENTY-FIFTH AMENDMENT

Ratified in 1967 by three-quarters of the states, the Twenty-fifth Amendment specifically provides that either the president himself or the vice president and a majority of his cabinet (or some other body designated by Congress) can declare that the president is unable to discharge the powers and duties of his office, in which case the vice president becomes *acting* president (not president).[63] The president is also authorized to declare when his disability is over and to resume the powers and duties of the office. However, if the vice president and cabinet (or some other body designated by Congress) disagree with the president's decision, Congress is designated to decide the issue. Thus, the amendment deals directly with the issues of (1) who precisely determines whether presidential disability exists; (2) what responsibilities does the vice president succeed to—the powers and duties of the office, or the office itself; and (3) who decides if and when the president has recovered from his disability, and if there is a disagreement on this point, how it is resolved.

The amendment also resolves the problem of a vacancy in the vice presidency. Interestingly, the United States has always had provisions to assure presidential succession, but until 1967 it did not have any constitutional means to fill a vice presidential vacancy. Throughout the nation's history, Congress had designated some federal official to be first in line of succession—the president pro tempore of the Senate, 1792–1886; the secretary of state, 1886–1947; the Speaker of the House (1947 onward).[64] Seven vice presidents have died in office, two have resigned; and nine others have succeeded to the presidency, leaving the vice presidency vacant for a total period of nearly thirty-eight years—roughly 20 percent of the nation's existence (see Table 14.1).[65] The absence of any constitutional arrangement for more than 185 years suggests how little importance the Founding Fathers attached to the second office. But this indifference would have had untold consequences if something had happened to the new successor president during this interim, for the country would have had a double vacancy in the top two leadership posts. The Twenty-fifth Amendment removes this gap in the constitutional machinery. If the vice presidency is vacant under the new amendment, the president nominates a successor, who must be confirmed by a majority in each chamber of Congress.

Table 14.1
Vice Presidential Vacancies

Vice President	Reason for Termination	Years	Months	Days
George Clinton	Death		10	12
Elbridge Gerry	Death	2	3	9
John C. Calhoun	Resignation		2	4
John Tyler	Succession	3	11	0
Millard Fillmore	Succession	2	7	23
William R. King	Death	3	10	14
Andrew Johnson	Succession	3	10	17
Henry Wilson	Death	1	3	10
Chester Arthur	Succession	3	5	13
Tom Hendricks	Death	3	3	7
Garret Hobart	Death	1	3	11
Theodore Roosevelt	Succession	3	5	18
James Sherman	Death		4	5
Calvin Coolidge	Succession	1	7	2
Harry S. Truman	Succession	3	9	8
Lyndon Johnson	Succession	1	1	29
Spiro T. Agnew	Resignation		1	26
Gerald R. Ford	Succession		4	10
Total		37	9	1

Source: Reprinted in abridged form by permission of the publisher from John D. Feerick, *The Twenty-fifth Amendment* (New York: Fordham University Press, 1976), Appendix D2, 255.

Since adoption of the Twenty-fifth Amendment in 1967, two vacancies in the vice presidency have already occurred. After Spiro Agnew resigned, President Nixon nominated Representative Gerald Ford, the House GOP minority leader, to the vice presidency. Less than a year later, President Nixon resigned rather than face an impeachment trial, and when Ford moved into the White House, he nominated New York Governor Nelson Rockefeller as the new vice president. Thus for the first time in the nation's history, neither the president nor vice president had been elected to these positions.

PRESIDENTIAL DISABILITY: STILL AN ISSUE

Loopholes still remain in the Twenty-fifth Amendment. Especially the determination of presidential disability is unclear. As Goldstein has pointed out: "A Chief Executive may clearly be incapable of performing his duties, but if both he and the cabinet refuse to acknowledge his inability, the Vice-President cannot act."[66] Nor does the Twenty-fifth Amendment deal easily with the determination of presidential disability, if the president is gravely injured in an accident or badly wounded in an assassination attempt.

Fortunately, no major constitutional crisis occurred in the hours immediately after the attempt on President Reagan's life in March 1981. Although he was unconscious for more than two hours while surgeons removed a bullet lodged within an inch of his heart, saving his life, Reagan recovered quickly. Indeed, the next day he was able to meet with his top advisers at his bedside and sign a bill concerned with dairy price support subsidies.

But in connection with the attempt on President Reagan's life, columnist William Safire and others have called attention to a critical problem about presidential disability that may arise under Section 4 of the Twenty-fifth Amendment when the "president's men"—the White House staff—refuse to alert the cabinet about the seriousness of a president's disability.[67]

Instead of calling the cabinet together to consider invoking Section 4, Richard Darman, deputy to Chief of Staff James A. Baker III, persuaded the White House officials that he should lock up the vital documents in his safe and not convene a cabinet meeting. The public's attention over the failure to invoke Section 4 was unintentionally diverted by Secretary of State Alexander Haig's unfortunate effort to calm the nation with his brash assertion "I am in control here . . . pending return of the Vice President." Events moved swiftly over the next twenty-four hours. But according to a White House correspondent for *Time* magazine, Laurence Barrett, a single White House staff member, in effect, made the decision to ignore the Twenty-fifth Amendment because the truth about the precarious medical condition of the president might have seriously disturbed the citizenry, and the cabinet might have voted to strip the president of his powers temporarily.[68]

In retrospect, White House aides could say that there was no reason to panic, for no international crisis was brewing and Reagan was soon on the road to recovery. But four days later the president was running an unexplained fever, and his doctors recommended a bronchoscope examination, which ordinarily required sedation. In the meantime, the CIA reported its concern about a possible Soviet invasion of Poland to quash an anti-government protest movement. Reagan's top advisers, according to Barrett, secretly considered the wisdom of invoking the Twenty-fifth Amendment, but then decided "to do so would cause confusion . . . and would offset their effort to assure the country and the world that Ronald Reagan was on the mend."[69] Thus, in the midst of a potential international crisis, White House insiders kept the decision making on presidential disability in their own hands, rather than following the constitutional procedure outlined in the Twenty-fifth Amendment.

Did this White House staff decision on presidential disability have any serious impact on the government and the public? Probably not. Perhaps the cabinet and the vice president could have done nothing better but wait for further reports on the president's condition. But someday, if another president is stricken, it would seem prudent to follow the constitutional procedure set down in Section 4 of the Twenty-fifth Amendment, and not leave the matter of presidential disability in the hands of the president's palace guard.

President Reagan's second encounter with the Twenty-fifth Amendment occurred in July 1985 when he underwent colon cancer surgery. Before Mr. Reagan entered the operating room he signed a letter transferring his powers to Vice President George Bush. However, Mr. Reagan chose not to invoke the Twenty-fifth Amendment, even though he followed the procedures spelled out in it.

Despite President Reagan's disclaimer, several legal authorities, including former Senator Birch Bayh (D-IN), one-time chairman of the Senate Judiciary Committee and the chief drafter of the amendment, and Dean John Feerick of Fordham University Law School, said the president had indeed invoked the Twenty-fifth Amendment. "To suggest they didn't use the power of the Twenty-fifth Amendment—there isn't any other place to get the power," said former Senator Bayh. "The president (alone) doesn't have the power to give up his office and then reclaim it." Dean Feerick agreed: "I don't see any basis (for the transfer) without the Twenty-fifth Amendment." Both men were interviewed on ABC Television's *This Week with David Brinkley*.[70]

Nor did the temporary transfer of power from Reagan to Bush come exactly in the clockwork fashion that the White House Staff portrayed it. For some unexplained reason, Vice President Bush, who was on his way back to Washington from his summer home in Maine, was not notified of the temporary transfer of power for twenty-two minutes after President Reagan went under anesthesia.[71]

Overall, the Twenty-fifth Amendment clarifies the status of a vice president who takes over in case of presidential disability—the vice president succeeds only to the powers and duties of the office, not the office itself. Moreover, as Donald Young has observed, "An ailing President may now safely relinquish his duties secure in the knowledge that he can resume his duties upon conclusion of his disability."[72] Almost as important, the amendment offers an effective mechanism for filling the vice presidency when it is vacant.

ONE VOTE AGAINST THE VICE PRESIDENCY

Historian Arthur M. Schlesinger, Jr., writing in a major academic journal two decades ago, advocated that the vice presidency be abolished.[73] In the event of a presidential vacancy, Schlesinger argued that an "intermediate election" for president should be held to select a replacement, instead of elevating the vice president to the nation's highest office. While conceding that he may have discounted the potential for the vice presidency as a stepping stone to the presidency since his essay first appeared in 1974, Schlesinger nonetheless recently reaffirmed his belief that the office should be abolished.[74] Instead, he would return to the cabinet succession system as prescribed in the Presidential Succession Act of 1886, until a special election can be held to choose a new president. Aside from the pro and con arguments, the Schlesinger plan would, of course, require a constitutional amendment to implement. Prospects for this major constitutional revision, however, do not seem bright in the current era.

Arguments for retention of an elected vice presidency seem to be far more persuasive. Two major national traumas—the Kennedy assassination and Richard Nixon's forced retirement—and the relatively smooth governmental transitions afterward by experienced Vice Presidents Lyndon Johnson and Gerald Ford assured stability and helped restore public confidence in the nation's leadership.

Former Vice President Mondale's thoughtful observations about the importance of an experienced presidential understudy merit serious consideration. Mondale opposes the abolition of the vice presidency because, he argues, the present system provides valuable on-the-job training to the higher office that the vice president might have to assume.[75] Furthermore, as the only other federal official elected by the voters nationwide, the vice president possesses a popular mandate, second only to that of the president. Also, as the responsibilities of the president continue to expand in this crisis-ridden era, the vice president can, if he has the president's confidence, be a valuable aide. In Mondale's words, "If the vice president is taken seriously, he can be an extended arm of command for the president."[76]

Since President Jimmy Carter's early decision to rely heavily on Vice President Mondale's advice and help, the notion of making greater use of the vice president as a general "minister without portfolio" has been gaining increased acceptance.[77]

Most recently, President Bill Clinton gave Vice President Al Gore a wide variety of tasks, especially in dealing with environmental matters. Gore's biggest assignment to date has been chairmanship of the National Performance Review Task Force on "Re-Inventing Government" to reduce the size and cost of the federal bureaucracy. In early September 1993, Vice President Gore—"the commander in the war against mismanagement"—unveiled a set of more than 800 recommendations that he said would streamline "old-fashioned, outdated government," save $108 billion over five years, and cut 252,000 federal jobs by 1998.[78] But critics have seriously questioned these numbers.

Washington author and columnist Elizabeth Drew has described Gore as "the most influential Vice President in history."[79] As President Clinton's top adviser, Gore has been heavily involved in everything from internal staff changes to the North American Free Trade Agreement (NAFTA) and the high-tech "information highway." Gore's unprecedented influence with President Clinton was underscored as early as the first cabinet meeting, according to Drew, when Clinton said, "If Al asks you for something, you should consider it as me asking."[80]

The changing role of the vice president in recent years has been summarized by one presidential scholar in these words:

The past two decades have seen the transformation of the Republic's Second Citizen from a minor political figure into an important presidential adviser. The vice presidency now offers its incumbent the opportunity to be among that small circle of senior presidential aides and counselors—with all the other demands placed on the First Citizen by the post-modern presidency, the president can use the sort of help and advice that an activist vice president has to offer. So it is likely that the new vice presidency is here to stay.[81]

Beyond doubt, the recent institutional changes—the executive budget, the expanded support staff, the move to the West Wing of the White House, the establishment of a special residence for the vice president, and the integration of the vice president's staff into the White House policy process—have all contributed to the growing stature of the vice presidential office.

NOTES

1. Joel K. Goldstein, *The Modern American Vice Presidency* (Princeton, NJ: Princeton University Press, 1982), 207.

2. Paul C. Light, *Vice Presidential Power: Advice and Influence in the White House* (Baltimore, MD: Johns Hopkins University Press, 1984), 1.

3. The analysis in this section relies primarily on Michael Nelson, "Background Paper," in *A Heartbeat Away,* Report of the Twentieth Century Fund Task Force on the Vice Presidency (New York: Priority Press, 1988), 21–109. But Nelson's classification does not include a separate category for "the institutionalized vice presidency."

4. Joseph E. Kallenbach, *The American Chief Executive* (New York: Harper & Row, 1966), 200.

5. Nelson, "Background Paper," 62.

6. Erwin C. Hargrove and Michael Nelson, *Presidents, Politics, and Policy* (Baltimore, MD: Johns Hopkins University Press, 1984), 29.

7. Edward S. Corwin, *The President: Office and Powers, 1787–1984*, 5th ed., Randall W. Bland, Theodore T. Hindson and Jack W. Peltason, eds. (New York: New York University Press, 1984), 67.

8. Twentieth-century vice presidents, however, have cast tie-breaking votes on the average of only one every two years—chiefly because the growth of the Senate from the original twenty-six members to the present 100 lessens the chances of tie votes. Thomas E. Cronin, "Rethinking the Vice Presidency," in Thomas E. Cronin, ed. *Rethinking the Presidency* (Boston: Little, Brown, 1982), 327.

9. Kallenbach, *The American Chief Executive,* 77–78.

10. Neal R. Peirce and Lawrence D. Longley, *The People's President: The Electoral College in American History and the Direct Vote Alternative,* rev. ed., (New Haven, CT: Yale University Press, 1981), 36–41.

11. Goldstein, *The Modern American Vice Presidency,* 6.

12. Quoted by Cronin, *Rethinking the Vice Presidency,* 326.

13. Nelson, "Background Paper," 30.

14. Ibid.

15. Ibid., 31.

16. For a discussion and analysis of the Presidential Succession Act of 1947, see Edward S. Corwin, *The President: Office and Powers, 1787–1984*, 5th ed., 62–63.

17. Light, *Vice Presidential Power*, 63. The discussion in this section depends heavily on this excellent study.

18. Bradley H. Patterson, Jr., *The Ring of Power: The White House Staff and Its Expanding Role in Government* (New York: Basic Books, 1988), 286.

19. Paul T. David, Ralph M. Goldman, and Richard C. Bain, *The Politics of National Party Conventions* (Washington, DC: The Brookings Institution, 1960), 389.

20. Sidney M. Milkis and Michael Nelson, *The American Presidency: Origins and Development* (Washington, DC: CQ Press, 1990), 365; Donald Young, *American Roulette: The History and Dilemma of the Vice Presidency* (New York: Viking Press, 1974), 181–182.

21. Goldstein, *The Modern American Vice Presidency*, 81.

22. Jules Witcover, *Crapshoot: Rolling the Dice on the Vice Presidency* (New York: Crown Publishers, 1992), 404.

23. Goldstein, *The Modern American Vice Presidency*, 81.

24. Stephen J. Wayne, *The Road to the White House* (New York: St. Martin's, 1980), 122.

25. Herbert Eaton, *Presidential Timber: A History of Nominating Conventions, 1868-1960* (London: Free Press, 1964), 451–453.

26. James W. Davis, *National Conventions in an Age of Party Reform* (Westport, CT: Greenwood, 1983), 149.

27. Witcover, *Crapshoot*, 415.

28. Quoted in Witcover, *Crapshoot*, 416.

29. In 1977, Representative Albert Quie (R-MN) introduced another variation of this plan: a national presidential primary bill whereby candidates for president and vice president would be separately selected by the voters in a one-day nationwide primary. See James W. Davis, *National Conventions in an Age of Party Reform*, 222.

30. For further discussion of several proposals to eliminate the game of "vice presidential roulette," see Goldstein, *The Modern American Vice Presidency*, 271–299; see also Davis, *National Conventions in an Age of Party Reform*, 144–150.

31. Goldstein, *The Modern American Vice Presidency*, 306.

32. Ibid., 308.

33. Gerald R. Ford, "On the Threshold of the White House," *Atlantic Monthly*, 1974, 63–65, as cited by Light, *Vice Presidential Power*, 7–8.

34. Ibid., 66.

35. During this fateful period Roosevelt was in the nation's capital less than a month. Truman later estimated that he saw FDR only eight times in the twelve months before Roosevelt's death—and this time span included the entire 1944 presidential campaign. Emmet John Hughes, *The Living Presidency* (New York: Coward, McGann, & Geohegan, 1972), 123.

36. Light, *Vice Presidential Power*, 61.

37. Ibid., 138.

38. Ibid., 134–135.

39. Ibid., 238.

40. Paul C. Light, "The Institutional Vice Presidency," *Presidential Studies Quarterly* 13 (Spring 1983): 207.

41. Light, *Vice Presidential Power*, 131.

42. Cronin, "Rethinking the Vice Presidency," 326–327.

43. As cited in Goldstein, *The Modern American Vice Presidency*, 309.

44. Young, *American Roulette*, 276–278.

45. Paul David, "The Vice Presidency: Its Institutional Evolution and Contemporary Status," *Journal of Politics* 29 (November 1967): 737–738.

46. Actually, he generally chairs the Senate only thirty minutes or so a day. Usually he turns the gavel over to a junior senator each day—unless an important vote is coming. It was a tragic irony that the young thirty-two-year-old Senator Edward M. Kennedy was in the chair when word reached the Senate that President Kennedy had been shot in Dallas. Young, *American Roulette*, 378.

47. Goldstein, *The Modern American Vice Presidency*, 178.

48. As cited by Goldstein, *The Modern American Vice Presidency*, 181.

49. Ibid., 183.

50. Robert J. Donovan, *Eisenhower: The Inside Story* (New York: Harper & Row, 1956), 280, as cited in Goldstein, *The Modern American Vice Presidency*, 185.

51. Jules Witcover, *White Knight: The Rise of Spiro Agnew* (New York: Random House, 1972), 393.

52. Witcover, *Crapshoot*, 389.

53. Quoted in George C. Edwards III and Stephen J. Wayne, *Presidential Leadership*, 2nd ed. (New York: St. Martin's, 1990), 185.

54. Cronin, "Rethinking the Vice Presidency," 332.

55. Ibid.

56. Michael Dorman, *The Second Man* (New York: Dell, 1968), 235.

57. Ibid., 238.

58. Young, *American Roulette*, 392.

59. Ibid., see also Stephen W. Stathis, "Presidential Disability Agreements Prior to the Twenty-Fifth Amendment," *Presidential Studies Quarterly* 12 (Spring 1982): 208–215.

60. As cited by Young, *American Roulette*, 390.

61. Ibid.

62. The Senate passed its version of the Twenty-fifth Amendment on February 19, 1965, by a vote of 72 to 0. The House acted favorably on its version in April 1965 by a vote of 368 to 29. The report of the conference committee was approved in the House by a voice vote on June 30, 1965. Six days later the Senate approved it by a vote of 68 to 5. Goldstein, *The Modern American Vice Presidency*, 232.

63. Twenty-fifth Amendment, Sections 2 and 3.

64. Goldstein, *The Modern American Vice Presidency*, 229–230.

65. Ibid.

66. Ibid., 223.

67. William Safire, *The New York Times*, 6 June 1983.

68. Laurence I. Barrett, *Gambling with History: Reagan in the White House* (Garden City, NY: Doubleday, 1983), 120–122.

69. Ibid.; for an excellent discussion of the Twenty-fifth Amendment and events surrounding the hospitalization of President Reagan after the attempt on his life on March 30, 1981, see Herbert L. Abrams, "Shielding the President from the Constitution: Disability and the 25th Amendment," *Presidential Studies Quarterly* 23 (Summer 1993): 533–553.

70. *Seattle Post-Intelligencer*, 15 July 1985.

71. Ibid. Some Washington insiders reported that the White House staff's failure to notify Bush of the transfer of power immediately was not an oversight, but reflected a power struggle going on between Bush and White House Chief of Staff Donald Regan, who saw no need for Bush to return to Washington. Bush, however, according to the same sources, insisted that he be on hand in the nation's capital during the president's hospitalization.

72. Young, *American Roulette*, 393.

73. Arthur M. Schlesinger, Jr., "On Presidential Succession, *Political Science Quarterly* 89 (Fall 1974): 475–506.

74. *A Heartbeat Away*, Report on the Twentieth Century Fund Task Force on the Vice Presidency, 17–18.

75. Witcover, *Crapshoot*, 400–402.

76. Ibid., 403.

77. Unlike many earlier vice presidents who were largely ignored, Witcover points out, "Mondale was included in all cabinet and National Security Council meetings, he lunched every Monday with Carter, and was told explicitly that he was free to join any meeting in the Oval Office, even those the President was holding with foreign chiefs of states. Furthermore, Carter ordered that the full paper flow to his own desk should go to Mondale's as well. The Vice-President was also in charge of long-range planning of the President's agenda." Witcover, *Crapshoot*, 299.

78. *The New York Times*, 8 September 1993.

79. Elizabeth Drew, *On the Edge: The Clinton Presidency* (New York: Simon & Schuster, 1994), 227.

80. Ibid.

81. Ryan J. Barilleaux, "The Post Modern American Presidency," *Presidency Research* 10 (Fall 1987): 18.

CHAPTER 15

PROPOSED REFORMS OF THE PRESIDENCY

Proposals to reform the presidency are nearly as old as the Constitution itself. That proposed presidential reforms have appeared frequently throughout our history should occasion no surprise, since the Founding Fathers deliberated longer and debated more vigorously over the power and structure of the presidency—as well as the selection process—than any other part of the nation's fundamental document.

Though proposals to reform the presidency number in the hundreds, it is noteworthy that only four constitutional changes affecting the presidency—the Twelfth, Twentieth, Twenty-second, and Twenty-fifth Amendments—have been approved since the Bill of Rights was added to the Constitution in 1791. Significantly, all four of these amendments have dealt with mechanical problems—a joint presidential-vice presidential ticket, a shift in the date of the presidential inauguration, the two-term limitation, and presidential disability as well as vice presidential vacancies. But none of the amendments has altered the formal structure or power of the executive branch.

In this chapter we examine and evaluate a wide variety of institutional reforms that have been proposed over the years—parliamentary government, concurrent presidential-congressional elections, the no-confidence vote in the presidential amendment, the plural executive, the mandatory question period, the six-year nonrenewable term plan, the direct election of the president, and modification of the Electoral College system—and then assesses the prospects and desirability of presidential reform.

BACKGROUND

Early critics of the presidency usually sought to impose restraints on the chief executive. Prior to the Civil War, for example, several constitutional lawyers and powerful Whig leaders in Congress, such as Daniel Webster and Henry Clay, seriously disturbed about Andrew Jackson's strong presidency, argued that the chief executive was the major flaw in the American system and should be checked by Congress or a council of state. During the fateful years leading up to the Civil War, several proposed amendments were also introduced in Congress that would have provided for two or three presidents, chosen on a sectional basis and serving as co-equals in power.[1] Few observers at the time realized, however, that the real threat to the Union would lie in a succession of weak incumbents incapable or unwilling to use the executive power to halt the fragmenting forces within the young Republic.

In the aftermath of the Lincoln presidency and the Reconstruction years, one leading scholar concluded that only by replacing the president with an executive council, patterned after the Swiss model, could American liberty be preserved.[2]

Toward the end of the nineteenth century, public law scholars, undoubtedly influenced by a series of weak, passive incumbents in the post–Civil War era, thought the presidency was evolving into a ceremonial office. The leading scholar (and future president), Woodrow Wilson, suggested that a parliamentary system might be preferable, though shortly after the turn of the century he became convinced, after watching President Theodore Roosevelt in action, that the presidential system offered far more opportunity for executive leadership.

To make presidential candidates more responsive to the popular will, leaders of the Progressive movement, the major reformers of the early twentieth century, concluded that the machinery for selecting presidents—the national convention—should be overhauled, especially the delegate selection process, and, if possible, be replaced by a national direct primary. Even Woodrow Wilson, in his first message to Congress in 1913, urged passage of a constitutional amendment to establish a national presidential primary. But this proposal was soon forgotten as Wilson pushed ahead with his banking and tariff reforms. In recent years, however, this proposal has been revived by a few members of Congress.

In the half-century spanning the decades between World War I and United States involvement in the Vietnam War, a variety of presidential reforms—most of them favoring some form of the British parliamentary system—were advanced by a number of American scholars.[3] But the proposals failed to attract any serious public or congressional support.

During this era the only proposed reform to capture the fancy of Congress, state lawmakers, and the country at large was the Twenty-second Amendment, ratified in 1951, to limit a president to two terms. Since then, critics of this constitutional restriction on presidential tenure have from time to time urged the repeal of the amendment. But not until Representative Guy Vander Jagt (R-MI), chairman of the House Republican Campaign Committee, urged the repeal of the Twenty-second Amendment in late spring 1986, in the hope that President Reagan might be persuaded to seek a third term, did the proposed repeal of this amendment attract brief national attention.

Congressional inaction on this issue in recent years, however, should not be construed as a complete absence of interest in presidential reform in the halls of Congress or in academic circles. Indeed, various proposals to improve the effectiveness of the chief executive or to constrain the powers of the president have surfaced periodically over the past quarter-century, especially during the Watergate era. Thus, it seems appropriate at this point to analyze and assess some of the more widely publicized proposals before making a final judgment on their potential suitability and, equally important, their prospects for adoption.

PARLIAMENTARY GOVERNMENT

One of the oldest reforms proposed for the presidency is the substitution of parliamentary government for the separation of powers and balanced constitution—a tried and tested system that has been in operation for nearly two centuries. Proponents of the parliamentary system (which fuses executive and legislative powers under the leadership of a prime minister and cabinet) claim that an American parliamentary system would achieve democratic responsibility and accountability and improve the link between public opinion and public policy. Clearly, a parliamentary system would introduce the direct accountability of the president and the executive branch to the national electorate but virtually eliminate constitutional checks and balances. Defenders of the parliamentary system, James W. Ceaser has pointed out, "rely on an electoral check rather than institutional checks to guarantee against abuses of power."[4]

Critics of the existing system argue, however, that the separation of powers prevents the development of responsible party government. In other words, voters have no assurance when they elect a president that he can implement a specific legislative program, since the legislative branch may be controlled by the opposition party, or control of the two houses of Congress may be divided between the two major parties. Under these circumstances the president finds himself, in effect, a prisoner of the separation of powers and nearly powerless to act. Even if the president's party controls both houses of Congress, opponents of the presidential system point out that members of his party may sometimes defy party discipline and vote with impunity against the president's legislative program.

Theoretically, under a parliamentary system a president would be able to deal with the high public expectations issue far more directly than under the present separation of powers system. Under a parliamentary system responsibility is clearly fixed. The president and his cabinet would present their agenda to

Congress and, assuming their voting majority, pass the president's legislative program intact. Strong party discipline would assure the president and his cabinet that they are empowered to act quickly and decisively without fear, normally, of being repudiated by their legislators. If the president and cabinet fail to deliver on their program and lose a vote of confidence, they would resign. Presidential accountability to the electorate would be direct and unmistakable. The voters would get the legislative program for which they cast their ballots. But the British experience with the parliamentary system has not in recent years indicated that the British prime minister enjoys any special advantage over the American president operating under a separation of powers system in satisfying the public's high expectations of executive leadership.[5]

American critics of the parliamentary system argue that it would destroy the "multiplicity of representational mechanisms" that are presently operative in the relationship between Congress and the president.[6] These instruments serve as a necessary means of political representation in a large, heterogenous country like the United States, marked by a decentralized party system and a federal structure of government. Channeling representation of such diverse special interest groups and sectional concerns, even a quasi-parliamentary system would probably overload the circuits of the two major parties and lead to their fragmentation. In the resultant sea of multipartyism the president (or prime minister) would be rudderless, not strong enough to govern alone and incapable of building a stable coalition among unyielding rival party leaders. As political scientist Norman C. Thomas has commented, "In all probability . . . an American parliamentary system would be characterized by a multiplicity of political parties, given our social pluralism, and hence it might encourage chronic instability like that of the French Fourth Republic or the current Italian Republic."[7]

CONCURRENT PRESIDENTIAL-CONGRESSIONAL ELECTIONS

Several reformers of the national government have proposed concurrent presidential-congressional elections to help overcome frequent governmental stalemate produced by the separation of powers.

Lloyd N. Cutler, a White House adviser in the Carter and Clinton administrations, for example, recommended the adoption of Congressman Jonathan Bingham's plan, which would require in presidential election years that voters in each congressional district vote for a trio of candidates as a team—president, vice president, and a House of Representatives member. Under this plan the political fortunes of the party's presidential and congressional candidates would be tied to one another and provide some incentive for sticking together after they are elected. Furthermore, Cutler and Bingham would extend the term of House members to four years to foster greater teamwork and, hopefully, to provide House members with greater protection against the pressures of single-interest groups. Actually, Cutler would prefer to move a step further and elect two senators to four-year terms, along with the candidates for president, vice president, and the House of Representatives.[8] Thus, members of Congress would come into office as part of a presidential team.

Another variation of the unified team ticket plan—the so-called four-eight-four plan—would institute four-year terms for House members, eight-year terms for senators, and four years for presidents.[9] By forcing voters to ballot for a team ticket and denying them the opportunity to split votes between the president and members of Congress, each institution could be substantially changed by the public in election years. Best of all, presidents would be granted four full years to implement policy changes without the usual losses inflicted on their party in the off-year elections.

While the team ticket proposal is not a foolproof protection plan against divided government, the odds for electing a unified party government would be significantly enhanced. James L. Sundquist, a senior fellow at the Brookings Institution, insists that "the team ticket would have a profound effect on the conduct of politicians of the majority party in office."[10] Especially during the president's first term, the chief executive and lawmakers of his party would be clearly aware that when reelection time arrived, they would stand or fall together. Consequently, legislators in the president's party would have a special incentive to help him establish a positive record.[11] To put this plan in place, however, would require a constitutional amendment. Whether the Cutler-type of single-party government would enable the president to satisfy high public expectations of his performance more readily than the present system is an open question. Since high public expectations of the president generally revolve around the state of the economy—and to a lesser extent, foreign affairs—the type of institutional leadership machinery would appear to be less important than the rate of inflation, unemployment, and taxation.

Other reforms of the presidency have also surfaced over the past two decades. The uncertainty surrounding the Nixon presidency and his threatened impeachment in 1974 triggered a serious discussion of how to deal with a president who has lost the nation's confidence and respect but who refuses to resign. The most widely discussed proposal at the time was the so-called no confidence vote.

THE NO CONFIDENCE VOTE

The Constitution, critics have reminded us, does not cover the question of what to do about a failed president who, although not physically or morally disabled, has lost the capacity to lead the country, but is not removable under the disability provisions of the Twenty-fifth Amendment or the impeachment clauses of the nation's basic charter. Shortly before President Nixon's forced resignation, Representative Henry Reuss (D-WI) proposed a constitutional amendment that would permit the ouster of a president by a no confidence vote.

Borrowed from the parliamentary government system, the no confidence vote is a means of presidential removal on policy or performance grounds, without the complicated procedural arrangements of impeachment, coupled with a provision for the dissolution of Congress and the call for a special presidential election.[12] Reuss's no confidence proposal was one of the more drastic responses to the widespread belief that the presidency in modern times has become too powerful. Supporters of the no confidence proposal hold the view that presidential power has grown beyond the level where checks and balances can be used effectively to constrain the president.

How would the no confidence amendment operate? According to the Reuss plan, the House and Senate could vote no confidence in the chief executive by an extraordinary three-fifths (60 percent) majority of members present and voting. If called for, the no confidence resolution would take priority over any other pending issue before Congress. If adopted, the president would step aside at once. He would then be succeeded by the vice president—a member of his own party. The new president would serve until a special presidential election could be held. Meanwhile, Congress would fix a date between 90 and 110 days for a special election for president and vice president as well as for members of Congress.

Representative Reuss's plan allows considerable flexibility on the time for the special election. If the no confidence vote came during the last year of a president's term, Congress could decide against a special election. If the vote occurred in a year of midterm elections (for example, 1990 or 1994), the presidential election would simply be added to the congressional races. The president elected in this manner would assume office the following January and serve for four years. If the special election occurred at any other time, Congress would specify when the new term would start, but it could not be less than sixty or more than seventy-five days following the election. The Reuss plan also contains a unique provision: An ousted president would be able to run again. The theory is that a defeated president should be given the opportunity to win vindication.[13] The two-term limitation of the Twenty-second Amendment would also be repealed.

In short, supporters of the no confidence vote have concluded that impeachment is an inefficient check on the president, since it only protects the country against criminal violations of the public trust, but not against presidential incompetence. Advocates of the no confidence proposal have reminded the country that incompetence is not an indictable offense.[14] The no confidence vote, its supporters point out, does not take power away from the president; instead, it makes him more accountable for how he uses his powers.

James L. Sundquist believes that if Congress were granted the no confidence vote and the president were not given the power to dissolve the legislature, which the British cabinet has, the overall effect—contrary to its critics—would exert a restraining influence on the presidency and restore a needed balance of power between the branches.[15]

Sundquist is also certainly on sound ground when he observes, "An institutional principle applied almost universally in the English-speaking world is that major decisions should not be made by one man acting alone, but by a collective body of some kind."[16]

The no confidence vote would aim to produce more presidential-congressional cooperation, and it would seek to provide a method for ending deadlocked or leaderless government such as occurred in the 1919–1920, 1931–1932, and 1973–1974 periods.[17]

THE CASE AGAINST THE NO CONFIDENCE AMENDMENT

Critics of the Reuss proposals argue that "the cure is worse than the occasional ailment."[18] They remind enthusiasts that Congress is not without resources to hold a president in check, short of impeachment—the War Powers Act, the Case Act (requiring presidential notification of executive agreements), the Budget and Impoundment Control Act of 1974, the National Emergencies Act of 1976, and the power of the purse.

As Thomas E. Cronin has observed, "In certain situations it would seem that the vote of no confidence would give Congress the power to continually frustrate a president with whom it disagreed."[19] The alternative would seem to be a government of continuous presidential elections, not unlike the revolving door governments of post-war Italy, and "overall paralysis or a government in which the president and Congress are so close as to defeat the basic concept of the separation of powers so fundamental to our system."[20] The resulting instability would make the development and implementation of long-term programs very uncertain. Cronin also notes: "A vote of no confidence arrangement might lead presidents to avoid making significant changes in policy that would antagonize Congress."[21] Imaginative leadership might also be cast aside in favor of policies rated highly popular in the opinion polls, whether sound or not.

Government instability would likely be a probable consequence of the no confidence vote proposals. Indeed, political scientist Allan Sindler has posed the question: "What of the possibility that a highly popular and aggressive president, if opposed by Congress, might seek a special election to gain public re-endorsement by challenging the Congress to vote no confidence?"[22]

The danger of a plebiscitarian type of democracy emerging from the no confidence proposal should not be easily dismissed. Cronin has pointed out that "a vote of no confidence could actually be used to strengthen the hand of an already strong leader, much as Hitler and DeGaulle used plebiscites to weaken their opposition."[23] National leaders have rarely, if ever, lost plebiscite votes.

Indeed, these leaders can time and word their plebiscites in such a fashion that they automatically guarantee a favorable vote. As Cronin has commented, "One imagines, for example, Lyndon Johnson could have won a vote of no confidence on his Vietnam policy in 1966. Or, Richard Nixon might have won a vote of no confidence during the early stages, say, the spring or summer of 1973, of his Watergate crisis."[24]

Clearly, the no confidence proposal offers no guarantees of higher quality leadership or greater presidential accountability. As Norman C. Thomas noted, "The potential for both Congressional and presidential manipulation of the procedure for short-run political advantage makes it unduly risky."[25] Also, it is difficult to disagree with Cronin's final assessment of the no confidence vote proposal:

This measure might at some future time give us an endless line of unsuccessful short-term presidents and as a result a paralyzed nation. We risk the unwise weakening of the presidency by such an amendment. Abuses of presidential power do need to be curbed, but this proposal is not the way to do it. We need better leadership, not a weakened presidency.[26]

Opponents also insist that the no confidence dissolution reform is unnecessary because impeachment and other available checks and balances can and have worked effectively. For proof, they point to the forced resignation of President Nixon as a recent example. Would the "no confidence" vote enable the president to meet high public expectations more readily than the existing separation of powers system? No one can say with a high degree of certainty without experimenting with the proposed reform. But, on balance, it would appear that the American people would be exchanging stability for uncertainty and frequent government turnover.

PLURAL EXECUTIVE

Some reformers believe that the job of president has become too big to be entrusted to one person. Even the Founding Fathers were concerned about this problem; they seriously considered and then dropped the idea of a plural executive. As the complexities and demands of the presidency have multiplied in the twentieth century, the concept of the plural executive has received occasional attention. Several variations of the plural executive have been suggested. Some students of the presidency have advocated the election of two or three presidents, dividing domestic and foreign responsibilities, or splitting up the policy formation and implementation tasks of the presidency.

Tugwell's Plan

Some years ago, Rexford Tugwell, a member of FDR's original "Brain Trust," proposed a new constitution that provided for two vice presidents to be elected with the president. One would be designated as first successor should the president die or become incapacitated. The job of these two officials would be to relieve the president of the managerial, regulatory, and custodial duties that he presumably can no longer perform effectively. The chancellors of foreign, financial, military, and legal affairs would be responsible to the vice president for general affairs. Chancellors of other departments would report to the vice president of internal affairs at the president's discretion. The president, freed of many administrative responsibilities, would be able to function full time as a policymaker in the critical area of government. Under this system, Tugwell argued, responsibility would be easy to pinpoint.[27]

The Tuchman Plan

In the 1970s, noted historian Barbara Tuchman, suggested a six-person directorate elected on a party ticket for a period of six years. Each member would serve one year as chairperson. The chairperson's vote would carry the weight of two members to avoid a tie. In Tuchman's view, "Personal government can get beyond control in the United States because the President is subject to no advisers who hold office independent of him." According to the distinguished historian, "Spreading the executive power among six eliminates dangerous challenges to the ego." Each of the six executives would be designated from the time of nomination as secretary of a specific department of government affairs: foreign (including military), financial, judicial, business, physical resources, and human affairs."[28]

The Finer Plan

A far more radical departure—indeed almost a revolutionary proposal—is Professor Herman Finer's plan to elect a president and eleven vice presidents together for a four-year term to serve as a kind of ministry through which the executive functions of government would be discharged. All twelve would be nominated together by national party conventions and elected for four years. Congress would be elected at the same time for a four-year term. Under the Finer plan, the president would preside over his cabinet or vice presidents, assign them their respective jobs, dismiss any of them if he wished, and appoint others to their positions. Only persons who had served in Congress for at least four years would be eligible to run for the presidency or vice presidencies. The president-elect and his cabinet or vice presidents would be given seats in Congress and the duty of leading the "loyal opposition." If there were a vote of no confidence, the president could (with the concurrence of a majority of his cabinet or vice presidents) force the resignation of the entire team and thereby cause Congress to be dissolved. New elections would then be held for all seats in Congress as well as for the president-vice president "cabinet."[29] Thus, the

Finer plan would connect the executive and legislative branches through standard terms of office for Congress and cabinet.

Shortcomings of the Plural Executive

The flaws of most plural executive plans are not hard to find: competition and disputes within the executive, a splintering and confusion of responsibilities, and further growth of the executive branch. One of the great virtues of the single executive is the ability to reach a quick decision, if needed, and to move with dispatch. But could a collective presidency reach a unified agreement in times of crisis? Would the public have confidence in, say, split decisions within the executive branch? Also, it seems doubtful if this federal bureaucracy would operate as effectively under a divided executive council. Furthermore, as Thomas E. Cronin warns, "Might not a collectivized presidency court paralysis or indecision, or both in a nuclear attack or in an international monetary crisis, when swiftness and decisiveness are often most needed?"[30]

Other defects of the plural executive are plainly evident. The plural executive would probably compound the problems of an already top-heavy executive establishment. Undoubtedly each president and each vice president would want his or her own staff, legislative liaison team, public relations staff, and press secretary. Presidential bureaucratization would reach new heights. Nor is it difficult to visualize each of the executives engaged in headline-hunting and credit taking for every accomplishment within the executive branch.

Clearly, a plural executive could be expected to suffer from executive internal competition. Might not an intra-executive veto process emerge that could hamstring or undercut executive unity and dispatch? Cronin reminds us that our existing system of checks and balances and limited government already seems, according to many people, designed more for paralysis than leadership. The plural executive would just accentuate this shortcoming.[31]

To leading critics, the most serious objection to the plural executive concept is that it would be exceedingly difficult to assign accountability. The finger pointing would probably never end. As Alexander Hamilton argued two centuries ago, the restraints of public opinion on the president would lose their efficacy if there were several executives rather than one president. Who should the people blame for disastrous policies? Which set of executives should ultimately face impeachment? Hamilton wisely concluded that it would be far easier for the people to oversee a single chief executive.[32]

Beyond question, proposals for institutionalizing more assistance for over burdened presidents, such as strengthening presidential planning and evaluation staff services, by legislation or grafting onto the Constitution proposals for a plural executive should be scrutinized with extreme caution. As Norman C. Thomas noted, "Present structural arrangements result in a form of collective leadership, and a President can achieve many of its alleged advantages through use of his high-level assistants."[33]

All strong presidents of the twentieth century—Teddy Roosevelt, Wilson, Franklin D. Roosevelt, Truman, Kennedy, Johnson, and Reagan—have always been able to attract capable staffers to handle the heavy load of White House business. Co-chief executives or additional vice presidents have been neither needed nor wanted.

Corwin's Legislative Cabinet

Almost four decades ago, a leading authority on the presidency, Edward S. Corwin, suggested that more harmonious relations would develop between the president and Congress if the president would choose part of his cabinet from leading members of Congress. The restructured cabinet would be selected by the president from both houses of Congress. Added to this group would be as many executive department heads as were required by the nature of the activity.[34]

Corwin's proposal of a legislative cabinet to replace the presidential cabinet, however, takes little account of the political facts of life governing the American separation of powers system. The legislative cabinet idea is an attempt to change the recognized ineffective advisory role of the cabinet as it is presently constituted. But the possibility of developing a viable advisory relationship between a president and cabinet composed of independently elected senators and representatives who are firmly entrenched in a seniority system is extremely remote. Not only would this proposal weaken congressional political leadership, it would also undercut the president's independent sources of political authority.

To force the president to surrender his initiative in both domestic and foreign affairs and to limit his goals to what he can sell to a legislative cabinet of senior members would leave him at the mercy of a congressional cabal. In addition, the legislative cabinet idea gives the president no more support or clout than he can secure at present by direct negotiation with party leaders on Capitol Hill.[35]

Both the plural executive and the legislative cabinet proposals would appear to offer few opportunities for enhancing the president's ability to fulfill the public's high expectations of his leadership.

THE MANDATORY QUESTION PERIOD

In 1864, Representative George Pendleton (R-OH), who is better remembered for his civil service reform bill, proposed that cabinet members be given seats in the House of Representatives, with the privilege of entering debate and being present a certain number of days each month to answer questions. Almost a century later, Senator Estes Kefauver (D-TN) revised this plan for a question-and-answer period for the department heads on the floor of either house. More recently, former Vice President Walter F. Mondale, when he was a member of the Senate, offered the same proposal again.

Over the years, however, the proposal for mandatory questioning of the present and principal department and agency heads has not generated much public support. Gerald Ford's voluntary appearance before the House Judiciary Committee in late 1974 to explain his pardon of former President Nixon undoubtedly further deflated support for the mandatory question period proposal. Nevertheless, political scientist Philippa Strum and others have argued that the proposal deserves serious consideration because of the excessive claims of executive privilege and the executive department's heavy preoccupation with secrecy, especially the Johnson and Nixon administrations.[36] Also, Strum insists that the mandatory question period would be the proper antidote to the frequent reluctance of top-level officials, such as President Nixon's secretary of state, Henry Kissinger, to testify before congressional committees and especially their insistence on delineating the topics and areas to be discussed in the hearings.

Designed in part as a symbolic attack on the imperial presidency, the mandatory question period would, its supporters insist, help achieve two reform goals: restoration of constitutional balance and greater presidential accountability. Professor Strum argues that the proposal would not require amending the Constitution, since Article II, Section 3, can be interpreted as providing a basis for a statute mandating a question period.

Opponents of this plan doubt whether a mandatory question period is worth the price in terms of policy effectiveness and the possibility that the proposed reform might foster renewed secrecy by the White House. Critics have also made a case that constant questioning of the president and top-level members of the executive branch might seriously stifle presidential initiative and contribute to a further undermining of legitimacy in the American governmental system. Critics also insist that most objectives of the mandatory question period could probably be achieved by legislation spelling out the scope of executive privilege and the conditions under which it could be invoked. Furthermore, as James L. Sundquist has wisely observed, "To require officials to appear for questioning in the Senate or the House against their will would not contribute to harmonious relationships nor add significantly to the store of knowledge available to legislators."[37] As a "safety valve," the mandatory question period would offer members of Congress the opportunity to ask a host of questions to embarrass the president, but it is difficult to see how this procedure would improve the prospects of a president to satisfy the public's high expectation of his job performance.

THE SIX-YEAR NONRENEWABLE TERM PROPOSAL

From time to time reformers of the presidency have proposed that the office be limited to a single six-year nonrenewable term. This is not exactly a new

Table 15.1
Proposed Six-Year Presidential Term (Gallup Poll)

Year	Yes/Favor %	No/Oppose %	No Opinion %
1986 (September)	25	70	5
1983 (February)	31	61	8
1981 (January)[a]	30	63	7
1979	30	62	8
1973	28	64	8
1971	20	73	7
1969	18	75	7
1945[b]	25	68	7
1943[c]	29	59	12
1938	21	67	12
1936	26	74	--*

*"Don't Know" figures, which were allocated between favor and oppose, are not available. *Question variations*: (a) "Would you favor changing the term of the president of the United States to one six-year term with no reelection?"; (b) "Would you favor changing the term of office of the president of the United States in the future to one six-year term with no reelection?"; (c) "Would you favor changing the term of office of the president hereafter to one six-year term with no reelection?"

Source: *Gallup Report* No. 209, February 1983, 12; No. 253, October 1986, 25.

idea. Originally proposed in Congress in 1826, the single six-year term proposal has been reintroduced more than 150 times since then. In 1830, Andrew Jackson recommended a single term, stating the office of the president should "be placed beyond the reach of any improper influences." At least nine other presidents, including Lyndon Johnson, Nixon, and Carter have also endorsed the proposal.[38] According to the Gallup poll organization, however, less than one-third of those polled in 1983 favored changing to a six-year term (see Table 15.1). To achieve a six-year presidential term, it would be necessary, of course, to amend the Constitution.

Proponents of the single six-year term—or the "term and a half," as it is sometimes called—have argued that it has many advantages over the existing four-year, renewable term. First of all, it would enable the president to devote his full time and attention to the job. No time would have to be devoted to seeking renomination and reelection. Under the existing system the president must set aside the fourth year (and sometimes more time) of his first term for running for reelection. The six-year single term, its supporters argue, would remove this political pressure and give the president an additional two years to carry out his long-term plans. As columnist Tom Wicker commented some years ago, "The argument that running for reelection takes too much of a President's time may be the strongest for the single six-year term."[39] Former Secretary of

State Cyrus Vance has made the point in stronger language: "Every President needs eight or nine months to learn his job. Then he has about one and one-half years to feel comfortable in a job he knows. Then he's running again for twelve to eighteen months."[40] Also, not to be forgotten, there is a midterm congressional election that no president can afford to neglect.

Furthermore, six-year term advocates insist that the current four-year term is too short for the president to achieve the goals he has set during his successful drive for the White House. The nature of the budget process, for example, is such that he is well into his second year before the impact of his program can be felt. Supporters of the six-year term argue that the proposal permits long-term study, planning, and implementation of a president's program, without wasting the fourth year in reelection campaigning.

One of the strongest arguments in favor of a single six-year term is that it would "liberate a president from the pressures of special-interest groups and party-line politics, allowing him to exercise greater independence of judgment and nonpartisan leadership."[41] Advocates of the single six-year term want "to take the politics out of the presidency, to de-emphasize the divisive aspects of electoral and partisan politics, to elevate the presidency above selfish or factional ambitions."[42]

Other supporters of the one-term presidency have also argued that it would permit a president to make decisions free from the temptation of political expediency. Former President Carter has reported that near the end of a first term, when a president opens a reelection campaign, there is a "driving pressure" on his challengers to "dispute or contradict the president on the issues for strictly political reasons."[43] Carter also recalled how Gerald Ford, seeking renomination in 1976, had to back off from strategic arms agreements reached with the Soviet Union at the Vladivostok summit and from trying to obtain ratification of the Panama Canal treaties when both projects came under heavy fire from his conservative intraparty challenger, Ronald Reagan.[44] Nor was President Carter immune from such pressures; he withdrew SALT II from Senate consideration early in 1980 after the Soviet Union's invasion of Afghanistan.

THE CASE AGAINST THE SIX-YEAR TERM

Deceptively appealing at first glance, the single six-year term would probably create more problems than it would solve. First of all, as several critics have pointed out, the president would be a lame duck from the moment of his election. The one-term president would still have to engage in political bargaining in order to win congressional support, but his political firepower would be considerably less than if he could stand for reelection.[45] Eligibility for reelection, Alexander Hamilton argued two centuries ago, is necessary "to enable the people, when they see reason to approve of his conduct, to continue him in his station, in order to prolong the utility of his talents and virtues."[46]

Clearly, the required reelection of a chief executive after four years is one of the most democratic features of the presidency. The need to seek reelection enhances the likelihood that a president will carefully weigh his policy options and their possible effect on his reelection chances before moving ahead. Presidential accountability is best maintained when the president must answer again to the electorate. Furthermore, as Thomas E. Cronin reminds us, "A political party should retain the threat of dumping a president as a check upon the incumbent and the office, especially upon a president who refuses to honor his party pledges."[47]

In early 1913, President-elect Woodrow Wilson, in seeking to block a proposed constitutional amendment to establish a single, six-year presidential term (the amendment had already passed the Senate by a 48-to-23 vote), wrote a Democratic congressional leader that a four-year term was "too long for a President who is not the true spokesman of the people, who is imposed upon and does not lead. It is too short a term for a President who is doing or attempting a great work of reform and who has not had time to finish it." Switching to six years, he insisted, "would increase the likelihood of its being too long, without any assurance that it would, in happy cases, be long enough. A fixed Constitutional limitation to a single term of office is highly arbitrary and unsatisfactory from any point of view."[48]

Cronin's telling argument against a single six-year term is equally persuasive: "The president who cannot be reelected after four years is unlikely to accomplish anything of value if he is given a free ride for another two."[49] Likewise, a president who shirks his political responsibilities and refuses to face reelection is not likely to accomplish much in the way of program development and substantive policy. As Cronin has aptly put it,

Reeligibility, used or not, is a potentially significant political resource in the hands of a president; and denying that resource, even in the more limited way that the Twenty-second Amendment has done, will diminish the leadership discretion of future presidents who desire to be activist initiators of policy.[50]

George Reedy, who served as secretary to Lyndon B. Johnson and later wrote one of the more thoughtful treatises on the presidency, has argued that single-term proposals are

based on the belief that a President's authority is somehow separable from his political leadership. . . . The reality is quite different. A president whose political leadership has suffered from erosion is virtually helpless. [51]

Separating the president from the pressures of the public, Reedy observed, would only "tend to make him an ineffective voice issuing orders and decrees."

Clearly, the single six-year term would make presidential accountability and executive branch responsiveness more difficult to achieve than under the present two-term system.[52] Nor should the possibility be ignored that the single six-year term, with reelection precluded, would intensify the presidential selection process. Thomas E. Cronin has warned, "Certainly in a winner-take-more situation, there is the likelihood that ideological competition would be more aggressive and perhaps more bitter than at present. Conflict would assuredly be heightened."[53] More than eighty years ago, Senator John Sharp Williams of Mississippi put his finger on another significant reason for rejecting the six-year term. A single six-year term, Williams argued, would likely extend periods of divided government, such as existed in the 1910–1912 period (and more recently for twenty years out of twenty-four between 1968 and 1992) for two additional years, thus "emphasizing rather than diminishing the defect of our system as it is."[54]

What are the prospects for the proposed amendment to limit the president to one six-year term? While one hesitates to rely on the crystal ball, it would appear that, despite the support of several former presidents and a number of prominent national leaders, the prospects are not bright. The formidable obstacles of the amending process itself make any basic change in the Constitution unlikely. As the supporters of the original equal rights amendment and District of Columbia statehood question have painfully learned, it is almost impossible to amend the Constitution without massive public support.

Many supporters of the single six-year presidential term amendment also favor term limitations on members of Congress—twelve years for members of each house. Consequently, it seems rather unlikely that present members of Congress would support the single six-year presidential term if it meant that they would soon be pressured into supporting an amendment to shorten their own political lives.

It remains to be seen how much effect the term limits movement or state legislators, governors, and federal lawmakers now spreading across the country has upon the single six-year term for presidents proposal. By 1994, twenty-two states had adopted term limits on lawmakers (some states included both federal and state officials) via popular initiatives. Consequently, it does not seem unreasonable to expect the influence of the term limit movement to stimulate renewed interest in a single six-year term for presidents in the years ahead. But how this institutional "reform" would enhance the president's ability to fulfill more readily the excessive public expectations placed upon the nation's chief executive escapes this writer.

REPEAL OF THE TWENTY-SECOND AMENDMENT

Whether advocating repeal of an amendment previously added to the Constitution less than five decades ago constitutes reforming the presidency may be debatable. But it is the author's view that the Twenty-second Amendment two-term limitation on presidents should be repealed, primarily because it makes a chief executive a lame duck the day after he is reelected. The Founding Fathers provided indefinite eligibility for presidents; the four-year term represented a compromise between those who favored the president's serving during "good behavior," meaning indefinitely so long as he comported himself within constitutional guidelines, and those who favored a seven-year term. Some Framers thought a second term should be banned.

Long after the Founding Fathers left Philadelphia, the length of presidential service continued to occupy national attention. Between 1789 and 1947, Thomas E. Cronin reminds us, "No less than 270 resolutions to limit eligibility for reelection were introduced in Congress."[55] Why did the Twenty-second Amendment win favorable approval after World War II, despite many previous rejections? The explanation can be traced to the special political conditions existing at that time. During the 80th Congress (1946–1948), Republicans dominated both houses of Congress, and they were determined not to see a repeat performance of four successive presidential victories by another FDR-type candidate.

Ironically, the Twenty-second Amendment, ratified in 1951, first applied to Republican President Dwight D. Eisenhower, who was barred from running in 1960. If Eisenhower had been eligible to run and wished to seek a third term, however, most political pundits agreed that he would have easily won renomination and reelection.

This amendment is, according to some critics, antidemocratic, for it limits the national leadership choice of party and electorate alike. Furthermore, if the nation were in the midst of a major war or domestic crisis, it compels a rotation in office just when the electorate may wish to see an experienced president continue. Passed more as a result of political spite—"retroactive partisan vengeance against FDR"—rather than adherence to sound democratic doctrine, the Twenty-second Amendment turns a reelected president into a lame duck from the moment he is declared the winner.

Though we have the experience of observing only Presidents Eisenhower and Reagan in their second terms, most political experts seem to agree that the long-term effects of the amendment will undermine the effectiveness of most second-term presidents. President Harry S. Truman, although not prohibited by the amendment from seeking another term in 1952, testified that any officer who is ineligible for reelection loses a lot of political clout. In the words of the plain-spoken man from Independence, the American people put the president "in the hardest job in the world, and send him out to fight our battles in a life and death struggle—and you have sent him out to fight with one hand tied behind his back because everyone knows he cannot run for reelection."[56] Truman added: "If he is not a good President, and you do not want to keep him, you do not have to reelect him. There is a way to get rid of him and it does not require a constitutional amendment to do it."[57]

Defenders of the Twenty-second Amendment have advanced several persuasive arguments for retention of the two-term limit. First, eight years is sufficient time for a president and his administration to produce major policy changes.[58] During this period they will have had plenty of time to advocate and fight for their major programs. If these proposals have not been enacted into law in eight years, they are unlikely to see the light of day in a third or fourth term. Also, most presidents suffer a diminution of power and loss of energy, and sometimes deteriorating health, during the latter part of a second term.

Second, the two-term limit on presidents is healthy for the two-party system. Both major parties benefit and are rejuvenated by the challenge at least every eight years of discovering and nominating a new crop of national leaders. Moreover, the record of governors and mayors who have stayed for three or more terms often provides grounds for additional skepticism. These multiterm executives have frequently been less than accountable for their actions and susceptible to the arrogance of power or corruption, or both.

Third, a president who remains in office for twelve or sixteen years would most likely be able to pack the Supreme Court and lower federal courts, fundamentally altering the political philosophy of the entire federal judiciary. President Franklin D. Roosevelt appointed nine justices in twelve years (actually eight years since he did not make his first High Court appointment until his second term). President Nixon appointed four justices in five years. Briefly, then, the defenders of the Twenty-second Amendment insist that it can continue to serve as an invaluable check and balance mechanism in the future, without undermining the effectiveness of dedicated presidents.[59]

What does the future hold for the Twenty-second Amendment? While most citizens support the two-term tradition, they sometimes view it as too restrictive to be cemented into the Constitution. However, there has been no ground swell to repeal the limitation. Possibly an emergency near the end of a popular president's second term might trigger a major repeal drive. But it seems doubtful if enough time could be found to repeal it before the election, even discounting the additional obstacles that might arise if it became a partisan issue, as seems likely. Nor should the possibility be dismissed that the repeal drive might run head on into an equally strong constitutional amendment drive to adopt the single, six-year presidential term.

DIRECT ELECTION OF THE PRESIDENT

Direct popular election of the president is a reform proposal that would probably have the most far-reaching impact—and undoubtedly a number of unanticipated consequences—on the presidency and the American party system.

By far the most democratic electoral proposal, the direct popular vote amendment is deceptively appealing. This plan would give every voter the same weight in the presidential balloting, in accordance with the one-person, one-vote doctrine. On paper, at least, the winner would gain more legitimacy as a result of a clear-cut popular triumph. Furthermore, the shortcomings of the present system, especially the constitutional requirement that presidential choice will be made by the House of Representatives if no candidate receives a majority of the electoral votes, would be replaced by a simple, direct, and decisive method.

Advocates of the direct vote plan point out that three times in the nation's history (1824, 1876, and 1888) the Electoral College has failed to give the popular vote winner a victory. Nor do they believe that the direct vote plan will undermine the federal system in any way. "The vitality of federalism," columnist Neal Peirce writes, "rests chiefly on the constitutionally mandated system of congressional representation and the will and capacity of the state and local governments to address compelling problems, not on the hocus-pocus of the eighteenth-century vote count system."[60]

Andrew Jackson, a losing candidate in the 1824 electoral college deadlock, four years later in his first annual message advocated that the electoral college be abolished and the president chosen by popular vote, with a run-off election between the two high candidates if no one received a majority in the initial ballot.[61] More recently advocated by Senator Birch Bayh (D-IN), the main sponsor of the Twenty-fifth Amendment on presidential disability, the Bayh plan would have presidents elected directly by the voters just as governors are. Additionally, the Bayh version also contained a provision that called for a national run-off election between the two top vote-getters in the event that no candidate received 40 percent of all votes cast.[62]

The proposed direct vote amendment, after more than a decade of debate and parliamentary skirmishing, was finally put to a vote in the U.S. Senate in July 1979. With ninety-nine senators voting, the proposal received fifty-one votes— fifteen votes short of the sixty-six needed for a proposed constitutional amendment.[63] Opponents of the amendment consisted of an alliance of southern conservatives and northern liberals. They were responding especially to black and Jewish groups who feared they might lose their "swing" vote power under the existing system. Several senators from the small states, worried about possible diminution of their voting strength, also cast votes against the proposed constitutional amendment. Failure on this vote ended further attempts in Congress to win approval of the direct vote amendment.

Some analysts predict that once a direct election amendment has been ratified, it would soon be followed by the adoption of a nationwide presidential primary. The same arguments advanced in favor of direct election of the president also apply to a nationwide primary amendment:

1. The nominee of each major party, if a run-off primary were used between the two top vote-getters in each party, would represent a majority of the voters;

2. the proposal could be easily understood by the prospective voters;

3. the proposal would grant no particular favor to any special interest group or individual states (e.g., New Hampshire or Iowa);

4. national opinion polls have consistently shown over the past two decades that two-thirds of the public favor both direct election of the president and a nationwide presidential primary.[64]

ARGUMENTS AGAINST DIRECT ELECTION OF PRESIDENTS

The direct election plan, however, is fraught with numerous potential booby traps. Under the direct popular election plan, containing the provision of a run-off between the two top vote-getters in the event no candidate receives a majority, it is likely that a large number of candidates—perhaps a dozen or more—would enter the contest. Conceivably, most of the moderate candidates would receive a small percentage of the popular vote, say, 5 to 8 percent of the vote, while popular extremists from each end of the political spectrum would collect nearly 20 percent of the vote. As a result, the run-off election would be among the extremists while the mainstream candidates representing the middle-of-the-road majority, would be forced to the sidelines. Thus, the eventual winner would be truly a "minority" president. The run-off proposal might also encourage third-party, independent, or "spoiler" candidacies and seriously undermine the two-party system. The possibility that a defeated candidate from a national convention might obtain a ballot listing as a new party or an independent candidate cannot be easily dismissed.

Historian Arthur M. Schlesinger, Jr., has expressed the fear that minor parties or single-cause candidates could magnify their strength under the direct vote plan. "Anti-abortion parties, Black Power parties, anti-busing parties, anti-gun control parties, pro-homosexual rights parties—for that matter, Communist or Fascist parties—have a dim future in the electoral college. In direct elections they could drain away enough votes, cumulative from state to state, to prevent the formation of a national majority—and to give themselves strong bargaining positions in case of a run-off."[65]

Thomas A. Cronin has also raised another direct election specter: "The direct vote method could easily produce a series of forty-one percent presidents."[66] Though we have elected sixteen minority presidents (i.e., candidates elected by less than 50 percent of the popular vote), the present Electoral College system—a two-stage process in which popular votes are transformed into electoral votes—magnifies the popular vote margin of the winner. Thus, even though there have been a number of cliffhanger presidential election contests—Kennedy-Nixon in 1960, Nixon-Humphrey in 1968, and Carter-Ford in 1976—only once in the past century has a president failed to receive 55 percent of the Electoral College vote. Most recently, President Bill Clinton in 1992 received only 43 percent of the popular vote in the three-way race against President George Bush and Ross Perot, but the "multiplier effect" of the present electoral system transformed his 370 electoral votes into nearly 69 percent of the Electoral College vote.

Direct popular vote, if it were extremely close—say, within a few thousand votes nationwide—might easily lead to interminable recounts and challenges, leave open the possibility of electoral fraud in some states, and raise serious questions over the legitimacy of choice. Opponents insist that it would encourage unrestrained majority rule and probably political extremism. Lawyer Charles Black, a scholar not often given to exaggeration, stated that direct election would be the most deeply radical amendment ever to enter the Constitution.[67] The present Electoral College process, which rests on a federal system of choice, dampens electoral tensions, and for a century it has produced, without fail, a popular vote winner. Above all, it has helped preserve the two-party system.

To appreciate fully the contribution of the existing Electoral College to the maintenance of a viable two-party system, imagine a direct election presidential campaign conducted without two major parties but rather a host of candidate-centered minor parties. Instead of two major candidates having a reasonable chance of winning a majority of the popular vote, the field would be filled with a dozen or more presidential hopefuls all calculating that they have some chance of capturing the White House. Most of these candidates would draw support from special interest groups and small segments of the population. As visualized by political scientist Robert Weissberg, "The incentive to create broad-based coalitions to capture a voting majority in twenty or thirty major states would be considerably reduced and the two major parties would virtually disappear."[68] Most likely, the country would see an endless string of "minority" presidents.

Under the direct election plan, state electoral victories would not be important, only the single national mandate would count. In defending the present system, national columnist George Will observed some years ago, "The electoral college promotes unity and legitimacy by helping to generate majorities that are not narrow, geographically or ideologically, and by magnifying (as in 1960, 1968, 1976) narrow margins of victories in the popular vote."[69]

Opponents of the direct system also point out that the small states would be submerged and lose some of the power they presently enjoy in the federal system. Furthermore, the direct popular vote plan, among other things, necessitates some form of national administration of presidential elections, upsetting the present decentralized and economical state management of elections. Direct popular election would probably trigger demands for a uniform ballot in all states and uniform voter qualifications. Moreover, as Thomas E. Cronin cautions: "Once members of Congress attack details of this nature, they are also likely to regulate further the presidential primary process, the methods of voting, and hence, at least indirectly, to influence the national conventions."[70]

Some critics fear that the direct election plan would make the candidates more remote from the voters by transforming the campaigns into national election telethons, since the sole object would be to reach as many potential voters in the large populous states in the most efficient manner possible.

Judith Best, a leading critic of direct election of the president, has made perhaps the most damaging charge against the proposal. To make the president the recipient of the only direct national mandate, she argues, would change the balance in the executive-legislative relationship to the great advantage of the president. A truly plebiscitarian president who could claim to speak directly for the general will could destroy the authenticity of the voice of Congress which speaks only for federal concurrent majorities. Direct election of the president, far from enhancing democracy, could undermine democracy itself.[71] Under these circumstances the opportunities for a president to engage in demagogic appeals to the mass electorate and thereby ratchet the level of public expectations ever upward would seem to be virtually unlimited.

What are the prospects for the direct election plan? Until a major Electoral College crisis occurs in a close election—if a candidate won the popular vote and yet lost in the Electoral College, or if a third-party candidate should garner enough electoral votes to force the presidential choice into the House of Representatives and the lawmakers remained deadlocked on their choice—the prospects for the direct election amendment do not seem especially promising.

OTHER PROCEDURAL REFORMS

Dissatisfaction with the Electoral College over the years, however, has produced several other proposals to modify its operation. But support for these plans has been so splintered that they have failed to stimulate much public support. Each of these plans, however, deserves brief mention.

The first, called the *automatic plan*, would result in the least change to the existing system, and it would remove the possibility of "faithless electors"— those who refuse to support the electoral winner in their home state. Under the automatic plan the presidential electors would be abolished, and the state's electoral vote would be automatically cast for the popular vote winner in that state. If no candidate won a majority of electoral votes nationwide, a joint session of Congress would select the president, with each representative and senator having one vote.

Under the second proposal—the *district plan*—the nation would return to the method used in the states early in our history (and recently re-adopted in Maine and Nebraska). In the district plan the presidential candidate who wins a plurality vote in each congressional district receives its electoral vote, with the remaining two electoral votes (derived from the two U.S. Senate seats) going to the nationwide popular vote winner. If no presidential candidate receives a majority of the electoral votes, senators and representatives, meeting jointly and voting individually, would select the president from the three candidates having the highest number of electoral votes. By and large, most of the support for the district plan has come from conservative members of Congress and interest groups based in the rural areas.

The third proposal, called the *proportional plan*, would split each state's electoral vote in proportion to the division of the popular vote. Thus, a candidate receiving 60 percent of the popular vote in the state would collect 60 percent of its electoral vote. In 1950, such a proposal, the so-called Lodge-Gossett plan, named after its two leading sponsors—Republican Senator Henry Cabot Lodge, Jr., of Massachusetts and Democratic Representative Ed Gossett of Texas— passed the Senate but failed to survive in the House.[72] This plan, which would reduce the advantage of the large states by preventing them from giving all of their votes to one candidate, has usually been opposed by lawmakers from the populous states. Critics of the plan have also argued that the proportional division of the electoral votes would be complicated by a strong third-party candidate, thus likely denying any candidate a majority of the electoral votes. Under this plan there would be the frequent likelihood of presidential elections being thrown into the House of Representatives.[73]

The fourth proposal, developed by members of the Twentieth Century Fund task force, is known as the *national bonus plan*.[74] If adopted, the national bonus plan would retain the Electoral College, but it would be heavily weighted toward the popular vote winner. Under the plan a pool of 102 electoral votes (two for each state and the District of Columbia) would automatically be awarded to the candidate who won the popular vote, to be added to the candidate's electoral vote. In all, there would be a combined total of 640 national electoral votes (538 Electoral College votes, plus 102 national bonus votes). If a candidate collected a majority in the Electoral College (321 votes), he or she would be declared elected. If not, a run-off election would be held within thirty days between the two candidates winning the most popular votes.

Advocates contend the plan would ensure that the popular vote winner would usually be the electoral vote winner and thus make it unlikely that the popular vote winner would lose the election, as happened in 1888 and could have occurred in 1960 and 1976. Furthermore, proponents insist the plan would reduce the chances of electoral deadlock, encourage a two-party competition in one-party states, and eliminate the faithless elector who votes against the popular choice in his or her own state.

Critics of the bonus plan contend that, among other things, the plan would discourage minor parties and independent candidates. Small states, it has been noted, might lose some of their influence in a diluted electoral vote and control over state election law. One respected political scientist, Allan P. Sindler, has expressed concern that the national bonus plan might also allow a plurality leader with a highly sectional base of voting support to collect the 102 bonus votes and thereby capture the presidency.[75] The national bonus plan would, of course, require a constitutional amendment.

Finally, the most important lesson to be drawn from a study of the proposed reforms of the presidency is that for each remedy there are as many problems as solutions. No single, all-purpose reform exists to help the president cope with the unrelenting demands placed on him. Indeed, a careful analysis of the various reform proposals suggests that most of the remedies merely exchange one set of difficulties for another—or, worse yet, undermine the existing effectiveness of the American chief executive.

In summary, no major overhaul of the presidency, it would seem, is needed at the present time. However, we should be mindful that an institution over two hundred years old may from time to time need some fine tuning. Past experience suggests that "the presidency will be revived not by a few grand strokes of constitutional change, but by the accumulation of small improvements at the right points in the system."[76] In the meantime, we should turn down the thermostat on presidential expectations and rely more heavily on the judgment of the American electorate to choose presidents who can meet the challenges of the 1990s and the early years of the twenty-first century and yet operate within the constitutional framework of the American shared powers system.

NOTES

1. Joseph E. Kallenbach, *The American Chief Executive* (New York: Harper & Row, 1966), 571.

2. Henry C. Lockwood, *The Abolition of the Presidency* (1884), as cited by Edward S. Corwin, *The President: Office and Powers, 1787–1984*, 5th ed., eds. Randall W. Bland, Theodore T. Hindson, and Jack W. Peltason (New York: New York University Press, 1984), 25.

3. See, for example, William Y. Elliott, *The Need for Constitutional Reform: A Program for National Security* (New York: McGraw-Hill, 1942); Henry Hazlitt, *A New Constitution Now* (New York: McGraw-Hill, 1942); Thomas K. Finletter, *Can Representative Government Do the Job?* (New York: Reynal & Hitchcock, 1942); and C. Perry Patterson, *Presidential Government in the United States: The Unwritten Constitution* (Chapel Hill: University of North Carolina Press, 1947).

4. James W. Ceaser, "In Defense of Separation of Powers," in Robert A. Goldman and Art Kaufman, eds. *Separation of Powers: Does it Still Work?* (Washington, DC: American Enterprise Institute, 1986), 182–183.

5. Thomas O. Sargentich, "The Limits of the Parliamentary Critique of the Separation of Powers," *William and Mary Law Review* 34 (Spring 1993): 679–739.

6. Frank J. Sorauf and Paul Allen Beck, *Party Politics in America*, 6th ed. (Glenview, IL: Scott, Foresman, & Company, 1988), 452–455.

7. Norman C. Thomas, "Reforming the Presidency: Problems and Prospects," in Thomas E. Cronin and Rexford G. Tugwell, eds. *The Presidency Reappraised*, 2nd ed. (New York: Praeger, 1977), 329.

8. Lloyd N. Cutler, "To Form a Government—On the Defects of Separation of Powers," *Foreign Affairs* 59 (Fall 1980): 126–143.

9. See Donald L. Robinson, *To the Best of My Ability: The Presidency and the Constitution* (New York: W. W. Norton, 1987), 270–271.

10. James L. Sundquist, *Constitutional Reform and Effective Government* (Washington, DC: The Brookings Institution, 1986), 85.

11. Ibid.

12. H.D. Res. 903 (93rd Congress, 2nd Session) February 14, 1974, copy supplied by Representative Reuss. For a more detailed discussion of the Reuss plan, see Henry S. Reuss, "A No-Confidence Amendment," *Commonweal*, 12 April 1974, 127–129.

13. Two other no confidence proposals for removing a failed president, offered by Reps. Jonathan B. Bingham (D-NY) and Edith Green (D-OR) during the Watergate era, are discussed in Sundquist, *Constitutional Reform and Effective Government*, 65–66.

14. Thomas E. Cronin, *The State of the Presidency*, 2nd ed. (Boston: Little, Brown, 1980), 345.

15. James L. Sundquist, "Parliamentary Government and Ours," *New Republic*, 26 October 1974, 10–12.

16. James L. Sundquist, "Needed: A Workable Check on the President," *The Brookings Bulletin* 10 (Fall 1973): 11.

17. Thomas, "Reforming the Presidency: Problems and Prospects," 330.

18. Cronin, *The State of the Presidency*, 348.

19. Ibid., 347.

20. Ibid.

21. Ibid.

22. Allan Sindler, "Critique of the Reuss Proposal," in Donald L. Robinson, ed., *Reforming American Government*, 225.

23. Cronin, *The State of the Presidency*, 347.

24. Ibid.

25. Thomas, "Reforming the Presidency: Problems and Prospects," 330.

26. Cronin, *The State of the Presidency*, 348.

27. Rexford Tugwell, "Constitution for a United Republics of America," Version 37, *The Center Magazine* 3 (September-October 1970): 31–32.

28. Barbara Tuchman, "Should We Abolish the Presidency?" *The New York Times*, 13 February 1973.

29. Herman Finer, *The Presidency: Crisis and Regeneration* (Chicago: University of Chicago Press, 1960), Chapter 7.

30. Cronin, *The State of the Presidency*, 363.

31. Ibid.

32. *The Federalist*, No. 70 (New York: Modern Library, 1937), 460–467; see also Terry Eastland, *Energy in the Executive: The Case for a Strong Executive* (New York: Free Press, 1992).

33. Thomas, "Reforming the Presidency: Problems and Prospects," 338.

34. Edward S. Corwin, *The President: Office and Powers*, 4th ed. (New York: New York University, 1957), 297–299.

35. Rowland Egger, *The President of the United States* (New York: McGraw-Hill, 1967), 151–152.

36. See Philippa Strum, "A Symbolic Attack on the Imperial Presidency: An American 'Question of Time,' " in Cronin and Tugwell, *The Presidency Reappraised*, 248–264.

37. Sundquist, *Constitutional Reform and Effective Government*, 177.

38. Tom Wicker, "Six Years for the Presidency?" *The New York Times* Magazine, 26 June 1983, 18.

39. Ibid.

40. Ibid.

41. Cronin, *The State of the Presidency*, 356.

42. Ibid., 354.

43. As cited by Wicker, "Six Years for the Presidency?" 19.

44. Ibid.

45. See Thomas, "Reforming the Presidency: Problems and Prospects," 334.

46. *The Federalist*, No. 72.

47. Cronin, *The State of the Presidency*, 356.

48. Woodrow Wilson letter placed in the *Congressional Record*, 64th Cong., 2nd Sess., 15 August 1916, 53, pt. 13: 12620, as cited in Cronin, *The State of the Presidency*, 368, note 38.

49. Ibid., 359.

50. Ibid. Harry S. Truman, testimony before the Subcommittee on Constitutional Amendments of the U.S. Senate, Committee on the Judiciary Hearings on S.D. Resolution II: Presidential Term of Office, 86th Cong., 1st Sess., 1959, Part I, 7, as cited by Cronin, *The State of the Presidency*, 360. See also Bruce Buchanan, "The Six-Year One-Term Presidency: A New Look at an Old Proposal," *Presidential Studies Quarterly* 18 (Winter, 1988): 129–142.

51. George Reedy, *The Twilight of the Presidency* (New York: New American Library, 1970), 138–139.

52. Thomas, "Reforming the Presidency: Problems and Prospects," 334.

53. Cronin, *The State of the Presidency*, 366, note 40.

54. *Congressional Record*, 30 January 1913, 2265–2266, as cited by Sundquist, *Constitutional Reform and Effective Government*, 45.

55. Cronin, *The State of the Presidency*, 47.

56. Harry S. Truman, *Senate Judiciary Hearings*, 86th Cong., 1st session, 4 May 1959, 7, as cited by Cronin, *The State of the Presidency*, footnote 28.

57. Ibid.

58. The discussion in this section is drawn primarily from Thomas E. Cronin, "Two Cheers for the 22nd Amendment," *The Christian Science Monitor*, 23 February 1987, 16.

59. Ibid. In October 1986, the Gallup Poll showed that 33 percent of the respondents favored repeal of the Twenty-second Amendment, but 64 percent opposed the repeal. Approximately 3 percent had no opinion. *Gallup Report*, No. 253, October 1986, 26.

60. As cited by Cronin, *The State of the Presidency*, 65.

61. James L. Sundquist, *Constitutional Reform and Effective Government*, 42.

62. 96th Congress, 1st Sess., S.J. Res. 28.

63. Neal R. Peirce and Lawrence D. Longley, *The People's President: The Electoral College in American History and the Direct Vote Alternative*, rev. ed. (New Haven, CT: Yale University Press, 1981), 205.

64. In 1977, the Gallup organization asked respondents, "Would you approve or disapprove of an amendment to the Constitution which would do away with the electoral college and base the election of the President on the total vote cast throughout the nation?" The results show: approve, 75 percent; disapprove, 14 percent; and no opinion, 11 percent. On a similar question a Harris Survey conducted in May 1977 showed 74 percent in favor, 13 percent opposed, and 13 percent not sure. See Appendix N, National Polls on Instituting Direct Popular Vote, in Neal R. Peirce and Lawrence D. Longley, *The People's President*: 296–299. In early 1988 a Gallup Poll on a proposed nationwide presidential primary showed that 65 percent of the respondents favored the proposal; 25 percent opposed; and 10 percent had no opinion. *The Gallup Report*, March 1988, 10.

65. As cited by Cronin, *The State of the Presidency*, 61–62.

66. Ibid., 65.

67. *Direct Election of the President* (Washington, DC: American Enterprise Institute, 1977), citing Black's testimony before the Senate Judiciary Committee in 1970, 392.

68. Robert Weissberg, "In Defense of the Electoral College," in Robert E. DiClerico and Allan S. Hammock, eds. *Points of View*, 4th ed. (New York: Random House, 1989), 144.

69. George Will, "Don't Fool with the Electoral College," *Newsweek*, 4 April 1977, 96.

70. Cronin, *The State of the Presidency,* 64.

71. Judith Best, *The Case Against Direct Election of the President: A Defense of the Electoral College* (Ithaca, NY: Cornell University Press, 1975), 101.

72. For a discussion of the Lodge-Gossett plan, see Neal R. Peirce and Lawrence D. Longley, *The People's President*, 146–150.

73. Ibid., 152–156.

74. For a more detailed discussion of the plan, see *Winner Take All*, Report of the Twentieth Century Fund Task Force on Reform of the Presidential Election Process (New York: Holmes Meier, 1978); Thomas E. Cronin, "Choosing a President," *The Center Magazine* 11 (September-October 1978): 5–15.

75. As cited by Cronin, *The State of the Presidency*, 69–70.

76. Godfrey Hodgson, *All Things to All Men* (New York: Simon & Schuster, 1980), 259.

CHAPTER 16

THE ROAD AHEAD

Because the president can bring national power into focus and implement national policy energetically, the nation has come to expect him to address pressing national problems and international crises immediately. Indeed, the president is the only political official in the federal government with the entire nation as his constituency. No other Western democracy, it might be noted, entrusts to its leader as much constitutional and extraconstitutional responsibility as the United States. Whether it be earthquake damage in California, a flood in the Mississippi valley, or high unemployment, the public turns first to the president to respond to the emergency. Because millions and millions of Americans concentrate their hopes and fears directly and personally upon the president, most chief executives feel compelled to act, no matter what the cost. The president has indeed become the tribune of the American people.

Throughout this text the underlying theme has been that the public's high expectations of modern presidents far exceed the president's capacity to satisfy the impatient public's demands. This final chapter will reassess this phenomenon and also endeavor to summarize the remarkable political and technological changes over the past half-century that have transformed the contemporary American presidency into a far more complex, institutionalized office than existed in the pre-modern era.

COMPARISON WITH THE PAST

The modern presidency, most scholars agree, began with President Franklin D. Roosevelt (1933–1945).[1] But the contemporary presidency functions in a dramatically changed environment from FDR's New Deal era. Political parties then served as the principal intermediaries between the president and the public. Parties performed reasonably well as vehicles for translating presidential campaign promises into concrete public policy. In this bygone era presidents depended heavily upon their congressional party leaders to handle the administration's legislative agenda on Capitol Hill. Divided government—one party controlling the executive branch and the other party, Congress—was the exception rather than the dominant factor it has become in recent decades.

Lobbying in the nation's capital by special interest groups was still relatively low-keyed in the pre–World War II era. Political action committees did not exist. Even more important, network television had not become the pervasive influence in presidential campaigns that it came to be in the early 1960s. Presidential incumbents and their challengers still depended heavily upon their political parties to win the necessary electoral votes to reach the White House. Opinion polls to measure the public's attitudes toward presidential incumbents and their performance were still in their infancy.

Since then, however, a series of political, structural, and technological developments across America has added many dimensions to the modern presidency. Jeffrey Tulis and several of his colleagues, for example, have argued that the presidency in recent decades has undergone a significant transformation in function and emphasis from a constitutional, administrative office to an executive-centered rhetorical office. They attribute this shift to several major influences: (1) the modern doctrine of activist, presidential leadership; (2) the modern candidate-centered presidential campaign; and (3) swift advances in communications technology.[2]

More than ever, the contemporary presidency accentuates the independence of the office. As political scientist Stephen Skowronek recently observed, "The political foundations of presidential action have become increasingly independent over time, the incumbent drawing upon resources for action that are ever more directly tied to the executive branch itself."[3] Over the years this transformation occurred even before the nominee occupied the Oval Office during the nominating phase of the White House race. Presidential nominating politics became candidate centered, not party centered.

NOMINATING PROCESS WIDENS GAP BETWEEN PRESIDENT AND HIS PARTY

Beyond doubt, the democratization of the presidential nominating process, especially the adoption of presidential primaries in at least thirty-nine states, has widened the gap between presidential candidates and their parties. Stephen Skowronek has noted, "Primary elections are the cornerstones of the plebiscitary presidency. They strip away the veneer of party unity and expose the individuality of each candidate."[4] Successful nominees no longer win the White

House by relying chiefly on state and local party organizations to handle electioneering duties. Instead, the presidential candidates organize and build their own campaign team of strategists, field organizations, pollsters, media specialists, and advertising experts independently of national and state party organizations.[5]

Nor do the major party nominees have to depend any longer upon their political parties to collect the funds needed to conduct the general election campaign. Uncle Sam now picks up the tab, if the candidate agrees not to accept private contributions. Thus, in 1992 President George Bush and challenger Governor Bill Clinton each received $55.2 million in federal campaign funds under the Federal Election Campaign Act of 1974 to underwrite their campaigns. Small wonder that the successful presidential nominee feels little obligation to his party for his electoral victory.

In the absence of cohesive political parties, presidents now find that even after reaching the White House, they must campaign constantly for support for their programs. They have learned that they can no longer automatically count on members of their own party in Congress to back the administration's programs. Meanwhile, members of Congress, in turn, have become more insulated from traditional forms of presidential influence.

Members of Congress conduct their own campaigns largely independent of their political parties and the president. Consequently, the lawmakers do not feel a strong sense of obligation to back the president's initiatives, unless it is in their own interest to do so. Thus, in this age of congressional independence the president and members of his own party in Congress frequently have their own separate—and sometimes conflicting—agendas.

STRUCTURAL AND POLITICAL BARRIERS

Structural and political barriers standing directly in the president's path now seem more formidable than ever. Not only must the president contend with the Madisonian shared powers system, but party fragmentation in Congress, the spreading "subcommitteeization" of Congress, and the emergence of more than four score of special congressional caucuses (the "Frost Belt" Caucus, the Black Caucus, etc.) have all weakened the president's ability to engage in legislative consensus building on Capitol Hill. This congressional atomization has forced modern presidents to develop a mass popular base outside and beyond Congress.[6] As explained by political scientists Lester E. Seligman and Cary R. Covington,

The emergence of the public as a key component of presidential governing coalitions has led presidents to adopt new campaigning strategies for building coalitions and to expand and formalize components of the White House that facilitate communication with and mobilization of the public and interest groups.[7]

The growing frequency of media-sponsored polls on presidential approval ratings has added to the president's leadership burden. During President Bill Clinton's first four months in office, for example, one major media outlet measured his job approval rating every three days on average. Any sharp drop in these polls can of course undermine his leadership of Congress and the country.

SPECIAL INTEREST GROUPS

In recent years, the enormous growth of special interest groups in Washington has also complicated the president's governing role. According to one source, the number of people lobbying in the nation's capital increased from approximately 4,000 in 1977 to nearly 20,000 by 1982.[8] Ten years later, political scientist James Thurber, in a systematic study, concluded that more than 91,000 lobbyists and people associated with lobbying were operating in the nation's capital.[9] The number of lawyers belonging to the District of Columbia Bar Association (a requirement to practice in Washington) increased from approximately 1,000 in 1950 to 21,000 by 1975. And by 1993, the number had jumped to 61,000![10] Of the 23,000 national trade associations operating in 1989, approximately one-third made their national headquarters in metropolitan Washington.

This special interest list does not include many of the dozens of consumer protection, environmental, and various "good government" organizations that are headquartered in Washington. Furthermore, each group seems more determined than the next to push its own policy agenda and protect its operating turf, no matter what the cost. This pervasive special interest group environment has increasingly polarized policy debates and made it far more difficult for a president to find compromise solutions to urgent national problems.

Modern Washington has been described by one national reporter as "wired for quadraphonic sound and wide screen video, lashed by FAX, computer, 800 numbers, overnight polls, Fed Ex, grass roots mail, air shuttle, and CNN to every citizen in every village on the continent and Hawaii, too."[11] Political action committees will always be found in the epicenter of this "500-channel democracy."

POLITICAL ACTION COMMITTEES

To add to the president's headaches, more than 4,200 political action committees (PACs)—the political arms of these special interest groups—have sprouted up in Washington over the past two decades (see Table 16.1). With bulging exchequers, these political action committees, representing all shades of the political spectrum—from trade unions, to automobile dealers, to doctors—have provided nearly 50 percent of the campaign funds for incumbent

Table 16.1
Growth of PACs by Type, 1974–1989

Year End	Corporate	Labor	Membership	Non-connected	Other†	Total
1974	89	201	318*	---	---	608
1975**	139	226	357*	---	---	722
1976	433	224	489*	---	---	1146
1977	550	234	438	110	28	1360
1978	785	217	453	162	36	1653
1979	950	240	514	247	49	2000
1980	1206	297	576	374	98	2551
1981	1329	318	614	531	109	2901
1982	1469	380	649	723	150	3371
1983	1538	378	643	793	173	3525
1984	1682	394	698	1053	182	4009
1985	1710	388	695	1003	196	3992
1986	1744	384	745	1077	207*	4157
1987***	1779	382	797	1044	209	4211

†"Other" includes the PACs of cooperatives without stock; *These totals include not only membership PACs, but nonconnected PACs and PACs of cooperatives and corporations without stock; **The date for this year is November 24, rather than December 31; ***The data for 1987 are as of July 1, 1987.

Source: Frank J. Sorauf, *Money in American Elections* (Glenview, IL: Scott, Foresman, 1988),78. Copyright © 1988. Reprinted by permission of HarperCollins College Publishers.

House members and slightly smaller percentages for Senate incumbents and challengers. Their contributions, though limited to $5,000 for each lawmaker, can be spread to an unlimited number of legislators. In 1986, for example, political action committees contributed almost $140 million to Senate and House candidates (see Table 16.2).

Although PAC directors are well aware that it is no longer possible—indeed, it is illegal—to attempt to buy votes, their contributions to members of Congress can nevertheless buy valuable access and influence. Some critics insist that this cozy relationship frequently affects an incumbent's vote on key legislation pushed by the president.

PRESIDENTIAL COUNTERACTIONS

To counter the phalanx of opposition organized by special interest groups and PACs, presidents are forced to construct their own legislative coalitions. The president and the White House staff have not hesitated to recruit their own team of lawmakers and special interest group representatives to lobby the president's program on Capitol Hill, instead of their own agenda.[12]

Table 16.2
Contributions by PACs to All Candidates for the House and Senate, 1974–1986 (in millions of dollars)

Year End	Corporate	Labor	Membership	Non-connected	Other†	Total
1974	*	$6.3	*	$0.7	$1.0	$12.5
1976	*	8.2	*	1.5	2.8	22.6
1978	$9.8	10.3	$11.3	2.8	1.0	35.2
1980	19.2	13.2	15.9	4.9	2.0	55.2
1982	27.5	20.3	21.9	10.7	3.2	83.6
1984	35.5	24.8	26.7	14.5	3.8	105.3
1986	49.4	31.0	34.4	19.4	5.3	139.4

†An ambiguous and omnibus category in 1974 and 1976—after then it includes the PACs of cooperatives and corporations without stock; *Specific figures not available.

Source: Frank J. Sorauf, *Money in American Elections* (Glenview, IL: Scott, Foresman, 1988),79. Copyright © 1988. Reprinted by permission of HarperCollins College Publishers. Adapted from Table 9 of Joseph E. Cantor, *Political Action Committees: Their Evolution, Growth, and Implications for the Political System*, report 84.78 GOV of the Congressional Research Service of the Library of Congress (30 April 1984), 88; data for 1984 and 1986 come from FEC reports.

As indicated earlier in the text, the president could formerly count on his congressional leaders—generally a dozen or so senior members of the House and Senate—to organize the voting majority needed to push through the president's bill.[13] But no more. Now with almost 535 individual entrepreneurs on Capitol Hill, more than forty committee chairs, and some 200 subcommittee chairs, the president and his staff must conduct one-on-one "retail" vote solicitation constantly to gain support for White House initiatives.[14]

To add to the president's burden, coalition building for each major administration bill usually requires a different coalition of lawmakers. The reason is clear. Voting alliances are often short-lived. Members of Congress who agree or differ on matters of free trade may view other issues, such as gun control or universal health care, in an entirely different light. Consequently, the president and his White House staff must cobble together a different configuration of lawmakers before almost every major measure comes up for a vote.

Presidents can expect to encounter heavy special interest lobbying attacks each time an administration-supported measure is introduced on Capitol Hill. Only by fighting fire with fire can presidents hope to stand up to these highly coordinated special interest group campaigns. This often involves the White House in its own intensive marketing campaigns.

MARKETING THE PRESIDENT AND HIS AGENDA

Serious mass marketing of the president and his public agenda may be said to have begun during President John F. Kennedy's abbreviated term. Live telecasts of JFK's press conferences afforded the photogenic young president an unparalleled opportunity to communicate directly with millions of viewers. President Kennedy, who quickly perceived the unique value of national television, seldom missed an opportunity to appear before the network cameras. Presidents Nixon, Ford, and Carter were much less effective in communicating their agendas to the American public via television. But the arrival of former movie star and California governor Ronald Reagan in the White House in 1981 signaled a new chapter in marketing the president and his agenda.

With his friendly, relaxed on-camera delivery before national television audiences, President Reagan convinced millions of viewers that his policies merited widespread support. Especially in his first year in office, Mr. Reagan used his mass marketing messages to persuade a majority of members of Congress—even though the opposition Democrats controlled the House of Representatives—to pass his budget and tax cuts as well as a huge increase in the military budget. Throughout his two terms Mr. Reagan and his staff carefully staged media events to reinforce his leadership.

President George Bush conceded early on that President Reagan was a hard act to follow and therefore made less effort to market his presidency. To be sure, his leadership of the allied coalition in the victorious Persian Gulf War pushed his favorable opinion poll ratings to all-time highs—over 89 percent. But President Bush's failure, in the flush of his Gulf War triumphs, to confront the nation's economic recession and push corrective measures to turn the economy around, most commentators agreed, cost him reelection in 1992.

Political analysts who may not have fully comprehended the meaning of the term "marketing the presidency" soon learned it shortly after newly elected President Bill Clinton arrived in the White House. Elected with only 43 percent of the popular vote in a three-way race, President Clinton apparently concluded early on that if he were as a "minority president" to be a successful president, he would have to wage an almost nonstop televised marketing campaign to build public support for his key legislative initiatives: his five-year deficit-reduction budget, universal health care, gun control, the North American Free Trade Act (NAFTA), and welfare reform. Rarely did a week pass by during his first twenty months in office that President Clinton was not out on the campaign trail seeking support for his legislative programs.

In the final week of April 1994, for example, President Clinton mounted a special "blitz" marketing campaign, in conjunction with Democratic House leaders, to win another of his patented, cliffhanger victories (216 votes to 214) on a measure to ban nineteen types of assault weapons.[15] Two years earlier, this same controversial Brady bill, bitterly opposed by the National Rifle Association, had lost by seventy votes. While Mr. Clinton would legitimately claim only a share of the credit for this surprise triumph, there was little doubt among Washington insiders that Mr. Clinton's daily television appearances reciting the ever-present danger of these assault weapons— "Street Sweepers," Uzis, and Tec-9s—and his numerous phone calls to undecided House members carried the day. Clearly, the vote was another victory for presidential marketing.

Granted that the energy President Clinton has expended in network television appearances and town hall meetings has not always translated into legislative success, Mr. Clinton's track record during his first twenty months in office nevertheless suggests that the Clinton marketing campaign format to win support in Congress may well be the model by which future presidents will be measured.

Unlike Republican Presidents Nixon, Ford, Reagan, and Bush, however, President Clinton did not have to deal with another thorny problem—divided government—during his first two years in office. But his luck was short-lived. It ran out in November 1994, when the Republicans captured control of both houses of Congress for the first time in forty years.

DIVIDED GOVERNMENT

Over the past quarter-century divided government has generally weakened presidential leadership. As a result of this split-level government between the executive and legislative branches, presidents have had to find alternative strategies for building support in Congress and with the general public. Republican presidents Nixon, Ford, Reagan, and Bush faced one or both houses of Congress controlled by the opposition Democrats for twenty out of the past twenty-four years (1968–1992). Consequently, they had no choice but to seek other means than just their own party members on Capitol Hill to win support for their programs. Since public support for the president's agenda is the biggest weapon in the chief executive's arsenal to overcome congressional resistance to his programs, presidents generally turn to the mass media—"going public" is the standard term used—as a coalition-building mechanism to construct cross-party congressional majorities.[16]

This plebiscitarian approach represents, in a sense, a carryover from early twentieth-century Progressive doctrine that greater presidential involvement in the legislative process is required because the executive branch better represents the public interest than does Congress.[17]

Especially with the return of divided government to Washington in 1995, the "personalist," plebiscitarian type of presidency described by Theodore H. Lowi in his thought-provoking study of the nation's top leader published in 1985 can be expected to reemerge.[18] Because a president in a divided government cannot count on his minority party members in Congress to deliver the needed votes to enact his initiatives, presidents believe that they have no choice but to follow the route of "going public," over the heads of Congress to win popular support. In Samuel Kernell's view, "Going public is a leadership style consistent with the requirements of a political community that is increasingly susceptible to the centrifugal forces of public opinion."[19]

In this age of opinion polls, one veteran pollster has commented, "Presidential approval ratings have created a pseudo-parliamentary situation whereby the president faces a monthly vote of confidence from the total electorate."[20] This nationwide monthly report card on his performance—a "continuing election"— serves as an additional inducement to seek public approval at every turn. No wonder Theodore H. Lowi insists, "The lines of responsibility run direct to the White House where the president is personally responsible and accountable for the performance of government."[21]

Somewhere beyond this point the threat of a plebiscitary or "personal" presidency may become even more imminent. This personal presidency, moreover, as defined by Lowi, connotes "an office of tremendous personal power drawn from the people—directly and through Congress and the Supreme Court—and based on the new democratic theory that the presidency with all powers is the necessary condition for governing a large, democratic nation."[22]

PLEBISCITARY OR PERSONAL PRESIDENCY

If a major depression and massive unemployment should hit the country in the years ahead and Congress fails to respond to the president's urgent requests for legislative action on anti-depression measures, the door may be open to a plebiscitary president who operates on the basis of mass approval. This process might well be facilitated by the introduction of some form of "teledemocracy," such as suggested by independent presidential candidate H. Ross Perot in the 1992 campaign.[23] If this form of electronic democracy were adopted, voters could make their views on specific issues known immediately to Washington by telephone, fax, or electronic mail.

Ross Perot's "electronic town hall," based on instant "telepolling" would result, it seems fair to say, in incessant public pressure on the president and Congress without the mediating influence of political parties. Direct democracy leaves no room for amendment, negotiation, and reconciliation of differences among competing interest groups—the central function of political parties.

This form of plebiscitary democracy is indeed deceptively appealing: just pick up the telephone and dial Washington with your voter input, or walk over to the fax machine or computer and send a message to the nation's capital. But as political scientist Jean Bettke Elshtain warns, "Teledemocracy means once again the political world is fragmented."[24] The stabilizing role of the two major parties whose members debate substantive issues would be absent. Instead, every issue would be settled by adding up the totals of the telephone calls or electronic responses. Deliberation and thoughtful debate would be pushed aside. Furthermore, the president and Congress would be expected to follow the dictates of the viewers sitting in their living rooms. But what if the president and Congress received mixed messages? What if the president's programs were endorsed and the congressionally supported measures were rejected, or vice versa? This electronic plebiscite might lead to the breakdown of executive-legislative comity and encourage the president to ignore the separation of powers system and govern by popular referenda.

Jean Bettke Elshtain reminds us that "plebiscitary majoritianism is quite different from democratic debate sustained by reasoned discussion and judgment."[25] Under a Perotist-type of populist democracy the president, with his frequent appearances on television and his symbolic leadership position, would mostly likely capture the television sweepstakes from Congress. History shows that plebiscites have been used routinely by such populist dictators as the late Juan Peron of Argentina to shore up anti-democratic majoritarian movements. By cleverly wording the plebiscite, the dictators invariably win these "popular" votes, thus claiming a special mandate and reinforcing their grip on power. Nor should it be forgotten that the Founding Fathers' greatest fear was that the newly created office of president might, unless checked by the Constitution and public opinion, become an "elected king." Teledemocracy would be a big step in that direction.

With the decline of political parties, the potential emergence of a plebiscitary presidency has been made easier. Presidents can forge a direct link to the mass electorate through network television. Paradoxically, as the public plays a more direct role in electing a president, parties are less able to effectively hold the president accountable. Thus, parties are less able to restrain the president from engaging in unilateral actions that undermine our separation of powers system.[26] The case of President Ronald Reagan and the Iran-Contra scandal immediately comes to mind.

Finally, as we move rapidly toward the twenty-first century, the steady displacement of the president's cabinet and the executive departments as policy-formulating agencies by the White House staff—the presidential branch—will continue. As discussed in Chapter 7, the constant need for instantaneous decision making on international crises, the fact that most cabinet heads are not close personal associates of the president as are many White House staffers, and the close physical proximity of the White House staff to the president all point in the direction of further centralized decision making in the presidential branch. As Seligman and Covington have observed, "In the absence of reliable governing coalitions, presidents are increasingly motivated to act from within the White House."[27]

Unless the fragmented political parties stage a miraculous recovery—and prospects for this comeback at present seem extremely remote—the continuing centralization of power in the White House and the plebiscitarian trend of recent presidents, who frequently go directly to the people to win approval of their policies, will pose a growing threat to our existing two-hundred-year-old federal Republic.

INTERNATIONAL CHALLENGES

Since the late 1980s, revolutionary changes around the world have been unfolding at a dazzling rate. Indeed, the president's global responsibilities make it virtually impossible for any chief executive to ignore foreign affairs for even a day. Since mid-1989, for example, within the time span of slightly more than a single four-year presidential term, American presidents have had to confront power shifts that have altered the world's political landscape more than at any time since World War II. Few analysts, even in their brashest moments, would have dared predict the seismic changes that have taken place: the end of the Cold War; the fall of the Berlin Wall; the breakup of the Soviet Union; the election of the first democratically chosen government in Russia; the agreement between Israel and the Palestine Liberation Organization to self-rule in Gaza; and the end of apartheid and the establishment of a freely elected, multiracial government in South Africa. These events, especially the disintegration of the Soviet Union coupled with the rapid rise of Communist China as a major world power, have created a new set of foreign affairs challenges for American presidents remindful of those President Truman encountered soon after World War II.

Meanwhile the erosion of American hegemony in the international community, which began with President Johnson and the Vietnam War (1965–1975), now requires that American presidents bargain with our allies and other countries on a more equal footing than during the frigid years of the Cold War. In the new age of limits, the United States can no longer dominate the world economy or use military force unilaterally to impose its will on every continent. Interdependence among the free nations has replaced the superpower politics of the Cold War years.[28] Presidential success depends upon cooperation with the leaders of other nations.

President Bush demonstrated that he understood the new ground rules of American team leadership when he organized a powerful alliance of European and Middle Eastern countries, plus Japan, to drive Iraqi forces out of Kuwait, after Iraqi dictator Saddam Hussein occupied the oil-rich sheikdom.

President Bill Clinton, his critics argued, failed during his first twenty months in office to display sure-footed leadership of the United Nations and in dealing with the seemingly intractable international problems of Serbian aggression in Bosnia, the Haitian dictatorship and its refugees, North Korean nuclear reactors, and Somalian warlords. However, President Clinton's decision in mid-September 1994 to send a top-level mission to Haiti, led by former President Jimmy Carter, convinced the Haitian military junta to relinquish power or face imminent invasion by 15,000 U.S. troops. This action produced a sudden diplomatic breakthrough for the young president. The rapid, peaceful U.S. occupation of the Caribbean island and the return of exiled President Jean-Bertrand Aristide to power also slowed Clinton's downward slide in the opinion polls.

This diplomatic-military triumph was followed two weeks later by President Clinton's decision to send 34,000 U.S. troops to Kuwait and Saudi Arabia in response to Iraqi dictator Saddam Hussein's shift of several divisions of his army to the Kuwait border, threatening the oil-rich sheikdom once again. Clinton's quick response to the Iraqi dictator's renewed threat to Kuwait won widespread bipartisan support in Congress and even approval from former President George Bush and former Secretary of States James A. Baker III. By mid-October 1994, approximately 61 percent of the respondents of a *Time*/CNN poll gave Mr. Clinton a favorable rating for his handling of the Iraqi crisis.[29]

While American presidents, it is generally agreed, can operate with greater latitude in foreign affairs than on domestic matters, the overseas tasks and pitfalls that lie ahead will test Clinton, the first post–Cold War president, and other future presidents in untold ways that even the most clearheaded foreign policy advisers cannot visualize or anticipate. But who can say that these uncharted obstacles are of any greater magnitude than those faced in 1787 by the Founding Fathers when they sought to find a new model of government to replace the floundering Articles of Confederation?

NOTES

1. Fred I. Greenstein, "Change and Continuity in the Modern Presidency," in Anthony King, ed. *The New American Political System* (Washington, DC: American Enterprise Institute, 1979), 45–85. Greenstein lists four aspects of the modern presidency that differentiate it from the earlier traditional presidency: (1) the president serves as chief legislator seeking congressional approval of his agenda; (2) the president regularly engages in public policymaking through actions not requiring congressional approval; (3) the president directs an extensive White House bureaucracy to implement his policies; (4) the president serves as a personal, symbolic leader responsible for the nation's general welfare. Ibid., 45–46.

2. James W. Ceasar, Glen E. Thurow, Jeffrey Tulis, and Joseph M. Bessette, "The Rise of the Rhetorical Presidency," *Presidential Studies Quarterly* 11 (Spring 1981): 158–171. See also Jeffrey K. Tulis, *The Rhetorical Presidency* (Princeton, NJ: Princeton University Press, 1987).

3. Stephen Skowronek, *The Politics Presidents Make* (Cambridge, MA: The Belknap Press of Harvard University Press, 1993), 55.

4. Ibid., 431.

5. "Extra-personalism," is a new term coined by Andrew E. Busch and James W. Ceaser to describe the process whereby self-appointed presidential candidates offer themselves to the American electorate without utilizing the party machinery—primaries, caucuses, and national conventions. By relying almost exclusively on network television, talk shows such as *Larry King Live*, and satellite broadcasts, Ross Perot in 1992, for example, acquired virtually equal stature with President George Bush and Governor Bill Clinton in contesting for the nation's highest office. See Andrew E. Busch and James W. Ceaser, "Does Party Reform Have a Future?" in William G. Mayer, ed. *In Pursuit of the White House* (Chatham, NJ: Chatham House, 1995), 350–352.

6. Theodore J. Lowi, *The Personal President* (Ithaca, NY: Cornell University Press, 1985), 133.

7. Lester G. Seligman and Cary R. Covington, *The Coalitional Presidency* (Chicago: Dorsey, 1989), 105–106.

8. Robert H. Salisbury, "Interest Groups in Washington," in Anthony King, ed. *The New American Political System*, 2nd ed. (Washington, DC: American Enterprise Institute, 1990), 204–205.

9. Kevin Philips, *Arrogant Capital: Washington, Wall Street, and the Frustration of American Politics* (Boston: Little, Brown, 1994), 33–34.

10. Ibid., 32.

11. Michael Wines, *The New York Times*, 16 October 1994.

12. Martha Joynt Kumar and Michael Baruch Grossman, "Political Communication from the White House: The Interest Group Connection," *Presidential Studies Quarterly* 16 (Winter 1986): 96.

13. Norman J. Ornstein, "The Open Congress Meets the President," in Anthony King, ed. *Both Ends of the Avenue*, 189–194.

14. Thomas E. Mann, "Elections and Change in Congress," in Thomas E. Mann and Norman J. Ornstein, eds. *The New Congress*. (Washington, DC: American Enterprise Institute, 1981), 53.

15. *The New York Times*, 6 May 1994.

16. Samuel Kernell, *Going Public*, 2nd ed. (Washington, DC: CQ Press, 1993).

17. Seligman and Covington, *The Coalition Presidency*, 29–45.

18. Lowi, *The Personal President*, 97–133.

19. Kernell, *Going Public*, 212.

20. Irving Crespi, "The Case of Presidential Popularity," in A. H. Cantril, ed. *Polling on the Issues* (Cabin John, MD: Seven Locks Press, 1980), 42.

21. Lowi, *The Personal President*, 96.

22. Ibid., 20.

23. See Philip Elmer Dewitt, "Dial D for Democracy," *Time*, vol. 140, 8 June 1992, 43–44.

24. Jean Bettke Elshtain, "Issues and Themes: Spiral of Delegitimation of New Social Covenant?" in Michael Nelson, ed. *The Elections of 1992* (Washington, DC: CQ Press, 1993), 121.

25. Ibid.

26. However, Bert A. Rockman, a leading presidential scholar, seems to suggest that a more plebiscitary presidency may strengthen political accountability. Bert Rockman, "The Modern Presidency and Theories of Accountability: Old Wine and Old Bottles," *Congress and the Presidency* 13 (Autumn, 1988): 152–154.

27. Seligman and Covington, *The Coalitional Presidency*, 144.

28. Richard Rose, *The Postmodern President*, 2nd ed. (Chatham, NJ: Chatham House Publishers, 1993), 28–30; see also Michael A. Genovese, *The Presidency in the Age of Limits* (Westport, CT: Greenwood, 1993), 22–27.

29. *Time*, vol. 144, 24 October 1994, 35.

APPENDIX: THE CONSTITUTION—PROVISIONS ON THE PRESIDENCY

ARTICLE I

Section 3

(6) The Senate shall have the sole power to try all impeachments. When sitting for that purpose, they shall be on oath or affirmation. When the President of the United States is tried, the Chief Justice shall preside; and no person shall be convicted without the concurrence of two-thirds of the members present.

(7) Judgment in cases of impeachment shall not extent further than to removal from office, and disqualification to hold and enjoy any office of honor, trust, or profit under the United States; but the party convicted shall, nevertheless, be liable and subject to indictment, trial, judgment, and punishment, according to law.

Section 7

(2) Every bill which shall have passed the House of Representatives and the Senate shall, before it becomes a law, be presented to the President of the United States; if he approves he shall sign it, but if not he shall return it, with his objections, to that house in which it shall have originated, who shall enter the objections at large on their journal and proceed to reconsider it. If after such reconsideration two-thirds of that house shall agree to pass the bill, it shall be sent together with the objections, to the other house, by which it shall likewise be reconsidered, and if approved by two-thirds of that house it shall become a law. But in all such cases the votes of both houses shall be determined by yeas and nays, and the names of the persons voting for and against the bill shall be entered on the journal of each house respectively. If any bill shall not be returned by the President within ten days (Sundays excepted) after it shall have been presented to him, the same shall be a law, in like manner as if he had signed it, unless the Congress by their adjournment prevent its return, in which case, it shall not be a law.

(3) Every order, resolution, or vote to which the concurrence of the Senate and the House of Representatives may be necessary (except on a question of adjournment) shall be presented to the President of the United States; and before the same shall take effect, shall be approved by him, or being disapproved by him shall be repassed by two-thirds of the Senate and House of Representatives, according to the rules and limitations prescribed in the case of a bill.

ARTICLE II

Section 1

(1) The executive power shall be vested in a President of the United States of America. He shall hold his office during the term of four years, and, together with the Vice President, chosen for the same term, be elected as follows:

(2) Each state shall appoint, in such manner of the legislature thereof may direct, a number of electors, equal to the whole number of Senators and Representatives to which the State may be entitled in the Congress; but no Senator or Representative, or person holding an office of trust or profit under the United States shall be appointed an elector.

(3) The electors shall meet in their respective states and vote by ballot for two persons, of whom one at least shall not be an inhabitant of the same state with themselves. And they shall make a list of all the persons voted for, and of the number of votes for each; which list they shall sign and certify and transmit to the seat of the government of the United States, directed to the President of the Senate. The President of the Senate shall, in the presence of the Senate and House of Representatives, open all the certificates and the votes shall then be counted. The person having the greatest number of votes shall be the President, if such a number be a majority of the whole number of electors appointed; and if there be more than one who have such a majority, and have an equal number of votes, then the House of Representatives shall immediately choose by ballot one of them for President; and if no person have a majority, then from the five highest on the list the said House shall in like manner choose the President. But in choosing the President the votes shall be taken by states, the representation from each state having one vote; a quorum for this purpose shall consist of a member or members from two-thirds of the states, and a majority of all the states shall be necessary to a choice. In every case, after the choice of the President, the person having the greatest number of votes of the electors shall be the Vice President. But if there should remain two or more who have equal votes, the Senate shall choose from them by ballot the Vice President. [Superseded by the Twelfth Amendment.]

(4) The Congress may determine the time of choosing the electors and the day on which they shall give their votes, which day shall be the same throughout the United States.

(5) No person except a natural born citizen, or a citizen of the United States at the time of the adoption of this Constitution, shall be eligible to the office of President; neither shall any person be eligible to that office who shall not have attained to the age of thirty-five years, and been fourteen years a resident within the United States.

(6) In case of the removal of the President from office, or of his death, resignation, or inability to discharge the powers and duties of the said office, the same shall devolve on the Vice President, and the Congress may by law provide for the case of removal, death, resignation, or inability, both of the President and Vice President, declaring what officer shall then act as President, and such officer shall act accordingly until the disability be removed or a President shall be elected. [Modified by the Twenty-fifth Amendment.]

(7) The President shall, at stated times, receive for his services a compensation, which shall neither be increased nor diminished during the period for which he shall have been elected, and he shall not receive within that period any other emolument for the United States or any of them.

(8) Before he enter on the execution of his office he shall take the following oath or affirmation:

"I do solemnly swear (or affirm) that I will faithfully execute the office of President of the United States, and will to the best of my ability preserve, protect, and defend the Constitution of the United States."

Section 2

(1) The President shall be Commander in Chief of the Army and Navy of the United States, and of the militia of the several states when called into the actual service of the United States; he may require the opinion, in writing, of the principal officer in each of the executive departments, upon any subject relating to the duties of their respective offices, and he shall have power to grant reprieves and pardons for offenses against the United States, except in cases of impeachment.

(2) He shall have power, by and with the advice and consent of the Senate, to make treaties, provided two-thirds of the Senators present concur; and he shall nominate, and by and with the advice and consent of the Senate, shall appoint ambassadors, other public ministers and consuls, judges of the Supreme Court, and all other officers of the United States, whose appointments are not herein otherwise provided for, and which shall be established by law; but the Congress may be law vest the appointment of such inferior officers, as they think proper, in the President alone, in the courts of law, or in the heads of departments.

(3) The President shall have the power to fill up all vacancies that may happen during the recess of the Senate, by granting commissions which shall expire at the end of their next session.

Section 3

He shall from time to time give to the Congress information of the state of the union, and recommend to their consideration such measures as he shall judge necessary and expedient; he may, on extraordinary occasions, convene both houses, or either of them, and in case of disagreement between them with respect to the time of adjournment, he may adjourn them to such time as he shall think proper; he shall receive ambassadors and other public ministers; he shall take care that the laws be faithfully executed, and shall commission all the officers of the United States.

Section 4

The President, Vice President, and all civil officers of the United States shall be removed from office on impeachment for and conviction of treason, bribery, or other high crimes and misdemeanors.

AMENDMENT XII (RATIFIED 1804)

The electors shall meet in their respective states and vote by ballot for President and Vice President, one of whom, at least, shall not be an inhabitant of the same state with themselves; they shall name in their ballots the person voted for as President, and in distinct ballots the person voted for as Vice President, and they shall make distinct lists of all persons voted for as President, and of all persons voted for as Vice President, and of the number of votes for each, which lists they shall sign and certify, and transmit sealed to the seat of the government of the United States, directed to the President of the Senate. The President of the Senate shall, in the presence of the Senate and House of Representatives, open all the certificates and the votes shall then be counted. The person having the greatest number of votes for President shall be the President, if such number be a majority of the whole number of electors appointed; and if no person have such majority, then from the persons having the highest numbers not exceeding three on the list of those voted for as President, the House of Representatives shall choose immediately, by ballot, the President. But in choosing the President the votes shall be taken by states, the representation from each state having one vote; a quorum for this purpose shall consist of a member or members from two-thirds of the states, and a majority of all states shall be necessary to a choice. And if the House of Representatives shall not choose a President whenever the right of choice shall devolve upon them, before the fourth day of March next following, then the Vice President shall act as President, as in the case of the death or other constitutional disability of the President. The person having the greatest number of votes as Vice President shall be the Vice President, if such number be a majority of the whole number of electors appointed, and if no person having a majority, then from the two highest numbers on the list the Senate shall choose the Vice President; a quorum for the purpose shall consist of two-thirds of the whole number of Senators, and a majority of the whole number shall be necessary to a choice. But no person constitutionally ineligible to the office of President shall be eligible to that of Vice President of the United States.

AMENDMENT XX (RATIFIED 1933)

Section 1

The terms of the President and Vice President shall end at noon on the 20th day of January, and the terms of Senators and Representatives at noon on the 3rd day of January, of the years in which such terms would have ended if this article had not been ratified; and the terms of their successors shall then begin.

Section 2

The Congress shall assemble at least once in every year, and such meeting shall begin at noon on the 3rd day of January, unless they shall by law appoint a different day.

Section 3

If, at the time fixed for the beginning of the term of the President, the President elect shall have died, the Vice President elect shall become President. If a President shall not have been chosen before the time fixed for the beginning of his term, or if the President elect shall have failed to qualify, then the Vice President elect shall act as President until a President shall have qualified; and the Congress may by law provide for the case wherein neither a President elect nor a Vice President elect shall have qualified, declaring who shall then act as President, or the manner in which one who is to act shall be selected, and such person shall act accordingly until a President or Vice President shall have qualified.

Section 4

The Congress may by law provide for the case of the death of any of the persons from whom the House of Representatives may choose a President whenever the right of choice shall have devolved upon them, and for the case of the death of any of the persons from whom the Senate may choose a Vice President whenever the right of choice shall have devolved upon them.

AMENDMENT XXII (RATIFIED 1951)

Section 1

No person shall be elected to the office of the President more than twice, and no person who has held the office of the President, or acted as President, for more than two years of a term to which some other person was elected President shall be elected to the office of President more than once. But this article shall not apply to any person holding the office of the President when this article was proposed by the Congress, and shall not prevent any person who may be holding the office of President, or acting as President, during the term within which this article becomes operative from holding the office of President or acting as President during the remainder of such term.

AMENDMENT XXIV (RATIFIED 1964)

Section 1

The right of citizens of the United States to vote in any primary or other election for President or Vice President, or for Senator or Representative in Congress, shall not be denied or abridged by the United States or any State by reason of failure to pay any poll tax or other tax.

Section 2

The Congress shall have the power to enforce this article by appropriate legislation.

AMENDMENT XXV (RATIFIED 1967)

Section 1

In case of a removal of the President from office or of his death or resignation, the Vice President shall become President.

Section 2

Whenever there is a vacancy in the office of the Vice President, the President shall nominate a Vice President who shall take office upon confirmation by a majority vote of both Houses of Congress.

Section 3

Whenever the President transmits to the President pro tempore of the Senate and the Speaker of the House of Representatives his written declaration that he is unable to discharge the powers and duties of his office, and until he transmits to them a written declaration to the contrary, such powers and duties shall be discharged by the Vice President as Acting President.

Section 4

Whenever the Vice President and a majority of either the principal officers of the executive department or of such other body as Congress may by law provide, transmit to the President pro tempore of the Senate and the Speaker of the House of Representatives their written declaration that the President is unable to discharge the powers and duties of his office, the Vice President shall immediately assume the powers and duties of the office as Acting President.

Thereafter, when the President transmits to the President pro tempore of the Senate and the Speaker of the House of Representatives his written declaration that no inability exists, he shall resume the powers and duties of his office unless the Vice President and a majority of either the principal officers of the executive department or of such other body as Congress may by law provide, transmit within four days to the President pro tempore of the Senate and the Speaker of the House of Representatives their written declaration that the President is unable to discharge the power and duties of his office. Thereupon Congress shall decide the issue, assembling within forty-eight hours for that purpose if not in session. If the Congress, within twenty-one days after receipt of the latter written declaration, or, if Congress is not in session, within twenty-one days after Congress is required to assemble, determines by two-thirds vote of both Houses that the President is unable to discharge the powers and duties of his office, the Vice President shall continue to discharge the same as Acting President; otherwise, the President shall resume the powers and duties of his office.

SELECTED BIBLIOGRAPHY

The bibliography is categorized by the following sections:

General Works on the Presidency

Anthologies on the Presidency

Campaigns, Elections, Parties, and the Electoral College

Presidential Leadership

The Public Presidency

The President and Congress

Presidential War Making

National Security and Foreign Policy

Administrative Leadership and Managing the White House

Presidents, the Supreme Court, and the Constitution

The Vice Presidency

Remaking the Presidency

Biographies, Autobiographies, and Psychological Studies

GENERAL WORKS ON THE PRESIDENCY

Barger, Harold M. *The Impossible Presidency.* Glenview, IL: Scott, Foresman, 1984.

Burke, John P. *The Institutionalized Presidency.* Baltimore: Johns Hopkins University Press, 1992.

Corwin, Edward S. *The President: Office and Powers, 1787–1984*, 5th ed., eds. Randall W. Bland, Theodore H. Hindson, and Jack W. Peltason. New York: New York University Press, 1984.

Cronin, Thomas E. *The State of the Presidency*, 2nd ed. Boston: Little, Brown, 1980.

DiClerico, Robert E. *The American President*, 3rd ed. Englewood Cliffs, NJ: Prentice-Hall, 1990.

Edwards, George C. III and Wayne, Stephen J. *Presidential Leadership*. 2nd ed. New York: St. Martin's, 1990.

Funderburk, Charles. *Presidents and Politics: The Limits of Power*. Monterey, CA: Brooks/Cole, 1982.

Griffith, Ernest S. *The American Presidency: The Dilemmas of Shared Power and Divided Government*. New York: New York University Press, 1976.

Hargrove, Erwin, *The Power of the Modern Presidency*. New York: Knopf, 1974.

Hoxie, R. Gordon. *The Presidency of the 1970s*. New York: Center for the Study of the Presidency, 1973.

Hughes, Emmet John. *The Living Presidency*. New York: Coward, McGann, & Geohegan, 1972.

Hyman, Sidney. *The American President*. New York: Harper & Row, 1954.

James, Dorothy. *The Contemporary Presidency*. New York: Pegasus, 1974.

Kallenbach, Joseph E. *The American Chief Executive*. New York: Harper & Row, 1966.

Koenig, Louis W. *The Chief Executive*, 4th ed. New York: Harcourt, Brace & Jovanovich, 1981.

Laski, Harold J. *The American Presidency*. New York: Harper Brothers, 1940.

McConnell, Grant. *The Modern Presidency*, 2nd ed. New York: St. Martin's, 1976.

Milkis, Sidney, and Nelson, Michael. *The American Presidency: Origins and Development*. Washington, DC: CQ Press, 1990.

Mullen, William F. *Presidential Power and Politics*. New York: St. Martin's, 1976.

Page, Benjamin I., and Petracca, Mark P. *The American Presidency*. New York: McGraw-Hill, 1983.

Pfiffner, James P. *The Strategic Presidency: Hitting the Ground Running*. Chicago: Dorsey, 1988.

Pious, Richard M. *The American Presidency*. New York: Basic Books, 1979.

Ragsdale, Lyn. *Presidential Politics*. Boston: Houghton Mifflin, 1993.

Reedy, George. *The Twilight of the Presidency*. New York: New American Library, 1970.

Rossiter, Clinton. *The American Presidency*, rev. ed. New York: New American Library, 1960.

Sickels, Robert J. *The Presidency*. Englewood Cliffs, NJ: Prentice-Hall, 1980.

Skowronek, Stephen. *The Politics Presidents Make*. Cambridge, MA: The Belknap Press of Harvard University, 1993.

Strum, Philippa. *Presidential Power and American Democracy*, 2nd ed. Pacific Palisades, CA: Goodyear, 1979.

Tatalovich, Raymond, and Daynes, Byron W. *Presidential Power in the United States*. Monterey, CA: Brooks/Cole, 1984.

Thach, C. C., Jr. *The Creation of the Presidency, 1775–1789: A Study in Constitutional History*. Baltimore, MD: Johns Hopkins University Press, 1922.

Watson, Richard A., and Thomas, Norman C. *The Politics of the Presidency*. New York: Wiley, 1983.

ANTHOLOGIES ON THE PRESIDENCY

Bach, Stanley, and Sulzer, George T., eds. *Perspectives on the Presidency*. Lexington, MA: D. C. Heath, 1974.

Barber, James David, ed. *Choosing the President*. Englewood Cliffs, NJ: Prentice-Hall, 1974.

———, ed. *Race for the Presidency: The Media and the Nominating Process*. Englewood Cliffs, NJ: Prentice-Hall, 1978.

Berman, Larry, ed. *The American Presidency*. Boston: Little, Brown, 1987.

————, ed. *Looking Back on the Reagan Presidency*. Baltimore, MD: Johns Hopkins University Press, 1990.

Bessette, Joseph M., and Tulis, Jeffrey, eds. *The Presidency in the Constitution*. Baton Rouge: Louisiana State University Press, 1981.

Campbell, Colin, and Rockman, Bert A., eds. *The Bush Presidency: First Appraisals*. Chatham, NJ: Chatham House, 1991.

————. *The Clinton Presidency: First Appraisals*. Chatham, NJ: Chatham House, 1995.

Cronin, Thomas J., ed. *Rethinking the Presidency*. Boston: Little, Brown, 1982.

————, ed. *Inventing the Presidency*. Lawrence: University Press of Kansas, 1989.

Cronin, Thomas E., and Tugwell, Rexford G., eds. *The Presidency Reappraised*, 2nd ed. New York: Praeger, 1977.

Dolce, Philip C., and Skau, George H., eds. *Power and the Presidency*. New York: Scribner's, 1976.

Fausold, Martin, and Shank, Alan, eds. *The Constitution and the American Presidency*. Albany: State University of New York Press, 1991.

Franck, Thomas M., ed. *The Tethered Presidency*. New York: New York University Press, 1981.

Graff, Henry F., ed. *The Presidents: A Reference History*. New York: Scribner's, 1984.

Greenstein, Fred I., ed. *The Reagan Presidency*. Baltimore, MD: Johns Hopkins University Press, 1983.

Harmel, Robert, ed. *Presidents and Their Parties: Leadership or Neglect*. New York: Praeger, 1984.

Heclo, Hugh, and Salamon, Lester M., eds. *The Illusion of Presidential Government*. Boulder, CO: Westview, 1981.

Hinckley, Barbara, ed. *The Presidency as Symbolic Office*. Chatham, NJ: Chatham House, 1988.

Hirschfield, Robert R., ed. *The Power of the Presidency*, 3rd ed. New York: Aldine, 1982.

Jones, Charles O., ed. *The Reagan Legacy: Promise and Performance*. Chatham, NJ: Chatham House Publishers, 1988.

King, Anthony, ed. *Both Ends of the Avenue*. Washington, DC: American Enterprise Institute, 1983.

————, ed. *The New American Political System*, 2nd ed. Washington, DC: American Enterprise Institute, 1990.

Kozak, David C., and Ciboski, Kenneth N., eds. *The American Presidency: A Policy Perspective from Readings and Documents*. Chicago: Nelson-Hall, 1985.

Latham, Earl, ed. *J. F. Kennedy and Presidential Power*. Lexington, MA: D. C. Heath, 1972.

Lengle, James I., and Shafer, Byron E., eds. *Presidential Politics: Readings on Nominations and Elections,* 2nd ed. New York: St. Martin's, 1983.

Malbin, Michael J., ed. *Money and Politics in the United States*. Washington, DC: American Enterprise Institute, 1981.

Mann, Thomas F., and Ornstein, Norman J., eds. *The New Congress*. Washington, DC: American Enterprise Institute, 1981.

Ornstein, Norman J., ed. *President and Congress: Assessing Reagan's First Year*. Washington, DC: American Enterprise Institute, 1982.

Palmer, John L., and Sawhill, Isabel V., eds. *The Reagan Record*. Cambridge, MA: Ballinger, 1984.

Polsby, Nelson, ed. *The Modern Presidency*. New York: Random House, 1973.

Ranney, Austin, ed. *The Past and Future of Presidential Debates*. Washington, DC: American Enterprise Institute, 1979.

Roberts, Charles, ed. *Has the President Too Much Power?* New York: Harper & Row, 1974.

Salamon, Lester M., and Lund, Michael S., eds. *The Reagan Presidency and the Governing of America*. Washington, DC: Urban Institute Press, 1984.

Thomas, Norman C., ed. *The Presidency in Contemporary Context.* New York: Dodd, Mead, 1975.

Thomas, Norman C., and Baade, Hans W., eds. *The Institutionalized Presidency.* Dobbs Ferry, NY: Oceana, 1972.

Waterman, Richard W., ed. *The Presidency Reconsidered.* Itasca, IL: F. E. Peacock, 1993.

Wilcox, Francis, and Franck, Richard, eds. *The Constitution and the Conduct of Foreign Policy.* New York: Praeger, 1976.

Wildavsky, Aaron, ed. *The Presidency.* Boston: Little, Brown, 1969.

————, ed. *Perspectives on the Presidency.* Boston: Little, Brown, 1975.

CAMPAIGNS, ELECTIONS, PARTIES, AND THE ELECTORAL COLLEGE

Abbott, David W., and Levine, James P. *Wrong Winner: The Coming Debacle in the Electoral College.* Westport, CT: Praeger, 1991.

Abrahamson, Paul R., Aldrich, John H., and Rohde, David W. *Change and Continuity in the 1992 Elections.* Washington, DC: CQ Press, 1994.

Aldrich, John H. *Before the Convention.* Chicago: University of Chicago Press, 1980.

Alexander, Herbert E. *Financing Politics: Money, Elections and Political Reform.* Washington, DC: CQ Press, 1980.

Asher, Herbert. *Presidential Elections and American Politics,* 3rd ed. Homewood, IL: Dorsey, 1984.

Best, Judith. *The Case Against the Direct Election of the President: A Defense of the Electoral College.* Ithaca, NY: Cornell University Press, 1975.

Bickel, Alexander. *The New Age of Political Reform: The Electoral College, the Convention, and the Party System.* New York: Harper & Row, 1968.

Bishop, George F., et al. *The Presidential Debates: Media, Electoral and Policy Perspectives.* New York: Harper & Row, 1978.

Brace, Paul, Harrington, Christine B., and King, Gary, eds. *The Presidency in American Politics.* New York: New York University Press, 1989.

Brams, Steven. *The Presidential Election Game.* New Haven, CT: Yale University Press, 1978.

Broder, David S. *The Party's Over.* New York: Harper & Row, 1971.

Burns, James MacGregor. *The Deadlock of Democracy: Four-Party Politics in America.* Englewood Cliffs, NJ: Prentice-Hall, 1963.

Ceaser, James W. *Presidential Selection: Theory and Development.* Princeton, NJ: Princeton University Press, 1979.

————. *Reforming the Reforms.* Cambridge, MA: Ballinger, 1982.

Chester, Lewis, Hodgson, Godfrey, and Page, Bruce. *An American Melodrama: The Presidential Campaign of 1968.* New York: Viking, 1969.

Crotty, William J., ed. *America's Choice: The Election of 1992.* Guilford, CT: Dushkin Publishing Group, 1993.

Crotty, William, and Jackson, John S. III. *Presidential Primaries and Nominations.* Washington, DC: CQ Press, 1985.

David, Paul T., Goldman, Ralph M., and Bain, Richard C. *The Politics of National Party Conventions.* Washington, DC: The Brookings Institution, 1960.

Davis, James W. *Presidential Primaries: Road to the White House,* 2nd ed. Westport, CT: Greenwood, 1980.

————. *National Conventions in an Age of Party Reform.* Westport, CT: Greenwood, 1983.

————. *President as Party Leader.* Westport, CT: Praeger, 1992.

DiClerico, Robert E., and Uslaner, Eric M. *Few Are Chosen: Problems of Presidential Selection.* New York: McGraw-Hill, 1984.

Germond, Jack W., and Witcover, Jules. *Blue Smoke and Mirrors: How Reagan Won and How Carter Lost the Election of 1980*. New York: Viking, 1981.

————. *Mad as Hell: Revolt at the Ballot Box in 1992*. New York: Warner Books, 1993.

Goldman, Peter, and Fuller, Tony. *The Quest for the Presidency, 1988*. New York: Simon & Schuster, 1989.

Keech, William R., and Matthews, Donald R. *The Party's Choice*. Washington, DC: The Brookings Institution, 1976.

Lammers, William W. *Presidential Politics: Patterns and Prospects*. New York: Harper & Row, 1976.

Longley, Lawrence, and Braun, Allen. *The Politics of Electoral College Reform*. New Haven, CT: Yale University Press, 1972.

Marshall, Thomas R. *Presidential Nominations in a Reform Age*. New York: Praeger, 1981.

Mayer, William G., ed. *In Pursuit of the White House*. Chatham, NJ: Chatham House, 1995.

Milkis, Sidney M. *The President and the Parties*. New York: Oxford University Press, 1993.

Nelson, Michael, ed. *The Elections of 1992*. Washington, DC: CQ Press, 1993.

Novak, Michael. *Choosing Our King*. New York: Macmillan, 1974.

Page, Benjamin I. *Choices and Echoes in Presidential Candidates*. Chicago: University of Chicago Press, 1978.

Peirce, Neal R., and Longley, Lawrence D. *The People's President: The Electoral College in American History and the Direct Vote Alternative*, rev. ed. New Haven, CT: Yale University Press, 1981.

Polsby, Nelson W. *Consequences of Party Reform*. New York: Oxford University Press, 1983.

Polsby, Nelson, and Wildavsky, Aaron. *Presidential Elections: Strategies of American Electoral Politics*, 6th ed. New York: Scribner, 1984.

Pomper, Gerald, ed. *The Election of 1980*. Chatham, NJ: Chatham House, 1981.

————, ed. *The Election of 1992*. Chatham, NJ: Chatham House, 1993.

Ranney, Austin. *Curing the Mischiefs of Faction*. Berkeley: The University of California Press, 1975.

Roseboom, Eugene H. *A History of Presidential Elections*. New York: Macmillan, 1964.

Sayre, Wallace S., and Parris, Judith H. *Voting for President*. Washington, DC: The Brookings Institution, 1970.

Schram, Martin. *Running for President, 1976: The Carter Campaign*. New York: Stein & Day, 1977.

Sorauf, Frank J. *Inside Campaign Finance*. New Haven, CT: Yale University Press, 1992.

Watson, Richard. *The Presidential Contest*, 2nd ed. New York: Wiley, 1984.

Wayne, Stephen. *The Road to the White House*, 4th ed. New York: St. Martin's, 1992.

White, Theodore H. *The Making of the President: 1960, 1964, 1968, and 1972*. New York: Atheneum, 1961, 1965, 1969, and 1973.

Witcover, Jules. *Marathon: Pursuit of the Presidency*. New York: Viking, 1977.

PRESIDENTIAL LEADERSHIP

Bailey, Thomas A. *Presidential Greatness*. Englewood Cliffs, NJ: Prentice-Hall, 1966.

Barrett, Laurence I. *Gambling with History: Reagan in the White House*. New York: Doubleday, 1983.

Brace, Paul, and Hinckley, Barbara. *Follow the Leader: Opinion Polls and the Modern Presidency*. New York: Basic Books, 1992.

Buchanan, Bruce. *The Presidential Experience: What the Office Does to the Man*. Englewood Cliffs, NJ: Prentice-Hall, 1978.

Burns, James Macgregor. *Presidential Government: The Crucible of Leadership.* Boston: Houghton Mifflin, 1966.

Califano, Joseph A., Jr. *A Presidential Nation.* New York: Norton, 1975.

Corvitz, L. Gordon, and Rabkin, Jeremy A., eds. *The Fettered Presidency: Legal Constraints on the Executive Branch.* Washington, DC: American Enterprise Institute, 1989.

Donovan, Robert J. *Tumultuous Years: The Presidency of Harry S. Truman, 1949–1953.* New York: Norton, 1982.

Drew, Elizabeth. *On the Edge: The Clinton Presidency.* New York: Simon & Schuster, 1994.

Eastland, Terry. *Energy in the Executive: The Case for the Strong Executive.* New York: Macmillan, 1992.

Fishel, Jeff. *Presidents and Promises.* Washington, DC: CQ Press, 1985.

Greenstein, Fred I., ed. *Leadership in the Modern Presidency.* Cambridge, MA: Harvard University Press, 1988.

Halberstam, David. *The Best and the Brightest.* New York: Random House, 1972.

Hargrove, Erwin C., and Nelson, Michael. *Presidents, Politics, and Policy.* Baltimore, MD: Johns Hopkins University Press, 1984.

Jones, Charles O. *The Presidency in a Separated System.* Washington, DC: The Brookings Institution, 1994.

Kellerman, Barbara and Barilleaux, Ryan J. *The President as World Leader.* New York: St. Martin's, 1991.

Leuchtenburg, William E. *Franklin D. Roosevelt and the New Deal.* New York: Harper & Row, 1963.

————. *In the Shadow of FDR: From Harry Truman to Ronald Reagan.* Ithaca, NY: Cornell University Press, 1983.

Lichtman, Allan J., and DeCell, Ken. *The Keys to the Presidency.* New York: Madison Books, 1990.

Neustadt, Richard E. *Presidential Power and the Modern Presidents.* New York: The Free Press, 1990.

O'Brien, Lawrence. *No Final Victories: From John F. Kennedy to Watergate.* Garden City, NY: Doubleday, 1974.

Rockman, Bert. *The Leadership Question: The Presidency and the American System.* New York: Praeger, 1984.

Rose, Richard. *The Postmodern President,* 2nd ed. Chatham, NJ: Chatham House, 1993.

Safire, William. *Before the Fall: An Inside View of the Pre-Watergate White House.* Garden City, NY: Doubleday, 1975.

Schlesinger, Arthur M., Jr. *The Coming of the New Deal.* Boston: Houghton Mifflin, 1958.

Shull, Steven A., ed. *The Two Presidencies: A Quarter Century Assessment.* Chicago: Nelson-Hall, 1991.

Sorenson, Theodore C. *Watchman in the Night: Presidential Accountability and Watergate.* Cambridge, MA: MIT Press, 1975.

Tiefer, Charles, *The Semi-Sovereign Presidency: The Bush Administration's Strategy for Governing Without Congress.* Boulder, CO: Westview, 1994.

Woodward, Robert and Bernstein, Carl. *All the President's Men.* New York: Simon & Schuster, 1974.

THE PUBLIC PRESIDENCY

Brody, Richard A. *Assessing the President: The Media, Elite Opinion and Public Support.* Palo Alto, CA: Stanford University Press, 1991.

Cornwell, Elmer E., Jr. *Presidential Leadership of Public Opinion.* Bloomington: Indiana University Press, 1965.

Edwards, George C. III. *The Public Presidency.* New York: St. Martin's, 1983.

Edwards, George C. III, Shull, Steven A., and Thomas, Norman C., eds. *The Presidency and Public Policy Making.* Pittsburgh: University of Pittsburgh Press, 1985.

Graber, Doris A. *Mass Media and American Politics.* Washington, DC: CQ Press, 1980.

Grossman, Michael Baruch, and Kumar, Martha Joynt. *Portraying the President.* Baltimore, MD: Johns Hopkins University Press, 1981.

Hodgson, Godfrey. *All Things to All Men.* New York: Simon & Schuster, 1980.

Kellerman, Barbara. *The Political Presidency.* New York: Oxford University Press, 1984.

Kernell, Samuel. *Going Public*, 2nd ed. Washington, DC: CQ Press, 1993.

Lowi, Theodore J. *The Personal President.* Ithaca, NY: Cornell University Press, 1985.

Maltese, John. *Spin Control: The White House Office of Communications and Management of Presidential News.* Chapel Hill: University of North Carolina Press, 1992.

McGinniss, Joe. *The Selling of the President, 1968.* New York: Pocket Books, 1969.

Minow, Newton N., Martin, John Bartlow, and Mitchell, Lee M. *Presidential Television.* New York: Basic Books, 1973.

Miroff, Bruce. *Pragmatic Illusions: The Presidential Politics of John F. Kennedy.* New York: McKay, 1976.

Paletz, David L., and Entman, Robert M. *Media Power Politics.* New York: The Free Press, 1981.

Patterson, Thomas E. *The Mass Media Election: How Americans Choose Their President.* New York: Praeger, 1980.

Patterson, Thomas E., and McClure, Robert. *The Unseeing Eye: The Myth of Television Power in National Elections.* New York: Putnam's, 1976.

Ranney, Austin. *Channels of Power.* Washington, DC: American Enterprise Institute, 1984.

Rimmerman, Craig A. *Presidency by Plebiscite.* Boulder, CO: Westview, 1993.

Robinson, Michael J., and Sheehan, Margaret A. *Over the Wire and on TV: CBS and UPI in Campaign '80.* New York: Sage, 1983.

Rubin, Richard L. *Press, Party, and Presidency.* New York: Norton, 1981.

Saldich, Anne Rowley. *Electronic Democracy.* New York: Praeger, 1979.

Seligman, Lester G., and Covington, Cary R. *The Coalitional Presidency.* Chicago: Dorsey, 1989.

Spear, Joseph C. *Presidents and the Press.* Cambridge, MA: MIT Press, 1986.

Spragens, William C. *The Presidency and Mass Media in the Age of Television.* Washington, DC: University Press of America, 1978.

Stuckey, Mary E. *The President as Interpreter in Chief.* Chatham, NJ: Chatham House, 1991.

Tulis, Jeffrey K. *The Rhetorical Presidency.* Princeton, NJ: Princeton University Press, 1987.

THE PRESIDENT AND CONGRESS

Binkley, Wilfred E. *The President and Congress*, 3rd ed. New York: Vintage, 1962.

Bond, Jon R., and Fleisher, Richard. *The President in the Legislature.* Chicago: University of Chicago Press, 1990.

Cox, Gary W., and Kernell, Samuel, eds. *The Politics of Divided Government.* Boulder, CO: Westview, 1991.

Davidson, Roger H., and Oleszek, Walter J. *Congress and Its Members*, 2nd ed. Washington, DC: CQ Press, 1985.

Edwards, George C. III. *Presidential Leadership of Congress.* San Francisco: W. H. Friedman, 1980.

————. *At the Margins: Presidential Leadership of Congress.* New Haven, CT: Yale University Press, 1989.

Fisher, Louis. *President and Congress.* New York: Free Press, 1972.

————. *Constitutional Conflicts between Congress and the President.* Princeton, NJ: Princeton University Press, 1985.

LeLoup, Lance T., and Shull, Steven A. *Congress and the President: The Policy Connection.* Belmont, CA: Wadsworth, 1993.

Mann, Thomas E. *A Question of Balance: The President, Congress, and Foreign Policy.* Washington, DC: The Brookings Institution, 1990.

Mansfield, Harvey C., Jr., ed. *Congress against the President.* New York: Praeger, 1975.

Mayhew, David R. *Divided We Govern.* New Haven, CT: Yale University Press, 1991.

Mezey, Michael L. *Congress, the President and Public Policy.* Boulder, CO: Westview, 1989.

Moe, Ronald, ed. *Congress and the President: Allies and Adversaries.* Pacific Palisades, CA: Goodyear, 1971.

Peterson, Mark A. *Legislating Together: The White House and Capitol Hill from Eisenhower to Reagan.* Cambridge, MA: Harvard University Press, 1990.

Shull, Steven A. *Domestic Policy Formation: Presidential-Congressional Partnership.* Westport, CT: Greenwood, 1983.

Shuman, Howard E. *Politics and the Budget: The Struggle between the President and Congress,* 3rd ed. Englewood Cliffs, NJ: Prentice-Hall, 1992.

Spitzer, Robert J. *The Presidential Veto: Touchstone of the American Presidency.* Albany, NY: State University of New York Press, 1988.

————. *President and Congress: Executive Hegemony at the Crossroads of American Government.* Philadelphia: Temple University Press, 1993.

Sundquist, James L. *The Decline and Resurgence of Congress.* Washington, DC: The Brookings Institution, 1981.

Thurber, James. *Divided Democracy.* Washington, DC: CQ Press, 1991.

Watson, Richard A. *Presidential Vetoes and Public Policy.* Lawrence: University Press of Kansas, 1993.

Wayne, Stephen J. *The Legislative Presidency.* New York: Harper & Row, 1978.

Wilson, Woodrow. *Congressional Government (1885),* 2 vols. New York: Meridian Edition, 1918.

PRESIDENTIAL WAR MAKING

Corwin, Edward. *Total War and the Constitution.* New York: Knopf, 1947.

Dawson, Joseph E. III, ed. *Commanders in Chief.* Lawrence: University Press of Kansas, 1993.

Eagleton, Thomas. *War and Presidential Power.* New York: Liveright, 1974.

Fisher, Louis. *Presidential War Power.* Lawrence: University Press of Kansas, 1995.

Hassler, W. W., Jr. *The President as Commander in Chief.* Reading, MA: Addison-Wesley, 1971.

Holt, Pat M. *The War Powers Resolution.* Washington, DC: American Enterprise Institute, 1978.

Javits, Jacob. *Who Makes War?* New York: Morrow, 1973.

Mueller, John. *War, Presidents and Public Opinion.* New York: Wiley, 1973.

Pusey, Merlo. *The Way We Go to War.* Boston: Houghton Mifflin, 1969.

Rossiter, Clinton. *Constitutional Dictatorship.* Princeton, NJ: Princeton University Press, 1948.

NATIONAL SECURITY AND FOREIGN POLICY

Barilleaux, Ryan J. *The President and Foreign Affairs: Evaluation, Performance, and Power.* New York: Praeger, 1985.

Crabb, Cecil V., Jr., and Holt, Pat. *Invitation to Struggle: Congress, the President and Foreign Policy,* 4th ed. Washington, DC: CQ Press, 1992.

Destler, I. M. *Presidents, Bureaucrats, and Foreign Policy.* Princeton, NJ: Princeton University Press, 1972.

Genovese, Michael A. *The Presidency in the Age of Limits.* Westport, CT: Greenwood, 1993.

George, Alexander L. *Presidential Decision-Making in Foreign Policy: The Effective Use of Information and Advice.* Boulder, CO: Westview, 1980.

Glennon, Michael J. *Constitutional Diplomacy.* Princeton, NJ: Princeton University Press, 1990.

Henkin, Louis. *Foreign Affairs and the Constitution.* Mineola, NY: The Foundation Press, 1972.

Hunter, Robert E. *Presidential Control of Foreign Policy.* New York: Praeger, 1982.

Koh, Harold H. *The National Security Constitution.* New Haven, CT: Yale University Press, 1990.

Kolko, Gabriel. *The Roots of American Foreign Policy.* Boston: Beacon, 1969.

Neuchterlein, Donald E. *National Interests and Presidential Leadership: The Setting of Priorities.* Boulder, CO: Westview, 1978.

Plischke, Elmer. *Diplomat in Chief.* Westport, CT: Greenwood, 1986.

ADMINISTRATIVE LEADERSHIP AND MANAGING THE WHITE HOUSE

A Heartbeat Away. Report of the Twentieth Century Fund Task Force on the Vice Presidency. New York: Priority Press, 1988.

Anderson, Patrick. *The President's Men.* Garden City, NY: Doubleday, 1968.

Berman, Larry. *The Office of Management and Budget and the Presidency, 1921–1979.* Princeton, NJ: Princeton University Press, 1979.

Califano, Joesph A., Jr. *A Presidential Nation.* New York: W. W. Norton, 1976.

Campbell, Colin. *Managing the Presidency: Carter, Reagan and the Search for Executive Harmony.* Pittsburgh: University of Pittsburgh Press, 1986.

Durant, Robert F. *The Administrative Presidency.* Ithaca: State University of New York, 1993.

Fenno, Richard F., Jr. *The President's Cabinet.* Cambridge, MA: Harvard University Press, 1959.

Fisher, Louis. *Presidential Spending Power.* Princeton, NJ: Princeton University Press, 1975.

Hart, John. *The Presidential Branch,* 2nd ed. Chatham, NJ: Chatham House, 1994.

Heineman, Ben W., Jr., and Hessler, Curtis A. *Memorandum for the President.* New York: Random House, 1980.

Henderson, Phillip G. *Managing the Presidency: The Eisenhower Legacy—From Kennedy to Reagan.* Boulder, CO: Westview, 1988.

Hess, Stephen. *Organizing the Presidency,* 3rd ed. Washington, DC: The Brookings Institution, 1993.

Johnson, Richard T. *Managing the White House.* New York: Harper & Row, 1974.

Kernell, Samuel, and Popkin, Samuel L., eds. *Chief of Staff: Twenty-Five Years of Managing the Presidency.* Berkeley: University of California Press, 1986.

Light, Paul C. *The President's Agenda: Domestic Policy from Kennedy to Carter.* Baltimore, MD: Johns Hopkins University Press, 1982.

Nathan, Richard P. *The Plot that Failed: Nixon's Administrative Presidency.* New York: Wiley, 1975.

————. *The Administrative Presidency.* New York: Wiley, 1983.

Patterson, Bradley H., Jr. *The Ring of Power: The White House Staff and Its Expanding Role in Government.* New York: Basic Books, 1988.

Pfiffner, James P. *The President, the Budget and Congress: Impoundment and the 1974 Budget Act.* Boulder, CO: Westview, 1979.

Tufte, Edward R. *Political Control of the Economy.* Princeton, NJ: Princeton University Press, 1978.

Williams, Walter. *Mismanaging America: The Rise of the Anti-Analytic Presidency.* Lawrence: University of Kansas Press, 1990.

PRESIDENTS, THE SUPREME COURT, AND THE CONSTITUTION

Abraham, Henry J. *Justices and the President: A Political History of Appointments to the Supreme Court.* New York: Penguin, 1974.

————. *The Judicial Process,* 4th ed. New York: Oxford University Press, 1980.

Barnum, David G. *The Supreme Court and American Democracy.* New York: St. Martin's, 1993.

Berger, Raoul. *Impeachment: The Constitutional Problems.* Cambridge, MA: Harvard University Press, 1973.

Bowen, Catherine Drinker. *Miracle at Philadelphia.* Boston: Atlantic-Little, Brown, 1966, 1986.

Fisher, Louis. *The Constitution Between Friends.* New York: St. Martin's, 1978.

Genovese, Michael A. *The Supreme Court, the Constitution, and Presidential Power.* Lanham, MD: University Press of America, 1980.

Jensen, Merrill. *The Articles of Confederation.* Madison: The University of Wisconsin Press, 1940.

O'Brien, David M. *Storm Center: The Supreme Court in American Politics.* New York: W. W. Norton, 1986.

Pritchett, C. Herman. *The American Constitution,* 2nd ed. New York: McGraw-Hill, 1968.

Rossiter, Clinton. *The American Presidency,* rev. ed. New York: Mentor, 1960.

Schlesinger, Arthur M., Jr. *The Imperial Presidency.* Boston: Houghton Mifflin, 1973.

Schubert, Glendon. *The Presidency in the Courts.* Minneapolis: University of Minnesota Press, 1957.

Scigliano, Robert. *The Supreme Court and the President.* New York: The Free Press, 1971.

THE VICE PRESIDENCY

Bayh, Birch. *One Heartbeat Away: Presidential Disability and Succession.* Indianapolis: Bobbs-Merrill, 1968.

Dorman, Michael. *The Second Man.* New York: Dell, 1968.

Feerick, John D. *The Twenty-Fifth Amendment.* New York: Fordham University Press, 1976.

Goldstein, Joel K. *The Modern Vice Presidency.* Princeton, NJ: Princeton University Press, 1982.

Light, Paul C. *Vice Presidential Power: Influence in the White House.* Baltimore, MD: Johns Hopkins University Press, 1984.

Nathan, Richard P. *The Administrative Presidency.* New York: Wiley, 1983.

Natoli, Marie D. *American Prince, American Pauper: Contemporary Vice Presidency in Perspective.* Westport, CT: Greenwood, 1985.

Sindler, Allan P. *Unchosen Presidents.* Berkeley: University of California Press, 1976.

Witcover, Jules. *Crapshoot: Rolling the Dice on the Vice Presidency.* New York: Crown Publishers, 1992.

Young, Donald. *American Roulette: The History and Dilemma of the Vice Presidency.* New York: Viking, 1974.

REMAKING THE PRESIDENCY

Best, Judith. *Direct Election of the President: A Defense of the Electoral College.* Ithaca, NY: Cornell University Press, 1971.

Finer, Herman. *The Presidency: Crisis and Regeneration.* Chicago: University of Chicago Press, 1960.

Hardin, Charles M. *Presidential Power and Accountability: Toward a New Constitution.* Chicago: University of Chicago Press, 1974.

Mondale, Walter F. *The Accountability of Power: Toward a Responsible Presidency.* New York: McKay, 1975.

Robinson, Donald L., ed. *Reforming American Government: The Bicentennial Papers of the Committee on the Constitutional System.* Boulder, CO: Westview, 1985.

———. *To the Best of My Ability: The Presidency and the Constitution.* New York: W. W. Norton, 1987.

Rose, Richard, and Suleiman, Ezra. *Presidents and Prime Ministers.* Washington, DC: American Enterprise Institute, 1980.

Shogan, Robert. *None of the Above.* New York: New American Library, 1982.

Sorenson, Theodore C. *A Different Kind of President.* New York: Harper & Row, 1984.

Sundquist, James L. *Constitutional Reform and Effective Government.* Washington, DC: The Brookings Institution, 1986.

Tugwell, Rexford. *The Enlargement of the Presidency.* New York: Doubleday, 1960.

BIOGRAPHIES, AUTOBIOGRAPHIES, AND PSYCHOLOGICAL STUDIES

Ambrose, Stephen E. *Eisenhower the President,* 2 vols. of *Eisenhower.* New York: Simon & Schuster, 1984.

———. *Nixon.* New York: Simon & Schuster, 1987.

Bailey, Thomas A. *Presidential Greatness: The Image of the Man from George Washington to the Present.* New York: Appleton-Century-Crofts, 1972.

Barber, James David. *The Presidential Character,* 3rd ed. Englewood Cliffs, NJ: Prentice-Hall, 1985.

Boyarsky, Bill. *Ronald Reagan: His Life and Rise to the Presidency.* New York: Random House, 1981.

Cannon, James. *Time and Chance: Gerald Ford's Appointment with History.* New York: HarperCollins Publishers, 1994.

Cannon, Lou. *President Reagan: The Role of a Lifetime.* New York: Simon & Schuster, 1991.

Donovan, Robert J. *Eisenhower: The Inside Story.* New York: Harper & Row, 1956.

Evans, Rowland, and Novak, Robert. *Lyndon Johnson: The Exercise of Power.* New York: New American Library, 1966.

Fairlie, Henry. *The Kennedy Promise.* Garden City, NY: Doubleday, 1973.

Ford, Gerald. *A Time to Heal: The Autobiography of Gerald R. Ford.* New York: Harper & Row, 1979.

Freidel, Frank. *Franklin D. Roosevelt: A Rendezvous with Destiny.* Boston: Little, Brown, 1990.

Glad, Betty. *Jimmy Carter: In Search of the Great White House.* New York: W. W. Norton, 1980.

Goldman, Eric. *The Tragedy of Lyndon Johnson*. New York: Knopf, 1969.

Greenstein, Fred I. *The Hidden Hand Presidency*. New York: Basic Books, 1982.

Haldeman, H. R. *The Haldeman Diaries: Inside the Nixon White House*. New York: G. P. Putnam's Sons, 1994.

Hargrove, Erwin C. *Presidential Leadership: Personality and Political Style*. New York: Macmillan, 1966.

Hill, Dilys M., and Williams, Phil. *The Bush Presidency: Triumphs and Adversities*. New York: St. Martin's, 1994.

Johnson, Lyndon B. *The Vantage Point: Perspectives of the Presidency*. New York: Holt, Rinehart & Winston, 1971.

Kearns, Doris. *Lyndon Johnson and the American Dream*. New York: Harper & Row, 1976.

Link, Arthur S. *Woodrow Wilson*, 5 vols. Princeton, NJ: Princeton University Press, 1917–1955.

McCullough, David. *Truman*. New York: Simon & Schuster, 1992.

Nixon, Richard M. *Six Crises*. Garden City, NY: Doubleday, 1962.

Parmet, Herbert S. *Eisenhower and the American Crusades*. New York: Macmillan, 1972.

———. *JFK: The Presidency of John F. Kennedy*. New York: Penguin, 1984.

Philips, Cabell. *The Truman Presidency*. New York: Macmillan, 1966.

Reeves, Richard. *President Kennedy: Profile of Power*. New York: Simon & Schuster, 1993.

Schlesinger, Arthur M., Jr. *A Thousand Days*. Boston: Houghton Mifflin, 1963.

Sorenson, Theodore C. *Kennedy*. New York: Bantam, 1966.

INDEX

About the Author

JAMES W. DAVIS is Professor Emeritus of Political Science at Western Washington University. Davis has followed American presidents for more than forty years as an observer and sometimes participant in the political process. In addition to the previous edition of *The American Presidency* (1987), he is the author of *Presidential Primaries: Road to the White House*, 2nd ed. (Greenwood, 1980); *National Conventions in an Age of Party Reform* (Greenwood, 1983); and *The President as Party Leader* (Greenwood, 1992). Several of his former students in Minnesota and Washington have served or are now serving on the staffs of governors or members of Congress. He is currently working on a sourcebook on presidential primaries and the caucus-convention system (forthcoming from Greenwood).

ISBN 0-275-94874-9

90000>

9 780275 948740

HARDCOVER BAR CODE